The Origin of Mind

The Origin of Mind

EVOLUTION OF BRAIN, COGNITION, AND GENERAL INTELLIGENCE

David C. Geary

AMERICAN PSYCHOLOGICAL ASSOCIATION • WASHINGTON, DC

Published by
American Psychological Association
750 First Street, NE
Washington, DC 20002
www.apa.org

To order
APA Order Department
P.O. Box 92984
Washington, DC 20090-2984
Tel: (800) 374-2721
Direct: (202) 336-5510
Fax: (202) 336-5502
TDD/TTY: (202) 336-6123
Online: www.apa.org/books/
E-mail: order@apa.org

In the U.K., Europe, Africa, and the Middle East, copies may be ordered from
American Psychological Association
3 Henrietta Street
Covent Garden, London
WC2E 8LU England

Typeset in Goudy by World Composition Services, Inc., Sterling, VA

Printer: Edwards Brothers, Inc., Ann Arbor, MI
Cover Designer: Berg Design, Albany, NY
Technical/Production Editor: Gail B. Munroe

The opinions and statements published are the responsibility of the author, and such opinions and statements do not necessarily represent the policies of the American Psychological Association.

Library of Congress Cataloging-in-Publication Data

Geary, David C.
    The origin of mind : evolution of brain, cognition, and general intelligence / by David C. Geary.
      p. cm.
    Includes bibliographical references and index.
    ISBN 1-59147-181-8
    1. Cognitive neuroscience. 2. Brain—Evolution. 3. Evolutionary psychology. I. Title.

QP360.5.G43 2004
153—dc22
                                       2004007707

British Library Cataloguing-in-Publication Data
A CIP record is available from the British Library.

Printed in the United States of America
First Edition

CONTENTS

LIST OF FIGURES

PREFACE

As with my last book, *Male, Female: The Evolution of Human Sex Differences* (Geary, 1998), the theme of the current volume is in many ways based on several ideas discussed in Darwin's (1871) *Descent of Man and Selection in Relation to Sex*. In this book, Darwin not only proposed some of the mechanisms of sexual selection (e.g., female choice of mating partners) and the evolutionary origin of many sex differences, but also discussed the evolutionary origin of humans (*Homo sapiens sapiens*) and corresponding changes in mind and brain, following Huxley's (1863) lead. Among other things, Darwin suggested that the human brain evolved from the basic blueprint found in other mammals and that many features of the human mind were continuous with those of other species—that is, the human mind differs from that of other mammalian species as a matter of degree, not kind. These were, of course, controversial proposals in his day, and they remain so. I have chosen the evolution of brain, cognition, and general intelligence, or g, as topics for this book, because these remain interesting and largely unsolved puzzles.

I have, on occasion, been accused of choosing topics that will provoke and irritate, and I have to say that I wish that this were true. I have chosen these topics not to irritate and offend, but rather because they represent a good set of problems to attempt to solve; the reader will have to judge for himself or herself whether I have succeeded in any significant way. I have cast these topics in an evolutionary framework because I believe that this is the correct metatheory from which to approach these and many other issues in psychology. I also wanted to at least attempt to integrate the evolution of behavioral biases with brain and cognitive evolution, and ultimately with general intelligence, because I assumed that they must all be interrelated in significant ways.

I worked under the assumption that motivational, affective, behavioral, cognitive, and brain systems have evolved to process social and ecological information patterns (e.g., facial expressions) that covaried with survival or reproductive options during human evolution. My specific proposal is that all of these systems are ultimately and proximately focused on supporting attempts by the individual to gain access to and control of the social (e.g., mates), biological (e.g., food), and physical (e.g., demarcation of territory) resources that supported survival and improved reproductive prospects during human evolutionary history.

In writing this book, I contacted experts in a number of fields to ensure that I had not missed an important study or simply to ask questions, and I asked many others to read drafts of one or more chapters. I would like to thank all of these individuals for their assistance: Mark Ashcraft, Dan Berch, Gary Brase, Kristin Buss, Nelson Cowan, Mark Dubin, Randy Engle, Mark Flinn, Ralph Holloway, Kevin MacDonald, Mike O'Brien, Steve Pinker, Todd Preuss, Amanda Rose, and Carol Ward. I'd also like to acknowledge my lab group who listened as I thought through some of the issues discussed herein and who read and commented on most of the book: Mary Hoard, Jennifer Byrd-Craven, Jacob Vigil, Lara Nugent, and Chattavee Numtee. I thank Travis Mason for translating sections of Brodmann's (1909) treatise on brain anatomy and Lansing Hays of APA Books for convincing me that the time was right to write a book on this topic, as well as Dave Bjorklund and Judy Nemes for a thoughtful vetting of the entire book. Finally, I thank Kelly Huffman and acknowledge her important contributions to the Evolution and Brain Organization section of chapter 4; an earlier version of this material appeared in Geary and Huffman (2002). Of course, the conclusions drawn in this book are my own and not necessarily those of any of the above-mentioned individuals.

The Origin of Mind

1

INTRODUCTION AND OVERVIEW

Charles Darwin and Alfred Wallace (1858) independently discovered the mechanisms of natural selection, that is, the processes that act in nature to create change within a species (microevolution) and to result in the origin of new species (macroevolution). More often than not, the processes are harsh and unforgiving and were thus described as a "struggle for existence" (Darwin & Wallace, 1858, p. 54). Human evolution was filled with many such struggles, and life remains a struggle in many parts of the world and for many people. As Alexander (1989) proposed, humans do not have to struggle quite as hard as most other species do simply to exist—that is, to stay alive. Humans differ from other species in their extraordinary ability to modify (e.g., build dams) and extract resources (e.g., use other species as food) from the ecology and then use these resources for survival and reproductive ends. In other words, humans are ecologically dominant, and once this was achieved, there was an important shift such that the competing interests of other people and coalitions of other people became, and remain, the central pressure that influences human evolution.

From this perspective, natural selection remains a "struggle for existence" but becomes primarily a struggle with other human beings for control of the resources that support life and allow one to reproduce (Geary, 1998). Human behavior, and at an abstract level the behavior of all species, can thus be conceptualized in terms of an evolved motivation to control. I am not in any way arguing that individuals of all species have a conscious, explicit motive to control other members of their species (e.g., mates) or other species (e.g., prey species). Rather, the result of natural and sexual selection (e.g., competition for mates) will be the evolution of brain, perceptual, cognitive, and affective systems that are sensitive to and process the types of information that have been correlated with survival and reproductive outcomes during the species' evolutionary history. The operation of these systems will bias behavior so it is directed toward the corresponding features of the ecology (e.g., prey) and focused on attempts to achieve control (e.g., capture of prey) of these potential resources. In most species, and often for humans, the processes typically occur implicitly (i.e., below conscious awareness) and automatically.

Whether these processes operate automatically and implicitly or at a conscious and explicit level, the unifying theme is that individuals of all species have evolved to attempt to organize their world in ways that eliminate predatory risks (e.g., evasion behaviors) and enhance survival and reproductive options, or at least to do so in ways that facilitated these outcomes during the species' evolutionary history. My shorthand for these behavioral biases is a *motivation to control*. My argument is that the foci of control-related behavioral biases and the supporting brain, perceptual, cognitive, and affective systems are three general forms of resource: social, biological, and physical. The corresponding competencies are captured by the domains of folk psychology (Baron-Cohen, 1995; Brothers, 1990; Humphrey, 1976), folk biology (Atran, 1998), and folk physics (Pinker, 1997; Povinelli, 2000). When applied to humans, these domains refer to an inherent and intuitive understanding of other people (folk psychology), other species (folk biology), and the physical world (folk physics). When meshed with ecological dominance and a struggle with other people to control these ecologies, the result is an evolutionary arms race. An arms race refers to the evolutionary change that results from the competing interests of individuals, within or between species, as they attempt to achieve competitive advantage (Dawkins & Krebs, 1979). For instance, a fast predator will capture slower prey more easily than faster prey, such that the average running speed of this prey species will increase across generations. Faster prey in turn puts slower predators at a disadvantage, such that the average running speed of this predatory species will increase across generations. And so it will continue. With respect to humans, an arms race will result in the elaboration of folk psychological systems that support social competition and cooperation and of the folk biological and folk physical (e.g., as related to tool use) systems that support ecological dominance.

A within-species arms race is particularly important, as it allows one to understand why and in what domains humans are different from related species. I argue that one result of this arms race was an evolutionary advantage for individuals who could compete in ways that differed from the routine.

This unpredictability—variant in behavior—is important, because it renders implicit and automatic heuristic-based processes less effective and places a premium on conscious, explicit problem-solving mechanisms (J. S. B. T. Evans, 2002; Stanovich & West, 2000). Later in this chapter, I touch on my predictions regarding the evolution of the brain and cognitive systems that support these explicit mechanisms and the associated ability to form conscious-psychological simulations or mental models (Johnson-Laird, 1983) of control-related behavioral strategies; these predictions will be elaborated in chapter 7. These explicit mechanisms then provide the theoretical and empirical link to general intelligence (chap. 8) and the use of general intelligence to learn evolutionarily novel competencies, such as reading (chap. 9). I believe the result is an integrated theoretical framework that accommodates the evolution of implicitly functioning modular systems (e.g., for processing facial features), explicit and controlled problem solving, and general intelligence, along with many other psychological phenomena (e.g., in-group, out-group dynamics).

OVERVIEW OF THIS BOOK

Chapter 2: Natural and Sexual Selection

In chapter 2, I introduce the basic mechanisms of natural selection and explain how these mechanisms operate. The processes are simple and mechanical, as Darwin and Wallace (1858) and later Dennett (1995) deftly explained. The ingredients needed for natural selection to operate are individual differences in a trait that are, in part, heritable; a correlation between individual differences in the trait and individual differences in survival or reproductive prospects; and ecological or social conditions that maintain this correlation over successive generations. As I explain, even small heritable differences can lead to substantive evolutionary change and can do so more quickly than most people realize (P. R. Grant, 1999). Heritable individual differences exist in a host of traits for species ranging from invertebrates to primates (Mousseau & Roff, 1987), and many of these same traits have been shown to covary with survival or reproductive prospects in natural ecologies (Kingsolver et al., 2001).

In these ecologies, there are three basic classes of selection pressure: climatic, ecological, and social. *Climatic pressures* refer to changes in ambient temperature or rainfall or the occurrence of less common events, such as volcanic eruptions, that significantly change the conditions under which the species evolved and is thus adapted. *Ecological pressures* typically involve interactions with other species, as in predator–prey relations. The corresponding adaptations are those that allow the organism to extract food from the ecology or to avoid being extracted as food, as well as an array of supporting adaptations (e.g., navigational competencies needed for prey search). *Social pressures* are composed of the competitive and cooperative relations among members of the same species—called *conspecifics*—as these relations influence survival or reproductive options. By outlining these forms of selection pressure, I set the stage for understanding the conditions that drove the evolution of the human brain and mind.

Chapter 3: Hominid Evolution and the Motivation to Control

Hominid Evolution

In the dynamic field of paleontology, new fossil finds often shake the human family tree, pruning or adding a branch here and there (Aiello & Collard, 2001; B. Wood & Collard, 1999). Despite the occasional shake-up, much is known about the major species of *Homo* and those of the predecessor genus *Australopithecus*. As far as I am concerned, the most interesting features of these species are brain volume and encephalization quotient (EQ). The latter provides an estimate of brain size relative to that of a mammal or primate of the same body size (Jerison, 1973). An EQ of 2.0 indicates that brain volume is double that of the average species of the same body weight. Since the emergence of australopithecines about 4 million years ago, brain volume has roughly tripled, and EQ estimates have increased two- to threefold (Jerison, 1973; Ruff, Trinkaus, & Holliday, 1997). The brain has also been reorganized in important ways (Holloway, 1973b; Tobias, 1987). We are now at a point in our evolutionary history in which there has been a very rapid (over a relatively few 100,000 years) increase in brain volume and EQ: Important and interesting changes have occurred in our recent evolutionary past.

Adaptation and Selection

Why have there been recent and rapid increases in brain size and EQ? I explore and evaluate a variety of climatic (Vrba, 1995a, 1995b), ecological (Kaplan, Hill, Lancaster, & Hurtado, 2000; Wrangham, Holland-Jones, Laden, Pilbeam, & Conklin-Brittain, 1999), and social (Alexander, 1989; Humphrey, 1976) selection pressures that have been proposed as the forces that drove the evolution of the human brain and mind. The general theme that runs through all of the proposals is that the human brain and mind have evolved to anticipate and thus better cope with unpredictable climatic, ecological, or social change within a lifetime. I conclude that climatic variability is not likely to have been the primary form of selection pressure driving these evolutionary changes. There is, in contrast, evidence that our ancestors became increasingly skilled in their ability to extract resources from the ecology through hunting and use of tools (Foley & Lahr, 1997;

Wrangham et al., 1999). This is where Alexander's (1989) ecological dominance proposal becomes important: As our ancestors improved in their ability to secure resources from the ecology, the primary problem became staying in control of the best ecologies—that is, keeping other humans from securing the same ecological resources.

I provide a framework that outlines the basic social and cognitive competencies needed to support ecological dominance and the changes in social dynamics that would have logically followed the achievement of ecological dominance. As mentioned, these conditions set the stage for a within-species arms race (Alexander, 1989; Humphrey, 1976). The predicted result is the evolutionary elaboration of the social, cognitive, and brain systems that enable individuals to compete in the arms race. This intense social competition results in conditions that will favor the evolutionary elaboration of a host of sociocognitive competencies, such as the ability to make inferences about the intentions of other people (i.e., theory of mind), as I describe in chapter 5. These modular systems are not enough, however, as people are tricky. Sometimes one needs to anticipate and mentally simulate what they might do next, just to stay even or get a bit ahead of the competition. This requires explicit problem-solving processes and an array of supporting brain and cognitive systems, as I describe in chapters 6 and 7.

Motivation to Control

As stated, my working hypothesis is that the brain and mind of all species have evolved to attend to and process the forms of information, such as the movement patterns of prey species, that covaried with survival and reproductive prospects during the species' evolutionary history. These systems bias decision making and behavioral responses in ways that allow the organism to attempt to achieve access to and control of these outcomes. I start this section with a brief review of how social status and resource control (e.g., money, land, cows) covary with mortality risks in traditional and preindustrial societies (Hed, 1987). In all of these contexts, individuals who control social and material resources realize substantive benefits (e.g., reduced mortality risks for their children). I then propose that attempts to achieve control will be dependent on modular brain and cognitive systems in the domains of folk psychology, folk biology, and folk physics and on affective, conscious-psychological, and executive cognitive systems.

Chapter 4: Evolution and Development of Brain and Cognition

I switch gears in chapter 4 and focus on issues related to the development and experiential modification of brain organization and cognitive functions during a lifetime, as contrasted with evolutionary change across generations. Plasticity in brain and cognitive systems is important because it is one outcome predicted to result from an evolutionary history of having to cope with variation in social and ecological conditions.

Current Debate and Theoretical Framework

Current debates are largely the same as old debates: Is the primary influence on brain organization and cognitive functions nature or nurture? Most theorists agree it is some combination of genetic and experiential influences that mold brains and influence cognition, but there is still a tendency to emphasize one type of influence or the other. In an attempt to bring some order to the confusion, or perhaps add to it, I outline a framework for understanding when evolutionary pressures should result in genetic constraints on brain organization and cognitive functions, and when these pressures should result in the evolution of systems that are plastic, or modifiable, in response to experiences (Geary & Huffman, 2002).

The gist is that inherently constrained and modular brain and cognitive systems should evolve for processing information patterns associated with those social and ecological conditions that are *invariant* across generations and lifetimes, if these conditions covaried with survival or reproductive outcomes. Plastic systems are modifiable within broader inherent constraints and should evolve for processing more *variant* information patterns—specifically, information patterns that are of survival or reproductive significance but vary across or within lifetimes. An example of an invariant information pattern is that generated by the organization of the human face (e.g., placement of eyes), and a variant information pattern results from individual differences in the shape of facial features.

Evolution and Brain Organization

In this section, I set the stage for considering how the human brain and mind are similar to and different from those of other species, and thus I get right at the heart of knotty philosophical issues that arose from Huxley's (1863) and Darwin's (1871) initial evolutionary forays into this arena. Comparative similarity is particularly divisive, as it provides strong evidence in support of the proposal that the human brain and mind are products of natural and sexual selection. The evolution of the human mind was, in fact, an issue that led to the scientific and sometimes personal estrangement between Darwin (1871) and Wallace (1869). In any event, there is a common blueprint for brain organization across mammalian species, including humans, as well as species-specific adaptations (Jones, 1985; Krubitzer, 1995). Similarities in brain organization, and presumably cognitive function, may be related to similarities in the genes that influence the prenatal development of the brain (Holland & Holland, 1999), although the specific mechanisms that influence prenatal brain development are debated. The points of contention are similar to those noted above—that is, whether the prenatal organization of the neocortex is largely due to experience (Schlagger & O'Leary, 1991)—input from the firing of subcortical neurons—or to inherently constrained patterns of neural migration and region-specific gene expression (Fukuchi-Shimogori & Grove, 2001; Rakic, 2000). The truth appears to be somewhere between these end points: The basic organization of the neocortex is molded by inherent constraints, but pre- and postnatal experiences fine-tune brain organization and function within these constraints (L. E. White, Coppola, & Fitzpatrick, 2001).

I next link brain organization to the ecological conditions that covary with survival and reproductive prospects, and again comparative studies are useful in this regard (Huffman, Nelson, Clarey, & Krubitzer, 1999), although not without limitations (Povinelli & Bering, 2002; Preuss, 2000a). We now know that there is a link between the size of areas of the somatosensory cortex involved in representing environmental patterns that create bodily sensations and the survival-related importance of the corresponding body region. For example, species that use their forepaws for food manipulation, such as raccoons (*Procyon lotor*), have more neocortical area devoted to these areas of the body than do their less dexterous cousins (Huffman et al., 1999). The section concludes with a discussion of the likely relations between brain–ecology links and brain development and evolution (Rakic & Kornack, 2001).

Experiential Modification of Brain Organization

The first topic in this section is whether evolutionary expansion of the brain was the direct result of specific selection pressures or an incidental result of pressures acting on other traits. An incidental expansion could occur because of allometric, or correlated, relations among the size of different regions of the body and among the size of different regions of the brain. If selection pressures resulted in expansion of one region of the neocortex, then other unrelated regions could, in theory, also expand. If this occurred during human evolution, then the organization and functions of the neocortex have not been influenced by evolutionary selection per se and thus should be highly plastic (Finlay & Darlington, 1995). These issues are hotly contested and not yet resolved (de Winter & Oxnard, 2001; Finlay, Darlington, & Nicastro, 2001).

In any case, it has been known since the seminal contributions of Rosenzweig and colleagues that postnatal experiences influence the size and functioning of the neocortex (Rosenzweig, Krech, Bennett, & Diamond, 1962). Subsequent studies of learning, developmental experiences, and the effects of injury consistently support this relation (Buonomano & Merzenich, 1998; Kaas, 1991; Ramachandran, 1993), especially during the developmental period (Stiles, 2000; Wiesel, 1982). Current debate and research are focused on the timing of these experiences and their relative influence (in comparison to inherent constraints) on the size, organization, and functions of the neocortex. At this point, it appears that experiential influences are small to moderate, although normal functioning requires an interaction between inherent constraint and experiential patterns. The combination fine-tunes the corresponding brain systems and functions of mind to the specifics of the ecology (Gottlieb, Wahlsten, & Lickliter, 1998; Greenough, 1991; Wiesel, 1982).

Soft Modularity

The interaction between inherent constraints on and openness to experiential modification of the neocortex can be understood in terms of three forms of soft modularity that can be linked to the invariant–variant information patterns introduced in the first section of the chapter. The first form of modularity follows an earlier proposal by R. Gelman (1990) and is conceptualized in terms of an exoskeleton with soft internal structures. The exoskeleton represents those brain and cognitive systems that have evolved to process invariant information patterns, and the soft internal structures represent systems that have evolved to accommodate individual differences within the constraints of the exoskeleton. The latter systems are perforce modifiable by experience. The second form of soft modularity encompasses the ability to form categories within broader constraints, as in the human ability to demarcate the social world into in-groups and out-groups. The final form of soft modularity involves experience-dependent redistributions of caloric and other resources from one area of the brain to another in response to patterns of use and disuse.

Chapter 5: Modular Domains of the Human Mind

I flesh out an earlier taxonomy of the evolved domains of the human mind (Geary, 1998; Geary & Huffman, 2002). The taxonomy is an integration of the work of many other scientists (Baron-Cohen, 1995; Dunbar, 1993; Hirschfeld & Gelman, 1994; Humphrey, 1976; Mithen, 1996; Pinker, 1997; Premack & Premack, 1995) and is an organized collection of modular systems that coalesce around the domains of folk psychology, folk biology, and folk physics. The taxonomy provides a means to link studies of human mental faculties with neurobiological studies of brain development, functioning, and evolution and to integrate modular systems with the less modularized cognitive processes (e.g., working memory) that I describe in later chapters.

Functional Taxonomy of the Human Mind

For folk domains, I outline the corresponding cognitive competencies, discuss potential neural correlates, and then make proposals regarding potential evolutionary functions. The most basic function is to guide the individual's behavior toward attempts to achieve access to and control of the social, biological, and physical resources that tended to covary with survival or reproductive outcomes during human evolution. Achieving control, of course, is not an easy task. As I describe in chapter 6, the motivation to control and associated behaviors are typically implicit and achieved only incrementally, if at all. As an example, the formation of friendships is supported by folk psychological competencies but does not, on the surface, appear to be guided by a motivation to control the behavior of these people. At the very least, there is often no explicit or conscious desire to do so. However, the development of these relationships and the associated social support are correlated with physical and psychological health and in some contexts mortality risks (e.g., Geary & Flinn, 2002; Taylor et al., 2000). These friendships are thus social resources that can enhance survival and reproductive prospects under the types of conditions found in traditional societies today and presumably throughout human evolution.

Building on the work of others, I propose that there are three sets of folk psychological modules. These direct attention toward and process social information related to the self, other individuals, and group formation (Gardner, 1983; Tulving, 2002). The former include awareness of the self as a social being and awareness of one's relationships with other people. The individual-level modules process the forms of information, such as nonverbal behavior (e.g., gestures), facial expressions, and language, that guide one-on-one social dynamics and foster one-on-one social relationships (Bugental, 2000). The group-level modules enable individuals to break their social world into categories of people, including kin and members of favored in-groups and disfavored out-groups. People also have the comparatively unique ability to form in-groups on the basis of ideology, such as nation. The group-level systems enable the formation of large-scale cooperative communities and coalitions, which in turn often compete with other coalitions for ecological and resource control (Horowitz, 2001).

The folk biological modules support the ability to develop taxonomies of other species and very elaborate knowledge systems about the behavior, growth pattern, and "essence" of these species (Atran, 1998; Berlin, Breedlove, & Raven, 1966). In traditional societies, these competencies support behavioral activities that are directed toward ecological control and dominance, such as hunting and horticulture (Kaplan et al., 2000). The folk physical systems support navigation, the formation of mental representations of physical features of the ecology, and the construction of tools. Some of these competencies, especially the ability to navigate, are similar to those found in other species and thus are not uniquely human (Tomasello & Call, 1997). The ability to construct and use tools, in contrast, far exceeds the competencies found in other species (Povinelli, 2000), and the evolution of this ability almost certainly contributed to the achievement of ecological dominance.

Development and Soft Modularity

As mentioned, soft modularity means that folk systems emerge from an interaction between inherent constraints and patterns of experience, especially developmental experiences. In theory, the most plastic modular systems are those that process information patterns that tend to be variant across generations and within lifetimes. These variant patterns will result from interactions between biological organisms, as in predator–prey relations, and social dynamics (Maynard Smith & Price, 1973), and thus it follows that the development of folk psychological and folk biological systems will be guided by inherent constraints but also show considerable plasticity. As described in chapter 4, the central function of the developmental period is to enable organisms to adapt neural, perceptual, cognitive, and behavioral systems to variation in these domains, if such sensitivity (e.g., the ability to discriminate one individual from another) resulted in survival or reproductive advantages during the species' evolutionary history. These evolutionarily expectant experiences are assumed to occur automatically through the organism's natural play, exploration, and social experiences and are predicted to adapt evolved modular systems to local conditions, such as the local language (Bjorklund & Pellegrini, 2000; D. G. Freedman, 1974; Greenough, 1991; MacDonald, 1992; Scarr, 1992). I suggest that the adaptation of these systems to local conditions occurs, at least in part, by means of the exoskeleton and the rule-based category formation forms of soft modularity.

Chapter 6: Heuristics and Controlled Problem Solving

Bounded Rationality and Heuristics

Among Simon's many contributions was the concept of bounded rationality (Simon, 1955, 1956), that is, a proposed link between cognitive and decision-making mechanisms and the ecological contexts in which these mechanisms evolved. These cognitive mechanisms enable the organism to automatically and implicitly attend to and process evolutionarily coupled ecological information and guide rational behavioral decisions in these contexts. *Rational* does not mean that the organism has evolved to make optimal (e.g., maximize number of offspring) or even conscious behavioral choices. Rather, the cost–benefit trade-offs associated with optimizing would lead to the evolution of cognitive and behavioral systems that result in "good enough" outcomes (Gigerenzer & Selten, 2001a; Simon, 1990a). For instance, the search for the "perfect" mate may extend for decades, if not longer, and any associated motivational, cognitive, or other mechanisms thus carry a very large reproductive cost. Satisfaction with a "good enough" mate, in contrast, would result in a shorter search and thus a higher probability of reproducing. More important, I link Simon's bounded rationality and related research (Gigerenzer, Todd, & ABC Research Group, 1999) to the invariant–variant continuum introduced in chapter 4. Bounded rationality and associated behavioral heuristics—decision-making rules of thumb— represent the evolution of brain, cognitive, and behavioral systems that direct attention toward and process information patterns that tend toward the invariant end of this continuum. These behavior–cognition–ecology links operate automatically and implicitly and recreate the behavioral outcomes that resulted in good enough survival or reproductive outcomes in the specific ecological context.

Controlled Problem Solving

Humans are not driven simply by implicit, automatically functioning behaviors that are triggered by specific ecological or social contexts. At times, individuals can inhibit the operation of these more automatic processes (Bjorklund & Harnishfeger, 1995) and approach the social or ecological situation using explicit, conscious processes (Stanovich & West, 2000). The systems that enable the inhibition of automatic processes and support conscious, controlled problem solving evolved to cope with information patterns that tend toward the variant end of the invariant–variant continuum. By definition, variant information patterns are somewhat unpredictable, rendering the behavior–cognition–ecology links that define bounded rationality less effective.

To illustrate explicit problem solving and reasoning in real-world, knowledge-rich domains, I chose the knowledge base, assumptions, inferences, and so forth that contributed to Darwin's and Wallace's discoveries of the principles of natural selection (Darwin, 1859; Darwin & Wallace, 1858; Wallace, 1855). To be sure, most people do not reason as logically and problem solve as systematically as did Darwin and Wallace (J. S. B. T. Evans, 2002; Stanovich, 1999), but the illustration seems appropriate to this book and captures the basics of explicit, controlled cognitive processes. I close with discussion of Johnson-Laird's (1983) mental models—that is, cognitive simulations of problem-solving situations.

Chapter 7: Evolution of Control-Related Mental Models

Cognitive and Brain Systems

Controlled problem solving and the ability to engage in rational analysis are correlated with general intelligence (Stanovich, 1999) and appear to require the inhibition of heuristic-based responding and the formation of a conscious, explicit representation of the corresponding information (J. S. B. T. Evans, 2002). The issues addressed in chapter 7 are centered on the cognitive systems and processes that allow people to become consciously aware of externally and internally generated information and to mentally change and reorganize these representations. These cognitive systems are understood in terms of executive control (Baddeley, 1986; Moscovitch, 2000) and working memory (Miyake & Shah, 1999). Working memory is composed of a central executive that controls attentional allocation and at least two slave systems, the phonological loop and the visuospatial sketchpad (Baddeley, 1986; Baddeley & Logie, 1999). The slave systems process auditory and visual–spatial information.

The key to understanding the operation of the central executive, as related to conscious awareness, is attentional control (Engle, 2002) and an attention-driven amplification of the activity of the brain regions processing information represented in the slave systems (Dehaene & Naccache, 2001; Posner, 1994). As an illustration, to become consciously aware of the face of someone with whom one is conversing, the central executive directs attention toward the face, which in turn is represented by portions of the visual system. This focusing of attention appears to result in a synchronizing of the brain regions that support executive functions and the brain regions that are processing the facial features, as well as an amplification of the activity of the latter brain regions. The result is a representation of the face in working memory and a corresponding conscious awareness of the face.

Attentional and executive control are dependent on several regions of the prefrontal cortex, such as the dorsolateral regions. Other regions of the prefrontal cortex support social cognition, including a sense of self (Tulving, 2002). The brain regions that support self-awareness are intimately tied to memories of personal experiences, called *episodic memory,* and the ability to mentally time travel (Wheeler, Stuss, & Tulving, 1997). The latter is the ability to project the self back in time to recreate a personal experience and to project the self forward in time to create simulations of situations that might arise in the future. Individuals who do not have a sense of self and who cannot mentally time travel because of brain injury have a very difficult time dealing with complex, dynamic situations that vary from the routine. These situations are typically social in nature and mesh perfectly with the variant forms of information emphasized in earlier chapters.

The prefrontal cortex and corresponding executive and working memory systems thus enable individuals to form conscious representations of a variety of social and ecological situations and to explicitly change the form of these representations. When these representations are infused with a sense of self and the ability to mentally time travel, the result is a mental capacity that may be uniquely human. I propose that self-awareness and other functions associated with the prefrontal cortex and executive control can be integrated with the motivation to control. Specifically, the motivation to control is facilitated by the ability to mentally simulate potential future social scenarios (Alexander, 1989; Humphrey, 1976) or changes in ecological conditions (Potts, 1998), and then rehearse a variety of potential responses to these situations (Geary, 1998). In other words, one way to deal with unpredictable situations is to mentally generate potential variations of these conditions and then rehearse behavioral strategies for controlling outcomes associated with each of these variations.

Problem Solving and Human Evolution

In this section, I integrate the climatic, ecological, and social pressures described in chapter 3 with evolution of executive and attentional control, self-awareness, and mental time travel. As noted, all of these competencies are heavily dependent on various regions of the prefrontal cortex, as well as the anterior cingulate cortex, and appear to be active primarily with tasks or social dynamics that vary from the routine. It follows that the selection pressures that contributed to the evolution of these cognitive competencies and the supporting brain systems required the individual to cope with information patterns that were toward the variant end of the invariant–variant continuum. Four forms of selection characteristic (e.g., time scale of information change) are then described and used to evaluate the plausibility that climatic, ecological, or social selection pressures drove the evolution of executive and attentional control, working memory, functioning of the prefrontal cortex, and some of the modular competencies described in chapter 5. I conclude that climatic pressures do not provide a sufficient explanation for the evolution of these human traits, but a combination of ecological and social pressures do.

But how is the struggle for control related to the evolution of executive functions, explicit and conscious awareness of the self, mental time travel, and the ability to engage in controlled problem solving, as well as the evolution of the supporting brain systems? The theme that helps to tie all of these together with the proposals of many other scientists emerges from a fusion of Tulving's (2002) self-awareness—termed *autonoetic awareness*—and Johnson-Laird's (1983) mental models—specifically, an autonoetic mental model, whereby the individual creates a self-centered mental simulation of the "perfect world" (Geary, 1998). A perfect world is one in which the individual is able to organize and control social (e.g., social dynamics), biological (e.g., access to food), and physical (e.g., shelter) resources in ways that would have enhanced survival or reproductive options during human evolution. The simulation of this perfect world is, in effect, the conscious-psychological component of the motivation-to-control model. A conscious-psychological simulation is advantageous in situations that cannot be readily addressed by heuristic-based responses. These are conditions in which the dynamics of the situation are not entirely predictable based on the individual's past experiences or the species' evolutionary history. These conditions require an explicit and conscious representation of the situation and some degree of problem solving and reasoned inference to cope with the dynamics.

Folk Psychology and Social Cognition

Social cognition is an integral feature of folk psychology and is predicted to be focused on the self, relationships and inferences about the behavior and internal states of other people, and group-level processes. On the basis of my motivation-to-control model and the work of Heckhausen and Schulz (1995), folk psychological mechanisms that facilitate control-related behaviors are also predicted to evolve. In this final section of chapter 7, I outline evidence related to the existence of control-related cognitions and attributions and discuss some of the social-psychological literature related to cognitions about the self and other people and as related to group-level interactions. My goal is to illustrate how this literature is readily accommodated within an evolutionary framework and to describe how many of these phenomena are the result of the social selection pressures described in earlier chapters.

Chapter 8: Evolution of General Intelligence

Psychometrics and Mental Abilities

In the latter half of the 19th century, Galton (1865, 1869) sought to determine if eminence, as defined by success in law, science, and other professions, runs in families: It does. He proposed that the abilities that contribute to this talent, or "genius," are largely hereditary and include a general mental ability. In 1904, Spearman published the first definitive empirical evidence for the existence of a general mental ability. The basic finding is that above-average performance in one academic domain is associated with above-average performance in all other academic domains and with peer ratings of intelligence and common sense. Spearman concluded "that all branches of intellectual activity have in common one fundamental function (or group of functions)" (p. 285), which he termed general intelligence, or g.

In the ensuing 100 years, the study of general intelligence has emerged as an active and thriving specialty within psychology. Researchers now understand that general intelligence is better conceptualized as general fluid intelligence, or gF, and general crystallized intelligence, or gC (Cattell, 1963). Fluid intelligence represents those functions or cognitive processes that support the ability to reason and problem solve as a means to cope with novel and complex conditions (Cattell, 1963; Embretson, 1995). Crystallized intelligence represents the individual's store of knowledge (e.g., facts, concepts). There are, in addition, competencies that require both gF and gC and processes that are confined to more restricted domains of ability, such as language-related and spatial abilities (J. B. Carroll, 1993; Spearman, 1927; Thurstone, 1938).

Cognitive and Brain Correlates

Recent research on general intelligence, and particularly gF, has been focused on identifying the cognitive processes and brain systems that define Spearman's (1904) function or functions (Deary, 2000; Jensen, 1998). These processes include speed of processing basic pieces of information—for example, speed of retrieving the letter name A from long-term memory (Jensen, 1982)—consistency in the speed of processing the same information from one time to the next (Jensen, 1992), speed and accuracy of identifying subtle variations in information (Nettelbeck & Lally, 1976), working memory capacity (Kyllonen & Christal, 1990), and ability to focus attention (Engle, 2002). The bottom line is that intelligent individuals identify subtle variations in external information quickly and accurately. Once the information is represented in the perceptual system (e.g., as a word), it is processed quickly and is accurately represented in short-term memory. Subsets of the information active in short-term memory are, by means of attentional focus, explicitly represented in working memory and made available to conscious awareness. In comparison to other people, intelligent individuals can hold more information in working memory and are better able to reason about and draw inferences from the associated patterns. The combination of a large working memory capacity and the ability to reason defines several of the core cognitive competencies that underlie fluid intelligence.

Above average performance on measures of g, and particularly gF, is associated with a larger neocortex (Rushton & Ankney, 1996), especially the dorsolateral area (Raz et al., 1993); activation of the dorsolateral prefrontal cortex and the anterior cingulate cortex during the solving of IQ test items (Duncan et al., 2000); and lower overall metabolic activity in the brain during complex problem solving (Haier et al., 1988). In short, many of the same brain regions associated with working memory and complex problem solving that I describe in chapter 7 support fluid intelligence (Kane & Engle, 2002). It appears that intelligent individuals are, through attentional focus, able to engage only those brain regions needed to solve the problem at hand. The attentional focus prevents the activation of task-irrelevant brain regions and thus results in less overall metabolic activity, and at a cognitive level this focus prevents task-irrelevant information from entering conscious awareness. The result is an enhanced ability to use working memory to engage in the problem-solving processes needed to cope with novel situations.

Origins of General Intelligence

Because general intelligence is an asset in many contexts (Gottfredson, 1997; Jensen, 1998), discussion of the origins of associated individual differences often generates considerable debate and obfuscation, as was recently illustrated by the firestorm surrounding Herrnstein's and Murray's (1994) *The Bell Curve*. It is not my goal to reignite this firestorm. Rather, I simply review the decades of research on genetic and environmental influences on the development and expression of general intelligence. The results of this research are clear: Genetic influences on individual differences in general intelligence are important and increase in magnitude from the preschool years to adulthood (E. G. Bishop et al., 2003; Bouchard & McGue, 1981). Although the research is not as conclusive, the same pattern may be evident for the cognitive processes (e.g., working memory) and brain systems that underlie g.

In no way do these genetic findings mean that environmental influences are not important. In fact, it appears that some amount of environmental stimulation is necessary for the full development of one's intellectual potential. Cross-generational increases in mean IQ scores (Flynn, 1987; Teasdale & Owen, 2000) and recent behavior genetic studies (e.g., Neiss & Rowe, 2000) suggest that environmental factors may suppress the development of general intellectual abilities for individuals living in difficult circumstances. In these populations, genetic influences on individual differences in g are smaller and environmental influences larger than in populations living in better circumstances. Environmental influences include those shared among family members (e.g., number of books in the home) and influences that are unique to each individual. Shared environmental influences appear to be an important contributor to individual differences in g during the preschool years and early childhood, whereas unique experiences exert an important influence on individual differences in g throughout the life span.

Mental Models, Evolved Modules, and g

My proposal in this section is that research on general fluid intelligence, gF, has identified many of the core cognitive processes and brain systems that support the use of autonoetic mental models and that gF evolved as a result of the social and to a lesser extent the ecological pressures I describe in earlier chapters. The ability to use these mental simulations is dependent on working memory, attentional control, and a brain system that includes the dorsolateral prefrontal cortex and the anterior cingulate cortex. These executive brain and cognitive systems function to deal with variation and novelty in social and ecological conditions and thus should be engaged when individuals must cope with conditions and information that cannot be automatically and implicitly processed by the modular systems described in chapter 5 and the heuristics described in chapter 6. In other words, the 100 years of empirical research on g has isolated those features of auto-noetic mental models that are not strongly influenced by content and that enable explicit representations of information in working memory and an attentional-dependent ability to manipulate this information in the service of strategic problem solving. Horn's and Cattell's (1966) definition of fluid intelligence and subsequent research on the underlying cognitive and brain systems are consistent with this view: There is considerable overlap in the cognitive and brain systems that support autonoetic mental models and those that support fluid abilities (Duncan et al., 2000; Kane & Engle, 2002).

One important discrepancy involves self-awareness, which is a core feature of autonoetic mental models but not an aspect of fluid intelligence. The reason for the discrepancy lies in the initial development and goal of intelligence tests—specifically, to predict academic performance, not social functioning or awareness of the self. Finally, I propose that crystallized general intelligence can be decomposed into two general classes. The first includes knowledge—facts, concepts, problem-solving procedures—that is learned during an individual's lifetime, as proposed by Cattell (1963). The second class includes inherent modular competencies and folk knowledge. As an example, language is almost certainly an evolved modular domain (Pinker, 1994), and many of the paper-and-pencil tests that measure crystal-lized knowledge "involve language either directly or indirectly" (J. B. Carroll, 1993, p. 599). Many of the other tests of crystallized knowledge measure a mix of learned and inherent competencies.

Chapter 9: General Intelligence in Modern Society

Evolution and Social Competition

I begin with an argument that the pressures associated with the evolu-tion of the motivation to control and the accompanying nexus of brain, cognitive, conscious-psychological, and affective traits, including g, are not much different from the day-to-day demands of modern societies. If social cooperation and competition were the driving forces in the evolution of this nexus, as Alexander (1989) proposed, then the core social dynamics that contributed to human evolution are no different than social dynamics today (Caporael, 1997). To be sure, the nuances of these dynamics may differ from one culture or historical period to the next, but the same male–female, parent–offspring, and other common relationships that I describe in chapter 3 are found in modern societies today, as well as in all other societies (D. E. Brown, 1991). The motivation to control is focused, in part, on organizing these relationships and the behavior of other people in ways that are consistent with one's best interests. People are also motivated to gain control of biological and physical resources, which include food, medicine, and shelter, and in most traditional contexts these resources are concrete (e.g., cows). In modern societies, resources are symbolic (e.g., money or stocks) but are important because they enable access to and control of concrete biological and physical resources and enhance the ability to influence the behavior of other people. At this level, the struggle for resource control is no different in modern societies than in traditional societies or throughout human evolution.

If the nexus of traits associated with the motivation to control was indeed driven by social competition and perhaps to a lesser extent pressures associated with ecological dominance (e.g., hunting), then these traits have evolved to cope with variant and unpredictable social behaviors and other variable conditions, as noted earlier. The associated variation creates conditions that favor the evolution of brain and cognitive systems that can be adapted during the individual's life span. The evolved function of the autonoetic mental models that I describe in chapter 7 is to anticipate, mentally represent, and devise behavioral responses to these variant conditions. Fluid intelligence and the cognitive components (e.g., working memory) represent an essential part of these models and are key to understanding the adaptation of modular systems for academic and occupational learning and thus the ability to compete in modern societies. I also emphasize that general intelligence is only one of many components of the motivation-to-control nexus and is thus predicted to explain a portion, but not all, of the individual differences in the ability to compete in the modern world. Other components include individual differences in modular competencies (Gardner, 1983), self-awareness (Tulving, 1985, 2002), and sensitivity to affective states in other people and oneself (Damasio, 2003).

General Intelligence and Social Outcomes

It has been well established that performance on IQ tests and other measures of *g* are correlated with an array of life's outcomes (Herrnstein &

Murray, 1994; Jensen, 1998; Lubinski, 2000). I cannot review and analyze all of these correlates and thus focus only on educational attainment, occupational status, and income. In combination, these define socioeconomic status (SES), which in turn provides a widely used index of social status in modern societies. General intelligence is the best single predictor of academic achievement currently available (Walberg, 1984), explaining roughly 50% of the individual differences in academic test scores and grades. General intelligence is also the best single predictor of years of schooling completed (Jensen, 1998) and of occupational status and job-related performance across the broad swath of jobs in modern societies (Gottfredson, 1997; Hunter & Hunter, 1984; Schmidt & Hunter, 1998). Outcomes in these areas are also influenced by motivational, personality, family, and general social conditions, but the importance of *g* cannot be refuted.

On average, more intelligent individuals obtain more schooling than other people, and those with more schooling enter higher-status and better-paying occupations more easily than other people. Studies that have simultaneously examined these relations indicate that both intelligence and schooling make independent contributions to occupational status (e.g., Scullin, Peters, Williams, & Ceci, 2000; Webb, Lubinski, & Benbow, 2002). Intelligence is also moderately correlated with wages, even for individuals with the same level of education (Ceci & Williams, 1997; Murray, 2002). The relation between IQ and wages appears to be due to the relation between IQ and educational outcomes, as well as between IQ and job-related performance (Gottfredson, 1997). When all is said and done, high fluid intelligence makes it easier to obtain the education needed to enter high-status and high-paying occupations and then to excel in these occupations.

Academic Learning

If the evolution of the components of autonoetic mental models, including fluid intelligence, was driven by social competition and the associated need to cope with variant and unpredictable conditions, then the evolved function of these models is to identify, anticipate, represent, and reason about evolutionarily novel information patterns. The components of fluid intelligence, especially working memory and attentional control, appear to be at the core of the ability to anticipate, represent, and reason about these patterns, and thus they are the keys to understanding how humans can construct novel cognitive competencies, such as reading, writing, and the ability to understand Newtonian physics. In other words, the evolution of fluid intelligence, though driven by social competition, opened the door to the ability to develop evolutionarily novel competencies during the life span (Geary, 1995; Rozin, 1976).

Support for this hypothesis comes from detailed studies of the relation between fluid intelligence and the cognitive (Ackerman, 1988) and neural

(Duncan & Owen, 2000) changes that occur during the process of learning. I make several proposals as to how the cognitive (e.g., working memory) and brain (e.g., the dorsolateral prefrontal cortex) mechanisms that compose fluid intelligence operate to construct evolutionarily novel competencies. However, fluid intelligence is involved only during the initial phase of learning: The fully developed competencies appear to reside in a network of cognitive and brain systems that differ from those that support gF (Gevins & Smith, 2000; Raichle et al., 1994). This network of systems represents one of the two classes of crystallized intelligence, or gC, I propose in chapter 8, specifically knowledge constructed during the individual's lifetime. Knowledge construction is possible because inherent modular systems evince some degree of plasticity and because independent modular systems can be interconnected to form unique neural networks and functional competencies (Edelman, 1987; Garlick, 2002; Sporns, Tononi, & Edelman, 2000). I discuss how fluid intelligence might interact with this plasticity in the construction of novel competencies.

I close the chapter with some thoughts on motivational issues as related to the pursuit of learning in evolutionarily novel contexts. I tie this to the domains of folk knowledge and suggest that these were the foundation for human intellectual history. As examples, Darwin's and Wallace's (1858) initial understanding of and interest in the biological world was almost certainly based on inherent, folk biological knowledge. They, of course, went well beyond this knowledge and did so using the problem-solving, reasoning, inference-making, and other explicit mechanisms—components of autonoetic mental models—described in chapter 6. The point is that human intellectual history emerged from and developed around the social, biological, and physical folk domains and did so because humans are inherently motivated to pursue understanding in these domains. The minority of individuals who push scientific, technological, and intellectual boundaries beyond folk knowledge create a knowledge gap.

One result of this gap is an accompanying change in the type and level of academic competency needed to live successfully (e.g., gainful employment) in the society in which these advances emerged. Today, there is an ever-widening gap between folk knowledge and scientific and technological advances and a corresponding increase in the need for people to acquire novel academic competencies. A crucial implication for education is that folk knowledge, though necessary, is no longer sufficient for occupational and social functioning (e.g., understanding interest on debt) in modern society. I illustrate the importance of this gap with discussion of the relation between evolved motivational biases to learn in folk domains and children's motivation, or lack thereof, to learn in school.

2

NATURAL AND SEXUAL SELECTION

To fully understand the evolution of brain, cognition, and g, a brief foray into the mechanisms of natural and sexual selection is necessary. The necessity arises because many social scientists are unfamiliar with the theoretical elegance of Darwin's (1859, 1871) seminal contributions and the considerable supporting evidence amassed during past decades (Endler, 1986; Kingsolver et al., 2001). At the same time, natural selection and sexual selection are the mechanisms that have driven the evolution of brain, cognition, and g, and thus description of the associated classes of selection pressure provides the foundation for subsequent chapters. For now, I will consider the basics of natural and sexual selection in the first and second sections, respectively.

NATURAL SELECTION

Mechanisms

The fundamental observations and inferences that led to Charles Darwin's and Alfred Wallace's (1858; Darwin, 1859) insights regarding natural selection and evolutionary change are shown in Table 2.1. Of particular importance are individual differences, which largely are a consequence of sexual reproduction (Hamilton & Zuk, 1982; Williams, 1975)

TABLE 2.1
Darwin's and Wallace's Observations and Inferences

Observation	Inference
1. All species have such high potential fertility that populations should increase exponentially.	More individuals are born than can be supported by available resources, resulting in competition for those resources that covary with survival prospects.
2. Except for minor annual and rare major fluctuations, population size is typically stable.	
3. Natural resources are limited, and in a stable environment they remain constant.	
1. No two individuals are exactly the same; populations have great variability.	1. Prospects for survival are not random but covary with the heritable characteristics (genetics) of individuals. The resulting differential survival is natural selection.
2. Much of this variability, or individual differences, is heritable.	2. Over generations, natural selection leads to gradual change in the population—that is, microevolution—and production of new species—that is, macroevolution or speciation.

Note. Observations and inferences are based on Darwin and Wallace (1858), Darwin (1859), and Mayr (1982). Although genetics were not yet understood, Darwin inferred that traits were passed from parent to offspring through, among other things, what was then known about the effects of selective breeding (artificial selection) on the emergence of various domestic species.

and to a lesser degree mutations (Crow, 1997). Whatever the cause, heritable individual differences are the backbone upon which selection acts and evolutionary change occurs.

As illustrated in Figure 2.1, the process is a simple yet powerful mechanism of change (Dennett, 1995). The first component is the heritability of the trait, namely the degree to which individual differences in the trait are influenced by individual differences in the genes that influence the expression of the trait. The second component is the strength of the relation between individual differences in the trait and individual differences in social (e.g., finding a mate) or ecological (e.g., finding food) outcomes that covary with survival or reproductive prospects (G. R. Price, 1970). The strength of selection and the rapidity of evolutionary change are determined by the product of these two components. As an example, if the trait has a heritability (h^2) estimate of 0.25, then 25% of the individual differences in the trait are due to variation in the associated genes (Plomin, DeFries, McClearn, & McGuffin, 2001), and if the strength of the relation between individual differences in the trait and survival prospects is 0.20 (in standard deviation [SD] units), then the strength of evolutionary selection is 0.05 (.25 × .20). Although this latter value seems small, it will result in a 1 SD

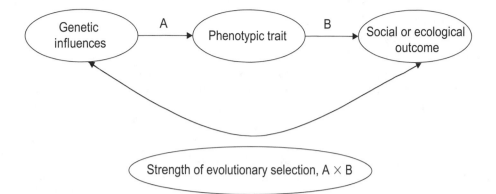

Figure 2.1. Evolution of a trait occurs when two conditions are present. First, individual differences in the trait must have a heritable component, represented by line A. Second, individual differences in the trait must covary with individual differences in survival or reproductive outcomes, represented by line B. The strength of evolutionary change is the product (A × B) of these two components.

change in the trait in 20 generations ($20 \times .05 = 1$), but only if these relations hold for all 20 generations.

Sometimes the adaptive advantage of a trait is so consistent and strong that heritable variability is eliminated, as with bipedal locomotion in humans (i.e., all genetically normal humans have two legs, an inherited but nonvariable trait). However, for a variety of reasons, many of the traits that covary with survival or reproductive outcomes show small to moderate heritable variability and are thus continually subject to evolutionary change (see Roff, 1992, for discussion of why heritable variability is maintained). Mousseau's and Roff's (1987) comprehensive review of the heritable variability of life history (e.g., age of maturation), physiological (e.g., cardiovascular capacity), behavioral (e.g., mating displays), and morphological (e.g., body size) traits provided an assessment of the first component shown in Figure 2.1 (i.e., line A) for 75 invertebrate and vertebrate species. Although there was considerable variability across species, contexts, and traits in the magnitude of the heritability estimate, the analysis indicated that "significant genetic variance is maintained within most natural populations, even for traits closely affiliated with fitness" (Mousseau & Roff, 1987, p. 188). Across species, the median heritability values were 0.26 for life history traits, 0.27 for physiological traits, 0.32 for behavioral traits, and 0.53 for morphological traits.

An analysis of the second component shown in Figure 2.1 (i.e., line B) was provided by Kingsolver and colleagues' (2001) review of field studies of the relation between the types of traits that Mousseau and Roff (1987) analyzed and survival and reproductive outcomes (see Sexual Selection and Social Dynamics section) in wild populations (see also Endler, 1986). Across species and traits, the median effect size—that is, the correlation between individual differences in the trait and individual differences in the survival or reproductive outcome—indicated that being one standard deviation above (e.g., later maturation) or below (e.g., earlier maturation) the mean was associated with a 16% increase in survival (e.g., probability of surviving to the next breeding season) or reproductive (e.g., number of offspring) fitness. If the heritability of any such trait was only 0.25, "then selection of this magnitude would cause the trait to change by one standard deviation in only 25 generations" (Conner, 2001, p. 216), or in 12 to 13 generations with a heritability of 0.50. A human trait with a heritability of 0.50 and a fitness advantage of 0.16 could, if selection acted in the same direction across generations, result in a one standard deviation change in the mean of the trait in about 300 years.

The basic point is that the principles of natural selection that Darwin and Wallace (1858; Darwin, 1859) discovered have been empirically evaluated in many species and for many different traits. It has been demonstrated that many of these traits fit the pattern of relations shown in Figure 2.1, namely that the traits both show heritable variability and covary with survival and reproductive outcomes and therefore exhibit the conditions necessary for evolutionary change.

Climatic and Ecological Selection Pressures

The second component shown in Figure 2.1 (i.e., line B) represents an integral coupling of heritable variation in a given trait and variation in social and ecological outcomes. Although the arrows in the figure point from genetic influences to social and ecological outcomes, the coupling can also be viewed as moving in the other direction. When the ecology changes, the usefulness of the trait may change as well, potentially gaining or losing advantage. Whatever direction the relations are viewed in, one of the clearest empirical documentations of a coupling of ecological change and trait evolution—natural selection—is provided by the work of Peter and Rosemary Grant (B. R. Grant & Grant, 1989, 1993; P. R. Grant & Grant, 2002a, 2002b). For more than 30 years, the Grants have been studying the relation between ecological change on two Galápagos islands—Daphne Major and Genovesa—and change in the survival rates and physical characteristics of several species of finch that reside on these islands, often called Darwin's finches. In addition to demonstrating a relation between climatic and ecological variation and evolutionary change, research on Darwin's finches also illustrates two important concepts—natural selection acting on variability to create within-species change (microevolution) and speciation or adaptive radiation (macroevolution).

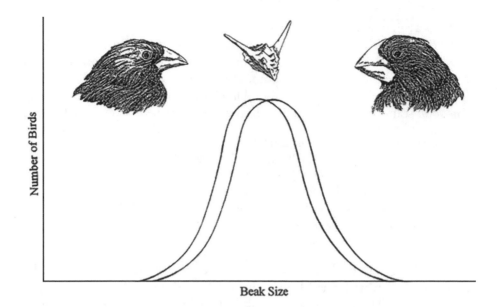

Figure 2.2. Cross-generational change in average beak size in the medium ground finch (*Geospiza fortis*). Illustration by Christopher Nadolski.

Variation and Natural Selection

Studies of the medium ground finch (*Geospiza fortis*), a species that resides on Daphne Major, illustrate how variability in a trait can covary with survival and reproductive outcomes and thus evolve. Figure 2.2 shows that individual medium ground finches naturally vary in beak size; differences are moderately to highly heritable for beak length ($h^2 = 0.65$), depth ($h^2 = 0.79$), and width ($h^2 = 0.90$; Boag, 1983; Boag & Grant, 1978). To the left is an individual with a relatively small beak, and to the right is an individual of the same age and sex with a relatively large beak. The distributions show that the beak size of most individuals falls between these two extremes.

When food (e.g., seeds, insects) is plentiful and varied, there is little relation between beak size and survival prospects. Under these conditions, the value of the second component in Figure 2.1 (i.e., line B) is close to 0.0, and thus natural selection does not operate on beak size. When food is scarce, however, the value of this component becomes larger than 0.0, because the size and shape of an individual's beak determines which foods it can eat and which foods it cannot (B. R. Grant & Grant, 1993). Individual birds that can specialize in abundant food sources because of beak size and shape survive in greater numbers than do individuals whose beak size and shape force them to specialize in a scarce food source. As an example, in 1973 a drought on Daphne Major resulted in an 84% decline in the quantity of foods available to Darwin's finches and a sharp increase in finch mortality. One of the relatively plentiful foods was the seeds of the caltrop plant (*Tribulus cistoides*). These seeds are encased in mericarps, shown in the center of Figure 2.2, which are armored with spikes and relatively large, at least for a finch. Some medium ground finches, or *fortis*, were able to exploit this food source, whereas others were not. As described by Weiner (1995),

> *fortis* with bigger beaks can crack the mericarp and gouge out the seeds faster than those with smaller beaks. Tiny variations are everything. A *fortis* with a beak 11 millimeters long can crack caltrop; a *fortis* with a beak only 10.5 millimeters long will not even try. "The smallest grain in the balance" can decide who shall live and who shall die. Between a beak big enough to crack caltrop and a beak that can't, the difference is only half a millimeter. (p. 64)

For Darwin's finches, life or death depended greatly on beak size. To make matters worse, small-beaked males that survived were at a mating disadvantage. These males were weaker than their better-fed large-beaked peers, which appeared to result in a difference in the vigor of their courtship displays. Female medium ground finches choose mates based on the vigor of these displays and thus preferred large-beaked males. The combination of differential survival rates and female choice (see Sexual Selection and Social Dynamics section) resulted in a measurable shift in the next generation's average beak size, as illustrated in Figure 2.2. The left distribution represents the beak size characteristics before the drought, and the right distribution represents these characteristics after the drought. Just after the drought, individual differences in beak size were still evident, but the average beak size increased, and there were fewer individuals with extremely small beaks and more individuals with extremely large beaks.

Having a beak that is larger than average is not, however, inherently better than having a beak that is smaller than average. It is beneficial only during periods of drought, that is, when foods available to small-beaked individuals become scarce. In 1982 to 1983, an especially strong El Niño event resulted in a 14-fold increase in rainfall on Daphne Major (B. R. Grant & Grant, 1993). Following this heavy rainfall, the number of caltrop plants and their mericarps decreased significantly, and the number of smaller seeds available on the island increased significantly. Small-beaked individuals were able to handle seeds more deftly than their large-beaked peers. The result was that small-beaked individuals survived in greater numbers than did large-beaked individuals, and small-beaked males were preferred as mating partners. After several generations of differential survival and mating success, the average beak size of medium ground finches was now smaller than it was just after the drought—the distribution had shifted back to the left (for an overview of the entire study, see P. R. Grant & Grant, 2002b).

Adaptive Radiation and Speciation

In the Daphne Major study, cross-generational changes in average beak size and shape were coupled to cross-generational changes in the distribution of available foods and with mating dynamics. Over the course of 30 years and seven generations, the evolutionary effects were significant reductions in the body size of medium ground finches and a significant change in beak shape, from somewhat blunted to moderately pointed (P. R. Grant & Grant, 2002b). These adaptations resulted in microevolutionary (i.e., within-species) changes in the medium ground finch such that the average individual in the population looked, in terms of body size and beak shape, somewhat different than did the average individual seven generations earlier. In other cases, sustained and directional (i.e., having the same effect such as favoring large beaks) selection, often combined with geographic isolation, can result in a single species diverging into two or more separate but related species, a process termed *macroevolution, speciation,* or *adaptive radiation*. Confirming Darwin's (1846) early speculation, recent DNA studies suggest that all 13 species of Darwin's finch arose during the past 3 million years from a single ancestral species that originated from the South American mainland (P. R. Grant, 1999; Petren, Grant, & Grant, 1999; Sato et al., 1999).

To envision how multiple species can evolve from a single species, consider again the two medium ground finches depicted in Figure 2.2. It is easy to imagine medium ground finches at the two extremes of the distribution consistently specializing in different foods. After many generations of such specializations, the evolutionary emergence of three distinct species is possible. In fact, such a process readily explains the three species of ground finch that currently reside on the Galápagos islands, that is, small (G. *fuliginosa*), medium, and large (G. *magnirostris*) ground finches (Petren et al., 1999). These species specialize in different sources of food and, in addition to body size, differ primarily in beak size and shape, the morphological specializations that allow them to exploit one type of food source or another. However, there is some overlap in the beak sizes of these related species. There is no overlap in the distribution of beak sizes of small and large ground finches, but the beak sizes of the smallest medium ground finches overlap those of the largest small ground finches. The beak sizes of the largest medium ground finches overlap those of the smallest large ground finches. These overlapping distributions are exactly what would be expected for species with a very recent common ancestor. In other words, the distributions of beak size in the three species of ground finch are understandable in terms of a common ancestor that was likely similar in size to the medium ground finch, with the large and small ground finches evolving from the tails, so to speak, of the distribution of medium ground finches. I elaborate on this and describe how Darwin and Wallace discovered the mechanisms of natural selection in the Controlled Problem Solving section of chapter 6.

Social Selection Pressures

In the same way that climate-driven changes in food availability influenced the evolution of body size and beak morphology in Darwin's finches, competition among members of the same species (i.e., conspecifics) can result in natural and sexual selection acting on traits that facilitate this competition to the extent that these traits covary with survival or reproductive outcomes (Mayr, 1974). One of the best examples of how such social competition can influence evolutionary outcomes is provided by the coalitional behavior of females of many species of Old World (Africa and Asia) monkey (Wrangham, 1980).

Coalitional behavior is most common in species in which high quality food sources, such as fruit trees, are clustered in one or a few locations (Sterck, Watts, & van Schaik, 1997). In these species, related females cooperate with one another to compete with other female kin groups for access to and control of these high quality food sources. The most common outcome is that larger and thus socially dominant matrilineal coalitions are able to gain access to these foods. The combination of social dominance—associated with the ability to influence the behavior of conspecifics—and better nutrition results in increased survival rates for individuals of successful coalitions and significant changes in reproductive patterns. In comparison to females in less successful coalitions, females in dominant coalitions mature earlier and have shorter interbirth intervals, and their offspring have higher survival rates (Silk, 1993). The result is significantly higher lifetime reproductive success for dominant as opposed to subordinate females.

Given the strong coupling between coalitional dominance and this array of survival and reproductive outcomes, selection will perforce favor individuals with the social and cognitive competencies needed to develop, maintain, and successfully use such coalitions (e.g., Bergman, Beehner, Cheney, & Seyfarth, 2003). Moreover, Silk, Alberts, and Altmann (2003) demonstrated that within matrilineal coalitions, the infants of female baboons (*Papio cynocephalus*) with larger social networks (e.g., as indicated by grooming) have higher survival rates than the infants of more socially isolated mothers. Stated somewhat differently, the survival and reproductive advantages associated with between- and within-coalitional behavior create a social ecology that influences the evolution of social competencies (Dunbar, 1993, 2003), just as the foraging ecology (i.e., available foods) influences the evolution of beak morphology in Darwin's finches.

Many features of this social ecology can influence the evolution of social and sociocognitive (e.g., attention to facial expressions of conspecifics)

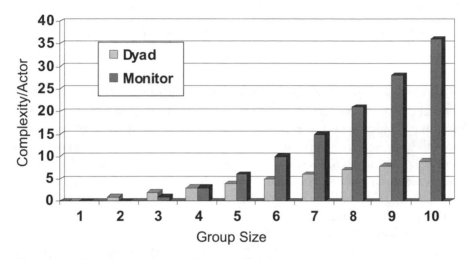

Figure 2.3. Social and sociocognitive (e.g., facial recognition) demands increase with increases in group size. The top half represents the actor and the number of potential relationships that he or she could develop in three-person and four-person groups, represented by the solid lines. The dashed lines represent the number of other dyadic relationships the actor must potentially monitor. The bottom half shows that as group size increases, the number of potential dyadic relationships the actor might enter increases linearly and the number of dyadic relationships the actor might monitor increases exponentially (see also Exhibit 2.1).

competencies (Dunbar, 1998). One of these features is coalition size, given that larger coalitions are better able to gain access to and control of essential resources and are better able to influence mating and other social dynamics. As shown in Figure 2.3 and Exhibit 2.1, the social and presumably sociocognitive demands of developing and maintaining coalitional relationships increase dramatically as group size increases. The potential number of dyadic relationships each individual could develop increases with each additional group member, and the number of other dyadic relationships the individual must potentially monitor increases exponentially. Not all other dyadic relationships are monitored, of course, but relationships associated with within-

At the most basic level, social complexity is determined by (a) the number of dyadic relationships in which the actor (shaded in Figure 2.3) is engaged and (b) the number of other relationships the actor must monitor. The latter refers to all dyadic relationships in which the actor is not directly engaged.

As an example, consider the top section of Figure 2.3. In a three-actor group, each actor is engaged in two dyadic relationships (solid lines) and must monitor one other relationship (dashed line). In a four-actor group, each actor is engaged in three dyadic relationships and must monitor up to three other relationships.

As shown in the bottom section of Figure 2.3, the number of potential dyadic relationships grows linearly with group size, whereas the number of other relationships the actor must potentially monitor grows more rapidly. Algebraically, the number of dyadic relationships is group size $(n) - 1$, the number of other relationships is $0.5n^2 - 1.5n + 1$, and the total number of dyadic and monitored relationships is $0.5n^2 - 0.5n$.

coalition social politics and furtive mating typically are (de Waal, 1982; Goodall, 1986). As an example of the latter, it is common for socially dominant males to monitor the social activities of females and other males, and they typically disrupt any resulting dyads (e.g., a male grooming a female). In addition to such within-group relationships, sociocognitive competencies, such as those needed to coordinate the defense of valued resources (e.g., a fruit tree), are needed to support the cooperative behavior associated with coalitional competition.

It follows that under conditions in which coalitions enable greater access to resources that covary with survival prospects and reproductive success, the supporting social and sociocognitive competencies will evolve (Dunbar, 1993). In keeping with this prediction, comparative studies indicate that species that form complex social groups tend to have a larger neocortex, more complex sociocognitive competencies, and a longer developmental period than do evolutionarily related species that are more solitary (Barton, 1996; D. A. Clark, Mitra, & Wang, 2001; Dunbar, 1993; Joffe, 1997; Kudo & Dunbar, 2001; M. L. Wilson, Hauser, & Wrangham, 2001). The general pattern is found for species that form long-term and highly interdependent social relationships and engage in some level of coalitional behavior and is not related to simple social proximity (Dunbar & Bever, 1998). The latter refers to herding, which is presumably related to decreased predation risk (T. Clutton-Brock & McComb, 1993).

SEXUAL SELECTION AND SOCIAL DYNAMICS

Sexual selection involves the social dynamics that define the species' reproductive activities (Darwin, 1871). To the extent that these activities involve social manipulation, deception, and coalitional activities, sexual selection is an important influence on brain and cognitive evolution (e.g., Sawaguchi, 1997). The implications for understanding the evolution of brain and cognition in hominids are described in the Social Pressures section of chapter 3. My goal in this section is to provide a primer on the basics of sexual selection—specifically, the processes associated with competition for mates, termed *intrasexual competition*, and those associated with choosing mates, termed *intersexual choice* (see Andersson, 1994; Darwin, 1871; Geary, 1998).

Mating or Parenting?

As shown in Figure 2.4, reproductive activities are distributed across mating and parenting, as well as nepotism (e.g., aiding siblings or cousins) in some species (Emlen, 1995). The key to understanding why males and females distribute reproductive behavior across mating and parenting is the biology of parental investment (Trivers, 1972; Williams, 1966). *Parental investment* is any cost (e.g., time) associated with raising offspring that reduces parents' ability to produce or invest in other offspring (Trivers, 1974), and the nature of this investment creates the basic dynamics of sexual reproduction and sexual selection.

The bottom line is that if one sex provides a larger parental investment, then members of that sex become an important reproductive resource for members of the opposite sex. The reproductive success of members of the lower investing sex is more strongly related to the number of mating partners than to care of individual offspring, whereas the reproductive success of members of the higher investing sex is more strongly influenced by care of offspring than by number of mating partners. Sex differences in the degree to which reproductive effort is allocated to competition for mates or to

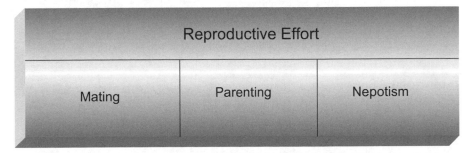

Figure 2.4. Reproductive effort is distributed between mating effort (e.g., competing for mates), parental effort (e.g., provisioning and protecting offspring), and in some species nepotism (i.e., behaviors that aid the survival or reproductive prospects of more distant relatives, such as cousins).

parental investment are found in the vast majority of species (Andersson, 1994; Geary, 1998; Trivers, 1972; Williams, 1966). These differences, in turn, are related to the potential rate of reproduction and to social and ecological influences on mating opportunities. These influences are discussed elsewhere and thus will not be detailed here (T. H. Clutton-Brock & Vincent, 1991; Emlen & Oring, 1977; Geary, 2000, in press; Krebs & Davies, 1993).

The basic points are that the sex with the higher potential rate of reproduction typically invests more in mating effort than in parental effort, whereas the sex with the lower rate of reproduction invests more in parental effort than in mating effort (T. H. Clutton-Brock & Vincent, 1991). The pattern arises because members of the sex with the higher potential rate of reproduction can rejoin the mating pool more quickly than can members of the opposite sex, and it is often in their reproductive best interest to do so (G. A. Parker & Simmons, 1996). For species with internal gestation and obligatory postpartum female care, as with mammals, the rate with which females can produce offspring is considerably lower than the potential reproductive rate of males (T. H. Clutton-Brock, 1991). Internal gestation and the need for postnatal care result in a strong bias in mammalian females toward parental investment and in a sex difference in the benefits of seeking additional mates (Trivers, 1972). Males can benefit from seeking and obtaining additional mates, whereas females cannot. Thus, the sex difference in reproductive rate, combined with offspring that can be effectively raised by the female, creates the potential for large female–male differences in the mix of mating and parenting, and this difference is realized in more than 95% of mammalian species (T. H. Clutton-Brock, 1989).

Social and ecological factors can also influence the potential rate of reproduction. As an example, male callitrichid monkeys (*Callithrix*) have a higher potential rate of reproduction than conspecific females do. However, shared territorial defense, female-on-female aggression that drives away the males' potential mating partners, the frequent birth of twins, and other factors negate this physiologically based sex difference and result in monogamy and high levels of paternal investment (see Dunbar, 1995; Saltzman, 2003).

Intrasexual Competition

Competition over mates, whether it is male–male competition or female–female competition, is an integral feature of the social dynamics of most species. The dynamics arise when members of one sex compete with one another for control of the reproductive potential (e.g., resources provided to offspring) of members of the opposite sex. In many cases this dynamic simply translates into competition for mating privileges. In most mammals, this involves male–male competition over sexual access to females. The result is that successful males monopolize the sexual behavior of females that, in turn, provide high levels of parental care to resulting offspring. Thus, on an abstract level intrasexual competition is ultimately about capturing the reproductive potential of members of the opposite sex.

Sex differences in the traits supporting intrasexual competition evolve to the extent that capturing the reproductive potential of members of the opposite sex requires different social and behavioral strategies for females and males (Andersson, 1994; Darwin, 1871). Studies of intrasexual competition have revealed that the associated traits can be physical, behavioral, social, cognitive, or neural and commonly affect only those traits that facilitate competitive ability (Andersson, 1994; Geary, 1998). One of the more common expressions of intrasexual competition involves physical threats and fights over access to mates or for control of the territory that members of the opposite sex need to raise offspring (e.g., nesting spots) competition that can be one-on-one or coalitional.

One-on-One Competition

Physical one-on-one intrasexual competition is very common across species of insect, fish, reptile, and mammal and occurs more frequently among males than females (Andersson, 1994). The typical result is that physically larger, healthier, and more aggressive males monopolize the reproductive potential of the majority of conspecific females. The accompanying individual differences in reproductive success—some individuals have many offspring, others few or none—result in the evolution of sex differences in physical size, armament and weaponry, and behavioral aggressiveness. A few examples of this form of evolved sex difference are shown in Figure 2.5. More relevant to the current discussion is competition that is highly dependent on cognitive competencies (e.g., spatial cognition, as in searching for mates; Gaulin & Fitzgerald, 1986, 1989; Gilliard, 1969). In these situations, cognitive and associated behavioral traits that facilitate intrasexual competition evolve in the same way that the physical traits shown in Figure 2.5 evolved (Geary, 1998).

Gaulin and Fitzgerald (1986, 1989; Gaulin, 1992) provided one of the best-documented examples of the influence of intrasexual competition on the evolution of cognitive sex differences; bird song is another example (Ball & Hulse, 1998; Hauser, 1996). The approach in Gaulin's studies was to compare evolutionarily related species—those with a recent common ancestor—of voles (small rodents, *Microtus*). The comparison of species with a recent common ancestor is a common approach in evolutionary biology and is important because existing differences across related species cannot be attributed to their distant evolutionary history. Rather, these

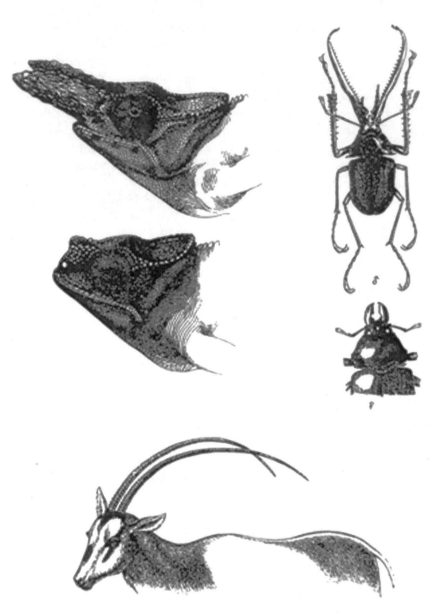

Figure 2.5. Examples of sexually selected characteristics used in physical male–male competition. To the upper left are the male (top) and female (bottom) of the *Chamaeleon bifurcus,* to the upper right are the male and female of the beetle *Chiasognathus grantii,* and at the bottom is a male *Oryx leucoryx,* a species of antelope. From *The Descent of Man, and Selection in Relation to Sex,* by C. Darwin, 1871, London: John Murray, p. 35, Vol. 2; p. 377, Vol. 1; and p. 251, Vol. 2, respectively.

differences are more likely to reflect current differences in reproductive strategy or adaptations to different social or ecological niches (see also the Evolution and Brain Organization section of chap. 4). The primary difference across these species of vole is that some are monogamous and some polygynous. By comparing related species of monogamous and polygynous voles, Gaulin and Fitzgerald studied the effects of sexual selection, which operates more strongly in polygynous species (Andersson, 1994), on sex differences in spatial cognition and at least one underlying brain region.

In the polygynous meadow vole (*Microtus pennsylvanicus*), males compete with one another by searching for and attempting to mate with females, who are dispersed throughout the habitat, rather than competing through physical contest. Prairie and pine voles (*Microtus ochrogaster, Microtus pinetorum*), in comparison, are monogamous, and males do not search for additional mates once paired. For meadow voles, intrasexual competition—through differential reproduction—will favor males who court the most females, which is possible only through an expansion of the home range. This form of male–male competition should, in theory, result in larger home ranges for male than female meadow voles, but no such sex difference should be evident in prairie or pine voles. Indeed, field studies indicated that male meadow voles have home ranges that cover 4 to 5 times the area of the home ranges of females, but only during the breeding season and only in adulthood (Gaulin, 1992; Gaulin & Fitzgerald, 1986). The latter pattern indicates that the sex difference in the size of the home range is related to the reproductive strategy of the male (i.e., searching for females) and suggests that this difference is mediated by sex hormones. As predicted, the home ranges of male and female prairie and pine voles overlap and do not differ in size (Gaulin & Fitzgerald, 1986).

The sex difference in the size of the home range means that male meadow voles should have better developed spatial abilities—abilities needed for navigation—than female meadow voles and male prairie and pine voles. Moreover, there should be no sex difference in the spatial abilities of monogamous prairie and pine voles. A series of laboratory and field studies confirmed these predictions. The polygynous male meadow vole showed better navigational skills than conspecific females and better navigational skills than males of evolutionarily related monogamous species (Gaulin, 1992; Gaulin & Fitzgerald, 1986, 1989). An equally important finding is that this same pattern of differences was found for the overall and relative volume of the hippocampus, which supports spatial cognition, among other cognitive abilities (L. F. Jacobs, Gaulin, Sherry, & Hoffman, 1990). The hippocampus of male meadow voles is larger than that of female meadow voles and larger than that of male prairie and pine voles.

Although these examples focused on male–male competition, the same effect is evident for female–female competition: Intrasexual competition results in the evolutionary elaboration and a hormonally influenced proximate expression of those traits associated with the competition, whether the traits are physical, behavioral, cognitive and neural, or some combination (Andersson, 1994; Geary, 1998; J. D. Reynolds, 1987; J. D. Reynolds & Székely, 1997). In addition to sexual selection, natural selection can also influence the evolution of brain and cognition and sometimes results in the evolution of sex differences in these domains.

Studies of the brown-headed cowbird (*Molothrus ater ater*) nicely illustrate this point (Sherry, Forbes, Khurgel, & Ivy, 1993). Brown-headed cowbirds are brood parasites—that is, females lay their eggs in the nests of other species that then hatch and feed the cowbird nestlings. Female cowbirds must use the home range in more complex ways than male cowbirds, because the females must locate suitable hosts for their eggs. Moreover, many hosts will accept cowbird eggs only after they have started laying eggs of their own. Thus, female cowbirds not only need to locate potential hosts but also must remember their locations and return to them at a suitable time. The sex difference in the spatial demands of reproduction should then result in a larger hippocampus in female relative to male cowbirds. This is exactly the pattern that Sherry and his colleagues (1993) found. As with voles, no sex differences in hippocampal size were found for species of bird that are evolutionarily related to the cowbird but whose males and females share a home range (e.g., red-winged blackbirds, *Agelaius phoeniceus*).

Coalitional Competition

In addition to competition for high quality foods, the evolution of coalitionary behavior can also be related to intrasexual competition (Wrangham, 1999). Two well-studied examples are the lion (*Panthera leo*) and the chimpanzee (*Pan troglodytes*). Just as beak size covaries with survival and reproductive outcomes in Darwin's finches, coalitional behavior covaries with the reproductive prospects of males of these two species.

To reproduce, male "coalitions must compete successfully against other coalitions in order to gain and retain residence in prides. . . . Larger coalitions oust smaller ones from prides and chase nomadic coalitions from their prides' ranges" (Packer et al., 1988, pp. 371–372). The formation of coalitions thus enhances reproductive outcomes in a social ecology where coalition size covaries with access to prides. The primary cost of this form of coalitional behavior is that sexual access to females must be shared among coalitional males, with a corresponding decline in the number of offspring sired by each male. The reproductive costs of coalition formation are, however, reduced if coalition members are related, because two offspring sired by a brother or brothers are genetically equivalent to one offspring sired by the individual; the *inclusive fitness* of each male is determined by the number of his offspring and by how his behavior contributes to the number of offspring sired by each of his brothers (Hamilton, 1964). This leads to a very specific prediction regarding the evolution of coalitionary behavior in lions: Selection should favor individuals who tend to form coalitions with brothers, and this is indeed the case (Packer, Gilbert, Pusey, & O'Brien, 1991). At times, male lions form coalitions with non-kin, but these coalitions tend to be small, as would be expected given the associated reproductive costs (i.e., low genetic relatedness to offspring sired by non-kin males).

The chimpanzee, one of our closest living relatives, provides an example of social dynamics that are more complex than those of the lion (de Waal, 1982; Goodall, 1986). Chimpanzee communities are defined by coalitions of related males that defend a territory against the incursions of other coalitions of male chimpanzees. Situated within this territory are subgroups of females and their offspring (Wrangham, 1986). Although social relationships among females can be quite intense (de Waal, 1993; Pusey, Williams, & Goodall, 1997), the focus here is on the cooperative behavior of male coalitions as related to the sexual politics of intra- and intercommunity relationships (de Waal, 1982; Goodall, 1986). Within communities, small coalitions of males cooperate to achieve social dominance over other coalitions of males, and successful coalitions gain some level of control over the social and sexual behavior of other community members (Mitani, Merriwether, & Zhang, 2000; Riss & Goodall, 1977). The associated activities are largely related to attempts to monopolize sexual access to estrous females (Goodall, 1986).

These smaller coalitions often merge to form larger coalitions that then patrol the border of the territory and make incursions into the territory of neighboring communities (Goodall et al., 1979). When members of such patrols encounter one another, the typical response is pant-hooting (a vocal call) and physical displays on both sides, with the smaller group eventually withdrawing (M. L. Wilson et al., 2001). At other times, meetings between patrols from one group and members of neighboring communities are deadly. Goodall (1986) described a series of such attacks by one community of chimpanzees on their southern neighbor. Over a 4-year period, the southern group was eliminated, one individual at a time, by the northern community. Members of the northern community then expanded their territory to include that of the now extinct southern group. The result for the successful group was the acquisition of prime feeding areas and the recruitment of young females into the community.

As with lions, chimpanzees, and females of many species of Old World monkey, social cooperation and competition covary with survival and reproductive outcomes in other species that tend to form coalitions (e.g., Foley, 1999; Hamilton, 1964; Wrangham, 1999). As I describe in the Sexual Selection and Population Genetics section of chapter 3, there is clear evidence for coalitional male–male competition in humans. For all of these species, coalitional behavior, or any form of social networking, can be readily understood as an aspect of the survival and reproductive strategies of each individual in the coalition, and not as an adaptation for the good of the species or even the wider group (Alexander, 1979; Williams, 1966). This is because individuals of successful coalitions gain survival and reproductive benefits beyond what could be achieved if they acted individually, despite the costs of sharing resources with other coalition members.

Intersexual Choice

The sex that invests more in parenting tends to be more choosy with regard to mating partners than the other sex (Trivers, 1972). Because females tend to invest more in parenting than males, female choice is predicted to be and is more common than male choice (Andersson, 1994). Male choice is predicted for species with paternal investment, although this prediction has not been as thoroughly tested as female choice (see Geary, 2000). In any case, female choice has been studied most extensively in birds but is also evident in some species of insect, fish, reptile, and mammal, including humans (Andersson, 1994; Buss, 1994).

Several examples of male traits that have been shaped by female choice are shown in Figure 2.6; in some species these traits may also be involved in male–male competition, as in dominance displays. These traits often involve elaborate physical displays, such as the long, elaborate tail of the male hummingbird (*Spathura underwoodi*), the crest along the back and tail of the male crested newt (*Triturus cristatus*), and the dorsal fin of the male dragonet (*Callionymus lyra*). In many species, males are often more elaborately colored than are females. Darwin described the male dragonet as having "brilliant gem-like colors . . . the body is yellow of various shades, striped and spotted with vivid blue on the head, [whereas the female] is of a dingy reddish-brown" (Darwin, 1871, Vol. II, p. 8). Traits such as those shown in Figure 2.6 are indicators of the physical, genetic, or behavioral fitness (e.g., ability to provision) of the male. These traits are termed *honest indicators* because they commonly cannot be expressed by unfit males without considerable cost (Zahavi, 1975).

Equally important, female choice can also influence social and behavioral evolution and often intensifies male–male competition. Some of the best examples are provided by studies of bowerbirds (Gilliard, 1969). In about 3 out of 4 of these species, the principal focus of competition and choice is the bower, although courtship displays and calls, as well as physical fights among males, are involved as well (Borgia & Coleman, 2000). Darwin (1871) described the bower of one such species (*Chlamydera maculata*), shown in Figure 2.7. More recently, Borgia and his colleagues have

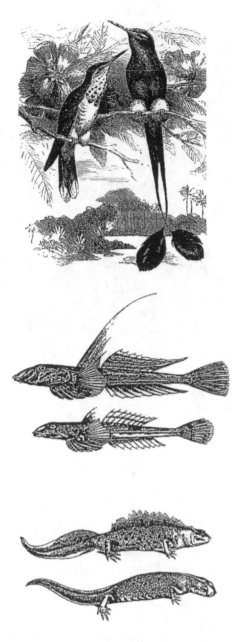

Figure 2.6. Indicators of male fitness shaped by female choice for selected species of bird, fish, and amphibian. At the top are female (left) and male (right) hummingbirds (*Spathura underwoodi*), in the center are male (top) and female (bottom) *Callionymus lyra,* and at the bottom are male (top) and female (bottom) *Triton cristatus* from *The Descent of Man, and Selection in Relation to Sex,* by C. Darwin, 1871, London: John Murray, p. 77, Vol. 2; p. 8, Vol. 2 and p. 24, Vol. 2, respectively.

Figure 2.7. Bower building and behavioral male–male competition in the bowerbird (*Chlamydera maculata*). From *The Descent of Man, and Selection in Relation to Sex,* by C. Darwin, 1871, London: John Murray, p. 70, Vol. 2.

extensively studied the bower building of a related species, the satin bower-bird (*Ptilonorhynchus violaceus*; e.g., Borgia, 1985a, 1985b; Collis & Borgia, 1992). These studies indicate that about 16% of males sire the majority of offspring and that female choice of these males as mating partners is strongly influenced by the complexity and symmetry of the male's bower, as well as by the number of decorations around the bower. The most important point is that the very complex social (e.g., defending the bower from attacks by other males) and behavioral (i.e., bower building) competencies evident in most species of bowerbird are readily understood in terms of the evolutionary mechanisms associated with sexual selection, although developmental in-fluences (e.g., practice of bower building) are important as well.

Sexual Selection and Brain and Cognitive Evolution

The preceding sections illustrate how the complexity of social relation-ships and social competition, such as male–male competition, is influenced by the struggle to reproduce. Darwin (1871) speculated that these features of sexual selection may have contributed to brain and cognitive evolution in primates, and others have elaborated on this proposal (Alexander, 1989; Geary, 1998, 2002c; Geary & Flinn, 2001; Pawlowski, Lowen, & Dunbar, 1998; Sawaguchi, 1997). As noted earlier, there is now consistent evidence for a relation between the complexity of social relationships in general and the size of the neocortex across species of primates and at least some other species, such as carnivores (Dunbar & Bever, 1998). The relation between sexual selection in particular and size of the neocortex has not been as extensively evaluated, although preliminary studies confirm Darwin's prediction. Pawlowski et al. and Sawaguchi found a relation between the intensity of male–male competition and the size of the neocortex across species of primate. Sawaguchi found that the cross-species correlation between relative size of the neocortex (controlling for overall brain size) and indexes of the intensity of male–male competition was quite high (rs = .65 to .66). The specific social, behavioral, and cognitive competencies that drive this relation between brain size and the intensity of male–male competition are not well understood but in theory should include the ability to maintain, monitor (e.g., for sexual fidelity), and manipulate social relationships in ways that facilitate access to estrous females. Observations of the sexual politics of male chimpanzees seem to be consistent with this prediction.

In any case, whenever social competencies—including those associated with female–female competition and maintaining spousal relationships, as with humans—enhance reproductive prospects, the result will be an evolutionary elaboration of these competencies and changes in the supporting brain and cognitive systems. These predictions have not been evaluated, although Geary (1998, 2002c) presented evidence in keeping with the view that female–female competition in humans (see Social Pressures section of chap. 3), which largely involves manipulation of social relationships, has resulted in specific sociocognitive and brain adaptations (e.g., for language fluency).

Although there is much to be learned, the pattern emerging from these studies is that complexity of social relationships, including intensity of social competition over social (e.g., mates) and other (e.g., food) resources, can be an important selective pressure associated with brain and cognitive evolution. I explore the implications for understanding brain and cognitive evolution in hominids in chapter 3 and present a taxonomy of supporting sociocognitive modules in humans in chapter 5.

CONCLUSION

Despite frequent and often heated remonstrations to the contrary, Darwin's (1859, 1871) principles of natural and sexual selection are well understood and have been empirically evaluated and supported through studies of hundreds of species (Andersson, 1994; Kingsolver et al., 2001; Mousseau & Roff, 1987). Whenever individual differences in a physical, developmental (e.g., maturational age), behavioral, or cognitive trait are heritable and covary with survival or reproductive outcomes, evolution of that trait will occur (G. R. Price, 1970). Some of the strongest evidence for the elegance and power of Darwin's principles comes from studies of physical traits that enhance survival prospects (natural selection), as illustrated by the beak size and shape of Darwin's finches, or that enhance reproductive potential (sexual selection), as illustrated by the sex differences shown in Figure 2.5. Although more difficult to study, behavioral and cognitive traits, and supporting brain systems, have also been submitted to evolutionary analyses (e.g., Krebs & Davies, 1993). The results are consistent with the view that these traits are subject to evolutionary modification through the same mechanisms that shape the evolution of physical traits (e.g., Gaulin, 1992).

Regardless of which specific traits are affected, selection pressures are commonly conceived of as climatic, ecological (e.g., food availability), social, or some combination, examples of which were provided in this chapter. There is every reason to believe, and no sound evidence to refute, Darwin's (1871) proposal that similar selection pressures, especially social pressures, were responsible for the evolutionary emergence of humans and our predecessor species (macroevolution) and for microevolutionary changes since the emergence of our species. My focus in the next chapter is on changes in brain size during the evolution of humans and predecessor species and on various models of climatic (e.g., Vrba, 1974, 1975), ecological (e.g., Kaplan, Hill, Lancaster, & Hurtado, 2000), and social (e.g., Alexander, 1989) pressures that may have driven these evolutionary changes.

3

HOMINID EVOLUTION AND THE MOTIVATION TO CONTROL

My goals for this chapter are to apply the principles of natural and sexual selection to questions related to brain and cognitive evolution in humans and our ancestors. In the first section, I focus on hominid evolution—hominids are bipedal apes—and the rapid expansion of brain size with the emergence of *Homo ergaster/erectus* and *H. sapiens* (Ruff, Trinkaus, & Holliday, 1997). In the second section, I provide an analysis and synthesis of the various theories regarding the selection pressures that drove this rapid increase in brain size and outline the basic thesis of the book. Specifically, building on the work of Alexander (1989), Humphrey (1976), and others, I propose that the rapid expansion of brain size can be understood in terms of the emergence of ecological dominance, possibly with *H. ergaster/erectus*, and a resulting shift from a primacy of ecological selection pressures (e.g., food) to social selection pressures. I close the chapter with a motivation-to-control theory that provides a framework for integrating issues related to brain and cognitive evolution with basic motivational, affective, and conscious-psychological systems.

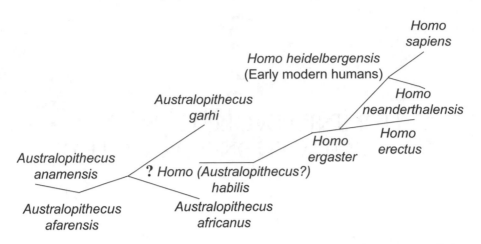

Figure 3.1. Simplified hominid family tree. The ? means that it is not known if the ancestor of *Homo habilis* was *Australopithecus garhi* or *A. africanus*.

HOMINID EVOLUTION

Origins

Although much is known about many of the species comprising the genus *Homo* and the apparent predecessor genus *Australopithecus*, there is controversy with respect to the classification of these species (McHenry, 1994; B. Wood & Collard, 1999). The debates include whether variation in fossils presumed to represent a single species in fact represent two or more species and the evolutionary relatedness of various species (Aiello, 1994; Aiello & Collard, 2001; T. White, 2003; B. Wood, 1992) and are fueled by the continual discovery of new fossils and potentially new hominid species (Asfaw et al., 1999; Haile-Selassie, 2001; Leakey et al., 2001; T. D. White et al., 2003; Zhu et al., 2001). There is, nonetheless, a general consensus with respect to major hominid species and their likely evolutionary relationships, as shown in Figure 3.1. The relations shown in the figure are simplified and do not include all species but still capture the essential pattern of hominid evolution, at least as it is currently understood (B. Wood & Collard, 1999). Of course, the ancestor common to modern humans and our closest living relatives, that is, chimpanzees (*Pan troglodytes*) and bonobos (*P. paniscus*), existed before the emergence of these species. Genetic analyses and the fossil record suggest that this common ancestor existed between 5 and 6 million years ago (e.g., Haile-Selassie, 2001; Horai, Hayasaka, Kondo, Tsugane, & Takahata, 1995).

Radiometric dating of sediments and other materials found with fossils allows for estimations of when the species represented in Figure 3.1 existed.

The results of such studies are represented in Figure 3.2 and suggest that *A. anamensis* existed about 4.0 million years ago and *A. afrarensis* from about 4.0 to 2.8 million years ago (Leakey, Feibel, McDougall, & Walker, 1995; Leakey, Feibel, McDougall, Ward, & Walker, 1998; McHenry, 1994). It was long thought that *A. africanus* was the likely link between *A. afarensis* and the line that eventually led to the evolution of humans, but the recent discovery of a contemporaneous species, *A. garhi*, makes this less certain (Asfaw et al., 1999). In any case, these species existed about 2.5 million years ago, and *A. africanus* existed from about 3.0 to 2.3 million years ago. The place of *H. habilis* in the evolutionary tree is also uncertain. In fact, this species has many features that are more similar to *Australopithecus* than to *Homo* (Dean et al., 2001; B. Wood & Collard, 1999), but in any case it existed from about 2.5 to 1.5 million years ago (B. Wood, 1992). The evolutionary relation of *H. ergaster* and *H. erectus* is debated, with the central issue being whether the associated fossils represent two distinct species or primitive and more advanced specimens of the same species, respectively. Recent evidence suggests that the fossils represent microevolutionary change in the same species, that is, earlier and later forms of the same evolving species (Asfaw et al., 2002).

Either way, *H. ergaster/erectus*, hereafter referred to as *H. erectus*, emerged in eastern Africa about 1.8 million years ago and began to move into Asia and possibly parts of southern Europe (Gabunia et al., 2000; Stringer, 1992). Evidence to date suggests that populations of *H. erectus* evolved into several species, including *H. neanderthalensis* and *H. sapiens* (McHenry, 1994). Although we must await more definitive results, the most recent common ancestor of *H. neanderthalensis* and *H. sapiens* may have existed more than 500,000 years ago (Ovchinnikov et al., 2000; Pääbo, 1999), but this is debated (Wolpoff, Hawks, Frayer, & Hunley, 2001). Genetic analyses suggest that modern humans evolved between 150,000 (Ke et al., 2001; R. Thomson, Pritchard, Shen, Oefner, & Feldman, 2000; Underhill et al., 2001) and roughly 50,000 years ago (Horai et al., 1995; Karafet et al., 1999). Early forms of the species (sometimes designated as *H. heidelbergensis*) appear to have emerged in eastern Africa, then migrated into Asia and later into Europe (Cavalli-Sforza, 1998; Semino et al., 2000; Stringer, 1992; see also T. D. White et al., 2003), although an initial migration by means of a sea route from southern Africa to India and east Asia is also possible (Underhill et al., 2001).

Whatever the migration route, it is important to note that many of our predecessor species, such as *A. afarensis* and *H. erectus*, existed for hundreds of thousands of years (McHenry, 1994), suggesting that these species were well adapted to the ecologies in which they were situated. In fact, *H. erectus* may have survived in some parts of the world until about 26,000 years ago, and Neanderthals survived in portions of Europe until

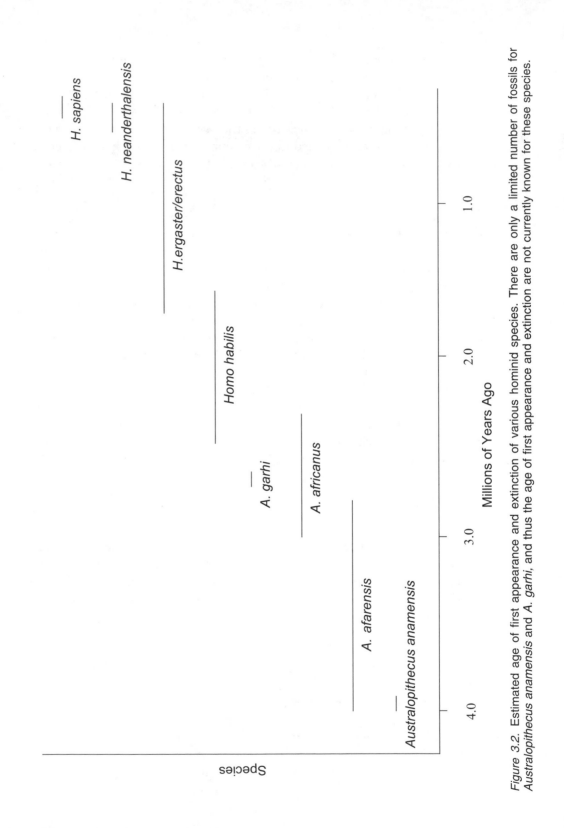

Figure 3.2. Estimated age of first appearance and extinction of various hominid species. There are only a limited number of fossils for *Australopithecus anamensis* and *A. garhi*, and thus the age of first appearance and extinction are not currently known for these species.

about 30,000 years ago (Stringer, 1992; Swisher et al., 1996). Fossils for both of these species have been found in the same geographic areas as fossils of early modern humans, although it cannot be stated with certainty whether these species had contact with early humans. Such contact, however, is plausible. At least with respect to the relation between H. erectus and modern humans, it is vigorously debated whether this contact resulted in interbreeding or aggressive replacement of H. erectus by early modern humans (e.g., Wolpoff, Hawks, & Caspari, 2000; Wolpoff et al., 2001). Genetic patterns for populations of modern humans are consistent with waves of migrations, within and between geographic regions, and suggest a combination of interbreeding and replacement (Templeton, 2002; Underhill et al., 2001), as discussed in a later section (Sexual Selection and Population Genetics).

Brain Evolution

My goal in this section is to provide an overview of gross changes in brain size over the past 5 million years of hominid evolution. Although it is almost certain that brain and cognitive specializations occurred independent of changes in brain volume during hominid evolution (Holloway, 1968, 1996), the relation between size of the neocortex and performance on measures of general intelligence makes it important to also consider evolutionary changes in brain volume (Rushton & Ankney, 1996; see also Gibson, Rumbaugh, & Beran, 2001). In the first section, I review research on changes in brain volume and potential changes in brain organization and in the second, changes in the encephalization quotient.

Brain Volume and Organization

A variety of techniques are available to estimate the brain volume of extinct hominids. One method involves reconstructing the fossilized cranium and then making a plaster cast of the inside of the cranium (e.g., Holloway, 1973b). These endocasts can be used to estimate cranial volume and thus brain volume, and in some cases they provide an impression of the architecture of the outer surface of the neocortex (e.g., Falk, 1983; Holloway & de la Coste-Lareymondie, 1982; Tobias, 1987). A representation of the outer surface of the left hemisphere of a human neocortex is shown in Figure 3.3. The gyri (folds) and sulci (valleys) leave impressions on the inner surface of the skull that can sometimes be recaptured in the endocast (for discussion, see Holloway, 1996).

The use of these and other methods has provided considerable information on the general pattern of evolutionary change in brain volume since and including A. afarensis. Figure 3.4 shows the mean values estimated

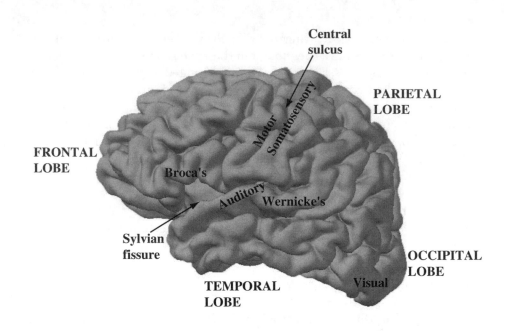

Figure 3.3. Outer surface of the left hemisphere of the neocortex of *Homo sapiens*. From *Words and Rules: The Ingredients of Language* (p. 244), by S. Pinker, 1999, New York: Basic Books. Copyright 1999 by Steven Pinker. Reprinted with permission.

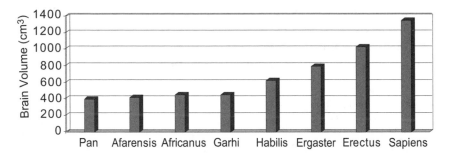
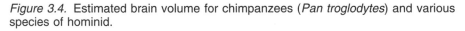

Figure 3.4. Estimated brain volume for chimpanzees (*Pan troglodytes*) and various species of hominid.

from multiple sources for all species (Falk et al., 2000; Holloway, 1973a, 1973b; McHenry, 1994; Tobias, 1987; B. Wood & Collard, 1999), with the exception of A. *garhi*, which is estimated from a single source (Asfaw et al., 1999). Although there is disagreement regarding the brain volume of some individual species, the overall pattern is clear. The australopithecines (A. *afarensis*, A. *africanus*, and A. *garhi*) show a significantly but modestly larger brain volume than extant chimpanzees and thus presumably a larger brain volume than the ancestor common to australopithecines, chimpanzees, and humans (McHenry, 1994; Tobias, 1987). There also appear to have been further but still modest increases in brain volume from A. afarensis to A. africanus and A. garhi.

Inferences about the brain morphology of the outer portion of the neocortex can be made only with caution but are nonetheless potentially instructive. Falk (1983) found that the brain morphology inferred from endocast patterns of a likely australopithecine skull was more similar to that of a chimpanzee and other great apes than to that of a human in terms of gyri and sulci patterns. However, Holloway and Kimbel (1986) questioned this interpretation and suggested that the brain morphology associated with this skull was in fact more humanlike. In any event, one pattern that is not found in great apes but is consistently found in australopithecines and other hominids, including humans, is a difference in the shape of the posterior portions of the left hemisphere and anterior portions of the right hemisphere. The visual area of the left hemisphere is smaller than expected on the basis of body and brain size (see next section), whereas portions of the left parietal area and right frontal area are larger than expected (Holloway & de la Coste-Lareymondie, 1982).

With the emergence of species of Homo, there were substantial changes in facial structure that may have enabled an increase in cranial size, and thus added potential for further evolutionary change in brain size and structure (Stedman et al., 2004). Indeed, increases in brain volume and added changes in the morphology of the outer surface of the neocortex are evident in H. habilis (Falk, 1983; Tobias, 1987). Included among the potential changes in the neocortex of H. habilis are expansions, albeit modest (see Problem Solving and Human Evolution section of chap. 7), of the frontal and parietal lobes and extensive remodeling—specifically, evidence of more folding and thus more surface area of the frontal lobes relative to A. africanus. As an example, one area of the frontal lobe that is implicated in human speech and gesture, Broca's area, appeared to have been expanded and had an architecture (e.g., pattern of sulcal and gyral folds) similar to that of modern humans. The increase in the size of the parietal cortex is interesting as well (Holloway, 1996), because it is coincident with increasingly sophisticated tool use with and after the emergence of H. habilis (see Ecological Pressures section later in this chapter) and because areas of the parietal cortex are engaged during tool use in modern humans (see Functional Ecological Systems section of chap. 5) and are involved in some components of controlled attention as related to working memory (see Cognitive and Brain Systems section of chap. 7). I discuss potential functional correlates of changes in the right frontal cortex, among other areas, in the Problem Solving and Human Evolution section of chapter 7.

As shown in Figure 3.4, further increases in brain volume, as well as morphology, are evident with the emergence of H. erectus and continuing to modern humans (McHenry, 1994; Ruff et al., 1997; B. Wood & Collard, 1999). The threefold increase in brain volume comparing A. *afarensis* to modern humans belies another important pattern, that is, relative stasis for very long periods of time. Although there was a modest increase in brain volume from A. *afarensis* to A. *africanus* and A. *garhi*, the changes evolved over the course of 1.5 million years. In other words, there was comparatively little change in brain volume from about 4 million years ago until the emergence of H. *habilis* about 2.5 million years ago (McHenry, 1994; B. Wood & Collard, 1999). As described in the next section, another period of relative stasis occurred from about 1.8 million years ago until about 500,000 years ago (Ruff et al., 1997). Stasis in size, however, does not mean there were no changes in the specialized functions of one or more brain regions (Holloway, 1996).

Encephalization Quotient

An understanding of changes in absolute brain volume during hominid evolution is important but can be misleading, because the absolute size of the brain increases with increases in overall body size and thus confounds cross-species comparisons (Harvey & Clutton-Brock, 1985). For instance, an adult male A. *africanus* weighed about 30% less than a modern adult human male. As discussed in chapter 4 (Allometry and Size of the Neocortex section), one result is that some proportion of the difference in absolute brain volume comparing these two species is due to differences in overall body size and not to selection pressures for increased brain size (McHenry, 1994). One measure used to control for this confound is the encephalization quotient (EQ), which is an index of brain size relative to that of an average mammal of the same body weight (Jerison, 1973; for discussion, see Holloway, 1996). As an example, McHenry estimated the EQ of chimpanzees to be 2.0—that is, the brain volume of chimpanzees is twice that of an average mammal of the same body weight.

EQ values for modern humans range from less than 5.0 (Aiello & Wheeler, 1995) to more than 7.0 (Jerison, 1973; Tobias, 1987), with estimates commonly ranging between 5.0 and 6.0 (McHenry, 1994; Ruff et al., 1997). The values vary from one analysis to the next because of different assumptions regarding the scaling relation between body size and brain size. Despite this variability, the overall evolutionary pattern is clear: EQ has increased dramatically over the past 4 million years of hominid evolution. I estimated EQ values for various hominid species as a percentage of the EQ of modern humans by taking the brain volumes shown in Figure 3.4 and interpolating these with EQ estimates Tobias (1987) derived. As shown in Figure 3.5, the EQ of chimpanzees, although double that of the typical mammal, is estimated to be 34% that of modern humans. The EQ of

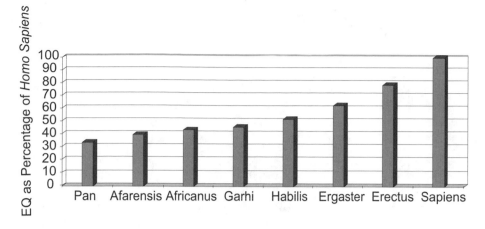

Figure 3.5. Encephalization quotients (EQs) for chimpanzees (*Pan troglodytes*) and various species of hominid as a percentage of the mean EQ of modern humans (*Homo sapiens*).

australopithecines was less than half that of modern humans, and the EQ of *H. habilis* was slightly more than half that of modern humans. Substantive increases in EQ are evident with the emergence of *H. erectus*, with values at the high end close to 80% that of modern humans. Figure 3.6 shows the general EQ trend over the past 1.8 million years, that is, since the emergence of *H. erectus* (based on data in Ruff et al., 1997). As with absolute brain size, EQ values indicate a long period (about 1.2 million years) of stasis, followed by a modest increase (about 12%) from 500,000 to 400,000 years ago, and then more rapid increases until about 35,000 to 20,000 years ago.

On the basis of Ruff et al.'s (1997) and Holloway's (1996) estimates, the EQ of modern humans appears to have peaked between 20,000 and 35,000 years ago and declined 3% to 4% during the past 10,000 to 20,000 years. The gradual decline in EQ values suggests that the selection pressures that resulted in the rapid increase in EQ beginning about 500,000 years ago have been relaxed during the past 10,000 to 20,000 years (Brace, 1995). During this time frame, agriculture, economic specialization, city-states, and other changes were becoming increasingly central features of human subsistence activities and social organization in many parts of the world (J. Clutton-Brock, 1992; Hole, 1992). The implication is that changes in social organization resulted in a relaxation of the selection pressures that drove the rapid increase in EQ from 400,000 to about 20,000 years ago. In other words, the evolved competencies associated with changes in brain size and organization were not as strongly correlated with survival or reproductive prospects over the past 20,000 years in comparison to the 450,000 years prior to this epoch. The implications for interpreting research on *g* are discussed in chapter 8.

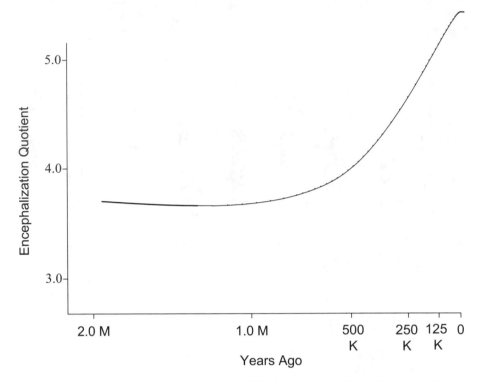

Figure 3.6. Estimated changes in encephalization quotient from *Homo erectus* to modern humans. M = million; K = thousand.

ADAPTATION AND SELECTION

My goal for this section is to review and evaluate models of potential selection pressures and adaptations associated with changes in EQ during hominid evolution. Specifically, I discuss climatic, ecological, and social pressures.

Climatic Pressures

Climatic variations and geological changes (e.g., volcano eruptions) are common and can result in short- and long-term changes in ambient temperature, rainfall, and other ecological conditions. As described for Darwin's finches in chapter 2 (Climatic and Ecological Selection Pressures section), these changes can influence the mix of vegetation, woodland, and so forth that support other species (e.g., deMenocal, 2001; Rutherford & D'Hondt, 2000; Tudhope et al., 2001; Vrba, Denton, Partridge, & Burckle, 1995). The most influential model of climatic and geologic influences on the evolution of flora and fauna is that proposed by Vrba, specifically the turnover pulse hypothesis (1974, 1975, 1995a, 1995b). The gist of the hypothesis is that large-scale climatic changes, such as those associated with glaciations and global cooling, can result in large-scale changes in habitat (e.g., change in the distribution of food sources) and in physical ecology (e.g., ambient temperature). The result is pulses of speciation and extinction events. Adaptive radiation and speciation occur, in theory, as habitat change results in geographic isolation—due, for instance, to deforestation and resulting pockets of woodlands within savanna—of populations of the same species and subsequent adaptations of these populations to local conditions. Extinction follows for species that are unable to adapt to change in habitat or physical conditions (e.g., temperature).

The issue I address in this section is whether such climatic changes contributed to hominid evolution in general and to the accompanying changes in brain volume and EQ in particular. Vrba (1995b) argued that significant glaciation between 2.8 and 2.5 million years ago resulted in decreased temperature and rainfall in Africa and a corresponding turnover pulse of many species of large fauna, including hominids. Evolutionary responses to decreasing temperature often include increases in physical size to enable greater retention of body heat and a prolonged period of physical development to enable growth of a larger body. Vrba argued that these physical adaptations resulted in an accompanying change in brain volume and EQ: "The conclusion is inescapable that hominine encephalization in the latest Pliocene started a new trend, of higher evolutionary rates than before" (Vrba, 1995b, p. 406). The specific mechanisms driving or at least maintaining the increase in hominid EQ are not detailed, but the implication is that EQ changes were not the direct result of ecological or social pressures but rather an incidental effect of broader physical adaptations (see Allometry and Size of the Neocortex section of chap. 4).

Vrba's (1974) turnover pulse hypothesis is difficult to test, given the incompleteness of the fossil record, among other issues (see Vrba, 1995a). Nonetheless, the model in general and as related to hominid evolution has attracted much attention and has been vigorously debated (Behrensmeyer, Todd, Potts, & McBrinn, 1997; Kimbel, 1995; Kingston, Marino, & Hill, 1994; Potts, 1998; Turner & Wood, 1993; T. D. White, 1995). Although the 2.8- to 2.5-million-year time frame has been questioned, there is evidence for the emergence of many new species of fauna in Africa between 3.0 and 2.0 million years ago, including as many as 4 to 6 new species of hominid, 3 of which are shown in Figure 3.2 (Behrensmeyer et al., 1997; Kimbel, 1995). However, inconsistent with the model is evidence that some groups of species did not show the predicted speciation and extinction pulses (T. D. White, 1995), and the change in mix of savanna and woodland may not have been as drastic as predicted (Kingston et al., 1994). Moreover, most of the changes in brain volume and EQ in H. habilis and H. erectus occurred less than 2 million years ago and do not appear to have been coupled with periods of rapid climatic change (T. D. White, 1995).

Another approach that can be used to address this issue involves determining if the increases in brain volume and EQ of early species of *Homo* were associated with similar increases in other African hominids and primates that lived in the same regions and during the same time frame. If there is a general relation between climatic changes and changes in body size and brain volume, then these other species should have experienced the same selection pressures and thus a similar change in brain volume and EQ as *H. habilis* and *H. erectus*. In one test of this hypothesis, Falk et al. (2000) compared the brain volumes of these early species of *Homo* to the brain volumes of three sister species of African hominids (*Paranthropus robustus*, *P. boisei*, *P. aethiopicus*) from roughly 2.0 to 1.5 million years ago. With the possible exception of *P. boisei* (see Elton, Bishop, & Wood, 2001), the brain volumes of these species did not change substantively during this time frame. Elton et al. examined change in the brain volume of a species of now-extinct baboon (*Theropithecus*) that appears to have lived in the same localities as *H. habilis* and *H. erectus*. As with the findings of Falk and colleagues, there was no change in the brain volume of this species of baboon during the time frame when *H. habilis* and *H. erectus* were experiencing significant increases in brain volume and EQ.

At this point, Vrba's (1974) turnover pulse hypothesis and related models (e.g., Potts, 1998) may explain the apparent increase and adaptive radiation of hominid species from 3.0 to 2.0 million years ago, including the evolutionary emergence of the line that eventually led to modern humans. Patterns of climatic variation and geologic change are not, however, consistent with the pattern of increased brain volume and EQ during hominid evolution, especially the very rapid changes during the past 500,000 years; see Calvin (2002) for an alternative interpretation. This is not to say that climatic events, such as glaciations, have not influenced human migration patterns or population expansions and contractions; it appears that they have (Underhill et al., 2001). Rather, patterns of climatic change do not correspond well to evolutionary change in EQ since the emergence of *Homo* and thus are not likely to have been the principal force driving the evolution of brain and cognition in humans.

Ecological Pressures

Darwin (1859) argued that relationships and competing interests among species were the driving force of natural selection. Among these are predator–prey relationships, competition among different species for the same food source, and the effects of parasites on physical vigor and health.

Parasites, food shortages, and occasional predator attacks do indeed covary with mortality risks for humans in traditional societies today and those who lived in preindustrial Europe and the United States (e.g., Hed, 1987; Hill & Hurtado, 1996; Morrison, Kirshner, & Molho, 1977). These factors have almost certainly been important components of natural selection during human evolution but are not in and of themselves sufficient explanations of the increases in hominid brain volume and EQ. If they were, then many species would have evidenced the same increases in brain volume and EQ given that parasites, predators, and food shortages are common selection pressures across species.

Instead, models of the relation between ecological pressures and brain and cognitive evolution in hominids have focused on the ability of hominids to extract biological resources from the ecology and through this improve survival prospects and support accompanying population increases and geographic expansions. The basic idea is supported, in part, by a common pattern across nonhuman species: Species with complex foraging or predatory demands have a larger brain volume and higher EQ than related species with less complex foraging or predatory demands (e.g., Barton, 1996; Barton & Dean, 1993; T. H. Clutton-Brock & Harvey, 1980; Kaplan & Robson, 2002). For instance, species that rely primarily on leaves and other plentiful foods have smaller brains than their cousins that rely on foods that are spatially dispersed and not always available, such as fruits. The argument is taken one step further with hominids; specifically, hominids evolved into superpredators that had (and still have) an extraordinary ability to capture (e.g., hunting) and process (e.g., cooking) other species for use as foods and medicines (Martin, 1967; Wrangham et al., 1999).

Kaplan, Hill, Lancaster, and Hurtado (2000) clearly demonstrated that humans in traditional societies—at least groups that have not been forced by other humans into resource-poor environments—are highly efficient at extracting life-supporting biological resources from natural ecologies through hunting and foraging (Hill et al., 2001). If the ability to extract and process biological resources was the driving force in the evolution of brain and cognition, then improvements in the ability of hominids to extract these resources should correspond to changes in brain volume and EQ during hominid evolution. To assess this hypothesis, several questions must be answered. Specifically, which social, behavioral, and other adaptations (e.g., manual dexterity associated with tool use; Trinkaus, 1992) allowed hominids to extract and process biological resources? When did these adaptations evolve? Were these adaptations likely to be a sufficient explanation of the changes in brain volume and EQ during hominid evolution?

As an example of how these questions can be approached, consider Teaford and Ungar's (2002) analysis of tooth size, shape, and wear patterns of australopithecines. Their analysis suggests that A. *afarensis* and other australopithecines evidenced a shift in diet relative to their predecessors (see also Jolly, 1970). Recent finds by Semaw and colleagues (2003) suggest that A. *garhi* constructed a variety of stone tools, including tools used to cut and process meat. These features of tooth morphology and behavioral adaptation suggest that australopithecines were able to eat a wider range of foods (largely seeds and soft fruits, and apparently some meat) than their predecessors and were thus able to occupy a wider range of ecologies. The associated behavioral (e.g., foraging strategy) and cognitive (e.g., determining growth patterns of fruit; Barton, 1996) adaptations may have contributed to the apparent increase in the EQ of australopithecines (see Figure 3.5) relative to their predecessors, but these adaptations occurred millions of years before the rapid rise in EQ associated with the emergence of H. *erectus* and H. *sapiens*.

Wrangham, Holland-Jones, Laden, Pilbeam, and Conklin-Brittain (1999) presented evidence consistent with the position that H. *erectus* used fire for cooking, which enables the use of a wider range of plant and animal species as foods; hominids appear to have been using fire for more than 800,000 years (Goren-Inbar et al., 2004). Foley (1987; Foley & Lahr, 1997) and others (de Heinzelin et al., 1999) have detailed the relation between advances in the sophistication of tools used for food extraction (e.g., digging sticks) and hunting and the appearance of species since A. *afarensis*. There is evidence that H. *habilis* used simple stone tools and that increases in the complexity of stone tools and their geographic distribution coincided with the emergence and migration patterns of H. *erectus*. J. D. Clark et al. (2003) provided evidence that early modern humans used even more complex stone tools about 150,000 years ago. Nonetheless, the most complex stone tools are found in archeological sites dating less than 50,000 years ago and are found with the fossils of modern humans, H. *heidelbergensis*, and H. *neanderthalensis* (Foley & Lahr, 1997). The pattern of tool "evolution" and the likely function of these tools, including hunting and food extraction (e.g., digging up roots), appear to be consistent with Kaplan et al.'s (2000) hypothesis.

Evidence that these changes resulted in the evolution of a superpredator comes from patterns of human migration and subsequent mass extinctions of other species. Following the conclusion of Wallace (1911)—"the rapidity of the extinction of so many large Mammalia is actually due to man's agency" (p. 264)—Martin (1967, 1973) presented evidence that mass extinctions of megafauna (prey species weighing 40 kg or more) were evident in Africa about 50,000 years ago, and later mass extinctions occurred in Australia, Asia, America, and New Zealand after the migration of humans into these regions. Although determining the precise dates of human migration and the extinction of other species poses some technical challenges, Wallace's and Martin's conclusion has been supported by a series of recent analyses that used multiple methods for determining these dates (Alroy, 2001; Ceballos & Ehrlich, 2002; G. H. Miller et al., 1999; R. G. Roberts et al., 2001).

As an example, evidence presented by R. G. Roberts et al. (2001) indicates a continent-wide mass extinction of Australian megafauna about 46,000 years ago, that is, roughly 5,000 years after the arrival of humans. Martin (1973) and Alroy (2001) presented evidence suggesting that the mass extinction of megafauna in North America occurred about 12,000 years ago, that is, roughly 1,000 to several thousand years after the arrival of humans. These mass extinctions have not been correlated with climatic or other ecological changes (e.g., glaciers; G. H. Miller et al., 1999), although the extinction of some species can, of course, be related to climate and ecological changes and not to human activity (Guthrie, 2003). In any case, analyses of declines in populations of species of large fish and mammals have directly linked these declines to human hunting and fishing from the time humans were primarily hunter-gatherers to the modern day (e.g., R. A. Myers & Worm, 2003; Pandolfi et al., 2003; Walsh et al., 2003).

Further evidence for a co-evolving relation between EQ and hunting and other dietary changes comes from the metabolic requirements of the human brain (Armstrong, 1990). Specifically, there is evidence that the evolutionary increase in brain volume was associated with a corresponding decrease in the mass of the metabolically expensive gastrointestinal tract (Aiello & Wheeler, 1995), although this evidence is not conclusive (Aiello, Bates, & Joffe, 2001). Evolutionary reduction in the size of the gastrointestinal tract requires change from a low quality (e.g., leaves, plants, grasses) to a high quality (e.g., fruits, meat) diet. The above noted shift in the australopithecine diet is thus consistent with the corresponding change in EQ, as is the rapid increase in EQ associated with the increasingly effective hunting competencies of H. erectus and H. sapiens.

Improvements in hunting efficiency and the ability to acquire other high quality foods were presumably supported by corresponding changes in brain and cognition. Indeed, as I describe in chapter 5 (Functional Ecological Systems section), there is evidence for an evolved folk biology in humans—specifically, brain and cognitive systems that are specialized for the categorization of plants and animals used as food sources and cognitive specializations for acquiring (e.g., by means of hunting) these foods (Atran, 1998). As Aiello and Wheeler (1995) noted, these relations do not, however, provide conclusive evidence that the changes in brain volume and EQ during hominid evolution were related solely to improvements in foraging and hunting competencies, only that they were necessary to support the evolutionary increase in brain volume.

Social Pressures

Ecological Dominance

The patterns described in the preceding section suggest a gradual improvement during hominid evolution in the ability to extract food from the ecology (Kaplan & Robson, 2002). These competencies became exceptional, in relation to other species, with the emergence of *Homo*, perhaps beginning with *H. erectus*. The trend continued with *H. erectus* and *H. sapiens*, as these species became exceptionally skilled at extracting biological resources from a variety of ecologies and at manipulating and changing these ecologies (e.g., through fire and tool use) in ways that almost certainly had survival and reproductive consequences. As *H. erectus* and later *H. sapiens* became increasingly skilled at exploiting and manipulating these ecologies, ecological dominance was achieved (Alexander, 1989). Once achieved, an evolutionary Rubicon was crossed: "The ecological dominance of evolving humans diminished the effects of 'extrinsic' forces of natural selection such that within-species competition became the principle 'hostile force of nature' guiding the long-term evolution of behavioral capacities, traits, and tendencies" (Alexander, 1989, p. 458).

The pattern of human migration and overkill of megafauna (Martin, 1967) is one example of ecological dominance and parallels Mac Arthur's and Wilson's (1967) analysis of island biogeography. When a species first migrates into an unexploited region, such as an island, that supports the survival and reproductive needs of the species and offers few constraints on population expansion (e.g., few predators), then there are low levels of social competition and a rapid increase in population size. As the population expands, the quantity or quality of the region's resources necessarily declines, and competition for access to these diminishing resources necessarily intensifies. The result is an added selection pressure—social competition over survival-related ecological resources.

Ecological dominance results in the same pattern, as it is the ability to very efficiently extract biological resources from the ecology and manipulate the ecology in ways that reduce mortality risks and support subsequent population expansions (Hill et al., 2001; Kaplan et al., 2000). However, as the population expands beyond the carrying capacity of the ecology, the inevitable result is a population crash, as was argued by Malthus in 1798. The combination of ecological dominance, population expansions, and the elevated mortality that defines population crashes results in a fundamental shift in selection pressures. Darwin's and Wallace's (1858, p. 54) conceptualization of natural selection as a "struggle for existence" becomes in addition a struggle with other human beings for control of the resources that support life and allow one to reproduce (Geary, 1998). Social competition is, of course, endemic across species but becomes an especially potent selection pressure for species that achieve ecological dominance (Alexander, 1989). These species have evolved adaptations that reduce ecological constraints on population expansions, creating cycles of expansions and contractions, although overall population levels may remain relatively constant when averaged across these cycles. During contractions, social competition for diminishing resources necessarily increases in intensity (Malthus, 1798).

In this situation, the stage is set for a form of runaway selection, whereby the more cognitively, socially, and behaviorally sophisticated individuals are able to outmaneuver and manipulate other individuals to gain control of resources in the local ecology and to gain control of the behavior of other people (West-Eberhard, 1983). To the extent that access to these resources covaries with survival and reproductive outcomes—and it does in many contexts (Betzig, 1986; Hed, 1987; Malthus, 1798; United Nations, 1985)—the associated sociocognitive competencies, and supporting brain systems, will necessarily evolve. The point is that Kaplan et al.'s (2000) and others' (e.g., Tiger, 1969) theory of the relation between ecological pressures and hominid brain evolution is consistent with Alexander's (1989) and others' (e.g., Humphrey, 1976) theory of the relation between social pressures and hominid brain evolution. Alexander's proposal implies that ecological pressures were more salient earlier in hominid evolution and social pressures were more salient later in hominid evolution.

Social Complexity

As noted in the Ecological Pressures section and elaborated in chapter 4 (Comparative Ecology and Brain Evolution section), comparative (i.e., cross-species) evidence supports the view that hunting, foraging, and other food acquisition behaviors are often related to the evolution and proximate development of brain and cognition, as are other activities such as predator avoidance (e.g., Barton, 1996; Catania, 2000; Dukas, 1998a). These brain, cognitive, and accompanying social and behavioral competencies function to maintain a territory and extract survival-related resources from this territory. These brain and cognitive competencies define the domains of folk biology and folk physics, which I describe for humans in chapter 5 (Functional Ecological Systems section). My point for now is that these brain and cognitive systems are integral to the human ability to achieve ecological dominance but must also be considered within a wider social context, as represented in Figure 3.7.

As represented in the bottom section of Figure 3.7, there may also be a co-evolving increase in the length of the developmental period (Kaplan et al., 2000; Kaplan & Robson, 2002) and an evolved bias to engage in developmental activities (e.g., play) that result in the proximate adaptation of hunting, foraging, and related behaviors to the demands of the local

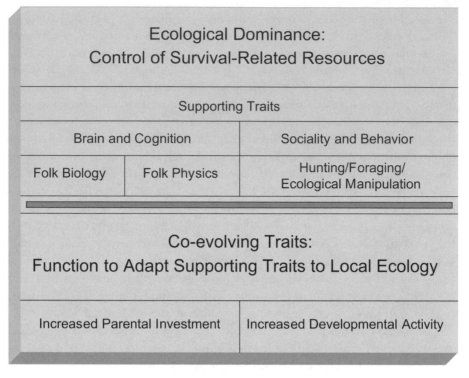

Figure 3.7. Ecological dominance results from the ability to efficiently extract resources from the ecology and to change and manipulate the ecology (e.g., use of fire for slash and burn agriculture) in ways that improve survival and reproductive prospects. The achievement of ecological dominance is dependent on folk knowledge, social cooperation, and the co-evolving traits of parental investment and developmental activity.

ecology (Bock & Johnson, 2004; Groos, 1898). If an increase in the length of the developmental period and associated activities does in fact result in better-adapted competencies, then an additional premium is placed on parenting. At the very least, the length of time during which parents provision and protect offspring must increase to give offspring the opportunity to practice hunting and foraging and other ecological skills (e.g., tool use). The relations shown in Figure 3.7 are not, however, perfectly coupled. The human developmental period and apparently that of *H. erectus* are actually shorter than would be expected on the basis of brain size alone (Allman & Hasenstaub, 1999; Dean et al., 2001). These findings do not invalidate the general relations shown in the figure, but rather suggest that other selection pressures, such as adult mortality risks (Stearns, 1992), operated to reduce the length of the developmental period.

In any case, the message is that ecological dominance cannot be achieved without cooperative relationships, including collective hunting and reciprocal sharing of meat, a division of labor, and so forth (Hill, 2002; Kaplan et al., 2000; Kaplan & Hill, 1985). At the same time, these relationships create the potential for larger-scale competition. As noted, an important result of ecological dominance is an expansion of population size. Expansions, in turn, result in diminishing ecological resources and thus create the potential for between-group competition over control of resource-rich ecologies and the forced migration of less competitive groups (Hamilton, 2001). Chagnon (1997) documented this very dynamic in the Yanomamö, and Horowitz (2001) documented many instances of similar forms of group-level conflict in human populations throughout the world. It is plausible that the same basic dynamic of between-group competition over resource-rich ecologies contributed to the earlier described migration of *H. erectus* and other species of *Homo* into Asia, Europe, and later Australia and America, although climatic changes likely contributed to migration patterns as well (deMenocal, 2001).

Social Dynamics

Social dynamics required to achieve ecological dominance and to support group-level conflict over preferred ecologies should favor the evolution of the suite of co-evolving traits shown in Figure 3.8 and elaborated in Table 3.1 (see S. B. Carroll, 2003, for related discussion). The basic human social structure is presumed to consist of kinship groups that cooperate to compete with other kinship groups over control of resource-rich ecologies and to manipulate reproductive dynamics (Geary & Flinn, 2001). Within-group relationships will entail a balance of cooperation to meet shared goals and conflict because of divergent goals. In theory and typically in practice, the relative bias toward cooperation or conflict varies directly with the degree of genetic relatedness between the individuals (e.g., Chagnon, 1997; Hamilton, 1964, 1975; Segal & Hershberger, 1999; Trivers, 1974; West-Eberhard, 1975). When combined with the potential for group-level conflict, these within-group dynamics create pressures for the evolutionary elaboration of a folk psychological system, as many contemporary scientists have emphasized (e.g., Barton, 1996, 1999; Brothers & Ring, 1992; Cosmides, 1989; Dunbar, 1993, 1998; Geary & Flinn, 2001; Humphrey, 1976; Pinker & Bloom, 1990; Premack & Woodruff, 1978; Sawaguchi, 1997) and as Darwin (1871) suggested more than 130 years ago.

The competencies that support human social dynamics are similar in many respects to those common in other species (see Table 3.1). Across species of primate, the complexity of social dynamics is positively correlated with brain size, and both social complexity and brain size are correlated with length of developmental period and maximum life span (Allman & Hasenstaub, 1999; Allman, McLaughlin, & Hakeem, 1993; Dunbar, 1993,

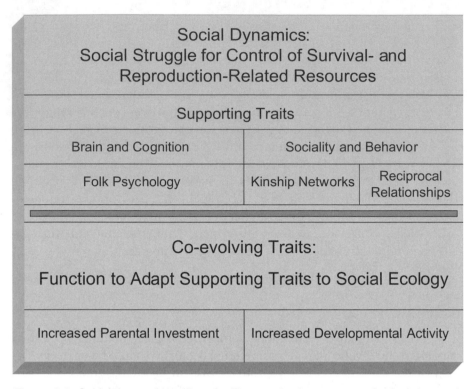

Social Dynamics: Social Struggle for Control of Survival- and Reproduction-Related Resources		
Supporting Traits		
Brain and Cognition	Sociality and Behavior	
Folk Psychology	Kinship Networks	Reciprocal Relationships
Co-evolving Traits: Function to Adapt Supporting Traits to Social Ecology		
Increased Parental Investment	Increased Developmental Activity	

Figure 3.8. Social competition is a significant selection pressure for humans and centers on attempts to achieve access to and control of resources that covary with survival and reproductive outcomes in the local ecology. These control-related activities are dependent on folk knowledge, social cooperation, and the co-evolving traits of parental investment and developmental activity.

1998; Joffe, 1997). Maximum life span, in turn, is associated with levels of parental investment (Allman, Rosin, Kumar, & Hasenstaub, 1998). In short, larger brains and higher EQs are generally associated with complex social systems, a long developmental period and long adult life span, and high levels of parental investment, as well as complex foraging and hunting demands (Kaplan & Robson, 2002).

For humans, extended parental investment typically occurs in the context of a wider kinship network that facilitates the feeding and protection of children and supports the extended developmental period. The latter allows individuals to engage in activities such as peer relationships and rough-and-tumble play (Bjorklund & Pellegrini, 2002; Groos, 1898; P. K. Smith, 1982). Although the issue is debated, one proposed function of these activities is to enable children to adapt social and sociocognitive competencies to the social conditions of the local group (Geary, 1998). Children learn, based on their personality and social and other skills (e.g.,

TABLE 3.1
Coevolving Traits Associated With Human Social Competition

Trait	Description
Large brain and complex social competencies	The overall size of the human neocortex is larger than expected for a primate of the same body and brain size (Rilling & Insel, 1999), and this difference is accompanied by expansions in size or changes in complexity of many specific areas of the neocortex (Rilling & Insel, 1999; Semendeferi, Lu, Schenker, & Damasio, 2002).
	Although results are preliminary, the neocortex appears to be larger than expected in those areas that support social competencies (Rilling & Insel, 1999), such as language (discussed more fully in chap. 7).
High levels of paternal investment	Paternal investment is evident in only 3% to 5% of mammalian species (T. H. Clutton-Brock, 1989).
	Even for these species, humans are unique in that paternal investment occurs in a social context of large multimale–multifemale communities where most adult members reproduce (Alexander, 1990).
	In nonindustrial societies, paternal investment reduces child mortality rates and, in many societies, contributes to children's ability to acquire social-competitive competencies (Geary, 2000).
Long developmental period and adult life span	Relative to other mammals and primates, children have a very long developmental period that is characterized by slow development during middle childhood and high dependency on adult caregiving (Bogin, 1999).
	During this period of slow growth, children engage in many activities, such as peer play, that likely facilitate social and sociocognitive competencies (e.g., Pellegrini & Bartini, 2001).
	Relative to other great apes, humans have a very long adult life span and low juvenile and adult mortality rates (Allman et al., 1993; Hill et al., 2001).
	The extended adult life span, including menopause in women, allows parents to invest in children during the long developmental period (Hawkes, O'Connell, Blurton Jones, Alvarez, & Charnov, 1998; Williams, 1957).

athletic), how to influence the behavior of other people and how to obtain culturally valued resources (e.g., meat obtained though hunting or money), competencies, and knowledge. These are predicted to enhance survival and reproductive prospects in adulthood.

The gist is that in traditional societies today (e.g., Chagnon, 1997), and presumably during recent hominid evolution, kinship groups and reciprocal relationships—called *friends* by psychologists (Hartup & Stevens, 1997)—

create social coalitions. The individuals that compose these coalitions cooperate to compete with other coalitions over ecological control and to manipulate reproductive dynamics. Within kinship groups, high levels of parental investment give children the opportunity to engage in activities (e.g., peer relationships; Harris, 1995) that allow the competencies needed to achieve ecological dominance (e.g., play hunting; Kaplan et al., 2000; Kaplan & Robson, 2002), compete for mates, manipulate and control social relationships, and parent, among other activities, to be practiced and adapted to local conditions (Bjorklund & Bering, 2003; Geary, 2002b, 2002c).

Forms of Social Relationship

A complete description and analysis of the many forms of human social dynamics is beyond the scope of this volume (for a few examples, see Bugental, 2000; Buss, 1994; Caporael, 1997; Geary, 1998; Horowitz, 2001). My goal is more modest, specifically, to provide a framework for organizing and conceptualizing the most fundamental of these dynamics and to do so within a broader comparative background. At its root, and as elaborated in the Motivation to Control section later in this chapter, the social behavior of individuals is ultimately focused on attempts to organize the social and material world so as to direct resources to themselves and their kin. Social cooperation results when resource control requires collective effort, and conflict results as different individuals and kinship groups compete to maintain control of or gain access to the same resources.

However packaged, social dynamics are centered on survival and reproductive activities, and parental investment and associated components of sexual selection are the core of these activities, as I describe in the first section below. In the second and third sections, I provide examples of how male–male competition and female–female competition result in social dynamics that, in theory, should place a premium on sophisticated sociocognitive competencies. My point in this section is that humans are a highly social species, and the accompanying relationships are the most demanding and complex endeavors that people must cope with day after day to be successful in life. Most other primates are highly social as well, but the most important result of runaway social competition during human evolution—following the achievement of ecological dominance—is an evolutionary elaboration of social competencies and a ramping up of social complexity, which in turn results in another evolutionary elaboration of social competencies, and so the cycle continues.

Parenting and Sexual Selection

Parenting and the reproductive dynamics that define sexual selection provide a way to organize the most fundamental human social dynamics and those of many other species (Andersson, 1994; T. H. Clutton-Brock, 1991; Darwin, 1871; Geary, 1998). Human fatherhood provides a particularly interesting segue into this framework, because there is little or no such in investment in 95% to 97% of other mammalian species (T. H. Clutton-Brock, 1989; for an exception, see Dunbar, 1995) and because it greatly complicates human reproductive dynamics. As described in chapter 2 (Sexual Selection and Social Dynamics section), when one sex invests in parenting, the other sex competes over access to this investment (Trivers, 1972). When both sexes parent and all parents are not equal, then both males and females compete for the parental investment of the opposite sex. Fatherhood then results in female–female competition over this investment and male choice of spousal partners, alongside male–male competition and female choice. To further complicate matters, paternal investment results in the formation of families and extended spousal relationships, and the long developmental period results in more extensive and extended parent–child relationships than in nearly all other species. As outlined in Table 3.2, these dynamics can be boiled down to three categories: intrasexual competition, intersexual choice, and family relationships (Geary, 2002b). The combination results in a degree of social complexity that is extreme, even among primates.

Male–Male Competition

Male–male competition occurs within men's social groups and between their social groups. The former is associated with attempts to achieve social status and dominance and thus the ability to influence the behavior of other members of the group, and the latter is typically focused on achieving control of resource-rich ecologies and facilitating competition for mates, as in raiding to capture wives or social politics in negotiating marital partners (Chagnon, 1997). The resulting competition is often lethal (Chagnon, 1988, 1997; Daly & Wilson, 1988), especially when it involves between-group competition (Horowitz, 2001). This form of competition requires the development and maintenance of male coalitions, as I described in chapter 2 (Coalitional Competition section; de Waal, 1993). The dynamics involved in creating and maintaining coalitions is universal and is colloquially known as *politics* (D. E. Brown, 1991). The formation of a within-coalition dominance hierarchy not only determines men's relative social status and how resources acquired by the coalition are distributed, but also is necessary for effective coalitional competition.

My point is that social dynamics for men require striking a balance between maintaining a cooperative relationship with a large number of other men and at the same time competing with these same men for in-group social dominance. Political activities and coalitional competition thus

TABLE 3.2
Forms of Social Conflict and Competition

Form of conflict or competition	Examples
Intrasexual competition	
Male–male competition	In traditional societies, men form kin-based coalitions that compete for control of mating dynamics (e.g., exchange of brides) and control of the resources that covary with survival and reproductive outcomes in the local ecology (Chagnon, 1988; Geary, 1998). Men also form dominance hierarchies within the in-group coalitions and compete for position (and influence) in the hierarchy. Competition is often physical and deadly (Keeley, 1996).
Female–female competition	Women form social networks that are commonly nested within the kin-based coalition of men. In these and other contexts, women compete for access to resources, including access to resource-holding or socially influential men. Relative to men, this competition is less physical (Campbell, 1999) and involves subtle manipulation of social relationships, with the goal of organizing these relationships so as to maximize the woman's access to resources that covary with survival and reproductive outcomes in the local ecology (Geary, 2002c).
Intersexual choice	
Male choice	Paternal investment leads to the prediction that men will be selective in their mate choices (Trivers, 1972), and this is the case. Men's mate choices are influenced by fertility cues (e.g., age), as well as by indicators of women's social and maternal competence (Geary, 1998).
Female choice	Women's mate choices are influenced by men's social and parental competence. More so than men, women also focus on men's social status, including material resources, social influence, and cues to their ability to acquire and maintain these resources (Buss, 1989, 1994). Women are also sensitive to indicators of their ability to influence potential mates and thus gain access to their resources.
Family relationships	
Spousal	Spouses, of course, cooperate in raising children, but extended maternal and paternal investment also results in strong potential for conflicts of interest (Kaplan et al., 2000; Svensson & Sheldon, 1998). The nature of these relationships can vary from one culture to the next (Draper, 1989; Draper & Harpending, 1988), but the same central conflicts are predicted: extent of maternal versus paternal investment, resource control (e.g., spending on children or status-oriented objects), and marital fidelity.

(continues)

TABLE 3.2 *(Continued)*

Form of conflict or competition	Examples
	Family relationships
Parent–offspring and sibling	Parents, of course, invest time and resources to promote the well-being of offspring, but offspring typically press for additional resources (Trivers, 1974), sometimes with accompanying morbidity and mortality costs to parents (Westendorp & Kirkwood, 1998). The long developmental period of humans results in an extended parent–child relationship and thus the potential for extended conflicts over parental allocation of resources. Finally, siblings compete for parental resources.

Note. From "Sexual Selection and Human Life History," by D. C. Geary, 2002b, *Advances in Child Development and Behavior, 30,* p. 66. Copyright 2002 by Academic Press. Adapted with permission.

require considerable social competency, although these skills differ from those that support women's relationships (Geary & Flinn, 2002).

Female–Female Competition

Women, of course, form cooperative social groups (Taylor et al., 2000), but typically within territory defined by men's coalitions (D. E. Brown, 1991; Pasternak, Ember, & Ember, 1997). Participation in these social networks provides women with social and emotional support and stability for themselves and their children. Stability of the social network, including the marital relationship, improves physical (Flinn & England, 1995) and psychological (Leadbeater, Blatt, & Quinlan, 1995) health and, through this, survival prospects of children in some contexts (United Nations, 1985). Unlike that of men, female–female competition is not coalitional but is still related to attempts to achieve access to desired resources, including mates. Rather than physical competition or direct status-related activities, female-on-female aggression is more commonly relational. It involves learning about the emotional states, secrets, intentions, and so on of other women and, if necessary, using this information to manipulate the web of social relationships within which the women are embedded (Björkqvist, Lagerspetz, & Kaukiainen, 1992; Björkqvist, Osterman, & Lagerspetz, 1994; Crick, Casas, & Mosher, 1997; Feshbach, 1969).

The successful use of this form of aggression perforce requires considerable sociocognitive competencies (Geary, 2002c). As an example of the complexity of this competition, consider again Figure 2.3 and Exhibit 2.1. As group size increases, the number of dyadic relationships each individual must potentially monitor increases exponentially. Not only does relational aggression require gathering information about all of the other individual girls and women in the social group, but information on the nature of dyadic relationships between these other girls and women must be gathered as well. If this were not complex enough, the successful use of relational aggression requires that girls and women manipulate their relationships with other girls and women and manipulate the nature of the relationships between dyads of other girls and women.

Summary

The complexity of intrasexual competition and other forms of relationship arises from the behavior and social activities of individuals as they attempt to organize the social and material world in terms of their own best interests. Conflicts are inevitable because the best interests of any two individuals, except perhaps monozygotic twins (Segal, 1993; Segal & Hershberger, 1999), do not completely overlap. Social competencies evolved to facilitate cooperation when interests do overlap (Trivers, 1971) and to facilitate the ability to outmaneuver individuals with competing interests (Humphrey, 1976). In this view, the earlier noted runaway selection occurred as a result of these dynamics, specifically because access to and control of significant resources require some level of influence over the behavior of other people, people whose self-interests differ and who thus attempt to organize the social world in different ways.

As a brief aside, it might be argued that cultural activities, such as art, music, and literature, do not at first glance seem to fit this bare-bones view of human nature. However, the theme of many of these works is the human condition—that is, affective (e.g., emotions) and social dynamics that covary with survival and reproductive outcomes in traditional societies (e.g., love, suffering; Whissell, 1996), and the production of these works often has an element of social competition among artists in the genre (G. F. Miller, 2000).

Sexual Selection and Population Genetics

Genetic studies of human populations and related species not only allow inferences to be drawn about the timing and pattern of human evolution as described earlier (Origins section), they also allow inferences to be drawn about human social dynamics, including migration patterns (Seielstad, Minch, & Cavalli-Sforza, 1998) and patterns of social competition (Underhill et al., 2001; Wyckoff, Wang, & Wu, 2000). The basic method involves comparing the geographic distribution and variability of mutations in mitochondrial DNA (mtDNA) genes and genes on the Y chromosome. mtDNA genes are inherited from the mother, and males inherit the Y chromosome from their father. Because of this, differences in the geographic distribution and variability of mtDNA and Y chromosome genes can be used to make inferences about ancestral maternal and paternal migration patterns and reproductive dynamics. Although there are other potential reasons, restricted variance in Y chromosome genes could result from male–male competition and female choice of mating partners. These common features of mammalian reproductive dynamics result in fewer males than females reproducing in any given generation (Andersson, 1994; T. H. Clutton-Brock, Harvey, & Rudder, 1977) and thus less variability in paternal than maternal ancestry. If male–male competition and female choice—that is, sexual selection— influenced human evolution, then there should be less variance in Y chromosome genes than in mtDNA genes in most human populations, and this is the case (Anagnostopoulos, Green, Rowley, Lewis, & Giannelli, 1999; Dorit, Akashi, & Gilbert, 1995; Hammer et al., 2001; Underhill, Jin, Zemans, Oefner, & Cavalli-Sforza, 1996; Underhill et al., 2000; Wells et al., 2001; J. F. Wilson et al., 2001).

Further evidence for sexual selection comes from mtDNA and Y chromosome patterns that indicate that ancestral males were often from geographically distant populations (Bortolini et al., 1999; Carvajal-Carmona et al., 2000; Merriwether et al., 1997; Mesa et al., 2000; J. F. Wilson et al., 2001). Carvajal-Carmona and colleagues reported one of the more extreme results; they assessed mtDNA and Y chromosome patterns for a Colombian (South America) population that was established in the 16th to 17th centuries. The results revealed that the maternal ancestry of this population was largely (more than 90%) Amerindian (i.e., native South American), whereas the paternal ancestry was largely (94%) European. When combined with historical records, these genetic patterns paint a picture of male–male competition in which European men displaced Amerindian men to the reproductive benefit of the former and at a large cost to the latter. Related studies have found similar though less extreme patterns in other South and North American populations (Bortolini et al., 1999; Merriwether et al., 1997). Underhill et al.'s (2001) analysis of Y chromosome genes from 1,062 men from various parts of the world suggest a repeating pattern of one population of men replacing another population of men in Africa, Europe, and Asia (see also J. F. Wilson et al., 2001), although the extent of replacement varies from one region to the next (e.g., Capelli et al., 2003).

Most of these genetic studies also reveal that men in most local communities are more closely related to one another than are women, but women have more kin ties to other communities in the region (e.g., Seielstad et al., 1998; Wells et al., 2001; J. F. Wilson et al., 2001). These genetic footprints, so to speak, support the proposed social structure for male–male competition noted in Table 3.2 and often documented in ethnographic studies (D. E. Brown, 1991; Chagnon, 1988)—specifically, that men tend to form kin-based coalitions. The pattern is also consistent with ethnographic studies of marriage patterns, whereby men typically stay in their birth group—a necessary feature of kin-based male coalitions—and women emigrate to the group of their husband (Murdock, 1981). At the same time, genetic and historical records suggest that more distant migrations are initiated by men who are migrating in search of material resources, social status, and reproductive opportunity (Hammer et al., 2001; Semino et al., 2000).

When these genetic patterns are combined with historical, anthropological, and archeological information (e.g., Chagnon, 1988; Keeley, 1996), a picture of recent human evolutionary history comes into focus. A central, but certainly by no means the only, feature of this history has been the formation of male kin-based social coalitions. These coalitions engaged, and still engage, in group-level male–male competition—that is, warfare—over control of life-supporting ecologies and control of reproductive dynamics. In many societies, the combination of coalitional warfare and within-group dominance hierarchies resulted—and still results—in polygyny, which, in turn, results in fewer men reproducing than women. As I just noted, women often migrate to the group of their husband, and once they have migrated they should, in theory, attempt to organize social relationships in ways that enhance their own well-being and that of their children (Geary, 2002c). Attempts to organize these relationships contribute to female–female competition (sometimes with co-wives) and spousal conflict.

Sexual selection might also be the mechanism by which both interbreeding and replacement models of human evolution can be reconciled (see Origins section in this chapter). Replacement would occur among males through coalitional male–male competition. Interbreeding would occur among males of successful coalitions and the females that resided with the males of unsuccessful coalitions. Of course, social dynamics are not always hostile and are often cooperative in terms of economic trade and exchange of marital partners from one group to another. The point is that these genetic studies are consistent with the view that social competition and reproductive dynamics contributed to human evolution. To the extent that these dynamics were dependent on social and sociocognitive competencies, they contributed to the evolution of brain and cognition, as I describe in later chapters.

MOTIVATION TO CONTROL

There is general consensus among clinical and research psychologists that humans have a basic motivation to achieve some level of control over relationships, events, and resources of significance in their lives (Fiske, 1993; Heckhausen & Schulz, 1995; Shapiro, Schwartz, & Astin, 1996; Taylor & Brown, 1988; S. C. Thompson, Armstrong, & Thomas, 1998), although there is no consensus as to whether this motivation to control has evolved. My proposal is that the mechanisms of natural and sexual selection operate such that a motivation to control will necessarily evolve if the associated behavioral biases contribute to the ability to achieve access to and control of resources that tend to covary with survival and reproductive outcomes and if individual differences in this motivational tendency are heritable. The thesis here and elsewhere (Geary, 1998) is that the human motivation to control is indeed an evolved disposition and is implicitly focused on attempts to control social relationships and the behavior of other people and to control the biological and physical resources that covary with survival and reproductive prospects in the local ecology. My proposal in this volume is that the combination of mechanisms represented in Figure 3.9 guides and supports attempts to achieve access to and control of these resources. In the first section that follows, I present evidence for a relation between achieving control and survival and reproductive outcomes, and in the second I flesh out the mechanisms that enable the achievement of this end.

Benefits of Control

The same relation between resource control and survival and reproductive outcomes described for other species in chapter 2 (e.g., Social Selection Pressures section) is evident in most human societies (Ellis, 1993, 1994), although this relation is not always apparent in resource-rich Western culture. For humans and other species, the resources that covary with these evolutionary outcomes fall into three categories: social, biological, and physical (for related discussion, see Henriques, 2003). Biological resources include food and medicine, and physical resources include the territories that contain biological resources and that support homes, agriculture, pastures, and so on. Coalitional control of biological and physical resources results in ecological dominance, as described earlier.

Although humans have mechanisms that obscure the fact that they often use social relationships and other people for their own ends (Alexander, 1989), they do indeed use them in this way. Other people are resources if they have reproductive potential (e.g., young females; Buss, 1994; Singh, 1993), social power, or access (e.g., through monetary wealth) to the biological and physical resources that covary with well-being and status in the culture (Irons, 1979). The goal of developing a relationship with an individual who has social power and wealth is fundamentally an attempt to influence the behavior of this individual and through this to achieve access to power and wealth (Fiske, 1993; Geary & Flinn, 2001).

In most contexts and for most people, the motivation to control is constrained by formal laws, informal social mores (enforced, e.g., through gossip; Barkow, 1992), and affective mechanisms (e.g., guilt) that promote

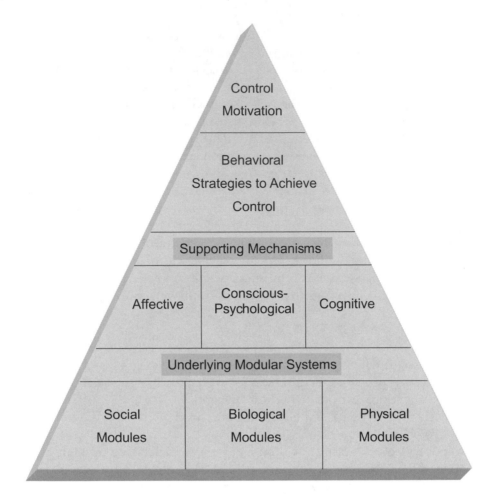

Figure 3.9. The apex and section below it represent the proposal that human behavior is basically driven by a motivation to control the social, biological, and physical resources that have tended to covary with survival and reproductive outcomes during human evolution. The midsection shows the supporting affective, conscious-psychological (e.g., attributional biases), and cognitive (e.g., working memory) mechanisms that support the motivation to control and operate on the modular systems shown at the base.

social compromise and reciprocal social relationships (Baron, 1997; Trivers, 1971). For most people, adherence to these laws and mores provides benefits that are sufficient to avoid the risks associated with attempts to achieve, for instance, absolute despotic control (Simon, 1990b). Still, consideration of history's despots allows a peeling away of these constraints and a more direct glimpse at the motivation to control. By definition, despots are individuals who have considerable social power and whose behavior is not typically constrained by affective or social consequences; they are also likely to differ from other people in terms of empathy for others, and in terms of the intensity of their need for social dominance.

With the absence of reciprocal cultural mores (i.e., democracy) and a professional police force and military to suppress despotic behavior, these individuals and their coalitions gained control of the first six human civilizations—ancient Mesopotamia, Egypt, the Aztec and Inca empires, and imperial India and China (Betzig, 1986, 1993). Across these and many other civilizations, the activities of despots were (and still are) centered on diverting the material and social resources of the culture to themselves and to their kin, typically to the detriment of many other people. On the basis of the historical record, they lived in opulence, and the men almost always had exclusive sexual access to scores—sometimes thousands—of women (Betzig, 1986, 1992).

Regardless of how one might morally evaluate these activities, despots and their kin were better fed, had better health, and had more children than their subjects (e.g., Betzig, 1992). In addition to the historical record, a recent genetic study provides direct evidence for the reproductive benefits of despotism. In this study, Zerjal et al. (2003) analyzed the Y chromosome genes of 2,123 men from regions throughout Asia. They found that 8% of the men in this part of the world have a single common ancestor who emerged from Mongolia and lived about 1,000 years ago. The geographic distribution of these genes fits well with the historic boundaries of the empire of Genghis Khan (c. 1162–1227), who was known to have had hundreds of wives and many, many children. They estimated that Genghis Khan and his close male relatives are the direct ancestors of 16 million men in Asia, ranging from northeast China to Uzbekistan, and the direct ancestors of about 0.5% of the world's total population.

Genghis Khan is, of course, an extreme example. As with other traits, it is almost certain that there are individual differences in the intensity of the motivation to control and individual differences in the manner in which it is expressed (e.g., Pratto, 1996). Heritable personality differences, for instance, might reflect the evolution of different strategies for obtaining access to social and material resources (Buss, 1991; MacDonald, 1995; McCrae & Costa, 1997; D. C. Rowe, 1994), with the desire for despotic control being only one of these alternative strategies (D. S. Wilson, Near, & Miller, 1996). However it is achieved, gaining some level of control over the activities of daily life, important social relationships, and material resources affords many of the same benefits, albeit on a much smaller scale, as those enjoyed by despots. Even in resource-rich Western culture, socioeconomic status (SES)—that is, the ability to influence other people and control material resources—is associated with a longer life span and better physical health (e.g., Adler et al., 1994; R. H. Bradley & Corwyn, 2002; Reid, 1998; Rodin, 1986), although it is not correlated with happiness or the subjective evaluation of well-being (Diener & Diener, 1996; Lykken & Tellegen, 1996; D. G. Myers & Diener, 1995).

In preindustrial and industrializing Western societies, and in traditional societies today (Hill & Hurtado, 1996; United Nations, 1985), SES was considerably more important than it currently is in Western culture (Hed, 1987; Herlihy, 1965; Klindworth & Voland, 1995; Morrison et al., 1977; H. Schultz, 1991; Vallin, 1991; Voland, 1988). In fact, parental SES often influenced which infants and young children would live and which would die. As just one example, during the 1437 to 1438 and 1449 to 1450 epidemics in Florence, Italy, child mortality rates increased 5- to 10-fold and varied inversely with parental SES even at the high end of the continuum (Morrison et al., 1977). As another example, in an extensive analysis of birth, death, and demographic records from 18th-century Berlin, H. Schultz (1991) found a strong correlation ($r = .74$) between parental SES and infant and child mortality rates. Infant (birth to 1 year) mortality rates were about 10% for aristocrats but more than 40% for laborers and unskilled technicians:

> A senior official of the welfare authorities (*Armenbehörde*) observed in 1769 that among the poor weavers of Friedrichstadt 75 out of every 100 children borne died before they reached "adulthood" (presumably twelve years of age). . . . He rightly regarded the poverty or affluence of the parents as the decisive factor in determining whether the children thrived or died. (H. Schultz, 1991, p. 243)

Given these relations, it is not surprising that individual and group-level conflicts of interest are invariably over access to and control of social relationships, other people, and the biological and physical resources that covary with survival or reproductive prospects in the local ecology and culture (Alexander, 1979; Chagnon, 1988; Horowitz, 2001; Irons, 1979; Keeley, 1996). Although these relations are often masked by the wealth and low mortality rates enjoyed in Western societies today, the implication is clear: In most human societies and presumably throughout hominid evolution, gaining social influence and control of biological and physical resources—that is, food, medicine, shelter, land, and so forth—covaried with reproductive opportunity (i.e., choice of mating partner), reproductive success (i.e., number of offspring surviving to adulthood), and survival prospects. In other words, heritable individual differences in human, and presumably earlier hominid, social competencies and behavioral strategies that enable achievement of social influence and resource control resulted in the evolution of these traits and the evolution of supporting affective, conscious-psychological (described in the Conscious-Psychological Mechanisms section, this chapter), and cognitive mechanisms. A fundamental motivation to control has evolved in humans, and probably all species at an abstract level, because success at achieving control of social relationships and biological and physical resources very often meant the difference between living and dying.

Modules and Mechanisms

The bottom sections of Figure 3.9 show the affective, conscious-psychological, and cognitive mechanisms and underlying modular systems that support control-related behavioral strategies. I describe the modular systems at the base of Figure 3.9 in chapter 5. The brain and cognitive systems that compose these modules are predicted to have evolved to process information (e.g., facial features) in the domains of resource control—that is, social (conspecifics), biological (e.g., other species that serve as food or medicine), and physical (e.g., demarcation of the group's territory). As I noted earlier and will elaborate on in chapter 5, biologically oriented anthropologists and psychologists refer to these modular systems as components of folk psychology, folk biology, and folk physics, respectively (e.g., Atran, 1998; Baron-Cohen, 1995; Brothers & Ring, 1992; Carey & Spelke, 1994; Coley, 2000; R. Gelman, 1990; Hirschfeld & Gelman, 1994; Humphrey, 1976; Pinker, 1997; Povinelli & Preuss, 1995; Premack & Woodruff, 1978). The point for now is that these systems draw attention to and process information patterns that have covaried with survival and reproductive outcomes during hominid evolution and are thus integral features of the behavioral strategies needed to achieve these outcomes.

Conscious-Psychological Mechanisms

As I describe in greater detail in chapter 7 (in sections on Mental Models and the Motivation to Control and on Social Cognition and Folk Psychology), these psychological mechanisms are conscious, explicit mental representations of situations that are centered on the self, one's relationship with other people, and one's access to biological and physical resources that are of significance in the culture and ecology in which one is situated. The representations are of past, present, or potential future states and might be cast as visual images, in language, or as memories of personal experiences (i.e., episodic memories). In chapter 7, I emphasize the ability to create a mental representation of a desired or fantasized state, such as a relationship with another individual, and to compare this to a mental representation of one's current state, such as the nature of the current relationship with this other individual. These are explicit, conscious-psychological representations of present and potential future states that are of personal significance and are the content to which more general reasoning and problem-solving processes are applied. These conscious-psychological representations might also result in the generation of feelings associated with the current state or potential changes in this state (Damasio, 2003).

Explicit attributions about the self or other people provide further examples of conscious-psychological representations. As an illustration, it is common for people to make attributions about the cause of failures to achieve social influence or other desired outcomes. An attribution of this type might involve an explicit evaluation of the reason for one's failure to achieve a desired outcome—for example, that the failure was due to bad luck—and would function to direct and maintain control-related behavioral strategies in the face of any such failure (Heckhausen & Schulz, 1995). Another example involves attributions about favored in-group members and disfavored members of an out-group. These attributional biases have been extensively studied under laboratory conditions and are particularly salient during times of intergroup competition and hostilities (e.g., W. G. Stephan, 1985). Horowitz's (2001) seminal analysis of ethnic conflict in the real world is consistent with these laboratory studies and with the position that conflict is invariably over resource control. Hostile and otherwise unfavorable attributions about the character and intentions of the out-group often include rumors of an intended out-group attack or conspiracy to, for instance, poison the in-group's food supply, attack the women, and so forth. These attributional biases justify, facilitate (e.g., by gaining support of other members of the in-group), and precede violence. The resulting conflict is often deadly and just as often results in the self-serving elimination of economic or social competitors. The attributional biases not only justify this self-serving violence, but also simultaneously protect individuals from the affective consequences, such as guilt and remorse, that could result if the violence were directed against a member of the in-group.

Cognitive Mechanisms

I also describe in chapter 7 the cognitive mechanisms that operate on conscious-psychological content (Cognitive Systems section), including working memory, attentional control, and the ability to inhibit automatic processing of external information (e.g., Baddeley, 2000a; Bjorklund & Harnishfeger, 1995; Cowan, 1988). I describe associated reasoning and problem-solving competencies in chapter 6 (Newell & Simon, 1972). These cognitive and problem-solving processes are the mechanisms that allow individuals to mentally represent and manipulate information processed by sensory and perceptual systems (e.g., sounds and words; Baddeley & Hitch, 1974) and the more complex forms of information processed by the social, biological, and physical modules. Working memory, for instance, enables the short-term retention of spoken utterances, which may facilitate vocabulary learning and other specific competencies.

However, the most important function from the perspective of this book concerns the relation between these cognitive and problem-solving mechanisms and the generation of and manipulation of conscious-psychological representations. In other words, working memory and attentional and inhibitory control are the content-free mechanisms that, for instance, enable the integration of a current conscious-psychological state with memory representations of related past experiences and the generation of mental models or simulations of potential future states (Alexander, 1989; Baddeley, 1994; Johnson-Laird, 1983). Perhaps this fine a distinction between cognitive and conscious-psychological processes is unnecessary, but I have done so to emphasize that the content of mental representations (the psychological component) is important from an evolutionary perspective. In much of the research in experimental psychology, the focus is on cognitive mechanisms, such as working memory, and not so much on the content on which these mechanisms operate (Miyake & Shah, 1999).

Evolutionary Function

My proposal in chapter 7 (Problem Solving and Human Evolution section) is that the evolved function of these cognitive mechanisms and conscious-psychological mechanisms is to generate a mental representation of the social, biological, and physical world. I assume that humans are biased to generate a fantasy representation of how the world "should" operate, that is, a representation of the world that would be most favorable to the individual's reproductive (e.g., fantasy of the "perfect" mate; Whissell, 1996) and survival interests. This mental representation serves as a goal to be achieved and is compared against a mental representation of current circumstances. Working memory mechanisms then serve as a platform for simulating social and other behavioral strategies that will reduce the difference between the ideal and actual states. These problem-solving (Newell & Simon, 1972) activities are ultimately directed toward the goal of attempting to achieve access to and control of social and other resources, as noted.

Following Damasio's (2003) distinction, affective mechanisms are separated into emotions, which are observable behaviors (e.g., facial expressions or social withdrawal), and feelings, which are nonobservable conscious representations of an emotional state or other conditions that can potentially influence the individuals' well-being (see Mental Models and the Motivation to Control section of chap. 7). Affective mechanisms guide behavioral strategies. The associated emotions provide feedback to other individuals (e.g., a frown may automatically signal disapproval), and feelings provide feedback to the individual (Campos, Campos, & Barrett, 1989). The latter provide an indicator of the effectiveness of control-related behavioral strategies. Positive feelings provide reinforcement when strategies are resulting in the achievement of significant goals, or at least a reduction in the difference between the current and desired state, and punishment (negative feelings) and disengagement occur when behaviors are not resulting in this end (J. A. Gray, 1987; Henriques, 2000).

The associated brain systems should function, in part, to amplify attention to evolutionarily significant forms of information, such as facial expressions, and to produce emotions, feelings, and corresponding behavioral tendencies that are likely to recreate outcomes that have covaried with survival or reproduction during hominid evolution (Damasio, 2003; Lazarus, 1991; Öhman, 2002). For instance, positive affect should function, in part, to maintain the forms of social relationship that are commonly associated with the achievement of survival and reproductive ends, and this appears to be the case. Happiness is strongly related to the strength of reciprocal and romantic relationships (Diener & Seligman, 2002), the former being sources of social support and allies during times of social conflict and the latter obviously related to reproductive goals.

As Darwin (1872/1998) argued and contemporary scientists (e.g., Ekman, 1992) have confirmed, emotions are effective social signals that influence the emotions, feelings, and behavior of other people. Hagen (1999, 2003) cogently argued that affective states, such as depression, can result in a host of social and behavioral changes that may be a form of social manipulation, that is, a strategy to organize the social world in ways that enhance the individual's self-interest. As an example, postpartum depression involves social withdrawal and a shutting down of behavioral systems associated with care of the newborn and the self. This form of depression is expressed through behaviors and emotional signaling and often occurs when the new mother does not have adequate social or economic support (Hagen, 1999). The behavioral depression is a reaction to this lack of support and is simultaneously analogous to a labor strike, whereby the woman signals that she will not invest in the well-being of the newborn. The newborn's father and other kin are, of course, invested in the well-being of the newborn and often respond to the mother's depression by providing additional social or economic support to the mother and the newborn. In this view, postpartum depression can be an emotional–behavioral strategy that elicits investment in the newborn and the mother that they otherwise would not receive. Moreover, because the mother is suffering, the risk of social retribution for not providing the expected level of maternal care is reduced.

CONCLUSION

Much is now known about human origins and our hominid ancestors, notwithstanding the sometimes rancorous debates about the associated evidence and its implications for understanding human nature (e.g., Templeton, 2002; Wolpoff et al., 2000). To be sure, the fossil record is incomplete and subject to legitimate scientific disagreement, but if one peers through the dust raised by these disagreements, an interpretable pattern can be seen. Whether our ancestral line stretches back to A. garhi or to A. africanus matters little to the issues addressed in this book. Individuals of these and other australopithecine species had larger brains than extant chimpanzees but brain volumes that were about one third that of modern humans and EQs that were less than half that of modern humans. Given that one of these, or some yet to be discovered sister species, was the ancestral species of modern humans, a high level of confidence can be placed on the conclusion that substantial changes in brain volume, EQ, and brain organization have occurred since the emergence of the genus Homo. Whether H. habilis was a member of this genus or an australopithecine is less important than the clear and substantial increases in brain volume and EQ that were associated with the emergence of H. erectus—there is general agreement that this was indeed an ancestor of modern humans (B. Wood & Collard, 1999)—and further increases with the emergence of humans.

The primary concern here is the selection pressures that drove these changes, and this is where the issues become more clouded. In fact, as I noted earlier and will discuss more fully in chapter 4 (Allometry and Size of the Neocortex section), there is debate as to whether the increases in brain volume and EQ during hominid evolution were the result of evolutionary selection at all or simply a byproduct of the evolution of other traits. The gist of Vrba's (1974, 1995b) climate-driven turnover pulse hypothesis is that much of the change in brain volume and EQ during hominid evolution was an incidental effect of increases in body size. There are many reasons, as I described earlier in this chapter, for questioning this conclusion, not the least of which being that the calculation of EQ controls for changes in body size. Nonetheless, the speciation events predicted by the model might explain the adaptive radiation and emergence of several species of hominid 3.0 to 2.0 million years ago, one of these species being the ancestor of modern humans.

My conclusion and that of most other scientists is that some combination of ecological and social pressures drove the evolution of brain and cognition during human evolution. The basic issues concern whether the primary selective pressures were largely ecological or social in nature. There is a tendency for anthropologists to emphasize ecologically based adaptations, such as those involved in acquiring (e.g., through hunting) and processing (e.g., cooking) food (e.g., Kaplan et al., 2000) and a tendency for primatologists and psychologists to emphasize social adaptations, such as those required to maintain reciprocal relationships or to socially manipulate conspecifics (e.g., Dunbar, 1993; Humphrey, 1976). Alexander's (1989; see also Flinn, Geary, & Ward, in press) model of ecological dominance combines the two classes of selection pressure, with adaptations to ecological pressures being primary earlier in human evolution and adaptations to social pressures being primary later in human evolution.

My motivation-to-control framework builds on Alexander's (1989) proposal and attempts to bundle these different forms of selection pressure together and link them to the affective, conscious-psychological (e.g., attributional biases; W. G. Stephan, 1985), and cognitive (e.g., working memory; Baddeley, 2000a) processes that psychologists traditionally study. The gist is that affective, conscious-psychological, and cognitive processes support behavioral attempts to gain access to and control of the types of social (e.g., mates), biological (e.g., food), and physical (e.g., territory) resources that have tended to covary with survival and reproductive outcomes during human evolution (Geary, 1998). The framework also provides a means to link these conscious-psychological and cognitive mechanisms to general intelligence and thus to link ecological and social selection pressures to the evolution of general intelligence. The basic argument is that many of the same mechanisms that support the motivation to control, such as efficiency of working memory and problem-solving mechanisms, appear to contribute to individual differences in general intelligence. The motivation to control thus provides the link between models of brain and cognitive evolution and empirical research on general intelligence, as I describe in chapters 8 and 9. Before these links can be fully integrated into an evolutionary perspective, discussion of research and theoretical issues associated with the evolution and development of the brain and cognitive modularity must be addressed and are thus the subject of the next two chapters.

4

EVOLUTION AND DEVELOPMENT OF BRAIN AND COGNITION

Controversy over the evolution of the human mind and brain has raged since naturalists began debating the implications of the principles of natural selection set forth in Darwin's and Wallace's first publication in 1858 and all but proved in 1859 with Darwin's masterwork, *Origin of Species*. Among other ensuing debates was the theoretical clash between these two great naturalists. Darwin (1871) argued that the mental faculties of the human brain, such as language, had evolved by means of natural and sexual selection and, although qualitatively different in some ways, showed many continuities with the faculties of mind and brain of other species. Wallace, in contrast, did not believe that the mental faculties of the human brain, especially as related to intelligence and morality, could be the result of mindless, so to speak, organic evolution. One of the first places in which Wallace's (1869) argument was articulated was at the conclusion of a review of Lyell's *Principles of Geology* (1867):

> But let us not shut our eyes to the evidence that an Overruling Intelligence has watched over the action of those laws [natural selection] so directing variations and so determining the accumulation [of favored traits], as finally to produce an organization sufficiently perfect to admit of, and even to aid in, the indefinite advancement of our mental and moral nature. (p. 205)

Contemporary debates have a less theological flavor, but the basic issue still concerns whether the human mind and brain are composed of specific faculties, now called *modules*, that evolved as a result of specific selection pressures (Hauser, Chomsky, & Fitch, 2002; Pinker & Jackendoff, in press). An example of how the brain could evolve in the absence of specific selection pressures is provided by Vrba's (1995b) proposal that climatic changes resulted in increased body size during hominid evolution that incidentally resulted in a corresponding increase in brain size (see Climatic Pressures section of chap. 3). Of course, models such as Vrba's are not the same as Wallace's "Overruling Intelligence," but they nonetheless touch on the same theme—that the specific faculties of the human mind and brain cannot be understood in terms of specific selection pressures. Rather, the human brain is largely uncommitted in terms of past selection pressures and thus is more of a *tabula rasa* organ, with faculties of mind emerging from developmental experiences. At first blush, general intelligence (g) would seem to be consistent with this experiential view, as g indexes the ability to cognitively and socially adapt to novelty, complexity, and change (Gottfredson, 1997; Jensen, 1998) and thus appears to be a very different form of cognitive ability than that implied by specific and evolved faculties (e.g., spatial, language) or modularity.

As noted in the introductory chapter, my ultimate goal is to develop a theory that not only is consistent with Darwin's (1871) evolved faculties but also integrates contemporary theory and research on modularity with the competencies that define g. In chapter 5, I present a taxonomy of cognitive modules that appear to have evolved as a result of the ecological and social pressures described in chapter 3. The model that integrates these evolved modules with more general cognitive systems (e.g., working memory) and thereby sets the stage for understanding the evolution of g is presented in later chapters. Before stepping into these literatures, I need to touch on a few foundational issues. In the first section, I get right at the heart of one of the more contentious of these issues—the extent to which the organization of brain and functions of mind result from inherent, gene-driven constraints or from the pattern of developmental experiences. The interaction of constraint and openness to experiential modification defines the issue of brain and cognitive plasticity, and in the fourth section I propose different forms of modularity that accommodate different forms of plasticity. In the second and third sections, I provide reviews of empirical and theoretical work related to the issues of gene-driven and experience-driven influences, respectively, on the organization of brain and functions of mind and corresponding evolutionary mechanisms.

CURRENT DEBATE AND THEORETICAL FRAMEWORK

There is continuing debate regarding the relative importance of inherent gene-driven constraints versus patterns of developmental experience on the organization and functioning of human mental faculties, such as language (for extended discussion, see Bjorklund, 2003; Lickliter & Honeycutt, 2003; Tooby, Cosmides, & Barrett, 2003). Nonetheless, most theorists agree that some combination of constraint and experience—that is, epigenesis—results in the phenotypic expression of these faculties (Elman et al., 1996; Geary & Bjorklund, 2000; Pinker, 1994, 1997; Tooby & Cosmides, 1995). Following R. Gelman (1990), *plasticity* refers to the balance of inherent constraint and developmental experience that results in the ability to adapt brain and cognitive systems and processes to socially and ecologically salient information, such as the basic shape of the human body and differences in the body shape (e.g., height, weight) of one person to the next. The mix of constraint and experience that produces brain and cognitive plasticity is shown in Figure 4.1. The areas above and below the dashed lines in the figure represent theoretical space in which few theorists wander; few argue that all functions of brain and mind are due exclusively to inherent constraints or to the pattern of experiences. The plasticity area of the triangle represents the current focus of debate, namely the extent to which inherent constraints or developmental experiences are emphasized. There are, of course, many nuances, and some degree of characterization is necessary to define the range of theoretical positions.

At one extreme is the position that brain and mind are composed of a constellation of modular systems that have a high degree of inherent constraint (Lenneberg, 1967; Pinker, 1994; Tooby & Cosmides, 1995), although the expression of different features of these systems can be contingent on early experiences (Greenough, Black, & Wallace, 1987). As an example, the brain and cognitive systems involved in processing phonemes (e.g., "ba," "da") are conceptualized as inherent, but the phenotypic expression of one phonemic system or another is contingent on early exposure to associated language sounds (Vouloumanos & Werker, in press; Werker & Tees, 1992). Gallistel (2000) suggested that inherent navigational systems can include mechanisms that enable the formation of relevant memory patterns, such as the memory of star patterns that migratory birds later use to guide navigation back to the birth site for breeding. The ability to form experience-dependent memories is, however, assumed to occur within the constraints of an evolved modular system.

At the other extreme is the position that the organization and functions of brain and mind emerge through an interaction between more minimal inherent constraints and the potent effects of developmental experience,

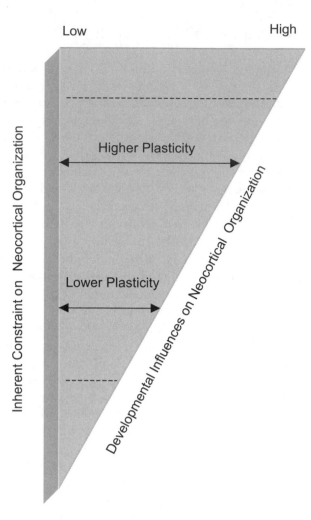

Low   High

Inherent Constraint on Neocortical Organization

Higher Plasticity

Lower Plasticity

Developmental Influences on Neocortical Organization

High/Low

Figure 4.1. The triangle represents the relation between inherent constraint and the influence of developmental experience on brain organization and cognitive functions. As degree of inherent constraint increases, the potential for experiential modification decreases. The length of the lines in the center of the triangle represents the corresponding degree of brain and cognitive plasticity. The area above the first dashed line represents the position that organization of the neocortex is almost completely dependent on developmental experiences, whereas the area below the second dashed line represents the position that organization of the neocortex is almost completely determined by genetic constraints. Few theorists hold either of these positions. From "Brain and Cognitive Evolution: Forms of Modularity and Functions of Mind," by D. C. Geary and K. J. Huffman, 2002, *Psychological Bulletin, 128,* p. 668. Copyright 2002 by the American Psychological Association. Reprinted with permission.

because the latter influence gene expression and brain organization (Elman et al., 1996; Heyes, 2003; La Cerra & Bingham, 1998; Lickliter & Honeycutt, 2003; Quartz & Sejnowski, 1997). The ability to process language-specific phonemes, for instance, results from constraints on the range and form of sounds that can be processed rather than an evolved system for specifically processing language sounds (Hauser et al., 2002). Within these broad constraints, regularities in spoken language interact with a largely uncommitted—in terms of past selection pressures—neocortex. The eventual result is the creation of modular systems that support language-specific processing (Paterson, Brown, Gsödl, Johnson, & Karmiloff-Smith, 1999).

Arguments by scientists at both extremes tend to focus on the benefits of inherent constraint or openness to experiential modification, often without full consideration of attendant costs. Cost–benefit trade-offs are, nonetheless, common to biological systems (Williams, 1957), and any potential cost of inherent constraint or openness to experiential modification will influence the evolution of brain and cognitive plasticity (Kaas, 2000). The most basic of these cost–benefit trade-offs are illustrated in Figure 4.2 and can be appreciated only in the context of the ecologies in which the species evolved (Dukas, 1998a). From this perspective, the mind and brain provide the interface between the organism and the ecology and function to guide the organism's behavior so as to achieve outcomes that enhance survival or reproductive prospects in these ecologies. Selection favors brain and cognitive systems that are open to experiential modification to the extent that information related to survival or reproduction is variant across generations and life spans. Selection favors inherent constraint to the extent that these information patterns are invariant across generations and life spans. From this perspective, different brain and cognitive systems are predicted to vary with respect to relative degree of openness and constraint to the extent that associated information patterns are variant or invariant, respectively.

My proposal is that Darwin's (1871) faculties of mind and brain are indeed the direct result of specific selection pressures. These pressures, in turn, can be understood in terms of patterns of information that have enabled organisms to achieve behavioral outcomes that have generally enhanced survival or reproductive prospects during the species' evolutionary history. Some of these information patterns, such as the shape of a face, are largely the same (invariant patterns) from one situation or generation to the next, and thus constrained brain and cognitive systems that direct attention to and process these patterns are predicted to evolve. For some information patterns, a sensitivity to individual differences (variant patterns) is essential. An example is the ability to distinguish the cry of one's own baby from the cry of all other babies. For these forms of information, some degree of inherent constraint is needed to distinguish the acoustical features of crying

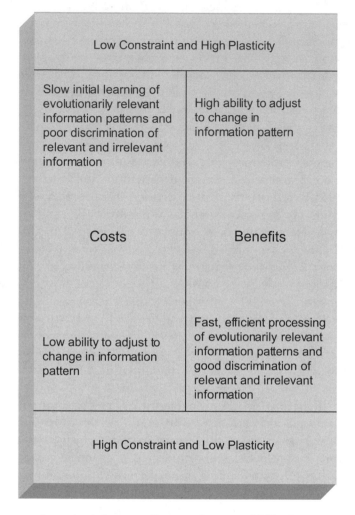

Variant Across Generations and Life Spans

Low Constraint and High Plasticity

Slow initial learning of evolutionarily relevant information patterns and poor discrimination of relevant and irrelevant information

High ability to adjust to change in information pattern

Costs

Benefits

Low ability to adjust to change in information pattern

Fast, efficient processing of evolutionarily relevant information patterns and good discrimination of relevant and irrelevant information

High Constraint and Low Plasticity

Invariant Across Generations and Life Spans

Figure 4.2. The rectangle highlights cost–benefit trade-offs that are predicted to influence the evolution of brain and cognitive plasticity. From "Brain and Cognitive Evolution: Forms of Modularity and Functions of Mind," by D. C. Geary and K. J. Huffman, 2002, *Psychological Bulletin, 128,* p. 668. Copyright 2002 by the American Psychological Association. Reprinted with permission.

from all other sounds, but plasticity of these systems is crucial for distinguishing one baby's cry from another. Because the specific features of one's own baby's cry cannot be coded in the genes, the brain and cognitive systems that process this information must be plastic, that is, modifiable in response to hearing the baby's cry.

EVOLUTION AND BRAIN ORGANIZATION

Comparative—that is, across species—research on brain organization and cognitive functions speaks directly to the crux of Darwin's (1871) and Wallace's (1869) debate over whether human mental faculties are continuous with those found in other species, especially other primates. My goal is to present the evolutionary logic and supporting evidence for understanding the implications of Darwin's argument—that is, how the human brain can show continuities with the brains of other species and yet be different in ways that are uniquely human. In the following sections, I provide a description of what appears to be the basic architecture of the brain, specifically the neocortex, and the possible genetic and developmental mechanisms that regulate constraint in the central nervous system (CNS). This, in turn, provides a framework for understanding how evolution can operate on brain systems that are common across species (due to a common ancestor) to create species-specific specializations, such as those faculties that Wallace argued set humans apart from all other species.

To achieve this goal, I provide in the first section a brief overview of research comparing various cross-species similarities in CNS subdivisions in an attempt to illustrate similarity because of a common ancestor, that is, to establish *homology* (for an accessible review, see Swanson, 2003). In the second and third subsections, I provide a brief survey of the cross-species similarity in genes that code for the prenatal organization of the CNS and a description of theories of neocortical development and evolution (for an accessible review, see Marcus, 2004). In the final subsection, I describe a framework for understanding cross-species continuities in brain development and evolution. The framework helps to clarify how the brains of different species can be at once similar, different, and modifiable in response to evolutionary pressures. The literature in these areas is, of course, large and growing, and thus an exhaustive survey is not possible; I do, however, provide a sampling.

Comparative Neurobiology

Comparing the brains of different species can be used to better understand brain evolution (Brodmann, 1909; Holloway, 1968; Krubitzer, 1995;

Krubitzer & Huffman, 2000; Supèr & Uylings, 2001). The most common approach is to examine extant species whose lines branched off the evolutionary tree at different points in evolutionary history. Although extant species have continued to evolve independently, they provide the best means to make inferences about the history of brain organization and evolution. For example, in mammalian evolution, three major lines have emerged: prototheria (extant example: duck-billed platypus, *Ornithorhynchus anatinus*); metatheria (extant example: eastern gray kangaroo, *Macropus giganteus*); and eutheria (i.e., placental mammals; extant example: human being). Comparative neurobiologists examine the brain organization of example species from these lines in an attempt to deduce similarities (constraints conserved from a common ancestor) and differences (species-specific adaptations) in species that share recent to very distant common ancestors.

Analyses of many species have uncovered much constraint or conservation in the architecture of the CNS. Many brain structures, such as the diencephalon (including the thalamus and hypothalamus) of all mammals studied, including prototherian, metatherian, and eutherian mammals, appear highly similar. The organization of the thalamus, a brain structure that is the relay for sensory information from the periphery to the neocortex, is highly conserved across mammals. Many of the sensory nuclei of the thalamus—that is, groups of cells that relay specific forms of sensory information (e.g., sounds)—are not only architectonically (i.e., organized) alike, they are also functionally similar in terms of cellular physiology and connectivity (Jones, 1985). Apparently homologous nuclei are found comparing a mouse (*Mus musculus*) and human thalamus, suggesting that this organizational feature of the thalamus evolved in a very early mammalian species; the ancestor common to the mouse and human lived about 75 million years ago (Mouse Genome Sequencing Consortium, 2002). Similarities such as these exist in other positions along the neural axis as well. For instance, similarities in brainstem nuclei have been identified in all mammals studied, including humans (Butler & Hodos, 1996).

Conservation of CNS subdivisions is not limited to subcortical regions. For example, many divisions of the hippocampus (a brain structure that supports certain forms of memory and spatial cognition) are also conserved across mammalian lineages (Butler & Hodos, 1996). All mammals, including humans (Disbrow, Roberts, & Krubitzer, 2000; S. A. Engel, Glover, & Wandell, 1997), have basic auditory, visual, and somatosensory neocortical regions (Krubitzer, 1995; Northcutt & Kaas, 1995), and reptiles and birds have *analogous*—same function, but independent evolution—and perhaps homologous regions in the telencephalon, the analog to the neocortex (Aboitiz, Morales, & Montiel, 2003; Doupe & Kuhl, 1999; Karten, 1997).

Several examples of conserved areas in the neocortex are illustrated in Figure 4.3. This figure shows the homologous primary sensory areas—

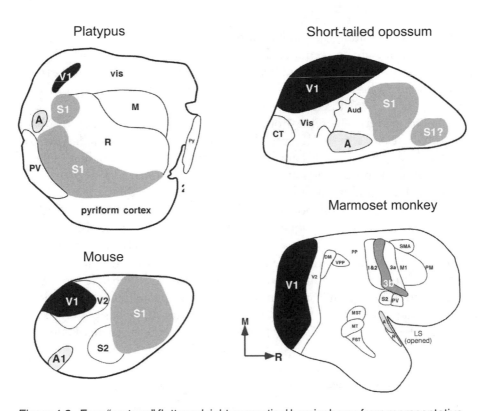

Platypus

Short-tailed opossum

Mouse

Marmoset monkey

Figure 4.3. Four "cartoon" flattened right neocortical hemispheres from representative animals from the three major mammalian lineages: a. prototherian platypus (*Ornithorhynchus anatinus*), b. metatherian short-tailed opossum (*Monodelphis domestica*), c. eutherian mouse (*Mus musculus*), and d. eutherian marmoset monkey (*Callithrix jacchus*). All of these mammals have a primary somatosensory cortical area (dark gray), a primary visual area (black), and a primary auditory area (light gray) that are likely to have been present in the common mammalian ancestor. A = presumptive primary auditory area; Aud = secondary auditory area; CT = caudal temporal area; DM = dorsal medial area; FST = fundal superior temporal; LS = lateral sulcus; M = presumptive motor cortex; M1 = primary motor area; MT = medial temporal area; MST = middle superior temporal area; PM = premotor area; PP = posterior parietal area; PV = parietal ventral area; R = rostral somatosensory region; S1 = primary somatosensory area; S2 = secondary somatosensory area; SMA = supplementary motor area; V1 = primary visual area; V2 = secondary visual area; vis = visual cortex; VPP = ventoposterior parietal area; 1 & 2, 3a, 3b = regions of somatosensory cortex; ↑ M = medial; → R = rostral. From "Brain and Cognitive Evolution: Forms of Modularity and Functions of Mind," by D. C. Geary and K. J. Huffman, 2002, *Psychological Bulletin, 128,* p. 670. Copyright 2002 by American Psychological Association.

including primary visual (V1), somatosensory (S1), and auditory (A/A1) cortices—in prototherian (platypus), metatherian (short-tailed opossum, *Monodelphis domestica*), and eutherian (mouse and marmoset monkey, *Callithrix jacchus*) mammals. That these areas are homologous, that is, the result of a common early ancestor, has been established using multiple methods that are both anatomical and functional. In addition, Disbrow et al. (2000), using brain imaging techniques, demonstrated the presence of multiple areas in the somatosensory cortex of humans (see Figure 3.3). They demonstrated these areas to be analogous and likely homologous to areas previously described in the somatosensory parietal cortex of monkeys.

The pattern emerging from current research suggests that the basic architecture and some of the specialized functions of the mammalian neocortex and subcortical regions are conserved across species, including humans. The results of these studies are inconsistent with Wallace's (1869) position that the brain and mind of humans are fundamentally different from those of other species. This is not to say that there are not brain and cognitive specializations that are uniquely human; there clearly are. Rather, as illustrated in a later section (Comparative Ecology and Brain Evolution), species-specific specializations can be readily understood as being built from the basic architecture of the mammalian brain (Holloway, 1968). There is every reason to believe that the brain and cognitive specializations that define human mental faculties have also been built from this basic architecture and can be understood in terms of the evolutionary pressures that I described in chapter 3.

Comparative Genetics

Many subdivisions of the brain and nervous system appear to be conserved across different branches of the evolutionary tree. In addition, it has been suggested that many genes that code for the prenatal development of these different subdivisions are also conserved across these species, including humans (Cavaillé et al., 2000; Chan & Jan, 1999; Gilbert, Opitz, & Raff, 1996; Holland & Holland, 1999; Katz & Harris-Warrick, 1999; Krubitzer & Huffman, 2000; Manzanares et al., 2000; Reichert & Simeone, 1999). As noted, many of the basic building blocks and presumably specializations (e.g., for processing sounds) are the same for the human brain and other brains (Karten, 1997). The prenatal development of these common CNS subdivisions must of course be genetically mediated, and thus it is likely that many of the same genes mediated the development of these subdivisions in the ancestor common to all living mammals and for some genes in the ancestor common to many living organisms. Although there is much to be learned and definitive conclusions cannot be drawn at this time, recent research suggests that at least some of the genes that establish or regulate the generation of these subdivisions may be conserved, or at least variants of the same gene may have similar functions with respect to early brain development (Grove & Fukuchi-Shimagori, 2003; Hatten, 2002).

Reichert and Simeone (1999), for instance, reported the existence of what appear to be homologous genes that guide the development of the

CNS in the fruit fly (*Drosophila*), mouse, and human; there are, of course, many genetic differences across these species (Venter et al., 2001). Abnormalities in the CNS are found in *Drosophila* mutants in which these genes are not expressed, and replacement with homologous human genes "rescue the brain and other defects" (Reichert & Simeone, 1999, p. 591). These same *Drosophila* genes have been shown to influence cortical development in the mouse, and additional studies suggest that other apparently homologous genes may control the development of the basic structure of the CNS in invertebrates and vertebrates (Holland & Holland, 1999; Rubenstein, Shimamura, Martinez, & Puelles, 1998).

There are also transcription factors (proteins that bind to specific DNA segments and control the expression of specific genes), growth factors, and secreted molecules that influence prenatal brain development and appear to be conserved in at least two species that have been compared, the chick (*Gallus domesticus*) and mouse (Puelles et al., 2000). The associated genes appear to function to regulate the genesis of subdivisions of the brains in both species (see Intrinsic Model section below), and some of the genes are also responsible for a similar function in nonmammals (Lee, Danielian, Fritzsch, & McMahon, 1997). There are many more examples of genes that seem to be homologous as well as analogous in terms of their function in CNS development across species as diverse as the fruit fly, chick, and mouse (Brose & Tessier-Lavigne, 2000; Chan & Jan, 1999), and many of these genes have been identified in the human genome (Venter et al., 2001).

The conservation of homologous genes for brain development suggests that the functional capabilities of the human brain and mind, including the neocortex, are similar in some respects to the functional capabilities of the brain and mind of other mammals and probably many nonmammalian species (Karten, 1997). There are, of course, many differences across these species, particularly for humans. The number of genes responsible for the development of the human brain appears to be several-fold larger than that of other species in which comparisons have been made (Venter et al., 2001). Recent studies also suggest that the same genes may be expressed differently in the brains of even closely related species, including comparisons of chimpanzees (*Pan troglodytes*) and humans (Enard et al., 2002).

In fact, Cáceres and his colleagues (2003) examined the frequency with which about 90 of the same or very similar genes are expressed throughout the neocortex of macaques, chimpanzees, and humans. Among other things, the results suggest that one way the human neocortex differs from that of the chimpanzee is in the frequency with which these genes are expressed, with humans showing a much higher frequency of gene expression. In other words, the human neocortex is "revved up," showing higher rates of neuronal and related activities (e.g., metabolic processes, synaptic change) than that of one of our closest relatives (see also Preuss, 2004). At the same time, in a related analysis in which 7,645 genes in the mouse, chimpanzee, and human were compared, A. G. Clark et al. (2003) found evidence for natural selection modifying a set of specific genes involved in neural development, speech, and hearing, among other traits, during human evolution (see also, Evans et al., 2004; Piao et al., 2004; Zhang, 2003).

My point is that there is accumulating evidence that many of the same genes that regulate the building of the human brain are involved in the building of other brains, as anticipated by Darwin (1871), and there are also very important species-specific differences. Still, it remains to be fully established that brain and functional continuities are indeed due to conserved genes and that species-specific differences can be traced to selection acting on specific genes. It is possible, for instance, that Cáceres et al.'s (2003) results were influenced by the effect of experience on frequency of gene expression, as contrasted with an inherent bias for the human brain to be "revved up" (Lickliter & Honeycutt, 2003).

The issue for now is how these genetic studies fit with my proposal that the brain and mind evolved to process invariant and variant information patterns that covaried with survival and reproduction during the species' evolutionary history. In theory, ecological conditions that are invariant across species should result in conditions that will favor the conservation of genes that support the prenatal development and later functioning of the associated brain and cognitive systems. For instance, on the basis of the three-dimensional organization of physical space and the physics of information transmission—such as the conduction of sound through air and water—brain and cognitive systems that are sensitive to these forms of information would be expected to evolve in many species (Shepard, 1994). Once evolved in an ancestral species, the stability of this ecological information should favor the conservation of these brain systems and associated genes with adaptive radiations, that is, when other species evolved from this ancestral stock. The result would be the conservation of these genes and homologous brain and cognitive systems in all species, such as all mammals, that evolved from the ancestral species.

Similar brain and perceptual systems may be expected to evolve independently in different lineages as well, although the genes that build these systems may differ. For example, portions of the mammalian temporal cortex (area A in Figure 4.3) and its analog in reptilian and avian species are involved in processing sounds, including acoustical patterns generated by conspecifics and other species. At a perceptual level, these systems appear to be very similar across mammalian and these nonmammalian species. At the same time, there are also more specialized regions for processing conspecific vocalizations (Doupe & Kuhl, 1999; Karten, 1997; Preuss, 2000a). The similarities could evolve in independent lineages because of the physics of information transmission and because of the presumed evolutionary importance of auditory information for communicating with other members of the same species or for locating other species (e.g., prey; Hauser, 1996).

Whether the systems are homologous or analogous, plasticity is expected to the extent that sensitivity to variability is important, as in the ability to distinguish one individual from another on the basis of vocalizations. As an example, T. Q. Gentner and Margoliash (2003) demonstrated that there are neurons in an area of the auditory region of the brain of European starlings (*Sturnus vulgaris*) that selectively respond to the songs of different starlings after they are exposed to these songs (plastic regions), whereas other areas of the auditory brain respond to all song-related sounds. Genes that support the development and functioning of brain and cognitive systems that are plastic would be conserved across species or evolve in independent lineages to the extent that sensitivity to individual differences is important in each of these species. Again, species-specific adaptations would be expected as well (e.g., to accommodate species differences in vocalization patterns).

Development of the Neocortex

Evolutionarily, change often results from changes in developmental processes, and as a result it is difficult to separate theories of neocortical evolution and neocortical development. In this section, I describe current theories of neocortical development, and in the Neocortical Evolution section below I relate these to theories of brain evolution. It has been understood for nearly a century that the human neocortex is subdivided into many functionally and architectonically distinct areas (Brodmann, 1909). *Arealization* refers to the prenatal formation of these areas and is best understood in the sensory cortices, such as those involved in vision, audition, and touch (Kaas, 1982). It is not yet fully understood how these areas are established either evolutionarily or within the development of a single brain (O'Leary, 1989; Rakic, 1988; Rubenstein et al., 1999).

Nevertheless, what was once a very hard-lined distinction between two different theoretical models of prenatal neocortical arealization is now emerging as a new theory of neocortical development that accommodates features of both models. One view, first proposed by Rakic (1988, 1995) and referred to as the *protomap hypothesis*, states that the development of discrete neocortical areas is dependent on a mechanism or mechanisms intrinsic to the neocortex. Molecules in the developing neural plate prespecify the tissue that will become a certain cortical area (e.g., a visual cortical area) by setting up columns of neurons—radial units—that are later organized into cortical areas (Levitt, 2000; Rakic, 2000; Rakic & Kornack, 2001). In this view, the neurons that compose these neocortical areas receive and generate genetically prespecified inputs and outputs to and from other cortical and subcortical areas and will later respond to a restricted class of stimuli, such as features of conspecific vocalizations. The opposing idea, referred to as the *protocortex hypothesis,* emphasizes the role of thalamic input in the determination of neocortical areal fate (for a review, see O'Leary, Schlaggar, & Tuttle, 1994). This hypothesis rests on the idea that cortical precursor cells are nonspecific—that is, they establish their identity later in development, giving the developing cortex more of a tabula rasa character.

Intrinsic Model

Consistent with the general idea of Rakic's (1988) proposal, recent results have shown that the developing neocortex is "patterned" early in development, with a graded expression of different genes in different cortical areas (Donoghue & Rakic, 1999; Grove & Fukuchi-Shimogori, 2003). These gene expression patterns are found in mice lacking thalamocortical inputs, suggesting that some degree of cortical arealization may occur without external, thalamic input (Miyashita-Lin, Hevner, Wassarman, Martinez, & Rubenstein, 1999; Nakagawa, Johnson, & O'Leary, 1999; see also K. M. Bishop, Goudreau, & O'Leary, 2000). It has been postulated that patterning centers in the developing telencephalon—brain tissue that will include the neocortex—have a primary role in regulating neocortical arealization (Miyashita-Lin et al., 1999; Rubenstein et al., 1999). Gene mutations in at least one such patterning center result in defects in the organization and functioning of many cortical regions (Furuta, Piston, & Hogan, 1997; Grove, Tole, Limon, Yip, & Ragsdale, 1998; S. M. Lee, Tole, Grove, & McMahon, 2000).

One section of the telencephalon expresses high levels of FGF8, a protein that is expressed by a gene that is a member of the family of mammalian genes that regulate growth and patterning in multiple embryonic tissues (Crossley & Martin, 1995; S. M. Lee et al., 1997; Reifers et al., 1998; A. S. Tucker, Yamada, Grigoriou, Pachnis, & Sharpe, 1999). This domain may regulate patterning of the many components of the developing brain, including the neocortex (Crossley, Martinez, Ohkubo, & Rubenstein, 2001; Fukuchi-Shimogori & Grove, 2001; Rubenstein et al., 1999). Indeed, a recent study suggests that FGF8 may play a general role in anterior–posterior organization of the neocortex (Fukuchi-Shimogori & Grove, 2001). In sum, there is emerging evidence that the largely prenatal development of areas in the neocortex is at least to some extent dependent on intrinsic, genetically mediated properties of the neocortex (Grove & Fukuchi-Shimogori, 2003).

Extrinsic Model

Intrinsic influences on the prenatal organization of the neocortex are not the whole story. When cells from the location of the visual cortex—

presumably destined to be visual cells—are transplanted into the developing somatosensory cortex, these cells develop into cells that are common in the somatosensory cortex (Schlagger & O'Leary, 1991). Also, in an elegant series of experiments, Sur and his colleagues demonstrated that if input from the retina (eye) is rerouted to the auditory cortex, the brain region that normally includes the auditory cortex develops many of the same properties of the visual cortex (A. W. Roe, Pallas, Hahm, & Sur, 1990; A. W. Roe, Pallas, Kwon, & Sur, 1992, Sharma, Angelucci, & Sur, 2000). Additionally, in early development, the removal of all cells "destined" to be visual cortical cells prior to the thalamic innervation of the neocortex results in a shift of the corresponding thalamic connections to a new location in the neocortex (Huffman, Molnar, et al., 1999). In other words, neurons in the region of the neocortex in which the visual cortex is not normally situated respond to visual stimuli and receive input from the thalamic nucleus that transmits visual information to the neocortex. These studies, and others (e.g. Catalano & Shatz, 1998), suggest that input from the thalamus and synaptic activity play a major role in the determination of organization of the neocortex.

On the basis of this evidence and that described in the previous section, most developmental neurobiologists now agree that normal and largely prenatal (in most species) development of the neocortex appears to depend on both internal (e.g., graded gene expression across areas of neocortex) and external (e.g., inputs from the thalamus) influences (Gao & Pallas, 1999; Levitt, 1995; for a review, see Pallas, 2001; Ragsdale & Grove, 2001). However, the mechanisms guiding the interaction between internal and external influences to produce the highly complex functional organization of the neocortex are not yet known. The message is that the basic organization of the neocortex and presumably the pattern of information to which different areas of the neocortex will eventually (i.e., postnatally) respond appear to be influenced by both inherent, gene-driven constraints and experiential inputs (e.g., firing of retinal cells) during prenatal and early postnatal development.

Comparative Ecology and Brain Evolution

There is clearly some degree of similarity in the organization of the human neocortex and that of other mammals. There are, however, unique species-specific differences in the organization of the neocortex and in many subcortical areas (Holloway, 1968). As Preuss (Preuss & Kaas, 1999; Preuss 2000a, 2001, 2004) aptly articulated, neurobiological studies of brain organization and development have been based largely on the assumption of cross-species similarities; have been restricted to only a few presumably modal species, such as lab rats (*Rattus norvegicus*) and rhesus macaques (*Macaca mulatta*); and have not systematically explored cross-species differences from an evolutionary perspective. As a result, more is known about similarities across a few well-studied species than about species-specific specializations. On the basis of what is known, a reasonable conclusion would be that many fundamental organizational (e.g., radial units, auditory cortex) and functional (e.g., sound processing) features of the neocortex and subcortical regions are the same across species, including humans. At the same time, there are many species-specific variations within the constraints of these conserved features (Dukas, 1998a; Moss & Shettleworth, 1996), although the relative balance of inherent constraints and experiential patterns that result in these cross-species differences cannot yet be determined.

Comparative Ecology

The clearest evidence for species-specific brain and cognitive specializations comes from studies of the cortical architecture of evolutionarily related species that have different physical and behavioral specializations (e.g., Barton, 1996; Barton & Dean, 1993; Barton, Purvis, & Harvey, 1995; Catania, Lyon, Mock, & Kaas, 1999; Dunbar, 1993; Hof, Glezer, Nimchinsky, & Erwin, 2000; Huffman, Nelson, et al., 1999; Moss & Simmons, 1996). The comparison of species with a recent common ancestor is important, because existing differences cannot be attributed to their distant evolutionary history. Rather, these differences more likely reflect current differences in reproductive strategy or adaptations to different social or ecological niches, factors that can be empirically studied and related to brain organization and cognitive functions (Catania, 2000).

Huffman, Nelson, et al. (1999) provided one example with their comparison of the somatosensory cortex of three species of marsupial. All of these related species have the same basic cortical architecture, but cortical areas associated with physical or behavioral specializations are enlarged (referred to as *cortical magnification*). In the striped possum (*Dactylopsila trivirgata*), the fourth digit is 30% larger than the other digits and is used for prey capture, specifically for locating and extracting insects from the bark of trees. The cortical area corresponding to this digit occupies about 33% of the somatosensory cortex devoted to the forepaw and 10% of the entire somatosensory cortex. There is also an overrepresentation of the tongue, which is used in a specialized way similar to the long digit. The northern quoll (*Dasyurus hallucatus*) does not have this physical or behavioral specialization, and only 3% to 5% of the somatosensory cortex is devoted to this digit. The northern quoll uses whiskers on the snout and other parts of the face to locate prey, whereas the striped possum is much less dependent on whiskers. The cortical representations of these whiskers occupy about 55% more somatosensory cortex in the northern quoll than in the striped possum.

There are many other examples as well, and a few of these are illustrated in Figure 4.4. The somatosensory cortex is enlarged for the associated physical specializations involved in foraging and prey capture (see Catania, 2000, for a similar analysis of related species of *Insectivora*). Huffman, Nelson, et al. (1999) argued that these species' differences are evolved and genetically mediated specializations associated with the different foraging activities of the species. On the basis of Rakic's model (e.g., Rakic, 1988) and the finding of some degree of prenatal organization to the mammalian neocortex (Miyashita-Lin et al., 1999), cross-species differences in the number of radial units supporting these evolved specializations are likely (Grove & Fukuchi-Shimogori, 2003). For this example, the number of prenatally generated radial units and cortical areas within the somatosensory cortex is assumed to differ across the species shown in Figure 4.4. For the raccoon (*Procyon lotor*), the number of prenatally determined neocortical areas devoted to the forepaws is expected to be considerably higher than those devoted to forepaws in the squirrel (*Sciurus caroliniensis*), reflecting different foraging specializations. The number of cortical areas devoted to the lips is expected to be much higher in the squirrel than the raccoon.

At the same time, a "second factor that can account for the differences we observe in the neocortical organization in mammals is the ability of the neocortex to change its pattern of organization throughout an individual's life" (Huffman, Nelson, et al., 1999, p. 27), as elaborated in the next section. In other words, initial, genetically mediated neocortical differences would result in cross-species differences in the sensitivity of the corresponding body regions. When these differences in sensitivity are combined with cross-species differences in early attentional and behavioral activities associated with the practice of different foraging strategies during play, the result would be the large cross-species differences observed by Huffman, Nelson, et al. and by others (e.g., Barton, 1996; Catania, 2000).

Neocortical Evolution

My goal in this section is to describe how selection could act on the basic organization of the neocortex to create species-specific brain and cognitive specializations (see also Preuss, 2000a, 2001). In the context of Rakic's (1988) protomap hypothesis, sexual reproduction and mutations should result in within-species variability in many traits potentially related to brain development and evolution. Included among these are the number of radial units composing any given neuroanatomical region; the cytoarchitectonic features, or connectivity of radial units or clusters of neurons (e.g., the number and type of interconnections within layers of radial units; Holloway, 1968); and the degree and pattern of connectivity between different neocortical and subcortical regions. Alteration of the genes that code

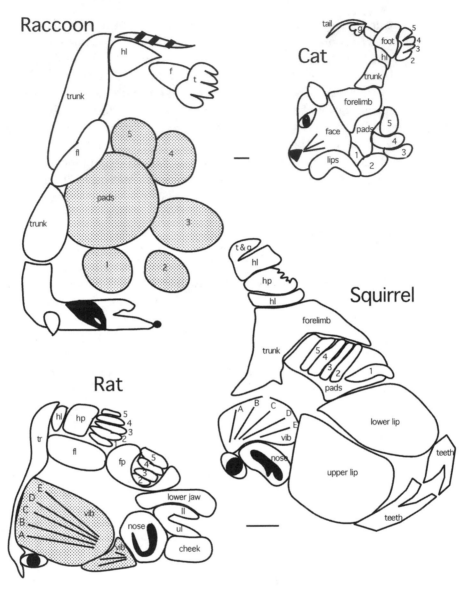

Figure 4.4. Examples of body representations in the somatosensory cortex. f = foot; fl = forelimb; fp = forepaw; g = glabrous; hl = hind limb; hp = hind paw; ll = lower lip; ul = upper lip; t = tail; t & g = tail and glabrous; tr = trunk; vib = vibrissae (whiskers); A–E = individual vibrissae representations; 1–5 = paw digits. From "Organization of Somatosensory Cortex in Three Species of Marsupials, *Dasyurus hallucatus, Dactylopsila trivirgata,* and *Monodelphis domestica:* Neural Correlates of Morphological Specializations," by K. J. Huffman, J. Nelson, J. Clarey, and L. Krubitzer, 1999, *Journal of Comparative Neurology, 403,* p. 29. Copyright 1999 by Wiley-Liss, Inc.

for the prenatal generation of neurons is a likely mechanism resulting in these individual differences (Caviness, Takahashi, & Nowakowski, 1995). For instance, individual variability in the timing or mode of cell division of the progenitor cells that produce neurons could result in significant individual, as well as species-level, differences in the number of radial units in a given region of the brain (Chenn & Walsh, 2002; Piao et al., 2004; Rakic, 1998). Selection could then act on the resulting variability, across individuals, in the fidelity and sensitivity of the associated sensory, cognitive, and behavioral systems and result in the evolutionary modification of these systems and corresponding differences across species (Kornack, 2000; Krubitzer & Huffman, 2000; Rakic, 1995).

Indeed, Kornack and Rakic (1998) found that differences in the size of the neocortex of the mouse and rhesus macaque could be explained, at least in part, by "substantially *more* successive rounds of cell division . . . during the neurogenetic period" (p. 1245) in macaques than in mice. These differences resulted in more progenitor cells in macaques than in mice and an accompanying increase in the number of radial units that compose the same area of the visual cortex. Differences were also found in the number of neurons that were produced and that migrated to different layers of the visual cortex. Preuss, Qi, and Kaas (1999) found considerable variability across various species of monkey, ape, and humans in the microcircuitry of regions of the primary visual cortex, although it is not clear (but it seems likely) that these differences arise through the same mechanisms described by Kornack and Rakic. Evans et al. (2004) and Zhang (2003) independently discovered a gene that may influence the generation of progenitor cells in the human brain and through this contribute to the large size of the human neocortex. In any event, there also appear to be differences in the dynamics of progenitor cell division and neuron generation for different regions of the neocortex within the same species, which, in turn, would result in different anatomical and presumably functional capacities of these different cortical regions (see also Barone & Kennedy, 2000; Rakic & Kornack, 2001).

Changes in genes (e.g., novel genetic interactions that can result from sexual reproduction) that regulate the prenatal dynamics of neurogenesis (i.e., the development and migration of neurons) thus provide one plausible mechanism that could account for evolutionary increases in the number of radial units and thus increases in the size of the neocortex. The same mechanism can accommodate change in the architecture of radial units and cortical fields (i.e., constellations of radial units that respond to a particular class of stimuli) and can account for cross-species differences in the number of radial units composing distinct brain regions and within-species differences in the number and specialization of radial units composing different brain regions (Kornack, 2000; Kornack & Rakic, 1998). If any such change in the genes that regulate the prenatal development and migration of neurons is heritable and if the accompanying change in perceptual, cognitive, or behavioral systems covaries with survival or reproductive outcomes, then the result will be an evolutionary modification of this brain region (Evans et al., 2004; Zhang, 2003).

In theory, these mechanisms could also result in the formation of hybrid radial units. These units appear to emerge at the border of preexisting, functionally distinct neocortical areas and consist of neurons that show processing characteristics of both areas (see Krubitzer & Huffman, 2000; Rakic, 1988). One potential result of the emergence of hybrid radial units is the evolution of functionally distinct neurocognitive systems, although this has been debated. For instance, some scientists suggest that human language is a unique form of conspecific communication and arose from the evolution of distinct, hybrid areas, such as Broca's area (Killackey, 1995; Northcutt & Kaas, 1995). Other scientists argue that human language is better conceived as being continuous, albeit more complex, with the communication systems of other primates and that brain regions homologous to Broca's and Wernicke's areas exist in other primates (Cantalupo & Hopkins, 2001; Gannon, Holloway, Broadfield, & Braun, 1998; Preuss, 2000a). The issue is not resolvable until more detailed maps of the physical and functional architecture of these brain regions are available for humans and multiple species of monkey and ape (Preuss, 2004). However it is resolved, selection acting on variation in brain organization and function created by modification of the pattern of gene expression governing early brain development is likely to be an essential component of brain and cognitive evolution, including the evolution of the human mind and brain.

EXPERIENTIAL MODIFICATION OF BRAIN ORGANIZATION

Even if changes in the dynamics of early brain development are the key to brain and cognitive evolution, the issue of the selection pressures that resulted in the retention of any such changes has been vigorously debated. In the first section, I focus on the issue of whether the evolutionary expansion of the neocortex was the direct result of specific selection pressures, such as the social pressures described in chapter 3 (Adaptation and Selection section), or an incidental effect of selection acting on other traits. An incidental expansion of the neocortex is of considerable importance, as it would imply that much of the neocortex is unspecialized in terms of past selection pressures, as I noted earlier. An unspecialized neocortex, in turn, would presumably respond to a broad range of information within the limits of the underlying sensory and perceptual systems and thus evince a high degree of plasticity (Quartz & Sejnowski, 1997). In the second section, I focus on empirical research on the degree to which injury and postnatal experience can influence neocortical organization and functioning.

Allometry and Size of the Neocortex

Allometry refers to systematic relations among different features of body morphology, architecture, and development (Harvey, Martin, & Clutton-Brock, 1987), relations that complicate the determination of whether any particular trait is the direct result of specific selection pressures (Deacon, 1990; A. Larson & Losos, 1996). Vrba's (1995b) model of hominid brain evolution, for instance, is based on the allometric relation between body size and brain size (Climatic Pressures section of chap. 3). Although this relation is not perfect, larger bodies are generally associated with larger brains. Selection that favored an increase in body size might also result in an incidental increase in brain size, that is, an increase in brain size in the absence of direct selection for improved perceptual or cognitive competencies. The body–brain allometry is, however, a crude index of any potential incidental expansion of the neocortex. A more central issue is the potential for allometric relationships among different regions of the brain, specifically whether selection that operated to increase the size of one brain area could result in increases in the size of other areas. The question has been vigorously debated (Barton, 1999; Barton & Harvey, 2000; D. A. Clark, Mitra, & Wang, 2001; de Winter & Oxnard, 2001; Finlay & Darlington, 1995; Finlay, Darlington, & Nicastro, 2001) and, as noted, is highly relevant to the broader issue of brain plasticity.

Allometric Expansion

Finlay and Darlington (1995) analyzed the relations among the absolute size of 12 brain regions across 131 species of mammal and found that a single factor accounted for 96% of the similarities in region size. Results for this factor suggest that a single mechanism may account for the absolute size of many different brain regions and thus provide evidence inconsistent with the position that there are specific faculties of brain and mind that evolved as a result of specific social or ecological selection pressures. Finlay and Darlington conceded that specific brain and cognitive adaptations are found but argued that they appear to be less important than a more general mechanism that influenced the evolution of the absolute size of all brain regions.

Finlay's and Darlington's (1995) proposed mechanism involves the genes regulating prenatal neocortical development (Kaskan & Finlay, 2001). As I noted, a several-fold increase in the size of the neocortex could occur as a result of genetic changes that prolonged the division of the progenitor cells that give birth to neurons (Rakic, 1988, 1995), which according to Finlay and Darlington could significantly increase the size of the neocortex in the absence of specific selection pressures. More precisely, selection that favored an increase in the size of one brain region could result in a corresponding increase in the size of all other brain regions, if change in the number of progenitor cell divisions was general. The implication is that much of the neocortex is underspecified with respect to past selection pressures and thus highly open to modification through developmental experience.

Brain Specialization

The analytic techniques Finlay and Darlington (1995) used, as well as their basic conclusion, have been questioned by several research teams that have analyzed the same data set (Barton & Harvey, 2000; D. A. Clark et al., 2001; de Winter & Oxnard, 2001). In contrast to Finlay and Darlington, who focused on absolute volume of different brain regions, these other scientists focused on the relative volume of different brain regions, or each region's volume as a percentage of total brain volume. In addition, these other scientists analyzed systems of brain regions that often operate together—*cerebrotypes*—to determine if these integrated systems were related to identifiable social or ecological conditions, such as demands associated with prey capture (D. A. Clark et al., 2001; de Winter & Oxnard, 2001). These techniques controlled for the allometric relation between brain size and body size and among different brain regions and allowed inferences to be drawn about the selection pressures that may have influenced the evolution of integrated systems of brain regions.

Using this approach, D. A. Clark et al. (2001) found that distinct cerebrotypes emerged for species of insectivore, shrew, and primate and were consistent with adaptations to specific ecological and social conditions (see also de Winter & Oxnard, 2001). For example, complex social dynamics are associated with larger neocortical volumes across species of primate (Barton, 1996; Dunbar, 1993; Sawaguchi, 1997) and carnivore (Dunbar & Bever, 1998), as described in chapter 2 (Sexual Selection and Brain and Cognitive Evolution section). The critical social variable is not simply aggregation in large groups, as in herding, but rather dynamics that involve developing long-term relationships with conspecifics and competition that involves, for instance, social deception (e.g., furtive mating). Most species of Old World (Africa and Asia) monkey tend to live in large social groups that encompass this form of social dynamic, whereas most species of New World (South America) monkey do not. In keeping with the prediction that this form of social dynamic encompasses a class of selection pressure that can influence brain evolution, D. A. Clark et al. found that Old World monkeys have a proportionally larger neocortex than do New World monkeys.

A more rigorous test of the adaptation hypothesis was provided by a comparison of New World monkeys, such as one species of spider monkey (*Ateles geoffroyi*), that live in social groups similar to those found in Old World monkeys (D. A. Clark et al., 2001). These New World species have higher neocortical volumes (69% of total brain volume) than less social New World species (62%) and volumes similar to those of Old World species (70%). Although de Winter and Oxnard's (2001) assumptions differed in some respects from those of D. A. Clark et al., both sets of analyses provided examples of convergent evolution. In other words, species without a recent common ancestor but that occupy similar ecological and social niches "converge in their brain proportions" (de Winter & Oxnard, 2001, p. 711); *brain proportion* refers to the percentage of total brain volume allocated to one region or another in a manner analogous to that shown in Figure 4.4. Finally, Piao et al. (2004) identified a gene that may more substantively influence the prenatal development of the human frontal cortex than other neocortical areas. Although these findings are preliminary, they suggest regional differences in the prenatal development of the human brain, contra the predictions of Finlay and Darlington (1995).

Cost–Benefit Trade-Offs

The potential for allometric expansion of the neocortex must also be evaluated in terms of cost–benefit trade-offs (Deacon, 1990). Not only does expansion of brain size result in higher basal metabolic costs, consuming about 20% of calories in the average human (Armstrong, 1990), it also results in a number of trade-offs regarding neuronal size and organization (Hofman, 2001; Kaas, 2000). Doubling the size of a neocortical region cannot be achieved by doubling the size of neurons. To maintain the same conduction properties (e.g., speed of transmission), dendrites that are doubled in length must be quadrupled in diameter (Kaas, 2000). The costs associated with proportional increases in the size of neurons may account for the most common pattern of larger cortical areas being associated with more neurons, although there are some neuronal size differences across cortical regions and species (Preuss, 2004). The point is that with cortical expansions, each neuron must communicate with proportionally fewer neurons than before the expansion. The result appears to be increased specialization of interconnected clusters of neurons. Stated somewhat differently, the microarchitecture of expanded regions of neocortex necessarily becomes more modularized and specialized for processing finer-grained pieces of information (Hofman, 2001; Kaas, 2000), even with simple allometric expansions of region size (Changizi, 2003).

Discussion of the many other changes associated with neocortical expansion is beyond the scope of this volume but has been provided in detail by Changizi (2001, 2003; Changizi, McDannald, & Widders, 2002). One of these complexities is nonetheless of interest, especially when it comes to humans. Cortical expansions result in an increase in the number of neurons, although not proportionally (Changizi, 2001; Holloway, 1968). As noted in chapter 3 (Brain Evolution section), the volume of the human brain, largely the neocortex, is about three times that of the chimpanzee brain, but Holloway estimated that the number of neurons in the human neocortex is only about 25% higher than the number of neurons in the chimpanzee neocortex. The increase in the size of the human neocortex may be more strongly related to increases in the extent of neuronal interconnections (i.e., number of axons and size of dendrites) within and between neocortical and subcortical areas than to an increase in number of neurons (see also Hofman, 2001; Preuss, 2004). I discuss these issues and implications more fully in chapter 7 (in the sections on Cognitive and Brain Systems and on Problem Solving and Human Evolution).

My point for now is that the metabolic and developmental costs of maintaining and constructing allometrically expanded neocortical areas or maintaining extensive connections within and between these areas should result in added selection pressures. Specifically, these costs should result in an evolutionary reduction to the smallest size and the smallest number of connections necessary for any allometrically expanded regions. Nonetheless, specializations associated with cortical expansion confer benefits such as increased specialization of neuronal circuits and a corresponding increase in the fidelity of information the region can process and an increased ability to integrate information within and across areas. These benefits could maintain an allometric expansion or result in an area-specific expansion, if they outweighed costs. One result, in theory, would be the evolution of differences in the microarchitecture of analogous (due to convergent evolution) or homologous (due to a common ancestor) regions of the same neocortical area (Kaas, 2000). In other words, niche-related expansions in the proportional size of specific brain regions, such as areas of the neocortex, might also be accompanied by niche-related modifications in the microarchitecture of these regions.

Preuss et al. (1999) found differences in the microarchitecture of at least one area of the primary visual cortex when they compared monkeys to apes and apes to humans, as I mentioned earlier. The functional and evolutionary significance of these results is not yet clear (see Preuss, 2000a, 2004, for related discussion), but they do suggest that the primary visual cortex of different species of primate is differentially sensitive to different forms of visual information. Despite these intriguing differences in microarchitecture and the finding of apparently niche-related differences in cerebrotypes across mammalian species (D. A. Clark et al., 2001; de Winter & Oxnard, 2001), the issue of whether and, if so, to what degree there has been a nonselected allometric expansion of the neocortex is far from resolved. It is very likely that there are considerably more niche-related brain and cognitive specializations than suggested by the analyses of Finlay and Darlington (1995; Finlay et al., 2001), but some proportion of unspecialized neocortex cannot be ruled out (Barton, 1999; Deacon, 1990). Moreover, the recent findings of Cáceres et al. (2003) indicating higher levels of gene expression and neural activity in the human brain relative to that of the chimpanzee suggest an evolutionary change that enhanced the functioning of many neocortical regions. These findings do not preclude region-specific differences in brain organization and neural activity but do suggest that there have been changes that have "revved up" the activity patterns of wide regions of the human neocortex.

Experience and Brain Organization

There is considerable evidence that many brain regions show molecular, neuronal, and organizational changes in response to injury and postnatal experience and learning (Buonomano & Merzenich, 1998; Kaas, 1991; Palleroni & Hauser, 2003; Ramachandran, 1993) and that such changes are more readily achieved during development than in adulthood (Stiles, 2000; Wiesel, 1982). The potential for experience-driven change in brain functioning and organization is evident across a wide range of species, indicating that the underlying mechanisms are evolutionarily old. At the same time, limits on the extent to which any such experience-driven change is possible and whether the potential for reorganization varies from one brain region to the next are not fully understood. As a result, these are areas of intense theoretical interest (La Cerra & Bingham, 1998) and empirical study (Dinse, Ragert, Pleger, Schwenkreis, & Tegenthoff, 2003).

Injury

Evidence regarding how accidental injury and experimental manipulations (e.g., anesthetization of skin areas) may influence brain organization and functioning comes from studies of adults of nonhuman and human species (Buchner, Kauert, & Radermacher, 1995; K. Fox, Glazewski, & Schulze, 2000; Jain, Catania, & Kaas, 1997; Moore et al., 2000; Ramachandran, 1993; Röricht, Meyer, Niehaus, & Brandt, 1999; Witte, 1998). For instance, therapeutic amputation of a digit or limb in monkeys results in an immediate suppression of activity of the corresponding somatosensory cortex, but regained functioning of many of these cells sometimes occurs within a few hours (Kaas, 1991). These cells typically fire in association with stimulation of adjacent digits, nearby body regions, or body regions represented in adjacent neocortical areas. The suggestion is that the injury resulted in the disinhibition of preexisting neuronal connections into these cortical regions (Buchner et al., 1995; Buonomano & Merzenich, 1998). There are also longer-term reorganizations of disrupted cortical areas, whereby adjacent cortical regions expand into the area associated with an injury or into more remote cortical areas that are horizontally connected to the disrupted region (e.g., Florence & Kaas, 1995; Witte, 1998). These results demonstrate injury-related modifications of the organization of the adult brain but also suggest that these organizational changes are restricted to the neural regions associated with the injury and that subsequent functioning of these regions is limited to preexisting connections.

The effects of injury on brain functioning and organization, as well as on associated functional competencies, are more difficult to study in developing organisms than in adults (Stiles, 2000). One complication is that different brain systems may support the same skill at different points in development. For instance, early injury may result in little initial functional loss, suggesting compensatory changes in brain functioning and organization, but functional deficits or failure to show normal developmental change may be evident at a later age, suggesting less compensatory change (e.g., Goldman, 1971). Moreover, the research of Stiles and her colleagues (see Stiles, 2000, for a review) suggests that different competencies may show different degrees of compensatory change in brain functioning and organization following early brain injury. In this longitudinal study, children who experienced neocortical injury prenatally or prior to 6 months of age were assessed on measures of language competence, spatial cognition, and ability to express emotion (e.g., on the basis of facial expressions). Through early childhood, these children tended to show less severe deficits than corresponding lesions would produce in adulthood, suggesting partial but incomplete compensatory changes. Some of the improvements in cognitive competencies appeared to reflect change in strategies used during task performance, whereas other improvements may have resulted from compensatory change in brain functioning and organization (Stiles, 2000).

For the spatial and emotion measures, the relation between lesion site and functional deficits was similar to that associated with brain injury in adulthood, suggesting that other cortical systems did not assume the functions normally supported by the injured tissues. The relation between lesion site and language deficits was more complicated, however. During the early stages of language acquisition, pervasive delays and deficits were evident regardless of lesion site, but as these children matured some lesion–deficit relations (e.g., poor vocabulary associated with left temporal lesions; see Figure 3.3) were similar to those associated with lesions in adulthood. The results suggest that "there is no simple or uniform pattern of deficit and recovery that can be captured by the traditional models" of compensatory change in brain functioning and organization following early injury (Stiles, 2000, p. 264).

Experience and Learning

Repeated sensory stimulation and other types of experience and learning are associated with a variety of molecular and other cortical changes in the somatosensory, auditory, and visual cortices in adulthood (Bao, Chan, & Merzenich, 2001; Buonomano & Merzenich, 1998; Dinse et al., 2003; Kaas, 1991; Recanzone, Merzenich, Jenkins, Grajski, & Dinse, 1992). Although nearly all of this research has been conducted with nonhuman species, Draganski et al. (2004) found a similar pattern of experience-dependent cortical change in adult humans. Most generally, it appears that experience—that is, repetitive stimulation or repetitive activity—results in cortical and subcortical modifications within the limits of preexisting systems. For instance, repeated sensory stimulation can result in a several-fold increase in the size of the corresponding somatosensory cortex, and simultaneous stimulation of adjacent body regions can result in overlapping cortical fields—that is, cortical areas that respond to stimulation of both body regions (Jenkins, Merzenich, & Recanzone, 1990; X. Wang, Merzenich, Sameshima, & Jenkins, 1995). These changes appear to reflect, at least in part, changes in the efficiency of preexisting synapses or the generation of new synaptic connections among preexisting neurons (Witte, 1998), although experience can also maintain newly generated neurons in at least one brain region, the hippocampus (Kempermann, Kuhn, & Gage, 1997).

Experience-based change in brain organization and functioning has also been demonstrated in normally developing brains, beginning with the seminal studies of Rosenzweig and colleagues (e.g., Rosenzweig & Bennett, 1972; Rosenzweig, Krech, Bennett, & Diamond, 1962; Rosenzweig, Krech, Bennett, & Zolman, 1962), and Greenough and colleagues (see Greenough et al., 1987). In the former studies, newly weaned rats were exposed to varying degrees of social and environmental enrichment or impoverishment. Many of the enrichment conditions included spending as much as 23 hours per day in an environment with other rats and many objects to explore, whereas impoverishment involved social isolation and no objects to explore. Enrichment conditions were associated with higher cortical and subcortical weights and changes in some enzymatic activity. The changes in brain weight were, however, modest. Animals experiencing enriched environments had neocortices that were about 4% heavier and subcortical weights that were 2% heavier than littermates experiencing impoverished conditions. In one manipulation, Rosenzweig and Bennett found that active exploration of an enriched environment without social contact led to similar changes in brain weight and enzymatic activity and, in fact, resulted in a 10% increase in the weight of the occipital (visual) cortex. Follow-up research suggested that the change in cortical weight was due to increased dendritic branching (Holloway, 1966). It was also found that brain weight differences across genetic strain of rat were two to four times larger than the brain weight differences when comparing rats that experienced enriched versus impoverished conditions (Rosenzweig et al., 1962); as I describe in chapter 8 (Brain Structure section), there are also genetic influences on individual differences in human brain weight, volume, and organization (Baaré et al., 2001; P. M. Thompson et al., 2001).

More recent studies have focused on experience-independent and experience-dependent influences on the architecture of specific brain regions (e.g., Chang & Merzenich, 2003; Crowley & Katz, 2000; Hersch & Stryker, 2004; L. E. White, Coppola, & Fitzpatrick, 2001) following the early work of Wiesel and Hubel (1965; Wiesel, 1982) and Rakic (1976). As an example, L. E. White et al. assessed the response patterns and microarchitecture of circuits of neurons in the visual cortex that respond to the angular orientation of presented objects. In this experiment, the development of orientation selectivity was compared across groups of normally reared, dark-reared, and lid-sutured ferrets (*Mustela putorius furo*). The dark-reared group was deprived of normal experiences during the time when these neural circuits showed a rapid increase in sensitivity to object orientation, and the lid-sutured group experienced an abnormal pattern of visual experiences (some light passed through the lid). The dark-reared group responded to angular orientation, and the microarchitecture of the associated neural circuits was near normal. However, fine-grained behavioral, electrophysiological, and anatomical assessments indicated that the dark-reared group showed less specificity in orientation responses (e.g., distinguishing between objects of similar orientation) and smaller neuronal circuits with fewer within-circuit interconnections than did the normal-experience group. The lid-sutured group showed the poorest levels of specificity in behavioral and electrophysiological orientation responses and the least complex circuits.

The results are consistent with findings of earlier studies of the visual cortex in other species, namely that the basic organization of this area of the neocortex is achieved without sensory experience, but that normal experiences—in terms of the species' evolutionary history (Greenough, 1991)—are needed to achieve optimal organizational and functional skills (Wiesel, 1982). Abnormal experiences, especially during the critical period of development, can result in abnormal or muted neuronal responses (e.g., Wiesel & Hubel, 1965). The mechanisms underlying the interaction between experience-independent architecture and experience-dependent modifications are not fully understood. One view is that overgeneration of synaptic connections in the neocortex of some mammals results in an increased sensitivity to early experiences (Huttenlocher, 1990) and that actual experience patterns result in competition among synaptic connections such that active connections are maintained and inactive connections degenerate (Greenough et al., 1987). Some recent work suggests that the mechanism may be more complex, whereby experiential patterns dynamically influence the organization of cortical fields rather than simply maintaining preorganized fields (L. E. White et al., 2001; see also Edelman, 1987). Either way, the maintained or generated pattern of connections appears to result in a more optimal sensitivity to the specifics of the organism's ecology than would presumably be achieved in the absence of experience-dependent change. These studies are consistent with the combination of intrinsic and extrinsic influences on neocortical arealization described earlier and suggest that postnatal experiences influence, within constraints, the organization and functioning of at least some neocortical areas.

SOFT MODULARITY

The research described in the preceding sections suggests that brain organization and most functions of mind are dependent on a mix of gene-driven constraints and patterns of early experiences. The mix of constraint and experience produces brain and cognitive plasticity, or the potential for experiences to influence brain organization and cognitive functions, but only within the confines of inherent constraints (R. Gelman, 1990). On the basis of the cost–benefit trade-offs described in Figure 4.2, my assumption is that information patterns that covary with survival and reproductive outcomes and that are invariant across generations and life spans favor the evolution of inherent, gene-driven constraints and thus relatively little brain and cognitive plasticity. Variant information patterns, in contrast, favor the evolution of brain and cognitive systems that are open to experience-driven modifications and thus considerable plasticity. As noted in the Motivation to Control section of chapter 3, both invariant and variant information patterns fall into three classes: social, biological, and physical; associated modules are described in chapter 5.

My goal in this section is to consider how variability within and across these different classes of information might be conceptualized, and to do this I propose three forms of plasticity—exoskeleton, rule-based category formation, and resource distribution. Each form of plasticity represents an evolved response to a different type of variability. Figure 4.5 illustrates this concept. The distributions represent evolutionarily significant domains that contain both invariant and variant information patterns, with the means representing invariant patterns and the tails variant patterns. As an example, the mean of the top distribution represents the basic structure of the human

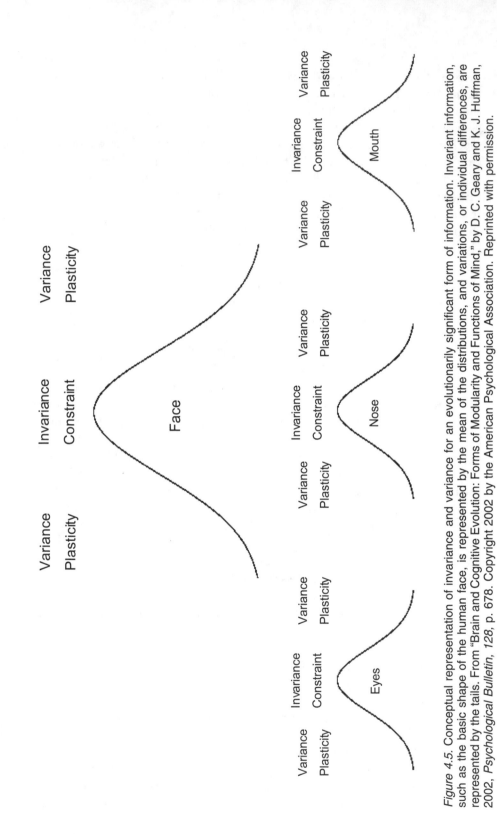

Figure 4.5. Conceptual representation of invariance and variance for an evolutionarily significant form of information. Invariant information, such as the basic shape of the human face, is represented by the mean of the distributions, and variations, or individual differences, are represented by the tails. From "Brain and Cognitive Evolution: Forms of Modularity and Functions of Mind," by D. C. Geary and K. J. Huffman, 2002, *Psychological Bulletin, 128*, p. 678. Copyright 2002 by the American Psychological Association. Reprinted with permission.

face, including shape and position of eyes, nose, and mouth. The tails represent variation, or individual differences, in this basic structure (e.g., distance between eyes). The smaller distributions represent the same concept, but for more discrete pieces of information.

In other words, the basic pattern of the human face is invariant, and thus inherent constraints on the brain and cognitive systems that are sensitive to these patterns are predicted to evolve, because these constraints would enable the fast, efficient identification of conspecifics (e.g., parents). Sexual reproduction, mutations, and development perturbations (e.g., poor nutrition) result in variation around this basic pattern. Brain and cognitive systems that are sensitive to this variation, and thus support the identification of specific individuals, are predicted to evolve to the extent that the ability to discriminate one individual from another results in a selective advantage. Systems associated with sensitivity to variation must perforce be plastic, as a new cohort of individuals is produced each generation. The combination of inherent constraint and openness to experience-driven modification is captured by the concept of soft modularity, as I detail in the following section. In the second section, I provide examples of the relations among constraint, developmental experiences, and plasticity.

Model of Soft Modularity

Forms of Modularity

Neurobiologists, psychologists, and philosophers use the term *module* differently (Cosmides & Tooby, 1994; Fodor, 1983; Krubitzer & Huffman, 2000). Definitions range from circumscribed cortical or subcortical areas that process distinct and limited forms of sensory information (Krubitzer & Huffman, 2000) to complex systems that involve cognitive, affective, and social components (Cosmides, 1989). To provide structure, four general forms of modularity are defined in Table 4.1, although a finer-grained analysis would produce more than four distinct categories. In any case, the different forms are assumed to represent information processing at different levels of abstraction and complexity, with systems at successive levels (e.g., face recognition at the cognitive level) integrating patterns of information processed at lower levels (e.g., perceptual mechanisms for processing distinct facial features). As a general rule, Marcus (2004) proposed that brain systems that process limited forms of information (e.g., angular orientation)—neural modules—can be used by multiple higher-level perceptual modules; each perceptual module in turn is potentially usable by multiple cognitive modules. In other words, lower-level modules can be used as building blocks for multiple higher-level modules, meaning that complex modular skills (e.g., face recognition) emerge (developmentally and evolutionarily) through a template that organizes pre-existing lower-level modules. In this way, each

TABLE 4.1
Forms of Modularity

Form	Description
Neural module	At this lowest level, modularity describes the relation between circumscribed sensory regions and the corresponding radial unit or units. As an example, consider the raccoon paw in Figure 4.4. Each of the forepaw pads, 1–5, and the supporting regions of somatosensory cortex represent one neural module. Each module provides limited information regarding the environment.
Perceptual module	Perceptual modules arise from the dynamic integration of activity patterns across individual neural modules and provide a more complex and abstracted representation of the environment and the organism's relation to the environment. Integration across the individual neural modules defining the raccoon forepaws results in the perception of a manipulated object, such as a food item.
Cognitive module	The next level of abstraction represents the ability to form meaning-based representations (e.g., meaning of an utterance) from perceptual modules. These processes also appear to include the ability to generate and mentally manipulate these representations in the absence of sensory input and to simulate manipulations of organism–environment relations. If raccoons had such modules, they could generate a mental representation of a food item, in the absence of manipulating it, and mentally test various means of manipulating the item to, for instance, better extract food.
Functional module	Functional modules represent the integration of lower-level modules with affective and motivational systems and direct the behavior of the organism toward evolutionarily significant goals. Affective and motivational systems lead raccoons to approach food sources or mates and avoid predators. For humans, the integration is across a complex mix of modular systems (described in chap. 5). As an example, one's sense of self is influenced by one's implicit and explicit group-level identifications (e.g., ethnicity, political affiliation).

From "Brain and Cognitive Evolution: Forms of Modularity and Functions of Mind," by D. C. Geary and K. J. Huffman, 2002, *Psychological Bulletin, 128,* p. 698. Copyright 2002 by the American Psychological Association. Adapted with permission.

complex cognitive module does not have to evolve *de novo*, but rather can emerge with an evolutionary duplication or modification of an existing template; the template organizes the expression of lower-level systems in a novel way, with no need for evolutionary change in the lower-level systems.

In the here and now, the end is a functional module that creates a mental representation of the environment. As I elaborate in chapter 6 (Reasoning section) and chapter 7 (Cognitive and Brain Systems section), the representation provides the interface between the organism and the environment in which the organism is situated and supports attempts to achieve behavioral control of significant resources, such as food, or the avoidance of negative outcomes, such as being eaten by a predator.

Ecological and Social Variability

As stated, I am assuming that the degree of plasticity covaries with the relative mix of variant or invariant information patterns in the domain. Invariant patterns are a common focus in evolutionary psychology and are defined in terms of stable problems that have recurred during the species' evolutionary history (Tooby & Cosmides, 1992, 1995). Stable and recurrent problems are assumed to result in the evolution of inherently constrained modular systems that process the associated information patterns and support a suite of decision-making and behavioral solutions, as I elaborate in the Bounded Rationality and Heuristics section of chapter 6. One pattern of information can result in the facultative expression of one prespecified behavioral solution and another pattern in the expression of an alternative solution (Cosmides, 1989; Tooby & Cosmides, 1995).

The three-dimensional structure of the physical world is the most stable feature of most ecologies (Shepard, 1994). As described by Gallistel (1990, 2000) and Dyer (1998), the evolved function of associated brain and cognitive systems should be to support navigation and accompanying behavioral activities, such as finding prey or migrating seasonally (e.g., Alerstam, Gudmundsson, Green, & Hedenström, 2001). Invariant features of physical space should favor the evolution of inherent, gene-driven brain and cognitive systems that are sensitive to the associated information, as well as mechanisms for accommodating feature variations within physical space. These variations include, as examples, the specific configuration of landmarks in which the organism is born or the position of celestial bodies (e.g., the sun) at various latitudes. These featural variations cannot be prespecified, but sensitivity to associated information patterns (e.g., star pattern) can, as can mechanisms that enable the organism to remember these configurations and navigate in this specific ecology (Gallistel, 2000).

The other primary class of evolutionarily significant information is generated by the dynamic relations among biological organisms, as Darwin (1859) noted. When survival and reproductive outcomes are dependent on the relationships and competing interests among biological organisms, some degree of unpredictability should, in theory, confer survival or reproductive advantage (Maynard Smith & Price, 1973). Important classes include host–parasite (Hamilton & Zuk, 1982) and predator–prey (Dawkins & Krebs, 1979) relationships, as well as the various forms of cooperative and competitive relationships described in Table 3.2 (e.g., spousal relationships; Geary,

2002b). Host–parasite relationships involve a never-ending and co-evolving interplay between the host's immune system defenses and the parasite's defense-evasion mechanisms (Van Valen, 1973). Variability in immune system defenses—achieved through sexual reproduction and mutation—is needed to avoid the rapidly evolving evasion mechanisms in the parasite. Variable defenses, in turn, create pressures for the co-evolution of the parasite's evasion mechanisms (e.g., Hamilton, Axelrod, & Tanese, 1990). For co-evolving features of predator–prey relationships and social relationships, variability is more likely to be at the behavioral level and at the level of supporting brain and cognitive systems. Behavioral and immune system variability must, however, occur in the context of stable forms of information, such as specific immune system molecules or the morphology and movement patterns of prey or predator species.

Architecture

My point in the preceding section is that most evolutionarily significant information patterns (e.g., prey evasion behavior) will show some degree of variance and invariance, but that the extent of invariance (e.g., features of physical space) or variance (e.g., social dynamics) differs from one domain to the next. Thus, a framework for capturing potential differences in the relative degree of inherent constraint and openness to experiential modification should be useful. The three forms of plasticity that define the concept of soft modularity provide the beginnings of such a framework. As described in Table 4.2, the first form is conceived as supporting the processing of stable classes of information and accommodating variability within these classes. The second form involves cognitive mechanisms for demarcating, expanding, or even constructing new categories of information (e.g., different species), but within broader constraints (e.g., animate beings). The final form enables the expansion and contraction of neural modules based on patterns of use and disuse.

For the first form of plasticity, my analogy is a perceptual or cognitive module with a hard exoskeleton and soft internal structures. The exoskeleton defines the range and forms of domain-specific information that is processed by neural and perceptual modules and any constraints within this range. For instance, perception of human speech sounds falls in the range of roughly 200 Hz to 6500 Hz (Hirsh, 1988), the range that allows for maximal communication of acoustical information (Kiang & Peake, 1988), as noted in Table 4.2. The bandwidth for perception of speech sounds creates boundaries, that is, an exoskeleton, that result in constraints on the form of communication system that can evolve. For humans, the exoskeleton will presumably include mechanisms that are specific to the acoustical patterns that can be produced by the human vocal apparatus (Liberman & Mattingly,

TABLE 4.2
Soft Modularity and Three Forms of Plasticity

Type of plasticity	Predicted and defining features
Exoskeleton	*Exoskeleton* refers to inherent constraints on the types of information the organism attends to and processes. The absolute boundaries are determined by the basic physics of information conduction, with the constraints for individual species falling within this range. An example is the bandwidth for human speech perception, 200 Hz to 6500 Hz, which is the range that allows for maximal communication of acoustical information within the physiological constraints of the auditory system (Hirsch, 1988; Kiang & Peake, 1988).
	Plasticity occurs within the constraints of the exoskeleton, and the associated "soft" mechanisms would evolve for species and domains in which within-category discriminations result in survival or reproductive advantage. An example is the ability to discriminate different acoustical patterns generated by different speakers.
	For some domains, the exoskeleton may include mechanisms that result in information-processing and behavioral constraints within the domain but enable a degree of functional plasticity. Examples include the rules of grammatical language (Pinker, 1999) and the rules of engagement for competition with conspecifics (Jackendoff, 1992). At the cognitive level, these constraints can be conceptualized as abstract rules.
Rule-based category formation	Features of the exoskeleton include inherent biases that result in the creation of evolutionarily significant classes of living and nonliving things, including conspecifics, prey species, and tools (Barton & Dean, 1993; Blake, 1993; Dennett, 1990).
	For some species, the exoskeleton may include additional mechanisms that result in the creation of subcategories within these broader classes. The resulting abstract rules (at the cognitive level) would enable finer-grained social and behavioral discriminations within broad categories. One example is in-group–out-group formation in humans.
Resource distribution	For many species, the brain is one of the most expensive organs to maintain (Armstrong, 1990), and thus mechanisms for energy conservation and redistribution are expected to evolve.
	These mechanisms would be fast acting and respond to learning, behavioral activities, and peripheral injury. The result would be the redistribution of calories and other resources from infrequently used neural modules to more frequently used modules. Examples would include changes in the size or fidelity of specific somatosensory areas that result from repeated stimulation of specific peripheral areas (e.g., whiskers; Buonomano & Merzenich, 1998; Polley, Kvašòák, & Frostig, 2004).
	Such mechanisms would result in more efficient perceptual, cognitive, and behavioral competencies through experience-driven expansions of the supporting brain regions, increased fidelity of the information processed by these regions, and reductions in the size of brain regions supporting less frequently used cognitions and behaviors. These changes, however, would occur within the limits imposed by any inherent, species-specific brain morphologies (Huffman et al., 1999).

From "Brain and Cognitive Evolution: Forms of Modularity and Functions of Mind," by D. C. Geary and K. J. Huffman, 2002, *Psychological Bulletin, 128,* p. 680. Copyright 2002 by the American Psychological Association. Adapted with permission.

1989). The soft internal structures operate within these constraints and accommodate within-category variability if the ability to make discriminations within the category enhances survival or reproductive prospects. In this example, soft internal structures are the mechanisms that allow the individual to discriminate the voice patterns of one person from another.

I predict that an exoskeleton form of modularity will evolve when survival or reproductive outcomes are dependent on the fast, efficient processing of stable (across generations and life spans) information patterns in a restricted domain and on the discrimination of variation within the domain or category. The clearest example is for species in which long-term social relationships are related to survival and reproductive outcomes, which includes nearly all species of primate (Foley, 1996). For these species, selection should favor the evolution of some degree of inherent constraint in the neural and perceptual and, in some species, cognitive modules involved in recognizing conspecifics, as well as plastic mechanisms for learning about specific individuals. Within-category plasticity would support the recognition of individuals or discriminations between individuals within the category of conspecifics and provides a mechanism for remembering past social episodes with specific individuals.

Another example is provided by a contrast of fruit-eating versus leaf-eating primates. Both classes of species must focus on specific categories of food, but the former must deal with greater variation within these categories. In particular, fruit-eating primates must discriminate between ripe and unripe fruit, must remember the location of spatially dispersed food sources, and must adjust foraging strategies to seasonal variations in the availability of these foods (Barton, 1996).

Deecke, Slater, and Ford (2002) provided another example by demonstrating that harbor seals (*Phoca vitulina*) are sensitive to the vocalizations of a potential predator, the killer whale (*Orcinus orca*), and make discriminations within this category. Different social groups of killer whale have different and readily identifiable vocalization patterns and differ in their preferred diet. Harbor seals discriminate between the vocalizations of killer whales who are fish eaters and those who are mammal eaters and avoid areas in which the latter are vocalizing. The seals also avoid areas in which unfamiliar whales who may or may not be mammal eaters are vocalizing. This suggests that the seals learn to discriminate safe and unsafe killer whale groups on the basis of experience with these individuals. Of course, a strictly modular system that did not allow these discriminations would also allow the seals to avoid predatory whales, but at a cost of avoiding whales that were not a threat. This cost includes avoidance of areas in which seals would normally feed and increased demands of attending to all whale calls. The ability to discriminate allows them to ignore, in a sense, the vocalizations of nonthreatening whales and to feed in the same locale as these groups. The ability to discriminate is thus more adaptive than would occur with a modular system that did not evidence this form of plasticity.

For at least some domains, the exoskeleton (i.e., inherent constraints) may also result in perceptual and cognitive biases that functionally result in abstract rules, or heuristics (described in chap. 6, Bounded Rationality and Heuristics section). These rules are descriptions of common patterns of behavior that can be interpreted as guiding organisms' interactions with other biological organisms or the physical world. One example comes from the dynamics of social competition, as in male–male competition for mates. The dynamics of such competition tend to be structured by "rules of engagement" or a form of social grammar (e.g., Andersson, 1994; Jackendoff, 1992). A common sequence would involve coordinated vocal threats and physical displays. If one male does not retreat, then the competition escalates to minor physical bouts and, from there, to more serious physical bouts. The rules of engagement allow individuals to make judgments (implicit decision making; see chap. 6) about the abilities of would-be competitors. These rules, along with memories of previous bouts with the same individual or similar individuals, provide an advantage in that they enable less competitive individuals to retreat before suffering real injury and allow more competitive individuals to defend resources with minimal effort. At the same time, a competitive advantage can be achieved by behavioral unpredictability within the constraints of these rules. Unpredictability would, for instance, partially negate advantages that experienced competitors have as a result of their larger repertoire of memories and strategies accrued during previous competitions.

The second form of plasticity is assumed to occur within the context of the exoskeleton and involves perceptual and cognitive biases that result in the creation of categories and mechanisms for acquiring information about the characteristics of objects or organisms in these new categories. The specific rules are likely to differ from one domain or species to the next, but the basic principles may be the same (Schusterman, Reichmuth, & Kastak, 2000). Consider, for instance, the survival demands of herbivores and carnivores. Both herbivores and carnivores likely show some inherent specializations for detecting meaningful species, such as the motion patterns of conspecifics or predators (Blake, 1993). At the same time, herbivores are likely to show perceptual and cognitive specializations for processing information about flora, especially species used as food sources, whereas carnivores should, and apparently do, show adaptations for processing information about fauna, especially prey species (Barton & Dean, 1993).

For highly specialized species, the systems for detecting and obtaining food are likely to show a high degree of inherent specification and comparatively little plasticity. For species in which food sources change across seasons, years, or even generations, selection should favor a different form of adaptation. Rather than specific modules for the detection and capture of specific prey, more general, but still inherent, constraints that bias attention to and the processing of a wider category of biological information is predicted (e.g., small mammals; R. Gelman, 1990), along with an ability to quickly learn patterns, such as motion patterns of different prey species, within those constraints (Giese & Poggio, 2003). In addition to these constraints, mechanisms—conceptualized as the rules for category formation—for creating categories of prey species or edible species of flora are expected. Categorization would include perceptual and cognitive systems for discriminating, for example, related prey species, as well as for acquiring knowledge about the behavior, growth patterns, and so forth of these species. Bergman, Beehner, Cheney, and Seyfarth (2003) demonstrated that female baboons (*Papio hamadryas*) are sensitive to the rank and the kinship of other troop members, suggesting that they categorize other individuals as within their family or within another, unrelated family.

A study conducted by D. J. Freedman, Riesenhuber, Poggio, and Miller (2001) provided preliminary support for the existence of neural systems that create cognitive categories on the basis of experience, systems that appear to be distinct from those that enable discrimination of individuals within each category. D. J. Freedman and his colleagues demonstrated that monkeys (species was unspecified, but presumably macaques) are able to form categories of never-before-seen dogs and cats (see also Neiworth, Parsons, & Hassett, 2004). On the basis of repeated exposure to pictures of dogs and cats, the monkeys formed distinct categories, dogs versus cats. Groups of cells in the lateral prefrontal cortex were active during the categorization of examples of dogs or cats but were not active in discriminating one dog (or cat) from another. Using similar methods, Sigala and Logothetis (2002) demonstrated that the pattern of neuron firing in a visual area of the temporal cortex changed as macaques learned to categorize faces and fish, suggesting that this area is involved in defining category features (e.g., oval shape for face, dorsal fin for fish). Studies of category formation in humans suggest the existence of several neural systems for category formation, including one for conscious, explicit category formation and the other for implicit (outside the individual's awareness) category formation (Ashby & Waldron, 2000). The explicit system appears to engage the same prefrontal regions identified by D. J. Freedman et al. (see Cognitive and Brain Systems section of chap. 7), and the implicit system may include the same region identified by Sigala and Logothetis.

The final form of plasticity would involve changes in the distribution of caloric (glucose) and other resources within the very "expensive" brain (Armstrong, 1990). As I mentioned above, brain tissue is costly, and mechanisms that reduce these costs and divert resources to those areas that subserve critical survival and reproductive functions, as needed, will be adaptive. A clear example is the seasonal change in the behaviors, cognitions, and size of the underlying brain regions that facilitate mating, as in seasonal changes in the complexity of bird song (Ball & Hulse, 1998) or spatial competencies associated with finding mates, as described in the Intrasexual Competition section of chapter 2 (Gaulin, 1992; Gaulin & Fitzgerald, 1989). With this form of plasticity, expensive brain tissue is not maintained during times of the year when the associated social and cognitive competencies do not provide a selective advantage.

The research described in the Experience and Brain Organization section on the relation between experience and changes in the size of the somatosensory cortex provides examples of changes that occur on a shorter time scale (Buonomano & Merzenich, 1998; Dinse et al., 2003). Experience results in increases in the size or the fidelity of brain regions supporting frequently engaged in behaviors or frequently active sensory or perceptual systems and decreases in the size or fidelity of brain regions that are less frequently engaged (e.g., Polley, Kvašóák, & Frostig, 2004). This form of plasticity enables fast changes in neural modules—and presumably in the corresponding perceptual, cognitive, and functional systems—in response to short-term fluctuations in the local ecology. It is likely that this form of plasticity will be found even for systems subject to the first two forms of plasticity, as well as for highly constrained modules of the type described by Tooby and Cosmides (e.g., Tooby & Cosmides, 1995) and others (e.g., Gallistel, 2000).

Development and Plasticity

As noted in Figures 4.1 and 4.2, plasticity implies brain and cognitive systems that are open to experiential modification, especially during the developmental period. The benefits of developmental plasticity are, of course, balanced by costs associated with delayed maturation, specifically the risk of death before having the opportunity to reproduce. The benefits associated with a long developmental period and the corresponding increase in plasticity must therefore be significant. On the basis of the model described above, my prediction is that the primary benefit of developmental plasticity is likely to be the ability to accommodate information patterns that have been variant during the species' evolutionary history and that this variation largely results from dynamic interactions among biological organisms. Although foraging demands can be complex and are related to neocortical size (Barton, 1996), for many species of primate, and especially for humans, complexity results primarily from social living (Alexander, 1989; Dunbar, 2003; Geary, 2002a, 2002b). Primate species that occupy complex social niches have a longer developmental period and a larger neocortex than do their cousins who occupy less complex niches (Dunbar, 1993; Joffe, 1997; Kudo & Dunbar, 2001; Sawaguchi, 1997).

For these domains, I predict that prenatal brain organization results in an exoskeleton that comprises neural and perceptual modules that process stable forms of information in these domains (e.g., the general shape of the human face). The result is biases in early postnatal attentional, affective, and information processing capacities, as proposed by R. Gelman (1990), as well as biases in self-initiated behavioral engagement of the environment (Scarr, 1992; Scarr & McCartney, 1983). The latter generate evolutionarily expectant experiences, that is, experiences that provide the environmental feedback needed to adjust modular architecture (the soft internal structures) to variation in information patterns in these domains (Greenough, 1991; Greenough et al., 1987). These behavioral biases are expressed as common juvenile activities, such as social play and exploration of the ecology (Bjorklund & Pellegrini, 2002; Geary, 1995; Geary & Bjorklund, 2000). I propose that these experience-expectant processes are features of the first two forms of plasticity described in Table 4.2.

As an illustration, the strong bias of human infants to attend to human faces, movement patterns, and speech reflects, in theory, the initial and inherent organizational and motivational structure of the associated modules (D. G. Freedman, 1974). These biases reflect the evolutionary significance of social relationships (Baumeister & Leary, 1995) and in effect recreate the microconditions (e.g., parent–child interactions) associated with the evolution of the supporting folk psychological modules (Caporael, 1997). Attention to and processing of this information provides the exposure to within-category variation that is needed to adapt the architecture of these modules to variation in parental faces, behavior, and so forth (R. Gelman & Williams, 1998). It allows the infant to discriminate the parent's voice from the voices of other potential parents with only minimal exposure to the parent's voice. By examining how heart rate patterns changed when human fetuses (gestation age of about 38 weeks) were exposed in utero to human voices, Kisilevsky et al. (2003) demonstrated that they are sensitive to and learn from the in utero speech of their mother and can discriminate her voice from that of other women.

CONCLUSION

The perspective I have taken in this chapter is clearly in keeping with Darwin's (1871) proposal that the mental faculties of the human brain, and all other brains, evolved by means of the same processes—natural and sexual selection—that shaped all other organs. My goal was to articulate more fully the general features of the ecology that influence brain and cognitive evolution and associated patterns of constraint and plasticity. In a nutshell, the function of brain and mind is to process socially and ecologically salient information and to guide the organism's behavior in ways that result in survival (e.g., prey capture) or reproductive (e.g., mate detection) advantages. When related to the motivation to control (chap. 3), the ultimate function of brain and cognition is to guide the organism's attempts to organize the social ecology in ways that benefit the individual and his or her kin and to gain access to and control of physical (e.g., territory) and biological (e.g., food) resources that enhance survival and reproductive prospects.

When viewed in this light and in terms of the cost–benefit trade-offs that are common to evolved systems (Williams, 1957), debate over the relative contributions of nature and nurture to the anatomical and functional organization of brain and mind center on two questions: What are the information patterns that have covaried with survival and reproductive outcomes and supported attempts to gain behavioral control of these outcomes during the species' evolutionary history? And to what degree are these patterns invariant or variant across generations and life spans? Invariant patterns are those that provide reliable and consistent information about conditions that have covaried with survival or reproductive outcomes during the species' evolutionary history. Examples include motion patterns generated by conspecifics or predators (e.g., Blake, 1993) and acoustical patterns generated by the human voice (Doupe & Kuhl, 1999), among many others. My prediction is that an evolved sensitivity to variant information patterns will occur when discriminations within broader, invariant categories result in survival or reproductive advantages. Examples include the ability to discriminate one human face from another (D. G. Freedman, 1974) or one species of related plant from another (e.g., edible vs. poisonous mushrooms; Atran, 1998).

The benefits of fast and efficient processing of invariant information patterns and the potential cost of failing to attend to this information or discriminate it from related patterns should favor the evolution of inherently constrained and modular neural, perceptual, and cognitive systems, as Cosmides and Tooby (1994) and Gallistel (2000) aptly articulated. The prediction of inherent constraint is supported by research in comparative neurobiology, comparative genetics, and developmental neurobiology. Included among these findings are cross-species similarities in the organization and physiological functioning of many neocortical and subcortical regions (Jones, 1985; Krubitzer, 1995), the possibility that some of these similarities and associated differences across regions may reflect the operation of conserved genes (Krubitzer & Huffman, 2000), and recent findings suggesting that aspects of neocortical arealization may be driven by region-specific gene expression (Miyashita-Lin et al., 1999).

Variation in patterns of socially and ecologically important information is common, and in fact behavioral variability is a predicted feature of relationships among biological organisms with competing interests (Maynard Smith & Price, 1973). Variation, in turn, would favor the evolution of neural, perceptual, and cognitive systems that are open to experiential modification to the extent that sensitivity to this variation results in survival or reproductive advantages. For instance, the dynamics of social relationships (i.e., cooperation and competition) can result in a selective advantage for the ability to discriminate one individual from another if the behavior of individuals differs and these individual differences have potential survival or reproductive consequences (Cosmides, 1989; Trivers, 1971), as they do in many species (e.g., Goodall, 1986). These more plastic mechanisms would enable, among other things, the discrimination of one individual from the next based on movement patterns, voice, and "how they think."

My proposal is that at all levels—neural, perceptual, cognitive, and functional—the degree of inherent constraint and openness to experiential modification is the evolutionary result of the degree to which the associated information patterns have been invariant or variant during the species' evolutionary history. The combination of constraint and openness is captured by the two forms of soft modularity described in this chapter—that is, the exoskeleton and rule-based category formation forms of modularity. My goal for the next chapter is to apply this basic framework of soft modularity to expand and elaborate on a proposed taxonomy of the mental faculties of the human mind (Geary, 1998; Geary & Huffman, 2002). The combination accommodates universal features of the human brain and mind (e.g., language; Pinker, 1994) and includes mechanisms (i.e., soft modularity) that allow for experience-driven differences to emerge within these broader constraints.

5

MODULAR DOMAINS OF THE HUMAN MIND

Darwin was a firm Darwinian, believing that most traits could be understood in terms of the principles of natural and sexual selection. As I mentioned in the previous chapter, mental faculties, such as language, were included among these traits, and Darwin (1871) argued that they were the evolutionary result of identifiable selection pressures such as group-level competition. During Darwin's time, evidence regarding the evolution of the human mind and brain rested, in part, on comparative studies. In particular, debates raged over whether there existed mental and anatomical continuities between the human mind and brain and those of great apes. Some early evolutionists and anatomists such as Huxley (1863) vigorously espoused evolved continuity, as illustrated in Figure 5.1. It was clear to these proponents of an evolved mind and brain that humans were different in many respects from even closely related species, but they held firm on the position that the mind and brain of humans were fundamentally similar to those of other primates and even other mammals. The debate continues to this day, as illustrated by the discussion as to whether Broca's area is found in apes or is unique to humans (see Neocortical Evolution section of chap. 4).

Even with the continuing debate, much has been learned about the brain systems that support many mental functions, including language (e.g., Cabeza & Nyberg, 1997, 2000). At the same time, much of this research has been conducted outside of the theoretical lens of evolution, and this

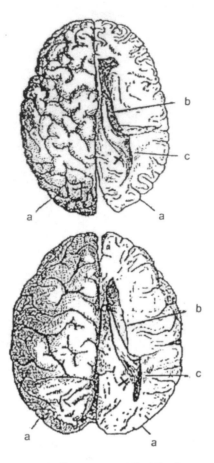

Figure 5.1. Huxley's response to the argument that the human brain was unique and thereby nonevolved—that is, created by an intelligent designer—was to illustrate homologous areas in the human (top) and chimpanzee (*Pan troglodytes,* bottom) brain. The size of the brains is scaled to allow for comparisons. From *Evidence as to Man's Place in Nature* (p. 121), by T. H. Huxley, 1863, New York: D. Appleton and Company. a = posterior lobe; b = lateral ventricle; c = posterior cornu; x = hippocampus minor.

in turn has contributed to the substantive divide between neurobiological research on the developmental and organizational properties of the brain, described in chapter 4, and cognitive research on the functional properties of the mind, described in chapters 6 and 7 (e.g., working memory and representational systems). The divide results, in part, from different levels of analysis, ranging from the mechanisms guiding the physical development of the brain to cognitions (e.g., attributional biases) that influence social dynamics. The former are tightly wedded to observable physical changes in brain organization and physiological functioning, and the latter are more abstract models of the functions of complex cognitive and behavioral systems.

Still, all of these features of mind and brain can be integrated within an evolutionary frame that accommodates the similarities between humans and related species as well as features of mind and brain that are unique to humans (Povinelli & Bering, 2002; Preuss, 2004; Tomasello & Call, 1997).

In this vein, the current chapter fleshes out a taxonomy of the evolved domains of the human mind—Darwin's (1871) mental faculties—that I and my colleague proposed in earlier work (see Geary, 1998; Geary & Huffman, 2002). The taxonomy is an integration of the work of many other scientists (cited in following sections) and provides structure to my earlier proposal that nearly all forms of information that covary with survival and reproductive outcomes fall into the categories of social, biological, and physical information (see the Motivation to Control section of chap. 3). The taxonomy of social, biological, and physical modules should provide a top-down structure for linking studies of human mental faculties with neurobiological studies of brain development, functioning, and evolution. I describe some of these links in this chapter. The taxonomy and associated selection pressures also provide a framework for integrating modular systems with the domain-general cognitive processes (e.g., working memory) that appear to define general intelligence, as described in chapter 7 (Problem Solving and Human Evolution section; for related discussion, see Chiappe & MacDonald, in press). I overview the taxonomy in the first section, and describe corresponding social and ecological modules in the second and third respective sections. In the final section, I discuss the relation between these proposed modular domains and developmental experience.

FUNCTIONAL TAXONOMY OF THE HUMAN MIND

The taxonomy of the human mind described in this chapter was constructed based on the assumptions of both continuity and uniqueness of the human brain and mind. I am not talking about uniqueness in the sense that Wallace (1869) argued for the uniqueness of the human mind. Rather, as Povinelli and Bering (2002) and Tomasello and Call (1997) aptly discussed, any unique features of the human mind (e.g., theory of mind) and brain must be understood in terms of human evolutionary history. As described in the Evolution and Brain Organization section of chapter 4, an optimal analysis of this history would require comparison of human brain anatomy and mental functions to closely related species, which would include *Homo erectus*, *H. neanderthalensis*, and australopithecines, among others (see Hominid Evolution section of chap. 3).

It is unfortunate that all of these sister species are extinct, leaving us only with much more distantly related extant great apes, such as chimpanzees (*Pan troglodytes*). Since the last common ancestor of chimpanzees and humans (5 to 6 million years ago), there has been considerable evolutionary change in encephalization quotient (EQ) and presumably mental functions, as reviewed in chapter 3. As a result, the mental faculties of chimpanzees and other great apes provide a foundation for understanding basic evolutionary continuities that are evident in humans, such as use of vocalizations and facial expression to socially communicate, but these continuities may say little about the evolution of other mental functions (Povinelli & Bering, 2002; Tomasello & Call, 1997), such as group formation according to social and cultural ideology (described in later sections).

Figure 5.2 presents a taxonomy of modular domains that captures most functional human mental faculties—there are some other domains, such as number counting (Geary, 1995; R. Gelman & Gallistel, 1978); Mithen (1996) independently constructed a similar, though less differentiated, taxonomy. These classes of modular domain coalesce around the areas of folk psychology, folk biology, and folk physics (Baron-Cohen, 1995; Baron-Cohen, Wheelwright, Stone, & Rutherford, 1999; Hirschfeld & Gelman, 1994; Medin & Atran, 1999a; Pinker, 1997; Spelke, Breinlinger, Macomber, & Jacobson, 1992) and are assumed to have evolved as a consequence of the social and ecological selection pressures described in the Adaptation and Selection section of chapter 3. More specifically, the modular systems support the evolved motivational disposition to attempt to gain access to and control of the types of social, biological (e.g., food), and physical (e.g., territory) resources that have tended to covary with survival and reproductive outcomes during human evolutionary history. The second level of the figure—social information and ecological information—reflects the evolutionary salience of other people and their behavior (Barton, 1996; Brothers, 1990; Brothers & Ring, 1992; Byrne, 2000; Dunbar, 1998; Gardner, 1983; Geary & Flinn, 2001; Humphrey, 1976) and the biological and physical ecologies that support survival and reproductive activities (e.g., Caramazza & Shelton, 1998; Kaplan, Hill, Lancaster, & Hurtado, 2000; Santos & Caramazza, 2002).

The third level represents functional modules as defined in Table 4.1 and encompasses the domains of folk psychology, folk biology, and folk physics. For folk biology and folk physics, the fourth level represents cognitive modules, which, in turn, would be supported by perceptual and neural modules (not shown in Figure 5.2). Folk psychology is more differentiated, given the complexity of human social relationships and the fact that more is known about these domains than the domains of folk biology and folk physics. Folk psychology can be further demarcated into cognitions focused on the self, other people, and group relationships—elaborated in chapter 7 (Social Cognition and Folk Psychology section)—and these in turn are supported by the corresponding cognitive modules shown in Figure 5.2. The modules represent, in a sense, nodes that represent biases in the type of

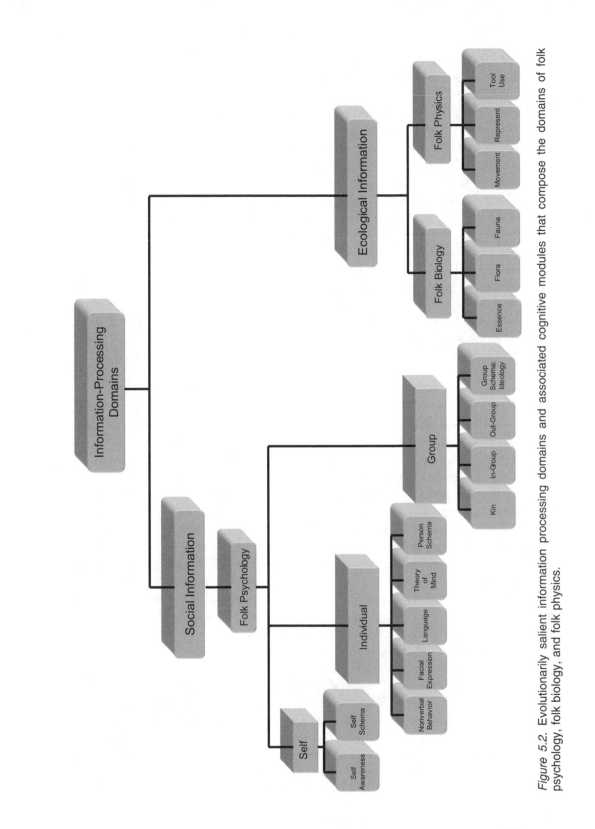

Figure 5.2. Evolutionarily salient information processing domains and associated cognitive modules that compose the domains of folk psychology, folk biology, and folk physics.

information that is processed (e.g., facial expressions) and around which knowledge about the self, others, and groups is organized.

Functional modules are goal related and represent the dynamic engagement of an array of neural, perceptual, and cognitive modules and an integration of the associated processing with affective and motivational systems. As an example, the individual-level functional module represented in Figure 5.2 (i.e., Folk Psychology: Individual) is instantiated during one-on-one social discourse and engages systems for processing and responding to nonverbal behavioral cues, language, and so forth. These cognitive systems are integrated with affective and motivational systems and function to direct behavioral strategies toward the achievement of social goals. In the two sections that follow, I focus on functional social and ecological systems, respectively. Each section includes subsections on predicted forms of cognitive modules, potential neural correlates, and potential pressures associated with their evolution. Each section ends with discussion of the relation between these functional systems and the forms of soft modularity outlined in chapter 4 and in Table 4.2.

FUNCTIONAL SOCIAL SYSTEMS

On the basis of differences across self-, individual-, and group-based social behavior, distinct cognitive modules are predicted to support these different forms of social cognition and dynamic (Bugental, 2000; Caporael, 1997; Dunbar, 1998; Gardner, 1983; Tulving, 2002). Self-awareness is the ability to consciously represent the self as a social being and to mentally project a representation of the self through time (Tulving, 1985), and the self schema is knowledge of one's personality, relationships with other people, and so forth (Markus, 1977). These are called *autonoetic awareness* by Tulving and *intrapersonal intelligence* by Gardner, respectively. The cognitive, memory, and brain systems that are involved in self-awareness are described in chapter 7 (Cognitive and Brain Systems section) as are the specifics of the self schema (Social Cognition and Folk Psychology section). Thus, I will not consider these further in this chapter.

In the first and second sections, I provide an elaboration of the individual- and group-level modules. The taxonomy of sociocognitive modules shown in Figure 5.2 was developed to accommodate both forms of social dynamic and, as noted, was derived from comparative studies of the forms of information used in social communication and that govern patterns of group dynamics, as well as social competencies that are more uniquely human (e.g., Altmann et al., 1996; Hauser, 1996; Leavens & Hopkins, 1998; Pinker, 1994). Most generally, the individual-level systems support social dynamics and relationships with other individuals, whereas the group-level systems are concerned with cognitions related to groups of other people and group-related social dynamics. Although I have termed these *modular systems,* because the prediction is some degree of difference in the brain systems processing these different forms of information (e.g., about the self vs. social categorization), overlap is expected, especially at the functional level. One's sense of self, for instance, is influenced by one's group memberships, such as ethnicity or political affiliation (Ashmore, Deaux, & McLaughlin-Volpe, 2004). Functional modules, as defined in Table 4.1, involve the integration of these different forms of information as they relate to the context in which the individual is currently situated.

Folk Psychology: Individual

Cognitive Modules

Caporael (1997) and Bugental (2000) described patterns of recurrent and universal one-on-one relationships in humans, including attachments between parent and child and friendships. Although there are motivational and affective differences associated with different forms of one-on-one relationship, they all appear to be supported by the same suite of sociocognitive competencies, including the ability to read nonverbal communication signals, facial expressions, language, and theory of mind (e.g., Adolphs, 1999; Brothers & Ring, 1992; Humphrey, 1976; Leslie, 1987; Moscovitch, Winocur, & Behrmann, 1997; Pinker, 1994; Premack & Woodruff, 1978). Theory of mind is especially salient in humans and represents the ability to make inferences about the intentions, beliefs, emotional states, and likely future behavior of other individuals (Baron-Cohen, 1995; Gopnik & Wellman, 1994). The integration of sociocognitive information processed by these modules with motivational and affective systems provides the basis for the development and maintenance of long-term relationships. These modules (e.g., processing facial expressions) are also engaged during the dynamics of one-on-one social interactions, providing cues to the on-line emotional states and intentions of other people. These sociocognitive competencies may also be used to manipulate and deceive other people as related to the goal of controlling social relationships in self-serving ways.

My suggestion is that the person schema (Fiske & Taylor, 1991) might be considered a fifth individual-level module. These schemata are discussed in chapter 7 (Social Cognition and Folk Psychology section) but may not be modular in the same sense as the four other individual-level modules. The associated schemata are probably built from specific memories of episodes with other people and inferences about the underlying traits (e.g., emotionally warm to distant) of these people. The modular component reflects a bias to attend to and organize these memories around specific other people and likely includes knowledge of how they are networked within the wider social group. The latter follows naturally from the complexity of human social relationships and on the basis of social dynamics described in Figure 2.3 and in Exhibit 2.1. The gist is that dyadic interactions and relationships are influenced by the social networks within which each individual is situated. Humans and individuals of at least some other species of primate are sensitive to the kin group and other social groups in which other individuals are networked (Bergman, Beehner, Cheney, & Seyfarth, 2003; Goodall, 1986), and in these species kin of high-status individuals are often treated better than kin of lower-status individuals (Geary & Flinn, 2001; Silk, 1987). Cognitive systems that result in detailed information about other people and that enable the monitoring and representation of the individual's relationships with other individuals in the social group are thus predicted to have evolved and are represented by the person schema module in Figure 5.2.

Neural Correlates and Potential Modules

There is a substantive body of research on biases in the forms of social information that humans, and many other species, process and some indications that these biases may be the result of modular neural, perceptual, and cognitive systems (e.g., Bentin, Sagiv, Mecklinger, Friederici, & von Cramon, 2002; Kanwisher, McDermott, & Chun, 1997). Whether any such modularity results from inherent constraints, developmental experiences, or some combination of the two is not entirely clear and is vigorously debated, as described in chapter 4. Whatever the combination of inherent and experiential influences, cognitive studies suggest distinct and potentially modular systems for the processing of facial and nonverbal communication cues (Rosenthal, Hall, DiMatteo, Rogers, & Archer, 1979), language (Pinker, 1994), and theory of mind (Adolphs, 1999; Baron-Cohen, 1995; Frith & Frith, 1999). As an example, J. Liu, Harris, and Kanwisher (2002) found evidence for distinct stages associated with the categorization of the basic shape of a human face and the identification of individual faces. Both stages occur quickly and automatically (in about 100 milliseconds for the first stage and 170 milliseconds for the second stage) and do not appear to be explainable in terms of more general visual processes.

The processing of this facial and other social information engages an integrated and distributed system of neocortical and subcortical systems, and the parallel operation of these systems results in functional social competencies. Included among these regions are the following:

- the fusiform gyrus (temporal cortex) and portions of the prefrontal cortex for face processing (Cox, Meyers, & Sinha, 2004; George et al., 1999; Halgren, Raij, Marinkovic, Jousmäki, &

Hari, 2000; Kanwisher et al., 1997; Nakamura et al., 2000; Ó Scalaidhe, Wilson, & Goldman-Rakic, 1997);

- portions of the left temporal and frontal cortices for processing aspects of human language (Belin, Zatorre, Lafaille, Ahad, & Pike, 2000);
- the right lateral occipitotemporal cortex for processing information patterns associated with the human body (e.g., shape; Downing, Jiang, Shuman, & Kanwisher, 2001);
- portions of the right posterior superior temporal sulcus (STS) for processing human biological motion (Grossman et al., 2000); and
- the amygdala and other limbic regions, as well as neocortical regions, for the parallel processing of the emotional valance and potential reward or punishment value of these cues (Adolphs, Damasio, Tranel, & Damasio, 1996; Aharon et al., 2001; Buchanan et al., 2000; Canli, Sivers, Whitfield, Gotlib, & Gabrieli, 2002; Kampe, Frith, Dolan, & Frith, 2001; Öhman, 2002).

As an example, in adults, portions of the left STS selectively respond to the phonetic aspects of human voice patterns (Belin et al., 2000), and the right temporal cortex is engaged during the processing of the prosody aspects of speech (Buchanan et al., 2000; J. S. Morris, Scott, & Dolan, 1999). Dehaene-Lambertz, Dehaene, and Hertz-Pannier (2002) found that many of these same brain regions are engaged when awake and sleeping 3-month-olds are exposed to human speech. Speech processing, especially of socially and emotionally salient speech, also engages areas in the prefrontal and frontal cortices as well as several subcortical areas, including the amygdala (D. M. Tucker, Luu, & Pribram, 1995). The amygdala appears to process aspects of human speech that signal threats and other human vocalizations that convey negative feelings, especially fear (Isenberg et al., 1999; J. S. Morris et al., 1999). One interpretation of this research is that different elements of human voice patterns and speech convey different types of information and that specialized and distributed neural and perceptual modules support the processing of this information. Other prefrontal and limbic systems appear to subserve motivational features of social information processing (Öhman, 2002), with threat cues, for instance, prompting a behavioral fight-or-flight response or increased social affiliation (Geary & Flinn, 2002; Taylor et al., 2000).

The results of many of these studies are, however, open to interpretation, given that a single brain region may process different forms of information (Cabeza & Nyberg, 2000). In addition to voice patterns, regions of the

STS are also involved in processing other forms of social information, such as the detection of human movement (Giese & Poggio, 2003), and the amygdala is involved in a variety of social competencies, such as theory of mind (Siegal & Varley, 2002) and in processing facial expressions in which the emotional signal is ambiguous (Adams, Gordon, Baird, Ambady, & Kleck, 2003). The finding that the same brain regions may be involved in the processing of different forms of information is consistent with Marcus' (2004) proposal that lower-level systems may be used in the construction of many higher-level modular competencies. The higher-level modules (e.g., for processing facial features) may thus be composed of a unique *constellation* of lower-level systems, but none of these lower-level systems need be unique to any specific higher-level module.

In any case, the integration across these neural, perceptual, and cognitive modules appears to engage portions of the right prefrontal cortex and limbic system, with current on-line content and social-emotional cues and information being integrated with memories for related situations (Damasio, 1995; Prabhakaran, Narayanan, Zhao, & Gabrieli, 2000; Siegal & Varley, 2002; D. M. Tucker et al., 1995). It is far from certain, but the endpoint of the integration of this information may be instantiated as a mental model (Johnson-Laird, 1983) in Baddeley's (2000a) episodic buffer—that is, an explicit and conscious working memory representation of the social discourse. In theory, the mental model supports functional social competencies, such as responding to a question or planning a social tactic. In short, the parallel processing of various forms of social information and the integration and representation of these information patterns in episodic working memory results in a functional module, as defined in Table 4.1 and elaborated in chapter 6 (Bounded Rationality and Heuristics section) and chapter 7 (Cognitive and Brain Systems section).

Evolutionary Considerations

As I described in chapter 2 (e.g., Sexual Selection and Brain and Cognitive Evolution section), the complexity of social relationships covaries with brain size, especially the volume of the neocortex (D. A. Clark, Mitra, & Wang, 2001; Kudo & Dunbar, 2001). For highly social species, the nature of these relationships influences survival and reproductive prospects (Goodall, 1986; Silk, Alberts, & Altmann, 2003). From a comparative perspective, language, theory of mind, and a sense of self are the most highly developed sociocognitive competencies in humans (Frith & Frith, 1999; Pinker, 1994; Tulving, 2002) and are hypothesized to be the co-evolutionary result of the increase in the complexity of human social dynamics associated with the shift from primarily ecological to primarily social selection pressures that should have followed the emergence of ecological dominance (Alexander, 1989), as I explained in the Social Pressures section of chapter 3. Recall, one predicted outcome of the achievement of ecological dominance is a ramping up of social selection pressures and thus the potential for these dynamics to result in the evolution of uniquely human social competencies that provide a competitive advantage over other people.

To be sure, other primates use and respond to conspecific facial expressions, vocalizations, and body language (Ghazanfar & Logothetis, 2003; Hauser, 1996; Leavens & Hopkins, 1998; Nahm, Perret, Amaral, & Albright, 1997), but none of these primates has a grammatical language (Fitch & Hauser, 2004). Moreover, there is little evidence to suggest that monkeys have a theory of mind or sense of self as a social being, although great apes may have a prototheory of mind, but this is vigorously debated (S. T. Parker & McKinney, 1999; Povinelli & Preuss, 1995; Premack & Woodruff, 1978). At the very least, chimpanzees, bonobos (*Pan paniscus*), and gorillas (*Gorilla gorilla*) display competencies that include the ability to behave and react strategically (e.g., deceptively) in social contexts and to do so in ways that exceed the competencies of monkeys. There is, however, no definitive evidence that these great apes have the specific ability to make inferences about the inferences of conspecifics or have a sense of self as a social being (Tomasello & Call, 1997), although the issue is far from resolved (Povinelli & Vonk, 2003).

In any event, it follows from the relation between neocortical volume and social complexity that the neocortical areas that support the unique aspects of human language and theory of mind will be larger in absolute size or evince more complex microcircuitry than homologous areas in other primates, or both, just as cross-species differences in foraging strategies are associated with differences in the size and organization of the somatosensory cortex (Comparative Ecology and Brain Evolution section of chap. 4). Rilling and Insel's (1999) neuroimaging study of individuals from 11 primate species indicated that the human neocortex has more surface area than predicted, on the basis of overall body and brain size, in areas that support aspects of human language (i.e., the left temporal cortex) and theory of mind (i.e., portions of the prefrontal cortex; see Adolphs, 1999; Baron-Cohen et al., 1994; Frith & Frith, 1999; Sabbagh & Taylor, 2000; see also Holloway, 1996). Semendeferi, Lu, Schenker, and Damasio (2002), in contrast, found that the absolute size of the frontal cortex was larger for humans than for chimpanzees, bonobos, orangutans (*Pongo pygmaeus*), and gorillas, but the relative size of the frontal cortex (compared to the rest of the neocortex) did not differ across these species. The differences across these studies may be due to a different comparison—relative volume (Semendeferi et al., 2002) versus surface area (Rilling & Insel, 1999).

Despite the different findings, both research teams agreed that there are likely to be similarities as well as differences in the microarchitecture and organization of the frontal and prefrontal cortices of humans compared to great apes; further discussion of functions of the prefrontal cortex is provided in chapter 7 (sections on Cognitive and Brain Systems and on Problem Solving and Human Evolution). Rilling and Insel's (1999) findings, for instance, converge with related comparative studies. Rauschecker, Tian, and Hauser (1995) reported that cells in the STS that are activated during the processing of phonetic features of human voice patterns selectively respond to conspecific vocalizations in the rhesus macaque (*Macaca mulatta*; see also Belin et al., 2000). Gannon, Holloway, Broadfield, & Braun (1998) found that the planum temporale—associated with speech comprehension in humans—shows the same hemispheric asymmetry in chimpanzees as in humans (N. Geschwind & Levitsky, 1968), although it is not known if this area subserves the processing of conspecific vocalizations in chimpanzees (see also Cantalupo & Hopkins, 2001).

Whether these portions of the STS or other areas of the left temporal cortex are homologous areas for the processing of conspecific vocalizations is not currently known, but it is a possibility (Poremba et al., 2004; Preuss & Kaas, 1999). On the basis of Rakic's (1988) model described in chapter 4 (Development of the Neocortex section), a gradual evolutionary expansion or modification of these areas could readily accommodate both the similarities (Doupe & Kuhl, 1999) and the differences (Preuss, 2004) in human speech and vocal communication in other primates and mammals. For instance, the evolution of the unique features of human language could have entailed, at least in part, an increase in the number of radial units in the STS and changes in the microcircuitry of these units to accommodate the greater complexity of human vocalizations.

We must also keep in mind that all of these comparative analyses are hampered by the extinction of species (e.g., *H. erectus*) that were more closely related to humans than are extant primates and great apes. As a result, the comparative data may never be definitive (Povinelli & Bering, 2002) but are nonetheless suggestive of continuities in the brain and cognitive systems that support social dynamics across primate species and are in line with an evolutionary expansion and modification of the systems that are most unique to humans. I elaborate in the Brain Evolution section of chapter 7.

Folk Psychology: Group

Cognitive Modules

A universal aspect of human social dynamics involves the parsing of the social world into groups (Alexander, 1989; Geary & Flinn, 2001; Horowitz, 2001; Premack & Premack, 1995). At a social-psychological level, the features of group-level parsing and identification (e.g., extent of emotional attachment to the group) are complex and beyond the scope of this volume (see Ashmore et al., 2004). My point is that social parsing is universal, and at a broad level the most consistent of these groupings are shown in Figure 5.2. The groupings reflect the categorical significance of kin, the formation of in-groups and out-groups, and a group schema, specifically an ideologically based social identification. The categorical significance and preferential treatment of kin is evident in a wide range of species (Hamilton, 1964) and is most strongly reflected in the motivational disposition for humans to form families and wider kinship networks of one form or another in all cultures (D. E. Brown, 1991; Caporael, 1997). For humans and some other species (e.g., chimpanzees; de Waal, 1982; Wrangham & Peterson, 1996), social parsing also involves the formation of in-groups and out-groups (Bornstein, 2003). For humans, and presumably other species, this parsing is often automatic and occurs without conscious awareness (Amodio et al., 2004; Phelps et al., 2000).

In traditional societies, in-group members are kin and social allies who share beliefs, such as origin myths, that distinguish them from other groups and who assign special significance to their own group (D. E. Brown, 1991). In all societies, in-groups and out-groups are defined by differing social and moral ideologies that favor in-group members and, under extreme conditions, devalue and even dehumanize out-group members (Fiske, 2002; W. G. Stephan, 1985). It is also clear that the dynamics of in-group–out-group formation are influenced by social ideologies that support a larger in-group (Horowitz, 2001). The social ideologies define a group schema, or system of shared beliefs, rules of conduct (e.g., the Ten Commandments or the U.S. Constitution), and so forth, that enables individuals to identify with a defined group and thus be part of a larger in-group than would be possible in the absence of a group schema. In short, identification with a group ideology facilitates cohesion and cooperation among members of the in-group and may confer other intrapersonal benefits such as reductions in anxiety associated with awareness of mortality (Solomon, Greenberg, Schimel, Arndt, & Pyszczynski, 2004).

Neural Correlates and Potential Modules

In many species, kin recognition mechanisms involve olfactory cues (e.g., Pfennig & Collins, 1993), and there is clear evidence for similar mechanisms in humans. For instance, many human mothers recognize the odor of their infant within 24 hours of giving birth (Fleming, Steiner, & Corter, 1997), and infants, in turn, recognize their mothers' breast odors in this same time frame (Porter & Winberg, 1999). Among other things, Weisfeld and his colleagues found that children could identify the odor of their full siblings but not of their half-siblings or stepsiblings (Weisfeld,

Czilli, Phillips, Gall, & Lichtman, 2003). These findings suggests that the human olfactory bulb is specialized for the detection of human pheromones and other odor-carrying molecules and may contribute to the ability to recognize kin and to discriminate kin from non-kin. As mentioned previously, fetuses also recognize the voice of their mother (Kisilevsky et al., 2003). However, the mechanism underlying this ability to recognize kin on the basis of odor and voice cues is not fully understood, although it must involve an epigenetic mechanism, that is, an interaction between inherent biases and exposure to these cues (see Porter & Winberg, 1999). Moreover, little is known about other brain or cognitive systems that support kin biases, although it is likely that these engage basic motivational and affective systems.

Similarly, little is known about the brain systems underlying in-group–out-group social psychology, the associated social categorizations, and the tendency to rally around ideologies. Nonetheless, there are several recent studies that indicate that the amygdala is often activated when individuals process the faces of unfamiliar out-group members (different race in these studies; Phelps et al., 2000; M. E. Wheeler & Fiske, in press). Specifically, the results suggest that out-group members may automatically and unconsciously trigger negative feelings and emotional displays, including fear, in many people.

Evolutionary Considerations

As I stated, kin-biased relationships are found across many species ranging from invertebrates to primates and are readily understandable in terms of inclusive fitness (e.g., Altmann et al., 1996; Hamilton, 1964). *Inclusive fitness* refers to the effect that an individual's behavior has on his or her own reproduction outcomes and those of his or her kin. Although the dynamics are complicated by self-interest and competition among relatives (Clutton-Brock, 2002; S. A. West, Pen, & Griffin, 2002), selection will typically favor individuals who facilitated the survival and reproductive prospects of kin, because the reproductive success of kin would perforce increase the altruist's genetic contributions to the next generation (Hamilton, 1975). The selective advantages of a kin bias would favor cognitive, affective, and other (e.g., pheromonal) mechanisms that enabled the parsing of conspecifics into kin and non-kin and the preferential treatment of the former.

Across species, the proximate benefit and presumed evolutionary function of in-group–out-group formation is predicted to be related to coalitional competition (Wrangham, 1999). As I described in chapter 2 (Intrasexual Competition section), when these social coalitions form in nonhuman species, they function to compete with other coalitions to gain access to or control of the resources that covary with survival (e.g., food; Silk, 1987) or reproductive outcomes (i.e., mates; Packer, Gilbert, Pusey, & O'Brien, 1991). When such coalitional behavior covaries with survival or reproductive prospects, any affective, motivational, or cognitive system that supported coalitional behavior would evolve.

When applied to humans, the general dynamics of in-group–out-group formation are predicted to be the evolutionary result of coalitional competition and function to enable the formation of large competition-related in-groups (Alexander, 1989; Geary & Flinn, 2001). The proximate benefit is the corresponding ability of larger coalitions to better control social and ecological resources than smaller coalitions (e.g., Chagnon, 1997). W. G. Stephan's (1985) review of the social psychology of intergroup relations supports this position, as do numerous studies on the social identification processes underlying group formation, categorization, and competition (e.g., Macrae & Bodenhausen, 2000; Sherif, Harvey, White, Hood, & Sherif, 1961). Humans readily form in-groups and out-groups and process information about members of these groups in ways that are favorably biased toward the in-group, particularly when the comparisons are made between groups that are competing for the same resource or in reaction to an out-group that potentially threatens resources held by the in-group (Fiske, 2002; W. G. Stephan, 1985). Considerable evidence for coalitional competition can be found outside of the social psychology laboratory, and in many instances the outcomes of this competition are brutal and covary with survival and reproductive outcomes (Chagnon, 1988; Horowitz, 2001; Keeley, 1996).

An in-group–out-group social psychology, which likely evolved in the context of competition between relatively small kin-based groups, more likely than not provided the foundation for the evolution of social ideologies and the tendency to form group-level schemata (Alexander, 1989; for an alternative explanation, see Solomon et al., 2004). As I stated above, the evolutionary root of these ideologies is the tendency for humans to generate shared belief systems, such as origin myths, that help to define in-groups, as exemplified in traditional societies today (D. E. Browne, 1991). As with other coalition-forming species, the function and ultimate selection pressure is likely to have been the resulting ability to increase group size and the accompanying competitive advantage (Wrangham, 1999). These ideologies are important because they appear to be the basis for the formation of large nation-states, that is, the social organization of individuals who have never met, and never will, and thus are unable to develop one-on-one reciprocal relationships (i.e., friendships). Such ideologies define the perceived mutual self-interest of individuals who compose these groups. The ideologies are the basis for the cultural evolution of large-scale societies and large-scale group conflict, as well as the cooperative division of labor and trade that are common within and between these societies.

Soft Modularity

Individual-Level Modules

If one evolved function of the proposed individual-level modules is to enable the formation and maintenance of social relationships, then these modules should show the exoskeleton form of soft modularity described in Table 4.2. For humans, it follows that the exoskeleton will be composed of neural, perceptual, and cognitive modules that are sensitive to the basic and universal features (e.g., general shape of the human face) that define the structure of human communication and the dynamics of one-on-one relationships. The latter would include inherent motivational biases to form relationships with other people (Baumeister & Leary, 1995), affective mechanisms (e.g., warmth, guilt) needed to maintain these relationships (Trivers, 1971), and inferential and attributional biases that guide social dynamics (e.g., Cosmides, 1989). By definition, the exoskeleton of the modules should include features that are sensitive to invariant information patterns conveyed in each of the individual-level areas shown in Figure 5.2—nonverbal behavior (e.g., gestures), facial processing, language, theory of mind, and person schema. At the same time, some degree of plasticity within the exoskeleton constraints would be needed to enable the identification and understanding (e.g., how they think) of specific individuals and maintain relationships with these individuals.

As an example, gestures appear to be a universal and apparently inherent mode of human communication (Rosenthal et al., 1979) but show a regional "dialect" (McNeill, 2000). McNeill demonstrated that both English-speaking and Spanish-speaking children use gestures to communicate but by 3 years of age adopt the movement styles of the region. Regional and individual variation in gesture patterns expressed in the context of a universal communication system is analogous to the pattern found for human language (Doupe & Kuhl, 1999) and apparently human facial expressions as related to emotion displays (Elfenbein & Ambady, 2003), and this variation is consistent with both inherent constraints and plasticity within these constraints. Specifically, constraint in the form of an exoskeleton (e.g., resulting in implicit knowledge that gestures convey social information; Iverson & Goldin-Meadow, 1998) and plasticity in the form of soft internal structures can accommodate the universal communicative features of gestures and body language, as well as of regional dialects and the unique gestural styles and body language (e.g., walking gait) of specific individuals.

Although not definitive, results from several recent neuroimaging studies are consistent with the exoskeleton form of modularity. The studies indicate that the left and right fusiform gyri, as well as other areas of the temporal cortex, are selectively activated when people process conspecific faces (Kanwisher et al., 1997). George and colleagues (1999) found that only portions of the right fusiform gyrus were activated when processing highly familiar faces, and Nakamura and colleagues (2000) found that the right fusiform gyrus was activated during the processing of faces and that the right temporal pole was activated during the discrimination of familiar and unfamiliar faces. Thus, there appear to be specific areas of the temporal cortex that are highly sensitive to invariant forms of information conveyed by human faces (e.g., eye position)—the exoskeleton (including the bilateral fusiform gyrus)—and subareas within and adjacent to this region that change in response to repeated exposure to the same face—the soft internal structures (including the right fusiform gyrus). Bentin et al. (2002) found that the processing of perceptual stimuli such as "●●" could activate the same neural systems that are activated by faces, but only if these stimuli were repeatedly presented in the context of a face. In other words, the perceptual, cognitive, and neural systems that process facial stimuli may be activated by stimuli that the individual interprets as facelike.

A general-learning interpretation of face processing in these regions has been offered, however. Gauthier, Tarr, Anderson, Skudlarski, and Gore (1999) trained adults to discriminate between different novel objects, called *greebles*. After extensive training, the right fusiform gyrus was activated while discriminating different greebles. Gauthier et al. concluded "that the face-selective area in the middle fusiform gyrus may be most appropriately described as a general substrate for subordinate-level discrimination that can be fine-tuned by experience with any object category" (p. 572). The difficulty with this interpretation is that the greebles had several facelike attributes (e.g., a round facelike shape on top of a more slender necklike base). If the bilateral fusiform gyrus is the exoskeleton for processing facelike information and portions of the right fusiform gyrus are the soft internal structures that encode memories of the distinct features of familiar faces, then Gauthier et al.'s results are not unexpected. In support of this interpretation, these same areas do not generally respond to other types of objects or environmental scenes that do not have facelike features, except in individuals with inherent sociocognitive deficits, such as autism (Nakamura et al., 2000; R. T. Schultz et al., 2000).

Theory of mind is also predicted to show general constraints on the types of information processed (e.g., a mismatch between vocal intonation and facial expression) and on the types of inferences drawn from this information (e.g., deception). Plasticity in the form of memory mechanisms for representing characteristics of familiar minds is expected as well, as these representations are a necessary feature of long-term relationships. Just as one recognizes the face and voice of a familiar person, one also comes to understand how each individual thinks. In addition, theory of mind may show a form of functional plasticity analogous to the rules of grammar (Jackendoff, 1992). A grammarlike feature of theory of mind would result in an exponential increase in the complexity and flexibility of social behavior that follows from the social selection pressures described in chapter 3. At the same time, the link to more basic motivational and affective systems would be preserved, as mediated, in part by the amygdala (Humphrey, 1976; Öhman, 2002; Siegal & Varley, 2002; D. M. Tucker et al., 1995). In this view, theory of mind is used to achieve many of the same social goals, such as mating or dominance, as are found in other primates. The means to achieve these goals are highly adaptive but constrained by a social grammar, in much the same way as was described for the rules of engagement during male–male competition (Architecture section of chap. 4).

Group-Level Modules

As I stated, the parsing of the social world into favored and disfavored groups is a universal dynamic in humans (e.g., Fiske, 2002; Horowitz, 2001) and in many other species (Altmann et al., 1996; Bergman et al., 2003; de Waal, 1982; Packer et al., 1991). The flexibility of parsing might be understood in terms of the rule-based category formation form of plasticity described in Table 4.2. The mechanisms that underlie the operation of such rules are not currently known but are likely to operate implicitly and automatically and are predicted to act on specific forms of information, such as groups of conspecifics, with different rules for forming different types of categories (e.g., Bugental, 2000). As I describe in chapter 7 (Social Cognition and Folk Psychology section), the output of these processes can become conscious and may be expressed as attributional biases and heuristics (i.e., "rules of thumb" for interacting with in-group members). As an example, the attributions regarding in-group members and out-group members clearly differ, as do the rules that define relationships among friends, spouses, and family members.

For highly social and political species, such as humans, category formation should show a high degree of functional plasticity. My prediction is that an evolved plasticity in the ability to vary the nature of group-level relationships was enhanced by the cycle of population expansions and contractions described by Malthus (1798) and in chapter 3 (Ecological Dominance section) and the corresponding changes in costs and benefits associated with group size. Large groups provide a competitive advantage but at the cost of having to share resources among more people. Thus, the mechanisms supporting group formation should be sensitive to the costs and benefits of group size and should result in the dissipation of large groups when benefits are low or do not outweigh the cost of resource sharing.

Whatever the specific cognitive mechanisms, at a behavioral level group-level relationships range from endemic conflict with the goal of exterminating the out-group to relatively low levels of conflict combined with tolerance and social exchange (Alexander, 1989; Chagnon, 1988; Macrae & Bodenhausen, 2000). If an in-group–out-group social psychology did in fact evolve in the context of coalition-based competition, then the patterns of in-group–out-group relationships—especially the degree of hostility and conflict—should, and do, have some relation to resource availability in the local ecology (Fiske, 2002; Sherif et al., 1961; W. G. Stephan, 1985), and, as predicted, the dynamics of intergroup relationships are related to control of these resources (Horowitz, 2001). Moreover, the rules for category formation should reflect perceived self-interest and perceived sources of threat to that interest. When resources are plentiful and coalitions are not needed, then the contextual pull for in-group–out-group formation is weak and group-level conflict is low in frequency and intensity (Alexander, 1989). When resources are limited and coalitions help to obtain access to and control of such resources, then an in-group–out-group social psychology is invoked, and these groups are formed on the basis of a categorical rule: "Those who assist me in achieving the desired goal are members of the in-group, and those who cooperate to thwart the achievement of this goal are members of the out-group."

Just as the rules of grammar can be supplemented by knowledge of individual words in the lexicon (e.g., irregular verb forms such as *went* instead of *goed*; Pinker, 1999), human coalitional politics can be transcended by knowledge of individual people. There can be hostility toward members of a defined out-group, but more friendly relationships can develop with specific individuals who might otherwise be defined as a member of this out-group (W. G. Stephan, 1985). These individual relationships are defined by the rules of friendship and thus are predicted to have little or no effect on more general out-group dynamics or attributions. Just as irregular verbs stored in a separate lexicon have no influence on the rules of grammar, as aptly described by Pinker (1999), friendly relationships with individual members of an out-group will have no influence on the rules of in-group–out-group formation or accompanying patterns of attributions or conflict (Macrae & Bodenhausen, 2000).

Results from cognitive and neuroimaging studies provide some support for this interpretation (Phelps et al., 2000; M. E. Wheeler & Fiske, in press). It was found that when participants processed the faces of well-liked and familiar individuals (e.g., celebrities) who might otherwise be categorized in an out-group or were instructed to make inferences about the individual as a person, the cognitive categorization of these individuals into an out-group was inhibited, as was activation of the amygdala. Inhibition of amygdala activation would presumably result in the inhibition of fear reactions to these potential out-group members. M. E. Wheeler and Fiske's study also suggests that the suppression of what would normally be automatic cognitive (i.e., categorization and stereotyping) and neural (e.g., amygdala activation) responses to members of an out-group often requires a conscious inhibition of these processes; specifically, categorization of potential out-group members occurs implicitly and without effort, but thinking about these people as individuals involves effortful processing (see also Amodio et al., 2004). I elaborate on implicit versus explicit, effortful processing in chapter 6.

FUNCTIONAL ECOLOGICAL SYSTEMS

Most species require behavioral systems for negotiating relationships with other species and movement in physical space. These behaviors require supporting neural, perceptual, and cognitive modules that are sensitive to the accompanying forms of information. The constellation of modular systems is captured by the notions of folk biology and folk physics (e.g., Gallistel, 1990; R. Gelman, 1990; Verbeek & de Waal, 2002). In the first and second subsections that follow, I discuss these classes of module (see Figure 5.2), and the third section I provide related discussion of soft modularity.

Folk Biology

Cognitive Modules

As Medin and Atran (1999b) noted, in "subsistence cultures, survival depends on a detailed appreciation of the habits, affordances, and interactions linked to the biological world" (p. 1). As described for other species in chapter 4 (Comparative Ecology and Brain Evolution section), humans in traditional societies are highly dependent on cognitive and behavioral specializations that support foraging and other forms of interaction with the natural world. Although the source of these specializations is currently debated (e.g., Keil, Levin, Richman, & Gutheil, 1999), the accompanying functional competencies are manifest as hunting, gathering, and horticulture, among other activities. At the most basic level, the supporting cognitive and functional modules are predicted to result in the ability to categorize and process information in the general domains of flora and fauna and to develop a supporting knowledge base that can be used in the service of obtaining foods and medicines (Atran, 1998; Malt, 1995).

Consistent with the view that these are universal features of folk biology, humans throughout the world are able to categorize the flora and fauna in their local ecologies (Atran, 1998; Berlin, Breedlove, & Raven, 1966; Carey & Spelke, 1994). In fact, humans living in natural environments develop very elaborate and complex classification systems of the flora and fauna in the local ecology and develop mental models of the behavior (e.g., growth patterns) of these plants and animals (for examples, see Medin & Atran, 1999a). Through ethnobiological studies, "it has become apparent that, while individual societies may differ considerably in their conceptualization of plants and animals, there are a number of strikingly regular structural principles of folk biological classification which are quite general" (Berlin, Breedlove, & Raven, 1973, p. 214). People's classification of plants and animals in traditional societies is similar to the scientific classification of these same organisms (Atran, 1994; Diamond, 1966), although the degree to which particular aspects (e.g., one species or another) of the classification system is more or less elaborated is contingent on the social and biological significance of the plants or animals to people in the culture (Atran, 1998; Malt, 1995).

People in traditional societies classify flora and fauna on the basis of common features (i.e., information patterns) of morphology, behavior, growth patterns, and ecological niche (e.g., arboreal vs. terrestrial). The combination of these cues and inferential biases (e.g., self-initiated movement implies a living organism; R. Gelman, 1990) helps to define the essence of the species (Atran, 1994; Malt, 1995). The *essence* is organized knowledge of the salient characteristics of the species and appears to be analogous, in one sense, to peoples' theory of mind and in another sense to the self and person schemata; knowledge of flora and fauna enable one to represent and predict the likely behavior of these organisms (e.g., seasonal growth in plants), just as theory of mind enables one to form representations of the intentions of other people and thus improves one's ability to predict their behavior. The knowledge for individual and related species may be organized in a way similar to that associated with self and person schemata—that is, there is a bias to attend to certain forms of information (e.g., self-initiated movement; R. Gelman, 1990) and then to organize information generated through experiences around these core attributes.

However the mechanisms are organized, knowledge of the essence of familiar species also allows people to make inferences about the essence of unfamiliar species (Berlin, 1999), that is, to generalize within the specific category of flora or fauna. For example, knowledge of one species of frog can be used to make predictions about the characteristics of a novel species of frog but not a novel species of bird (Atran, 1994). These mental models and other aspects of folk biological knowledge presumably manifest as working-memory representations that enable the integration of this knowledge and related memories with perceptions and cognitions generated during functional activities, such as hunting. It is possible that this information is integrated with related memories in the episodic buffer (Baddeley, 2000a). In any case, the working memory representations support a functional module, as defined in Table 4.1 and elaborated in the Problem Solving and Human Evolution section of chapter 7.

Neural Correlates and Potential Modules

Some research in the cognitive neurosciences is consistent with the prediction of neural, perceptual, and cognitive modules for processing distinct information patterns generated by plants, animals, and artifacts, although there is not a consensus on the meaning of these studies (Farah, Meyer, & McMullen, 1996; Forde & Humphreys, 2002; Gaffan & Heywood, 1993; Hart & Gordon, 1992; Laws & Neve, 1999; Low et al., 2003; Warrington & Shallice, 1984). Some of the studies suggest distinct perceptual, cognitive, and brain mechanisms for the categorization of living and nonliving things (Gerlach, Law, Gade, & Paulson, 1999; Ilmberger, Rau, Noachtar, Arnold, & Winkler, 2002; Lloyd-Jones & Humphreys, 1997; Perani et al., 1995). As an example, it is often found that bilateral damage to the posterior portions of the neocortex, especially the anterior portions of the temporal cortex (Gainotti, 2002), results in disruptions in the ability to name living things, but not nonliving things (Farah et al., 1996; Warrington & Shallice, 1984). However, occasionally the reverse is found. Sacchett and Humphreys (1992) reported a case study of an individual with a brain injury who could name living things but not manufactured, nonliving things (see Caramazza & Shelton, 1998). The double dissociation across individuals is important because it strengthens the argument for distinct brain and cognitive systems for the categorization of living and nonliving things. Hart and Gordon (1992) reported another injury-related dissociation, but for this individual the distinction was between the categorization of fruits and vegetables versus animals, consistent with the argument for different brain and cognitive systems for representing flora and fauna.

The results of brain imaging studies of normal individuals are not conclusive, however (C. J. Price & Friston, 2002). J. T. Devlin et al. (2001) found that the same brain regions were engaged when individuals made decisions during the categorization of names of animals, fruits, tools, and vehicles. Gerlach et al. (1999) and Perani et al. (1995), in contrast, asked individuals to make categorizations based on illustrations, not names, and found that different brain regions were engaged during the categorization of animals and manufactured artifacts. Low et al. (2003) found evidence that different but adjacent regions of the left temporal cortex represented categories of plants, animals, clothes, and furniture but did not find a clear distinction between the ease of categorizing living things versus manufactured artifacts. Many cognitive studies indicate that there are differences in the perceptual and cognitive mechanisms involved in the categorization of living and nonliving things and that the categorization processes involve distinct naming and visual mechanisms (Lloyd-Jones & Humphreys, 1997).

In addition to being inconclusive with regard to an inherent folk biology, nearly all of these studies were conducted with adults and thus do not directly address the issue of whether any modularity results from inherent constraint or patterns of developmental experience. Thus, debate continues as to whether such results are consistent with inherent, modular systems; stem from more general learning mechanisms operating on perceptual and functional differences across living and nonliving things; or, most likely, involve some combination (Caramazza & Shelton, 1998; Farah et al., 1996; Gaffan & Heywood, 1993; Warrington & Shallice, 1984).

Evolutionary Considerations

Neural, perceptual, cognitive, and inferential systems for processing information about other species should evolve to the extent the resulting functional and behavioral biases covary with survival outcomes (e.g., predator avoidance). As I described in chapter 4 (Comparative Ecology and Brain Evolution section), there is evidence for these types of specializations across a wide range of species (Barton & Dean, 1993; Huffman, Nelson, Clarey, & Krubitzer, 1999). As with these nonhuman species, folk biological knowledge covaries with survival prospects for humans living in traditional societies. As an example, Atran's (1994) finding of a highly differentiated taxonomy of fauna for Itza-Maya (Guatemala) hunters is in keeping with the view that the function of this folk biological knowledge is, at least in part, survival related. This taxonomy was "related to features of behavior, habitat, diet, and functional relationships to people" (p. 331), which very likely facilitate the hunting of these animals. The same pattern has been found for plants that serve as foods and medicines in other traditional societies (D. Clement, 1995; Figueiredo, Leitão-Filho, & Begossi, 1993, 1997).

Research on Western children's formation of biological taxonomies is also consistent with the existence of inherent, and possibly evolved, biases that guide the development of folk biological modules (Keil, 1992; Santos & Caramazza, 2002). For instance, preschool children and infants for some tests have an implicit understanding of some differences between living and nonliving things, implicitly understand the difference between plants and animals, and appear to have rudimentary mental models of the essence of animals, models that become increasingly sophisticated during childhood (Coley, 2000; Coley, Solomon, & Shafto, 2002). Included in this folk biological knowledge is the implicit understanding, and sometimes explicit attribution, that living things and nonliving things have different types of innards and that living things are capable of self-initiated movement (R. Gelman, 1990; Hickling & Gelman, 1995). Later, children understand that animals must eat to survive and that they produce offspring that share characteristics with their parents (Carey & Spelke, 1994; Coley, 1995). Children also exhibit similar forms of knowledge about plants, although this knowledge appears to emerge at a later age (Coley et al., 2002). As with the brain injury and imaging studies described previously, there is no consensus regarding the meaning of this research (e.g., Au & Romo, 1999)—that is, whether it is best understood in terms of inherent modular constraints or as the result of general learning mechanisms. My position and that of Caramazza and colleagues (Caramazza & Shelton, 1998; Santos & Caramazza, 2002) is that the initial sources of children's implicit knowledge are inherent, modular systems that are components of an evolved folk biology.

Folk Physics

Cognitive Modules

Neural, perceptual, and cognitive systems that enable organisms to act on, respond to, and in some cases mentally represent the physical world are evident across a wide range of species—from invertebrates to humans—and are likely to show a fair degree of inherent modularity (Gallistel, 1990; Shepard, 1994). These systems appear to be sensitive to many invariant features of physical space and can accommodate variation (e.g., movement of trajectories, shading in color perception; Shepard, 1994) within these constraints. For humans and a few other species, one additional aspect of folk physics includes the ability to mentally represent physical objects and mentally manipulate these representations as they relate to the practice of tool use (Baron-Cohen et al., 1999; Lockman, 2000). However, people's understanding of many such physical phenomena, such as tool use, is considerably more sophisticated than that of other species, including chimpanzees (Johnson-Frey, 2003; Povinelli, 2000). In any case, a useful conceptualization of the most general classes of functional physical module is in terms of movement (Andersen, Snyder, Bradley, & Xing, 1997), representation (Shepard, 1994), and tool use (Pinker, 1997), as shown in Figure 5.2.

The distinction between movement and representation is based on Milner and Goodale's (1995) framework for the functional and anatomical organization of the visual system, although analogous mechanisms are evident in other systems (Dukas, 1998b), as exemplified by the bat's (e.g., brown bat, *Eptesicus fuseus*) use of echolocation to guide prey capture (Moss & Simmons, 1996). Neural and perceptual modules that process movement-related information allow the organism to track and behaviorally respond to current information in the external world. Among other things, the associated perceptual and cognitive systems enable the generation of three-dimensional analogue maps of the environment (Gallistel, 1990), support the tracking of the movement of objects in space (Shepard, 1994), and enable adjustments for the influence of gravity on the trajectory of falling objects, as when these objects are tracked behaviorally (e.g., caught; McIntyre, Zago, Berthoz, & Lacquaniti, 2001). There is also some evidence for distinct visuomotor systems involved in distinct activities that require movement in physical space, such as prey location and capture versus preda-tor avoidance, in keeping with a modular perspective (see Barton, 1996).

In addition to systems for supporting movement, some species also appear to have systems that support the representation of features of the physical environment when they are not directly engaging the environment. Kuhlmeier and Boysen (2002) demonstrated that many, but not all, chim-panzees are able to form a correspondence between the location of a minia-ture object in a scale model of an enclosure and the location of the actual object in the enclosure, suggesting that some chimpanzees are able to gener-ate a mental representation of the location of objects that are not currently being viewed. Other experimental manipulations suggested that these chim-panzees form a mental representation of the location of objects on the basis of landmark information (e.g., the object is next to another object) and geometric coordinates (e.g., the object is northeast of another object). Studies in human cognition indicate that performance on tasks that involve the judgment of movement in physical space (e.g., visually tracking a moving object) is only weakly related to performance on tasks that involve generating a mental representation of physical space (e.g., a map; Schiff & Oldak, 1990; Watson & Kimura, 1991), in keeping with the distinct movement and representational modules in the taxonomy presented in Figure 5.2. As with chimpanzees, the representational systems for humans include, among others no doubt, the ability to generate a mental model of the physical layout of the habitat (i.e., the geometric coordinates) and for remembering the relative location of landmarks within this habitat (Matthews, 1992).

Tool use is found in one form or another in all human cultures and enables people to more fully exploit biological resources in the local ecology (Murdock, 1981). The neural, perceptual, and cognitive systems that enable tool use have not been as systematically studied as the systems supporting movement and representation, although researchers are beginning to under-stand some of these mechanisms (Johnson-Frey, 2003; Lockman, 2000). On the basis of research by Povinelli (2000) on how chimpanzees understand tool use, among other aspects of folk physics, it appears that the feature that distinguishes humans from this other tool-using species is the human ability to use mental simulations of how objects can be used as tools to achieve a particular goal and to constrain these simulations by folk physical knowledge (e.g., how rotating an object can influence its effectiveness as a tool, or the effects of gravity on tool manipulation).

As with folk psychology and folk biology, it is possible that the functional modules associated with folk physics also entail mental models (Johnson-Laird, 1983) that engage Baddeley's (2000a) episodic buffer, along with other working memory systems such as those that support visuospatial processing and representations. In other words, the actual use of tools, navigation from one place to another, or capturing prey all involve the integration of implicit (potentially inherent) knowledge and memories for related past experiences with information patterns in the current environment. As elaborated in chapter 6 (Reasoning section) and chapter 7 (Cognitive and Brain Systems section), such integration is necessary for functional and behavioral competence and in some situations—those that entail novelty—may require the generation of an explicit mental model for simulating behavioral strategies to cope with these situations. It is the ability to use these mental simulations to generate potential behavioral responses to variant and novel social and ecological conditions that separates humans from other species, as I elaborate in later chapters.

Neural Correlates and Potential Modules

The processing of information patterns associated with physical space and mental representations of this space appear to engage the parietal cortex, the hippocampus, and several other brain regions (Andersen et al., 1997; Ekstrom et al., 2003; Maguire, Frackowiak, & Frith, 1997), and different patterns of information or representation appear to engage relatively distinct systems of brain regions. As an example, memory for the relative location of landmarks is dependent on a spatial memory system that appears to be distinct, in some respects, from the system that generates an abstract representation of three-dimensional space. In a neuroimaging study, Maguire et al. (1997) contrasted the brain regions involved in navigating a complex route through London—taxi drivers imagined and described these routes during brain imaging—with the brain regions associated with imagining highly salient landmarks. The route and landmark tasks engaged many of the same brain regions, such as parts of the parietal cortex, but the route task also engaged the hippocampus, whereas the landmark task did not (see also Maguire, Frackowiak, & Frith, 1996). Maguire et al. (1998) also provided evidence for distinct brain systems involved in representing physical space (especially the right hippocampus and right inferior parietal cortex) and for tracking speed of movement in this space (especially the right caudate nucleus).

Nakamura et al. (2000) found that regions of the left and right parietal–occipital junctions and portions of the left and right hippocampi were engaged during the processing of scenes and that these regions differed from those engaged during the processing of faces or objects. Ekstrom et al. (2003) placed electrodes in the hippocampus and adjacent brain regions of patients with severe epilepsy as part of the procedure to determine the foci of the seizures. These individuals then navigated in a computer-generated virtual town. Cells in the hippocampus were found to be selectively responsive to geometric location in the town, whereas cells in the adjacent parahippocampal region were responsive to specific landmarks. The results provide evidence for distinct brain regions for processing geometric place information and landmark information.

Recent demonstrations of injury-related functional dissociations between knowledge about tools (e.g., name, description of their use) and the actual use of tools suggest that distinct systems of brain regions support these distinct competencies (Hodges, Spatt, & Patterson, 1999; see also Lockman, 2000). In a review of neuroimaging and brain injury research, Johnson-Frey (2003) concluded that homologous brain regions in the parietal and motor areas are involved in object grasping and manipulation in humans and other primates. He also concluded that humans differ from these other species in terms of the ability to mentally reason about how tools might be used to solve practical goals and that the ability to reason about tool use depended on other regions of the parietal cortex and some regions of the temporal cortex (see also C. J. Price & Friston, 2002). Relatedly, Hodges et al. (1999) concluded that

> there are clearly more sophisticated [than object location] processes that facilitate the plausible—if not always correct—manipulation and usage of objects. It seems likely that parietal lobe areas are responsible for the transformation of spatial representations of attended objects into the motor coordinate frame for action, which entails an element of mechanical problem solving. (p. 9447)

In a neuroimaging study of humans and monkeys (presumably macaques), Vanduffel et al. (2002) found evidence for engagement of different areas of the parietal cortex during the solving of a complex three-dimensional spatial task. They interpreted these findings as suggesting that humans are more sensitive to certain forms of environmental motion than monkeys and suggested that the competency might have evolved for "manipulating fine tools" (Vanduffel et al., 2002, p. 415). Whether this is the case remains to be seen, but the results of of these studies (Hodges et al., 1999; Maguire et al., 1996; Vanduffel et al., 2002) suggest that distinct systems of brain regions in the parietal cortex, hippocampus, and other regions are engaged during the processing of information patterns associated with different aspects of folk physics. However, it is not known if these specialized functions are the result of inherent constraint, developmental experiences, or more likely some combination.

Evolutionary Considerations

On the basis of an evolutionary and comparative analysis of spatial cognition, Dyer (1998) concluded,

> On the most general level, the adaptive significance of spatial orientation is obvious: It is easy to imagine why natural selection has equipped animals with mechanisms that enable them to (1) acquire information

about their position and orientation relative to fitness-enhancing resources, such as food or mates; and (2) guide movements in search of
better conditions. (p. 201)

In other words, the neural, perceptual, and cognitive systems that enable
movement in physical space, and that in some species enable the mental
representation of physical space, will necessarily covary with survival and
reproductive outcomes and thus evolve.

The ability to use tools to manipulate and to better control the environment is evident in a few species. Some groups of chimpanzees, for instance,
use stones in a hammer–anvil manner to crack open nuts (Mercader, Panger,
& Boesch, 2002). Human tool use, however, is extraordinary in comparison
(Pinker, 1997). As I described in chapter 3 (Ecological Pressures section),
there is a very long evolutionary history of tool use in hominids and a
pattern of increasing sophistication of these tools beginning with *H. habilis*
and continuing to modern humans (de Heinzelin et al., 1999; Foley &
Lahr, 1997; Gowlett, 1992). Accompanying the long history of tool use in
hominids is a host of supporting anatomical changes, such as the human
thumb, that support the physical construction and use of tools (Trinkaus,
1992). I also noted in chapter 3 (Brain Evolution section) that endocasts
made from the skulls of early hominids allow inferences to be drawn about
evolutionary change in the outer surface of the neocortex (Holloway, 1973b).
Although these methods do not allow definitive conclusions to be drawn,
it is of interest that there appear to have been changes in the organization
and size of the parietal lobes—the brain regions involved in tool use (Hodges
et al., 1999)—with the emergence of *H. habilis* (Tobias, 1987).

As outlined in various sections in chapter 3 (e.g., Ecological Pressures),
the advantages associated with tool use include an increase in the range of
foods available to the individual, such as with the use of stone hammers to
extract marrow from bone, and an enhanced ability to control some physical
resources, as with tools used to start fires (Wrangham, Holland Jones, Laden,
Pilbeam, & Conklin-Brittain, 1999). Stated otherwise, tool use enabled
early hominids to more fully exploit and control biological and physical
resources, and their use must have covaried with survival and reproductive
(e.g., weapons related to male–male competition) outcomes, as tool use
does today in all human cultures. The evolution of tool use and underlying
brain and cognitive systems almost certainly contributed to the eventual
ecological dominance of *Homo* and helped to set the stage for the within-
species arms race that likely drove much of brain and cognitive evolution
since *H. erectus* (see Ecological Dominance section of chap. 3). A pattern
of increasingly effective tool use during hominid evolution and corresponding changes in brain and cognitive evolution would also help to explain

Povinelli's (2000) findings that chimpanzees have a poor understanding of physical phenomena, including tool use, relative to human children.

Soft Modularity

Folk Biological Modules

The pattern of cross-cultural similarities and differences in folk biological knowledge—as well as the nature of the task itself (i.e., to categorize and learn about other living things)—appears to be most readily understandable in terms of the rule-based categorical plasticity described in Table 4.2. Inherent and modular constraints (the exoskeleton) can be predicted in terms of neural and perceptual systems that are sensitive to invariant forms of information regularly produced by other living things, such as self-initiated biological motion and basic morphological prototypes (e.g., the basic body plan for mammals is the same across species; R. Gelman, 1990). Plasticity may occur at the level of cognitive modules, specifically as a form of categorical rule that acts on these forms of information. Categorical plasticity would be a necessary feature of any folk biological functional module, at least for humans. Biological categorization would be a reflection of the operation of rules that, for instance, resulted in the broad clustering of objects in the world into animate and inanimate sets (R. Gelman, 1990): One associated categorical rule might be "If the object shows a basic morphology associated with animals or plants and self-generated growth or movement, then it is animate." Other categorical distinctions would be generated by different rules. For example, animals can be distinguished from plants on the basis of morphology and ease of self-initiated movement (Atran, 1998; Coley, 2000).

Inherent information-processing biases in the form of an exoskeleton and categorization rules, including mechanisms for developing knowledge systems about individual species (including their essence), would result in similarities in the folk biology of people in different cultures, as well as differences. As an illustration, even though American college students and Itza-Maya hunters produce highly similar taxonomies for common mammalian species on the basis of morphology and behavior, they often differ in some of their more functional categorizations (Atran, 1994, 1998). For example, "Itzaj form a group of arboreal animals, including monkeys as well as tree-dwelling procyonids (kinkajou, cacomistle, raccoon) and squirrels (a rodent)" (Atran, 1998, p. 558). The clustering of these species is based on their occupation of a similar ecological niche rather than morphological similarities, which in turn is functional for these hunters because it aids them in locating these animals.

There are also differences in the inferences drawn by Itzaj hunters and American college students. The differences are related, in part, to degree of expertise (elaboration of folk biological knowledge) with the species in question and the relevance of these species for day-to-day activities (Medin, Coley, Storms, & Hayes, 2003). For instance, Itzaj hunters consider large predatory mammals (e.g., jaguars) as the standard prototype for mammals, whereas American college students consider smaller mammals (e.g., raccoons) as the standard prototype (Atran, 1998). The standard prototype, or primary exemplar, then provides the ideal against which inferences about other animals are drawn and provides a functional anchor for making decisions that are useful for the particular ecology. For Itzaj, the exemplar of large and potentially dangerous mammals likely speeds the identification of these animals and allows fast inferences to be drawn about similar species (e.g., cougars).

Folk Physical Modules

As I stated, some aspects of the physical environment, especially its three-dimensional structure, are invariant across time and place, and thus genetically prespecified information processing biases that are sensitive to these forms of information should be favored by selection pressures, as Gallistel (1990), Shepard (1994), and Tooby and Cosmides (1992) argued. However, other aspects of the physical ecology can be highly variant across locations, as in mountainous terrain versus arctic tundra. For species that occupy a wide range of physical ecologies, some degree of plasticity of the associated neural, perceptual, and cognitive systems is predicted (Potts, 1998). More precisely, mechanisms of the exoskeleton (see Table 4.2) that support the formation of memories for the specific features of the local ecology would be highly adaptive for such a species, in keeping with Gallistel (1995, 2000). This form of soft modularity would include constraints (i.e., an exoskeleton) on the type of information processed (e.g., landscapes) and more plastic systems (i.e., soft internal structures) that enable the formation of memories for and the development of a knowledge base of the physical ecologies within which the individual lives. Ecologies that are subject to fluctuations in weather patterns and climate, as in seasonal changes, would also create pressures that would favor the same form of soft modularity.

Cognitive and brain research on tool use is less abundant than research on other systems that process folk physical information. Nonetheless, it is clear that tool use is highly plastic in humans (Murdock, 1981) but may have modular constraints (Hodges et al., 1999; Johnson-Frey, 2003). Modular constraints would include attentional, neural, and perceptual systems that result in an orientation toward inanimate objects; brain and cognitive systems that support the ability to grasp and manipulate these objects; and, for humans, systems that enable the generation of mental representations of these how these objects might be used as tools. The latter might occur in an episodic buffer that guides the mental manipulation of tool-related representations and integrates these within an action frame, that is, a behavioral system (functional module) for using the objects as tools (Hodges et al., 1999; Lockman, 2000). At the same time, the wide range of tools used by humans suggests that the categorization and mental representation of objects as potential tools is not highly constrained. In fact, the finding that people are able to readily create functional categories of tools, such as those used in domestic activities versus those used in hunting or warfare (Lockman, 2000; Murdock, 1981), suggests that the rule-based categorical form of plasticity described in Table 4.2 may apply to tool use. The fundamental rule governing the categorization of tools and other artifacts appears to be the intent of the creator of the tool—that is, children and adults categorize manufactured artifacts on the basis of their intended function (e.g., sitting, as in chairs) rather than other attributes, such as shape (Bloom, 1996; Dennett, 1990; S. A. Gelman & Bloom, 2000). Still, there are physical constraints (e.g., based on shape) on how one object or another can be used as a tool.

There is also evidence for the third type of plasticity described in Table 4.2, resource distribution. In a neuroimaging study, Maguire et al. (2000) found that the posterior hippocampus, which appears to support large-scale navigation, was larger in taxi drivers than in age-matched men who were not taxi drivers. Moreover, hippocampal "volume correlated with the amount of time spent as a taxi driver (positively in the posterior and negatively in the anterior hippocampus)" (Maguire et al., 2000, p. 4398). The authors suggested that the right posterior hippocampus is one of the brain structures involved in storing and using complex spatial maps of familiar environments, whereas the anterior hippocampus is involved in encoding the spatial configuration of novel environments. The implication is that the repeated and often complex navigation of taxi drivers resulted in adaptive changes in the relative size of these different areas of the hippocampus. However, the study is not in itself conclusive but is consistent with the predictions of the resource distribution form of plasticity and with the earlier described research on brain plasticity in other species (Experience and Brain Organization section of chap. 4; Buchner, Kauert, & Radermacher, 1995; Buonomano & Merzenich, 1998). The brain is, in effect, a highly dynamic organ with inherent constraints that anchor the organism's interactions with the world but at the same time can change its organization and functions, within these constraints, in response to changing conditions.

DEVELOPMENT AND SOFT MODULARITY

As I noted in the Development and Plasticity and other sections of chapter 4, there is debate regarding the extent to which cognitive and other competencies result from genetic constraints on brain organization and patterns of developmental experiences (e.g., Lickliter & Honeycutt, 2003). These debates remain to be fully resolved. My working assumption is that one function of juvenility is to enable organisms to adapt neural, perceptual, cognitive, and behavioral systems to variation in domains in which sensitivity to variation—such as discriminating one individual from another—resulted in survival or reproductive advantages during the species' evolutionary history. These evolutionarily expectant experiences are assumed to accrue through the organism's natural play, exploration, and social experiences and are predicted to adapt evolved modular systems to local conditions, such as the local language (Bjorklund & Pellegrini, 2000; D. G. Freedman, 1974; Geary, 2002b; Geary & Bjorklund, 2000; Greenough, Black, & Wallace, 1987; MacDonald, 1992; Scarr, 1992). These evolutionarily expectant experiences may be needed for the normal development of the exoskeleton.

As an example, Le Grand, Mondloch, Maurer, and Brent (2001) found that obstructed vision due to congenital cataracts during the first few months of life was associated with a later inability to distinguish between similar configurations (e.g., spacing of eyes) of the same face. Their findings are consistent with results described chapter 4 (Experiential Modification of Brain Organization section) and suggest that normal development of even highly modularized and likely evolved cognitive systems may require early exposure to evolutionarily expectant information. The broader adaptation of these systems to local conditions likely occurs, at least in part, through modification of the internal structures of the exoskeleton and through the rule-based category formation. These forms of plasticity are predicted to be most evident in domains that support relationships between biological organisms, that is, the social and biological modules shown in Figure 5.2, because relationships among biological organisms necessarily result in more variation in information patterns than do activities that engage the physical world.

Language is one well-known example whereby the features of individual languages (e.g., phonemes) are accommodated within what appear to be inherent neural, perceptual, and cognitive constraints such that individuals develop the language to which they are exposed (R. Brown, 1973; Kuhl, 1994; Kuhl et al., 1997; Pinker, 1994), although whether the inherent constraints are minimal (Hauser et al., 2002) or more extensive (Pinker & Jackendoff, in press) is vigorously debated. Aspects of this accommodation appear to involve the exoskeleton form of plasticity (e.g., for phoneme recognition) and occur as an experience-expectant feature of language development (Doupe & Kuhl, 1999; Vouloumanose & Werker, in press). Similar processes are predicted to occur for the other social domains, as reflected for example in the recognition of one's parents—the exoskeleton ensures that infants attend to human faces, and the soft internal structures are modified to allow recognition of frequently processed faces.

Developmental experiences may also facilitate later category formation, as related to social activities. Boys' group-level competition (e.g., team sports) provides one example of the early formation of competition-based in-groups and out-groups and the coordination of social activities that may provide practice for primitive group-level warfare in adulthood (Geary, 1998; Geary, Byrd-Craven, Hoard, Vigil, & Numtee, 2003). Although comparative studies suggest that play fighting does not always correspond to improved fighting competencies in adulthood (e.g., Pellis & Iwaniuk, 2000; Pellis & Pellis, 1998), my suggestion is that for humans these natural games provide the practice needed for the skilled formation and maintenance of social coalitions in adulthood and result in the accumulation of memories for associated activities and social strategies. In other words, and in keeping with the comparative analyses of Pellis and colleagues, these games may be more strongly related to learning about the skills of other boys and acquiring the social competencies for coordinated group-level activities than to learning specific fighting behaviors, such as hitting. My assumption is that these activity biases and the accompanying effects on brain and cognition are related to the ecological and social selection pressures described in chapter 3.

Experiences during development also appear to result in the fleshing out of many other features of folk psychological, biological, and physical knowledge. Children's implicit folk biological knowledge and inherent interest in living things result, in theory, in the motivation to engage in experiences that automatically create taxonomies of local flora and fauna and in the accrual of an extensive knowledge base of these species. In traditional societies, these experiences include assisting with foraging and play hunting (e.g., Blurton Jones, Hawkes, & O'Connell, 1997). As described in chapter 3 (Ecological Pressures section), anthropological research indicates that it often takes many years of engaging in these forms of play and early work to learn the skills (e.g., how to shoot a bow and arrow) and knowledge needed for successful hunting and foraging (Hill & Hurtado, 1996), although this is not the case with all hunting and foraging activities (Bliege Bird & Bird, 2002; Blurton Jones & Marlowe, 2002). The complexity of hunting and foraging activities varies with the ecology in which the group is situated, a situation that should select for plasticity in the associated brain, cognitive, and behavioral systems.

Another example is provided by the ability to mentally form maplike representations of the large-scale environment that occurs more or less automatically as organisms explore this environment (Gallistel, 1990; Poucet, 1993). For humans, the ability to form these representations is evident by 3 years of age (DeLoache, Kolstad, & Anderson, 1991), improves gradually through adolescence, and often requires extensive exploration and exposure to the local environment (Matthews, 1992). More precisely, research by Matthews clearly shows that children automatically (without conscious awareness that they are doing so) attend to geometric features of the large-scale environment and landmarks within this environment and are able to generate a cognitive representation of landmarks and their geometric relations at a later time (e.g., they can later draw a map of the environment). Children's skill at generating these representations increases with repeated explorations of the physical environment (see also Landau, Gleitman, & Spelke, 1981; Mandler, 1992). Thus, learning about the physical world is a complex endeavor for humans and requires an extended developmental period, in comparison with the more rapid learning that occurs in species that occupy a more narrow range of physical ecologies (Gallistel, 1995, 2000). A recent study by Chen and Siegler (2000) suggests that similar processes occur for tool use. They demonstrated that 18-month-olds have an implicit understanding of how to use simple tools (e.g., a hooked stick to retrieve a desired toy) and with experience learn to use these tools in increasingly effective ways.

In sum, a long developmental period is presumed to be an evolved feature of human life history and appears to function to enable the fleshing out of folk psychological, biological, and physical knowledge. The necessity of a long developmental period results from the complexity and variability of social relationships and social competition (Alexander, 1989; Geary, 2002b; Geary & Flinn, 2001) and the wide range of biological and physical-ecological (e.g., mountainous vs. desert) niches occupied by humans (Kaplan et al., 2000). In each domain, there is evidence for both inherent and presumably gene-driven constraints that guide attention to and the early processing of invariant information patterns, such as human biological motion or the shape of a human face (D. G. Freedman, 1974; R. Gelman, 1990; Grossman et al., 2000), as well as experience-based modifications of the associated systems to accommodate variation, such as recognition of individual faces, within broader constraints (Pascalis, de Haan, & Nelson, 2002). The concept of soft modularity described in chapter 4 seems to capture the basic pattern of invariant and variant information patterns, with developmental experiences functioning to accommodate variant information patterns in the domains of folk knowledge.

CONCLUSION

I argued in chapter 4 and elsewhere (Geary & Huffman, 2002), as have others (e.g., Gallistel, 1995; R. Gelman, 1990; Tooby & Cosmides,

1992), that the evolution of brain and mind can be understood in terms of information patterns (e.g., motion patterns of predators) that have covaried with survival (e.g., predator avoidance) and reproductive (e.g., mate identification) outcomes during the species' evolutionary history. I further proposed that invariant information patterns will result in the evolution of gene-driven constraints and modularity, whereas variant information patterns will result in the evolution of brain and cognitive systems that are open to experiential modification (Geary & Huffman, 2002). These basic assumptions were applied to a taxonomy of the human mind (Geary, 1998), specifically to domains captured by research in the areas of folk psychology (Baron-Cohen, 1995; Premack & Woodruff, 1978), folk biology (Atran, 1998; Caramazza & Shelton, 1998), and folk physics (Gallistel, 1990; Johnson-Frey, 2003; Shepard, 1994). Associated neuropsychological and brain imaging research is not definitive, but some of this research is consistent with modular systems for processing invariant information patterns in each of these domains, including systems for detecting and processing human movement patterns (Downing et al., 2001), discriminating flora from fauna (Hart & Gordon, 1992), and representing physical space in the service of navigation (Maguire et al., 1998), among others. However, the relation between the neurobiological and genetic findings described in chapter 4 and the cognitive research on folk knowledge described in this chapter remains to be fully explored.

Variation in evolutionarily significant information patterns during human evolution should have resulted in the evolution of modular folk psychological systems that are complemented by systems that can accommodate variation within each of these domains. These more plastic mechanisms would enable, among other things, the discrimination of one individual from the next on the basis of movement patterns, voice, and how they think. Again, the current research is not conclusive, but neural and perceptual systems that accommodate these and other forms of variability (e.g., dialect differences) within broader constraints are evident for speech (Doupe & Kuhl, 1999), face recognition (Nakamura et al., 2000), emotion recognition (Elfenbein & Ambady, 2003), and gesture (McNeill, 2000). Social and cognitive research suggests plasticity in the ability to form categories related to tool use (Bloom, 1996) and social competition (Fiske, 2002; W. G. Stephan, 1985), among other things. An openness to organizational and functional modification related to experience, learning, and injury has also been demonstrated for the developing (Stiles, 2000) and mature brain (Bao, Chan, & Merzenich, 2001), as I described in chapter 4, but again the relation between this neurobiological research and cognitive research associated with folk knowledge is unclear.

My proposal here and elsewhere (Geary & Huffman, 2002) is that at all levels—neural, perceptual, cognitive, and functional—the degree of inherent constraint and openness to experiential modification is the evolutionary result of the degree to which the associated information patterns have been invariant or variant, respectively, during the species' evolutionary history (see also Tooby & Cosmides, 1992). In a sense, constraints provide an anchoring for the organism's attending to and responding to the social and ecological world. For humans, the absence of such constraints, as in autism or other neurological disorders, results in identifiable deficits that compromise the individual's ability to succeed in social and other domains of life (Baron-Cohen, 1995; Lawrence et al., 2003). The combination of constraint and openness is captured by the two forms of soft modularity described in chapter 4, that is, exoskeleton and rule-based category formation. For both forms, constraint would evolve for guiding attention to and processing invariant information patterns in the domains of folk psychology, biology, and physics (R. Gelman, 1990), and openness to experiential modification would evolve to capture variation at the level of the individual (soft internal structures) or category (e.g., in-group–out-group, rule-based) within these broad domains.

Variation in information patterns would also result in pressures for an extended developmental period, which in turn should enable neural, perceptual, cognitive, and functional (e.g., social behaviors) adaptations to variation across social (e.g., local language) and ecological (e.g., food sources) conditions (Geary, 2002b; Kaplan et al., 2000). In other words, brain and cognitive plasticity during the developmental period is, in theory, an adaptation to accommodate variation in social and ecological conditions, but within the broader constraints of folk knowledge (for an alternative view, see Lickliter & Honeycutt, 2003). From an evolutionary perspective, brain and cognitive systems associated with folk knowledge would also be modifiable to some degree in adulthood, a concept captured by the resource distribution form of soft modularity (Table 4.2).

In closing, an evolutionary perspective provides a framework for linking research on brain and cognitive organization and functions from the level of conserved genes that guide the organization of the central nervous system described in chapter 4, on one hand, to folk biological knowledge that guides hunting in traditional societies described in this chapter, on the other. More precisely, conserved brain and cognitive systems in complex animals, in theory, serve similar functions across species—that is, to negotiate relationships with conspecifics, other species (e.g., prey, or predators), and the physical world. Species-specific adaptations within these broad domains of folk psychological, biological, and physical knowledge are also found, as are mechanisms to accommodate variation within each of these domains. The goal of the next two chapters is to place these folk systems in the context of more general cognitive mechanisms, including working memory, and to link these general mechanisms to the selection pressures and the motivation-to-control model outlined in chapter 3. The melding of these cognitive mechanisms with those that underlie individual differences in general intelligence is provided in chapter 8.

6

HEURISTICS AND CONTROLLED PROBLEM SOLVING

In previous chapters I have outlined climatic, ecological, and social selection pressures that potentially contributed to the evolution of the human brain and mind (chap. 3); reviewed neurogenetic and neurobiological research as related to inherent constraints on and experiential modification of brain organization and cognitive functions (chap. 4); proposed three forms of soft modularity that accommodate inherent constraint on and experiential modification of brain organization and cognitive functions (chap. 4); and presented a taxonomy of human cognitive modules (chap. 5). An essential but missing piece of the puzzle concerns the relation between these brain and cognitive systems and the cognitive processes that support the organism's behavioral engagement of the ecology. In other words, if the function of behavior is to bring about evolutionarily significant outcomes, such as capturing prey or finding a mate, then these behaviors must be systematically linked to brain development, organization of the neocortex, cognitive modules, and so forth. The link is forged if the function of brain and mind is to process information patterns that tended to covary with survival or reproductive outcomes during the species' evolutionary history and that then guide behavioral strategies that result in the achievement of these outcomes. An example is the shape and movement patterns of a potential meal, that is, information conveyed by prey, and the corresponding behaviors that are directed toward the goal of capturing this meal.

The link between brain and cognitive systems that attend to and process this information and the corresponding behaviors can be understood in terms of a motivation to control, as I proposed in chapter 3. In the first section of the current chapter, I present an initial look at how the motivation to control interfaces with the implicit (i.e., outside of conscious awareness) and explicit (i.e., in conscious awareness) cognitive processes that guide organisms' behavioral engagement of the ecology and illustrate how this perspective melds well with research in psychology, cognitive science, economics, and other disciplines (Gigerenzer & Selten, 2001a; Johnson-Laird, 1983; Simon, 1955, 1956, 1990a). In the second section I focus on implicit cognitive processes and in the third section on explicit cognitive processes. The latter are involved in controlled problem solving and reasoning and provide the segue to chapter 7, in which I focus on the cognitive and brain systems that support explicit, controlled problem solving and discuss pressures that might have contributed to their evolution; explicit and controlled problem solving and the underlying cognitive and brain systems are at the heart of the evolution of general intelligence, the topic of chapter 8. For now, I want to stress the importance of implicit cognitive processes as they relate to evolution and the motivation to control and to contrast these implicit systems with the explicit systems that support controlled problem solving.

MOTIVATION TO CONTROL

As I argued in earlier chapters, the evolved function of brain, cognitive, affective, and other systems is to attend to, process, and respond to the types of information that covaried with survival or reproductive outcomes during the species' evolutionary history. The corresponding behaviors are directed toward actually achieving these outcomes. The combination of brain, cognitive, and other systems as they are linked to behavioral engagement of the environment represents a functional module, as defined in Table 4.1. A functional module dynamically arises as information generated by current ecological circumstances activates the brain, cognitive, and affective systems that guide the organism to behave in ways that will bring about some level of control in this ecology, such as prey capture. In effect, the evolved function of behavior is to recreate outcomes that facilitated survival or reproduction during the species' evolutionary history (Caporael, 1997; Geary, 1992). Of course, not every behavior results in evolutionarily significant outcomes; most in fact do not. As I describe later in this chapter, many behaviors result in outcomes (e.g., developing a social reputation) that incrementally build toward outcomes (e.g., gaining access to resources) that are of significance.

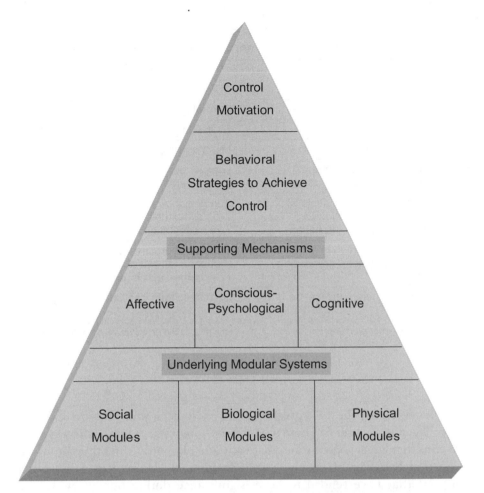

Figure 6.1. Behavioral attempts to achieve access to and some level of control of the resources that tended to covary with survival or reproductive options during hominid evolution are supported by affective, conscious-psychological, and cognitive systems.

The nexus of traits that compose the motivation to control were introduced in Figure 3.9, which is presented again here as Figure 6.1. The figure is reproduced because my focus is on the implicit cognitive processes—features of the modular systems at the base of the triangle in Figure 6.1—that guide behavioral engagement of the environment and the explicit cognitive processes (center of the figure) that support problem solving about potentially important outcomes or relations in the environment. In chapter 7, I provide a few examples of the affective and conscious-psychological mechanisms represented by the center of Figure 6.1 (Social Cognition and Folk Psychology section) and the brain and cognitive systems underlying problem solving. For now, focus is on the base of the triangle,

TABLE 6.1

Characteristics of Implicit and Explicit Cognitive Systems

Implicit System	Explicit System
Unconscious	Conscious
Automatic	Controllable
Evolved early	Evolved late
Common across species	Might be unique to humans
Pragmatic, context-dependent expression (e.g., social discourse)	Logical, decontextualized, abstract representations (e.g., chess)
Parallel processing of multiple sources of contextual information (e.g., face, body posture, vocal intonation)	Sequential processing of decontextualized abstract representations
Parallel processing results in high but effortless information-processing capacity	Sequential processing is limited by attentional and working memory resources and is therefore effortful
Unrelated to general intelligence	Correlated with general intelligence

Note. From "Logic and Human Reasoning: An Assessment of the Deduction Paradigm," by J. S. B. T. Evans, 2002, *Psychological Bulletin, 128*, p. 989. Copyright 2002 by the American Psychological Association. Adapted with permission of the author.

which represents the folk psychological, biological, and physical modules introduced in chapter 5. These modules are composed of brain and cognitive systems that largely operate automatically and implicitly, directing the attention and behavior of people toward features of the ecology (e.g., other people) that have tended to be of significance during human evolution. Affective systems also tend to operate implicitly, automatically, and in conjunction with folk modules (Gray, 2004), although individuals are often explicitly aware of the outcome of affective processes (e.g., the experienced feeling, such as joy; Damasio, 2003).

The basic characteristics of these implicit systems are shown in the first column of Table 6.1, and to be fully appreciated, these are contrasted with characteristics of explicit systems in the second column (J. R. Anderson, 1990; Dennett, 1987; J. S. B. T. Evans, 2002; Johnson-Laird, 1983; Reber, 1993; Stanovich & West, 2000). I describe how implicit systems appear to operate in the Bounded Rationality and Heuristics section and discuss the explicit systems in the Controlled Problem Solving section, as well as in the Cognitive and Brain Systems section of chapter 7. Before getting to these sections, I want to provide a link between implicit and explicit cognitive systems and the cost–benefit trade-offs and variant–invariant issues introduced in chapter 4.

Cost–Benefit Trade-Offs

The evolution of cognitive and other systems that guide behavioral attempts to control significant outcomes, such as prey capture, must have been balanced by a host of cost–benefit trade-offs (Simon, 1990a). The most basic trade-off involves balancing the speed of behaviorally responding to the ecology against the accuracy of identifying ecological information. Fast responding is often at a cost of information accuracy, and vice versa. In other words, fast behavioral responses are possible if there are brain and cognitive systems that react to the ecology based on partial and often fleeting information, such as prey movement caught out of the corner of the eye. These brain and cognitive systems are likely to evolve to capture information that has been consistently associated with survival or reproductive outcomes throughout the species' evolutionary history. As I described in chapter 4 and illustrated in Figure 4.2, this is information that tends to be invariant from one generation to the next and across the life span. Information that is less consistent, or variant, across generations or within lifetimes and that can be of evolutionary significance, as in the specifics of social dynamics, often requires closer attention and thus slower responding.

In Figure 6.2, I link invariant and variant forms of information to implicit and explicit cognitive mechanisms, respectively. The x axis places the invariant-to-variant information patterns on a continuum, and the y axis and the inner area of the rectangle show the general features of the cognitive mechanisms that should evolve to process and respond to information along this continuum. Information patterns that tend to be invariant across generations, such as the basic shape of the human face, should result in the evolution of brain and cognitive systems that operate quickly, implicitly, and with a minimum amount of information, and this appears to be the case. As I mentioned in chapter 5, J. Liu, Harris, and Kanwisher (2002) found that people automatically and quickly (one tenth of a second) identify and categorize human faces. Schyns, Bonnar, and Gosselin (2002) demonstrated that the categorization of faces in terms of sex, emotional expression, and personal identity is based on different bits of facial information. Sex can be determined by the shape of the eye and nose and facial expression by configuration of the mouth. The processes that focus attention on and process these bits of information operate implicitly—that is, people are not aware of these brain and cognitive operations, although they are sometimes aware of the outcome of these processes (e.g., explicitly determining that the person is happy on the basis of facial expression). Other information patterns differ across relationships, contexts, and generations. These more variant patterns, such as the intentions of a would-be mate during the courtship process, often require conscious, explicit problem solving to generate

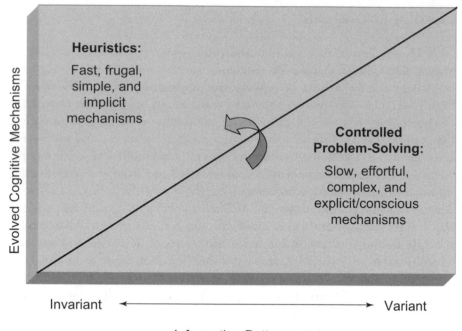

Figure 6.2. The types of cognitive mechanisms that operate on ecological or social information are predicted to vary with the extent to which that information tended to be invariant (resulting in evolved heuristics) or variant (resulting in evolved problem-solving mechanisms) during the species' evolutionary history and during a typical life span.

behavioral responses or long-term behavioral strategies—in this example, to make inferences about the potential mate's likely intentions regarding the relationship.

The inner section of the rectangle is not in and of itself novel, as a similar contrast of fast and implicit mechanisms with slow, effortful, and explicit mechanisms has been argued by other cognitive and evolutionary scientists, including Dennett (1987), J. S. B. T. Evans (2002; J. S. B. T. Evans & Over, 1996), Cosmides and Tooby (2000), Johnson-Laird (1983), Reber (1993), and Stanovich (1999; Stanovich & West, 2000), among others. The contribution here, to the best of my knowledge, is the proposal that the evolution of implicit and explicit cognitive systems can be tied directly to evolutionarily significant information patterns that have tended toward the invariant and variant ends, respectively, of the continuum shown in Figure 6.2. The curved arrow at the center of the figure represents the process of learning—specifically, how the ability to explicitly engage in controlled problem solving can result in knowledge acquisition during the life span. I discuss how this process might work to create evolutionarily novel competencies, such as the ability to read, in chapter 9 (Academic Learning section).

Variance–Invariance

Many evolutionary scientists (e.g., Cosmides & Tooby, 1994; Gallistel, 1995) have predicted that implicit systems will evolve and be expressed in situations that produce information patterns or dynamics (e.g., social exchange) that have invariant features across generations and have tended to covary with evolutionary outcomes. As I noted above, evolutionary invariance must not be confused with completeness of these information patterns in real-world settings. Fast responding is often achieved at a cost of gaining incomplete information, and even with unlimited time, many implicitly guided decisions, inferences, and behaviors are based on incomplete information, which results in some degree of uncertainty (Hastie & Dawes, 2001; Oaksford & Chater, 1998; Shepard, 1994). Heuristics and other fast, implicit mechanisms would thus be triggered in situations in which the individual's sensory, perceptual, and cognitive systems capture significant aspects, albeit not 100%, of these information patterns.

Moving toward the other extreme, information patterns become increasingly variant—that is, they become more novel in terms of the species' evolutionary history. Novelty, however, is a matter of degree. As I described in chapter 4 (Soft Modularity section), many of the constrained features of exoskeletons respond to invariant information patterns, such as the basic shape of the human face, but show some degree of plasticity. Plasticity evolves in these domains when sensitivity to individual differences, as in the ability to recognize individual faces, covaries with survival or reproductive outcomes. However, this form of plasticity is restricted to the modules at the base of the triangle in Figure 6.1 and described in chapter 5. Functional behaviors, in contrast, emerge from the simultaneous activity of many of these cognitive modules, as well as from the activation of context relevant affective systems (Gray, 2004). As the number of activated cognitive modules increases, the complexity of the mental representation that integrates activity across all of these modules necessarily increases. This moves us toward the rightmost—controlled problem solving—section of Figure 6.2.

To illustrate, when conversing with another person, one simultaneously tracks changes in this individual's facial expressions across time and integrates these with temporal changes in other forms of social information, such as gestures, vocal intonation, and language. This information, in turn, is simultaneously integrated with other forms of social cognition described in chapter 7 (Social Cognition and Folk Psychology section), such as memories of previous conversations with this person. The integration results in a functional behavioral system that allows one to engage in the conversation and, if necessary, make judgments about the interaction (e.g., the other person's intentions). The integration of all of this information, such as facial expressions with vocal intonation, and the changing dynamics of the conversation create more variability than that associated with individual modules (e.g., for face processing). One automatically and implicitly processes the emotion signaled by the other person's facial expression and by his or her vocal intonation. However, as I describe in chapter 7 (Cognitive and Brain Systems section), if the emotion signaled by the facial expression and vocal intonation differs, then one's attention is drawn to the discrepancy, and the information becomes consciously and explicitly represented in working memory. At this point, one can engage in controlled problem solving and make an inference—"Is the person being deceptive?"—about the cause of the discrepant information.

The variation at this functional level also creates the potential for behavioral unpredictability. Indeed, as I described in the Ecological and Social Variability section of chapter 4, Maynard-Smith and Price (1973) and others (Dawkins & Krebs, 1979) argued that a proneness toward unpredictability should evolve during the co-evolutionary arms race that often characterizes relationships between biological organisms with competing interests. These relationships include those between predator and prey and with members of one's own species. In the latter circumstance, the heuristics that guide many social interactions will be less effective in predicting and responding to the behavior of an unpredictable competitor. The only recourse is to use a counter-strategy that is not dependent on heuristics—specifically, to use more effortful and controlled problem solving to determine the intentions and the best ways to respond to this type of competitor (e.g., Chiappe & MacDonald, in press). In this view, the mechanisms that support slow, conscious, explicit, and controlled problem solving evolved as a consequence of the selective advantages associated with social and behavioral (e.g., predator avoidance) unpredictability, as elaborated in chapter 7 (Problem Solving and Human Evolution section). Unpredictability in turn creates information patterns that are toward the variant end of the continuum shown in Figure 6.2.

BOUNDED RATIONALITY AND HEURISTICS

I suggested with Figure 4.2 that invariant information patterns should result in the evolution of inherently constrained brain, perceptual, and cognitive mechanisms that compose the exoskeleton (see also Gallistel, 2000; Tooby & Cosmides, 1995). These constraints will result in fast, efficient, and generally accurate information identification and processing and are represented by the left portion of Figure 6.2. The constraints should not only compose attentional and information processing systems but also guide decision making and behavioral processes such that outcomes that tend to facilitate survival or reproductive options are quickly, automatically, and effortlessly attempted, and sometimes achieved (success is never guaranteed). In cognitive science, economics, psychology, and related disciplines, the combination of mechanisms that enable information to be identified and processed quickly and that enable fast and frugal decision making are called *heuristics*, or decision-making rules of thumb (Gigerenzer & Selten, 2001a; Simon, 1955, 1956; Tversky & Kahneman, 1974).

I provide extended discussion in the Heuristics section later in this chapter, but for now I note that these may involve implicit (see Table 6.1) and inherent biases that do not require extended learning or are acquired with minimal experience (Gigerenzer, Todd, & ABC Research Group, 1999), as in the ease of acquiring a fear of snakes. As noted in the Controlled Problem Solving section and in chapter 7 (Cognitive and Brain Systems section), heuristics may also develop more slowly and as a result of repeated controlled problem solving, as in the effort required to learn the procedures used to solve algebra problems (Geary, 2001; Greeno & Simon, 1988). In any event, heuristics often represent an evolved link between the organism's sensory, perceptual, cognitive, affective, and behavioral systems and the ecological conditions in which these systems evolved. In the first section that follows, I provide an introduction to the basics of this link, and in the second section I discuss how this relation maps onto my definition of a functional module. These sections provide the contextual background that will help to illustrate the usefulness of cognitive heuristics as behavioral and decision guiding mechanisms.

Bounded Rationality

Behavior–Cognition–Ecology Links

Many decades ago, Simon (1955, 1956) proposed that the ability to achieve significant goals, such as obtaining a mate, requires mechanisms within the individual and complementary information patterns in the environment (see also Brunswik, 1943). In other words, behaviors, cognitions, brain functions, and so forth are fully understandable only when placed in the type of ecological context that drove their evolution. This is the link between evolutionarily significant information patterns and the brain and cognitive systems that have evolved to process and respond to this information. The information and linked brain and cognitive systems are toward the invariant end of the continuum shown in Figure 6.2. From the perspective I am developing in this book, these links involve the implicit brain and cognitive systems that compose the exoskeletons for folk psychology, folk biology, and folk physics (see Soft Modularity section of chap. 4). Simon called the relation between these exoskeleton systems and information in the ecology *bounded rationality* (e.g., Gigerenzer & Selten, 2001b; Simon, 1990b). As Timberlake (1994) aptly argued, the relation can also be understood in terms of Pavlovian conditioning, specifically the relation between an ecological stimulus and an evolved, unconditioned response. To be consistent, I will use the term *bounded rationality*.

The gist is that there is a relation between the here-and-now mechanisms that guide behavioral decision making and the ecologies in which these mechanisms have evolved, a type of lock-and-key relationship (Tooby & Cosmides, 1995). To illustrate, consider again the human face. As noted in chapter 5 (Folk Psychology: Individual section), there are brain and cognitive systems that attend to and process information generated by human faces and facial expressions (Kanwisher, McDermott, & Chun, 1997). One pattern is generated by the shape of the eyes and nose, which provides information on the sex of the individual, whereas another pattern is generated by the configuration of the mouth, which provides information about the individual's emotional state (Schyns et al., 2002). This information is automatically and implicitly processed by the receiver, who in turn expresses corresponding emotion and other social signals (e.g., smile).

The receiver may also make decisions regarding the dynamic. The decisions do not, however, need to be conscious and explicit. They can be based on feelings that are automatically generated by the facial expressions and other social information generated by the other person. Negative feelings, such as fear elicited by an angry expression, may prompt withdrawal, and positive feelings, such as happiness generated by a smile, a continuance of the interaction (Damasio, 2003; Öhman, 2002). In any case, these automatically and implicitly generated reciprocal relations are illustrated in Figure 6.3, and the mechanisms associated with conscious awareness of other people's facial expressions are discussed in the next chapter.

When considered in terms of the trade-offs noted above, cognitive mechanisms that support decision making and behavioral engagement of the environment are not predicted to be optimal in the sense that the best possible choices are always made. Optimal choices are commonly inferred through mathematical and statistical methods that are applied to more information than is commonly available to organisms in real-world settings (Gigerenzer & Selten, 2001a). Even if organisms had all relevant information available, there are cognitive limits on the ability to process and manipulate all of the information needed to make an optimal decision (e.g., in working memory; see Cognitive and Brain Systems section of chap. 7). There are time costs associated with optimizing as well (Simon, 1955). The combined costs of limited ecological information, limited cognitive resources, and delayed behavioral responding to the ecology make the evolution of brain and cognitive systems that optimize unlikely.

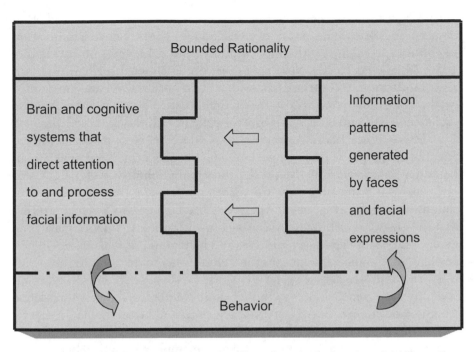

Figure 6.3. Bounded rationality is a coupling of ecological and social information patterns that occurred regularly during the species' evolutionary history and complementary brain and cognitive systems that have evolved to direct the organism's attention to and processing of this information. The coupling often results in automatic behavioral responses that act on the ecological or social information.

Instead of optimization, evolution should favor what economists term *satisficing* and *aspiration level* (Selten, 2001; Simon, 1956). *Satisficing* means that motivational and behavioral systems will be directed toward achieving an ecological goal that satisfies a basic need (e.g., hunger). It results in an outcome that is typically "good enough" but not always optimal. *Aspiration level* means that the organism may continually adjust the definition of what is "good enough" on the basis of the most immediate successes or failures or on the lifetime pattern of successes and failures. B. F. Skinner's (1938) operant conditioning thus moderates the expression of the mechanisms that support satisficing—shaping what is good enough—and aspiration level. Successes mean that the behavior of the organism has been rewarded through the achievement of the ecological goal (e.g., having a proposal for a date accepted), which in turn can result in an increasing aspiration level. Failures mean that the behavior of the organism has been punished through a failure to achieve the goal (e.g., having a proposal for a date rejected), which in turn can result in a decreasing aspiration level. When combined with a fundamental motivation to control, continual success can result in rapacious behavior and "megalomania," at least in humans. Genghis Khan and other despots provide extreme examples of what might happen when a motivation to control is combined with unfettered success at achieving control (Betzig, 1986; Zerjal et al., 2003). Most people are not like Genghis Khan, and thus their motivation to control, satisficing, and aspiration level are constrained by the competing interests of other individuals, resulting in very dynamic social ecologies and complex cognitive demands (Kenrick, 2001).

Mate choice illustrates the point (Todd & Miller, 1999). With the possible exception of despots, no individual could attract and evaluate all potential mates and only then make the optimal choice or choices. Once one potential mate is rejected, the option of choosing that mate at a later time has typically evaporated. Moreover, the cost of this lost opportunity and the cost of searching for and evaluating all potential mates makes the evolution of motivational, cognitive, and behavioral systems that result in optimal mate choices unlikely. Rather, such costs should result in the evolution of systems that achieve good enough or satisficing outcomes. Aspiration level, in this example, refers to those features of potential mates that define what is good enough. Success at attracting potential mates should, in theory, and it does in practice, result in increasing aspiration levels, such as preferring increasingly attractive or successful mates or multiple mates (Buss, 1994; Gangestad & Simpson, 2000). Failures, in contrast, should result in decreasing aspiration levels. As described in chapter 2 (Sexual Selection and Social Dynamics section) and chapter 3 (Forms of Social Relationship section), these features of mate choice are an integral part of sexual selection and create behavioral and social dynamics that are ubiquitous across sexually reproducing species and are of obvious evolutionary significance.

Barnacle Geese

To clarify the point, let me step back from humans and review what might be considered intelligent, rational behavior of another species, barnacle geese (*Branta leucopsis*). Pairs of barnacle geese bond for many breeding seasons and choose mates according to similarities in age and size (Black, Choudhury, & Owen, 1996). Smaller females are reproductively better off when paired with smaller than with larger males, and larger females are reproductively better off when paired with larger than with smaller males. Some mates are thus better than others, which in turn creates conditions that will favor the evolution of brain, cognitive, and behavioral mechanisms that will guide mate choice decisions. These mechanisms must enable the birds to assess the relative age and size of potential mates and a mechanism to stop searching once a mate of roughly of the same age and size is found— that is, once a good-enough mate is found.

Black et al. (1996) found that individuals that sampled many potential mates and switched mates if a marginally better one was found had a 50% reduction in the probability of successfully breeding during that season. The cost of mate switching and the cognitive demands of comparing potential mates on one or more dimensions (e.g., size) place serious limits on the potential for the evolution of socially and cognitively sophisticated optimizing mechanisms. A good-enough choice can be made with limited sampling and a form of bounded rationality (or an unconditioned stimulus response; Timberlake, 1994) that cues into specific features of other geese, such as size, coloration, and movement patterns (e.g., Blythe, Todd, & Miller, 1999). Geese of similar age, health, and size should more readily synchronize the mating dance than other pairs. Synchronization may thus serve as a simple mechanism for assessing other geese and a mechanism for stopping the mate search. Aspiration levels would vary with the number of times the individual is courted. Thus, what appears to be a complex mate choice decision may be achieved by implicit neural and perceptual systems as defined in Table 6.1, mechanisms that are sensitive to a few cues (e.g., size), and a mechanism that stops the mate search when a compatible (e.g., as determined by synchronized movements) partner is found.

In other words, the mate choice decisions of barnacle geese, and most other species, are not as intelligent as might be inferred from their behavior. This is because the behavior can be explained in terms of evolved brain, perceptual, and cognitive systems that automatically and implicitly cue into relevant information and guide the behavior of the individual such that an evolutionarily significant outcome is achieved, or at least outcomes are achieved that eventually have a significant result. This is bounded rationality: There is no need for conscious awareness of these cues or controlled problem solving. After all, geese have rather small brains and are not considered to be among the most intelligent creatures on the planet, but they nonetheless survive and make effective reproductive decisions. Much of human behavior and decision making and those of other species can be explained by the same types of bounded-rationality mechanisms (Gigerenzer & Selten, 2001a).

Functional Modules

The coupling of the exoskeleton with corresponding ecological information—bounded rationality and unconditioned stimulus response relations—generally results in behavioral decisions that are good enough to achieve evolutionarily significant outcomes, such as finding a mate (Simon, 1956; Timberlake, 1994). The basic features of bounded rationality can be mapped onto the domains represented in Figure 6.1. Satisficing corresponds to the motivation to control, that is, the motivation to gain access to the forms of resource that represented good-enough outcomes during the species' evolutionary history. More precisely, these outcomes and satisficing behaviors should be clustered around the social (e.g., mates), biological (e.g., food), and physical (e.g., nesting site) resources that covaried with survival or reproductive outcomes during the species' evolutionary history.

For humans, these resources (e.g., mates and group affiliation) are the ecological half of bounded rationality, and the most basic internal and implicit mechanisms are the exoskeleton systems that result in the attention to and processing of information in the domains of folk psychology, folk biology, and folk physics. These mechanisms largely conform to the features of implicit systems described in Table 6.1 and can be organized in terms of the social, biological, and physical modules described in chapter 5, as I mentioned earlier. The automatic and implicit operation of these brain and cognitive systems and corresponding behavior generate a functional module, as defined in Table 4.1.

Heuristics

Implicit Decision Making

Heuristics are the cognitive representations (e.g., memory patterns) and biases (e.g., tendency to weight some memories more than others) that result in decision-making rules of thumb. For barnacle geese, one rule of thumb is, "choose a mate of roughly the same age and size." The rule of thumb is not, of course, explicit but can be inferred from the rational behavioral choices of these animals. For humans, heuristics and implicit decision making can be approached in terms of the seminal contributions of Tversky and Kahneman (1974; Kahneman, Slovic, & Tversky, 1982). These scientists demonstrated how cognitive biases can result in systematic errors in judgment, such as underestimating or overestimating the probability of an event occurring. These biases often result from how a problem is framed (e.g., in terms of gains or losses) or how the events are described (e.g., globally or specifically; C. R. Fox, 1999; C. Heath, Larrick, & Wu, 1999; Tversky & Koehler, 1994). Tversky and Kahneman also noted that these biases occur because people tend to draw inferences and make decisions based on their intuitive understanding of the situation and typically disregard statistical or other relevant mathematical information. However, the forms of statistical and mathematical information Tversky and Kahneman used in their experiments are not part of human evolutionary history, and thus people would not be expected to automatically use this information in their decision making.

For heuristics that have an evolved basis, the intuitions that influence decision making are very likely to be features of folk knowledge, that is, biases that evolved in natural ecologies but that may also lead to judgment errors in modern society (Brase, Cosmides, & Tooby, 1998; Geary, 2002a, 2003). As an example, people judge the risk of dying in a plane crash on the basis of how easily they recall examples of plane crashes from long-term memory, called the *availability heuristic*. This heuristic probably results in a good intuitive sense of risk in natural settings, but mass media reporting of plane crashes results in memories that distort this heuristic and result in an overestimate of this risk (Lichtenstein, Slovic, Fischhoff, Layman, & Combs, 1978).

Building on the early work of Simon (1955, 1956, 1990a), Gigerenzer and his colleagues pioneered the study of natural, or folk, decision-making heuristics (e.g., Gigerenzer, 2001; Todd, 2001). The accompanying research has provided empirical support for the thesis that heuristics often lead to near optimal and typically good-enough decisions in many real-world situations, that is, the types of situations in which these decision-making mechanisms likely evolved (e.g., Czerlinski, Gigerenzer, & Goldstein, 1999; Davis & Todd, 1999). As noted in Figure 6.2, heuristics are composed of mechanisms that operate quickly, frugally (i.e., with minimal information), and implicitly, or outside of the individual's awareness. Figure 6.4 fleshes out the internal mechanisms associated with bounded rationality, the exo-skeleton (e.g., for processing facial features), and heuristics. With the exception of controlled attention and controlled problem solving (described later in this chapter), these mechanisms seem to capture the gist of folk heuristics (Gigerenzer, 2001). When a bounded rationality match between internal systems (e.g., perceptual biases) and ecological conditions is achieved, heuristic-based decisions and behavioral responses are executed quickly, effortlessly, and often without the need for conscious awareness or reflection.

Elaboration

To clarify the processes that compose folk heuristics, I will walk through the steps represented in Figure 6.4. The top of the figure represents a social or ecological goal, many of which are driven by the implicit motivation to achieve access to the types of resource that tended to facilitate survival or reproductive prospects during the species' evolutionary history. These goals are not typically conscious, nor are they easily achieved. Achievement is often incremental, if it occurs at all, and results as individuals engage in natural activities. I assume that these activities are largely focused on the achievement of subgoals, the accumulation of which will lead to the achievement of the ultimate, evolutionary goal. As an illustration, in nearly all species of primate, seemingly mundane day-to-day activities, such as grooming, occur more or less automatically and presumably without awareness of any proximate or ultimate goal (de Waal, 2000; Dunbar, 1993; Foley, 1996).

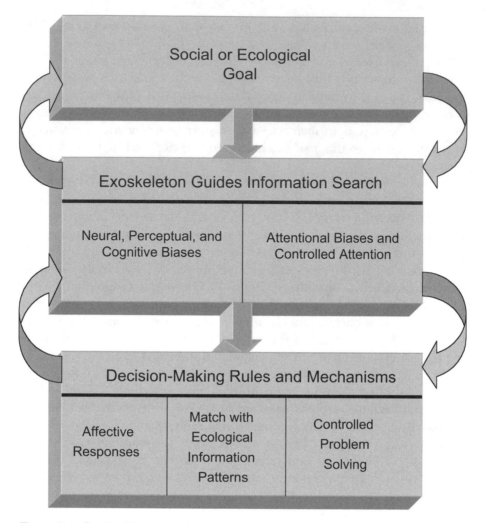

Figure 6.4. Goal achievement is an incremental and iterative process. Each step requires a search for and processing of associated information (e.g., attending to facial expressions) and decision-making rules and mechanisms (e.g., emotional responses to facial expression) that enable dynamic behavioral responses to this information.

Nonetheless, these activities are an integral feature of the survival and reproduction of individuals of these species. In addition to removal of parasites, grooming facilitates the maintenance of cooperative social relationships (Dunbar, 1993); the analog for humans is "festive social chatter." The function of these social coalitions is to influence wider social and reproductive dynamics (Goodall, 1986) or to maintain control of valued resources, such as fruit trees (Silk, 1987). The bottom line is that the ultimate function of these seemingly mundane activities is to allow the individual to form social relationships that in turn, when necessary, facilitate the individual's attempts to gain access to reproductive (mates) or material (food) resources.

The exoskeleton and information search level of Figure 6.4 represents brain and cognitive systems that operate implicitly and guide the behaviors that result in the achievement of significant goals, such as developing a social alliance. The exoskeleton is composed of the modules described in chapter 5 and includes mechanisms for processing facial cues, body movements, and so forth. These mechanisms function to process information toward the invariant end of the continuum shown in Figure 6.2. Decision-making rules and mechanisms result when a bounded rationality match is achieved between the social information generated by conspecifics and the exoskeleton systems that have evolved to process this information. I illustrated such a match earlier, with the description of how people cue into, process, and respond to different bits of information generated by the human face.

As a specific example, humans and other primates have inherent biases to attend to the faces of conspecifics and automatically respond with negative emotional signals (e.g., frown) and feelings (e.g., fear or anger) to facial expressions that suggest aggressive intent (Öhman, 2002). There is a match between exoskeleton systems internal to the individual and social information patterns—bounded rationality (Simon, 1955)—that results in emotional responses (e.g., facial expressions) and in inherent biases in behavioral responding. A lower-status individual may respond to this aggressive facial display with fear and behavioral withdrawal, whereas a higher-status individual may respond with anger and behavioral approach or attack. These behavioral responses appear to operate more or less implicitly and automatically and can be described in terms of decision-making heuristics.

Complex Social Dynamics

The dynamics of reciprocal exchange allow me to elaborate on how bounded rationality and heuristics can be used to understand complex social behavior. On the basis of Trivers's (1971) model of reciprocal altruism, Cosmides (1989) argued that humans have evolved heuristics that guide reciprocal social exchanges. The specific heuristic-based mechanisms that govern social exchanges are not fully understood, but to be effective they must involve cognitive mechanisms that guide attention to the dynamics of the trade, monitor for equality of exchanged goods, and result in social decisions (Cosmides, 1989; C. Heath et al., 1999). There must also be affective mechanisms that trigger emotions (social cues, such as a facial expression) and feelings (consciously felt emotions) as these relate to the equality of the exchange. If one is cheated, the response might include negative emotions (e.g., threatening body posture) that provide a context-appropriate social signal, as well as internal feelings (e.g., anger) that prompt one to retaliate or avoid future exchanges (Damasio, 2003; Sanfey, Rilling, Aronson, Nystrom, & Cohen, 2003; Trivers, 1971). This form of heuristic should evolve in all social species that engage in reciprocal exchanges.

Indeed, Brosnan and de Waal (2003) demonstrated that capuchin monkeys (*Cebus apella*) have a sense of fair play—that is, they appear to have implicit heuristics that influence the process of social exchange and reflect an expectation of equal exchanges. When this sense of fair play is violated, such as when a researcher gives a monkey less food reward than a social partner for the same amount of work, these monkeys respond by refusing to cooperate with the human who "shortchanged" them: "Monkeys refused to participate if they witnessed a conspecific obtain more attractive reward for equal effort, an effect amplified if the partner received such a reward without any effort at all. These reactions support an early evolutionary origin of inequity aversion" (Brosnan & de Waal, 2003, p. 297).

Experimental studies of humans are also consistent with an intuitive sense of fair play. Cosmides (1989) and Gigerenzer and Hug (1992) demonstrated that college students had difficulty solving abstract reasoning problems but easily solved the same problems when they were recast as social exchanges; these social scenarios involved an individual receiving a benefit but only if a required cost is paid or that involved a violation of this conditional arrangement, as with Brosnan and de Waal's (2003) monkeys. In other words, these students easily understood these problems when they were presented in ways that tapped their fair play heuristic. Sugiyama, Tooby, and Cosmides (2002) found the same pattern with Shiwiar hunter-horticulturalists from the Ecuadoran Amazon. These unschooled adults performed as well as Harvard undergraduates on tests that assessed their ability to detect violations—cheating—of reciprocal social exchanges. At a behavioral level, children are also very sensitive to cheating and will avoid relationships with other children who do not reciprocate or "play fair" (Hartup & Stevens, 1997; Newcomb, Bukowski, & Pattee, 1993).

An alternative argument is that the cognitive and affective mechanisms that guide social exchanges emerge as general learning systems that pick up recurrent patterns during exchange experiences (e.g., Cheng & Holyoak, 1989). The positions are the same as those explained in chapter 4—specifically, the debate as to whether human cognition is best understood in terms of inherent modular systems or as resulting from a relatively uncommitted neocortex that can develop social modules (e.g., for face processing) and heuristic-like mechanisms through repeated experiences. Stone, Cosmides, Tooby, and Knight (2002) tested Cosmides's (1989) predictions. Specifically, they assessed the cheater detection competencies of an individual with damage to areas of the prefrontal neocortex that typically support social cognitions, such as theory of mind (Baron-Cohen, 2000), and the amygdala, which responds to affect-eliciting social information (Öhman, 2002). This individual performed very poorly on these cheater-detection tasks but performed with only minor impairments or normally on several other complex cognitive or decision-making tasks that should not require use of cheater-detection heuristics. Two other individuals with brain injury to one, but not the other, of these areas performed as well as college students on the cheater detection tasks. The results suggest that cheater detection is supported by a specialized neural system that requires the coordinated functioning of areas of the prefrontal cortex and the amygdala, among other regions.

In a related study, Sanfey et al. (2003) used neuroimaging techniques to determine the brain regions engaged when adults participated in the Ultimatum Game. The game involves a proposer and a responder. The proposer makes an offer as to how to split $10, and the responder can either accept or reject the offer. Each pair interacts only once, so there is no opportunity for negotiation. The proposals were made either by another individual or by a computer. Some of the offers were fair ($5 each), whereas the rest varied in degree of unfairness ($7/$3 to $9/$1). For blatantly unfair offers ($8/$2 or $9/$1) from another individual (but not the computer), responders rejected 50% or more of the offers. This is an irrational response, because rejection always entails a $0 payoff, whereas acceptance of one of these unfair offers would have resulted in a payoff of $1 or $2. For these trials, areas of the brain that are normally active with pain, disgust, and other negative physical states associated with a threat to one's well-being (i.e., the insula; see also Damasio, 2003) were especially active, as were other areas associated with cognitive conflict and explicit decision making (i.e., the anterior cingulate cortex and dorsolateral prefrontal cortex; see Cognitive and Brain Systems section of chap. 7). With unfair offers, it appeared that the implicit affective processes that biased the individual to reject the offer were in conflict with the rational processes that biased the individual to accept the offer for at least some gain. When the former brain regions were the most active, offers tended to be rejected. When the latter brain regions were the most active, offers tended to be accepted.

The results seem to be similar to those found by Brosnan and de Waal (2003) and suggest that humans' sense of fairness and corresponding behaviors are moderated by automatic and implicit affective processes. The results are also in keeping with social exchanges in capuchin monkeys in that human cheater-detection heuristics can be consciously stated as decision-making rules that describe how individuals avoid being cheated—"Stay away from people who don't reciprocate, or don't play fair"—but many of the processes that govern the accompanying emotions (and feelings), cognitions, and behaviors occur in accordance with the implicit systems described in Table 6.1. Stated a little differently, the processes operate implicitly and automatically, but individuals are often consciously aware of the endpoint (e.g., the felt emotion) of these processes. The extent to which these heuristics emerge from evolved and inherent constraints or through recurrent patterns of experience is not currently known. It seems likely that some combination of constraint and plasticity is needed to explain the ubiquity of social exchange, the need to detect cheaters, and the many different ways in which humans can engage in reciprocal exchanges.

When considered in terms of the continuum shown in Figure 6.2, reciprocal exchanges may, at times, result in the need for explicit, conscious, and effortful processing, as Sanfey et al. (2003) found. Effortful processing should be most evident in conditions that deviate from expectations, whether these expectations are an implicit and inherent sense of fairness or differ from culture-specific exchange rituals (e.g., the specifics of monetary exchanges differ from the exchange of cows for land). With respect to the latter, experience with these specific rituals becomes integrated with the more inherent features of social exchange. Gradually, the effortful processing becomes implicit, automatic, and effortless and results in the formation of culturally specific exchange heuristics. As noted earlier, I discuss the potential mechanisms through which explicit processing results in the formation of implicit, automatic heuristics and other forms of learning in chapter 9 (Academic Learning section).

CONTROLLED PROBLEM SOLVING

Laboratory studies of how people solve problems occupied cognitive psychologists throughout much of 20th century (e.g., Luchins, 1942; Newell & Simon, 1972) and continue to do so (J. S. B. T. Evans, 2002). These endeavors have borne considerable insights into the ways in which people (and some other species) approach and solve problems that require the explicit system described in Table 6.1 and that I explain more fully in the next chapter (Cognitive and Brain Systems section). Although the content of these lab-based problems differs from that of problems that confront people living in traditional societies and the forms of ecological and social selections pressures described in chapter 3, some of the basic problem-solving processes are very likely to be the same. In fact, as I describe in chapter 8 (Cognitive and Brain Correlates of Intelligence section), the processes described in the following sections appear to capture many of the core competencies measured on intelligence tests.

Problem Solving

Knowledge-Lean Domains

To fully understand the processes underlying controlled problem solving, one has to strip the problem to the bone, that is, to ask people to solve problems to which they have had little prior exposure (Greeno & Simon, 1988; Newell & Simon, 1972; VanLehn, 1989). These knowledge-lean domains are important because they allow cognitive psychologists to study problem-solving processes that are not influenced by prior knowledge. In this situation, people cannot rely on the types of heuristics described in the preceding sections, but must instead use more conscious and effortful problem solving processes.

An example of one such problem is shown in Figure 6.5 (Luchins, 1942). The initial state of the problem is shown at the top of the figure: The 8-oz container is full, and the 5-oz and 3-oz containers are empty. The goal is to move from this initial state to the end state shown at the bottom of the figure, that is, a state in which container 1 and container 2 hold exactly 4 oz each. *Operators* are the rules that define how people can change the initial state into the successive intermediate states that ultimately lead to the goal. In this example, the only allowable operation is to pour liquid from one container into another, with the constraints that all of the liquid must be poured from the initial container or poured until the second container is full. The combination of (a) an initial state, (b) a desired goal or end state, (c) a system of operations (rules for pouring in this example) that can transform the initial state to the end state, and (d) a form of state representation defines the *problem space*. *Representation* refers to the mental or physical form of the initial, intermediate, and final states and can be, for instance, linguistic, visual, spatial, or some combination (Johnson-Laird, 1983; Kosslyn & Thompson, 2000). One sequence of operations and visual representations of the corresponding states that leads to the desired goal of having four ounces in the first and second containers is shown in Figure 6.6.

With the use of these types of knowledge-lean tasks and a combination of experimental studies and computer simulations, Newell and Simon (1972) discovered that a common approach to solving such problems involves a *means–ends analysis*. First, the current state is compared to the desired end state. Next, memory is searched to identify operations that can be used to reduce the difference between the current state and the desired state. An operation is chosen and executed, and the resulting state is then compared to the desired state. The sequence is repeated until the goal is reached, although achievement of the final goal often requires the solving of a series of subgoals. A means–ends analysis is often more complex than the example shown in Figure 6.6, but the same general approach has been shown to be

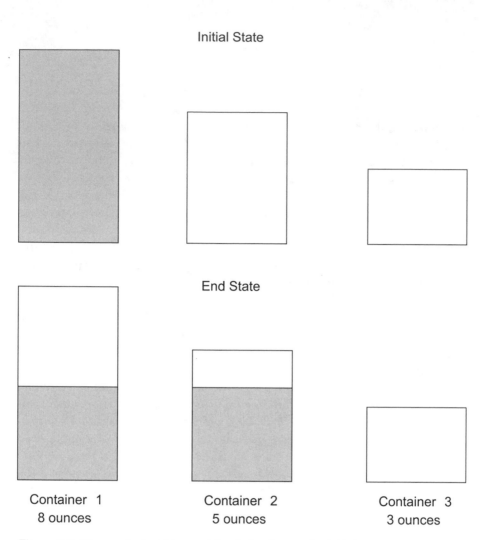

Figure 6.5. The goal of problem solving is to change the initial state to the desired end state.

an effective problem-solving method across many domains ranging from simple puzzles to integral calculus (Greeno & Simon, 1988).

With experience solving a particular type of problem, people can develop heuristics or rules of thumb that simplify movement through the problem space (e.g., by eliminating a subset of allowable but not often useful operations) and thus that result in faster and more accurate problem solving. As shown in Figure 6.2, any such heuristics will be most useful for those features (e.g., the most effective operations) that are similar—tending toward the invariant end of the continuum—across problems. Stated more generally, information (e.g., operations) that is the focus of conscious and effortful

Problem Space

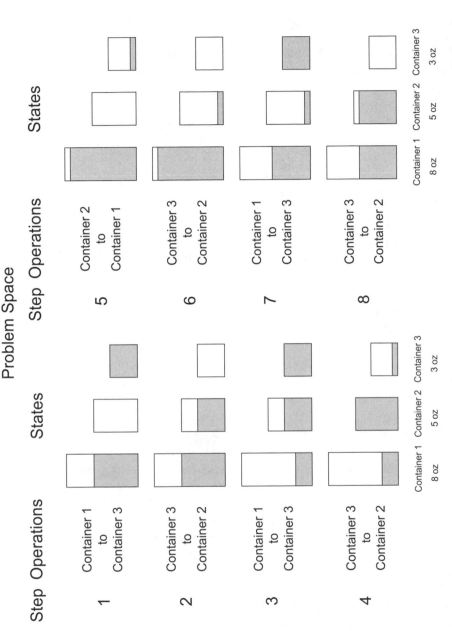

Figure 6.6. Problem space is the representation (visual in this example) of the initial, intermediate, and end states, as well as the operations (pouring from one container to another) and sequence of operations that transform the problem from the initial state to the desired end state. Step 1 is the first operation; 3 oz of liquid are poured from Container 1 to Container 3, resulting in the adjacent state. Steps 2 through 8 are the sequence of operations that ultimately result in the desired end state at Step 8.

problem solving and that is similar across problem-solving episodes will result in the formation of implicit, automatic, and effortlessly executed problem-solving heuristics (J. R. Anderson, 1982). As contrasted with the evolved heuristics described earlier for barnacle geese or the fundamentals of social exchange, these learned heuristics are formed during the individual's lifetime. An example is learning the sequences needed to solve complex arithmetic problems, such as 34 + 45. Initial problem solving is slow and effortful and requires consciously representing the information (e.g., 4 + 5) in working memory while moving through the sequence of steps. After extensive practice, the sequences are automatically and effortlessly executed (Frensch & Geary, 1993), as I elaborate in chapter 9 (Academic Learning section).

Knowledge-Rich Domains

Most problem solving in the real world and with many laboratory tasks (e.g., mathematics problems) occurs for domains in which individuals have varying degrees of experience and knowledge. Problems in these domains are, in addition, often ill structured—that is, the solution requires knowledge that spans multiple domains, or the desired end state is not clear. The study of problem solving in these areas is thus many times more complicated than the study of how people solve the water jar example but gets right to the heart of human problem solving. Problem solving in these knowledge-rich domains involves many of the same processes engaged during the solution of knowledge-lean tasks, specifically, a problem space, operations, representational states, and goals (Greeno & Simon, 1988; Newell & Simon, 1972; VanLehn, 1989).

Problem solving in knowledge-rich domains is also influenced by the nature and extent of the individual's *declarative knowledge* (i.e., explicitly known facts, principles, and so forth) in the domain and the nature and types of operations (or procedures) the individual has learned or inferred from previous problem-solving attempts (J. R. Anderson, 1982; Medin, Coley, Storms, & Hayes, 2003). Problem solving in these domains can also be influenced by previously learned strategic plans for approaching these tasks (Greeno & Simon, 1988). Cognitive psychologists sometimes call the latter *schemata*. These consist of a memory system of linked operations and the sequence in which they were executed in previous problem-solving situations. Schemata are essentially heuristics that are acquired through the repeated solving of similar forms of complex problems. The entire body of knowledge, including facts, procedures, schemata, that is stored in the individual's long-term memory is a form of intelligence called *crystallized general intelligence* (Cattell, 1963), which I discuss in various sections of chapters 8 and 9.

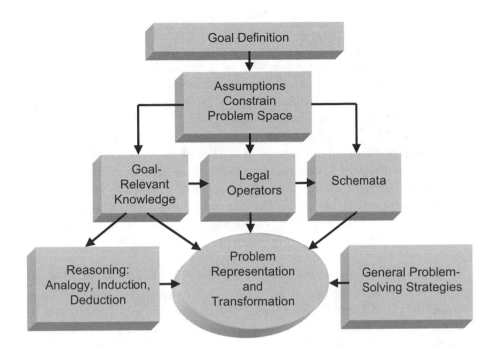

Figure 6.7. Problem solving in knowledge-rich domains involves a problem space, goal-relevant knowledge, legal operators (rules for transforming the problem space), and schemata (an integrated system of operators). These interact with reasoning and general problem-solving strategies (e.g., means–ends analysis) during the successive transformations of the problem space and representational state until the goal is achieved.

As an example of complex, explicit problem solving in a knowledge-rich domain, consider the goal that many 19th-century naturalists set for themselves: specifically, to determine the mechanisms responsible for the origin of new species or speciation (see Desmond & Moore, 1994; Raby, 2001). This was an ill structured problem in that the solution required knowledge that spanned many domains (e.g., the fossil and geologic records), and the knowledge and operators needed to ultimately solve the problem were not known. As a result, it was not possible to solve this problem by means of inherent or previously learned heuristics.

Figure 6.7 shows the cognitive resources that were likely used to solve this and other ill-structured problems. Once the goal was defined, basic assumptions about the nature of the problem needed to be made. In the first half of the 19th century and before this time, most naturalists, such as the anatomist and paleontologist Richard Owen (1860), assumed that the origin of species was driven by some form of divine intervention (Ospovat, 1981). This assumption was crucial because it defined the problem space and the relevant operations, knowledge (e.g., scripture), and schemata that could be applied in attempts to solve the problem. Owen's assumption of divine intervention placed legal operators that involved material causes, and thus the actual mechanisms involved in speciation, outside of the problem space and thus rendered the problem unsolvable. Darwin and Wallace, in contrast, assumed that the origin of species was due to material causes acting in nature (Browne, 2002; Darwin, 1846; Desmond & Moore, 1994; Raby, 2001). Once this assumption was made, the next issues concerned the problem-solving processes and goal-relevant knowledge that Darwin and Wallace used to tackle this problem, that is, to discover the mechanisms of natural selection. Although my discussion is, of course, speculative, it provides an appropriate and interesting illustration of explicit, complex problem solving and use of the explicit system described in Table 6.1. The description also lays the groundwork for my proposals in the Problem Solving and Human Evolution section of chapter 7.

Some aspects of how Darwin and Wallace solved the problem of speciation are more certain than others, especially with respect to basic assumptions and some of the background knowledge that contributed to their discovery. The relevant knowledge was not scripture for Darwin or Wallace, but rather arose (I assume) from evolved folk biological systems (see Folk Biology section of chap. 5) as these were applied to extensive observations of nature and as elaborated by associated academic learning, such as through the reading of Lyell's (1830) *Principles of Geology* (F. Darwin, 1893/2000). On the basis of fossils found throughout the geologic record, Lyell (1839) noted,

> It appears, that from the remotest periods there has been ever a coming in of new organic forms, and an extinction of those which pre-existed on the earth; some species having endured for a longer, others for a shorter time; but none having ever re-appeared after once dying out. The law which has governed the creation and extinction of species [is not known]. (p. 161)

The observations and hypotheses of Malthus (1798) also contributed greatly to Darwin's and Wallace's goal-relevant knowledge and to the construction of associated legal operators, that is, the mechanisms that operate in nature; Darwin's understanding of these operators emerged slowly between 1838 and 1856 to 1857 (Ospovat, 1979, 1981). Malthus's insightful monograph described a pattern of oscillating expansions and contractions of the size of human populations in preindustrial Europe and in other regions of the world. As I described in chapter 3 (Ecological Dominance section), human populations have tended to expand (i.e., before birth control) when there is excess land and food. Expansion often continues beyond the carrying capacity of these resources, at which point the population crashes. The crashes represent a sharp increase in mortality, largely because of famine, epidemics, and conflicts with other people (e.g., wars) over control of land and other life-supporting resources. The increased mortality reduces the population to a level below carrying capacity, that is, to a point where there are once again excess resources, and thus another cycle of population expansion ensues. With respect to Malthus's description, Wallace noted the following in a letter written in 1887 and reprinted in Darwin's autobiography (F. Darwin, 1893/2000):

> This had strongly impressed me, and it suddenly flashed upon me that all animals are necessarily thus kept down—"the struggle for existence"— while *variations*, on which I was always thinking, must necessarily often be *beneficial*, and would then cause those varieties to increase while the injurious variations diminished. (italics in original, pp. 200–201)

A few of the observations and inferences of Malthus (1798) and of Darwin and Wallace (1858; see Table 2.1) are recast as the legal problem-solving operators shown in the top section of Table 6.2. The operators could easily be transformed into a computer simulation (Newell & Simon, 1972) or mathematical representation (Mac Arthur & Wilson, 1967) of the common oscillating pattern of population expansions and contractions that Malthus (1798) described for humans and that later were documented for other species (e.g., Witting, 2000). The operators represent the reproductive and survival-related mechanisms and dynamics that act in natural populations. In addition to reading Lyell (1830) and Malthus, Darwin (1846) and Wallace (1855) acquired goal-relevant knowledge through their extensive collection and taxonomic organization of species of many different kinds (Stott, 2003) and through careful observation of these species in natural ecologies. The knowledge placed important constraints on how the problem was represented and therefore constraints on where in the problem space the legal operators could act. Some of the goal-relevant knowledge is shown in the second section of Table 6.2.

As an example, the observation that population size tends to be stable across generations meant that the first operator in Table 6.2—number of offspring produced is greater than the number of parents—could not act such that population size increased indefinitely (I explain this more fully in the Reasoning section below). The observation thus constrained the problem space and created the subgoal of identifying additional operators that either halted reproductive activity when the population reached carrying capacity or reversed population expansions by some other mechanism. It cannot be known with exactitude how Darwin and Wallace solved this subgoal, but a means–ends analysis is a distinct possibility. The subgoal was to identify the operators that maintain population size, given an initial state that resulted in a constantly increasing population size. The knowledge that was used to construct operators that reduced the distance between the initial

TABLE 6.2
Using Problem Solving to Discover Natural Selection

Criterion	Fact
Legal operators	Operator 1. For each reproductive cycle, the number of offspring produced is greater than the number of parents.
	Operator 2. The probability of offspring survival varies with ecological conditions, such as resource availability (e.g., land, food):
	A. When resources are plentiful, more offspring survive, and populations expand.
	B. When resources are scarce, more offspring die, and populations contract.
	Operator 3. Resource availability varies with population size:
	A. Expansion gradually reduces quantity of resources available per individual.
	B. Contraction gradually increases quantity of resources available per individual.
	Operator 4. The probability of mortality or survival is not entirely random; it is related to individual characteristics.
	Operator 5. Some specific traits are correlated with the ability to extract resources from the ecology (or, e.g., avoid predation) and thus with the probability of mortality or survival.
Goal-relevant knowledge	Fact 1. Populations tend to be stable across generations.
	Fact 2. Predation, disease, climate, and competition result in high mortality.
	Fact 3. Individuals of the same species vary on most traits.
	Fact 4. The fossil record suggests that species change gradually; some go extinct; and others emerge.
	Fact 5. Variations of the same species and related species are found in the same or contiguous geographic regions.
Schemata: Natural selection	Schema 1. Same as Operator 1: Populations will expand if unchecked.
	Schema 2. Schema 1 is linked with Operators 2 and 3, coupling the oscillating pattern of population expansions and contractions to ecological conditions.
	Schema 3. Schema 2 is linked to Operator 4, coupling population expansions and contractions with differential (i.e., not random) mortality and survival.
	Schema 4. Schema 3 is linked to Operator 4, coupling differential mortality and survival to individual characteristics.
	Schema 5. Schema 4 is linked with Operator 5, coupling specific individual characteristics that influence mortality and survival with ecological conditions.

(continues)

TABLE 6.2 *(Continued)*

Criterion	Fact
Analogy: Artificial Selection	Feature 1. People selectively breed other species in order to exaggerate desired traits within a species (microevolution).
	Feature 2. Selective breeding works because offspring are similar to parents on the selected trait.
	Feature 3. Offspring must somehow (genes were not yet understood) inherit the selected trait.
	Feature 4. Generations of selective breeding can lead to the emergence of different varieties of the same species (e.g., different breeds of dog) or the emergence of new species, such as domestic species from their wild ancestors (macroevolution).

state (increasing population size) and the end state (stable population size) of the subgoal included Fact 2—that is, predation, disease, climate, and competition result in high mortality. The pattern that Malthus (1798) described and Darwin and Wallace (1858) appreciated—specifically, that the fluctuations in mortality rate varied with ecological conditions— contributed to the creation of Operator 2 and Operator 3. Coupling these operators results in Schema 2, which is shown in the third section of Table 6.2. The formation of this schema solved the subgoal; population size is kept in check through high mortality.

The solving of this subgoal created the foundational schema for natural selection. More precisely, when Schema 2 is constrained by Fact 2 (predation, disease, climate, and competition result in high mortality), the result is a system that creates large numbers of individuals, most of whom perish before becoming parents. The next important constraint on the problem space arose from the observation that the probability of mortality or survival is not entirely random, creating a fourth legal operator (Malthus, 1798). Operator 4 is important because it links differential mortality or survival to population expansions and contractions, that is, Schema 3. Schema 4—mortality risk is correlated with characteristics of the individual—results when this operator is linked to Schema 3. The fifth operator is crucial, as it indicates that there must be mechanisms that operate such that beneficial variations increase in frequency and injurious variations decrease in frequency, to paraphrase Wallace (1887/2000). As described in chapter 2 (Natural Selection section), the result is a recurrent pattern of population expansions and selective contractions. With each contraction, the individuals with traits (e.g., beak size) best suited to the change in conditions survive and reproduce in greater numbers than do individuals with injurious traits.

Analogical reasoning contributed to Darwin's (1859) linking of Operator 5 to Schema 4—specifically, the analogy provided by the breeding of domesticated species, as show in the bottom section of Table 6.2. Domestic breeding highlighted how variability could be coupled with selection of favored traits to produce change within a species (microevolution) and to create new species (macroevolution). In the concluding chapter of *Origin of Species*, Darwin (1859) noted the importance of this analogy:

> Man does not actually produce variability. . . . But man can and does select the variations given to him by nature, and thus accumulate them in any desired manner. He thus adapts animals and plants for his own benefit or pleasure. . . . It is certain that he can largely influence the character of a breed by selecting, in each successive generation, individual differences. . . . This process of selection has been the great agency in the production of the most distinct and useful domestic breeds. . . . There is no obvious reason why the principles which have acted so efficiently under domestication should not have acted under nature. In the preservation of favoured individuals and races, during the constantly-recurrent Struggle for Existence, we see the most powerful and ever-acting means of selection. . . . More individuals are born than can possibly survive. A grain in the balance will determine which individual shall live and which shall die, —which variety or species shall increase in number, and which shall decrease, or finally become extinct. (pp. 466–467)

In this quote, all of the legal operators (e.g., "More individuals are born than can possibly survive") and goal-relevant knowledge (e.g., breeders selectively breed other species according to individual differences in preferred traits) are pulled together to form a coherent framework of operators represented as Schema 5. The organized system of legal operators—that is, Schema 5—defines the mechanisms and processes of natural selection and explains all of the facts in Table 6.2, among many others. Once it was fully understood, Darwin appeared to have used Schema 5 in an heuristic-like manner—that is, it implicitly and of course often explicitly guided his subsequent thinking and experimental investigations of natural phenomena (Browne, 2002).

In contrast to Darwin, Wallace did not believe that artificial selection provided a useful analogy for understanding natural selection and the origin species. Rather, he appeared to have approached the final step through other forms of inductive reasoning and through deductive reasoning; Darwin used these processes as well but also relied on analogical reasoning. Some of the underlying processes are described in the next section. For now, an illustration of how Wallace appeared to have explicitly reasoned about the problem is provided in an 1855 article titled "On the Law Which Has Regulated the Introduction of New Species." In this article, he proposed the following hypothesis: *"Every species has come into existence coincident both in space and time with a pre-existing closely allied species"* (p. 186, italics in original). In other words, new species arise from extant species. Induction—formulating a general principle according to observable facts—played an important part in Wallace's formulation of this conclusion.

During his expeditions in the Amazon and throughout Malaysia, Wallace (1855) observed that there is a pattern in the geographic distribution of species (Fact 5 in Table 6.2): "closely allied species in rich groups being found geographically near each other, is most striking and important" (p. 189). He also described how the same pattern is evident in the fossil record. When this pattern was combined with deductions based on a number of premises and facts described in the article, Wallace concluded that related species (e.g., of butterflies) are found in the same geographic location because they all arose from a common ancestor that resided in this location. Wallace further concluded that the creation of new species from existing species "must be the necessary results of some great natural law" (p. 195). Wallace discovered the great natural law—natural selection—three years later, when he linked Malthus's (1798) observations to the earlier noted favorable and unfavorable variations in traits (Darwin & Wallace, 1858).

Finally, I turn to the issue of how the problem space might have been explicitly represented and transformed by Darwin and Wallace. They both, of course, described the process in written form, thus casting it as a language-based representation (Darwin, 1859; Darwin & Wallace, 1858), but this is not necessarily how the problem was initially represented and transformed. Both Darwin and Wallace were keenly aware of variations within single species and across related species, suggesting that the early representations were visual, that is, based on how individuals from the same and related species looked (e.g., in terms of size; Darwin, 1846). Indeed, one biographer noted how important visualizing was to Darwin as a method to think through problems (Stott, 2003). A more abstract visual representation of these individual differences is shown in Figure 6.8. The center distribution represents individual differences in beak size of the medium ground finch (*Geospiza fortis*). As I described in chapter 2 (Natural Selection section), individual differences in beak size are heritable and covary with survival (i.e., through food acquisition) and reproductive (i.e., through female choice of healthy, well-fed males) outcomes during food shortages (P. R. Grant, 1999). The left and right distributions represent individual differences in the beak size of small (G. *fuliginosa*) and large (G. *magnirostris*) ground finches, respectively. Genetic analyses suggest that all three species arose from a single common ancestor about 3 million years ago (Petren, Grant, & Grant, 1999; Sato et al., 1999).

The point here, however, is to illustrate how Darwin and Wallace might have represented transformations of the problem space while constructing the mechanisms of natural selection. One series of transformations involves the emergence of small and large ground finches from the naturally

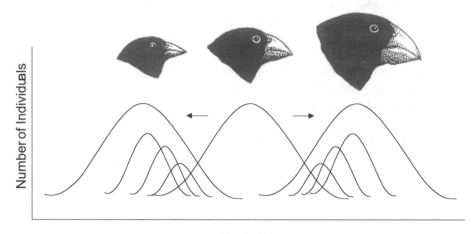

Beak Size

Figure 6.8. Visual representation of the origin of new species. From left to right, the species of small (*Geospiza fuliginosa*), medium (*G. fortis*), and large (*G. magnirostris*) ground finches are all descended from a common ancestor. Although the speciation events did not occur in this precise manner, beak size in the medium ground finches (center) illustrates how individual differences in one species can give rise to the evolution of new species. Finch illustrations from *Ecology and Evolution of Darwin's Finches,* p. 78, by P. R. Grant, 1999, Princeton, NJ: Princeton University Press. Reprinted with permission of the author and Princeton University Press.

occurring variability in the beak size of medium ground finches. The transformations occur as medium ground finches with smaller and larger beaks begin to specialize—due to geographic isolation or competition—in food sources that differ from one another and from finches toward the center of the distribution. The smaller distributions represent successive transformations of the problem space across generations and the corresponding increase in the frequency of medium ground finches with smaller and larger beaks. After many successive transformations—which Darwin (1846) appears to have visualized as he presumably mentally simulated the process of selection acting over many generations (see next section)—two new species eventually emerge from a single ancestral species.

Reasoning

The ability to engage in explicit rational analysis and to reason through difficult problems, as did Darwin and Wallace (1858), captures at least some aspects of general intelligence and what is measured on tests of intelligence (e.g., Raven, Court, & Raven, 1993). These processes are certainly not sufficient to explain all of the creative insights that resulted in Darwin's and Wallace's discovery (see Simonton, 1999, 2003), but they illustrate some of the more central features of the explicit system described in Table 6.2. In the first section that follows, I discuss the reasoning process and mental models that enable people to draw explicit inferences during problem solving, and in the second section I illustrate the processes. I describe the relation between explicit problem solving, mental models, and the motivation to control in the Problem Solving and Human Evolution section in chapter 7.

Reasoning and Mental Models

In many problem-solving contexts, people's decision making and inferences differ from those that would be arrived at if they reasoned on the basis of the rules of formal logic. Considerable theoretical debate and empirical work has focused on determining why most people do not reason as logicians do (e.g., Braine, 1978; J. S. B. T. Evans, 2002; Johnson-Laird & Byrne, 2002: Manktelow, 1999; Oaksford & Chater, 1996, 1998; Wason, 1966). The debate remains to be resolved, but there is now some consensus that people's decision making and inference drawing often results from bounded rationality and heuristics, as well as acquired task-relevant knowledge (Medin et al., 2003). As described earlier in this chapter, much of human behavior, like that of other species (e.g., barnacle geese), can be understood in terms of evolved brain and cognitive mechanisms that operate automatically and implicitly and enable fast and generally accurate decision making and behavioral responding to the environment.

Unlike nearly all other species, most humans have the crucial ability to inhibit heuristic-based responses (Bjorklund & Harnishfeger, 1995) and thus the ability to make decisions and draw inferences on the basis of explicit processes (Cosmides & Tooby, 2000; J. S. B. T. Evans & Over, 1996; Reber, 1993; Stanovich, 1999; Stanovich & West, 2000). As noted in Table 6.1, the explicit system is composed of those cognitive and brain mechanisms (described in chap. 7, Cognitive and Brain Systems section) that enable the formation of conscious, abstract, and decontextualized representations of social or ecological conditions or other forms of information such as the premises in a deductive reasoning task. The ability to mentally generate, maintain, and manipulate these abstract representations is limited by limitations in attentional and working memory resources (also elaborated in chap. 7) and is thus effortful. The pattern of representations is called a *mental model*, which is an analog simulation of a specific situation or state of affairs in the world. Mental models are commonly constructed through language or images (Johnson-Laird, 1983). The important language component is the most basic unit of meaning, called *propositions*, in the spoken utterance or written sentence (J. R. Anderson, 1990); "Joe is tall" is an example of a proposition. The images can be vivid and perceptual-like or composed of nonvisual spatial representations, or some combination (Kosslyn & Thompson, 2000).

Johnson-Laird (1983) argued that in most situations, people's reasoning is based not on the formal rules of logic, but rather on the construction of a mental model of the information presented, for instance, in a syllogism. The model is constructed on the basis of prior related knowledge and memories of relevant contexts. As an example, consider the following syllogism:

- All people taller than 6 feet 5 inches are basketball players.
- Joe is 6 feet 7 inches tall.
- Therefore, Joe is a basketball player.

The conclusion that Joe is a basketball player follows logically from the premises in the syllogism, but many people would state that the conclusion is false because they can recall or simply imagine tall individuals who are not basketball players. The ability to draw the correct inference in this example, as well as in many other contexts (Bjorklund, Cormier, & Rosenberg, in press), requires an inhibition of prior related experiences and a decoupling, to use Cosmides and Tooby's (2000) term, of this personal frame of reference to form a mental model of the two terms of the syllogism. Imagine that there are 300 people in the community, and 20 of them are 6 feet 5 inches tall or taller. Now imagine all 20 of these individuals in a group (say, a in gym) and that *all* of them are basketball players. The second premise—Joe is 6 feet 7 inches tall—can be mentally modeled by placing Joe among the latter group of individuals. Once this is done, the correct inference, that Joe is a basketball player, follows easily.

Reasoning About Natural Selection

Before approaching the issue of the evolution of mental models (discussed in chap. 7, Problem Solving and Human Evolution section), I consider an illustration of how mental models might be used in the context of complex problem solving. As noted, Figure 6.8 is an abstract, decontextualized representation of the process of natural selection as related to the origin of new species. To fully understand the emergence of smaller and larger finches from the population of medium finches, one can mentally simulate successive increases, across generations, in the number of smaller and larger finches represented by the series of increasingly larger distributions. It is likely that Darwin, as well as Wallace, engaged in a similar form of mental simulation in the discovery and subsequent use of the principles of natural selection (see Browne, 2002). The legal operators and schemata in

Table 6.2 are also abstract, decontextualized representations of the processes that result in natural selection. The inductive and deductive inferences that were necessary to formulate the theory of natural selection were based on these abstract representations and thus were also dependent on the explicit system and a form of mental model. A mental model of these premises and the logical conclusion of the following syllogism can be done in the same manner as was done for the basketball example:

- Reproduction will produce a steady increase in population size.
- In nature, population sizes tend to be stable.
- Therefore, more individuals are born than survive to adulthood.

Now consider that examples of analogical reasoning are evident in the routine and everyday activities of most people, and even some chimpanzees (Gillan, Premack, & Woodruff, 1981). However, complex and explicit analogies, such as that linking artificial and natural selection, do not occur as readily (D. Gentner & Markman, 1997; Holyoak & Thagard, 1997). It is clear that Darwin's (1859) analogy was based on explicit mappings between features of artificial selection and natural selection. To confirm these mappings, he sought out the expertise of pigeon breeders, as just one example, and conducted experiments himself (Desmond & Moore, 1994). To illustrate, pigeon breeders are sensitive to individual differences in traits (e.g., coloration, feather length) that they find of interest. The breeders then use these individual differences to determine which pigeons will be allowed to reproduce and which will not. The birds that are not allowed to breed are in effect removed from the population in a manner analogous to death or not being chosen as a mate (sexual selection) in wild populations. The effect of this selective breeding, as Darwin noted, is the exaggeration of the trait across generations. The actions of the breeders in turn map onto the relation between individual differences in traits that are associated with survival and reproduction in natural ecologies and the evolution of these traits.

Although an analysis of Darwin's reasoning is interesting in and of itself, the point that I am trying to make is that the ability to problem solve and draw inferences in ways that are associated with general intelligence (see chap. 8) requires the inhibition (Bjorklund et al., in press; Bjorklund & Harnishfeger, 1995) of heuristic-based folk systems and the use of explicit, decontextualized, and abstract representations of phenomena (J. S. B. T. Evans, 2002; Stanovich, 1999). These representations often compose mental models, that is, mental simulations of the phenomena of interest. Johnson-Laird (1983) proposed his mental model theory to explain how people reason and why they make certain types of reasoning errors. Mental models are, however, useful for understanding a much wider range of human endeavors, as I will elaborate in the next chapter.

CONCLUSION

Nearly everyone with whom I have discussed the matter has agreed with my conclusion that humans are more intelligent than barnacle geese. Yet many aspects of human behavior and that of all other species, including barnacle geese, are influenced by brain and cognitive processes that occur automatically and implicitly, that is, without conscious awareness. The processes bias decision making (e.g., as related to mate choice) and the ways in which the individual behaviorally engages the environment such that good-enough outcomes are typically achieved with little effort. These heuristics and the corresponding bounded rationality represent the link between information patterns that have tended to covary with evolutionary outcomes and the behavioral responses that have tended to bring about favorable outcomes (Gigerenzer & Selten, 2001a; Simon, 1990a). The evolution of these cognition–behavior–ecology links can only occur for ecological patterns and behavioral responses that tend to be invariant from one generation to the next and within life spans (Gallistel, 1990; Tooby & Cosmides, 1995). These links are highly adaptive, as they will result in the evolution of brain, perceptual, cognitive, and attentional systems that will result in the quick identification and processing of significant information patterns (see Figure 4.2 and Figure 6.2) and thus the ability to quickly respond to these patterns.

Imagine the advantage of a gazelle, for instance, that has perceptual and attentional systems that automatically focus it on the shape and movement patterns of lions, resulting in predator avoidance responses to these information patterns. The result of these heuristics is fast, efficient information identification and processing and automatic decision making and behavioral responding to the corresponding ecological conditions. The logical counterstrategy is to vary information patterns so as to disrupt the operation of the heuristic. A lion might do so by engaging in prey tracking behaviors that differ from the typical pattern. To achieve this variation, the expression of evolved heuristics must be inhibited and the associated behaviors must be modified during the individual's lifetime. The ability to modify heuristic-based processes is most likely to evolve in situations in which two species are in competition, as in predator–prey relationships (Dawkins & Krebs, 1979) or with intense social competition (Maynard Smith & Price, 1973). In both situations, some degree of behavioral unpredictability—variation from heuristic-like behaviors—will result in an adaptive advantage, whether this advantage involves an improved ability to capture prey or an improved ability to outwit conspecifics.

The ability to modify heuristic-based decision-making and behavioral patterns is achieved through the inhibition of automatic execution of these heuristics (Bjorklund et al., in press) and subsequent explicit, controlled problem solving (J. S. B. T. Evans, 2002; Stanovich, 1999; Stanovich & West, 2000). The problem solving often takes the form of a mental model, or a mental simulation of a current situation or state of affairs (Johnson-Laird, 1983). Mental models provide an important adjunct to heuristic-based responses, because these models enable behavioral strategies and potential counters to these strategies to be mentally simulated (i.e., projected into the future) before being attempted in the real world. These explicit and controlled processes also allow for a more systematic and reasoned evaluation of whatever patterns might be of interest (e.g., the behavioral biases of competing groups) and a mechanism to draw inferences about abstract representations of these patterns. Whether the behaviors or cognitions are heuristic based or result from controlled problem solving, my proposal is that the focus is generally on attempts to gain access to or control of the types of social (e.g., relationships), biological (e.g., food), or physical (e.g., territory) resources that have tended to covary with survival or reproductive options during the species', including humans', evolutionary history.

7

EVOLUTION OF CONTROL-RELATED MENTAL MODELS

In chapter 6, I provided an introduction to research on heuristics and controlled problem solving and began to link these to the cognitive and behavioral control strategies represented by the middle section of Figure 6.1. My first goal for the current chapter is to describe the cognitive and brain systems that support explicit, controlled problem solving. The descriptions flesh out the neurocognitive systems that support behavioral control and extend the concept to include a sense of self (Tulving, 1985). In the second section, I relate the brain regions that support controlled problem solving and a sense of self to changes in brain size and encephalization quotient (EQ) during human evolution and to the three forms of selection pressure (i.e., climatic, ecological, and social) described in chapter 3. In this section, I describe my proposal regarding the conscious-psychological mechanisms that evolved to support control-related behavioral strategies. In the final section, research in the area of social cognition and folk psychology is reviewed as it relates to social selection pressures and the motivation to control. Throughout the chapter, I attempt to incorporate the issue of variance–invariance as related to brain and cognitive evolution described in previous chapters.

COGNITIVE AND BRAIN SYSTEMS

I will now address the cognitive and brain systems that support the ability to generate and manipulate the representations that compose mental models and support complex problem solving. An exhaustive review of the substantial and growing literatures in these areas and the many debates therein is not my goal (see Gazzaniga, 2000; Miyake & Shah, 1999; Tulving & Craik, 2000). Rather, I highlight areas of consensus regarding the cognitive and brain systems that support conscious mental representations and the ability to manipulate these representations.

Cognitive Systems

From an evolutionary perspective, cognition encompasses the mechanisms that enable the organism to attend to, process, store in memory, and retrieve from memory the information patterns that have tended to covary with survival and reproduction during the species' evolutionary history (Dukas, 1998a). As I described in chapter 4, some of these information patterns vary across generations and within lifetimes. Variation in turn creates conditions that favor the evolution of phenotypic plasticity (Dukas, 1998b). The different forms of soft modularity described in chapter 4 (Model of Soft Modularity section) are examples of phenotypic plasticity as it relates to the ability to accommodate individual differences in significant modular domains (e.g., face recognition) and create categories within these domains.

Another critical form of plasticity is the ability to form mental models of past, present, and potential future states and manipulate the models in ways that enable the simulation of control-related behavioral strategies (Geary, 1998). Research in the related areas of memory and cognition is vast and expanding (e.g., Cowan, 1995; Miyake & Shah, 1999; Tulving & Craik, 2000), and thus I am able to highlight only areas related to the evolutionary model described later in this chapter. Of particular importance are processes that result in conscious, explicit memories and representations as related to the self (Tulving, 1993; M. A. Wheeler, Stuss, & Tulving, 1997; M. A. Wheeler, 2000) and the working memory processes that can operate on these representations (Baddeley, 1994, 2000a, 2000b). But first, it will be useful to consider more implicit processes.

Implicit Processes

Implicit refers to the neural, sensory, perceptual, and cognitive systems that automatically capture and process patterns of social or ecological information but operate below the individual's awareness (Hasher & Zacks, 1979;

Tulving, 2000). Consistent with Simon's (1955, 1956) bounded rationality and Gigerenzer's and colleagues' heuristics (e.g., Gigerenzer & Selten, 2001a), the types of information to which these systems automatically respond and the form of their output are linked in systematic ways to information patterns in the environment. An example of this link was provided by J. R. Anderson and Schooler's (1991, 2000) studies of the frequency and distinctiveness of social communications (e.g., e-mail, newspaper stories) and the memories that form according to these patterns:

> The basic idea is that at any point in time, memories vary in how likely they are to be needed and the memory system tries to make available those memories that are most likely to be useful. The memory system can use the past history of use of a memory to estimate whether the memory is likely to be needed now. (J. R. Anderson & Schooler, 1991, p. 400)

In a manner analogous to the mechanisms of natural selection (Siegler, 1996), memories of frequently occurring events are retained in long-term memory, and memories of infrequently occurring events are typically lost; the exceptions appear to be for infrequent events that are distinct or that result in intense negative feelings. For instance, people who have been frequently encountered in the past are likely to be encountered again in the future. The processes that result in the formation of memories of these people occur automatically and implicitly (Hasher & Zacks, 1979). One result is that memories associated with often-encountered people are more readily available to conscious awareness and more easily recalled than information associated with infrequently encountered people. Frequent social interactions with a co-worker will result in the automatic formation of memory representations of these episodes and related information, such as personality characteristics. When the person is encountered again, his or her distinctive features (e.g., facial structure) elicit the recall of relevant information stored in long-term memory. Because of frequent past encounters, the information is recalled quickly, effortlessly, and with little error and often results in conscious awareness of previous personal experiences with the co-worker and associated facts (Tulving, 1993).

The basic point is that memory systems appear to have evolved to be responsive to information patterns and changes in these patterns (e.g., frequency of encountering a person) during individual lifetimes, such that the most frequently encountered and affectively salient ecological information is automatically encoded and stored in long-term memory (Nelson, in press). One result is a link between commonly experienced events and memories for these events, which creates a recognition heuristic that can result in quick and efficient behavioral responses when similar events are again experienced

(Todd, 2000). Sometimes the corresponding memories influence behavior without the individual's conscious awareness of the operation of the heuristic, and at other times the memories become available to conscious awareness.

The modular information processing systems that compose the domains of folk psychology, folk biology, and folk physics also operate automatically and implicitly (Gelman, 1990; Kanwisher, 2001). The associated neural, perceptual, and cognitive systems result, for instance, in the automatic attention to and processing of the forms of information (e.g., eyes, gestures) needed to support social discourse and relationships (Baron-Cohen, 1995; Rosenthal, Hall, DiMatteo, Rogers, & Archer, 1979). The heuristic-based decisions and behaviors described in chapter 6 (Bounded Rationality and Heuristics section) also result from automatic, implicit processes. Simon's (1955, 1956) bounded rationality represents the relation between significant information patterns that have recurred across generations and corresponding behavioral responses that have resulted in improved survival or reproductive options, but bounded rationality can also include ecology–cognition–behavior links that are formed during the organism's lifetime.

Whether the result of inherent or learned ecology–cognition–behavior links, much of the behavior of the species, including much of human behavior, can be understood in terms of these automatic and implicit processes. Although these processes define much of what it is to be human and explain much of human behavior, individual differences in their operation (e.g., sensitivity to social cues) do not appear to be strongly correlated with general intelligence, as noted in Table 6.1 (Baron-Cohen, Wheelwright, Stone, & Rutherford, 1999; J. S. B. T. Evans, 2002; Stanovich, 1999).

Explicit Processes

Controlled problem solving and the ability to engage in rational analysis are correlated with general intelligence (Carpenter, Just, & Shell, 1990; Stanovich, 1999; Süß, Oberauer, Wittmann, Wilhelm, & Schulze, 2002) and appear to require the inhibition of heuristic-based responding and the formation of a conscious, explicit representation of the corresponding information (Bjorklund, Cormier, & Rosenberg, in press; Bjorklund & Harnishfeger, 1995; J. S. B. T. Evans, 2002; J. Johnson, Im-Bolter, & Pascual-Leone, 2003; Johnson-Laird, 1983; Pascual-Leone, 1987; Stanovich & West, 2000). The basic issues are centered on the cognitive and brain systems and processes that result in an individual becoming consciously aware of externally and internally generated information and the ability to mentally change and reorganize these representations. The accompanying issues have engaged philosophers for centuries and have attracted the attention of psychologists and neuroscientists in recent decades (Dehaene, 2001; Dennett, 1987; Pinker, 1997). There is, of course, debate on these issues, but an impressive level of agreement has been achieved with respect to the basic cognitive processes involved in conscious awareness.

Making the Implicit Explicit

A basic scheme for understanding the relation between implicit and explicit processes is shown at Time 1 in Figure 7.1. The outer sections of the oval represent the sensory and perceptual systems that capture information patterns from the external environment and the most basic forms of neural, perceptual and cognitive system that generate internal representations (e.g., of objects or faces) of these external patterns. These systems would be included in the neural, perceptual, and cognitive modules described in Table 4.1 and at the perceptual and cognitive level include the modular components of folk psychology, folk biology, and folk physics described in chapter 5 and shown at the base of Figure 6.1.

But how does one become explicitly aware of implicitly processed information patterns? How does a person become conscious of the social, biological, and physical worlds? As one example of how conscious awareness occurs, there are areas in the visual system that are particularly sensitive to the information patterns generated by human faces (Functional Social Systems section of chap. 5; Kanwisher, McDermott, & Chun, 1997). The associated neural (i.e., fusiform gyrus), perceptual (e.g., pulling out specific facial features), and cognitive (i.e., integrating specific features into a whole face) modules appear to operate automatically and implicitly. The result is an activation of inherently constrained exoskeleton systems that are sensitive to invariant facial features (e.g., basic shape of the face) and systems that have been shaped by previous experiences to represent memories of the faces of particular people, as described in chapter 4 (Soft Modularity section).

Social discourse results in an interaction between long-term-memory representations of familiar faces and the patterns generated by the face of the social partner. The interaction essentially involves, to some extent, matching current information patterns to patterns stored in long-term memory, which is possible because the same areas that process the information also store it in long-term memory (Barsalou, Simmons, Barbey, & Wilson, 2003; Cowan, 1995, 1999; Damasio, 1989; Ruchkin, Grafman, Cameron, & Berndt, 2003). When the interaction occurs, the systems that process this facial information are in an active state. The active state is achieved through an increase in the rate or pattern of firing of the neurons that process the corresponding information and by neuronal systems that are activated by the firing of the first neuronal system (Damasio, 1989; E. K. Miller & Cohen, 2001). Experimental studies indicate that neural activation is not in and of itself enough for the conscious recognition of the face (Kanwisher, 2001).

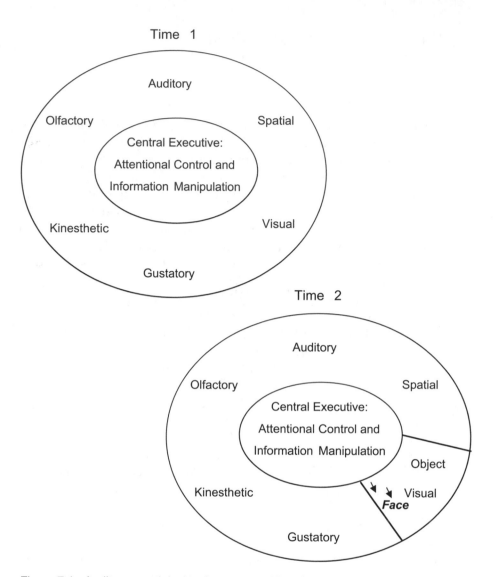

Figure 7.1. *Auditory, spatial, visual, gustatory, kinesthetic,* and *olfactory* in the outer section of the ovals represent neural, sensory, perceptual, and cognitive modules that process external information patterns in these domains. The central executive is composed of the mechanisms that direct attention to one of these domains and result in a conscious, explicit awareness and representation of the corresponding information. At Time 1 there is no specific focus of attention, but at Time 2 attention is focused on a face, which then becomes available to conscious awareness.

Conscious, explicit awareness and recognition of the face, and any other form of information represented by the outer section of the oval, requires that other systems direct attention to the activated information (Baddeley & Hitch, 1974; Cowan, 1988, 1995; Dehaene & Naccache, 2001; Driver & Vuilleumier, 2001; Engle, 2002). Sometimes the systems that direct shifts in attention and changes in the content of conscious awareness are triggered automatically by abrupt and novel changes in the environment, as when people orient toward a sudden and loud noise (Sokolov, 1963). At other times, apparently different systems, called the *central executive*, are involved in the explicit and controlled directing of attention (Baddeley & Logie, 1999; Cowan, 1999). The mechanisms by which the central executive creates conscious, explicit awareness are not fully understood, but the result is an attention-driven amplification of the activated information (Posner, 1994) and a synchronization of the brain regions that compose the central executive and the brain regions that are processing the external information (Damasio, 1989; E. K. Miller & Cohen, 2001; Ruchkin et al., 2003). The arrows at Time 2 in Figure 7.1 show the attention-driven amplification of the portions of the visual system that are activated by facial information (see Folk Psychology: Individual section of chap. 5). The result is that the face "pops" into conscious awareness.

Central Executive

The attentional systems of the central executive and the accompanying ability to mentally manipulate explicit representations (e.g., words) are important features of working memory. The details regarding the ways in which information is stored and manipulated in working memory and the limits of this system are debated (Baddeley & Logie, 1999; Cowan, 2001; Miyake & Shah, 1999). Nonetheless, it is now clear that individual differences in working memory capacity are related to individual differences in the ability to focus attention and prevent irrelevant information from diverting attention from the task at hand (Conway, Cowan, & Bunting, 2001; Conway & Engle, 1994; Engle, 2002; Engle, Conway, Tuholski, & Shisler, 1995; Kane & Engle, 2000; Rosen & Engle, 1998).

In addition to attentional control, performance on working memory tasks and on tests of general intelligence is also correlated with the speed of information processing, such as the speed of determining if two line segments are the same length (e.g., "<—" versus "—>"; Ackerman, Beier, & Boyle, 2002; Fry & Hale, 1996, 2000; Jensen, 1998; Kail, 1991; Luciano, Wright, et al., 2001; Salthouse, 1991, 1996). I provide extensive discussion of these cognitive correlates of intelligence in the next chapter. The point for now is that attention versus speed need not be competing views of the basis of working memory, because performance on speeded tasks appears to be dependent on sustained attention (Conway, Cowan, Bunting, Therriault, & Minkoff, 2002; Engle, personal communication, January 27, 2003). In any case, Engle (2002) proposed that the central executive and working memory are defined by the ability to use attentional resources to amplify and maintain goal-relevant internal representations (i.e., a pattern of neural activity associated with external information) and to inhibit irrelevant information patterns from entering conscious awareness. In this view, there is no separate working memory system. Rather, the combination of the brain regions (described in a later section) that control attention-driven amplification and the amplified perceptual and cognitive processes compose working memory (Cowan, 1999; Ruchkin et al., 2003).

Slave Systems

Although some of the details await resolution, Engle's model can accommodate the seminal contribution of Baddeley and Hitch (1974), although Baddeley and Logie (1999) were not convinced of this. Baddeley and Hitch proposed that working memory is composed of the central executive that controls attentional allocation and two slave systems, the *phonological loop* and the *visuospatial sketch pad* (see also Baddeley, 1986; Baddeley & Logie, 1999). In a very general sense, these slave systems correspond to the auditory and visual-spatial areas, respectively, of Figure 7.1. The phonological loop is composed of a phonetic buffer that holds acoustic information (e.g., the sounds *ba, pa, da*) in short-term memory and an articulatory rehearsal mechanism. Acoustical patterns represented in short-term memory quickly decay unless refreshed by articulating the sounds by speaking them aloud or mentally. The central executive engages the articulatory mechanism.

Baddeley and colleagues proposed that the evolved function of the phonological loop is to combine and form long-term memory representations of novel phonological combinations, that is, for vocabulary acquisition (Baddeley, Gathercole, & Papagno, 1998). The phonological loop would thus operate on an evolved system that processes the full range and form of sounds included in human speech—also processed by at least some other mammals (Doupe & Kuhl, 1999)—to create novel combinations or novel blends of these sounds (Kuhl et al., 1997). When combined with inherent constraints on the grammatical structure of utterances (R. Brown, 1973; Pinker, 1994, 1999), such a mechanism could easily explain differences in the surface structure of human languages (e.g., differences in the sounds of words) and regularities in how words are combined to communicate meaning. Although the visuospatial sketch pad has not been as extensively studied, the evolutionary functions are almost certainly related to navigation and movement in space as related to, for instance, prey capture and predator avoidance (Dyer, 1998; Gallistel, 1990, 2000). The visuospatial sketch pad may also be engaged when generating mental images and memories of objects, places, and people (Silverman & Eals, 1992) and for mentally manipulating or changing the form of these images (Logie, 1995).

More recently, Baddeley (2000a, 2002) proposed a third slave system, the *episodic buffer*. As with the other slave systems, the buffer is controlled by the central executive but does not process phonetic or visuospatial information per se. Rather, the buffer results in the conscious awareness of experiences that require an integration of information—potentially including that represented in the phonological buffer and visuospatial sketch pad—across space and sometimes across time. Looking out of one's office window and being simultaneously aware of trees, buildings, moving cars, and so forth would only be possible with the operation of something like Baddeley's episodic buffer. Such a buffer would also be necessary for the formation of long-term memories of personal experiences, termed *episodic memory* (Tulving, 1983): The "information of episodic memory could be said to concern the self's experiences in subjective space and time" (Tulving, 1993, p. 67).

Before turning to self-awareness, I note that Figure 7.1 includes sensory and perceptual systems for olfactory, kinesthetic, and gustatory information, despite the fact that most models of human memory and cognition are focused on the auditory, spatial, and visual systems. The focus on the three latter systems is, in my opinion, the result of a species-centric view of memory and cognition. The focus on visuospatial systems is understandable for a diurnal (active during the day) primate, as these systems appear to be elaborated in such species (Barton, 1996). The focus on the auditory system is understandable for a highly social species that uses language as a primary mode of communication. Humans can also form long-term and working memory representations of movement patterns (Reisberg, Rappaport, & O'Shaughnessy, 1984) and clearly have sensory systems and form memories for the other forms of information shown in Figure 7.1 (Cowan, 1988). My point and that of biologists who study cognition in other species (Dukas, 1998a) is that the organization and the extent of elaboration of memory and cognitive systems can differ from one species to the next, depending on the types of information (e.g., olfactory vs. visual) that most strongly covary with survival and reproductive options. The result would be analogous to the cross-species differences in the organization of the somatosensory cortex illustrated in Figure 4.4, but these differences would be across broader memory, cognitive, and brain systems.

Self-Awareness

When it comes to declarative knowledge, that is, knowledge that can be explicitly expressed, there are two classes of neurocognitive system, semantic and episodic (Tulving, 1983). Cognitive psychologists often study this knowledge by means of memory tests, and thus the systems are commonly referred to as *semantic memory* and *episodic memory*, respectively. Semantic memory refers to the retrieval of decontextualized facts and information, whereas episodic memory refers to the retrieval of time-based, contextualized memories of one's life history. A conscious representation of facts and decontextualized information is *noetic awareness,* and a conscious time-based representation of the self and personal experiences is *autonoetic awareness* (Tulving, 1985, 2002; M. A. Wheeler, 2000). Although a distinction between noetic and autonoetic awareness has been vigorously debated (see Tulving, 2002), the distinction has been demonstrated in experimental studies of memory (Tulving, 1985), neuroimaging studies of these memory processes (Craik et al., 1999; Düzel, Yonelinas, Mangun, Heinze, & Tulving, 1997), and research on the consequences of brain injury (Levine et al., 1998) and psychiatric disorder on memory and awareness (Danion, Rizzo, & Bruant, 1999).

More completely, autonoetic awareness is the ability to consciously consider the self across time, that is, to recall personal experiences, relate these experiences to current situations, and project oneself into the future (Levine, 1999; M. A. Wheeler, 2000). As Levine argued, autonoetic awareness includes the ability to "cast oneself as a player in scenarios emerging from various choices available at any given moment. . . . This capacity facilitates the self-regulation of behavior necessary for the achievement of personally-relevant goals" (p. 200). The generation of these mental scenarios requires the inhibition of heuristic-based biases and the integration of information across modalities and time and in this sense is similar to Baddeley's (2000a) episodic buffer. These scenarios can be understood as a form of mental model (Johnson-Laird, 1983) in which not only is the self the primary actor in the situation, but the individual is also aware that the self is the primary actor. Stated more plainly, the autonoetic mental model is experienced as daydreams and fantasies (M. A. Wheeler, 2000) but serves the more serious function of allowing individuals to consciously form future-oriented goals, regulate future-directed behavior, and integrate these within a seamless and self-aware knowledge of one's life history.

Of course, all species have future-oriented goals, namely to stay alive and to reproduce, but these goals are achievable through implicit, heuristic-based processes (Suddendorf & Busby, 2003). It may be that the potentially unique human ability to project oneself into the distant future is a side effect, so to speak (Gould & Vrba, 1982), resulting from the evolution of other cognitive and memory systems (Tulving, 2002). Another possibility is that the ability to generate self-centered mental models of potential future situations and potential behaviors in these situations is a direct result of one or several of the selection pressures I described in chapter 3 and elaborate below. For now it is important to note that autonoetic mental models are needed only in situations that differ from day-to-day routine (Levine, 1999) and that differ from the ecology–cognition–behavior links associated with bounded rationality and evolved heuristics (Gigerenzer & Selten, 2001a; Simon, 1956). Specifically, autonoetic mental models enable individuals to anticipate and mentally simulate potential behavioral strategies to deal with variation in social dynamics or ecological conditions.

Brain Systems

Brodmann's (1909) systematic and now seminal studies of the architecture of the neocortex of humans and several other species provided one of the earliest comprehensive attempts to understand not only the anatomy but also some of the functions of the brain. Brodmann's original map of some of the larger anatomical regions of the human neocortex is shown in Figure 7.2. Figure 7.3 shows these same regions, but a little more clearly. My goal in this section is to highlight the relation between the functioning of the prefrontal cortex, such as areas 9 and 46 shown in the top section of Figure 7.3, and executive functions and episodic memory. It is clear that other areas of the brain, such as the hippocampus and some posterior regions of the neocortex, also contribute to these competencies (Driver & Vuilleumier, 2001; Kanwisher, 2001; Moscovitch, 1994; Rees, Kreiman, & Koch, 2002). For instance, attentional focus and control are important features of complex problem solving and conscious awareness and are dependent on multiple areas of the prefrontal cortex, as well as the parietal cortex (e.g., areas 7 and 40 of Figure 7.3) and some subcortical systems (Andersen, Snyder, Bradley, & Xing, 1997; Bisley & Goldberg, 2003; J. D. Cohen, Perlstein, Braver, Nystrom, Noll, et al., 1997; Collette & Van der Linden, 2002; Posner, 1994; Posner & DiGirolamo, 2000).

The prefrontal cortex is of particular interest and the focus of this section. It is implicated in the competencies that define executive functions, episodic memory, and self-awareness, as well as general intelligence (Duncan et al., 2000; J. R. Gray, Chabris, & Braver, 2003). M. A. Wheeler et al. (1997) provided a useful heuristic for conceptualizing the cognitive functions of the prefrontal cortex. The first of three levels of function involves monitoring and integrating patterns of information generated by more posterior regions of the neocortex as related to the achievement of specific goals. A simple example is the sequencing and integration of the steps needed to solve arithmetic problems, such as 34×46 (Geary & Hoard, 2001; Luria, 1980). The second level is represented by attentional control and inhibition of irrelevant information, and the third level represents episodic memory and self-awareness. As described in the section that follows, there is evidence suggesting that the first two levels define the executive functions of the

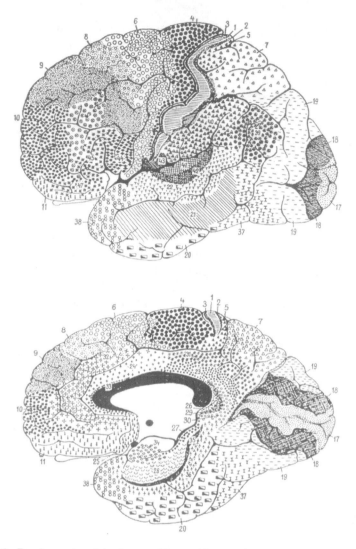

Figure 7.2. Brodmann's original map of the architectural units of the human neocortex. From *Vergleichende Lokalisationslehre der Grosshirnrinde in ihren Prinzipien dargestellt auf Grund des Zellenbaues* [Comparative localization of the cerebral cortex based on cell composition] (p. 131), by K. Brodmann, 1909, Leipzig, Germany: Barth. See caption of Figure 7.3 for description of the general cortical locations and basic functional competencies.

prefrontal cortex, which appear to be independent of the systems that support self-awareness. In any event, areas of the prefrontal cortex are highly interconnected with one another (E. K. Miller & Cohen, 2001; J. N. Wood & Grafman, 2003), and thus the executive and self-awareness systems function in a highly interdependent manner in most situations.

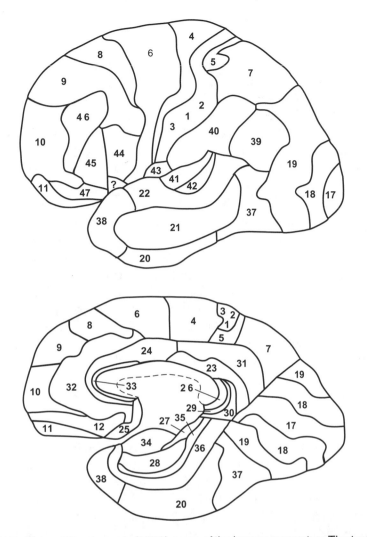

Figure 7.3. Maps of Brodmann's (1909) areas of the human neocortex. The top section is a lateral (outer) view of the cortex, whereas the bottom section is a medial (center, between the two hemispheres) view. Many of these areas can be subdivided into specialized subregions that process different forms of information. Very generally, areas 1, 2, 3, 5, 7, 31, 39, and 43 and regions of area 40 are part of the parietal cortex and support a variety of functions including sense of body position, attention, spatial competencies, and integration of information across modalities. Areas 17, 18, and 19 are part of the occipital cortex and support simple and complex visual perception. Areas 22, 41, 42, and subregions of areas 38 and 40 are part of the temporal cortex and support simple and complex auditory and speech perception. Areas 20, 21, 26 through 28, 34 through 37, and 52 are also part of the temporal lobe but support a variety of complex visual competencies. Areas 4, 6, and 8 are involved in complex motor movements and are part of the frontal cortex. Area 44 and subregions of area 45 are involved in speech generation and are part of the frontal cortex. Areas 9, 10, 11, 12, 25, 46, 47, and subregions of 45 are part of the prefrontal cortex and support behavioral control, executive functions, and many complex social competencies. Areas 23, 24, 29, 30, parts of 31, 32, and 33 are part of the cingulate and support attentional and emotional functions. Illustration by Mark Dubin.

An exciting and dynamic area of research in the cognitive neurosciences involves the study of the brain regions that support executive functions (Bunge, Klingberg, Jacobsen, & Gabrieli, 2000; Carpenter, Just, & Reichle, 2000; Dehaene & Naccache, 2001; Duncan, 2001; J. B. Rowe, Toni, Josephs, Frackowiak, & Passingham, 2000; E. E. Smith & Jonides, 1999; J. N. Wood & Grafman, 2003) and support the ability to explicitly reason and problem solve (Kane & Engle, 2002; Waltz et al., 1999). As with other domains, many of the details are yet to be resolved. Active debate and research are focused on determining whether specific areas of the prefrontal cortex are specialized for specific competencies (Goldman-Rakic & Leung, 2002; Koechlin, Ody, & Kouneiher, 2003; Moscovitch & Winocur, 2002; Normal & Shallice, 1986; Shallice, 2002) or are more general, nonspecialized systems (Carpenter et al., 2000); what the specific functions are of specific regions of the prefrontal cortex (Collette & Van der Linden, 2002; Passingham & Rowe, 2002); whether the prefrontal cortices of the right and left hemispheres support different functional competencies (K. E. Stephan et al., 2003; Tulving, Kapur, Craik, Moscovitch, & Houle, 1994) or support different forms of working memory content, specifically visual (right) or verbal (left: E. E. Smith, 2000; E. Smith & Jonides, 1999); and the degree to which posterior and subcortical regions of the cortex are involved in executive functions (Carpenter et al., 2000).

The debates arise because of differences in the methods used to study prefrontal functions (e.g., single-cell recordings vs. brain imaging) and because the rich interconnections among regions of the prefrontal cortex greatly complicate the experimental study of potential specific functions of one area or another (E. K. Miller & Cohen, 2001). These complications are not the central focus here; the central point is that the interconnections within the prefrontal cortex and with other areas of the brain make it well situated to serve as the center for executive functions (Baddeley, 2002) and for broader supervisory and behavioral control (Curtis & D'Esposito, 2003; Duncan, 2001; E. K. Miller & Cohen, 2001; Moscovitch & Winocur, 2002; Shallice, 2002; J. N. Wood & Grafman, 2003). However the details are eventually resolved, Duncan (2001), E. K. Miller and Cohen, and Kane and Engle (2002), among others (e.g., Goldman-Rakic & Leung, 2002), have agreed that areas of the dorsolateral region of the prefrontal cortex, including areas 9 and 46 (sometimes the prefrontal pole, that is, area 10) shown in the top section of Figure 7.3, are involved in the executive functions of working memory, as is the anterior cingulate cortex (area 24 in the bottom section of Figure 7.3).

These regions appear to be particularly important for active goal maintenance and the explicit inhibition of competing and goal-irrelevant internal (e.g., memories) and external distractions (M. C. Anderson et al., 2004; Duncan, 2001; Kane & Engle, 2002; E. K. Miller & Cohen, 2001; Petersen, Fox, Posner, Mintun, & Raichle, 1988; Shallice, 2002). These ends appear to be achieved by biasing, perhaps through attentional amplification (Dehaene & Naccache, 2001; Posner, 1994), the activation of posterior and subcortical pathways that represent the information needed for goal achievement and the inhibition of brain areas that represent (e.g., memory storage) or process goal-irrelevant information. However, the dorsolateral areas and the anterior cingulate cortex appear to be heavily involved only in achieving goals that are not readily achieved by means of heuristics (Ranganath & Rainer, 2003). The anterior cingulated cortex, in particular, is activated when goal achievement requires dealing with some degree of novelty or conflict (e.g., choosing between two alternatives). The result appears to be an automatic attentional shift to the novel or conflicted information and activation of the dorsolateral and other prefrontal areas (Botvinick, Braver, Barch, Carter, & Cohen, 2001). These areas in turn enable the explicit, controlled problem solving needed to cope with the novel situation or resolve the conflict (Kerns et al., 2004). Botvinick and colleagues' (2001) proposal that novelty and conflict result in automatic attentional shifts and activation of executive functions is important, because it addresses the homunculus question. The central executive does not activate itself, but rather is automatically activated when heuristic-based processes are not sufficient for dealing with current information patterns or tasks.

The description of the functions of these brain regions also meshes nicely with the descriptions of controlled problem solving described in chapter 6. As noted, controlled problem solving requires generation of an end state, or the desired goal, and the development of a strategy to achieve this goal. The processes involve moving, so to speak, from the current state to the desired end state and doing so using only goal-relevant information and only legal transformations of the associated information. Movement through problem space requires that the end goal or one of several subgoals is actively maintained in working memory while processing related pieces of information and engaging in the multiple steps required to solve the problem. The latter might involve retrieving solutions to similar problems from long-term memory or retrieving specific goal-related facts from long-term memory, as illustrated in the previous chapter with Darwin's and Wallace's discovery of natural selection (see Table 6.2 and related text).

When viewed from the perspective of controlled problem solving, the dorsolateral areas appear to be involved in maintaining the task goal in mind, guiding the sequencing of the multiple problem-solving steps, and suppressing the potential interfering effects of externally or internally generated distractions (Kane & Engle, 2002). The anterior cingulate cortex is activated in situations that involve conflicting information during the problem-solving process, such as detecting when competing alternatives to solving a particular subgoal are retrieved from long-term memory (E. K. Miller & Cohen, 2001). As I mentioned, activation of the anterior cingulate cortex appears to result in attentional shifts to and an explicit representation of this information in working memory, which enables the individual to evaluate and choose one of the alternatives or make other adjustments in the problem-solving process (Botvinick et al., 2001; Kerns et al., 2004).

The prefrontal cortex and the central executive are not, however, synonymous (Moscovitch & Winocur, 2002; Stuss & Levine, 2002). The prefrontal cortex encompasses a much broader range of competencies than those attributed to working memory and the central executive. Moscovitch and Winocur argued that these broader functions also include *working with memory*, not simply working memory. The hippocampus and other non-prefrontal brain regions are involved in acquiring memories and in the conscious experience of retrieved memories (Moscovitch, 1994). The pre-frontal cortex is involved in searching for, retrieving, and using these memories. One might work with these memories to, for instance, re-experience the past and infuse these memories with a sense of self, as I describe in the next section. Working with memory might also involve searching for the pattern of memories needed to solve a particular problem. Darwin's (1846) and Wallace's (1855) extensive knowledge derived from their explorations no doubt included a wealth of memories of many different species in many different habitats. They were very likely to have worked with these memories in the development of the principles of natural selection, in addition to having used their working memory during the problem-solving phases outlined in Table 6.2.

In any event, the broad executive control exercised by the prefrontal cortex and the anterior cingulate cortex not only guide controlled problem solving, but also concurrently learn the associated abstract rules that can be applied to novel but related situations (e.g., Wallis, Anderson, & Miller, 2001): An example of transferring abstract rules from one context to another is provided by Darwin's and Wallace's (1858) use of Malthus's (1798) model of population expansions and contractions to solve the problem of the origin of species. Controlled problem solving also appears to involve the synchronization of neural activity in the posterior and subcortical regions that process the goal-relevant information. The synchronization appears to involve an integration of information across sensory modalities (e.g., visual and auditory information) with motivational (e.g., reward value of the information) and affective systems (Damasio, 1995; Plutchik, 2001, 2002; Tucker, Luu, & Pribram, 1995; Watanabe, 2002), and with motoric-behavioral plans that guide the individual's goal-oriented behavioral engagement of the ecology (Curtis & D'Esposito, 2003). With repeated synchronization of neural activity, these regions eventually work together without the need for explicit, conscious problem solving (John, 2003; E. K. Miller & Cohen, 2001; Ruchkin et al., 2003). In other words, controlled problem solving can eventually result in the learning of heuristics and other forms of knowledge, as I discuss in chapter 9 (Academic Learning section).

Episodic Memory and Autonoetic Awareness

The brain and cognitive systems that support episodic memory and awareness of the self appear to differ from the brain and cognitive systems that support memory and awareness of other things (Craik et al., 1999; Düzel et al., 1997; Nyberg, Forkstam, Petersson, Cabeza, & Ingvar, 2002; Tulving, 2002) and that support the executive functions described in the previous section (M. A. Wheeler et al., 1997). Several lines of evidence converge on the conclusion that the right prefrontal cortex is involved in the retrieval of episodic memories (the left prefrontal cortex is involved in the initial encoding of these experiences; Tulving et al., 1994) and in self-awareness (Wheeler et al., 1997).

In one such study, Craik and colleagues (1999) used positron emission tomography (PET) to examine the brain regions that were activated when adults rated positive (e.g., friendly) and negative (e.g., selfish) personality traits as related to the self, famous personalities, people in general, and the number of syllables in the word (an experimental control condition). In comparison to the syllable condition, the three people-related conditions were associated with increased activity in the left frontal cortex. This result was most likely related to the semantic encoding and retrieval of the meaning of the trait words. The most interesting result involved a contrast of the self condition with the famous personalities and people in general conditions. The contrast revealed some activation of portions of the left prefrontal cortex but primarily activation of several areas of the right prefrontal cortex. It was concluded that the processing and retrieval of information that involved memories of personal experiences (e.g., as related to the traits presented in this study) and the person's self-concept are dependent on the functioning of the right prefrontal cortex.

Consistent with brain imaging studies (Nyberg et al., 2002), traumatic injuries to the right prefrontal cortex, perhaps areas 10, 11, and 25 (see Figure 7.3), as well as their connections to brain regions associated with memory formation, result in an array of deficits that differ from trauma-related deficits in executive functions (Levine, 1999; Levine et al., 1998; Moscovitch & Winocur, 2002; Stuss & Levine, 2002; Tulving, 1985). One such patient, KC, suffered severe injuries to these brain regions as a result of a motorcycle accident. After recovery from the initial trauma, KC performed normally on IQ tests and on tests of executive functions but "cannot recollect a single episode of his life from either before or after" the injury (Levine,

1999, p. 207). Nor could KC project himself into the future—that is, when asked to imagine his activities for the following day, he drew a blank (Tulving, 1985, 2002). He later learned, through the semantic memory system, facts about himself (e.g., his former job) but was unable to place these facts in the context of memories of his personal life history. Levine et al. reported a similar pattern for ML, another patient with severe damage to the same brain regions.

The associated deficits also include difficulties in self-regulation (e.g., judging risks) and with social activities in general. These people find it difficult to inhibit previously learned responses and thus cannot cope with situations that involve change from one type of response to another. In effect, they cannot problem solve when the task involves novelty and cannot make effective decisions that involve comparing current choices to future outcomes; comparing current choices to various alternative outcomes had they made a different decision; or integrating past experiences (e.g., negative outcomes, such as regret) with current decision making (Bechara, Damasio, & Damasio, 2000; Bechara, Damasio, Tranel, & Damasio, 1997; Camille et al., 2004; Damasio, 2003). Social activities are, of course, very complex and entail subtle and almost constant and concurrent change in multiple sources of information, including facial expression, vocal intonation, body language, and so forth. In addition, social activities are by definition intimately related to the self and, for humans, one's sense of self. In social situations, ML "reported difficulty knowing how to behave around family members and friends, and had to be taught socially acceptable behaviour" (Levine et al., 1998, p. 1956). These individuals can use the semantic memory system to learn how to behave in social situations (e.g., "Don't do x"). They recognize social deficits in other people but cannot understand these same deficits as related to the self (M. A. Wheeler et al., 1997).

Episodic memories are not stored in the right prefrontal cortex per se. Rather, the right prefrontal cortex is involved in the retrieval of personal experiences from the posterior regions of the neocortex and the subcortical regions that were engaged during the actual experience (Tulving, 2002). Regions of the right prefrontal cortex also appear to infuse these recollections with a sense of self that is continuous across time, and regions of the left prefrontal cortex interpret these recollections as a language-based narrative of one's life history (Roser & Gazzaniga, 2004). These brain regions appear to bind together, so to speak, the current situation with personal memories for related situations and as related to future goals. As I mentioned, if the sense of self is added, Tulving and colleagues' model of episodic memory (Tulving, 2002; M. A. Wheeler et al., 1997) is very similar to Baddeley's episodic buffer (Baddeley, 2000a), which has also been hypothesized as being supported by the right prefrontal cortex (Prabhakaran, Narayanan, Zhao,

& Gabrieli, 2000). The buffer holds perceptual and cognitive information generated by current ecological circumstances, integrates this information with memories of related situations, and enables the organism to behaviorally respond to the situation. The episodic buffer is probably common across species but may be uniquely human when infused with autonoetic awareness.

Summary and Integration

Explicit, controlled problem solving and reasoning are supported by the central executive and the executive control processes of the prefrontal cortex, with some assistance from other areas of the brain (E. K. Miller & Cohen, 2001; Posner, 1994). The central executive is largely defined by the ability to focus attention on goal-relevant tasks and information and to inhibit irrelevant information from entering conscious awareness (Bjorklund & Harnishfeger, 1995; Engle, 2002; Pascual-Leone, 1987). The functional result is the ability to consciously maintain, focus on, and mentally manipulate goal-relevant information that is represented in other cognitive systems (Baddeley & Hitch, 1974; Ruchkin et al., 2003). Examples of the sequence and nature of these working-memory manipulations, at least for humans and in its most complex form, were described in the Controlled Problem Solving section of chapter 6. It has been well established that regions of the prefrontal cortex in both the left and right hemispheres are engaged for tasks that require the conscious, attention-demanding executive control functions of working memory (Kane & Engle, 2002), whether the task involves complex reasoning or simply keeping a phone number in mind. It is not certain at this point, but it appears that different regions of the prefrontal cortex may be involved in maintaining representations of different types of information (Koechlin et al., 2003; E. E. Smith, 2000; E. E. Smith & Jonides, 1999).

The corresponding studies of working memory and executive control almost always involve the processing of information that is distinct from the self—that is, the studies do not require a sense of self. Tulving (1985, 2002) proposed that another form of working memory and conscious awareness exists, that involving knowledge of the self. This autonoetic awareness is not simply self-awareness; it involves the ability to mentally relive past experiences—episodic memory—and to project oneself into the future (Tulving, 2002). As with the other working memory systems, the supporting brain regions are also located in the prefrontal cortex, especially in the right hemisphere and in different regions in the right hemisphere (e.g., area 11 vs. 46) than for working memory tasks that do not involve the self (Craik et al., 1999; M. A. Wheeler et al., 1997). In any case, the ability to mentally project oneself through time while simultaneously being aware of self attributes, such as one's personality, preferences, and so forth, is a particularly important and potentially unique human capacity (Suddendorf & Busby, 2003).

My proposal is that autonoetic awareness and more general functions associated with the prefrontal cortex and executive control can be integrated with the motivation to control. Specifically, the motivation to control is facilitated by the ability to mentally simulate potential future social scenarios (e.g., Humphrey, 1976) or changes in ecological condition (Potts, 1998) and then rehearse a variety of potential behavioral responses to these situations (Geary, 1998). These are unpredictable, or variant, situations, and one way to deal with them is to mentally generate potential variations of these conditions and then mentally rehearse behavioral options for coping with each of these variations, as elaborated in the next section.

PROBLEM SOLVING AND HUMAN EVOLUTION

I now consider the selection pressures that may have resulted in the evolution of the capacity for executive control (including sustained attention), self-awareness, and mental time travel. Among other brain regions, all of these competencies are heavily dependent on various regions of the prefrontal cortex (e.g., area 46 in Figure 7.3), the frontal pole (area 10), and the anterior cingulate cortex (area 24), or some combination, and appear to be active primarily with tasks or social dynamics that vary from the routine. On the basis of the latter possibility, I assume that the selection pressures that contributed to the evolution of these cognitive and brain systems required the individual to cope with information patterns that were toward the variant end of the continuum shown in Figure 6.2.

Variation in the conditions that covaried with evolutionary outcomes would, by definition, reduce the effectiveness of heuristics and result in a selective advantage for the ability to inhibit heuristic-based responses and deal with variation through the explicit processes noted in Table 6.1, including working memory and controlled problem solving. Variation in these situations differs from variation in more specialized modular systems. The latter involves, for instance, individual differences in facial structure, whereas the former involves time-dependent and nonroutine change in more macro conditions. Examples are the strategies and counterstrategies that emerge during group-level conflict. Whether these involve national wars or more local conflicts, the unfolding dynamics of each situation are never entirely predictable, although there are predictable features across situations (Horowitz, 2001). For any condition that changes in unpredictable ways, explicit problem solving can be used to plan strategies to initiate change in conditions; to move from the new, changed state back to the conditions before the change; or to make adjustments to adapt to anticipated change.

In the Adaptation and Selection section of chapter 3, I reviewed the climatic, ecological, and social selection pressures that potentially contributed to the evolution of brain and cognition in humans. I evaluate these pressures in the first section that follows in terms of how well they fit with the need for explicit, controlled problem solving and related cognitive competencies. In the second section, I review comparative and paleontological evidence as related to the evolutionary expansion and reorganization of the human frontal cortex, and in the third section I integrate the issues addressed in the first two subsections with the motivation to control.

Selection Pressures

The cognitive and brain systems that define and support executive control and the corresponding ability to engage in explicit, controlled problem solving and abstract reasoning differ from the cognitive and brain systems that support awareness and the coupled ability to engage in mental time travel (Levine, 1999; Tulving, 2002). It is therefore possible that different selection pressures contributed to the evolution of the ability to engage in explicit problem solving and that support self-awareness. Another possibility is that the same type of selection pressure contributed to the co-evolution of all of these competencies, but that different features of the selection pressure contributed to the evolution of more specific competencies and brain regions. Either way, if variation is the key to understanding the evolution of these competencies, then the selection pressure or pressures should show at least some combination of the characteristics presented in the following section. I discuss the relation between these characteristics and climatic, ecological, and social selection pressures in the second, third, and fourth sections, respectively.

Selection Characteristics

The first type of characteristic concerns the time scale of information change, or how frequently and predictably climatic, ecological, or social conditions change. Most broadly, the time scale for which this change tends to occur must be within the limits of a single lifetime, and these changes should occur repeatedly during a lifetime. As Bjorklund and his colleagues emphasized, adapting to change requires the inhibition of heuristic-based responses and thus operation of the central executive (Bjorklund et al., in press; Bjorklund & Harnishfeger, 1995). Adapting to short-term change or variation is consistent with the operation of the central executive as it is traditionally defined (e.g., Baddeley, 1986). The ability to engage in mental time travel is probably also governed by the central executive but is most advantageous for adapting to change that occurs over a longer time scale, but still within the confines of a lifetime. The combination of the central executive as it is traditionally defined and mental time travel suggests that the better theoretical candidates for potential selection pressures are conditions that involve frequent and repeated changes across shorter- and longer-time scales within the length of a typical life span.

The second characteristic concerns the type of selection pressure that would drive the evolution of self-awareness and explain the finding that self-awareness tends to be coupled with the ability to engage in mental time travel (Tulving, 2002). The third characteristic is the potential for a co-evolutionary arms race that would favor brain and cognitive evolution. Consideration of such an arms race is important, given the rapid increase in absolute brain size (see Figure 3.4), increase in EQ (see Figure 3.6), and presumably change in brain organization during the past 500,000 years. The fourth characteristic concerns whether the three forms of selection pressure are substantially different comparing humans to apes and other primates. A comparative perspective is important, because the conditions that resulted in the substantive changes in brain and cognition during human evolution must have differed in important ways from the conditions experienced by related species and their ancestors (Povinelli & Bering, 2002).

Climatic Conditions

As I described in the Climatic Pressures section of chapter 3, climatic variation has been proposed as a factor that contributed to the expansion of brain volume and EQ during human evolution. Some theorists have argued that brain volume increased as a direct result of climatic variation, that is, to devise behavioral strategies to cope with climatic change (Potts, 1998). Other theorists have argued that change in brain volume was an incidental effect of increases in body size (Vrba, 1995b); cold climates favor larger body sizes for heat retention. Selection for larger body size, in turn, could have resulted in an allometric expansion of brain size in the absence of specific selection pressures acting on brain size and improved cognitive competencies (see Allometry and Size of the Neocortex section of chap. 4). The EQ estimates should, of course, control for any such allometric expansions, and on the basis of this and other considerations I concluded in chapter 3 that climatic variation was not a sufficient explanation for the expansion in brain size and EQ during human evolution.

In addition to the difficulties outlined in chapter 3, climatic variation does not fit many of the characteristics outlined in the preceding section. The time scale of climatic change tends to be longer than the time scale that governs the functioning of the working memory system. To be sure, memories for previous patterns of climatic variation could be used, in a working with memories sense (Moscovitch, 1994). These patterns would be based on the long-term episodic memory system and, in part, on executive control. Explicit recall of memories of these climatic patterns and use of these memory patterns for predicting and thus preparing for future climatic variation is consistent with explicit, controlled problem solving and mental time travel. However, the climatic variation itself occurs over a longer time scale than the time scale under which the short-term working memory system operates.

Regardless, it is not clear how climatic variation would result in conditions that favored the evolution of self-awareness or the coupling of self-awareness with the ability to engage in mental time travel. Moreover, the rapid increase in brain volume during human evolution is most consistent with an evolutionary arms race, but climatic variation does not fit the conditions normally associated with such an arms race; arms races occur among biological organisms with competing interests (Darwin, 1859; Dawkins & Krebs, 1979). Finally, as I described in chapter 3, other hominid and primate species that were subjected to the same climatic variation as our ancestors, including the ancestors of modern great apes, did not undergo the substantive changes in brain volume and EQ that characterize human evolution. I am not arguing that explicit processes, such as controlled problem solving and use of mental models, cannot be used to anticipate and thus behaviorally adapt to climatic variation. It is clear that humans are skilled in this regard. Rather, the preponderance of evidence is inconsistent with the hypothesis that climatic variation was incidentally (Vrba, 1995b) or directly (Potts, 1998) responsible for the increase in brain volume and EQ or the apparent changes in brain organization (see Brain Evolution section later in this chapter) during human evolution.

Ecological Conditions

Ecological selection pressures refer to the ability to extract resources (e.g., prey species) from the environment and, at the same time, avoid being extracted by other species (e.g., predator, parasite). As described in the Ecological Pressures section in chapter 3, there is compelling evidence that humans in traditional societies today are exceptionally skilled at extracting resources from the ecologies in which they are situated (Kaplan, Hill, Lancaster, & Hurtado, 2000). They then use these resources (e.g., meat obtained through hunting) to reduce mortality risks and, for men at least, to increase their mating and thereby reproductive options (Hill et al., 2001; Hill & Kaplan, 1988). I also reviewed evidence consistent with the position that there has been a gradual evolutionary improvement in the ability of our ancestors to exploit ecological resources. Broadly speaking, these improvements appear to track the pattern of change in brain volume and EQ during human evolution. Wallace (1911), Martin (1967, 1973), and others argued that the end result of these changes was that humans evolved into a superpredator. Alexander (1989) elaborated on this concept and proposed that evolution into a superpredator meant that humans, and perhaps *Homo erectus*, achieved ecological dominance. It follows that the achievement of ecological dominance would have been associated with the evolutionary elaboration of the folk biological and folk physical modules that support hunting, foraging, and tool-making competencies.

The issue here is whether there are features of human ecological activity that are consistent with the characteristics I outlined above. Although no studies have explicitly tested this hypothesis, the time scale for some aspects of hunting would seem to be consistent with both the shorter- and longer-term characteristics of the central executive and mental time travel. Hunting, of course, involves tracking or ambushing prey and dealing with corresponding prey evasion behaviors. It requires adapting to rapid changes in information patterns as prey attempt to avoid and evade capture. These are changes that I assume are represented in short-term and perhaps working memory, but these demands are not unique to humans. The act of hunting often requires the sustained attention that is an integral feature of executive control, but the ability to focus attention is also likely to be evident in most species that hunt.

Human hunting differs from that of other species in the use of sophisticated tools and in the extent to which hunting activities can be coordinated socially and planned in advance. Tool construction requires sustained attention and advanced planning. The latter is implicated in the construction and use of different tools for different purposes and different forms of weapon for different types of prey. This degree of tool specialization was particularly evident with the evolutionary emergence of modern humans and our most immediate ancestors (i.e., *H. heidelbergensis*), although more subtle improvements in tool construction were evident even before this time (J. D. Clark et al., 2003; Foley & Lahr, 1997). Whatever the level of sophistication, construction of hunting weapons in and of itself indicates advanced planning for the hunt. Planning a hunt likely involves executive control as related to the ability to mentally time travel, that is, to project oneself into the future and mentally simulate the planned hunting activity. It is unlikely that any other species plans hunts by means of mental time travel. Chimpanzee (*Pan troglodytes*) hunting, for instance, appears to be more opportunistic. Although it is socially organized, it appears to be largely triggered by the presence of a prey species (Goodall, 1986). Social activities are coordinated during the hunt by means of vocalizations and other social information, but chimpanzee hunts are probably not planned in advance, at least not on the same time scale that humans plan hunts. Foraging is also an important subsistence behavior but may be more dependent on the long-term episodic memory system than on executive control (Geary, 1998; Silverman & Eals, 1992).

In any event, hunting is by definition consistent with the potential for an evolutionary arms race, as it necessarily entails a predator–prey relationship (Dawkins & Krebs, 1979). A co-evolutionary arms race would, however, require that the predator and prey species remain constant across generations, and it is not known whether this constancy was a feature of hunting during hominid evolution. In traditional societies today, humans hunt a wide range of other species (Hill, 1982). If this same omnivorous pattern was the norm during human evolution, then it would weaken the argument for a co-evolutionary arms race.

A comparative analysis of the folk biological competencies that would support human ecological dominance is not easy to do, given the difficulty of assessing these folk competencies in nonhuman primates. Other primates, of course, have a wide range of neural, perceptual, and behavioral adaptations that allow them to discriminate plants and animals (e.g., Barton, Purvis, & Harvey, 1995), and some of these species, such as the chimpanzee, may have the ability to form more general categories of other species, such as those that serve as prey (Tomasello & Call, 1997). There is no evidence that chimpanzees, or any other species, can form the explicit, taxonomic organization of related species that is common for humans in traditional societies or that they have any competencies analogous to the human ability to understand the essence of other species (Atran, 1998; see the Folk Biology section of chap. 5).

The research literature on the folk physical competencies of primates is considerably more extensive than that associated with folk biological competencies. Tomasello and Call (1997) and Parker and McKinney (1999) reviewed much of this evidence for various species of ape and monkey, as did Povinelli (2000) for the chimpanzee. All of these species have visual, spatial, and navigational competencies that appear to be as good as and sometimes exceed that of humans. Some of these species appear to be able to form simple visuospatial representations of images and mentally manipulate (e.g., mentally rotate) these images. Thus, humans do not appear to stand out in the movement and simple representation areas described in the Folk Physics section of chapter 5. Comparative differences do, however, emerge for tool use and the ability to conceptually understand physical causality.

It is well known that chimpanzees use a variety of tools in wild settings (Goodall, 1986) and that all great apes, as well as gibbons (lesser apes; *Hylobates*) and some species of monkey (e.g., brown capuchin, *Cebus apella*), can learn to use a variety of different types of simple tools in captive settings (Tomasello & Call, 1997). In a series of more than two dozen experiments, Povinelli (2000) demonstrated that although chimpanzees are effective users of tools, they do not have a clue when it comes to understanding causal relations between tools and the effect of tool use on the environment. They readily learn how to use tools and appear to recall experiences with a particular tool and a particular outcome and may use this experience to guide tool use in highly similar situations. They do not, however, approach tool use with an abstract understanding of more general relations between, as examples, the shape or pliability of a tool and the shape of the container from which a piece of food must be retrieved. Nor do chimpanzees appear to use mental models based on physical principles (e.g., an intuitive understanding of gravity) to simulate how a tool might be used in a novel way to solve a novel problem; they do solve novel problems, but not in this way (see Povinelli, 2000).

The point is that aspects of the folk biological and folk physical competencies of humans appear to be qualitatively different than those of great apes and other primates. As I discuss in the Academic Learning section of chapter 9, this is not to say that untutored humans have a sophisticated, Newtonian understanding of physics or a Darwinian understanding of biological evolution; they do not (J. Clement, 1982; Geary, 2002a; McCloskey, 1983). Rather, humans have an implicit and often explicit understanding of relations within the physical and biological worlds and have naïve but effective conceptual models of how many phenomena in the physical or biological worlds operate. These models enable humans to exploit ecologies in ways consistent with Alexander's (1989) proposal. Whether unique or not, human folk biological and folk physical knowledge is consistent with the proposal that hunting and related ecological activities (e.g., cooking) contributed to the evolution of brain and cognition in humans (Hill, 1982; Hill et al., 2001; Kaplan et al., 2000).

Some of the other features described in the Selection Characteristics section earlier in this chapter do not appear to fit the ecological model, in particular self-awareness and the uncertainty regarding whether human hunting fits the pattern needed for a co-evolutionary arms race. Thus, in keeping with my conclusion in chapter 3 (Ecological Pressures section) and that of other scientists (e.g., Aiello & Wheeler, 1995), the evolution of the ability to achieve ecological control is an important piece of the human evolutionary puzzle: Ecological activity was likely to have been related to evolutionary change in brain size and EQ and to change in more specialized cognitive and brain systems that support some folk competencies. However, it does not appear that the activities associated with ecological control are sufficient for explaining all of the features of executive control and especially self-awareness.

Social Conditions

As Alexander (1989) proposed and I elaborated in chapter 3 (Social Pressures section), the achievement of ecological dominance shifts selection pressures to social competition for control of the best ecologies or for control of diminishing resources within ecologies. My goal in this section is to consider whether social competition is also consistent with the features I outlined in the Selection Characteristics section. First, the temporal dynamics of one-on-one and group-level social discourse and competition are consistent with the time scale under which the working memory system operates. In fact, one of the two primary slave systems, the phonological buffer and articulatory loop, is language based (Baddeley & Hitch, 1974), and Baddeley, Gathercole, and Papagno (1998) proposed that the primary, evolved function of this system is language acquisition. It is not likely that the visuospatial sketch pad is as intimately related to social discourse, although many aspects of social dynamics are visual, as in recognizing faces, interpreting body language, and monitoring the rapid temporal changes in these information patterns during social interactions. Preuss, Qi, and Kaas (1999) cautiously suggested that some of the apparently unique architectural features of the human brain systems that support visual processes may be adapted for lip reading and thus aid in language comprehension. Either way, many aspects of group-level competition and dynamics also involve rapid and often unpredictable changes in information patterns and thus often require sustained attention and other features of executive control.

As I described earlier in this chapter (Explicit Processes section), neuropsychological studies suggest that self-awareness, awareness of oneself as being continuous through time, and mental time travel are intimately linked on a neurological and cognitive level (Levine, 1999; Tulving, 1985, 2002). To again quote Levine, this autonoetic awareness involves the ability to "cast oneself as a player in scenarios emerging from various choices available at any given moment. ... This capacity facilitates the self-regulation of behavior necessary for the achievement of personally-relevant goals" (p. 200). The scenarios in which humans very often cast themselves are social, as emphasized by scientists from many different disciplines (Barton, 1996, 1999; Brothers & Ring, 1992; Cosmides, 1989; Dunbar, 1993, 1998; Geary & Flinn, 2001; Humphrey, 1976; Pinker & Bloom, 1990; Premack & Woodruff, 1978). Awareness of the self and a sense of that self as part of a continuum of past, present, and future experiences would seem to be most advantageous in contexts in which other actors can use this same knowledge as an aspect of their social strategies. In this sense, self-awareness is the ability to understand those features of the self that others might cue in on and use in their social interactions and strategies that involve one (Dennett, 1987). The relation to mental time travel is elaborated in the Mental Models and the Motivation to Control section. For now, my point is that of the three forms of proposed selection pressure, autonoetic awareness is most consistent with social pressures.

Intense social competition is also in keeping with the operation of a co-evolutionary arms race but within, rather than between, species. In fact, the achievement of ecological dominance and the resulting overexploitation and subsequent competition for control of life-supporting ecologies should accelerate any such arms race. Ecological dominance enables humans to reduce mortality risks better than other species (Hill et al., 2001) and thus experience more rapid population expansions. As Malthus (1798) described, rapid population expansions result in rapid consumption of the ecology's resources and thus the potential for sharp population crashes. The associated cycles were described in chapter 6 (Knowledge-Rich Domains section and Table 6.2) and create the potential for rapid evolutionary change in the traits that facilitate competition for ecological resources. The potential for rapid change increases because the sharp population crashes are, in effect, expressed as very high mortality among individuals who are unsuccessful in competing for resource control. The population on which the next expansion is based is thus more competitive than the previous population, but with the next crash those who are relatively less competitive suffer exaggerated mortality rates, and so it continues (Boone & Kessler, 1999; Geary, 2000). This type of social and population dynamic is consistent with the rapid changes in brain volume and EQ and with some of the potential changes in brain organization described in later sections.

Comparative analyses also provide strong support for a within-species arms race, because such an arms race would result in the evolution of sociocognitive competencies that are unique to humans. All primates, and great apes in particular, are capable of engaging in an array of complex social activities, including social deception and manipulation, cooperation, and coordinated group-level conflict, among others (Byrne, 1995; de Waal, 1982, 2000; Goodall, 1986; Tomasello & Call, 1997). At the same time, there are several social-cognitive modules associated with the folk psychological systems described in chapter 5 that appear to be uniquely human, including awareness of the self as a social being, language, and theory of mind (Adolphs, 2003; Gallagher & Frith, 2003; Tomasello & Call, 1997). I predict that humans will also have a comparatively unique understanding of their relationships with other people and will differ from other species in terms of some of the aspects of the group-level modules described in chapter 5. In particular, humans have the unique ability to form coalitions around abstract ideologies, such as nationality. I describe other relevant and potentially unique characteristics of human folk psychology in the Social Cognition and Folk Psychology section later in this chapter.

Brain Evolution

In this section, I return to the basic questions broached by Darwin (1871) and Huxley (1863) and mentioned briefly in the introductory section of chapter 5. These concern whether the human brain and mind are essentially continuous with those of other primates—the position of Darwin and Huxley—or whether there have been more qualitative changes in brain organization and functions of mind during human evolution. The issues are complicated and are the focus of historical (e.g., Brodmann, 1909; Holloway, 1968; Jerison, 1973) and more recent comparative analyses and debates (Holloway, 2002; Rilling & Insel, 1999; Semendeferi, Armstrong, Schleicher, Zilles, & van Hoesen, 1998, 2001; Semendeferi & Damasio, 2000; Semendeferi, Damasio, Frank, & van Hoesen, 1997; Semendeferi, Lu, Schenker, & Damasio, 2002; Tobias, 1987). Definitive answers cannot be drawn at this time (Preuss, 2000a, 2000b, 2001), but the possibilities have been narrowed since Darwin's and Huxley's time. In the following sections, I provide overviews of research and debate regarding evolutionary expansion and reorganization, respectively, of the human prefrontal cortex.

Expansion of Prefrontal Cortex

In a series of brain imaging studies of humans, great apes, and several other primate species, Semendeferi and her colleagues challenged the view that the frontal cortex has disproportionately expanded (e.g., Deacon, 1990, 1997) during human evolution (Semendeferi, 2001; Semendeferi & Damasio, 2000; Semendeferi et al., 1997; Semendeferi et al., 2002; see also Holloway, 2002). As with other studies (see Brain Evolution section of chap. 3), they found the absolute size of human frontal cortex to be larger than that of great apes and primates, but not larger than would be expected given the overall size of the entire neocortex. The pattern might be interpreted in terms of a simple allometric expansion of the entire neocortex, as described in chapter 4 (Allometry and Size of the Neocortex section). Semendeferi and colleagues' analyses largely focused on the entire frontal cortex, which includes the prefrontal (e.g., areas 46 and 9 in Figure 7.3) and motor areas (e.g., areas 4 and 6). In one analysis, they did separate motor from prefrontal areas and found that as a percentage of neocortical volume, the volume of the human prefrontal cortex was not larger than that of great apes (Semendeferi et al., 2002). The range for humans was, however, clearly toward the high end; for humans, 29% to 33% of the neocortex was occupied by the prefrontal regions, and the range for great apes was 26% to 30%. The differences were not statistically significant but are consistent with evidence that motor areas of the frontal cortex are comparatively—controlling for overall brain size—smaller in humans than in chimpanzees, suggesting that the human prefrontal cortex is comparatively larger (Preuss, 2000b).

Moreover, the human prefrontal cortex has more neural connections with subcortical regions than that of great apes (Preuss, 2004) and has greater gyrification than that of great apes. With respect to the latter, there are more folds and thus more surface area in this but not most other regions of the neocortex (Rilling & Insel, 1999; Zilles, Armstrong, Moser, Schleicher, & Stephan, 1989; Zilles, Armstrong, Schleicher, & Kretschmann, 1988). The folding allows for faster communication across adjacent regions that process similar forms of information, and the expanded surface area creates the potential for greater modularity and differentiation of functions within more specific areas of the prefrontal cortex (Deacon, 1990).

Whether the prefrontal cortex has differentially expanded, the absolute size of this area in and of itself may be important. Gibson, Rumbaugh, and Beran (2001) described a series of studies in which primates were rewarded for making one of two potential responses, such as pressing one lever and ignoring a second lever, to get a bit of food. Once the basic rule, or heuristic, was learned, the rule changed such that pressing the second lever was rewarded and pressing the first lever was not. Reward was now dependent on the ability to inhibit a well-learned response. As described in the Explicit Processes section earlier in this chapter, the ability to inhibit evolved as well as learned heuristics is a cognitive competency that is dependent on the prefrontal cortex. Across a variety of primate species, including human children and great apes, performance on this type of task is related to absolute brain size but not to EQ per se.

The evolutionary increase in absolute size of the human prefrontal cortex appears to have resulted in an increase in the interconnections among these regions and other regions of the brain (Hofman, 2001; Holloway, 1968). As absolute volume increases, the degree of interconnections among neurons (i.e., axons, white matter) increases more rapidly than do increases in the number of neurons (i.e., cell bodies, grey matter). Despite a threefold difference in volume, Holloway estimated that the number of neurons in the human neocortex is only about 25% higher than that of the chimpanzee neocortex. The human neocortex is thus less densely packed per volume with neurons but much more highly interconnected. The general relation between size and extent to which neurons are interconnected fits well with the finding that the human prefrontal cortex is richly interconnected (E. K. Miller & Cohen, 2001; J. N. Wood & Grafman, 2003) and suggests that humans may have an enhanced ability to integrate information across modalities in comparison to other primates (Hofman, 2001; Holloway, 1968).

Reorganization of the Prefrontal Cortex and Anterior Cingulate Cortex

An increase in absolute brain size also results in greater modularity within cortical regions and thus the potential for the evolution of species-specific specializations in these regions (Deacon, 1990; Preuss, 2000b, 2001). Greater modularity could result in the emergence of comparatively novel brain systems or (or perhaps and) greater differentiation within existing systems. Indeed, comparisons of human brain anatomy to that of great apes and other primates suggest evolution of regional specializations in areas of the human visual cortex (Holloway, 1996; Preuss et al., 1999), in areas of the temporal cortex that support some aspects of the language processing (Gannon, Kheck, & Hof, 2001; Rilling & Insel, 1999), and in areas of the posterior cortex that are associated with integrating information across sensory modalities (Holloway & de la Coste-Lareymondie, 1982), among other brain regions (Rilling & Insel, 1998). It is almost certain that the human prefrontal cortex and the anterior cingulate cortex have undergone substantive reorganizations during human evolution as well as changes in absolute size (Preuss & Kaas, 1999).

The anterior cingulate cortex (area 24 in Figure 7.3) is larger in primates than in other mammals (Vogt, 1987), and there is a form of neuron that is found only in the anterior cingulate cortex of great apes and humans (Nimchinsky et al., 1999). Although these neurons are common in gorillas (*Gorilla gorilla*) and chimpanzees, they are clustered into groups of three or more cells only in bonobos (*Pan paniscus*) and humans. These cells are slightly more abundant in humans than in bonobos, and the cell bodies range from almost 2½ times to more than 3½ times the volume of the cell bodies found in great apes. These cells appear to be involved in connecting the anterior cingulate cortex with the prefrontal cortex and other brain regions.

Koechlin et al. (2003) provided evidence for functional and architectural subdivisions, that is, modularization, within the dorsolateral prefrontal cortex for controlled processing of episodic, contextualized, and sensorimotor information. K. E. Stephan et al. (2003) found that the left and right dorsolateral regions and the left and right anterior cingulate cortex are used to control the processing of language and visuospatial information, respectively. Holloway and de la Coste-Lareymondie (1982; Holloway, 1996) found evidence that in *H. erectus* and modern humans, the left occipital area is smaller than the corresponding right occipital area, and the right frontal cortex is larger than the corresponding left frontal cortex. Zilles and his colleagues (1996) confirmed this finding for human right-handers and found no such asymmetry in chimpanzees. In particular, the dorsolateral prefrontal cortex (i.e., area 46) and the frontal pole (i.e., area 10) are larger in the right than the left hemisphere. Semendeferi et al. (2001) found that the human frontal pole is about twice as large as expected on the basis of overall size of the human brain. The size of the frontal pole is especially large in the right hemisphere and is estimated to be composed of nearly three times as many neurons as the corresponding area in chimpanzees, bonobos, and other great apes. Across species, there are both similarities and differences in the microarchitecture of this area. Humans differ from great apes in ways that suggest more neuronal interconnections within the frontal pole and with the prefrontal cortex.

However, not all areas of the prefrontal cortex are disproportionately larger in humans. In another anatomical comparison of the human brain and the brain of apes, Semendeferi et al. (1998) found that for humans, area 13, which appears to be a subdivision of Brodmann's (1909) area 11 (see Figure 7.3), is about half the size expected on the basis of overall brain size. They speculated that area 13 is comparatively small because adjacent areas, specifically other regions of area 11 and regions of area 47, may be composed of a large number of specialized subdivisions, each of which would process specific but related forms of information.

Summary and Integration

The EQ of the prefrontal cortex does not appear to be as extreme as once thought, but there is evidence for a modest (<10%) expansion in comparison to the size of the rest of the neocortex (Holloway, 2002). More important, however, are changes in absolute size of the prefrontal cortex and reorganizations of specific regions of the prefrontal cortex and other brain regions (Hofman, 2001; Holloway, 1968; Semendeferi et al., 2001). There is evidence for expansion and evolutionary change in the organization of the anterior cingulate cortex (Nimchinsky et al., 1999), and there is evidence for an evolutionary expansion of the dorsolateral prefrontal cortex, in particular area 46 in the right hemisphere (Holloway & de la Coste-Lareymondie, 1982; Zilles et al., 1996), and modularized subdivisions of the left and right dorsolateral prefrontal cortex (Koechlin et al., 2003). In combination, the anterior cingulate cortex and dorsolateral prefrontal cortex are important for maintaining attentional focus and control and for stopping task-irrelevant information from entering conscious awareness (Dehaene & Naccache, 2001; Kane & Engle, 2002). These regions are also essential for controlled problem solving (Duncan, 2001; Shallice, 2002; E. E. Smith & Jonides, 1999) and for generating internal goal-related representations (e.g., mental models) of behavioral plans for acting on the environment or for coping with novel or conflicting information (Curtis & D' Esposito, 2003; Kerns et al., 2004).

The disproportionate expansion of the right prefrontal cortex in general, at least in right-handed individuals, and the frontal pole in particular, as well as the potential reorganization of area 11, are of great theoretical importance, although other regions of the prefrontal cortex may be of greater importance (Gallagher & Frith, 2003). In any event, these areas appear to be involved in self-awareness, social problem solving, the ability to recall personal experiences, and the ability to mentally to project oneself into the future (Levine, 1999; Tulving, 1985, 2002). The anterior cingulate cortex is also involved in various forms of social cognition and in fact appears to be involved in the integration of neural activity in regions of the prefrontal cortex with neural activity in brain regions, such as the amygdala, that respond to emotion-laden and social information (Nimchinsky et al., 1999; Taketoshi & Nishijo, 2000; Yamasaki, LaBar, & McCarthy, 2002).

The picture that is beginning to emerge from these studies and the research described in the Cognitive and Brain Systems section at the beginning of this chapter is multifaceted. The increase in overall brain size during human evolution almost certainly resulted in an enhanced ability to integrate information within and across modalities, including enhanced executive control. The latter would be associated with gradual evolutionary expansion and potential reorganization of the dorsolateral areas of the left and right prefrontal cortices and the anterior cingulate cortex. The result would be accompanying improvements in the ability to inhibit evolved heuristic-based responses and instead internally represent and mentally manipulate ecological and social information explicitly and consciously in working memory. The absolute and potential EQ-based enlargements of the right prefrontal cortex and the frontal pole, as well as the potential reorganization of area 11 and the anterior cingulate cortex, are all consistent with important and substantive evolutionary changes in a host of social competencies, including self-awareness, social problem solving, the ability to cope with social novelty, and the ability to project oneself through time. These changes are consistent with discussion in the Selection Pressures section of this chapter and are integrated with the motivation to control in the next section.

Mental Models and the Motivation to Control

I proposed in chapter 3 that a single concept—the motivation to control—can be used to understand the evolution and proximate functioning of all species, from the level of the brain to complex social behavior. I am not saying that individuals of all species have a conscious and explicit goal to control other individuals and resources in their environment: They do not. I am proposing that natural and sexual selection will operate such that behavioral biases will evolve that focus on securing the types of social and ecological resources that have tended to covary with survival or reproductive outcomes during the species' evolutionary history. These biases will result from the activity of an array of brain, cognitive, and affective mechanisms that process the corresponding information (e.g., movement patterns of prey species) and guide the behavioral activities toward these features of the social and ecological world. As described in the Bounded Rationality and Heuristics section of chapter 6, most of these processes and behavioral activities occur automatically and implicitly.

Conscious-Psychological Evolution

How is the struggle for control related to the evolution of executive functions, explicit and conscious awareness of the self, mental time travel, and the ability to engage in controlled problem solving, as well as the evolution of supporting brain systems? The theme that ties all of these together with the proposals of many other scientists (Baddeley, 2002; Dehaene & Naccache, 2001; Dennett, 1987; Humphrey, 1976; Picton, Alain, & McIntosh, 2002; Strathman, Gleicher, Boninger, & Edwards, 1994) emerges from a fusion of Tulving's (2002) autonoetic awareness and Johnson-Laird's (1983) mental models—specifically, an *autonoetic mental model* whereby the individual creates a self-centered mental simulation of the "perfect world." A perfect world is one in which the individual is able to organize and control social (e.g., mating dynamics), biological (e.g., access to food), and physical (e.g., shelter) resources in ways that would have enhanced the survival or reproductive options of the individual and kin during human evolution. The simulation of this perfect world is, in effect, the conscious-psychological component of the middle section of Figure 6.1.

The simulation will be needed for conditions that cannot be addressed by means of a heuristic-based response. These are conditions in which the dynamics of the situation are not entirely predictable on the basis of the individual's past experiences or human evolutionary history. As I proposed in chapter 6 (e.g., Figure 6.2), these conditions require an explicit and conscious representation of the situation and may require some degree of controlled problem solving. My proposal and predictions regarding the cognitive and brain features of the conscious-psychological system that supports these explicit representations and the ability to engage in controlled problem solving are outlined in the first and second sections of Table 7.1.

The simulation of a perfect world requires the ability to decouple cognitive systems from engagement with the actual world (Cosmides & Tooby, 2000) and then to use these systems to either recreate a previous episode or create a more abstracted and decontextualized representation of social dynamics or other aspects of the world. Following Johnson-Laird (1983) and others (e.g., Deacon, 1997; Kosslyn & Thompson, 2000), the representations are typically language based or visuospatial, or some combination, and are an integral aspect of the explicit system described by J. S. B. T. Evans (2002), Stanovich (1999), and others (J. R. Anderson,

TABLE 7.1

Predicted Features of Conscious-Psychological Control Mechanisms

Mechanism	Predicted and defining features

Cognition	1. The most fundamental feature is the autonoetic mental model (Johnson-Laird, 1983; Tulving, 2002), that is, the ability to generate a self-centered mental simulation that recreates previous personal experiences or abstract representations of features that are common across experiences (e.g., Damasio, 1989; Dehaene & Naccache, 2001; Dennett, 1987; Humphrey, 1976).
	
	2. The simulations or fantasies are defined by a fundamental motive to organize the social, biological, and physical worlds in ways that are optimal for the individual and his or her kin (Geary, 1998). These are perfect worlds in which the individual is able to control other people, events, and access to material resources and to do so in ways that would have enhanced survival or reproductive outcomes during human evolution.
	
	3. Consciousness
	
	    a. emerges from an attention-driven amplification of the brain systems that are processing current social or ecological information patterns (Dehaene & Naccache, 2001; Posner, 1994).
	
	    b. for humans often involves awareness of the self as a part of the social or ecological dynamic (Tulving, 2002) and presumably emerges when the activity of the supporting brain systems is synchronized with the activity of the systems that are processing social or ecological information. The result is an explicit, conscious awareness of the self as a being that is situated in a social dynamic, relationship, or in some ecological circumstance.
	
	4. Self-awareness is predicted to provide an adaptive advantage for those traits, such as personality or physical characteristics, that influence social or ecological dynamics or that might be the foci of the social strategies of other people. Awareness would facilitate the ability to manipulate these cues (e.g., deception) and better use them to control these dynamics. It functions as a counterstrategy to other people's theory of mind abilities, among other advantages.
	
	5. The operation of the simulation is predicted to be dependent on both executive control (Baddeley, 1986; Moscovitch, 2000) and the ability to mentally time travel (Tulving, 2002). When fused with self-awareness, mental time travel enables the individual to recreate a previous episode or to project himself or herself into a future episode.
	
	6. Problem solving, as traditionally studied by cognitive psychologists (e.g., Greeno & Simon, 1988; Newell & Simon, 1972), describes processes that are engaged in to simulate strategies that will close the gap between the fantasized perfect world and the individual's current situation. Problem-solving strategies are predicted to be influenced by self-awareness and awareness of those traits that affect social or ecological dynamics. Reasoning is the related ability to draw inferences about the likely outcome of a simulated strategy or counterstrategy.

(continues)

TABLE 7.1   *(Continued)*

Mechanism	Predicted and defining features
Cognition *(continued)*	7. Controlled attention and working memory are necessary to maintain the simulation in an active and thus changeable state. The active and changeable states correspond to the problem space and the legal operations (e.g., social rules) that change the problem space, as described in the Controlled Problem Solving section of chapter 6.
	8. Feelings are an integral part of these conscious-psychological processes (Damasio, 2003) and provide adaptive feedback about the potential effectiveness of the simulated social or ecological strategies. Most basically, imagined success is reinforced with positive feelings, and failure or attempts by others to control one's behavior are accompanied by negative feelings (Campos et al., 1989). Feelings, such as guilt when violating a reciprocal relationship, also constrain social strategies (Trivers, 1971); these influence the form of legal operators or rules that can be used in social problem solving.
Brain	1. In keeping with Tulving's (2002) proposal, evolutionary expansion and reorganization of the regions of the prefrontal cortex, such as the frontal pole, that are related to self-awareness and the ability to mental time travel are predicted.
	2. In keeping with R. W. Engle's (e.g., Kane & Engle, 2002) proposal, evolutionary expansion and reorganization of regions of the prefrontal cortex, such as the anterior cingulate cortex and dorsolateral area (e.g., area 46), that are required for executive control and sustained attention and thus controlled problem solving are predicted.
	3. Autonoetic mental models require the integration of the functioning of the cognitive and brain regions in 1 and 2 above and thus their co-evolution. The resulting prediction is that these regions will be highly interconnected, as they are (E. K. Miller & Cohen, 2001), and their coordinated functioning will be needed to function day to day, especially in social situations.
	4. Evolutionary expansion or reorganization of those brain regions associated with the modular folk knowledge needed for social competition (e.g., theory of mind) or ecological control (e.g., theory of the essence of other species and tool construction) is predicted.
Foci of control	1. Autonoetic mental models are predicted to be focused on the folk biological and folk physical modules needed to achieve ecological dominance, specifically those associated with hunting and foraging (e.g., a species' essence) and with tool construction and use.
	2. The primary foci of autonoetic mental models are predicted to be social relationships and dynamics. These are predicted to correspond to the three levels of folk psychological module associated with the self, one-on-one relationships, and group-level relationships.

1990; Dennett, 1987; Reber, 1993; Stanovich & West, 2000; see Table 6.1). The mental reconstitution of a past episode allows the individual to consciously and explicitly evaluate the dynamics of the episode (e.g., "What did he mean when he said . . . ?") and to plan and rehearse strategies for anticipated future episodes that involve the same person or theme. Mental simulations can also involve abstractions of common features or themes across episodes. Many fictional characters and their relationships, as in action or romance novels (Whissell, 1996), are abstractions that recreate personalities and social dynamics, albeit in an exaggerated form, that are common across social situations.

The creation of conscious-psychological simulations is likely to be driven by executive control (Baddeley, 1986; Moscovitch, 1994) and associated brain regions in the prefrontal cortex. Recent brain imaging studies suggest that areas 32 and 9 (Figure 7.3) of the prefrontal cortex are particularly active in tasks that require people to mentally simulate the behavior of other people or to simulate future social or other scenarios (Gallagher & Frith, 2003). These systems appear to reconstitute the activity of the brain regions that were engaged during personal experiences or to activate more abstracted representations of common features of these experiences (Damasio, 1989). The reconstitution would, for instance, involve retrieving episodic memories and then working with these memories as the episode is explicitly and consciously examined. When the simulations are fused with Tulving's (1985, 2002) autonoetic awareness and integrated with the functioning of associated brain regions, such as the right frontal pole (area 10) and other prefrontal regions (e.g., area 32), an evolutionarily unique brain, cognitive, and conscious-psychological system emerges. As I noted in a previous section, the system places the self-aware individual at the center of a simulated construction or reconstruction of the social or ecological world and, more importantly, allows the individual to control outcomes in this world (Geary, 1998). The use of such a simulation, perforce, requires the ability to mentally time travel, both backward in time to reconstruct an episode and forward in time to simulate behavioral strategies.

As described in Table 7.1 and proposed by Tulving (2002), awareness of the self as a social being and as an actor in worldly dynamics may make human consciousness unique. As described in the Cognitive and Brain Systems section earlier in this chapter, conscious explicit awareness of information, situations, or objects that do not involve the self appears to result from an attention-driven amplification of activity of the brain systems processing this information, with the amplification being driven by the dorsolateral prefrontal cortex and perhaps the anterior cingulate cortex (Dehaene & Naccache, 2001; E. K. Miller & Cohen, 2001). If the same mechanisms are involved in conscious awareness of the self, then all that is required is an attention-driven amplification of the areas of the right frontal cortex that seem to be involved in representations of the self. If these latter areas are simultaneously amplified with areas that are processing other forms of information or involved in retrieving episodic memories, then the result is a conscious-psychological system in which an awareness and understanding of the self is insinuated in the awareness and understanding of other people, things, or dynamics.

In keeping with Dennett's (1987) arguments, my prediction is that self-awareness will provide a particular advantage for those traits, such as personality or physical attributes, that influence social dynamics and that might be the foci of the social strategies of other people. Awareness of one's personality or any trait that other people might use to their advantage would facilitate the ability to manipulate these cues (e.g., deception) and better use them to control social dynamics. Others people's ability to read one's mind, that is, rely on their theory of mind competencies, then becomes the counterstrategy to one's use of deceptive manipulation. The implication is that there might have been a co-evolving relation between self-awareness and theory of mind. Self-awareness is in effect the counterstrategy to other people's ability to see through one's social deceptions and make inferences about underlying goals and motives.

Controlled attention, working memory, and other executive functions, such as the ability to work with memories, are necessary supporting components of these conscious-psychological simulations. The result is the ability to generate an explicit simulation and maintain it in an active and changeable state in Baddeley's (2000a) episodic buffer. Problem solving involves successive and goal-related changes in this state and is understandable in terms of the features described in the Controlled Problem Solving section of chapter 6, such as problem space, legal operators, and means–ends analysis. The legal operators are the laws, other social influences (e.g., gossip), and feelings (e.g., guilt) that constrain or promote the types of behaviors that are deemed acceptable in striving to achieve the goal. The combination represents the explicit, controlled problem-solving mechanisms used to generate and simulate strategies to reduce the distance between one's perfect world and current circumstances.

Simulated behavioral strategies are in effect problem-solving exercises focused on ways to gain access to and control of social relationships and dynamics and the forms of resource that enhance survival or reproductive options in the current ecology. Affective systems are necessarily an integral feature of these simulations and mesh well with Damasio's (2003) distinction between emotional and feeling components of affect. His theory is sophisticated and nuanced and beyond my ability to completely describe here. Basically, emotions and feelings represent the physical and social well-being of the individual as this relates to the achievement (positive affect) or not (negative affective) of goals that covaried with outcomes during human evolution. In keeping with this prediction, Eisenberger, Lieberman, and Williams (2003) demonstrated that explicit social exclusion—a negative experience for a species that evolved in a social milieu—is associated with increased activation of the anterior cingulate cortex and areas of the right prefrontal cortex (e.g., area 12, Figure 7.3) that are active when the individual is physically distressed. As briefly mentioned in chapter 6 (Heuristics section), emotions are observable and often occur automatically and implicitly, as with the automatic triggering of a fear-signaling facial expression under threatening conditions (Öhman, 2002). Feelings, in contrast, are explicit and conscious representations of emotional states and the well-being of the individual. If the psychological simulations are built from episodic memories or abstract representations of common features across episodes, then recreation of episodes or common social themes should include associated feelings (Damasio et al., 2000). Imagined success at achieving a social goal or acquiring riches should result in a feeling that is similar, though perhaps a bit muted, to the feeling that would result from actually succeeding in these endeavors (Damasio, 2003). As in navigating life in the actual world (e.g., Campos, Campos, & Barrett, 1989), feelings that result during simulated activities provide feedback as to the value of the goal and the potential outcomes of control-related behavioral strategies.

Finally, reasoning involves the processes used to make inferences about the likely outcomes of instituting one strategy or another (e.g., as related to tool use) or for generating potential social strategies or counterstrategies of competitors. As noted in the Reasoning section of chapter 6, this is not to say that most people use these explicit simulations and problem-solving processes to reason as logicians do; it is clear that most human beings do not typically reason in this way (J. S. B. T. Evans, 2002). In fact, strictly logical reasoning may not be possible in the context of social dynamics that include multiple players with a combination of cooperative and competing interests and in the absence of perfect knowledge of the future choices of each player (Colman, 2003). Rather, their inferences are based on folk knowledge (illustrated in the next section), memories of related experiences, analogy, and so forth (see Stanovich, 1999). Nonetheless, individuals who are high in general intelligence can use these simulations to represent social, biological, and physical phenomena abstractly and often do reason logically (J. S. B. T. Evans, 2002; Stanovich, 1999), as I illustrated in chapter 6 (Problem Solving section).

Foci of Conscious-Psychological Control

Behavioral strategies are focused on gaining access to and control of the social, biological, and physical resources that tended to covary with survival or reproductive outcomes during the species' evolutionary history.

For humans, these resources can, of course, be more abstract, as in dollars, but they afford the same fundamental advantages that were important during human evolution. The advantages include, among others, the ability to influence social relationships and dynamics, gain access to foods and other biological resources (e.g., medicine), and secure a safe and often opulent physical environment (e.g., an air-conditioned home or office) for one's family. Achievement of these outcomes is associated with better health and lower mortality risks (e.g., Adler et al., 1994).

However, if my proposal is correct, then the foci of conscious-psychological simulations should be largely restricted to social, biological, or physical conditions that covaried with evolutionary outcomes but that also tend to be variant within lifetimes. As described in the Selection Pressures section, I concluded that these more restricted conditions are likely to include the ecological demands associated with hunting and tool construction (tools are variable in that they can be used for multiple functions; Dennett, 1990) but most often to deal with social dynamics (see bottom section of Table 7.1). The simulations should involve activation of the brain, perceptual, and cognitive systems that compose the modules that support hunting (e.g., for understanding the essence of other species), tool use, and social dynamics (e.g., theory of mind). These modular systems were described throughout chapter 5 (see Figure 5.2) and, for social dynamics, include representations of the self, other people, one-on-one relationships with other people, and group-related identifications and activities.

SOCIAL COGNITION AND FOLK PSYCHOLOGY

If the taxonomy of social modules I proposed in chapter 5 captures the fundamentals of folk psychology, then social cognitions, as an integral part of folk psychology, should be focused on the self, relationships and inferences about the behavior and internal states of other people, and group-level processes. On the basis of my motivation-to-control model and the work of Heckhausen and Schulz (1995) and others (Rothbaum, Weisz, & Snyder, 1982), folk psychological mechanisms that facilitate control-related behaviors are also predicted to evolve. In the first section that follows, I outline evidence related to control-related cognitions, and in the second section I touch on the literature related to cognitions about the self and other people and group-level interactions. As with other domains covered in this book, the area of social cognition and related research in neuroscience is vast, and thus an exhaustive review is not possible, nor is it my goal (see Adolphs, 2003; Bodenhausen, Macrae, & Hugenberg, 2003; Cacioppo et al., 2002; Fiske & Taylor, 1991; Kunda, 1999). Rather, I hope to demonstrate that many of these phenomena are consistent with the social selection pressures described in this chapter and in chapter 3. Before beginning this discussion, I note that a similar analysis can be done in the areas of folk biology (Caramazza & Shelton, 1998; Medin & Atran, 1999a) and folk physics (Povinelli, 2000), but less is known in these areas than in the area of social and folk psychology. The differences across these domains are a natural consequence of intense social selection pressures and the corresponding focus on other people and associated species-centric research agendas. In any case, my goal is to illustrate how social cognitions are an evolved form of folk knowledge.

Control-Related Conscious-Psychological Mechanisms

As I described in the Motivation to Control section of chapter 3, there is a consistent and linear relation—the more the better—between social influence, resource control, and the individual's and his or her family's health and psychological well-being (Adler et al., 1994). The relation is true even in resource-rich Western societies and at the higher end of the income continuum in these societies. In a review of the relations among wealth, mortality risks, and psychological factors (e.g., depression), Gallo and Matthews (2003) defined SES as "an aggregate concept defined according to one's level of resources or prestige in relation to others" (p. 11). This definition has a clear and substantive social component: The level of actual resources is important, but in addition, one's position in the social hierarchy influences and is influenced by physical health, life span, and psychological functioning (e.g., self-esteem), as with other primates (Sapolsky, 1993). Gallo and Matthews also proposed that the strength of the relation between SES and physical health is moderated by a sense of personal control of the circumstances of day-to-day living. Lachman and Weaver (1998) found that reported health varied with SES, but individuals in "the lowest income group with a high sense of control showed levels of health and well-being comparable with the higher income groups" (p. 763). Control over daily events is correlated with a number of physiological and health-related outcomes and is related to an extended life span in elderly people (Rodin, 1986).

But are there conscious-psychological mechanisms (e.g., attributing success to personal qualities) consistent with an evolved motivation to control? Although the question has not been addressed from an evolutionary perspective, studies conducted throughout much of the 20th century suggest that the answer is yes (Fiske & Taylor, 1991). The concepts of self-efficacy and personal control as related to the regulation of goal-related behavior capture the gist of these research endeavors (Bandura, 1986; Langer, 1975; Rothbaum et al., 1982). "Self-efficacy beliefs are conceptualized as highly specific control-related beliefs which concern one's ability to perform a particular outcome. The stronger one's perceived self-efficacy, the more one will exert effort and persist in a task" (Fiske & Taylor, 1991, p. 198). The beliefs involve, among other things, a conscious assessment of one's competencies vis-à-vis the desired outcome and vis-à-vis the perceived competencies of others who are attempting to achieve the same outcome, that is, potential competitors (Langer, 1975).

As described by Rothbaum et al. (1982) and Heckhausen and Schulz (1995; Schultz & Heckhausen, 1996), there are a myriad of conscious-psychological and implicit mechanisms that maintain self-efficacy and goal-directed behavior in the face of inevitable failures. The former mechanisms include self-serving attributions that allow people to interpret personal failure in ways that maintain their sense of self-efficacy. Such interpretations might involve attributing failure to external causes ("It wasn't my fault") or maintaining an illusion of control by interpreting the outcome as predictable ("I knew that this would happen"). These same mechanisms are engaged with rituals, belief in psychic powers, and so on and serve the function of attempting to predict and control potentially significant life events (e.g., finding a mate, the health of kin) and to mollify the fear and anxiety associated with not having complete control over these events. The importance of these conscious-psychological processes becomes clear when they fail; the individual is at risk for depression and behavioral inhibition—that is, a cessation of attempts to influence social dynamics and achieve control of desired resources (Seligman, 1991; Shapiro, Schwartz, & Astin, 1996).

Control-related conscious-psychological mechanisms can be integrated with other mechanisms discussed in this book. First, the focus of one's attempts to achieve control of personally important outcomes varies with physical, social, and cognitive competencies (Taylor & Brown, 1988; S. C. Thompson, Armstrong, & Thomas, 1998), which meshes nicely with Simon's (1955, 1956) concepts of satisficing and aspiration level (Bounded Rationality and Heuristics section of chap. 6). Decline in physical competencies associated with a terminal illness, as one example, is associated with changes in the focus of control-related behaviors and cognitions. What was once routine becomes a significant goal to aspire to and attempt to achieve. A sense of self-efficacy can be achieved with success in engaging in these routine activities (e.g., driving to the store). In other words, a good-enough outcome, aspiration levels, and control-related attributions change with one's successes and failures and with changes in one's physical, cognitive, or social condition (Schulz & Heckhausen, 1996; Taylor & Brown, 1988).

Second, control-related attributions might be integrated with models of explicit, controlled problem solving and with activity of the anterior cingulate cortex and other brain regions. These attributions appear to be more or less automatically engaged in situations in which heuristic-based behaviors do not lead to the desired outcome, and thus these situations elicit explicit, controlled processing of features of the self, the context, and the outcome. The engagement of explicit processes may occur because of the discrepancy between one's desired outcome and the actual outcome, which may result in the automatic activation of the anterior cingulate cortex (Botvinick et al., 2001) and automatic attentional shifts to representations of the self, the goal, and features of the situation that are thwarting achievement of the goal. Indeed, Posner and Rothbart (1998) reviewed neuroimaging and developmental evidence consistent with the view that the anterior cingulate cortex, the amygdala, and areas of the prefrontal cortex become active during physically, socially, or affectively distressing situations. The result is an automatic attentional shift to the distressing features of the situation, presumably as related to the self. The resulting representations would be active in working memory and subject to top-down evaluation and manipulation, as related to generation of control-related attributions as well as to detecting the source of the distress and simulating alternative routes to the goal. The attributions are constructed as one attempts to interpret the reason for the failure of heuristic-based behavior, or failure to meet expectations in the situations ("The test did not assess what I know").

Social Cognition

As I discussed in several earlier sections, self-awareness and the ability to self-regulate in social contexts, judge risks, and respond with affect to social conditions, among other real-world competencies, are supported by the frontal pole (area 10 in Figure 7.3) and the right ventromedial areas (e.g., area 11) of the prefrontal cortex, as well as other brain regions (Bechara et al., 1997; Damasio, 2003; Eisenberger et al., 2003; Moscovitch & Winocur, 2002; Stuss & Levine, 2002; Tulving, 2002). However, the preceding sections did not provide any details with respect to the implicit and explicit cognitions that relate to the self and others and to group-level dynamics. The three respective sections fill in some of these gaps (for reviews, see Fiske & Taylor, 1991; Kunda, 1999). For ease of presentation, I treat cognitions in these areas as separate, but at a functional real-world level they are often simultaneously activated, either implicitly or explicitly (Ashmore, Deaux, & McLaughlin-Volpe, 2004). For instance, self-evaluations and behavioral engagement with the environment may be influenced by contextual cues that trigger representations of group identification and membership, such as sex or ethnicity (Steele, 1997). In these and many other situations, aspects of the self schema, which include group identifications, are activated along with group-level categorical information.

As described in the Bounded Rationality and Heuristics section of chapter 6, selection pressures that tend to be similar across generations should result in attentional, information processing, and decision-making biases that operate automatically and implicitly (Gigerenzer & Selten, 2001a; Simon, 1956). At the same time, mechanisms that support explicit, controlled processing of social cognitions are predicted to have evolved as a consequence of intense social selection pressures and the corresponding advantages achieved by varying social behavior so that this behavior is not perfectly predictable. The reality of social cognition is a mix of implicit and explicit processes that researchers are only beginning to understand (e.g., Bechara et al., 1997; Lieberman, Ochsner, Gilbert, & Schacter, 2003), and thus aspects of the discussions that follow are necessarily speculative.

Self

One focus of social psychological research is on people's self schema (Fiske & Taylor, 1991; Kunda, 1999; Markus, 1977). The *self schema* is a long-term memory network of information that links together knowledge and beliefs about the self, including positive (accentuated) and negative (discounted) traits (e.g., friendliness), episodic memories, self-efficacy in various domains, and so forth. Most of the time, this knowledge is implicit. Although the evidence is not entirely consistent, self schemas appear to regulate goal-related behaviors, specifically where one focuses behavioral effort and whether one will persist in the face of failure (Sheeran & Orbell, 2000). Social regulation results from a combination of implicit and explicit processes that influence social comparisons, self-esteem, valuation of different forms of ability and interests, and the formation of social relationships (Drigotas, 2002). For instance, when evaluating the competencies of others, people focus on attributes that are central features of their self schema and prefer relationships with others who provide feedback consistent with the self schema. Athletes implicitly compare and contrast themselves to others on dimensions that involve physical competencies, whereas academics focus more on intellectual competencies (Fiske & Taylor, 1991). People value competencies in which they excel and discount competencies for which they are at a competitive disadvantage (Taylor, 1982).

Conditions that involve the self schema and cannot be addressed by means of heuristics or that violate beliefs about the self should, in theory, result in a conscious awareness of the corresponding aspects of the self. Awareness of these features of the self schema appears to contribute to the regulatory processes that allow people to examine competencies, behaviors, social attitudes, and the current situation as these relate to information that is inconsistent with the self schema or is not readily addressable with heuristic-based responses (Fiske & Taylor, 1991; Kunda, 1999). These are, by definition, social problems that must be solved, and self-awareness in these situations should be advantageous. An explicit and conscious representation of relevant information about the self in working memory is amenable to controlled problem solving and the ability to reason and make attributions about the social situation as it relates to features of the self schema. As I suggested earlier in this chapter (Mental Models and the Motivation to Control section), controlled problem solving involves an autonoetic mental model that centers around those features of the self schema that have been activated by the current situation.

Another potentially important feature of the self schema is the ideal self. Although a comparison of the current self with an imagined ideal self can result in negative affect if one falls short (Higgins, 1987), the combination provides a self-referenced problem space. The problem space, as defined in chapter 6 (Controlled Problem Solving section), provides a mechanism whereby individuals can evaluate current competencies, traits, and social strategies as these relate to achieving social and other goals. A means–ends analysis, for instance, would occur within this problem space and allow the individual to estimate which of his or her competencies or social strategies must be modified to reduce the distance between the current situation and the desired outcome. Anyone who has aspired to becoming a research scientist, chief executive officer, or any other socially valued position that requires long-term effort has probably engaged in such a process; for an example, see Desmond's (1997) biography of Thomas Huxley.

In short, the schema directs attention to features of the self that are socially or otherwise important and that relate to social comparisons, attributions regarding the self, and conditions that are not readily achieved by means of heuristics. My proposal is that the ability to become consciously aware of and mentally problem solve using self information represents social cognitions that are part and parcel of an evolved folk psychology that resulted from the social selection pressures emphasized by many other scientists (Alexander, 1989; Humphrey, 1976).

Others

People form person schemas of familiar people and people for whom future social relationships are expected (Fiske & Taylor, 1991; Kunda, 1999). The *person schema* is a long-term memory network that includes representations of the other person's physical attributes (e.g., age, race, sex), memories of specific behavioral episodes, and more abstract trait information; trait information often varies across two continuums, sociability (warm to emotionally distant) and competence (Schneider, 1973). It seems likely that the person schema also includes the types of information I described in chapter 5 (Folk Psychology: Individual section) and described by many others, such as theory of mind (Adolphs, 1999; Frith & Frith, 1999; Leslie, 1987). Theory of mind would include memories and trait information about how the person typically makes inferences (e.g., tends to attribute hostile intentions to others, called the *hostile attribution bias*) and responds to social cues, their social and other goals, and so forth. The person schema is also likely to include affective dimensions, including memory representations that elicit a sense of familiarity and specific feelings based on episodic memories (Brothers, 1990; Damasio, 2003).

During social interactions, the knowledge represented in the person schema is implicit—that is, there is no conscious representation of this information (e.g., where the person is on the sociability trait), but it can nonetheless influence the dynamics of the interaction (Fiske & Taylor, 1991). However, when the person's behavior is inconsistent with the schema, then attention is drawn to the inconsistency, and the behavior is explicitly and consciously represented in working memory. The explicit representation allows inferences to be drawn about the likely source of the inconsistency and facilitates incorporation of the behavior into the person schema. The person schema is also related to the use of mental simulations—called the *simulation heuristic*—to make judgments about how the person might react in various situations (Kahneman & Tversky, 1982). For instance, the individual's traits, such as warm to emotionally distant, influence how easy it is generate one type of behavioral sequence or another. It is easier to imagine—to mentally simulate the dynamics of—a socially warm friend making a good impression when first meeting your family than it is to imagine the same outcome with an emotionally distant friend.

The literature on person schema and related areas, such as person perception (e.g., stereotypes based on sex) and attributional biases, is considerably richer and more complex than implied in the preceding paragraphs (Bodenhausen et al., 2003; Fiske & Taylor, 1991; Kunda, 1999). My point is that much of this research is consistent with the proposal that social cognition has been shaped by social selection pressures (e.g., Brothers, 1990; Dunbar, 1998) and adds to these proposals by filling in the details, so to speak. The combination of the person schema and Kahneman's and Tversky's (1982) simulation heuristic is of particular importance, as it fleshes out some of the specifics of my autonoetic mental models. The person schema allows one to more easily simulate how other people will respond in potential future situations and thus enables better prediction of other people's behavior and the rehearsal of related social strategies.

Groups

As I explained in chapter 2 (Social Selection Pressures section), many species form cooperative groups and engage in coalitional competition for control of survival-related (e.g., fruit trees) or reproduction-related (e.g., mates) resources. Species in which these social groups form have a larger neocortex and more complex sociocognitive competencies than do evolutionarily related species that are more solitary (Barton, 1996; D. A. Clark, Mitra, & Wang, 2001; Dunbar, 1993; Dunbar & Bever, 1998; Kudo & Dunbar, 2001). As I described in chapter 3 (Social Pressures section), one consequence of the achievement of ecological dominance is increased social competition and a corresponding advantage associated with the ability to form cooperative groups, specifically groups that will eventually compete with other groups for control of ecological and social resources (Alexander, 1989; Geary & Flinn, 2001).

These selection pressures set the stage for the evolution of an in-group–out-group social psychology (Alexander, 1979) and group identification mechanisms that facilitate the formation of large and thus competitive coalitions, as I noted in chapter 5 (Folk Psychology: Group section). Although they tend not to consider the phenomena in terms of selection pressures, social psychologists have studied in-group–out-group dynamics and group identification for much of the 20th century and now have a considerable understanding of these dynamics at a cognitive and behavioral level (Bodenhausen et al., 2003; Bornstein, 2003; Fiske, 2002; Fiske & Taylor, 1991; Hewstone, Rubin, & Willis, 2002). Hewstone and colleagues concluded that "threat is a central explanatory concept in several of the theories . . . and literature on intergroup bias" (p. 586). The theories and literature focus on the details of prejudice, favorable evaluations of and identification with members of a perceived in-group, and derogation of and hostilities toward members of out-groups, as well as other forms of social cognition.

Under conditions in which a group's status or resources are threatened by the activities or perceived hostile intentions of other groups, the basic tendency of humans to form in-groups and out-groups and to process information about members of these groups in ways that are favorably biased toward the in-group and negatively biased against the out-group is exacerbated (Hewstone et al., 2002; Horowitz, 2001). These biases are evident with measures that assess explicit attitudes toward members of in-groups and out-groups—that is, people are sometimes consciously aware of these biases and consciously identify with the in-group (Abrams & Hogg, 1990). There is also evidence for biases that operate on an implicit level. Threats to one's physical well-being, even if it is below conscious awareness (e.g., when encountering the word *funeral*), result in an enhanced endorsement of in-group ideologies and harsher evaluations out-group members (Arndt, Greenberg, Pyszczynski, & Solomon, 1997; Greenberg, Pyszczynski, Solomon, Simon, & Breus, 1994). As I noted in chapter 5 (Folk Psychology: Group section), the amygdala is often activated when individuals process the faces of unfamiliar out-group members, suggesting that out-group members may automatically and unconsciously trigger negative feelings (presumably fear) in many people (Phelps et al., 2000; M. E. Wheeler & Fiske, in press).

As I described in the Sexual Selection and Population Genetics section of chapter 3, there is considerable evidence for group-level male–male competition among kin groups, with successful male groups reproductively displacing less successful groups (Carvajal-Carmona et al., 2000; Underhill et al., 2001). Given the complexity of group-level competition (Bornstein, 2003), there should be a corresponding sex difference in the tendency to form competition-related groups and in supporting patterns of social cognition (Geary, 1998; Geary, Byrd-Craven, Hoard, Vigil, & Numtee, 2003). Arndt and his colleagues found that under conditions of threat, even subtle threats, men but not women show enhanced focus on in-group ideologies (e.g., increased patriotism) and especially negative evaluations against perceived members of out-groups and against members of in-groups that militate against the in-group ideology (Arndt, Cook, & Routledge, 2004; Arndt, Greenberg, & Cook, 2002). These are exactly the forms of social cognitions that I predicted would evolve in response to group-level male–male competition (Geary, 1998).

My basic point is that the implicit and explicit cognitive and behavioral processes involved in the formation of in-groups and out-groups and in social identification are readily interpretable in terms of social selection pressures. These social-psychological phenomena are the proximate mechanisms that facilitate the formation of cooperative coalitions that, in turn, function to enable access to or control of the social and ecological resources that enhance the well-being of group members (see Horowitz, 2001). Enhancement is essentially about control of the resources that facilitate the health and well-being of the individual and his or her kin and about improving reproductive options, as with other species. When viewed in terms of mental models and the motivation to control, explicit representations of group-level dynamics allow for the simulation of potential future relationships among groups, as well as competitive strategies. These simulations are at the heart of military strategy and many competitive games (e.g., chess, many video games that appeal to boys).

CONCLUSION

As I described in chapter 6, controlled problem solving and the ability to engage in rational analysis are correlated with general intelligence (Stanovich, 1999) and require the inhibition of heuristic-based responding and the formation of a conscious, explicit representation of the corresponding information (Bjorklund et al., in press; J. S. B. T. Evans, 2002). The goal of this chapter was to describe the cognitive and brain systems that support controlled problem solving and conscious awareness and to propose a model of how these evolved and how they relate to folk psychological knowledge. These cognitive systems and processes are understood in terms of executive control (Baddeley, 1986; Moscovitch, 2000) and working memory (Miyake & Shah, 1999). Although the issue is debated, it appears that the key to understanding the operation of these systems, as related to conscious awareness, is attentional control (Engle, 2002) and an attention-driven amplification of the activity of the brain regions that are processing other forms of information (Dehaene & Naccache, 2001; John, 2003; Posner, 1994). This focusing of attention appears to result in a synchronizing of the brain regions that support executive functions and the brain regions that are processing other information, such as the facial features of someone with whom one is conversing. The result is a representation of the face in working memory and a corresponding conscious awareness of the face.

Attentional control and executive control are dependent on several regions of the prefrontal cortex (e.g., dorsolateral), which in turn are highly integrated with other regions of the prefrontal cortex (e.g., ventromedial). The latter support social cognition (Adolphs, 2003), including a sense of self as a social being (Suddendorf & Busby, 2003; Tulving, 2002; M. A. Wheeler et al., 1997), affective responses to social conditions (Eisenberger et al., 2003), and the ability to generate mental simulations of social and other behaviors (Gallagher & Frith, 2003). The combination results in an acute sensitivity to social information and dynamics and the ability to project the self back in time to recreate a personal experience and to project the self forward in time to create simulations of scenarios that might arise in the future. Individuals who do not have a sense of self and cannot mentally time travel due to brain injury have a very difficult time dealing with complex, dynamic situations that vary from the routine.

The prefrontal cortex and corresponding working memory systems thus enable individuals to form conscious representations of a variety of social and ecological situations and to explicitly manipulate—that is, change the form of—these representations. When the representations are infused with a sense of self and the ability to mentally time travel, the result is a mental capacity that appears to be evolutionarily unique (Tulving, 2002). My proposal is that self-awareness and more general functions associated with the prefrontal cortex and executive control can be integrated with the motivation to control. The evolutionary function is to support behavioral control and to do so through the ability to mentally simulate potential future social scenarios (Humphrey, 1976) or changes in ecological conditions (Potts, 1998), and then rehearse a variety of potential responses to these situations (Geary, 1998). The reasoning and problem-solving mechanisms described in chapter 6 capture the processes involved in predicting potential changes in social and ecological conditions and then generating potential behavioral responses. Social rules, for instance, are the legal operators that determine acceptable and unaccepted behaviors when simulating responses in the social problem space. At the same time, the benefit of behavioral unpredictability and thus the inability to perfectly predict social dynamics lead to the prediction that human evolution did not select for completely logical reasoning. This is because this form of reasoning would not, and does not, capture the actual pattern of social dynamics (Colman, 2003).

Analysis of the three general forms of selection pressure described in chapter 3—climatic, ecological, and social—suggests that the motivation to control, self-awareness, and the ability to mentally simulate future scenarios evolved as a result of ecological (e.g., as related to hunting) but especially social selection pressures. I suggest that the integration of these concepts and the proposals of many other scientists (Alexander, 1989; Baddeley, 2002; Dennett, 1987; Humphrey, 1976) emerges from a fusion of Tulving's (2002) self-awareness and Johnson-Laird's (1983) mental models. These autonoetic mental models allow the individual to create a self-centered mental simulation of the "perfect world." A perfect world is one in which the individual is able to organize and control social (e.g., social dynamics), biological (e.g., access to food), and physical (e.g., shelter) resources in ways that would have enhanced survival or reproductive success during human evolution. The use of these simulations is especially advantageous in situations that cannot be readily addressed by means of the automatic and implicit, heuristic-based responses described in chapter 6 (Bounded Rationality and Heuristics section). These are variant and dynamic conditions, in which heuristic-based responses would be ineffective in bringing about behavioral control. As I proposed in chapter 6, these conditions require an explicit and conscious representation of the situation and may require some degree of controlled problem solving and reasoned inference to cope with the accompanying dynamics.

Finally, if social selection pressures and a motivation to control were key components of human evolution, then social-psychological mechanisms that facilitate control-related behaviors will have evolved. These mechanisms, including attributions that facilitate control-related behavior in the face of failure, are clearly evident in humans, affecting both social and psychological (e.g., depression) functioning (Taylor & Brown, 1988) and health (Rodin, 1986). On the basis of the proposed taxonomy of cognitive modules described in chapter 5 and intense social selection pressures, the social cognitions of humans are predicted to have evolved to be focused on the self, other people, and group-level interactions. There is little doubt that this is indeed the case (Fiske & Taylor, 1991), although arguments over whether these reflect the expression of evolved biases or not can certainly be made. My point is that research on self schemas (Markus,

1977), person schemas (Bodenhausen et al., 2003), and group-related social behaviors and cognitions (Bornstein, 2003) is consistent with evolutionary research and theory (Alexander, 1989; Dunbar, 1998). The social-psychological research fills in many of the details of actual day-to-day social behaviors and cognitions and thus complements evolutionary models of the relation between social competition and brain and cognitive evolution.

8

EVOLUTION OF
GENERAL INTELLIGENCE

Psychologists have been studying human intelligence for more than 100 years and have done so using both psychometric and cognitive/experimental theory and methods. The psychometric tradition involves the study of individual differences on paper-and-pencil ability tests (e.g., spatial abilities) and on standardized achievement and IQ tests (Spearman, 1904; Thurstone, 1938) and is one of the most successful long-term research endeavors in the field of psychology. As I describe in the next chapter (General Intelligence and Social Outcomes section), individual differences on IQ tests, as well as other measures of g, are strong predictors of individual differences in achievement in school, the ability to learn in many nonschool settings, and outcomes in a variety of other modern-day contexts, including productivity at work (Gottfredson, 1997; Hunter & Hunter, 1984). Whatever is being measured by tests of g, it is an asset that matters, and thus issues associated with g often result in rancorous debate and obfuscation (Benbow & Stanley, 1996; Herrnstein & Murray, 1994; Pinker, 2002). The cognitive tradition has a more sedate history but sometimes involves the study of the processes underlying performance on the test of g and tests of more specific cognitive abilities (E. Hunt, Lunneborg, & Lewis, 1975). Included among these processes are working memory and attentional control, as I described in the Cognitive and Brain Systems section of chapter 7.

Excellent reviews of the psychometric and cognitive traditions and reviews of the history of the study of intelligence have been provided by J. B. Caroll (1993), Deary (2000, 2001), Jensen (1998), Lubinski (2000, 2004), and R. J. Sternberg (1984), and thus there is no need for an exhaustive review here. I do, however, provide some history and background on both of these traditions and their melding in the first two respective sections. In the second section, I also review research on the cognitive and brain correlates of g, and in the third section I address one of the issues that creates the most contention associated with the study of intelligence—specifically, the origins of these differences (Herrnstein & Murray, 1994; Pinker, 2002). It is not my goal to discuss the social and political implications of these differences, but rather to review the associated empirical studies. In several of these sections, I link research on g with a variety of evolutionary issues discussed in previous chapters. In the final section, I focus specifically on the relation between the motivation to control, autonoetic mental models, and g.

PSYCHOMETRICS AND MENTAL ABILITIES

Organization of Mental Abilities

In the latter half of the 19th century, Darwin's half-cousin Francis Galton (1865, 1869) was at the forefront of the systematic study of hereditary talent, including mental abilities. Galton was interested in whether intellectual ability, as defined by eminence in law, science, literature, among other talents (e.g., music), ran in families; Darwin's family was included in this study. On the basis of the study of these eminent men and their relatives, Galton concluded in 1865 "that hereditary influence is as clearly marked in mental aptitudes as in general intellectual power" (p. 320). The systematic measurement of this general intellectual power, or general intelligence (g), began with Spearman's (1904) classic study. He administered to groups of elementary and high school students as well as adults a series of sensory and perceptual sensitivity and discrimination tasks (e.g., the ability to discriminate one musical pitch from another). Teachers and peers also rated the students on their in-school intelligence and out-of-school cleverness or common sense. Scores on standard exams in classics, French, English, and mathematics were also available for the high school students. Correlations were then computed among all of the tasks, ratings, and examination scores, revealing that they were all positively correlated; above average performance on one task was associated with above average performance on all other tasks, on exam scores, and for ratings of intelligence and common sense. On the basis of these findings, Spearman (1904) concluded "that all branches of intellectual activity have in common one fundamental function (or group of functions), whereas the remaining or specific elements of the activity seem in every case to be wholly different from that in all the others" (p. 285).

Spearman (1927) later argued that individual differences in performance on paper-and-pencil mental ability tests reflected individual differences in the quantity of "mental energy" that persons could apply to specific tasks. The quantity of mental energy was indexed by a single factor, g, which, in turn, was indexed (and is still indexed) by performance that was weighted and summed across a variety of ability tests. The additional processes unique to each type of mental test (e.g., spatial vs. language fluency) were represented by a specific factor, s. Although abilities represented by g and s were part of his theory, Spearman argued that g was of primary importance in explaining individual differences across the wide array of human abilities. The major contemporary alternative to Spearman's theory was that proposed by Thurstone (1938; Thurstone & Thurstone, 1941). Using the newly developed method of factor analysis (a statistical method for clustering sources of variability across mental and other measures), Thurstone found that performance on paper-and-pencil ability tests tended to cluster into a set of primary abilities: Verbal Comprehension, Word Fluency, Numerical Facility, Spatial Abilities, Perceptual Speed, Memory, and Reasoning. These primary mental abilities were thought to represent the core domains of human intellectual competency. Performance across these measures was nonetheless correlated—above-average scores in Verbal Comprehension were associated with above-average scores in Reasoning—in support of Spearman's g.

Although they differed in the degree to which they emphasized g or specific mental abilities, Spearman's (1904) and Thurstone's (1938) pioneering work revealed that human intellectual abilities could be hierarchically organized. One such organization is illustrated in Figure 8.1, with Spearman's g representing processes that are used to solve problems across Thurstone's primary domains. The primary mental abilities, in turn, represent processes and knowledge that are common across more restricted domains. Numerical facility, for instance, represents the processes that span the four arithmetic operations, but each operation has knowledge that is not shared with the other operations (e.g., the table of multiplication facts differs from the table of addition facts). Several influential hierarchical conceptions of the organization of human abilities followed. Specifically, Burt (1940), G. H. Thomson (1951), and P. E. Vernon (1965) proposed influential hierarchical theories. Common to all of these theories was the identification of several strata of human intellectual ability (but see Guilford, 1972). The highest-stratum ability, influencing performance on all mental tests, is g. Lower-level strata represent abilities spanning more restricted domains of cognition.

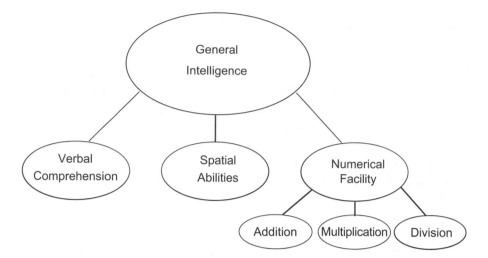

Figure 8.1. Studies of performance on paper-and-pencil ability tests indicate that they cluster into groups that assess broad to more restricted cognitive abilities. At the highest stratum are processes that are engaged when people are taking all types of ability tests. These processes (e.g., attentional focus) are represented by general intelligence. The second stratum represents processes (e.g., speed of retrieving words from long-term memory) that differ from general intelligence but influence performance on a range of tests, such as all verbal tests. The lower stratum contains processes that are unique to a particular competency.

In a series of important empirical and theoretical works, Cattell and Horn (Cattell, 1963; Horn, 1968; Horn & Cattell, 1966) argued that the single general ability proposed by Spearman (1904) should be subdivided into two equally important but distinct abilities. The first ability, called *crystallized intelligence* (gC), is manifested as the result of experience, schooling, and acculturation and is referenced by overlearned skills and knowledge, such as vocabulary. The second ability is called *fluid intelligence* (gF) and is thought to represent a biologically based ability that is referenced, in part, by the ability to learn—that is, the ability to acquire skills and knowledge. Additional lower-strata ability dimensions within the Cattell and Horn model include visualization (Gv), perceptual speed, and fluency skills (Horn & Cattell, 1966), although gC and gF are central to their theory. Refinements of these hierarchical models have followed these early works (e.g., J. B. Carroll, 1993; Gustafsson, 1984), but the basic message is still the same: There is a "fundamental function (or group of functions)" (Spearman, 1904, p. 285) that influences performance on all forms of mental ability test, as well as performance in school and in social situations (T. Hunt, 1928; Legree, 1995), and this function is general intelligence (W. Johnson, Bouchard, Krueger, McGue, & Gottesman, 2004).

Intelligence Tests

Spearman's (1904) early work and that of other experimental psychologists paralleled and contributed to work on the development of standardized intelligence tests, that is, IQ tests (Jensen, 1998). The first practical IQ test was that developed by Binet and Simon (Binet, 1905; Binet & Simon, 1916). Their goal was to develop an objective measure of children's readiness for school and to determine whether they were mentally delayed and thus not likely to benefit from schooling. The result was a battery of tests ranging from simple motor and perceptual tasks to tests of working memory (although it was not called this at the time), judgment, and reasoning. Terman (1916) standardized the test for use in the United States, the Stanford–Binet Intelligence Scale. Along with the influential scales developed by Wechsler (1949, 1955), the Stanford–Binet and the many revisions of these tests (e.g., Thorndike, Hagen, & Sattler, 1986) are widely used measures of intelligence, although other measures, such as the Raven's Progressive Matrices Test (Raven, Court, & Raven, 1993), are also widely used.

For all of these tests, average performance (based on age) is defined as a score of 100; half of individuals score higher and half score lower. A score of 115 represents performance at about the 82nd percentile, and a score of 85 is at about the 18th percentile. Mental giftedness is commonly defined by a score of 125 (95th percentile) or 130 (98th percentile) and mental retardation by a score below 70 (2nd percentile). Performance on these measures is highly stable from one year to the next, at least by age 5 (Deary, Whalley, Lemmon, Crawford, & Starr, 2000; Sattler, 1974); it is correlated with performance on the above described paper-and-pencil abilities tests (Jensen, 1998) and predicts functioning in a wide range of activities (Gottfredson, 1997), as I describe in chapter 9 (General Intelligence and Social Outcomes section).

However, the relation between measures of g and performance on mental ability tests is not uniform across the range of intelligence, according to Spearman's (1927) law of diminishing returns. For low-IQ groups, low performance on one type of test (e.g., vocabulary) is strongly predictive of low performance on a different type of test (e.g., spatial abilities). As intelligence increases, the strength of this relation diminishes (Detterman & Daniel, 1989; Jensen, 2003; Spearman, 1927). The basic finding is illustrated in Figure 8.2, which presents the pattern of test scores for vocabulary (V), spatial (S), and numerical (N) ability tests for three hypothetical (from left to right) low-, average-, and high-ability individuals. The scores of the low-ability individual are uniformly below average for all three tests, and those of the high-ability individual are above average. However, there is a greater

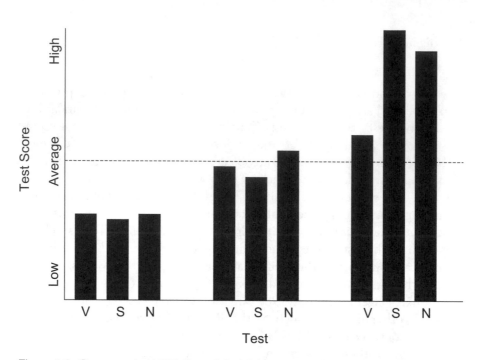

Figure 8.2. Spearman's (1927) "law of diminishing returns" means that as intelligence increases, within-individual differences in specific abilities increase. Individuals with low-IQ scores tend to score below average on all ability tests, whereas individuals with high-IQ scores might have near-average scores on one type of test but exceptionally high scores on another. N = numerical; S = spatial; V = vocabulary.

divergence between the level of ability in specific cognitive domains for the high-ability individual than for the average- and lower-ability individuals. The high-ability person is only slightly above average in vocabulary but significantly above average in spatial and numerical abilities. Thus, the fundamental functions that compose *g* are related to ability scores across a wide range of domains, but at the same time, there are also more restricted abilities that influence performance in one domain (e.g., verbal) but not another (e.g., spatial). Individuals who are exceptional in one of these more restricted domains are often less exceptional, though typically above average, in other domains.

COGNITIVE AND BRAIN CORRELATES OF INTELLIGENCE

The early study of mental abilities was not restricted to analyses of individual differences on paper-and-pencil tests. There were also experimental studies of the speed of reacting to various stimuli and other elementary processes that might underlie general intelligence, but the results were not encouraging (e.g., Wissler, 1901). Many decades later, with the development of computer technologies and accompanying conceptual advances, experimental psychologists were able to study and identify the elementary processes that contributed to a wide range of cognitive abilities. Included among these are measures of the speed of scanning visual information held in short-term memory (S. Sternberg, 1966), speed of retrieving basic facts (e.g., letter names) from long-term semantic memory (Posner, Boies, Eichelman, & Taylor, 1969; Posner & MacLeod, 1982), and speed of executing and coordinating the operations involved in analogical and other forms of reasoning (R. J. Sternberg, 1977; R. J. Sternberg & Gardner, 1983).

The initial foci of these methodological and conceptual advances was on identifying the elementary processes common to all people, but attention soon turned to the study of individual differences in these processes (e.g., speed of execution) as they related to psychometric abilities (E. Hunt, 1978, 1983; Pellegrino & Glaser, 1979). The use of these methods and the study of their relation to g generated and continues to generate methodological and critical debate and alternative ways of conceptualizing human intelligence (Gardner, 1983; R. J. Sternberg, 1984, 1997, 2000). The details are beyond the scope of this chapter, but a central issue is whether these elementary processes can be linked in any meaningful way to g. In the following sections, I review the relation between measures of these cognitive processes and measures of g.

Speed of Processing

The basic issue concerns whether speed of executing elementary processes is related to performance on measures of g. As an example of an elementary cognitive process, consider a simple task developed by Posner and his colleagues (1969). They presented upper- and lower-case combinations of various letters, such as AA, Ab, Aa, and CE one at a time on a computer monitor. The participants indicated (by depressing a response key) whether the letters were the same or different, with the time between the presentation of the letter pair and participants' response recorded by the computer. With the use of a bit of statistics and arithmetic, the difference in speed of responding—*reaction time*—to pairs that are physically identical compared to pairs that are identical in name (e.g., AA vs. Aa) provides an index of the speed of accessing the name code from long-term memory. College students can access these name codes in about 80 thousandths of a second (i.e., 80 milliseconds). In the following sections, I review the relation between performance on these and related cognitive measures and performance on ability tests.

Specific Abilities. In a now seminal study, Hunt and his colleagues (1975) found that speed of accessing letter names, word names, and other bits of language-related information from long-term memory was related to performance on a paper-and-pencil measure of verbal ability. The faster the speed of information access, the higher the score on this ability test. Follow-up studies of the relation between measures of these types of elementary processes and performance on various types of ability measures yielded promising but mixed results (Geary & Widaman, 1987, 1992; Keating, List, & Merriman, 1985; Lansman, Donaldson, Hunt, & Yantis, 1982; R. J. Sternberg & Gardner, 1983).

Widaman and I found that variables representing the speed of executing two basic processes—arithmetic fact retrieval and carrying from one column to the next (e.g., in 45 + 38, 10 is carried from the units to the tens column)—were strongly related to performance on paper-and-pencil tests of Thurstone's (1938) numerical facility (i.e., complex arithmetical) but were unrelated to performance on tests of spatial abilities (Geary & Widaman, 1987, 1992). Lansman and her colleagues found that a variable representing the speed of mentally rotating geometric images was related to performance on tests of spatial abilities but not to tests of language abilities. The basic finding in these studies is that the faster individuals execute elementary cognitive processes in specific domains, the higher they score on paper-and-pencil ability tests in these same domains. Despite other studies that found little relation between processing variables and ability measures (Keating et al., 1985), studies of this type generally support the hierarchical models of intelligence. More precisely, unique ability domains are supported, in part, by unique sets of underlying elementary processes.

General Intelligence. At the same time, other researchers were trying to determine if speed of executing elementary processes might be one of the components underlying *g* (e.g., J. B. Carroll, 1993; Eysenck, 1986; Horn, 1988; P. A. Vernon, 1987). For instance, the speed of accessing letter names from long-term memory is not only related to verbal ability, but also to performance on measures of *g*. Keating and Bobbitt (1978), as just one example, found that children who had average scores on an IQ test were slower at accessing letter names from long-term memory than were children with above-average IQ scores. Speed of accessing letter names was also correlated with IQ scores when the groups were combined. Across studies, faster access is associated with higher IQ scores, although the strength of the relation is modest (*r*s of about −0.3; Neubauer, 1997); the correlation is negative because faster processing speed is represented by lower numbers (e.g., 50 ms vs. 100 ms).

More than any other contemporary scientist, Jensen, with his colleagues, has examined the relation between performance on the letter-identification task and many other simple and complex reaction-time tasks and performance on standardized IQ tests and other psychometric measures of g (Jensen, 1982, 1987a, 1987b, 1992; Jensen, Larson, & Paul, 1988; Jensen & Munro, 1979; Kranzler & Jensen, 1991). Across these reaction-time tasks and variables that represent speed of executing cognitive processes, two basic patterns emerged. First, faster speed of cognitive processing is related to higher scores on measures of g, but the strength of the relation is moderate (rs of about −0.3 to −0.4). Second, variability in speed of processing across trials is related to scores on measures of g (rs of about −0.4). The variability measure provides an assessment of the consistency in speed of executing the same process multiple times, such as speed of retrieving the name code for A across multiple trials. Individuals who are consistently fast in executing these processes have the highest scores on IQ tests (Deary, 2000; Jensen, 1998; Neubauer, 1997), even after extensive task practice (Neubauer & Freudenthaler, 1994).

In a more recent and one of the most ambitious of studies in this tradition, Deary, Der, and Ford (2001; Der & Deary, 2003) administered an IQ test and simple and complex reaction-time tasks to a nationally representative sample of 900 adults from Scotland. This study is particularly important because of the large sample size and inclusion of the entire range of intellectual abilities. The relation between the associated speed-of-processing measures and performance on the IQ test was in the range found by Jensen and colleagues (e.g., Jensen, 1998) for the simple task (r = −0.31) and stronger than this for the complex task (r = −0.49). As Jensen (1992) found, a variable that represented intraindividual variability in speed of processing was also correlated with IQ scores (r = −0.26). For the simple task, Der and Deary found some evidence for Spearman's (1927) law of diminishing returns—that is, the relation between speed of processing and IQ did not hold well for individuals who scored above the 90th percentile on the IQ test (IQ > 120); speed was a predictor of IQ for individuals scoring lower than 120. A more linear relation between speed of processing and IQ was, however, found for the complex task: Across the entire range of ability, the higher the IQ, the faster the speed of processing. Spearman's law of diminishing returns may not hold for novel, complex tasks. For complex tasks, the more g an individual has at his or her disposal, the better he or she performs.

Finally, combinations of speed-of-processing and variability measures are sometimes found to be more highly correlated with measures of g (some rs > 0.6) than are single measures (e.g., Keating & Bobbitt, 1978; Kranzler & Jensen, 1991), suggesting that speed and variability are supported by different mechanisms. However, in other studies single speed-of-processing measures predicted IQ scores as well as combinations of measures, suggesting one fundamental mechanism underlying speed and variability (see J. B. Carroll, 1991; Neubauer, 1997). The issue of single or multiple mechanisms remains to be resolved.

Mechanisms. Studies of the mechanism or mechanisms underlying speed of processing and its relation to *g* have focused on a number of psychological and neurological factors. Among other factors, Horn (1988) suggested that speed of processing was related to (a) speed of identifying basic pieces of information (e.g., a contour) or patterns under conditions that require focused attention and (b) speed of making decisions. Jensen (1998) suggested that speed of making these identifications and decisions might be related to nerve conduction velocity. In the most extensive of these studies, P. A. Vernon and Mori (1992) found that faster peripheral nerve conduction velocities (e.g., measuring speed of reflexive responses from wrist to elbow) were associated with higher IQ scores (*rs* of about .45) and with faster reaction times on cognitive tasks (*rs* from about −0.2 to −0.3). However, additional analyses suggested that nerve conduction velocity did not mediate the relation between speed-of-processing on cognitive tasks and IQ scores. Moreover, other studies have found a much weaker relation between peripheral nerve conduction velocity and IQ (Reed & Jensen, 1992) or no relation at all (Barrett, Daum, & Eysenck, 1990). On the basis of a review of this literature, P. A. Vernon, Wickett, Bazana, and Stelmack (2000) tentatively concluded that faster peripheral nerve conduction velocities are associated with higher IQ scores, but only for men; the reason for this sex difference is not known.

Nerve conduction velocity in the central nervous system can be inferred through the use of electrophysiological recordings of brain activity during reaction-time tasks. Use of these methods has revealed higher IQ scores to be associated with faster central nerve conduction velocities, although the strength of the relation is moderate (*rs* of about .30; McGarry-Roberts, Stelmack, & Campbell, 1992; Reed & Jensen, 1991, 1992, 1993), and the overall pattern in the literature is inconclusive (P. A. Vernon et al., 2000). Furthermore, central nerve conduction velocities are not consistently correlated with speed-of-processing measures derived from these reaction-time tasks and thus do not appear to mediate the relation between speed of processing and IQ (Deary, 2000).

Jensen (1992, 1998) has proposed that individual differences in variability in speed of processing are related to synchronization of the brain systems that are engaged during reaction-time tasks. This hypothesis remains to be fully explored (R. D. Roberts & Stankov, 1999), but it is consistent with the cognitive neuroscience models I described in chapter 7 (Cognitive and Brain Systems section). It appears that synchronization of the brain regions that compose the central executive and the brain regions that are processing external information result in a conscious, explicit representation of the information in working memory (Damasio, 1989; E. K. Miller & Cohen, 2001; Ruchkin, Grafman, Cameron, & Berndt, 2003). I elaborate in the Evolved Modules, Mental Models, and g section later in this chapter. At this point, the mechanisms that underlie the relation between speed and variability of processing information and performance on measures of g are unclear.

Inspection Time

The methods involved in reaction-time tasks necessarily involve a motor component, even if it is only pressing a response key. The time needed for the motor response is incorporated into the overall reaction time, and thus these times cannot be unambiguously attributed to more central cognitive processes, although there are statistical and other ways to adjust for this. A method that is not influenced by motor responses is inspection time (Deary & Stough, 1996; Nettelbeck & Lally, 1976). The procedure is simple: As shown in Figure 8.3, the individual is instructed to fixate on an X presented at the center of a computer screen; the screen then goes blank, and the stimulus appears for, say, 70 milliseconds, and then the mask is displayed, which prevents the individual from responding using an afterimage of the stimulus. The task is to determine whether the line on the left or right of the stimulus figure is shorter by pressing a response

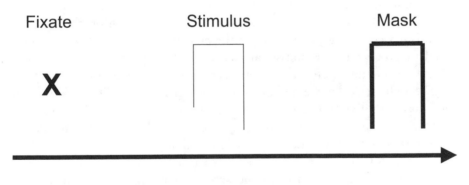

Figure 8.3. One method of measuring inspection time is to first have the individual fixate on an X presented at the center of a computer screen; the screen then goes blank, and the stimulus appears for a varying amount of time (e.g., 30 to 200 milliseconds), and then the mask is displayed. The mask prevents the individual from responding using an afterimage of the stimulus. The task is to determine, by pressing a response key, whether the line on the left or right is shorter. The score is the shortest stimulus duration (e.g., 70 milliseconds) under which the individual can accurately detect the shorter line.

key. This involves a motor component, but the motor component is not the measure of interest. Rather, what is measured is the amount of time the stimulus has to be viewed before the individual can reliably determine which line is shorter (e.g., correctly identify the shorter line 85% of the time). Some adults require a 50-millisecond exposure, and others require a 100-millisecond exposure or longer.

Inspection time is thought to represent the minimal amount of time needed for the individual's sensory and perceptual systems to encode and begin to process the presented information (Deary, 2000). Since Nettelbeck's and Lally's (1976) initial finding that inspection time was significantly correlated with performance on measures of g—short inspection times are associated with higher IQ scores—the procedure has been administered in more than 220 published studies (Nettelbeck, 2001). These studies confirmed the initial finding and have consistently shown a relation between inspection time and performance on measures of g. The strength of the relation is moderate (rs of about −0.4 to −0.5) and more strongly related to performance on nonverbal IQ measures than on verbal IQ measures (Deary & Stough, 1996; Grudnik & Kranzler, 2001; Kranzler & Jensen, 1989). The bottom line is that individuals who require only very brief exposures to detect details of visual displays and analogous auditory presentations score higher on IQ tests than do individuals who require longer exposures.

The source of inspection time performance is debated (e.g., Crawford, Deary, Allan, & Gustafsson, 1998; Deary, McCrimmon, & Bradshaw, 1997; G. Evans & Nettelbeck, 1993; Hutton, Wilding, & Hudson, 1997; Petrill, Luo, Thompson, & Detterman, 2001). Petrill et al. found that performance on inspection-time tasks was correlated with performance on the types of speed-of-processing tasks described in the preceding section. However, once speed of processing was statistically controlled, inspection time was still related to general intelligence. Nettelbeck suggested that inspection time may be influenced by the ability to focus attention and detect change on the basis of limited, time-constrained amounts of information. Hutton et al. found that inspection time was, indeed, correlated with performance on some measures of attention, but Crawford et al. found no such relationship. Deary et al. found that performance on the inspection-time task was correlated with performance on other measures that require rapid detection of visual information change, suggesting that visual inspection time is influenced by individual differences in very basic neurophysiological processes in the visual system.

Electrophysiological studies of the relations among inspection time, reaction time, and IQ provide support for Deary et al.'s (1997) hypothesis. The electrophysiological methods provide a measure of the timing of subcortical and cortical processing of the presented information, such as the inspection-time task shown in Figure 8.3. As reviewed by Deary (2000) and

P. A. Vernon et al. (2000), these studies have revealed that, as a whole, some electrophysiological measures are correlated with IQ scores (*r*s of about 0.3 to 0.5) and with inspection time performance (*r*s of about 0.3 to 0.6). The pattern suggests that individual differences in inspection time are due to individual differences in the speed and accuracy with which information is identified and classified by the associated perceptual systems.

In a related study, Deary, Simonotto, et al. (2001) used brain imaging techniques to identify the brain regions that were activated when healthy adults performed easy and difficult inspection-time tasks. Their results revealed similarities and differences in the brain regions activated during inspection time and those that support the explicit representation of information in working memory, as I described in the Cognitive and Brain Systems section of chapter 7 and the regions activated when people take IQ tests, as I describe later in this chapter (Brain Regions and *g* section). The anterior cingulate cortex was not involved in inspection time, as it is with many attention-demanding working memory tasks, but another area associated with attentional focus, area 40 in the parietal cortex (see Figure 7.3), was engaged. Some areas of the prefrontal cortex (e.g., area 47) were engaged during inspection time, and other areas were deactivated or suppressed. The suppressed regions included those that appear to be involved in self-awareness (e.g., area 10).

At this point, there is little doubt that inspection time is related to performance on IQ tests and other measures of *g*. However, the source of this relationship is not entirely clear. Inspection time performance may reflect the ability to sustain attention, speed of information detection in the visual and auditory perceptual systems, strategies for approaching these types of experimental tasks, or most likely some combination. The most promising results involve the electrophysiological measures, which suggest that individual differences in IQ are related, in part, to individual differences in the sensitivity and fidelity with which sensory and perceptual systems identify information patterns in the external world and represent these patterns in short-term memory. The result is that more intelligent individuals identify and respond to subtle variations in external information more quickly and accurately than do less intelligent individuals (P. A. Vernon et al., 2000). Inspection-time measures appear to tap these individual differences.

Working Memory

Working Memory and Fluid Intelligence

As I described in the Cognitive and Brain Systems section of chapter 7, working memory is composed of a central executive and multiple slave systems that process information in specialized domains, such as auditory or visual (Baddeley, 1986). The central executive is of particular importance, because it appears to represent in a domain-general system, that is, a system that can operate on information that is processed by and represented in many other brain and cognitive systems (Engle, Kane, & Tuholski, 1999). The central executive and supporting brain systems are, in fact, modularized but nonetheless are domain general in the sense that one function is to integrate information across more modularized (e.g., folk psychology) domains. The most important function of the central executive, and other executive functions, is to cope with novelty and change, specifically information and situations that cannot be handled by the heuristic-based systems that I described in chapter 6 (Bounded Rationality and Heuristics section). The central executive functions such that the novel or changing information is represented in working memory—that is, the information is mentally represented such that the individual is consciously aware of the novelty and is able to generate strategies to cope with the situation. An example of a laboratory task that is novel and thus requires working memory, strategic problem solving, and reasoning is the fluid container problem shown in Figure 6.6.

Research on the relation between performance on laboratory working memory tasks and performance on IQ tests and other measures of g have focused on Cattell's and Horn's fluid intelligence, gF (Cattell, 1963; Horn, 1968). As Cattell stated, "Fluid general ability . . . shows more in tests requiring adaptation to new situations, where crystallized skills are of no particular advantage" (p. 3). In theory then, performance on measures of gF should be strongly associated with individual differences in working memory, and this is indeed the case, whether the measure of gF is a standardized IQ test (Carpenter, Just, & Shell, 1990; Conway, Cowan, Bunting, Therriault, & Minkoff, 2002; R. W. Engle & Kane, 2004; R. W. Engle, Tuholski, Laughlin, & Conway, 1999) or scores on psychometric tests of complex reasoning that are highly correlated with IQ scores (Colom, Rebollo, Palacios, Juan-Espinosa, & Kyllonen, 2004; Kyllonen & Christal, 1990; Mackintosh & Bennett, 2003; Süß, Oberauer, Wittmann, Wilhelm, & Schulze, 2002). In fact, Horn (1988) and many other scientists (Carpenter et al., 1990; Stanovich, 1999; Süß et al., 2002) have argued that measures of strategic problem solving and abstract reasoning define gF, and the primary cognitive system underlying problem solving, reasoning, and thus gF is working memory. The strength of the relation between performance on working memory tasks and scores on measures of reasoning and gF ranges from moderate (rs about 0.5; R. W. Engle, Tuholski, et al. 1999; Mackintosh & Bennett, 2003) to very high ($rs > 0.8$; Colom et al., 2004; Conway et al., 2002; Kyllonen & Christal, 1990).

Embretson (1995) conducted one of the few studies that separated working memory capacity (i.e., the amount of information that can be held and manipulated in working memory) and the processes involved in making controlled, explicit inferences. She found that both of these competencies contributed to skill on an abstract reasoning measure (i.e., a measure of gF). The combination of working memory capacity and the ability to explicitly make inferences using information represented in working memory explained almost all of the individual differences in fluid intelligence across a group of 577 U.S. Air Force recruits. Skill at making inferences explained about two thirds of the individual differences in gF, and working memory capacity explained about one third of the individual differences in gF. This study suggests that many measures of working memory capacity are actually assessing multiple skills, specifically the ability to hold and manipulate information in working memory, draw inferences about relations among these pieces of information, and then apply these inferences during the act of controlled problem solving. (I described the latter set of processes in the Controlled Problem Solving section of chap. 6.)

Finally, performance on measures of working memory are sometimes correlated with performance on measures of gC, but the strength of the relation is typically weaker than that between working memory and gF (Engle, Tuholski, et al., 1999; Horn, 1988). In fact, Cattell and Horn (Cattell, 1963; Horn, 1968) hypothesized that individual differences in gF influence individual differences in the ability to acquire knowledge in school and in other novel situations and thus result in individual differences in gC: High scores on measures of gF are associated with high scores on measures of gC, although the strength of the relation varies with the specific tests used to measure these forms of g (J. B. Carroll, 1993; Mackintosh & Bennett, 2003) and varies across the lifespan (Li et al., 2004). Given that gF is correlated with the ability to learn in school, on the job, and elsewhere (Gottfredson, 1997), it is likely that individual differences in crystallized intelligence are indeed due, in part, to individual differences in fluid intelligence, as predicted (Horn, 1968; Lehrl & Fischer, 1988).

However, this is not the whole story. There are individual differences on measures of crystallized intelligence, such as vocabulary tests, that are unrelated to individual differences on measures of gF (Horn, 1988; Neubauer, Spinath, Riemann, Angleitner, & Borkenau, 2000). This suggests brain and cognitive systems, possibly those involved in the formation of long-term memories (e.g., the hippocampus), unique to the acquisition of crystallized knowledge as contrasted with fluid intelligence. Moreover, the dimension of personality known as openness to experience is also correlated with gC but not with gF (Bates & Shieles, 2003; Mackintosh & Bennett, 2003). Overall, it appears that the processes that define gF, the brain and cognitive systems associated with long-term memory formation, and the dimension of personality associated with interest in new experiences (e.g., as manifested in reading) interact to create crystallized knowledge (Rolfhus & Ackerman, 1999).

Components of Working Memory

As I discussed in chapter 7 (Cognitive and Brain Systems section), there is ongoing debate regarding the components of working memory and, on the basis of the strong relation between working memory and gF, the components of fluid intelligence. One position is that individual differences in working memory and gF are largely due to individual differences in the basic speed of information processing (Ackerman, Beier, & Boyle, 2002; Fry & Hale, 1996, 2000; Jensen, 1998). The major alternative view is that individual differences in working memory and gF are largely due to individual differences in attentional control (Engle, 2002; Kane & Engle, 2002). The finding that measures of working memory, attentional control, speed of processing, and gF are all correlated with one another complicates the testing of these alternative theories. As I described earlier in this chapter, faster and consistent speed of information processing is associated with higher fluid intelligence and a higher working memory capacity (G. E. Larson & Saccuzzo, 1989; Salthouse, 1991, 1996). However, attentional control is also associated with higher fluid intelligence and a higher working memory capacity (Engle, Tuholski, et al., 1999; Kane & Engle, 2002).

In one study that attempted to disentangle some of these relationships, Fry and Hale (1996) administered sets of speed-of-processing and working memory tasks and a measure of gF to children, adolescents, and young adults. This approach was used because with development, speed of information processing becomes faster (Kail, 1991) and working memory capacity (Case, 1992) and fluid intelligence (Raven et al., 1993) increase. If working memory underlies fluid intelligence, then age-related improvements in gF should be explained by age-related improvements in working memory capacity, and this is what the researchers found. About 40% of the developmental change in gF was due to age-related improvements in working memory capacity, and about 70% of the improvement in working memory capacity was due to age-related increases in speed of processing. These and other results suggest that individual differences in working memory are related to individual differences in speed of processing (Fry & Hale, 2000).

These findings are not as clear-cut as they might seem, because performance on speed-of-processing tasks requires attentional focus, and thus Fry and Hale's (1996) results and those of others (Salthouse, 1991, 1996) might be due to individual differences in the ability to focus attention rather than speed of processing per se. In one related study, Conway et al. (2002)

administered speed-of-processing, working memory, and short-term memory tasks and two measures of gF to 120 young adults. The short-term memory tasks assess how well information stays active in memory, but unlike working memory tasks they do not assess the ability to hold on to information while simultaneously engaging in other effortful mental tasks. Working memory thus requires short-term memory and additional processes, but most previous studies did not control for the contribution of short-term memory to working memory. It was found that speed of processing was related to performance on the short-term memory tasks but not on the working memory tasks. Moreover, when the short-term memory contributions to working memory were controlled, individual differences in working memory were still highly predictive of gF scores, but neither short-term memory nor speed of processing were related to gF.

These results suggest that speed of processing is related to the activation of information in short-term memory but not to the processes that distinguish short-term memory from working memory. As I described in chapter 7 (Cognitive and Brain Systems section), these working memory processes appear to be the ability to maintain attentional control and prevent irrelevant information from diverting attention from the task at hand (Conway, Cowan, & Bunting, 2001; Conway & Engle, 1994; Engle & Kane, 2004; Engle, Conway, Tuholski, & Shisler, 1995; Kane & Engle, 2000). At this point, it is clear that working memory capacity is one of the primary, if not *the* primary, cognitive competency underlying fluid intelligence. However, there is no clear resolution to whether the processes underlying working memory are basic speed of processing, attentional control, some combination of the two, or other yet unidentified mechanisms (Horn, 1988).

The question of where inspection time fits into this research also awaits resolution. Deary and Stough (1996) suggested that inspection time might tap one of the cognitive components of gF. Bates and Shieles (2003) found that shorter inspection times were indeed associated with better fluid intelligence ($r = -0.56$), but Burns and Nettelbeck (2003) found that inspection time was related to speed of processing but was not correlated with performance on a measure of gF. One possibility is that inspection time tasks are tapping the speed and fidelity with which basic sensory and perceptual systems represent information in short-term memory. If so, inspection time performance would be dependent on the speed with which these systems identified and processed information but would not require working memory per se and, as a result, would not be directly linked to gF. If inspection time taps the systems that eventually result in the representation of information in short-term memory, then inspection time would be indirectly related to gF, given that working memory processes operate on a subset of the information represented in short-term memory (Cowan, 1995).

Brain Regions

Size

In reviewing the literature on brain regions, my focus was on the study of brain volume, as determined by brain imaging techniques, and performance on standardized IQ tests or other measure of *g*, as contrasted with the literature on the relation between external head circumference and IQ. The reviews have revealed a consistent but modest relation between brain size and IQ scores (*r* of about 0.4); the bigger the better, after correcting for potential allometric confounds such as body size (Deary, 2000; Flashman, Andreasen, Flaum, & Swayze, 1998; Rushton & Ankney, 1996; P. A. Vernon et al., 2000). In one of the most comprehensive of these studies, Wickett, Vernon, and Lee (2000) examined the relations between total brain volume, as measured by a brain imaging technique, and performance on measures of *g*F, *g*C, short-term memory, and various reaction-time measures. Because many psychometric tests require both *g*F and *g*C, they used analytic techniques that enabled a separation of the contributions of fluid and crystallized abilities to performance on each measure and thereby gained a sharper estimate of the relation between brain volume and these abilities. Larger brain volumes were associated with higher fluid abilities (*r* = 0.49) and better short-term memories (*r* = 0.45) but were unrelated to crystallized abilities (*r* = 0.06). Larger brain volumes were also associated with faster reaction times (*r*s about −0.4) and less variability in reaction times (*r*s about −0.4).

The relation between the size of specific brain regions and IQ scores is less certain, although there is a tendency for size of the neocortex to be more consistently related to IQ scores than size of subcortical areas (Deary, 2000). A few studies have found relations between size of specific brain regions and IQ, although these findings should be considered preliminary. Flashman et al. (1998) found that larger frontal and temporal cortices, but not parietal or occipital cortices, were associated with higher standardized IQ scores. Raz et al. (1993) examined the relation between performance on measures of *g*F and *g*C and total brain volume, volume of the dorsolateral prefrontal cortex, the somatosensory cortex, portions of the parietal cortex, and the hippocampus. Higher *g*F scores were associated with larger total brain volume (*r* = .43), a larger dorsolateral prefrontal cortex (*r* = .51), and more white matter (i.e., neuronal axons) in the prefrontal cortex (*r* = .41) but were unrelated to size of the other brain regions. Performance on the *g*C measure, in contrast, was not related to size of any of these brain regions or total brain volume, in keeping with the findings of Wickett et al. (2000).

Regional Activation

A number of studies have used various imaging techniques to examine the brain regions that become activated or deactivated while individuals solve items on measures of gF or those regions that are active during novel problem solving comparing groups that differ in IQ (Duncan et al., 2000; Gray, Chabris, & Braver, 2003; Haier et al., 1988; Prabhakaran, Smith, Desmond, Glover, & Gabrieli, 1997). These are early and pioneering studies, and thus the most appropriate interpretation of their findings is not entirely certain (Deary, 2000). Most of the studies reveal a pattern of activation and deactivation in a variety of brain regions, much of which is likely due to task-specific content of the reasoning tasks (e.g., verbal vs. visual information). The overall results are mixed, but recent studies using the imaging methods most sensitive to regional change in activation and deactivation suggest that fluid intelligence may be supported, in part, by the same system of brain regions that supports working memory and attentional control (see Cognitive and Brain Systems section of chap. 7).

In one such study, Duncan et al. (2000) found the dorsolateral prefrontal cortex (e.g., area 46; see Figure 7.3) and the anterior cingulate cortex (area 24) to be particularly active while adults solved novel verbal and spatial reasoning tasks that are commonly used as measures of gF. In a similar brain imaging study, Gray et al. (2003) examined the relations among experimental measures of working memory, specifically measures of attentional control and the ability to inhibit irrelevant associations, and performance on a measure of gF. In keeping with Duncan et al.'s results and Engle's model of attention and working memory (Engle, 2002; Kane & Engle, 2002), the dorsolateral prefrontal cortex was active during tasks that involved controlled attention and inhibition, and the level of activation was correlated with fluid intelligence. The anterior cingulate cortex was also active, as were areas of the parietal cortex (e.g., area 40) that are associated with attentional control. However, parietal activation was more strongly related to gF scores than was activation of the anterior cingulate cortex.

Esposito and his colleagues also found that the dorsolateral prefrontal cortex was active when young adults solved reasoning and related working memory problems (Esposito, Kirkby, van Horn, Ellmore, & Berman, 1999). These same regions were active when older adults solved the same reasoning problems, although the older adults did not perform as well as the younger adults on the reasoning task. The lower performance of the older adults appears to have been due to the activation of several task-irrelevant brain regions that were suppressed (i.e., deactivated) in younger adults. At a cognitive level, activation of these normally suppressed brain regions would result in task-irrelevant thoughts intruding into working memory while attempting to reason. These results are consistent with Engle's attentional control and inhibition model (Engle, 2002; Kane & Engle, 2002) and with typical findings of inhibition difficulties and declines in gF with normal aging in adulthood (e.g., Baltes, 1997). The latter suggests that the declines are due to activation of task-irrelevant brain regions. Finally, Haier, White, and Alkire (2003) found gF scores to be related to brain activation during a nonreasoning memory task. Higher scores on an IQ test were associated with greater neural connectivity between posterior regions of the cortex (areas 37 and 19; see Figure 7.3) associated with identifying, naming, and categorizing objects and the anterior cingulate cortex and several regions of the prefrontal cortex.

Using electrophysiological measures, Gevins and Smith (2000) found that the dorsolateral prefrontal cortex was engaged during a complex working memory task. Moreover, individuals with high scores on a standardized IQ test were better able to engage this system, that is, focus attention on the task, and thus outperformed less intelligent individuals. With practice and learning, intelligent individuals relied less on the dorsolateral prefrontal cortex and more on posterior brain regions, suggesting that the focused attention and problem solving associated with higher IQ scores results in the rapid formation of implicit problem-solving strategies and more automatic processing of task demands. As I describe in chapter 9 (Academic Learning section), the rapid automatization of complex tasks is commonly associated with gF. The bottom line is that compared to less intelligent individuals, intelligent individuals require less practice to shift the processing demands of the task from the explicit system to the implicit system described in Table 6.1. In other words, gF is associated with the rapidity of learning novel information, thereby resulting in a shift in the processing of this information to brain and cognitive systems that do not require focused attention and working memory (Ackerman, 1988).

Injury

The evidence reviewed in the preceding sections and in chapter 7 (Cognitive and Brain Systems section) provide strong support for the position that areas of the prefrontal cortex and a few other brain regions (e.g., the anterior cingulate cortex) are integral to the functioning of the working memory system and the ability to reason and problem solve, and these in turn explain much of the individual differences on measures of g. In fact, neuropsychological measures of prefrontal functioning are highly correlated with IQ scores (Obonsawin et al., 2002). However, one apparent inconsistency in the literature is the finding that individuals with damage to the prefrontal cortex often perform normally on standardized IQ tests. In one large-scale study that included 656 individuals with brain injury, Warrington, James, and Maciejewski (1986) examined the relation between the location of these injuries, including the frontal cortex, and scores on a standardized IQ test, the Wechsler Adult Intelligence Scale (WAIS; Wechsler, 1955). There was little relation between lesion site and IQ scores, and the IQ scores of individuals with frontal lesions were average.

Duncan (1995) suggested that the lack of correlation between IQ scores and prefrontal damage was due to use of IQ tests, including the WAIS, that measure both gC and gF. More precisely, he proposed that damage to the prefrontal cortex should disrupt fluid abilities but not crystallized knowledge. To test this hypothesis, Duncan, Burgess, and Emslie (1995) assessed four individuals with prefrontal damage, IQ-matched normal controls, and a second group of control patients with damage to posterior regions of the cortex. They administered the WAIS and a second IQ test that does not assess gC and is particularly sensitive to individual differences in gF. For the control group and the individuals with damage to posterior regions of the cortex, the scores on WAIS and the measure of gF were comparable. By design, the WAIS IQ scores of the individuals with prefrontal damage and the IQ-matched normal control group did not differ. However, there was a 22 to 38 point IQ gap comparing the WAIS and gF scores of the individuals with prefrontal damage.

In a series of follow-up experiments, it was demonstrated that one of the fluid processes severely disrupted by prefrontal damage involves the management and coordination of goals and subgoals during controlled problem solving (Duncan, Emslie, Williams, Johnson, & Freer, 1996). Damage to the prefrontal regions of the cortex can severely disrupt fluid intelligence, that is, the ability to engage in controlled problem solving in novel domains or to even engage in simple nonroutine tasks. At the same time, damage to these regions does not severely disrupt crystallized intelligence, although the individual's ability to use this knowledge in novel conditions is often severely disrupted (Luria, 1980). It appears that the disruption of fluid abilities can be traced to an inability to maintain attentional resources on task-relevant goals and to organize and manipulate these goals in working memory (Carpenter et al., 1990).

Metabolic Activity and Mental Effort

The functioning of neurons requires glucose, and thus the brain's use of glucose during problem solving and other cognitive tasks provides a measure of the mental effort, so to speak, required to cope with the demand. In particular, the associated changes in the brain's metabolic activity appear to be a reflection of the number of neurons engaged during the task. Positron emission tomography (PET) is the brain imaging technique needed to measure metabolic activity while individuals perform cognitive tasks, and it is very expensive to operate. As a result, the number of studies that have assessed the relation between performance on IQ tests and metabolic patterns during cognitive processing is limited but nonetheless informative (Haier et al., 1988; Haier, Siegel, Tang, Abel, & Buchsbaum, 1992; G. E. Larson, Haier, LaCasse, & Hazen, 1995; Neubauer, Fink, & Schrausser, 2002; Parks et al., 1988).

Haier et al. (1988) contrasted brain metabolic activity while individuals were engaged in a simple cognitive task that required them to attend to a computer screen and another task that was a standard measure of gF. The gF task required greater glucose utilization than the simple task, as might be expected on the basis of differences in the complexity of the tasks. Individual differences on the gF measures were inversely related to glucose metabolism in most of the brain regions they assessed ($rs \geq -0.44$). More intelligent individuals used less glucose while solving the IQ items and by inference exerted less mental effort to achieve the same or superior performance during problem solving in comparison to their less intelligent peers. Haier et al. (1992) found that higher fluid intelligence was associated with rapid declines in glucose use while individuals learned a computer game. With practice, more intelligent individuals showed greater improvement on the task and a marked decline in glucose use. Among a few other brain regions, sections of the prefrontal cortex and the anterior cingulate cortex showed the most significant IQ-related declines in glucose metabolism during learning. Other studies suggest similar but more complex relations among glucose use, IQ, and cognitive performance (G. E. Larson et al., 1995; Neubauer et al., 2002).

At this point, the research on the relation between IQ and the brain's glucose utilization patterns during complex problem solving and learning cannot be considered conclusive (Deary, 2000; P. A. Vernon et al., 2000). The results to date are, nonetheless, consistent with the hypothesis that high fluid intelligence is associated with a more efficient and focused use of the brain systems needed for coping with a variety of cognitive demands. In particular, the results suggest that intelligent individuals are better able to focus attentional resources and thus engage only those brain and cognitive systems needed for the task at hand and simultaneously inhibit the activity of brain regions that are not needed for the task, in keeping with Engle's attentional control and inhibition system (Engle, 2002; Kane & Engle, 2002). At the level of brain activity, the associated neural efficiency would result in fewer neurons being engaged during the task and thus lower overall glucose metabolism.

General Fluid Intelligence	General Crystallized Intelligence
Performance Characteristics	
Controlled Problem Solving: Reasoning, inferring, and abstracting	Knowledge Base: Facts, procedures, and heuristics
Cognitive Mechanisms	
Working Memory: Attentional and inhibitory control; speed of processing; and, short-term memory	Long-Term Memory: Quantity and organization of information and speed of information access
Brain Mechanisms	
Dorsolateral prefrontal cortex; anterior cingulate cortex and other attentional systems and neurophysiological processes supporting short-term memory	Brain regions involved in the storage (e.g., the hippocampus) of evolved or learned information patterns

Figure 8.4. A schematic view of fluid and crystallized general intelligence. Performance characteristics are the most common manifestations of these forms of intelligence. Individuals who are high in fluid intelligence perform well on tasks that involve controlled problem solving, and individuals who are high in crystallized intelligence perform well on tasks that assess their knowledge in a variety of areas. The lower sections of the figure represent some of the primary cognitive and brain mechanisms, respectively, that appear to support these forms of general intelligence.

Summary and Integration

Performance Characteristics

Individual differences in general intelligence, *g*, can be understood in terms of individual differences in fluid intelligence, *g*F, and crystallized intelligence, *g*C (Cattell, 1963; Horn, 1988). Figure 8.4 shows some of the most basic performance characteristics associated with *g*F and *g*C and the some of the underlying cognitive and brain mechanisms. Intelligent individuals show a particular advantage over their less intelligent peers in the ability to cope with novel, complex, and dynamic circumstances. These tasks and conditions require problem solving, reasoning, making inferences, and forming abstractions. As I described in the Controlled Problem Solving section of chapter 6, these processes engage the explicit system described in Table 6.1 and elsewhere (e.g., J. S. B. T. Evans, 2002; Stanovich &

West, 2000). Intelligent individuals also know more facts, more procedures for solving problems (e.g., learned algebraic procedures), and more heuristics. I am assuming that this reflects a combination of inherent individual differences in folk knowledge, as well as knowledge acquired during the individual's lifetime. The ability to learn during a lifetime is related to gF, personality characteristics that influence the seeking of knowledge, and the brain systems that support the representation and access of information stored in long-term memory.

Cognitive Mechanisms

If controlled problem solving is the central competency that defines fluid intelligence, then many of the same cognitive and brain mechanisms that support controlled problem solving (Cognitive and Brain Systems section of chap. 7) should support performance on measures of gF, and this is indeed the case (Duncan et al., 2000; Kane & Engle, 2002). The most important of these cognitive systems is working memory, specifically the ability to explicitly and consciously represent information patterns, manipulate these patterns in a controlled fashion, and draw inferences about relations among the patterns (Embretson, 1995). There is debate as to the processes that support working memory and that mediate the relation between working memory and performance on measure of gF. The debates have, nonetheless, narrowed the mechanisms to individual differences in the ability to control attention and inhibit irrelevant information from intruding into conscious awareness (Engle, 2002) or (or perhaps *and*) individual differences in the speed of processing bits of information (Fry & Hale, 2000; Jensen, 1998). The latter would explain the consistent relation between performance on measures of gF and measures that assess the speed and consistency with which information is processed. Basically, high gF scores are associated with faster information processing and more consistency in the speed of executing the same process across time (Deary, 2000; Kranzler & Jensen, 1991; P. A. Vernon et al., 2000). However, performance on these measures also requires controlled attention, and thus the issue of whether attention, speed of processing, or a combination underlies individual differences in working memory capacity remains to be resolved.

Figure 8.4 also shows short-term memory as being related to fluid intelligence, even though Conway et al. (2002) found that individual differences on measures of short-term memory were not related to performance on measures of gF once the overlap between short-term memory and working memory was controlled. By definition, short-term memory is all of the information currently active above a baseline level, and working memory is that subset of short-term memory represented in the individual's conscious awareness (Cowan, 1995). Processes that facilitate the activation of information in short-term memory should thus be indirectly related to working memory, as the quantity and quality of information that can be simultaneously active in short-term memory is the foundation for forming explicit, working memory representations. Inspection time may be related to performance on IQ tests, and indirectly related to gF, through short-term memory: The evidence suggests that inspection-time measures assess speed and fidelity with which individuals' perceptual systems identify external information and represent these patterns in short-term memory (Deary, 2000; Deary et al., 1997).

High Intelligence

In all, it appears that highly intelligent individuals identify and apprehend bits of social and ecological information more easily and quickly than do other people, and their perceptual systems process this information such that it is activated in short-term memory more quickly and with greater accuracy than it is for other people. Once active in short-term memory, the information is made available for conscious, explicit representation and manipulation in working memory. Central characteristics of highly intelligent people are their ability to represent more information in working memory than other people and their enhanced ability to consciously manipulate this information. The manipulation in turn is guided and constrained by the reasoning and inference-making mechanisms I described in chapter 6 (Controlled Problem Solving section). Finally, gF is associated with the ability to learn new information (Ackerman, 1986, 1988). When high fluid intelligence and a strong long-term memory system is combined with an interest in seeking novel experiences, the result is the acquisition of a large store of crystallized knowledge, gC, over the life span (Bates & Shieles, 2003; Cattell, 1963; Horn, 1968; Li et al., 2004).

Brain Mechanisms

If controlled problem solving and supporting working memory resources are the heart of gF, then the same brain systems that underlie working memory should be engaged when people solve items on IQ tests, and these same systems should differ comparing groups of individuals with higher and lower IQ scores. The results of the associated brain imaging and neuropsychological studies, and especially the studies that used the most sensitive measures of regional brain activity, support this hypothesis (Deary et al., 2000; Duncan et al., 1995; Gray et al., 2003; Kane & Engle, 2002). High scores on measures of gF are associated with activation of the dorsolateral prefrontal cortex and several brain regions associated with attentional control, including the anterior cingulate cortex and regions of the parietal cortex. High fluid intelligence is also associated with the ability to inhibit irrelevant information from intruding into conscious awareness (Esposito et al., 1999). At the level of brain mechanisms, the result is suppression of the neural systems that process this irrelevant information. The ability to inhibit the activation of irrelevant brain systems explains the finding that high fluid intelligence is associated with lower glucose metabolism during complex problem solving—that is, the activity of unnecessary brain regions is suppressed, and therefore there is less overall brain activity (Haier et al., 1988).

Larger brain volumes are also associated with higher scores on measures of gF, faster and greater consistency on speed-of-processing tasks, and higher scores on measures of short-term memory (Deary, 2000; Jensen, 1998; Wickett et al., 2000). These relations are typically found when total brain volume or total volume of the neocortex is correlated with cognitive and information processing measures (Deary, 2000; P. A. Vernon et al., 2000), although Raz et al. (1993) found that high fluid intelligence was also associated with a larger dorsolateral prefrontal cortex and more white matter (i.e., axons) in this brain region. More white matter indicates more neuronal connections within the prefrontal cortex and a prefrontal cortex that is richly integrated with posterior and subcortical brain regions (E. K. Miller & Cohen, 2001).

As I described in the Allometry and Size of the Neocortex section of chapter 4, a gross expansion in the size of a brain region results in architectural changes such that there is more modularity within this region (Changizi, 2001; Kaas, 2000) and greater neuronal interconnections (i.e., white matter) between the modularized segments of the region and often with other brain regions (Hofman, 2001; Holloway, 1968). An expansion in the size of a brain region will thus result in a corresponding enhancement in the sensitivity of the region to externally generated information patterns and an enhanced ability to detect subtle variation in these patterns (Hofman, 2001; Kaas, 2000). At a cognitive level, these changes in microarchitecture should, in theory, result in faster and more reliable detection and processing of social and ecological information and an enhanced short-term memory for this information; enhanced short-term memory would result from the greater number of neurons that would be activated when the information is processed. In other words, changes in microarchitecture associated with cortical expansion may contribute to the relation between brain volume and performance on speed-of-processing and short-term memory measures, as Wickett et al. (2000) found, and in theory should result in shorter inspection times. Shorter inspection times follow from regional modularization because of the increase in the number of neurons specialized for detecting and contrasting one type of information from another.

Evolutionary Considerations

As a consequence of the cognitive and brain mechanisms described thus far, it appears that highly intelligent people, in comparison to other people, excel in the ability to quickly and accurately cope with novel and changing social and ecological situations and to consciously and explicitly represent these scenarios in working memory. The ability to cope with change and novelty is in fact one of the features of gF emphasized by Cattell and Horn (Horn & Cattell, 1966) and links directly back to the invariant–variant continuum that I introduced in chapter 4 and in Geary and Huffman (2002). The gist is that the function of brain and cognition is to process and enable behavioral responses to information patterns (e.g., facial expressions) that have tended to covary with survival or reproductive outcomes during the species' evolutionary history. Some of these information patterns, such as the basic shape of a human face, are invariant across generations, and therefore selection should result in the evolution of brain and cognitive systems that are inherently constrained to process these specific forms of information (see Figure 4.2 and corresponding text). For humans, these constrained systems are represented by the modules I described throughout chapter 5, as well as by heuristic-based decision-making mechanisms (see Bounded Rationality and Heuristics section of chap. 6) and attributional biases (see Social Cognition and Folk Psychology section of chap. 7).

In theory, variant forms of information are in the same folk domains as invariant forms, but the former can vary across generations and within lifetimes. As I described in chapter 3 (Adaptation and Selection section) and chapter 7 (Problem Solving and Human Evolution section), variant information patterns are most likely to be associated with ecological and social selection pressures, that is, pressures that involve interactions among two or more living organisms with competing interests. I elaborate on the potential relation between these pressures and the evolution of gF in a later section (Evolved Modules, Mental Models, and g). The point for now is that research on general intelligence can be placed within a wider evolutionary framework, and the most fundamental constraints (i.e., variant–invariant information patterns) associated with the evolution of brain and cognition are consistent with mechanisms that have been found to be associated with general fluid intelligence.

ORIGINS OF GENERAL INTELLIGENCE

As I noted in the introductory comments, the origins of individual differences in intelligence generate heated debate, as illustrated by the firestorm generated by Herrnstein and Murray's (1994) *The Bell Curve*. Underneath the social and political rancor, scientific psychologists have been studying these origins since the time of Galton (1865, 1869). As I discuss in the sections below, these efforts have focused on determining both the hereditary and environmental contributions to individual differences in intelligence.

Heredity

Galton (1869) demonstrated that eminent accomplishments in politics, literature, science, music, poetry, and so forth often run in families and, on the basis of this, concluded that the traits that result in exceptional talent, or "genius," are largely hereditary. Since Galton's time, the behavior genetic study of individual differences in behavior, personality, and cognition has become very sophisticated and focuses on both hereditary and environmental influences (for extended discussion, see Hay, 1999; Plomin, DeFries, Craig, & McGuffin, 2002; Plomin, Defries, et al., 2001), although the field itself is sometimes soundly criticized (see Gottlieb, 1995, 2003; for rebuttal, see D. C. Rowe, 2002; Segal & Hill, in press; Turkheimer, Goldsmith, & Gottesman, 1995). Critiques notwithstanding, the behavior genetic study of individual differences in intelligence has a long history and has revealed a very consistent pattern of findings for psychometric measures and standardized IQ tests. The study of the heritability of information processing measures (e.g., those indexing speed of processing) and brain size and structure is more recent, as is the search for genetic markers of individual differences in intelligence. The results in these latter areas are more mixed, but nonetheless of interest.

Before beginning, I must emphasize that the results reviewed in the following sections refer only to individual differences within a population, and not, for instance, to the proportion of an individual's IQ score that is due to genes or environment. If the heritability for performance on an IQ test is 50%, then 50% of the between-person or individual differences on the test can be attributed to differences in genes or in gene expression across individuals in this population. Furthermore, heritability estimates are not necessarily stable and in fact often vary across generations and populations (Plomin & DeFries, 1980; Sundet, Tambs, Magnus, & Berg, 1988). As environmental conditions within a population (e.g., nutrition, educational opportunity) become more similar, individual differences in any measured trait will necessarily become more strongly related to genetic influences. When environmental conditions vary within the population of interest, the potential for environmental influences on the trait will necessarily increase. The issues are complicated further by the fact that environments can influence gene expression (Gottlieb, 2003), and individuals with different genotypes sometimes seek different environments (Plomin, DeFries, & Loehlin, 1977; Scarr & McCartney, 1983; Segal & Hill, in press). The most important point is that for any given trait, the heritability estimate derived from one population living in one type of circumstance may differ from the heritability estimate for a different population living under different circumstances. I discuss these differences, as related to IQ, in the Environment section later in this chapter.

Briefly, environmental or experiential influences are typically considered to be shared among family members or unique to each individual. As an example, shared experiences for siblings may include living in the same home, having the same parents, going to the same school, and so forth. Nonshared experiences can reflect differences in the way parents treat different children, differences in relationships with peers, or interactions between the individual's traits and these social influences (Harris, 1995). The specifics of what constitutes a shared or unique environment are not well understood at this time.

General Intelligence

On the basis of twin, family, and adoption studies, it is clear that a significant portion of the individual differences in intelligence is heritable, although genetic influences on fluid intelligence might be stronger than those on crystallized intelligence (Bouchard, Lykken, McGue, Segal, & Tellegen, 1990; Bouchard & McGue, 1981; Jensen, 1998; McCartney, Harris, & Bernieri, 1990; McClearn et al., 1997; Plomin, DeFries, et al., 2001; Scarr & Weinberg, 1983; R. S. Wilson, 1983). In a classic review of the world literature of behavior genetic studies of intelligence, Bouchard and McGue found that closely related family members were more similar in their IQ scores than were distantly related family members. The correlation of the IQ scores of identical or monozygotic twins (100% shared genes) reared in the same household was .86 and for monozygotic twins reared apart, that is, in different households, .72. The corresponding values for dizygotic (50% shared genes) twins and nontwin siblings (50% shared genes) were .60 and .47. The respective values for half-siblings (25% shared genes) and between adoptive parents and their adopted children (0% shared genes) were .31 and .19. Their overall results indicated that about 50% (i.e., heritability, or $h^2 = .50$) of the individual differences in intelligence were related to genetic influences.

Subsequent studies have confirmed this pattern for populations outside of Western cultures (Elbedour, Bouchard, & Hur, 1997; Pal, Shyam, & Singh, 1997) and have revealed that genetic influences on intelligence are moderate during the preschool years and increase in importance as the individual moves into adulthood (E. Bishop et al., 2003; McCartney et al.,

1990; McGue, Bouchard, Iacono, & Lykken, 1993; Plomin & Spinath, 2002; Posthuma, de Geus, & Boomsma, 2002). During the preschool years and early childhood, roughly 40% (sometimes lower) of the individual differences in intelligence can be attributed to genetic influences and the remaining portion to shared and unique environmental influences. As one example, in a longitudinal assessment that combined results from twin and adoption studies, E. Bishop et al. found that genetic influences explained 40% to 50% of the individual differences in intelligence during the preschool years, but more than 70% of the individual differences by 7 years of age (see also Bartels, Rietveld, van Baal, & Boomsma, 2002). Swedish and U.S. studies of monozygotic twins reared apart indicate that by middle age, nearly 80% of individual differences intelligence are heritable (Bouchard et al., 1990; Pedersen, Plomin, Nesselroade, & McClearn, 1992). Bouchard et al. found that 80% of the individual differences on a measure of gF were heritable, as were about 70% of the individual differences for WAIS scores, which assesses both gF and gC.

The basic pattern in these twin studies and in adoption studies (e.g., Loehlin, Horn, & Willerman, 1989; Scarr & Weinberg, 1983) is clear, as illustrated in Figure 8.5. As individuals move from childhood to adolescence to adulthood, the genetic influences on individual differences in intelligence increase in importance. The reasons for the developmental increase in genetic influences are not known, but they likely include a mix of changes in gene expression and developmental change in niche seeking (McGue et al., 1993; Scarr & McCartney, 1983; Segal & Hill, in press). During early childhood, parents provide many of the environmental influences. As individuals mature, they are better able to seek niches consistent with their interests and abilities. As an example, intelligent individuals are more likely than less intelligent individuals to seek and benefit from experiences such as continued formal (e.g., college) and informal (e.g., reading) educational experiences that can result in improvements in performance on some subscales (e.g., vocabulary, general information) on some IQ tests.

Specific Cognitive Abilities

Consistent with hierarchical models of human abilities, behavioral genetic research has revealed genetic influences on individual differences in specific cognitive abilities (Alarcón, Plomin, Fulker, Corley, & DeFries, 1998; Bouchard et al., 1990; Cardon, Fulker, DeFries, & Plomín, 1992; Luo, Petrill, & Thompson, 1994; Pedersen et al., 1992; Reznick & Corley, 1999; Rietveld, van Baal, Dolan, & Boomsma, 2000; Segal, 2000). Like Bouchard and McGue (1981) for measures of general intelligence, DeFries et al. (1979) found that parents and their biological children resembled one another for several specific cognitive abilities, especially language-related and spatial

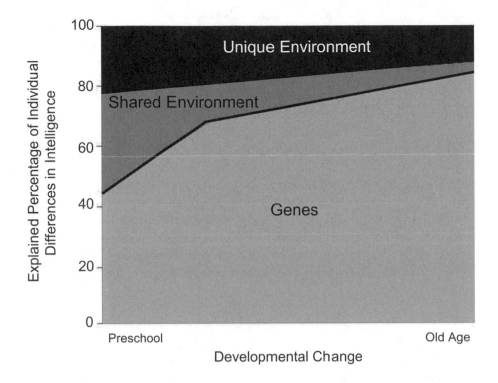

Figure 8.5. The relative contributions of genes, shared environmental experiences (e.g., shared among members of the same family, such as socioeconomic status), and nonshared environmental experiences to individual differences in *g*. The nonshared experiences are unique to each person.

abilities. In a 16-year-study of the similarity between adopted children and their adoptive and biological parents, Plomin and his colleagues found that as children matured, they became increasingly similar to their biological parents and less similar to their adoptive parents for measures of *g* and for measures of verbal abilities, spatial abilities, and short-term memory (Plomin, Fulker, Corley, & DeFries, 1997).

L. A. Thompson, Detterman, and Plomin (1991); Cardon et al. (1992); Luo et al. (1994); and Neubauer et al. (2000) estimated the extent to which familial resemblance for specific cognitive abilities might simply be due to the influence of *g* (Jensen, 1998). In all of the studies, the correlation between performance on IQ tests and on measures of specific cognitive abilities appeared to be related to shared genes. In other words, there is substantial overlap between the genetic influences on *g* and the genetic influences for specific cognitive abilities (Plomin & Spinath, 2002). At the same time, there was evidence, although not conclusive, for unique genetic influences on competencies in the areas of language, spatial cognition, and short-term memory. L. A. Thompson et al. estimated that about 50% of the genetic influences on these specific abilities overlapped the genetic influences on g, and the remaining genetic influences were unique to each of these specific abilities. Pedersen et al. (1992) found the same pattern for a sample of older adult twins and reported higher heritability estimates for some language and spatial measures than is typically found in younger samples, suggesting that genetic influences on specific cognitive abilities might show the same developmental increase found with measures of g. In contrast, intra-individual differences in specific abilities (e.g., verbal vs. spatial) appear to be largely due to unique environmental influences once the influence of g is controlled (Petrill, 2002). In other words, once the relation between specific abilities and g is removed, between-person differences in specific abilities are partly heritable, whereas much of the within-person differences in the level of ability in one domain (e.g., vocabulary) versus another (e.g., arithmetic) are largely due to the individual's unique experiences.

Speed of Processing

In comparison to behavior genetic research on g, there are fewer twin and family studies of the heritability of performance on information processing tasks, such as those that assess speed of processing and working memory. The studies that have been conducted have yielded estimates ranging from little to no genetic influences for performance on some speed-of-processing measures to genetic influences that explain more than 60% of the individual differences on other measures (Baker, Vernon, & Ho, 1991; Bouchard et al., 1990; Ho, Baker, & Decker, 1988; Luciano, Smith, et al., 2001; McGue, Bouchard, Lykken, & Feuer, 1984; Neubauer et al., 2000; P. A. Vernon, 1989). The results for composite measures (i.e., measures summed across tasks) are more consistent and indicate that genetic influences account for about 50% of the individual differences in inspection time, speed of processing, and variability in speed of processing, with most of the remaining individual differences related to unique environmental influences. Consistent with the pattern shown in Figure 8.5, it appears that genetic influences on individual differences in speed of processing and related competencies are smaller in childhood (Petrill, Luo, Thompson, & Detterman, 1996) than in adulthood (McClearn et al., 1997).

Several studies have also sought to determine whether the relation between information processing tasks and measures of g can be explained by shared genes (Baker et al., 1991; Ho et al., 1988; Luciano, Smith, et al., 2001; Neubauer et al., 2000). The results of these studies are consistent and indicate that shared genetic influences explain nearly all of the relation between information processing measures and measures of g (Plomin &

Spinath, 2002; Posthuma, de Geus, Baaré, Hulshoff Pol, Kahn, & Boomsma, 2002). As an example, Neubauer et al. (2000) found that about 50% of the variability on a composite speed-of-processing measure was related to genetic influences and 50% to unique environmental influences. The genetic correlation—the extent to which individual differences on two measures can be attribute to shared genes—between this composite and two measures of gF was .46 and .49, whereas the correlation was .40 with a measure of gC. These shared genes explained all of the phenotypic (i.e., measured) correlation (about −0.5) between speed of processing and fluid intelligence and about 80% of the correlation with crystallized intelligence. Stated more directly, these results suggest that the genetic influences that result in faster speed of processing, quicker inspection times, and greater consistency in speed of processing are the same genetic influences that contribute to high measured intelligence, especially fluid intelligence. These same studies also suggest genetic influences that are uniquely related to performance on information processing tasks and intelligence tests. The implication is that only a portion of the heritable influences on g can be explained by the heritable influences on speed of processing.

Working Memory

Working memory is, of course, an excellent theoretical candidate to explain some of the remaining heritable influences on g. It is known that between 30% and 60% of the individual differences on measures of short-term memory are heritable (Ando, Ono, & Wright, 2001; Pedersen et al., 1992), but much less is known about the heritable influences on working memory, which includes short-term memory and the executive functions involved in manipulating information represented in short-term memory (Baddeley, 1986; Cowan, 1995). Fortunately, the heritability of working memory and the genetic relation between working memory and intelligence has been recently explored in samples of adolescents and young adults from Japan (Ando et al., 2001) and Australia (Luciano, Wright, et al., 2001).

Both studies suggest that about 50% of the individual differences in working memory are related to genetic influences and the remaining 50% to unique environmental influences (Ando et al., 2001; Luciano, Wright, et al., 2001). The results for Ando et al. are particularly informative because these researchers used both verbal and spatial measures of working memory and were able to separate the short-term memory component from the executive component of working memory. In this study, genetic influences explained 49% and 43% of the individual differences in the executive processes for spatial and verbal working memory, respectively. There were genetic influences that were common to these executive competencies, short-term memory, and measures of gF and gC, as well as genetic influences that were unique to the spatial and verbal domains (see also Luciano et al., 2003). The common genetic influences explained 64% of the individual differences in gF but only 26% of the individual differences in gC. The results are preliminary but nonetheless suggest that the relation between working memory and fluid intelligence is mediated, in part, by a set of genes that is related to performance on both types of measures. The results also suggest that there are genes uniquely related to the ability to process and represent information in the language (i.e., verbal) and spatial domains, in keeping with hierarchical models of human abilities and in keeping with the finding that the left and right dorsolateral prefrontal regions are engaged during the processing of verbal and spatial information, respectively (E. E. Smith & Jonides, 1999; K. E. Stephan et al., 2003).

Brain Structure

Heritability Estimates. Twin and family studies of individual differences in the volume and structure of the whole brain and specific brain regions indicate moderate to substantial genetic influences, small to moderate unique environmental influences, and occasional shared environmental influences (Baaré et al., 2001; Bartley, Jones, & Weinberger, 1997; D. H. Geschwind, Miller, DeCarli, & Carmelli, 2002; Pennington et al., 2000; Posthuma et al., 2000; Posthuma, de Geus, & Boomsma, 2002; P. Thompson et al., 2001). Baaré and his colleagues used imaging techniques to determine the overall brain volume and corresponding volumes of gray (neurons) and white (axons) matter for twin and sibling young adults, specifically 54 monozygotic twin pairs, 58 dizygotic twin pairs, and 34 of their siblings. The inclusion of twins and siblings enabled a very sensitive assessment of shared and unique environmental influences on these features of brain anatomy, on top of genetic influences. Genetic influences explained 90% of the individual differences in total brain volume and 82% and 87% of the individual differences in volume of gray and white matter, respectively. The remaining differences were due to unique environmental effects; there were no significant shared environmental effects.

In a study of older (around age 70) twins, D. H. Geschwind and his colleagues (2002) found that 64% of the individual differences in total brain volume could be attributed to genetic influences, whereas 23% and 13% of the differences could be attributed to shared and unique environmental influences, respectively. They also found moderate genetic influences for the size of more specific brain regions (27% to 56%), as well as moderate unique environmental influences and some shared environmental influences. The most important shared environmental influences were for the left frontal (explaining 22% of the individual differences) and left temporal (explaining

26% of the individual differences) cortices, whereas the most important (explaining $\geq$ 45% of the individual differences) unique environmental effects were for the parietal and occipital cortices of both hemispheres. Overall, individual differences in the volume of the frontal lobes were more strongly related to genetic than to environmental influences, and individual differences in the volume of the posterior regions were more strongly related to environmental (largely unique) than to genetic influences. They also confirmed the findings of Zilles and his colleagues (1996) and of Holloway and de la Coste-Lareymondie (1982; Holloway, 1996) for the endocasts of *H. erectus*. Specifically, the right frontal cortex was larger than the left frontal cortex, whereas the right occipital cortex was smaller than the left occipital cortex. This pattern was highly heritable, especially for right-handed individuals.

In the most sophisticated of these brain imaging studies, P. Thompson et al. (2001) constructed three-dimensional maps of the entire brain for sets of monozygotic and dizygotic twins and were able to estimate the degree of anatomical similarity of the entire cortex for these twin pairs. The structure of the brains of both monozygotic and dizygotic pairs was highly similar and in some brain regions was indistinguishable comparing one monozygotic twin to the other. These latter regions included Broca's and Wernicke's areas, both associated with language functions; the parietal–occipital association cortices; and several prefrontal regions, including part of the dorsolateral prefrontal cortex (area 46; see Figure 7.3). The twins were also administered an IQ test and a battery of working memory and selective attention measures. Performance on all of these measures was weighted to provide an overall measure of g but would be biased toward gF with some contributions of gC. The relation between performance on the measure of g and volume of gray matter in the entire brain and in the frontal, temporal, parietal, and occipital cortices was then examined. Individual differences in g were related only to volume of the frontal cortex, while simultaneously controlling for volume of all other regions.

Allometry. Because individual differences in the volume of the entire brain and that of specific brain regions is moderately to strongly heritable, issues concerning allometric influences on brain size and structure need to be addressed. As I discussed in the Allometry and Size of the Neocortex section of chapter 4, selection that acted to increase the size of one brain region could result in an incidental, allometric expansion of all other brain regions (Finlay & Darlington, 1995). The implications are of central importance, because an allometric expansion would suggest that even if the size of most brain regions is highly heritable, the regions themselves might be not be related to a specific selection pressure. As a result, the function assumed by these regions would be largely determined by patterns of early experience (Quartz & Sejnowski, 1997). If this is the case, then brain volume and volume of all other brain regions would be governed by the same developmental processes (see Development of the Neocortex section of chap. 4) and genetic influences, but would not be of particular interest with respect to specific ecological and social selection pressures (Adaptation and Selection section of chap. 3).

Although the results cannot be considered conclusive, behavior genetic studies suggest both allometric and region-specific genetic influences on brain volume and structure. Using the sample of twins and siblings described by Baaré et al. (2001), Posthuma et al. (2000) sought to determine if the size of the cerebellum (involved in motor movement and some learning) was related to the same genetic influences that determine body size and cranial capacity. Overall, 88% of the individual differences in cerebellar volume were related to genetic influences, and 30% of the variation in cerebellar volume was related to the same genetic influences that determine body size and overall cranial capacity, that is, allometric influences. At the same time, they determined that "58% of the total variance in cerebellar volume is due to genetic factors that are unique to cerebellar volume" (Posthuma et al., 2000, p. 316). The cortical maps used by P. Thompson et al. (2001) suggest that genetic influences on individual differences in brain volume and structure are strong, but that the extent of these influences varies across brain regions. Their results are in need of replication but suggest genetic influences on the size and structure of the frontal cortex that cannot be explained by allometric relations, and are consistent with neurobiological research that suggests some differences in the pattern of gene expression in different regions of the cortex during prenatal development (Development of the Neocortex section of chap. 4), especially as related to the development of the frontal cortex (Piao et al., 2004).

Summary. Behavior genetic studies of brain volume and structure provide a link to the research described throughout chapter 4 and suggest both allometric and region-specific genetic influences on individual differences in brain anatomy and presumably function. The latter findings are consistent with the proposal that the structure and function of different brain regions have been shaped, to some degree, by different selection pressures (Barton & Harvey, 2000; D. A. Clark, Mitra, & Wang, 2001; de Winter & Oxnard, 2001). These same studies also suggest small to moderate allometric and environmental influences on individual differences in brain volume. The latter influences appear to be especially prominent in many of the posterior brain regions. Environmental influences are, of course, indicative of plasticity in the organization and perhaps functioning of these regions, as I described in the Experiential Modification of Brain Organization section of chapter 4. With respect to the issues I address in this chapter, the most intriguing finding is that individual differences in the volume and organization of the prefrontal cortex, including the dorsolateral prefrontal cortex, are highly heritable and have been linked to individual differences in general intelligence (P. Thompson et al., 2001).

Genetic Markers

Early estimates suggest that the human genome is composed of about 30,000 functional genes and many more functional proteins (International Human Genome Sequencing Consortium, 2001; Venter et al., 2001). Venter et al. estimated that differences between the human genome and those of at least a few other species are most pronounced for genes involved in the development and functioning of the brain and several other biological systems (e.g., those involved in immune functions). The number of genes involved in the construction and functioning of the human brain is not yet known but will be in the thousands. The vast number of genes influencing brain development and functioning greatly complicates the search for the perhaps 100 genes underlying the heritability of intelligence and related cognitive competencies (e.g., working memory). The difficulty is further complicated by evidence suggesting that each of these genes has small effects, that is, that individual differences in intelligence result from the additive effects of many genes. Detecting even one of these genes is analogous to searching for a needle in a haystack.

Nonetheless, several methods are currently being used in the search for these genes (see Plomin & Craig, 2001). The most ambitious and largest of these endeavors is the IQ QTL Project headed by Robert Plomin; QTL (quantitative trait loci) refers to multiple genetic loci that contribute to quantitative, or measurable, traits (Plomin, 2002; Plomin & Neiderhisher, 1991). Early results for this project and related studies were mixed. A genetic marker that appeared to be correlated with intelligence was identified in several studies (Plomin et al., 1995; Skuder et al., 1995), but a follow-up study failed to confirm this finding (Petrill et al., 1998). Other scientists have sought to determine if normal variation in genes—different copies of the same gene (i.e., alleles)—that influence brain development or functioning are linked to normal variation in IQ scores, but they have not found an association (Deary et al., 2003; Mazzocco & Reiss, 1997). More recently, Plomin and his colleagues have developed a sophisticated and conservative multistage approach for identifying the genes and alleles that differ comparing lower- and higher-IQ groups and that are transmitted from parents to children in the highest IQ group (Plomin, Hill, et al., 2001). Although not conclusive, it appears that this research group is close to identifying several genes that contribute to high general intelligence (see Plomin & Spinath, 2002).

Evolution and Heritability

In the Natural Selection section of chapter 2, I described the basic mechanisms of evolutionary change and research on the heritability of associated traits, that is, traits that covary with survival or reproductive prospects in natural populations. In these populations, strong selection pressures often reduce the heritability of the associated traits, although for a variety of reasons they do not typically reduce the heritability to zero (Stearns, 1992). As I described, the median heritability values suggest that between 26% and 53% of the individual differences in life history (e.g., age of maturation), physiological (e.g., cardiovascular capacity), behavioral (e.g., mating displays), and morphological (e.g., body size) traits are due to genetic influences (Mousseau & Roff, 1987). There are some instances of higher heritabilities (h^2s of 0.65 to 0.90) for traits that covary with survival or reproductive outcomes, such as beak size in Darwin's finches (Boag, 1983), but more typically the values are moderate.

The heritability estimates for specific cognitive abilities (e.g., spatial abilities), speed of processing, inspection time, working memory, size of many specific brain regions, and general intelligence during early childhood are all in the same range found for naturally or sexually selected traits in wild populations of other species. The heritability estimates for general intelligence in later childhood and in adulthood and for total brain size ($h^2 > 0.7$), in contrast, are higher than is typically found for selected traits. These high heritability estimates might reflect a relaxation of the pressures that resulted in the expansion of the human neocortex and in general intelligence during recent evolutionary history. A relaxation of pressures means that the strength of the relation between these traits and survival and reproductive outcomes is reduced, although not necessarily to zero. A relaxation of selection pressures could result in a cross-generational increase in the magnitude of heritability estimates, because individuals across a broader range of abilities would survive and successfully reproduce.

There would also be a gradual decline in total brain volume and in overall IQ scores. As I described in the Brain Evolution section of chapter 3, the EQ of modern humans appears to have peaked between 20,000 and 35,000 thousand years ago and has declined 3% to 4% since that time (Holloway, 1996; Ruff, Trinkaus, & Holliday, 1997). The pattern suggests that the pressures that resulted in the rapid increase in EQ beginning about 500,000 years ago have been relaxed during the past 10,000 to 20,000 years (Brace, 1995). During this time frame, agriculture, economic specialization, city-states, and other changes were becoming increasingly central features of human subsistence activities and social organization in many parts of the world (J. Clutton-Brock, 1992; Hole, 1992). The implication is that changes in social organization resulted in a relaxation, but not a negation, of the selection pressures associated with expansion of human brain size. Whether the decline in EQ and brain size has been associated with a decline in population-level intellectual abilities—after controlling for recent secular improvements—is not known but is a possibility, given the moderate relation between brain size and IQ (Rushton & Ankney, 1996). In any event, a relaxation of the pressures that selected for the evolution of general intelligence is consistent with a slight dysgenic effect in modern populations and during recent history—that is, lower-ability individuals have a higher reproductive success than higher-ability individuals (Lynn, 1996).

The high heritability estimates might also result from social and cultural changes that have improved the living conditions of large segments of the populations in modern, industrial societies. Improved living conditions appear to result in most individuals receiving the experiences needed to achieve their full potential (Scarr, 1992), and this in turn is associated with higher heritability estimates than found for populations living in less optimal conditions (D. C. Rowe, Jacobson, & Van den Oord, 1999; Turkheimer, Haley, Waldron, D'Onofrio, & Gottesman, 2003). The time scales associated with these recent environmental changes and those associated with the decline in EQ are very different—about 100 years for the former and 10,000 or more years for the latter. Thus, recent improvements in IQ may be comparatively minor when set against a longer-term decline (e.g., Loehlin, 1998; Lynn, 1996).

Environment

Behavior Genetic Studies

Behavior genetic studies suggest that individual differences in general intelligence and more specific cognitive abilities (e.g., spatial) are influenced by genes and by environmental experiences. The environmental effects are composed of influences shared by family members, such as the wealth of the family, and influences that are unique to each individual, as I mentioned earlier. Although it is clear that these environmental influences are important contributors to individual differences in mental abilities, the specific types of experiences that influence such abilities are not well understood. Nonetheless, I provide a brief review of some of the environmental experiences that might influence individual differences in general intelligence.

Prenatal Environment. In theory, many factors, such as maternal nutrition or alcohol use, may influence the prenatal environment in ways that can affect early brain development and, through this, intelligence. Indeed, in an analysis of 212 behavior genetic studies, B. Devlin, Daniels, and Roeder (1997) estimated that "maternal effects," including prenatal environment, could account for as much as 20% of the similarity in the IQ scores of pairs of monozygotic twins and 5% of the similarity of among other siblings. They suggested that these maternal effects have been incorporated into the genetic influences shown in Figure 8.5, and thus previous work has overestimated heritable influences on intelligence. However, their overall estimate that about 50% of the individual differences in IQ—across all ages—are due to genetic influences is in keeping with Bouchard and McGue's (1981) estimate. They also found evidence, though not conclusive, of age-related increases in heritable influences, as shown in Figure 8.5. In any case, if these maternal effects are confirmed, they would explain an important portion of the shared environment effects on intelligence.

One way to assess specific prenatal maternal effects is to examine the relation between maternal use of various drugs, such as alcohol, and children's later intelligence. One well-known example is fetal alcohol syndrome (FAS), in which maternal alcohol use during pregnancy is associated with brain malformations and lower IQ scores in their children (J. West, 1986). However, only a minority of fetuses exposed to alcohol develop FAS, and it is unclear whether prenatal exposure to moderate levels of alcohol and other potentially damaging chemicals have long-term influences on intelligence. Two longitudinal studies have addressed this issue for alcohol (Greene et al., 1991; Streissguth, Barr, Sampson, Darby, & Martin, 1989), and one of these addressed it for many other drugs (e.g., valium, barbiturates, marijuana). Both studies included more than 350 children and their mothers. The mothers were assessed during the pregnancy and the children were assessed at 4 years of age in one study (Streissguth et al., 1989) and multiple times through 5 years of age in the other (Greene et al., 1991). Streissguth et al. found that none of the multiple drugs used during pregnancy were significantly related to children's IQ scores at age 4 except alcohol. They found that maternal consumption of three or more drinks per day was associated with an estimated loss of five IQ points, but Greene et al. found no such effect. In an analysis that estimated the "worst case" situation, but excluded cases of FAS, Greene et al. estimated that moderate alcohol use may result in a two point loss in IQ scores, if any loss at all.

Another way to assess prenatal effects is to compare monozygotic twin pairs who differ in prenatal environment. About two of three such pairs share the same placenta and a prenatal blood supply that circulates between them. The remaining pairs develop with separate placentas and blood supplies. Of course, these latter pairs are exposed to a very similar prenatal environment and the same type of prenatal environment experienced by dizygotic twins. Still, these prenatal experiences are not as similar as those experienced by the monozygotic pairs who share a blood supply. In a large assessment (including 451 twin pairs) of the potential effects of these early environmental differences, N. Jacobs et al. (2001) found no relation between the type of prenatal environment experienced by monozygotic twins and IQ scores in childhood, although twins that shared a prenatal placenta and blood supply were slightly more similar than other monozygotic twins on an arithmetic and vocabulary test. In keeping with genetic influences, monozygotic twins with separate placentas and blood supplies were more similar for IQ scores and for scores on nearly all tests of more specific abilities than were dizygotic twins.

Family Environment. As shown in Figure 8.5, behavior genetic studies indicate important shared and unique environmental influences on intelligence, especially during the preschool years and early childhood. One potentially important class of shared environmental influences is the home environment, as indexed by parental attentiveness to the child, amount of conversation, and other measures. Evidence for the importance of these influences is provided by the finding that adopted children with intelligent adoptive parents score higher on IQ tests than do adopted children with less intelligent adoptive parents, but the strength of the relation is small (rs of about 0.2; Bouchard & McGue, 1981; Scarr, 1992; Scarr & Weinberg, 1977; Weinberg, Scarr, & Waldman, 1992). In an innovative study of shared experiences, Segal (2000) compared sets of virtual twins on various measures of cognitive ability and IQ. Virtual twins are formed when parents adopt a child and have a biological child of about the same age. These children thus grow up in the same household with the same parents, go to the same school, and likely have many of the same friends. The IQ scores of virtual twins, at least in childhood, are moderately related ($r = 0.26$). These adoption and virtual twin studies suggest a modest influence of shared environments on individual differences in intelligence, at least in childhood. They do not, however, tell us whether the influence of the family environment is more important for some families than for others or for some children than others (e.g., Collins, Maccoby, Steinberg, Hetherington, & Bornstein, 2000).

D. C. Rowe and his colleagues conducted a series of studies based on a national sample of 90,000 U.S. adolescents, the National Longitudinal Study of Adolescent Health (Neiss & Rowe, 2000; D. C. Rowe, Jacobson, et al., 1999). With the use of large numbers of twins and adoptees from this sample, they were able to address several issues that could not be fully assessed with previous studies. Neiss and Rowe identified 565 adopted adolescents and matched them to 565 adolescents living with their biological parents. The adolescents were matched on age, sex, race, and IQ and were all from two-parent families. Parental education was available for both parents for 392 pairs of matched families and did not differ comparing adoptive to biological families. As found in other adoption studies, parent–offspring correlations were higher for biological adolescents (rs 0.36 to 0.41) than for adoptive adolescents (rs 0.16 to 0.18). More important, the shared effect of family environment was significant and explained about 4% of the individual differences for performance on a measure of gC.

Using the same national sample but this time focusing on twins, siblings, half-siblings, cousins, and unrelated siblings (e.g., from blended families), D. C. Rowe, Jacobson, et al. (1999) again examined the relative contributions of genetic and environmental influences on individual differences in gC. In addition, they examined whether the importance of these influences varied across socioeconomic backgrounds (indexed by parental education). Overall, 57% of the individual differences in gC were estimated to be related to genetic influences and 13% to shared family environment. However, the estimates for the relative influence of genes and the shared environment varied by level of parental education. For parents with a high school diploma or better, about 75% of the individual differences in their children's gC scores were related to genetic influences and none of this variability was related to shared family environment. About 20% of the parents had not completed high school and for these families, 26% and 23% of the individual differences in their children's gC scores were related to genetics and shared family environment, respectively. In an analysis of a sample of largely lower-SES children, Turkheimer et al. (2003) found little genetic influences on individual differences in IQ scores (measuring gF and gC) for children in the lowest SES families and moderate shared family and unique environmental influences. As SES increased, the estimated genetic contributions to individual differences in gC and gF increased and environmental influences decreased.

These recent studies (D. C. Rowe, Jacobson, et al., 1999; Turkheimer et al., 2003) are consistent with two previous studies (Fischbein, 1980; Scarr-Salapatek, 1971) and support Scarr's (1992) prediction that environmental influences on cognitive abilities will be the largest in the least stimulating environments. In other words, families that provide an intellectually stimulating environment (e.g., more complex parent–child language discourse, availability of books) allow all of their children to develop their full intellectual potential. The beneficial effects of such family contexts are not detected in behavior genetic studies, because these studies focus on individual differences, and in optimal environments individual differences are more strongly related to genetic variability than to variability across families. It appears that the environments provided by these families can result in improvements in mean levels of competency, even when individual differences are more strongly related to genetics (D. Rowe et al., 1999; Stoolmiller, 1999). The finding for poorly educated parents provides direct evidence for the influence of shared family environment on individual and mean levels of general intelligence, although the strength of these effects are modest.

Unique Environment. As shown in Figure 8.5, the strongest environmental influences on individual differences in general intelligence, as well as specific cognitive abilities, are experiences that are unique to each individual. Although errors in measuring IQ are also subsumed under these effects, it is almost certain that unique experiences can influence the development and expression of intellectual abilities. Identifying unique effects has proved to be difficult, however (Turkheimer & Waldron, 2000). One class of unique effects may involve individual differences in niche seeking, that is, differences in the type of environment people create for themselves and in the types of experiences they seek (Scarr & McCartney, 1983). One such niche-seeking effect may be related to individual differences in openness to experience, which, as I mentioned earlier, is related to individual differences in gC (Bates & Shieles, 2003; Mackintosh & Bennett, 2003). Two individuals with the same potential to develop high crystallized intelligence will differ in the actual level of crystallized knowledge they acquire to the extent that they differ in openness to experience. No doubt, there are many other yet-to-be-identified traits and experiences that account for the unique environmental effects on general intelligence.

Interventions

There have been numerous environmental enrichment interventions, such as Head Start, designed to improve the cognitive and social competencies of children living in poverty or other difficult circumstances (see Ramey & Ramey, 1998a; Spitz, 1986). These types of interventions appear to result in a number of beneficial outcomes, including improved academic functioning (Lazar, Darlington, Murray, Royce, & Snipper, 1982). Many of these interventions were not designed to target children's general intelligence per se, but nonetheless have been used to assess whether such enrichment can improve intellectual functioning. The interpretation of these studies results is hotly debated and is beyond the scope of this book (e.g., Detterman & Thompson, 1997; Ramey & Ramey, 1998a; Spitz, 1999). The bottom line is that many of these interventions are initially associated with modest, and sometimes substantial, improvements in IQ scores, but most of these gains fade with time.

Children born into difficult circumstances and adopted into higher-SES families experience an intervention that lasts throughout their childhood and adolescence. In comparison to other children born into difficult circumstances and who remain with their birth parents, these adopted children have higher IQ scores in early childhood, although some, but not all, of these gains appear to fade by adolescence (Weinberg et al., 1992). Duyme, Dumaret, and Tomkiewicz (1999) identified a group of 69 children who were abused and neglected during the preschool years and adopted around age 5. All of these children had preadoption IQ scores below the 20th percentile. Sixty-five of these children were located 6 to 12 years later and reassessed. The average difference in IQ score was 14 points, meaning the typical child had a below-average score before adoption and a low-average score in adolescence. The gain in IQ scores was highest for the group of children adopted into professional homes and lowest, though still significant, for children adopted into working class homes. For children adopted into professional and working class homes, the gain in IQ was highest for children with the highest preadoption IQs, indicating that the brighter of the adoptees gained the most from their experiences in their adoptive families.

The intervention studies suggest that many children will not experience long-term improvements in general intelligence with early short-term environmental enrichment (Spitz, 1986), although some may achieve modest gains (Ramey & Ramey, 1998b). At the same time, many children living in the most difficult circumstances do not appear to achieve their full intellectual potential, and it is these children who can benefit substantively through adoption and perhaps other sustained interventions. At this point, the minimal amount and form of experiences that will result in the best outcomes within genetic-based limits for most children are unclear (Scarr, 1992). When considered in light of the recent studies by D. C. Rowe, Jacobson, et al. (1999), Turkheimer et al. (2003), and related research (Fischbein, 1980), it appears that the majority of children in modern societies receive these minimal experiences, but at the same time a significant minority of children are growing up in environments that do not allow for the achievement of their full intellectual potential.

Secular Trends

In a now classic analysis, Flynn (1987) demonstrated substantial cross-generational gains in mean IQ levels in 14 industrialized nations from the early part of the 20th century throughout the 1970s. These changes, called the *Flynn effect*, have been confirmed in numerous studies and are evident for measures of both gF and gC, but they tend to be larger for measures of fluid intelligence (Flynn, 1998; Jensen, 1998). The extent of the gains varied from one country to the next but was typically about 3 to 5 IQ points per decade from the 1930s to the 1970s. Kanaya, Scullin, and Ceci (2003) discussed the numerous legal, social, and educational implications. My focus is on the implications of these changes for understanding the evolution and proximate expression of g.

Flynn (1987) found no evidence that the rate of increase was slowing through the 1970s, but Lynn and Hampson (1986) found that the rate of increase had slowed in Japan by the 1970s, and Teasdale and Owen (2000) found that the rise had all but stopped in Denmark by the 1990s. Several studies by Teasdale and Owen (1989, 2000) provide an important illustration of the trend and address the issue of whether the increases are found for all levels of intellectual ability. These studies are of particular importance because the identical IQ test was administered to 90% to 95% of all 18-

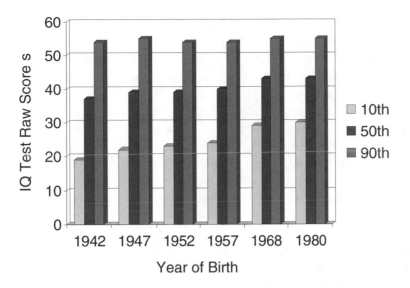

Figure 8.6. Changes in raw IQ scores across generations for individuals at the 10th, 50th, and 90th percentiles. The increase in mean IQ across generations appears to be largely due to improvements at the lower end of the range of intellectual ability. Based on data presented in "Continuing Secular Increases in Intelligence and a Stable Prevalence of High Intelligence Levels," by T. W. Teasdale and D. R. Owen, 1989, *Intelligence, 13,* p. 260. Copyright 1989 by T. W. Teasdale; and "Forty-Year Secular Trends in Cognitive Abilities," by T. W. Teasdale and D. R. Owen, 2000, *Intelligence, 28,* p. 117. Copyright 2000 by T. W. Teasdale. Adapted with permission of the authors.

year-old men born in eastern Denmark. These men were conscripted into the Danish military and represented about 40% of the Danish men born between 1939 and 1980. Teasdale and Owen (1989) selected a representative sample of about 10% of these men and examined IQ scores for groups broken into 5-year intervals (e.g., 1939–1943, 1944–1948). Each of these groups included at least 6,500 individuals. The follow-up study (Teasdale & Owen, 2000) included men born in 1970 and 1980 and tested in 1988 and 1998, respectively. Average raw scores for individuals at the 10th, 50th, and 90th percentiles are shown in Figure 8.6 for individuals born between 1942 and 1980. During this span of four decades, there was a modest improvement in mean IQ scores. However, there was no change for individuals at the 90th percentile and a substantial improvement for individuals at the 10th percentile.

The pattern suggests that during this time span there was little or no change in the general intelligence of the mentally gifted; the intellectual abilities of individuals with average potential showed small to moderate improvements, but no apparent changes in reaction or inspection times (Nettelbeck & Wilson, 2004); and the intellectual abilities of individuals with IQ scores that were significantly below average increased substantially.

Lynn and Hampson (1986) reported a similar trend for Great Britain. Teasdale and Owen's (1989, 2000) findings are in keeping with the analyses of Duyme et al. (1999); D. C. Rowe, Jacobson, et al. (1999); Turkheimer et al. (2003); and the predictions of Scarr (1992). More precisely, all of these findings indicate that growing up in difficult environments does not allow for the full expression of intellectual potential, especially for children with the highest intellectual potential (Duyme et al., 1999). The cross-generational pattern suggests that the environments of the lower strata of human populations in industrial societies improved the most during the 20th century, at least in terms of the factors that contribute to the expression of one's intellectual potential. The findings for early intervention studies appear contra to this conclusion, but these interventions might be applied on top of already potent secular changes, and thus the early enrichments might not add to these more general changes. Alternatively, the early interventions may move children closer to their potential earlier in life, but as other children enter school and thus receive enriched experiences, they catch up, and the effects of the interventions appear to fade.

In any event, a variety of mechanisms have been proposed as underlying the cross-generational increase in mean IQ scores, including poor tests (Flynn, 1987), improved nutrition and health care (Lynn, 1998), universal education (Ceci, 1991; Teasdale & Owen, 1989), increased complexity of the secular environment (e.g., increase in books, complex games; Greenfield, 1998), interactions between these environmental improvements (e.g., schooling), and individual niche seeking (Dickens & Flynn, 2001; but see D. C. Rowe & Rodgers, 2002; Loehlin, 2002). As might be imagined, these are vigorously debated and as yet unresolved issues (see Jensen, 1998; Neisser, 1998). At this point, it appears that the improvement in mean level of gC and especially gF is due to a combination of mechanisms, each of which contributes to the overall increase. These secular changes appear to be most beneficial to individuals with high intellectual potential who are living in the most difficult circumstances.

At first blush, these recent secular increases in mean IQ level appear to contradict my earlier suggestion that mean levels of g may have declined over the past 20,000 or so years, according to the 3% to 4% decline in mean EQ over this time period (Ruff et al., 1997). The changes in EQ occurred over a time scale that is 100 to 200 times longer than the time scale associated with the Flynn effect, and thus comparisons of these changes must be done with caution. At this point, it is likely that the Flynn effect is the result of improved environmental conditions interacting with phenotypic plasticity in the brain and cognitive systems that support gC and gF. These improvements would result in higher measured and actual mean levels of intelligence, which in turn would obscure the measurement of any longer term changes in the genotype that contributes to the development of the brain and cognitive systems that support gC and gF (Lynn, 1996).

EVOLVED MODULES, MENTAL MODELS, AND g

In several earlier sections, I touched on a few potential links between evolutionary issues and empirical and theoretical research on g, such as the potential relation between evolutionary expansion of the size of the neocortex and speed of processing. In the following sections, I focus on broader issues. In the first, I attempt to integrate research on g with the invariant–variant continuum that I introduced in chapter 4 and elaborated in chapter 6 and with the forms of selection pressure associated with information variability. In the second section, I make several proposals regarding the relation between fluid intelligence, autonoetic mental models, and the motivation to control, and in the final section, I discuss modularity and crystallized intelligence.

Variation and Selection Pressures

Invariance–Variance

The evolved function of brain and cognition is to process information patterns and guide associated behavioral responses that have tended to covary with survival or reproductive outcomes during the species' evolutionary history. As I proposed in chapter 4 and in Geary and Huffman (2002), these patterns vary along a continuum from invariant to variant. Invariant patterns, such as the basic shape of the human body, should result in the evolution of modular systems. Variant patterns can be understood on at least two levels. The first includes variant patterns within the constraints of modular systems, such as individual differences in body shape (e.g., height, weight). If sensitivity to this variation covaries with survival or reproductive prospects (e.g., if weight affects health of a prospective mate, as it does; Manson et al., 1995), then some degree of plasticity should evolve in the corresponding brain and cognitive systems. The second includes variant patterns at a more macro level, as in the behavioral dynamics of predator–prey and social relationships. If variation at this level requires integration of information across modular systems, then the potential for the emergence of executive brain and cognitive systems emerges, specifically systems for tracking and integrating changing information patterns across more modularized systems.

The evolved modular systems (chap. 5) associated with invariant information patterns, along with learning during the individual's lifetime, can be mapped onto Cattell's and Horn's (Cattell, 1963; Horn & Cattell, 1966) crystallized intelligence. As I suggest in chapter 9 (Academic Learning section), the ability to learn during a lifetime should be dependent, in part, on the extent to which modular systems are plastic and thus adaptable to novel conditions. For humans, the result is the potential for the acquisition of evolutionarily novel, or biologically secondary, competencies, such as reading (Geary, 1995; Rozin, 1976). Adapting to novelty and dealing with complex and varied information is the primary condition that Cattell and Horn found to be associated with fluid intelligence, and thus fluid intelligence can be linked to the selection pressures that create novelty and complexity, but at the macro level.

Selection Pressures

I discussed three classes of selection pressure—climatic, ecological, and social—in earlier chapters and concluded that a combination of ecological and social factors likely contributed to the evolution of the human brain and mind. Of these, I argued, as have many others (Alexander, 1989; Dunbar, 1998; Humphrey, 1976), that patterns of cooperation and competition among individuals and coalitions of individuals were the most potent of these pressures, at least during more recent human evolutionary history. More precisely, the complexity of these social dynamics and the advantages associated with some degree of behavioral unpredictability during social competition (Maynard Smith & Price, 1973) result in variation at the macro-level. These conditions are consistent with the three selection criteria I outlined in chapter 7 (Problem Solving and Human Evolution section); specifically, they generate recurrent and somewhat unpredictable patterns of change during the life span, they favor the evolution of self-awareness, and they have the potential for generating a within-species co-evolutionary arms race.

Of these three criteria, the first generates conditions that provide a plausible explanation for the evolution of fluid intelligence. The first criteria means that social dynamics generate recurrent and somewhat unpredictable conditions that, in turn, would favor the evolution of brain and cognitive mechanisms that enable the ability to anticipate these conditions, inhibit heuristic-based responses, and generate novel behavioral solutions. As I elaborate later in this chapter, several of the components of fluid intelligence, including the ability to deal with novelty and change, and the corresponding attentional, inhibitory, and working memory competencies are well matched to these conditions. Of course, the third criterion is needed to explain the rapid expansion in EQ, and presumably fluid intelligence, during human evolution, and the second is related to the evolution of autonoetic mental models, of which gF is only one component.

Mental Models and Fluid Intelligence

My proposal in this section is that the empirical and theoretical research on general intelligence and especially fluid intelligence has identified many of the core features that support the use of autonoetic mental models, which evolved as a result of the social and to a lesser extent ecological pressures described in previous chapters. The core function of autonoetic mental models is the ability to mentally generate a problem space that includes a representation of the "perfect world" (see Mental Models and the Motivation to Control section of chap. 7). In the perfect world, the individual is in control of the social, biological, and physical resources that have tended to covary with survival and reproductive prospects during human evolutionary history: The behavior of other people and the flow of resources align with the individual's best interest. The real world operates differently, however. The goal is to generate strategies that will reduce the difference between conditions in the real world and those simulated in the perfect world, that is, to generate ways to gain better control of important relationships and resources.

The problem-solving processes, inference making, and reasoning used to devise the corresponding social and behavioral strategies are dependent on working memory, attentional control, and the supporting brain systems, along with a sense of self. In this view, the mechanisms that support an explicit, conscious awareness of information represented in working memory evolved as a result of the same social pressures that drove the evolution of autonoetic mental models and gF. Autonoetic or self-awareness is important to the extent that one must cope with the maneuvering of other people (e.g., their ability to read one's mind through a theory of mind competency)—that is, the perfect world of most people will involve manipulating others to behave in ways that are counter to their best interest. When many people with divergent and competing interests are able to simultaneously anticipate and mentally simulate these moves and countermoves, the complexity of social dynamics explodes, and the predictability of the dynamics decreases accordingly.

The ability to use these simulations is dependent on working memory, attentional control, and the underlying brain systems that I described in the Cognitive and Brain Systems section of chapter 7. These brain and cognitive systems function to deal with variation and novelty in social and ecological conditions, and thus they will not be constrained to process a particular form of information, as are the modular systems I described in chapter 5. These executive systems should therefore be engaged when individuals must cope with conditions and information that cannot be automatically and implicitly processed by modular systems, including items on intelligence tests and other measures of g. This does not mean that intelligence tests are not useful and valid; they clearly are, as I describe in the next chapter. Rather, 100 years of empirical research on *g*, and especially *gF*, has isolated those features of autonoetic mental models that are not strongly influenced by content and that enable explicit representations of information in working memory and an attentional dependent ability to manipulate this information in the service of strategic problem solving.

Cattell and Horn's (Cattell, 1963; Horn & Cattell, 1966) definition of fluid intelligence and subsequent research on the underlying cognitive and brain systems are consistent with this view: There is considerable overlap in the systems that support autonoetic mental models and those that support fluid abilities (e.g., Duncan et al., 2000). One important discrepancy involves self-awareness, which is a core feature of my proposal but not an aspect of fluid intelligence. The reason for the discrepancy lies in the initial development and goal of intelligence tests, specifically to predict academic performance (Binet & Simon, 1916). Because the initial goal was to predict learning in an evolutionarily novel context (i.e., school), the content of the items that compose intelligence tests was largely asocial. There were hints of a social component in the early research on general abilities, but the field did not progress in this way, given the goal of predicting school performance. Spearman (1904) found that above-average performance in academic domains was associated with above-average ratings of "common sense" or out-of-school competencies, which presumably involve some social situations (see also Legree, 1995). Galton's (1865, 1869) criteria for indexing "genius" was intimately linked to social eminence and success. As I describe in the next chapter, fluid abilities are still related to success at social competition, albeit competition in the evolutionarily novel and complex world of modern schools and work environments (Gottfredson, 1997).

Before turning to *gC*, note that my explanation suggests that the evolution of *gF* was due to social and ecological pressures that are independent of the current uses of standardized intelligence tests in modern society. The evolved function of *gF* is to cope with change and novelty in social and ecological conditions. As I discuss in the next chapter, these competencies support the learning of evolutionarily novel competencies during the life span, including learning in school and on the job. The latter are what IQ tests are designed to predict in the modern world, but this is not the evolved function of *gF* (see also Kanazawa, 2004).

Modularity and Crystallized Intelligence

Classes of Crystallized Intelligence

In the most comprehensive review of the psychometric literature ever conducted, J. B. Carroll (1993) concluded that most of the psychometric tests that index *gC* "involve language either directly or indirectly" (p. 599).

Included among these are tests of vocabulary, listening comprehension, word fluency, reading, and spelling. The two latter skills are taught in school, as are some of the other competencies that index crystallized intelligence, such as complex arithmetic, other school-taught quantitative skills, and mechanical abilities. General cultural knowledge is also an indicator of gC, as are some measures of spatial and visual abilities; the latter are, in addition, related to a lower stratum spatial-visualization ability domain (see Figure 8.1).

In total, these tests appear to tap many of the modular domains I described in chapter 5, in particular language and spatial representation. They do not appear to tap all of these domains, but this is potentially because not all of the modular competencies have been assessed. When other modular competencies are measured and correlated with intelligence, there is a relation: Legree (1995) found that measures that assessed knowledge of social conventions and social judgments were related to psychometric g, a combination of gC and gF. T. Hunt (1928) found that individuals who were sensitive to social cues (e.g., facial expressions) and other forms of social information scored higher on measures that would now be considered to tap both gC and gF. In others words, I am suggesting that the inherent knowledge represented in the modular systems described in chapter 5 defines one class of crystallized intelligence. The other class of crystallized intelligence is represented by the knowledge (e.g., facts, concepts, procedures) learned during the individual's lifetime through formal or informal instruction or just incidentally, as proposed by Cattell (1963). I discuss how this evolutionarily novel knowledge might be constructed through the interaction of gF, plasticity in modular systems, and experiences in the Academic Learning section of chapter 9.

Diminishing Returns

An interaction between gF and plasticity in modular systems as this relates to the construction of biologically secondary competencies provides an explanation for Spearman's (1927) law of diminishing returns. There is more within-person variability across specific abilities, such as writing versus mathematics, for individuals with above-average IQs than for other individuals. If gF and plasticity within modular systems determine the extent to which these systems can be modified during academic learning, then limits in either fluid intelligence or modular plasticity, or both, will place limits on academic learning. Intelligent individuals have fewer limits on their potential to acquire academic competencies, and thus if they devote more time to learning in one domain or another, the result will be a divergence in the level of skill developed in the two domains, in keeping with the finding that within-person differences across specific abilities are related to unique environmental experiences (Petrill, 2002).

CONCLUSION

It has been a century since Spearman's (1904) discovery that above-average abilities in one academic domain are associated with above-average abilities in other academic domains and with high peer ratings of common sense. He concluded that there must be a function or group of functions that contribute to ability across these domains. The function is general intelligence, g. In the ensuing 100 years, Spearman's results and hypothesis have been supported and elaborated (J. B. Carroll, 1993; Jensen, 1998; Thurstone, 1938). Psychologists now understand that g can be decomposed into fluid intelligence (gF)—the ability to problem solve as a means to adapt to novel and complex situations—and crystallized intelligence (gC)—the inherent (evolved modular) and learned store of knowledge (Cattell, 1963; Horn & Cattell, 1966). There are also more specific abilities that overlap to some extent with gF and gC but that, in addition, are unique to some extent (G. H. Thomson, 1951; Thurstone, 1938; P. E. Vernon, 1965); examples include abilities in the verbal, spatial, and quantitative domains.

During the past several decades, research psychologists have focused on identifying the cognitive processes and brain systems—Spearman's (1904) function or functions—that underlie individual differences in g, especially gF (Deary, 2000; Duncan et al., 2000; Jensen, 1998), as well as individual differences in specific abilities (E. Hunt et al., 1975). These endeavors have revealed that intelligent individuals identify subtle variations in information quickly and accurately (Deary & Stough, 1996), and once the information is represented in the perceptual system (e.g., as a word), it is processed quickly (Jensen & Munro, 1979) and consistently (Jensen, 1992). Once identified and processed by the perceptual system, the information is represented in short-term memory, and by means of attentional focus, a subset of this information is explicitly represented in working memory and made available to conscious awareness (Cowan, 1995). In comparison to other people, intelligent individuals can hold more information in working memory and are better able to reason about and draw inferences from the associated patterns (Embretson, 1995; Kyllonen & Christal, 1990; Stanovich, 1999). The combination of a high working memory capacity and the ability to reason about information represented in working memory defines several of the core cognitive competencies that underlie fluid intelligence.

The processes that support working memory, in turn, have been narrowed to the ability to control attention and inhibit irrelevant associations from intruding into working memory (Engle, 2002; Engle et al., 1995), speed of information processing (Fry & Hale, 2000), or some combination of these mechanisms. Whatever the contributions of speed of processing, brain imaging and cognitive-experimental studies are consistent with Engle's and his colleagues' (e.g., Kane & Engle, 2002) hypothesis that individual differences in attentional and inhibitory control are an integral component of individual differences in working memory and gF. The brain regions that have been associated with fluid intelligence include those described in the Cognitive and Brain Systems section of chapter 7, specifically the dorsolateral prefrontal cortex and the anterior cingulate cortex, among other regions (Duncan et al., 2000).

Individual differences in gF, gC, working memory, speed of processing, brain size, and so forth are influenced by heritable and environmental factors (Ando et al., 2001; Bouchard & McGue, 1981; P. A. Vernon, 1989). For most of these competencies, roughly 50% of the individual variation within a population can be attributed to variation in the underlying genes or in gene expression, and most of the remaining variation can be attributed to experiences that are unique to the individual. Developmentally, genetic influences tend to increase with age, and environmental influences, especially those shared among family members, decrease with age (McGue et al., 1993). Whatever the reason for this developmental change, most of the heritability estimates are in the range found for traits (e.g., body size) that covary with survival and reproductive outcomes in wild, nonhuman species (Mousseau & Roff, 1987). This in and of itself does not necessarily mean that these human cognitive abilities have evolved, but it does mean that the raw material necessary for their evolution is present.

Indeed, my proposal is that general intelligence, in particular gF, evolved as a result of the same social and to a lesser extent ecological selection pressures that drove the evolution of autonoetic mental models, which in turn can be linked to the motivation to control (Problem Solving and Human Evolution section of chap. 7). More precisely, fluid abilities represent the attentional and working memory components of autonoetic mental models but do not include other equally important components of these models (e.g., self-awareness). The evolutionary function of fluid abilities is to support control-related problem solving. These mechanisms are designed to cope with the varied and often unpredictable nature of human social dynamics, specifically to simulate variation in these dynamics and to generate social and behavioral strategies that enable, if effective, better control of relationships and other resources. Crystallized intelligence results from the operation of gF as this facilitates the acquisition of biologically secondary competencies, such as reading, and from inherent individual differences in the modular systems outlined in chapter 5.

9
GENERAL INTELLIGENCE
IN MODERN SOCIETY

In this final chapter, I explore the relevance of my motivation-to-control model and the evolution of general intelligence in modern society. The first task in arguing for such relevance is to outline how evolutionary issues and mechanisms associated with the motivation to control and general intelligence might relate to outcomes in modern societies, and I do so in the first section. If the nexus of affective, cognitive, conscious-psychological, and brain systems that define the motivation to control and the evolution of the nexus was significantly influenced by social competition, then components of this nexus, including general intelligence, should be predictive of the ability to compete for resource control in modern societies. As I discuss in the second section, social status and resource control in modern societies are defined by socioeconomic status (SES), which in turn is indexed by a combination of years of education, occupational status, and income. Individual differences in general intelligence, especially gF, or fluid intelligence, predict individual differences in each of these areas, in keeping with predictions of the evolutionary model. In the final section, I make several proposals regarding the mechanisms that might underlie the relation between general intelligence and the ability to learn evolutionarily novel competencies in school and on the job.

EVOLUTION AND SOCIAL COMPETITION

Let me return to the selection pressures and motivation to control that I introduced in chapter 3. Alexander's (1989) proposal was that once our hominid ancestors achieved ecological dominance, the primary pressure that drove hominid and eventually human evolution was competition with other people. I cast this competition as a struggle with other people for control of the social, biological, and physical resources that tended to covary with survival or reproductive outcomes during human evolutionary history (Geary, 1998). The evolutionary changes that enabled hominids and eventually humans to achieve ecological dominance likely included elaboration of folk biological modular systems and aspects of folk physical modular systems (e.g., as related to tool construction). If Alexander's proposal is correct, then these elaborations would have evolved before the ramping up of social competition and would remain elaborated, given the continuing need to secure resources from the ecology (Kaplan, Hill, Lancaster, & Hurtado, 2000). The elaboration of folk psychological modular systems and the emergence, or substantive elaboration, of autonoetic mental models would follow as a result of social competition.

Evidence for a relation between social competition and evolutionarily salient outcomes was provided in the Sexual Selection and Population Genetics and the Motivation to Control sections of chapter 3. In the former section, I describe genetic footprints that suggest a pattern of one population of men reproductively displacing another population of men in all regions of the world (Carvajal-Carmona et al., 2000; J. F. Wilson et al., 2001). These studies are consistent with coalitional male–male competition over control of the reproductive potential of women and the resources needed to raise families. In the latter section, I describe a relation between social status, resource control, and mortality risks in traditional societies today (Hill & Hurtado, 1996; United Nations, 1985) and in preindustrial and industrializing Western societies (e.g., Hed, 1987; H. Schultz, 1991). In these societies, higher social status and better resource control (e.g., food, shelter, servants) are associated with improved survival prospects and better reproductive outcomes (e.g., Betzig, 1986; Zerjal et al., 2003). In fact, it has only been during the past 100 to 200 years in which the strength of the relation between social status, resource control, and premature mortality has abated in Western societies (Schofield, Reher, & Bideau, 1991). Even in these societies, high social status and resource control are still associated with better physical health and a longer life span (Adler et al., 1994).

Motivation to Control

My motivation-to-control model includes a nexus of affective, conscious-psychological (e.g., mental models), cognitive (e.g., working memory), and modular systems, as well as supporting brain regions. The evolved function of this nexus is to guide the simulation and generation of behavioral strategies directed toward gaining access to and control of social, biological, and physical resources. *Social resources* refer to the behavior of other people, and the motivation to control is manifested as attempts to influence other people to behave in ways consistent with one's best interest. These social strategies are varied and include slavery and political manipulation, as well as social cooperation. *Biological and physical resources* most generally refer to food, medicine, territory, shelter, and so forth. For humans, the nature of biological and physical resources can vary from one ecology and culture to the next (Irons, 1979) and can range from concrete (e.g., cows) to symbolic (e.g., money). Control of symbolic resources, such as money, is important because it enables access to more concrete resources and affords an enhanced ability to influence the behavior of other people. These symbols (e.g., jewelry, clothing) are also status displays, and their use may influence how well one is treated in day-to-day social interactions.

In Western and many other cultures, resource control is now pegged to money and other symbolic resources (e.g., stock shares). The motivation to control in these societies is therefore focused, to some degree, on gaining control of these forms of resource. Control of monetary and related resources can, of course, be achieved in many ways, including marriage, theft, inheritance, and employment. The latter is the most common strategy in modern societies—that is, one way to get access to resources is to secure a high-paying job. These occupations not only provide a higher income, but also often result in greater control over one's work environment and greater influence over the behavior of other people in the work environment. Because of these benefits, competition for higher-paying and higher-status jobs is greater than that for lower-paying jobs. One way to increase one's ability to compete for these jobs is through additional or specialized education. In fact, a combination of educational level, occupational status, and income represents the individual's or family's SES, which is a broad indicator of social status within modern societies.

What I am trying to convey is that in terms of day-to-day activities, the ecologies of modern societies may appear to be very different than the types of social and ecological contexts in which the motivation to control evolved. However, beneath the surface there are many similarities: The basic social dynamics and complexity that I outlined in Exhibit 2.1 and

Table 3.2 are essentially the same. The nuances of male–female, parent–child, and other relationships may vary from one context to the next, but these same forms of relationship are human universals (D. E. Brown, 1991). More important, the basic dynamics and forms of social cooperation and conflict evident today are almost certainly the same basic dynamics that contributed to the evolution of the motivational, affective, and other systems that support engagement in these relationships (Bugental, 2000; Caporael, 1997). The struggle for access to and control of symbolic resources such as money is really no different than the struggle for control of more concrete resources: As I noted above, the outcome is the same. My point is that if the nexus of systems that support the motivation to control evolved as a result of social and to a lesser extent ecological pressures, then the same motivational dispositions should be expressed in modern societies. Moreover, individual differences in the supporting competencies, such as gF, should be associated with individual differences in the ability to compete for resource control in these societies.

General Intelligence and Modularity

General Intelligence

In chapter 4 (Model of Soft Modularity section), I described how interactions among biological organisms with competing interests, as in predator–prey relations and social competition, favor the evolution of some degree of behavioral unpredictability (Maynard Smith & Price, 1973). The associated variability in behavior creates conditions that favor the evolution of brain and cognitive systems that can be adapted during the individual's life span, that is, less modularized, executive systems. Social competition appears to have created such conditions during human evolution and resulted in an evolutionary arms race (Alexander, 1989) and an accompanying evolutionary elaboration of the executive systems that support general intelligence, especially gF. These systems are decoupled to some degree from modularized systems and enable the generation of abstracted representations of social dynamics or ecological conditions (Cosmides & Tooby, 2000). I cannot elaborate here, because of space constraints, but the ability to decouple and engage in mental simulations and to form abstractions of social and ecological conditions likely contributed to the emergence of art and other symbols about 50,000 years ago (Bahn, 1992) and supported the technological (e.g., increasingly sophisticated tools) and social-organizational advances that have produced modern societies.

In any event, general intelligence captures only an aspect of the nexus of systems that support the motivation to control. Thus, performance on measures of gF and gC are predicted to be among many of the components of this nexus that should contribute to success in modern societies. As R. J. Sternberg (2000) and Gardner (1983) emphasized, success in life is also related to competencies in domains other than general intelligence. On the basis of the motivation-to-control nexus, individual differences in success in life should be related to individual differences in g, as well as individual differences in awareness of the self as an individual and in social contexts (Tulving, 2002; M. A. Wheeler, Stuss, & Tulving, 1997), affective sensitivity (Damasio, 2003), and in the modular competencies described in chapter 5.

Modularity

With respect to modularity and in keeping with some of Gardner's (1983) proposals, there are individual differences in the brain and cognitive systems that support folk psychology, folk biology, and folk physics, as well as individual differences in the motivation to pursue activities in these areas. Individual differences in modular domains, whether they are heritable or the result of experiences, should contribute to individual differences in academic focus and ease of learning in these domains. As extreme examples, the contributions of Wallace and Darwin, as well as those of their 18th-century predecessors, especially Linnaeus (i.e., Carl von Linné; Frängsmyr, 1983), were almost certainly initially based on the same cognitive systems and inferential biases that define folk biology. Of course, their contributions went well beyond this base of folk knowledge, but these contributions appear to have been built from this base and to have been driven by an interest in the natural world. For these people, it was a near-obsessive interest in the natural world (e.g., Lindroth, 1983).

In keeping with the results of Baron-Cohen, Wheelwright, Stone, and Rutherford (1999) for contemporary mathematicians and physical scientists, there is some evidence for elaborated modular systems in the domain of folk physics for highly eminent physicists and mathematicians (see also Shea, Lubinski, & Benbow, 2001). In his masterwork *The Principia* (i.e., *The Mathematical Principles of Natural Philosophy*), Sir Isaac Newton (1687/1995) relied heavily on spatial-geometric representations and made numerous references to spatial imagery. He also relied heavily on analogy, as did Darwin (1859), in combination with exacting logic and, according to biographers, an extended period of sustained effort and attention to this work (Berlinski, 2000; M. White, 1998). Although a functional relation can only be guessed, it is of interest that areas of the neocortex that are typically associated with spatial imagery and other areas of folk physics (i.e., the parietal lobe) were unusually large in Albert Einstein's brain (Witelson, Kigar, & Harvey, 1999). In response to a query by Hadamard (1945) as to how he approached scientific questions, Einstein replied,

The words of the language as they are written or spoken, do not seem to play any role in my mechanism of thought. The psychical entities which seem to serve as elements in thought are certain signs and more or less clear images which can be "voluntarily" reproduced and combined. . . . There is, of course, a certain connection between those elements and relevant logical concepts. (Hadamard, 1945, p. 142)

Hadamard also noted that Einstein "refers to a narrowness of consciousness" (p. 143), which appears to have referred to sustained attention and the inhibition of distracting information while working on scientific questions. Einstein's accomplishments are, of course, unusual, but his descriptions of how he achieved some of his insights are of interest because they are consistent with an attention-driven use of mental simulations and a reliance on the modular systems that support folk physics, as are some of Newton's (1687/1995) descriptions in *The Principia*. As with Wallace and Darwin, Newton and Einstein went well beyond folk knowledge. In fact, Newton explicitly stated, "I do not define time, space, place and motion, as being well known to all. Only I must observe, that the vulgar conceive those quantities under no other notions but from the relation they bear to sensible objects" (p. 13). In other words, the vulgar among us only understand physical phenomena in terms of folk knowledge, and Newton intended to and did go well beyond this.

I discuss how people move from the vulgarities of folk knowledge to academic or biologically secondary knowledge in the Academic Learning section later in this chapter. My point for now is that Newton's and Einstein's use of mental simulations is consistent with the autonoetic mental model, without the self aspect and with a focus on spatial–visual representations (folk physics), as contrasted with language-based representations (folk psychology). The logical competencies that contributed to their break-throughs were almost certainly based on the problem-solving, reasoning, and inference-making processes described in chapter 6, which in turn are supported by working memory, attentional control, and gF. In short, an interaction among enhanced folk systems, sustained effort and motivation along with high fluid intelligence, and a rich domain-relevant store of crystallized knowledge appear to have been essential components in these and other scientific breakthroughs (Geary, 2002a; Simonton, 2003).

GENERAL INTELLIGENCE AND SOCIAL OUTCOMES

I noted in a preceding section that general intelligence is only one component of the motivation "to" control nexus, and thus performance on IQ tests and other measures of g should be correlated with success in many domains of life but would not be expected to explain all of the individual differences in life's outcomes. I will not be able to review all of these correlates and so will focus on the domains of life that are used to determine one's SES, which, as I mentioned earlier, is an indicator of social status and success in modern societies. These domains are education, occupational status, and income. Before reviewing the relation between intelligence and outcomes in these areas, I want to briefly touch on some of the other areas in which intelligence provides an advantage. General intelligence is one of the better, if not the best, predictor of an array of important outcomes in life above and beyond education, occupation, and income, including physical health and lifespan (Deary, Whiteman, Whalley, Fox, & Starr, 2004; Gottfredson, 2004). On the basis of analyses of a large nationally representative (U.S.) study—the National Longitudinal Study of Youth (NLSY)—that included more than 10,000 individuals, among other sources, Herrnstein and Murray (1994) determined the odds of success in a variety of life's domains. One comparison involved the odds of experiencing a variety of negative life experiences, comparing individuals who scored between the 5th and 25th percentiles on measures of g to those who scored between the 75th and 95th percentiles. In comparison to individuals in the higher-IQ group, individuals in the lower-IQ group were 50% more likely to experience divorce within the first 5 years of marriage (22% vs. 15%), four times more likely to have a child out of marriage (17% vs. 4%), seven times more likely to be incarcerated (7% vs. 1%), and eight times more likely to need long-term welfare support (17% vs. 2%), among many other differences (see also Gottfredson, 1997). Of course, other factors, such as degree of behavioral impulsivity, also contribute to many of these outcomes (e.g., Caspi, 1993). The point is that in modern societies, individual differences in intelligence covary with individual differences in many of life's outcomes. This is not to say that these outcomes are inevitable or somehow genetically determined. As I described in the last chapter (Environment section), individual differences in IQ for individuals growing up in lower SES backgrounds (e.g., with poorly educated parents) is just as strongly or more strongly related to environmental as genetic influences (D. C. Rowe, Jacobson, et al., 1999).

Education

General Intelligence

Intelligence tests were designed to predict educational outcomes, and they do very well in this regard. Walberg (1984) reviewed 3,000 studies of the relation between performance on academic achievement tests and a variety of student attributes (e.g., intelligence), home environment factors (e.g., television viewing), and classroom variables. By far the best individual predictor of achievement was IQ ($r = 0.7$). Jensen (1998), Lubinski (2000), and Matarazzo (1972) also reviewed research on the relation between IQ scores and performance on academic achievement tests and reached the same conclusion. They estimated that the correlation between general intelligence and academic achievement ranges between 0.6 and 0.8, indicating that between 36% and 64% of the individual differences in performance on academic achievement tests can be explained by individual differences in general intelligence. The relation between IQ scores and academic achievement is found even when the IQ tests are administered years before academic achievement is assessed. Longitudinal studies indicate that preschool IQ scores predict academic achievement and grade-point average throughout the elementary and high school years, although domain-specific competencies (e.g., word recognition in preschool predicts later reading achievement) are also important to success in school (Gutman, Sameroff, & Cole, 2003; Stevenson, Parker, Wilkinson, Hegion, & Fish, 1976).

Jensen (1998) estimated that individual differences in general intelligence explain about 36% (rs of about 0.6) of the individual differences in years of education completed. Several long-term longitudinal studies of individuals scoring above the 99th percentile on IQ tests illustrate the relation and indicate that exceptionally high general intelligence is associated, on average, with exceptional educational outcomes (Terman, 1925/1959). Lubinski, Benbow, and their colleagues are currently studying mathematically and verbally gifted adolescents with estimated IQ scores above the 99th percentile. They have followed many of these individuals for more than 20 years (Lubinski, Webb, Morelock, & Benbow, 2001; Webb, Lubinski, & Benbow, 2002). By age 33, more than 20% of these individuals had earned doctoral degrees (e.g., PhD, MD), compared with 1% of the population as a whole. This pattern of exceptional educational attainment is even more dramatic for the most intelligent subgroup of this sample, that is, individuals with IQ scores that place them as 1 in 10,000 (Lubinski et al., 2001). By 23 years of age, nearly all of these individuals had graduated from college, 31% had received an MA or MS degree, and 12% had received a doctorate; many of the latter group entered college early. Of course, high intelligence is not a guarantee of success in school, but it does substantially increase the odds of earning an undergraduate degree, as well as advanced college degrees.

These studies also indicate that other personal attributes and some environmental factors are related to educational outcomes, but none of these factors in and of itself is as strong a predictor as IQ. Of the personal attributes, Walberg's (1984) analysis suggested that motivation was, in addition to IQ, significantly related to academic achievement and explained about 10% of the individual differences in achievement. Most of the studies Walberg reviewed did not simultaneously assess the influences of intelligence and motivation on academic outcomes, and thus the meaning of these results is not entirely clear. Recently, Gagné and St Père (2003) assessed intelligence, student motivation and persistence, and academic performance (e.g., in math) from the beginning to the end of an academic semester. For the 200 high school students who participated, intelligence and motivation and persistence were unrelated. A combination of performance on two IQ tests explained 40% of the individual differences in academic achievement, and persistence measures explained between 6% and 10% of these individual differences; the motivational measures were unrelated to achievement.

Although individual environmental factors are not always found to be strong predictors of academic achievement, composites of risk factors (e.g., low parental education, parental mental illness) or broader social conditions (e.g., opportunity to pursue higher education) are sometimes found to be potent influences on educational outcomes. Gutman et al. (2003) found that preschool children living in high-risk environments—defined using a composite of 10 risk factors—had lower grades than other children from 1st to 12th grade, independent of IQ scores. In a large-scale behavior genetic study of twins and their family of origin, A. C. Heath et al. (1985) found that family influences on years of schooling varied across generations. Before World War II, family background explained 47% of the individual differences in educational outcomes. Following the war and the liberalization of educational opportunity, family background explained less than 10% of the individual differences in years of schooling. For the younger generation, genetic influences (likely mediated by IQ) explained about 70% of the individual differences in years of schooling; Tambs, Sundet, Magnus, and Berg (1989) found a similar cross-generational pattern.

Mechanisms

A correlation between IQ scores and educational outcomes does not necessarily mean that high general intelligence is causally related to superior academic achievement. One way to establish a causal relation is to demonstrate that the same cognitive processes (e.g., attentional control, speed of processing) and genetic influences that contribute to individual differences in gF and gC also contribute to individual differences in educational outcomes. In a series of such studies, L. A. Thompson, Detterman, and their colleagues demonstrated just such a relation (Luo, Thompson, & Detterman, 2003a, 2003b; L. A. Thompson, Detterman, & Plomin, 1991). In the first of these twin studies, they found that individual differences in achievement in reading, language, and mathematics during the elementary school years were related to genetic and shared family influences. Intelligence and achievement were correlated, and they estimated that the relation between achievement and intelligence was almost entirely genetically mediated. In other words, the genetic influences on individual differences in academic achievement appear to be the same genetic influences that contribute to individual differences in general intelligence. In a related analysis of a large national (U.S.) sample of young adults, D. C. Rowe, Vesterdal, and Rodgers (1999) found that IQ predicted years of education (rs about 0.6) and that 64% and 68% of the individual differences in IQ and years of education, respectively, could be attributed to genetic influences. Moreover, about two thirds of the correlation between IQ and years of education could be attributed to shared genes and one third to shared environment.

Finally, Luo et al. (2003a, 2003b) found that many of the same elementary processes that underlie individual differences in general intelligence appear to underlie individual differences in academic achievement. The cognitive tasks used in this study assessed speed of processing, inspection time, short-term and working memory, and required attentional control. A composite of these measures was moderately correlated (rs about 0.5) with achievement in language, reading, and mathematics. The relation between these elementary processes and achievement was primarily mediated by genetic influences. In other words, the same genetic influences that contribute to better working memory also contribute to higher academic achievement. Performance on a measure of g was also found to predict achievement in each of these academic domains, and the relation between general intelligence and achievement was mediated by performance on the cognitive tasks.

In all, these studies suggest that the genetic influences that result in high general intelligence contribute to superior academic achievement and more years of formal education. The same elementary processes that underlie individual differences in g also contribute to individual differences in academic achievement, and the genetic influences that result in faster speed of processing, better working memory and so forth substantively overlap the genetic influences on academic achievement. The combination of results suggests that g is causally related to educational outcomes and that the relation is mediated by the elementary cognitive processes that underlie general intelligence, as I described in chapter 8 and elaborate in the Academic Learning section later in this chapter. Nonetheless, on the basis of findings such as those reported by A. C. Heath et al. (1985), it is clear that the relative contribution of heritable and environmental influences on these patterns can vary from one population and one generation to the next.

Work

A relation between general intelligence and work-related outcomes is widely recognized (e.g., Gottfredson, 1997; Herrnstein & Murray, 1994; Hunter & Schmidt, 1996; Jensen, 1998; Lubinski, 2000; Schmidt & Hunter, 2004). However, the importance of this relation and whether measures other than general intelligence, such as job-related knowledge, are preferable as indexes of work-related outcomes is vigorously debated (Ree & Earles, 1993; Schmidt & Hunter, 1993; Wagner, 1997). My goal is not to delve into the debate, but rather to review the empirical research on the relation between general intelligence and occupational status and performance on the job.

Status

In modern societies, there is considerable variation in occupational prestige and the accompanying level of income and social influence in the workplace. At the highest level are professional occupations, such as managerial executive or physician, and at the lowest level are semiskilled and unskilled occupations, such as manual laborer. There is no debate regarding the finding that higher levels of intelligence are associated with more years of education and higher occupational status (Gottfredson, 1997; Jensen, 1998; Nyborg & Jensen, 2001; C. R. Reynolds, Chastain, Kaufman, & McLean, 1987; Scullin, Peters, Williams, & Ceci, 2000). The debates arise when issues of causality are considered, such as whether occupational status is more strongly related to years of education or to intelligence. One argument is that years of education or training is the better predictor of eventual occupational status, whereas another argument is that intelligence influences the ability both to acquire the education needed to compete for high-status jobs and to function in these jobs (see Gottfredson, 1997; Scullin et al., 2000).

In any event, substantive differences in general intelligence are evident across occupations, such that individuals with higher IQ scores populate higher-status occupations (Gottfredson, 1997; Schmidt & Hunter, 2004). In an analysis of the nationally (U.S.) representative standardization sample for the Wechsler Adult Intelligence Scale—Revised (Wechsler, 1981), C. R. Reynolds et al. (1987) found that for 20- to 54-year-olds, the average IQ score of professional and technical workers was at about the 75th percentile, whereas that of unskilled workers was below the 25th percentile. It is certainly possible that working in demanding, high-status occupations improves performance on IQ tests, but longitudinal studies and the relation between intelligence and job performance suggest that the casual relation is from intelligence to occupational status.

Using the NLSY, Scullin et al. (2000) found that performance on a measure of *g* administered in high school showed a substantive and positive correlation (*r*s about 0.5) with occupational prestige 15 years later; Tambs et al. (1989) found the same relation in Norway. In the earlier mentioned study of mathematically and verbally gifted people, Webb et al. (2002) found that individuals scoring above the 99th percentile on a measure of *g* in adolescence clustered, as a group, in high prestige occupations by age 33; the average individual in this group was near the 95th percentile in terms of occupational status. Gottfredson (1997) provided an exceptional review of the relation between intelligence and occupational attainment and functioning. On the basis of this review, she concluded that high intellectual ability was required to obtain the education needed to enter and then to deal with the complexities of the most prestigious and best paying jobs in modern societies. Not all highly intelligent individuals choose to enter these demanding jobs or pay the cost of obtaining the needed education. High intelligence simply increases the odds of being able to successfully compete in these arenas.

Job Performance

General intelligence, especially gF, is the best single predictor of occupational performance (e.g., sales, scientific publications) across the broad swath of jobs available in modern economies (Gottfredson, 1997; Hunter & Hunter, 1984; Schmidt & Hunter, 1998, 2004). Predictive validity represents the economic value of using the test as a selection criterion, that is, increases in job-related productivity and reductions in training and retraining costs that accrue as a result of using the test to make employment decisions. For some jobs (e.g., mechanic, electrician), work samples have slightly higher predictive validities than IQ tests, but IQ is the best predictor of performance for most jobs and is the best predictor of the ability to learn on the job, including jobs in which work samples are a valid selection criterion. Across jobs, the validity coefficient for IQ tests is .51 for job performance and .56 for success in job training programs. Other measures, such as the Graduate Record Examination, show moderate validity coefficients (as high as .24) with other indexes of later job performance, such as number of scientific publications and publication citation count (Kuncel, Hezlett, & Ones, 2001).

In any case, the predictive validity of intelligence measures increases with increases in job complexity, and thus the usefulness of these measures for predicting performance varies from one occupation to the next. The coefficient is .58, on average, for professional jobs and .23 for unskilled jobs (Schmidt & Hunter, 2004). Analyses of the components of job complexity indicate that professional, high-status jobs in modern societies are characterized by demands that are variable from day to day, require the ability to learn new information and integrate it with existing job-related knowledge, use reasoning and make judgments, identify and solve problems quickly, and compare information across two or more sources (Gottfredson, 1997). The ability to cope with all of these demands is facilitated by the components of fluid intelligence, including working memory, attentional control, and speed of processing.

The most common domain in which these complex demands emerge is social. Specifically, many of these demands result from the requirements of having to coordinate the activities and cope with the competing goals of other people: "This should not be surprising, because other individuals are among the most complex, novel, changing, active, demanding, and unpredictable objects in our environments. Living and working with others is a complicated business" (Gottfredson, 1997, p. 107). The two other realms associated with job complexity involve working with complex things, as in architecture or engineering, and dealing with complex data patterns, as in mathematics. As I noted earlier, the ability to cope with these demands should be related to modular competencies in folk domains, as well as gF.

However, intelligence is not the only predictor of job performance. Several dimensions of personality, especially conscientiousness and integrity, add significantly to the predictive validity of intelligence (Ones, Viswes-varan, & Schmidt, 1993; Schmidt & Hunter, 1998, 2004). Conscientious-ness is a major dimension of human personality and reflects individual differences in the extent to which the individual is dependable, careful, and responsible in social relationships and day-to-day activities. Integrity tests appear to assess a combination of conscientiousness, emotional stability, and the extent to which the individual is socially cooperative. Individuals who score low on measures of integrity show more job-related theft, absentee-ism, and disciplinary problems than do other individuals. Individuals who score high in integrity perform better than other individuals on many dimen-sions of worked-related activity. These dimensions of personality are not strongly correlated with intelligence and are related to job performance for low- and high-complexity occupations. Finally, there is some evidence that self-efficacy, or the belief that one has the competencies to be successful at a given task, is related to job performance (Stajkovic & Luthans, 1998). For work settings low in complexity, self-efficacy is moderately correlated with performance (estimated $r = 0.5$) and significantly but weakly correlated with performance in high complexity settings (estimated $r = 0.2$). In all, performance on the job is related to a combination of fluid intelligence, integrity, and beliefs about one's competency, but the relative importance of these traits varies. As the complexity of job demands increases, the relative importance of fluid intelligence increases.

Income

The typical correlation between IQ and income in modern societies ranges between 0.3 and 0.4, a moderate relation (Jensen, 1998; Lubinski, 2000). The interpretation of this relation is made difficult by the fact that IQ, education, and income are all positively correlated, and thus the relation between IQ and income might simply reflect that fact that more intelligent individuals complete more schooling and people with more schooling earn more money. Several analyses have simultaneously estimated schooling and

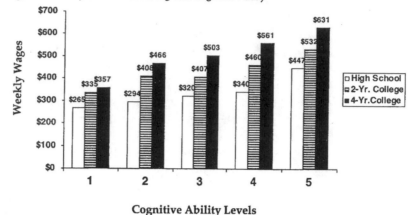

Weekly Wages in 1992 by Levels of Schooling and Cognitive Ability

Cognitive Ability Levels

Figure 9.1. Average wages are positively related to years of schooling and cognitive ability levels; cognitive ability levels were determined based on performance on a measure of general intelligence. The most economically successful group is college graduates with the highest intellectual ability. Yr. = year. From "Schooling, Intelligence, and Income," by S. J. Ceci and W. M. Williams, 1997, *American Psychologist, 52,* p. 1057. Copyright 1997 by American Psychological Association. Reprinted with permission.

IQ effects on income and have determined that both are important (Ceci & Williams, 1997; Nyborg & Jensen, 2001). As illustrated in Figure 9.1, weekly wages increase with increases in years of schooling and with increases in cognitive ability levels, that is, g. Moreover, there is evidence that as the modern economy shifted from a manufacturing base to an information base in the latter part of the 20th century, the wage benefits associated with additional years of schooling, especially in technical fields (Grogger & Eide, 1995; Rivera-Batiz, 1992), and higher intelligence (Herrnstein & Murray, 1994) increased. Although the research base is not as strong as that in modern societies, it appears that education and intelligence also contribute to wages in developing nations (Boissiere, Knight, & Sabot, 1985).

Murray (2002) tested the hypothesis that individual differences in general intelligence are causally related to individual differences in income. To do this, he again looked to the NLSY and compared the educational and occupational outcomes for full siblings from the same family, but only from families with parents who earned a middle-class or better income and who had not divorced. This approach identifies children growing up in privileged circumstances and controls for family socioeconomic background and other shared environmental influences on intelligence, education, and later income. Using individuals in the average range of intelligence as a comparison group, Murray found that by 30 to 38 years of age their siblings with higher IQ scores had obtained more formal education and earned more.

At the same time, their siblings with lower IQ scores received less formal education and earned less. The income differences were evident even for individuals with the same level of education. Overall, siblings with above-average IQ scores earned about 30% more than their siblings with an average IQ, whereas those with average IQ scores earned about 40% more than their siblings with below-average IQ scores.

Using the NLSY archive and analyzing patterns among full and half-siblings, D. C. Rowe, Vesterdal, & Rodgers (1999) found a relation between IQ and income ($r = .34$). They also found that 42% of the individual differences in income could be attributed to genetic influences and that 12% of the genetic influences on income overlapped with the genetic influences on IQ. In other words, a significant proportion of the individual differences in income are related to heritable influences, and a portion of these influences appear to be the same as those that contribute to general intelligence. These shared heritable influences must be expressed in terms of individual differences in the cognitive mechanisms, such as attentional control, that underlie IQ and facilitate job-related performance. At the same time, environmental influences on income are clearly important, as are heritable influences that are unrelated to intelligence. These latter influences are likely to include individual differences in personality, such as conscientiousness, and vocational interests (Lubinski, 2000; Schmidt & Hunter, 2004).

Summary and Integration

The gist of these sections is that higher general intelligence facilitates the acquisition of school-related competencies (see Academic Learning section) and, through this, increases the odds of obtaining an advanced education. These educational outcomes facilitate the ability to compete for high-status jobs and through them obtain higher wages. For groups with the same level of education, higher general intelligence is associated with higher wages, presumably because more intelligent individuals perform better than less intelligent individuals in most occupations and thus secure higher wages. Although the strength of the relation between intelligence and wages is moderate, it is important in terms of income earned over the course of a lifetime. According to the wages shown in Figure 9.1 and over a 30-year career, a college graduate in the highest category of general intelligence will earn $427,440 more than a college graduate in the lowest category.

The finding that general intelligence appears to be causally related to each of these components of SES—education, occupational status, and wages—and thus with the ability to compete with other people for social status and resource control is consistent with my earlier argument. Specifically, the executive competencies (e.g., working memory, attentional control) that define general intelligence are used in modern contexts in ways consistent with the motivation to control, that is, to secure the skills that will eventually lead to greater resource control and greater social influence. Nonetheless, general intelligence cannot be the whole story, as it is only one aspect of the motivation-to-control nexus and only one feature of the core of this nexus, the core being the autonoetic mental model and the ability to simulate future states.

General intelligence, as it is measured by psychometric and standardized IQ tests, does not capture the components of mental models that represent self-awareness or the ability to mentally time travel or the affective features of the motivation-to-control nexus. As Tulving and his colleagues described, brain injuries that result in a lost sense of self and an inability to mentally time travel severely compromise the person's ability to function in modern and presumably other societies, even with average or better IQ scores (Tulving, 1985, 2002; M. A. Wheeler et al., 1997). The lost sense of self is particularly devastating when it comes to the ability to cope with the complexities of social relationships (M. A. Wheeler, 2000), in keeping with the view that the complexity of these relationships drove the evolution of self-awareness (Alexander, 1989). Modular competencies, such as theory of mind and language, as well as affective systems (e.g., awareness of one's feelings) are also part of the motivation-to-control nexus, and deficits in these areas can compromise social and occupational functioning (e.g., Baron-Cohen et al., 1999; Damasio, 2003). Basically, individual differences in these competencies appear to contribute to individual differences in the ability to compete for resource control and social influence, above and beyond the influence of general intelligence.

ACADEMIC LEARNING

The final issue I wish to address concerns the mechanisms that allow people to start with the vulgarities, as defined by Newton (1687/1995), of the folk systems and construct from these an impressive array of biologically secondary abilities, such as reading and writing, as well as an ability to understand Newtonian physics. As I discuss in the first and second sections, respectively, these mechanisms include general fluid intelligence and plasticity in evolved, or biologically primary, folk systems. In the final section, I discuss several motivational issues related to academic learning.

Fluid Intelligence

If the evolution of general fluid intelligence was driven by behavioral and social variation and unpredictability in behavioral and social dynamics, then the mechanisms that compose fluid intelligence are designed to identify, anticipate, represent, and reason about evolutionarily novel information patterns. Novelty is a matter of degree, of course, because the variation involves social dynamics and perhaps dynamics associated with ecological dominance (e.g., hunting). Still, the mechanisms are not constrained to process highly specific forms of information (e.g., contour of a human face), as are modular systems described in chapter 5. The implication is that the evolution of fluid intelligence, though driven by social competition, opened the door to the ability to develop evolutionarily novel cognitive competencies—biologically secondary abilities—during the life span (Geary, 1995; Rozin, 1976). The relation between general intelligence and academic achievement, years of education, and on-the-job learning supports this hypothesis, as does empirical research on the cognitive and brain mechanisms that underlie the learning of secondary competencies.

Learning and Cognition

Training Studies. The relation between g, academic achievement and job-related training suggests that individuals who are high in general intelligence learn evolutionarily novel information more easily than do other individuals. These correlations, however, do not indicate how fluid intelligence actually affects the learning process. Ackerman has been at the forefront of efforts to link the psychometric and cognitive traditions to better understand the mechanisms of academic and job-related learning as these relate to general intelligence (Ackerman, 1986, 1988; Ackerman & Cianciolo, 2000, 2002; Rolfhus & Ackerman, 1999). On the basis of these studies and related research (J. R. Anderson, 1982), Ackerman (1988) proposed that the process of learning can be divided into three stages—cognitive, perceptual-speed, and psychomotor. The details are beyond the scope of this discussion, but the gist is that different abilities are related to individual differences in academic and job-related performance at different points in the learning process. One difference between evolved modular competencies and secondary competencies is the need for Ackerman's cognitive phase of learning. The inherent constraints associated with evolved competencies can be understood as putting them at Ackerman's second or third phase of learning, without the need for the first phase.

For academic and job-related learning, the cognitive stage refers to the relation between general intelligence, especially gF, and initial task performance. The prediction is that novel and complex tasks will require an attention-driven, explicit representation of task goals and information patterns in working memory: These mechanisms represent the explicit cognitive system described in Table 6.1 (J. S. B. T. Evans, 2002; Stanovich & West, 2000) and the attentional and working memory processes described in chapter 7 (Cognitive and Brain Systems section). During this phase, the problem space, legal operators, and task goals are learned, as is the sequence of steps needed to perform the task (e.g., to solve an algebra problem). This phase of learning would be involved when one is first introduced to the water-level problem I used to illustrate problem solving in chapter 6 (Figure 6.6) or as related to the goal of discovering the mechanisms of natural selection (see Table 6.2).

Once the task is understood, the problem space is defined, and the operations needed to solve the problem are sequenced, the perceptual-speed and then psychomotor phases commence. During these phases, the sequence of problem-solving steps is memorized and linked to the behavioral components of the task. With enough practice, the eventual result is the automatic, implicit processing of task features and automatic behavioral responses to these features. These phases of learning represent the shift from explicit representations and controlled problem solving to automatic, implicit, and sometimes heuristic-based processing of and responding to the task, as I illustrated in Figure 6.2.

Ackerman and his colleagues have extensively tested hypotheses related to his model of learning—specifically, that individual differences in gF and task-relevant crystallized knowledge will predict individual differences in the early phases of learning, whereas individual differences on measures of speed of perceptual and motor processes will predict individual differences after extensive task practice (Ackerman, 1988; Ackerman & Cianciolo, 2000, 2002). The results of these studies are generally consistent with the hypotheses, especially when it comes to g (largely gF) and ease of initial learning. Ackerman (1988, Experiment 2) found that when individuals first learn to make difficult meaning-based categorizations (e.g., monkey belongs to the category of animal), speed of making judgments about category membership was moderately correlated with general intelligence (r about 0.4), but not perceptual skills (r about 0.15). After 12 practice sessions, individual differences in speed of making category judgments were unrelated to g (r < 0.1) but moderately related to perceptual skills (r about 0.3). However, relations such as these hold only if the task requirements remain constant from one practice session to the next. If the task is modified—making it novel—then the importance of individual differences in perceptual abilities declines and the importance of individual differences in g reemerges.

Moreover, the importance of the attentional and working memory components of gF is particularly strong for complex tasks. If the task requires integration of information patterns that change across time and requires decision making, the importance of fluid intelligence remains strong even after extensive practice. A work-related example is provided by tasks that simulate the demands of an air-traffic controller. One task involves learning the rules that govern decision making, such as whether to keep a plane in a holding pattern or allow it to land on the basis of air traffic, wind, and so forth. Another task involves the especially complex demands of tracking and making decisions based on information patterns (e.g., multiple plane icons) represented on dynamic radar screens (Ackerman & Cianciolo, 2000, 2002). Performance on these tasks is indexed by the number of flights that are properly routed (e.g., landed or allowed to fly over the airport) and speed of making these decisions. Ease of initial rule learning is moderately correlated with fluid intelligence (rs of about 0.4 to 0.5) and remains so even after 6 hours of practice (r about 0.3).

Performance on the radar task is moderately to highly correlated with fluid intelligence (rs from 0.4 to 0.8) and remains so throughout training. A causal relation between performance and gF was experimentally demonstrated through the manipulation of task complexity; specifically by increasing or decreasing the number of planes the individual was required to simultaneously monitor. As the number of planes increases, the importance of fluid intelligence increases and becomes essential at the highest levels of task complexity. Performance on the radar task is also moderately related to perceptual abilities (rs about 0.4), presumably reflecting the importance of the ability to quickly and accurately detect and discriminate the multiple plane icons and related information (e.g., altitude, flight direction).

Mechanisms. Ackerman's (1988) theory and studies, as well as related research (e.g., J. R. Anderson, 1982), support the conclusion in the earlier Education and Work sections; general intelligence and especially gF is causally related to the ease of learning novel information and concepts. Individual differences in fluid intelligence are determined by individual differences in attentional control, speed of processing, working memory resources, and the ability to draw inferences from the information patterns represented in working memory (Embretson, 1995; Fry & Hale, 2000; Kane & Engle, 2002). It then follows that the initial learning of evolutionarily novel academic and job-related competencies is driven by the ability to control attention, simultaneously represent multiple pieces of information in working memory, and logically piece this information together. In many cases, the drawing of inferences about information represented in working memory is facilitated if the information is made available to conscious awareness, although pattern learning can occur without conscious awareness, but attention still appears to be needed (Stadler & Frensch, 1997). A more fundamental issue concerns how working memory, speed of processing, attentional processes, and activities of the supporting brain systems create competencies that do not have an evolutionary history (Karmiloff-Smith, 1992; Rozin, 1976). Researchers are only beginning to explore these issues (Geary & Bjorklund, 2000), and thus I can offer only speculation at this time.

To begin, I described in chapter 7 (Cognitive and Brain Systems section) how the dorsolateral prefrontal regions, the anterior cingulate cortex, and attentional regions of the parietal cortex are particularly important for explicitly representing goals and information to be manipulated in working memory (Duncan, 2001; Kane & Engle, 2002; E. K. Miller & Cohen, 2001; Shallice, 2002). These ends appear to be achieved through an attention-driven amplification of neural activity in the posterior and subcortical pathways that process the information needed for goal achievement (Dehaene & Naccache, 2001; Posner, 1994). The result appears to be a simultaneous and synchronized activation of all of these brain regions. Speed of processing may be related to synchronization: The synchronization appears to occur through neural connections that communicate back and forth between these different brain regions, creating feedback cycles (John, 2003). Faster speed of processing would facilitate synchronization, because faster processing would enable more accurate adjustments in synchronization per feedback cycle. With repeated synchronized activity, the result appears to be the formation of a neural network that automatically links the processing of these information patterns (Sporns, Tononi, & Edelman, 2000). Functionally, the result is a new cognitive competency.

To illustrate how the process might work, consider how children initially learn to read. One of the component skills underlying reading is phonemic decoding (L. Bradley & Bryant, 1983). Decoding requires an explicit awareness and representation in working memory of a basic language sound (e.g., *ba, da, ka*) and the association of this sound, as well as blends of sounds, with corresponding visual patterns, specifically letters (e.g., B, D, K) and letter combinations. Attentional focus on the relation between the sound and the letter should, in theory, result in the amplification of the activity of the brain regions that process both forms of information and the simultaneous representation of both forms of information in working memory. The process should result in the synchronization of this brain activity with activity in the dorsolateral prefrontal cortex and the anterior cingulate cortex and, with sufficient practice, the formation of a learned association between the sound and letter.

With extended practice, the association becomes represented in long-term memory and thus becomes implicit knowledge, representing Ackerman's (1988) final stages of learning. When this is achieved, the association between the sound and letter, or letter combination and word sound, is automatically triggered when the letter string is processed during the act of reading and thus no longer engages the prefrontal cortex, the anterior cingulate cortex, working memory, or related cognitive and brain systems and no longer requires gF. We now have an evolutionarily novel cognitive competency, the linking of a language sound with a visual pattern so that the visual pattern—such as the one you are currently reading—automatically triggers the word-sound and associated concept. This is reading.

The learning of phonetic decoding is a simple academic task and one that is not highly dependent on fluid intelligence, but it illustrates how the processes may work for the learning of more complex skills. The primary difference across task complexity would involve the length of the first phase of learning, to use Ackerman's (1988) model. More precisely, complexity is related to the extent to which the task is evolutionarily novel, the amount of information that must be identified and processed to deal with task demands, and the extent to which this information changes across time. As each of these features increases in complexity, there is an accompanying increase in the need for sustained attention, working memory, and the ability to reason and make inferences, that is, an increased reliance on gF. The practical result is that as the complexity of academic and job-related demands increases, the proportion of the population that can cope with these demands decreases (Gottfredson, 1997).

Learning and Brain Mechanisms

In a review of brain imaging studies of working memory, problem solving, and learning, Duncan and Owen (2000) concluded that all of these cognitive functions are dependent on the dorsolateral prefrontal cortex and the anterior cingulate cortex. Other areas are also active when people are engaged in these tasks, and there are, of course, different patterns of brain activity associated with learning one type of skill or another (Callan et al., 2003; McCandliss, Posner, & Givón, 1997). Nonetheless, the brain regions identified by Duncan and Owen are consistently engaged when people are learning novel information and or coping with complex tasks that require working memory resources and attentional control (see also Kane & Engle, 2002). Additional research is needed, but there is evidence suggesting that the dorsolateral prefrontal cortex and anterior cingulate cortex are engaged only during Ackerman's (1988) first phase of learning (Raichle et al., 1994), in keeping with the proposed mechanism described previously. Thereafter, brain activation is associated with the particular type of stimulus (e.g., visual vs. auditory) and the specifics of task demands.

Unfortunately, there are only a few studies that have combined learning and brain imaging with assessments of general intelligence. Haier, Siegel, Tang, Abel, and Buchsbaum (1992) assessed the brain's use of glucose during the learning of a novel spatial problem-solving task. Individuals with high IQ scores learned the task more quickly than their less intelligent peers and showed more rapid declines in glucose metabolism across learning trials; see also the Metabolic Activity and Mental Effort section in chapter 8. Using electrophysiological methods, Gevins and Smith (2000) found that the dorsolateral prefrontal cortex was initially engaged during the learning of a complex task that required working memory and attentional control, but engagement of this region declined as individuals learned the task. The decline was especially pronounced for intelligent individuals, who in turn appeared to shift the processing of task requirements to more posterior regions of the brain. The results of these studies are not conclusive but are consistent with studies of the relation between gF and ease of learning (Ackerman, 1988; Ackerman & Cianciolo, 2000, 2002): Through attentional control and inhibition, intelligent individuals use cognitive resources more efficiently than do other people.

At this point, it appears that one function of the dorsolateral prefrontal cortex, the anterior cingulate cortex, and the posterior attentional system is to ensure the synchronized activity of other brain regions, such that anatomical and functional links are formed among these regions. When couched in terms of gF, it appears that the associated ability to focus attentional resources and inhibit the activation of task-irrelevant information (Kane & Engle, 2002) results in the ability to synchronize only those brain regions needed for secondary learning. The result would be lower glucose use and faster learning for individuals high in gF, because fewer unneeded brain regions are activated and thus fewer regions are anatomically linked. Functionally, the result would be a sharper representation and better understanding of the new competency, because irrelevant information and concepts would not be linked to this competency. Once formed, an evolutionarily novel cognitive competency emerges.

Folk Systems

Plasticity

The acquisition of biologically secondary abilities, such as reading or air-traffic control, involves the brain and cognitive mechanisms associated with gF but must also involve other mechanisms. Fluid intelligence is involved during the initial phase of learning, but the fully developed abilities appear to reside in a network of cognitive and brain systems that differ from those that support gF (Gevins & Smith, 2000; Raichle et al., 1994). This network of systems represents crystallized intelligence, or gC (Cattell, 1963; Horn & Cattell, 1966). In chapter 8 (Modularity and Crystallized Intelligence section) I argued that gC was composed of two broad classes of knowledge. The first is folk knowledge and information processing biases constructed during human evolutionary history and built into evolved modular systems (chap. 5), and the second is knowledge constructed during the individual's lifetime. The latter is possible to the extent that inherent modular systems evince some degree of plasticity and to the extent that independent modular systems can be interconnected to form unique neural networks and functional competencies (Garlick, 2002; Sporns et al., 2000).

As I explained in the Experiential Modification of Brain Organization section of chapter 4, there is evidence for neural plasticity in most of the brain regions that are likely to support inherent, modular systems. Plasticity can result from allometric expansions of the corresponding brain region or from an evolved plasticity in the system. The evolutionary function of the latter is to enable these systems to be fine-tuned to the nuances of the ecologies in which the individual is situated, although the fine-tuning appears to occur within inherent constraints on the forms of information the brain and cognitive systems can process (e.g., visual contours, prototypical shape of a human face). Modular plasticity also indicates that these systems can be modified to process evolutionarily novel information if this novel information is similar to the forms of information the system evolved to process (Sperber, 1994). I give an example later in this chapter; my point for now is that variation in social and ecological dynamics during human evolution not only provides an explanation for the evolution of gF, but should also have resulted in a selective advantage for plasticity within modular systems, as I described in chapter 5. Modular plasticity, in turn, enables the formation of crystallized knowledge during the life span.

It is also likely that there are individual differences in modular plasticity and thus individual differences in the ease of forming crystallized knowledge in the associated domain: Several potential examples were described earlier in this chapter in the General Intelligence and Modularity section (see also Gardner, 1983). Whether individual differences in modular plasticity are correlated with individual differences in gF remains to be seen. On the one hand, the finding that the genes that support gF and gC overlap to some degree (Horn, 1988) suggests that higher-than-average levels of modular plasticity will be associated with higher-than-average fluid intelligence. On the other hand, there appear to be genes unique to gF and gC, suggesting some independence between modular plasticity and fluid intelligence.

Folk Psychology and Reading and Writing

In the Learning and Cognition section, I described how the initial phase of learning how to read might occur. I want to now expand on this discussion and consider how reading and writing might be more broadly related to inherent, folk psychological modules (see also Geary, 2002a).

Because the function of written and therefore read material is to communicate with other people, it follows that writing and reading emerged from and currently are based on evolved social communication systems, that is, folk psychology. Writing must have emerged (culturally) from the motivational disposition to communicate with and influence the behavior of other people (e.g., morals in the Bible) and must engage the same folk psychological systems, especially language and theory of mind. Stated somewhat differently, secondary activities, such as reading and writing, must involve co-opting or adapting evolved folk systems for culturally specific uses (Geary, 1995; Rozin, 1976, Rozin & Schull, 1988). If correct, then writing and reading should engage many of the same brain and cognitive systems that support folk psychology. I focus on reading because the research base is larger than that on writing.

The research to date is not definitive, but it is consistent with the hypothesis that the acquisition of reading-related abilities (e.g., word decoding) involves the co-optation of primary language and language-related systems, among others (e.g., visual scanning; Rozin, 1976). Wagner, Torgesen, and Rashotte (1994) reported that individual differences in the fidelity of kindergarten children's phonological processing systems, which are basic features of the language domain, are strongly predictive of the ease with which basic reading abilities (e.g., word decoding) are acquired in first grade (see also L. Bradley & Bryant, 1983; Talcott et al., 2000). Children who show explicit awareness of basic language sounds are more skilled than are other children at associating these sounds with the symbol system of the written language. In further support of the co-optation hypothesis, Pugh et al. (1997) found that the brain and cognitive systems that are engaged during the processing of language sounds are also engaged during the act of reading (see also Shaywitz et al., 2004).

It is also likely that reading comprehension engages theory of mind, at least for literary stories, poems, dramas, and other genres that involve human relationships (Geary, 1998). This is because comprehending the gist of these stories involves making inferences about the nuances of social relationships, which by definition involves theory of mind. It is also of interest that some of the more popular forms of literature are focused on interpersonal relationships and dynamics, typically reproductive relationships, as in the case of romance novels (e.g., Whissell, 1996) and the male–male competition (with unrestricted sexuality) in the case of spy novels and related genre. In these stories, a sense of self may also come into play to the extent that the individual identifies with the protagonist or antagonist in the story.

Motivation

I have argued for an inherent motivation to control, that is, a bias for individuals to organize their behavior in ways that facilitate their ability to gain access to and control of the behavior of other people, other species, and the physical environment. The corresponding motivation-to-control nexus is organized around the respective domains of folk psychology, folk biology, and folk physics. As I describe in the following sections, this motivational nexus provides a frame for understanding human intellectual history, the widening gap between academic and folk knowledge, and children's motivation to learn in school.

Human Intellectual History

If folk domains define the inherent biases that guide what people think about and where they direct their behavioral activities, then cultural (e.g., philosophy, poetry), technological, and scientific advances must have been initially constructed from the corresponding folk modular systems. As described previously, the construction of these novel, biologically secondary abilities can be understood as resulting from an interaction between gF and modular systems. In other words, human intellectual history and the emergence of modern scientific and academic domains largely coalesced around the areas of folk psychology, folk biology, and folk physics. Academic disciplines in universities do indeed fall into these three categories, with humanities and the social sciences developing from the area of folk psychology; biology, zoology, forestry, medicine, and so on developing from the area of folk biology; and much of mathematics as well as physics and engineering developing from the area of folk physics. Of course, some domains, such as biochemistry, emerged from a combination of areas, folk biology and folk physics in this example. Still other academic domains, such as linguistics, are focused on the study of specific adaptations (i.e., language), and some academic competencies, such as writing and reading, are built from a combination of evolved modules, as described above (Geary, 1995).

My point is that the historical development of scientific and academic disciplines is predicted to have been initially based on the evolved but often scientifically naïve cognitive, inferential, and attributional biases associated with the domains of folk psychology, folk biology, and folk physics. Stated somewhat differently, these folk domains are the three primary pillars on which intellectual advances were initially built. The building itself emerged from an interaction between these folk domains, gF, and the reasoning and problem-solving competencies described in chapter 6. In some cases, these evolved biases provided a solid frame for the emergence of the scientific discipline, and in other cases they led to false starts and scientifically incorrect conceptual models. As examples, implicit knowledge in the areas of folk biology and folk physics was explicitly articulated, codified (often incorrectly), and expanded on by Aristotle and other Greek intellectuals. Many of these explicit representations of implicit folk knowledge provided the initial foundation for the scientific development of academic disciplines, as with Euclid's contributions to geometry (K. Devlin, 1998). Other elaborations and conceptual models proved to be false starts, as in the Greek system of four basic elements (i.e., air, earth, fire, and water) that contributed to the development of the pseudo science of alchemy (e.g., Strathern, 2001). As I mentioned previously, the early classification system of Linnaeus was almost certainly based, to some degree, on the cognitive systems and inferential biases that define folk biology.

Linnaeus, of course, moved well beyond folk knowledge and did so with the development of explicit rules for systematically classifying species and the degree of relationship among species. His binomial methods explicitly organized the biological world in terms of genera (e.g., *Homo*) and species: Species of the same genera, such as *H. erectus* and *H. sapiens,* are related (for an accessible discussion, see Tudge, 2000). Of course, this early scientific taxonomy continues to be expanded and refined and most recently informed by genetic analyses of the relation between species (e.g., F.-G. R. Liu et al., 2001). A similar attention to observation, codification, and use of the scientific method resulted in the emergence of physics, chemistry, and other scientific domains and supports the continued growth of these fields. With the emergence of these disciplines, intuitive biases and naïve conceptualizations of the natural world were tested, evaluated, and often refuted and replaced with more scientifically accurate conceptual models of the world, as was done by Newton (1687/1995).

Academic and Folk Knowledge

As stated in chapter 5, folk biology represents the evolved ability to develop classification systems of flora and fauna and mental models of the essence of these species (Atran, 1998). Although folk biological knowledge provided the foundation for the emergence of the scientific classification system of Western biology, this folk knowledge is rudimentary in comparison to the vast knowledge of the modern-day biological sciences. As an example, people, even young children, infer that living things have "innards" that differ from the innards of nonliving things and that offspring will have the same appearance and "essence" of their parents (Carey & Spelke, 1994; Coley, 1995; R. Gelman, 1990). The scientific study of "innards" is, of course, anatomy and physiology, and the study of "essence" is behavioral ecology. Through the use of the experimental method and detailed observation, the associated knowledge bases in anatomy, physiology, and ecology have far surpassed people's intuitive understanding of folk biology.

Not only is the gap between people's intuitive understanding of the biological world and the knowledge base of the biological sciences widening at a rapid pace, the inferential biases of folk biology may sometimes interfere with the comprehension of scientific models of biological phenomena. The most fundamental of these are the principles of natural selection (Darwin

& Wallace, 1858). Yet inferential biases in folk biology, along with religious objections, may conspire to make the basic mechanisms of natural selection sometimes difficult to comprehend. First, one inferential bias results in a focus on similarities across members of the same and related species (see Atran, 1998). This bias facilitates the functional goal of being able to predict the behavior (e.g., growth patterns) of these plants and animals as related to procuring food and medicine. At the same time, the focus on within-species similarities runs counter to the insight that within-species differences, or variation, provide the grist for evolutionary selection. Second, folk biological knowledge is also implicitly focused on the behavior of flora and fauna at different points in a single life span (e.g., maturity of a plant relative to when it is best to harvest) and not the cross-generational time scale over which natural selection occurs. In other words, people are biased to think about and understand the biological world in ways that are at odds with the observations and principles of natural selection.

As I mentioned earlier, people have a naïve understanding of certain physical phenomena, and the initial emergence of physics as a domain of conscious intellectual activity was likely to have been based on this folk knowledge. For instance, when asked about the forces acting on a thrown baseball, many people (including many undergraduate physics students) believe that there is a force propelling it forward, something akin to an invisible engine, and a force propelling it downward. The downward force is, of course, gravity, but there is in fact no force propelling it forward once the ball leaves the player's hand (Clement, 1982). The concept of a forward-force, called "impetus," is similar to pre-Newtonian beliefs about motion prominent in the 14th to 16th centuries. The idea is that the act of starting an object in motion, such as throwing a ball, imparts to the object an internal force—impetus—that keeps it in motion until the impetus gradually dissipates. Even though adults often describe the correct trajectory for a thrown object, their explanations reflect this naïve understanding of the forces acting on the object. Although "impetus" is in fact a fictional force, it is a good-enough explanation of most everyday situations.

As Newton (1687/1995) noted, this and other naïve conceptions about the workings of the physical world interfere with learning the scientific principles associated with mechanics, as well as many other principles, such as those that represent centrifugal force, velocity, gravity, and motion (Clement, 1982; E. Hunt, 1993; E. Hunt & Minstrell, 1994; McCloskey, 1983). As with biology, the knowledge base of the physical sciences is exponentially larger than the knowledge base of folk physics, and in some cases (e.g., quantum mechanics) the accompanying conceptual models bear little resemblance to the naïve concepts of folk physics.

Motivation to Learn

One result of scientific and technological advances is an accompanying change in the type and level of academic competency needed to live successfully (e.g., gainful employment) in the society in which these advances emerged. Today, there is an ever-widening gap between folk knowledge and scientific and technological advances and a corresponding increase in the need for people to acquire novel academic competencies. A crucial implication for education is that folk knowledge, though necessary, is no longer sufficient for occupational and social functioning (e.g., understanding interest on debt) in modern society. I discuss many educational implications elsewhere (Geary, 1994, 1995, 2001, 2002a) and wish only to touch on one of these here, specifically the relation between evolved motivational biases and children's motivation to learn in school.

If the function of a long developmental period is to fine-tune folk systems to the particulars of the social, biological, and physical ecologies in which the individual is situated (Geary & Bjorklund, 2000), then children are predicted to be innately curious about and motivated to actively engage in activities that will produce the experiences needed for this fine-tuning. The associated motivational biases should direct children to engage in social relationships and explore the biological and physical world (Geary, 1995; R. Gelman, 1990; R. Gelman & Williams, 1998). Because intellectual, scientific, and technological advances have resulted in a gap between folk knowledge and these advances, there will also be a gap between the inherent motivational dispositions of children to engage in folk-related activities (e.g., play) and the need to engage in activities that will lead to the mastery of academic competencies. In other words, the gap between folk knowledge and the forms of competency needed for successful living in modern society is predicted to result in an accompanying mismatch between the inherent and preferred motivational and activity biases of children and the forms of activity needed for secondary learning.

For instance, if social competition was a driving force during hominid evolution, then children should have a strong and inherent motivational bias to engage in social activities, and these activities should recreate the forms of social competition that were important during hominid evolution (Geary, Byrd-Craven, Hoard, Vigil, & Numtee, 2003). The finding that a universal aspect of children's (and adults') self-directed activities are social and very often competitive in nature is consistent with this prediction (Baumeister & Leary, 1995); competition over friends, called *relational aggression,* is one example (Crick, Casas, & Mosher, 1997). A corollary prediction is that a burning desire to master algebra or Newtonian physics will not be universal, or even common. Surveys of the attitudes and preferences of American schoolchildren support this prediction and indicate that they value achievement in sports (a ritualized but primary form of social competition) much more than achievement in any academic area (Eccles, Wigfield, Harold, & Blumenfeld, 1993).

There are, of course, many individuals who pursue biologically secondary learning and engage in secondary activities on their own initiative, but this follows from the prediction of a continuity between folk knowledge and human intellectual history. To clarify, scholars in the humanities and social sciences are predicted to be (and are) fundamentally motivated to understand human social relationships and biologists and physicists to be motivated to understand the biological and physical worlds (A. Roe, 1956). The difference between scholars in these domains and other people is predicted to be related to several dimensions of human individual differences. It is individuals who are at the extreme end of all of these distributions, as with Darwin and Newton, who generate a disproportionate number of scientific and technological advances (Murray, 2003; Simonton, 1999, 2003). In addition to gF and modular plasticity, the areas in which these individual differences emerge include intellectual curiosity or openness to experience, a basic dimension of human personality (Goldberg, 1993); the willingness to engage in the long and often tedious training required to master the academic discipline (Ericsson, Krampe, & Tesch-Römer, 1993); and perhaps differences in the degree to which the underlying folk systems (including brain, cognitive, and motivational aspects) are elaborated, as I described earlier.

CONCLUSION

The pressures that drove the evolution of the motivation to control and the accompanying nexus of brain, cognitive, conscious-psychological, and affective traits, including g, are not much different from the pressures we all experience in modern societies. This is necessarily true if these evolutionary forces were largely social in nature, as the basic dynamics of these relationships will be recreated in each and every generation and will be centered around the same types of relationships (e.g., parent–child; male–female) and focused on the same fundamental issues (e.g., finding a mate). The motivation to control is focused, in part, on organizing these relationships such that other people behave in ways that are consistent with one's best interests. People, and individuals of all other species, are also motivated to gain access to and control of the biological and physical resources that improve survival and reproductive prospects. In modern societies, resources are symbolic (e.g., money or stocks), but gaining control of these resources is important because they enable access to and control of concrete biological (e.g., food) and physical (e.g., shelter) resources and facilitate the ability to influence the behavior of other people. When considered in these terms, the struggle for control, whether over symbolic or concrete resources, is no different across modern societies and traditional societies or throughout human evolution.

The most important dynamic that results from competition for resource control is behavioral unpredictability (Maynard Smith & Price, 1973), that is, the generation of behaviors and social conditions that differ to some degree across social episodes within each lifetime and across each generation. The associated variation in behavioral and social dynamics results in conditions that favor the evolution of brain and cognitive systems that can be adapted during the individual's life span, that is, less modularized, executive systems. As I described in chapters 6 and 7, the system that evolved to anticipate, mentally represent, and devise behavioral responses to these variable conditions is the autonoetic mental model. Fluid intelligence and the cognitive components (e.g., working memory) represent essential features of these models and are the key to understanding the human ability to adapt modular systems for academic and occupational learning and through this the ability to compete in modern societies. As I noted, general intelligence is only one of many features of the motivation-to-control nexus and autonoetic mental models and thus is not the whole story when it comes to understanding individual differences in the ability to compete. Nonetheless, g is an important part of the story.

Indeed, performance on IQ tests and other measures of g are correlated with an array of life's outcomes (Herrnstein & Murray, 1994; Jensen, 1998; Lubinski, 2000), including educational attainment, occupational status, and income, as well as a host of other socially relevant outcomes (e.g., divorce risk). I focused on education, occupation, and income because, in combination, these define that most commonly used measure of success in modern societies, socioeconomic status. General intelligence is the best single predictor of academic achievement (e.g., Walberg, 1984), years of schooling completed (Jensen, 1998), occupational status (Gottfredson, 1997), and performance on the job (Schmidt & Hunter, 1998). Intelligence is also moderately correlated with wages, even for individuals with the same level of education (Ceci & Williams, 1997; Murray, 2002). The relation between intelligence and wages appears to be due to the relation between intelligence and educational outcomes, as well as between intelligence and job-related performance (Gottfredson, 1997). When all is said and done, high general intelligence and especially fluid intelligence make it easier to obtain the education needed to enter high-status and high-paying occupations and then to excel in these occupations. In short, general intelligence, especially gF, evolved to facilitate competition with other people for social and resource control and it is still used in this way.

I make several proposals regarding the mechanisms that allow people to start with folk systems and construct the academic and job-related competencies that facilitate success in modern societies. If the evolution of autonoetic mental models, including fluid intelligence, was driven by the need to cope with variant and unpredictable social conditions, then the function of these models is to identify, anticipate, represent, and reason about evolutionarily novel information. The components of fluid intelligence, especially working memory and attentional control, appear to be at the core of these abilities and thus are the key to understanding how humans can construct evolutionarily novel cognitive competencies. Support for this hypothesis comes from cognitive (Ackerman, 1988) and brain (Duncan & Owen, 2000) studies of the relation between gF and the process of learning in evolutionarily novel domains. Fluid intelligence is, nonetheless, involved only in the first step of this learning process. Fully developed competencies appear to reside in a network of cognitive and brain systems that differ from those that support gF (Gevins & Smith, 2000) and can be understood in terms of crystallized intelligence, or gC (Cattell, 1963). The formation of this class of crystallized knowledge appears to be possible because of plasticity in inherent modular systems and because independent modular systems can be interconnected to form unique neural networks and functional competencies (Garlick, 2002; Sporns et al., 2000).

I close the chapter with some thoughts on motivational issues as related to the pursuit of learning in evolutionarily novel contexts. I tie this to the domains of folk psychology, folk biology, and folk physics and suggest that human intellectual history emerged from and developed around these three folk domains and did so because humans are inherently motivated to pursue understanding in these domains. The minority of individuals who push scientific, technological, and intellectual boundaries beyond folk knowledge, such as Darwin or Newton, create a knowledge gap. One result is an accompanying change in the type and level of academic and job-related competencies needed to live successfully in the society in which these advances emerged. Today, there is an ever-widening gap between folk knowledge and scientific and technological advances and a corresponding increase in the need for people to acquire novel academic and job-related skills. A crucial implication for education is that folk knowledge, though necessary, is no longer sufficient for successful occupational and social functioning. I illustrate the importance of this gap with discussion of the relation between evolved motivational biases to learn in folk domains and children's motivation, or lack thereof, to learn in school.

AFTERWORD

To close the book, I want to reiterate my basic proposal and then explore how this proposal can be extended to topics that I did not address in this work, specifically neurodevelopmental, mood, and anxiety disorders. Let us begin with a restatement of the theme of the book: The behaviors, cognitions, brain systems, and other traits of humans and individuals of all other species can be understood in terms of a motivation to control. Behavioral control is predicted to be focused on the forms of resource that tended to covary with survival or reproductive outcomes during the species' evolutionary history. The motivation to control is not explicit or conscious, but rather reflects the function of evolved traits. The primary dynamic that has driven and is currently driving human evolution is competition with other people and groups of other people for resource control, including control of the behavior of other people. Resources fall into three categories: social, biological, and physical. The brain, cognitive, affective, psychological, and behavioral biases that evolved to facilitate attempts to gain control of resources in these domains compose folk psychology, folk biology, and folk physics.

In addition to creating pressures for the elaboration of folk psychological systems (e.g., theory of mind), social competition results in variation in social dynamics and through this variation creates pressures for the elaboration of brain and cognitive systems that can anticipate, mentally represent, and devise behavioral strategies to cope with these dynamics. The autonoetic mental model is the conscious-psychological mechanism that evolved to cope with the variation created by complex social dynamics and to facilitate resource control under such conditions. The autonoetic mental model enables one to generate a self-centered simulation of the perfect world and to simulate strategies to reduce the difference between this perfect world and current conditions; a *perfect world* is one in which other people behave in ways consistent with one's best interest and biological and physical resources are under one's control. The systems that evolved to support the use of autonoetic mental models are known as general fluid intelligence, working memory, and attentional control. The combination of these systems and folk knowledge is the foundation on which human intellectual and cultural advances have been built.

In addition to providing a framework for better understanding the evolution of brain and cognitive systems, the model described in this book may also be applicable to a wider range of human phenomena. As I mentioned in chapter 5, the inherent constraints of exoskeletons provide anchors that orient people to features of the social and natural world that have been of significance during human evolution. The number and complexity of anchors in human folk knowledge provide humans with enormous benefits in terms of a wide of array specific cognitive skills. The benefits are, as always, coupled with potential risks. In terms of neurodevelopment, the building of these anchors must be a delicate and complex process and is bound to fail at times. The resulting neurodevelopmental disorders might be approached in terms of deficits in the exoskeleton of folk systems. The taxonomy of modules shown in Figure 5.2 might provide a starting point for classifying patterns of intact and disrupted folk systems with neurodevelopmental disorders. Many features of autism, for instance, can be understood in terms of poor competencies in many specific features of folk psychological anchors, such as failure to make eye contact and to understand the social significance of this behavior (Baron-Cohen, 1995).

Autonoetic mental models are essential for planning for the future and coping with the dynamic and ever-changing patterns of social relationships. Accompanying this benefit may be an increased risk for anxiety and depressive disorders. If an individual projects a future that is hopeless, sensing a lack of control, or believes that he or she lacks the self-efficacy to cope with projected future conditions, then depression and anxiety may result. The ability to project oneself into the future also adds the burden of understanding one's own mortality and that of one's significant others, which in turn can result in increased anxiety and other complications (see Solomon, Greenberg, Schimel, Arndt, & Pyszczynski, 2004). Another result may be obsessive rumination on potential future conditions. Some amount of rumination is likely to be an adaptive approach to generating strategies for coping with future conditions, but rumination may be debilitating in more extreme forms. Some symptoms of schizophrenia, such as delusions, may be derived from the ability to generate autonoetic mental simulations, but with schizophrenia there is a breakdown in the mechanisms that separate awareness of what is being simulated from awareness of the actual world (Cosmides & Tooby, 2000).

The maintenance of humans' highly complex brain and cognitive systems may require considerably more regulatory mechanisms than that of the brains of other species (Cáceres et al., 2003). The full implications of Cáceres et al.'s findings of higher rates of gene expression in the human brain compared to that of the chimpanzee and the associated increase in neural activity and necessary supporting systems remain to be determined. For instance, it is not known if there are individual differences in the rate of gene expression and, if so, whether they might be related to individual differences in speed of processing or fluid intelligence. Either way, regulatory mechanisms may be more intricate and thus more prone to disruption in humans than in other species. Failure of mechanisms that inhibit gene expression and neural activity may result in a "revving up" of neural activity that is outside of the normal range. In other words, the evolution of a brain that is "revved up" compared with that of other species may have the cost of increased risk of mania and bipolar disorder. The converse is a failure to maintain neural activity at normal "revved up" levels and thus depression. In theory, this type of depression may differ from that associated with projecting a hopeless future. Whether this is the case or not, the model presented in this book has many potential implications beyond those addressed in these chapters, and I have touched on only a few of these in these closing paragraphs.

REFERENCES

Aboitiz, F., Morales, D., & Montiel, J. (2003). The evolutionary origin of the mammalian isocortex: Towards an integrated developmental and functional approach. *Behavioral and Brain Sciences, 26,* 535–586.

Abrams, D., & Hogg, M. A. (Eds.). (1990). *Social identity theory: Constructive and critical advances.* New York: Springer-Verlag.

Ackerman, P. L. (1986). Individual differences in information processing: An investigation of intellectual abilities and task performance during practice. *Intelligence, 10,* 101–139.

Ackerman, P. L. (1988). Determinants of individual differences during skill acquisition: Cognitive abilities and information processing. *Journal of Experimental Psychology: General, 117,* 288–318.

Ackerman, P. L., Beier, M. E., & Boyle, M. O. (2002). Individual differences in working memory within a nomological network of cognitive and perceptual speed abilities. *Journal of Experimental Psychology: General, 131,* 567–589.

Ackerman, P. L., & Cianciolo, A. T. (2000). Cognitive, perceptual-speed, and psychomotor determinants of individual differences in skill acquisition. *Journal of Experimental Psychology: Applied, 6,* 259–290.

Ackerman, P. L., & Cianciolo, A. T. (2002). Ability and task constraint determinants of complex task performance. *Journal of Experimental Psychology: Applied, 8,* 194–208.

Adams, R. B., Jr., Gordon, H. L., Baird, A. A., Ambady, N., & Kleck, R. E. (2003, June 6). Effects of gaze on amygdala sensitivity to anger and fear faces. *Nature, 300,* 1536.

Adler, N. E., Boyce, T., Chesney, M. A., Cohen, S., Folkman, S., Kahn, R. L., et al. (1994). Socioeconomic status and health: The challenge of the gradient. *American Psychologist, 49,* 15–24.

Adolphs, R. (1999). Social cognition and the human brain. *Trends in Cognitive Sciences, 3,* 469–479.

Adolphs, R. (2003). Cognitive neuroscience of human social behaviour. *Nature Reviews: Neuroscience, 4,* 165–178.

Adolphs, R., Damasio, H., Tranel, D., & Damasio, A. R. (1996). Cortical systems for the recognition of emotion in facial expressions. *Journal of Neuroscience, 16,* 7678–7687.

Aharon, I., Etcoff, N., Ariely, D., Chabris, C. F., O'Connor, E., & Breiter, H. C. (2001). Beautiful faces have variable reward value: fMRI and behavioral evidence. *Neuron, 32,* 537–551.

Aiello, L. C. (1994, March 31). Variable but singular. *Nature, 368,* 399–400.

Aiello, L. C., Bates, N., & Joffe, T. (2001). In defense of the expensive tissue hypothesis. In D. Falk & K. R. Gibson (Eds.), *Evolutionary anatomy of the primate cerebral cortex* (pp. 57–78). Cambridge, England: Cambridge University Press.

Aiello, L. C., & Collard, M. (2001, March 29). Our newest and oldest ancestor? *Nature, 410,* 526–527.

Aiello, L. C., & Wheeler, P. (1995). The expensive-tissue hypothesis: The brain and digestive system in human and primate evolution. *Current Anthropology, 36,* 199–221.

Alarcón, M., Plomin, R., Fulker, D. W., Corley, R., & DeFries, J. C. (1998). Multivariate path analysis of specific cognitive abilities data at 12 years of age in the Colorado adoption project. *Behavioral Genetics, 28,* 255–264.

Alerstam, T., Gudmundsson, G. A., Green, M., & Hedenström, A. (2001, January 12). Migration along orthodromic sun compass routes by arctic birds. *Science, 291,* 300–303.

Alexander, R. D. (1979). *Darwinism and human affairs.* Seattle: University of Washington Press.

Alexander, R. D. (1989). Evolution of the human psyche. In P. Mellars & C. Stringer (Eds.), *The human revolution: Behavioural and biological perspectives on the origins of modern humans* (pp. 455–513). Princeton, NJ: Princeton University Press.

Alexander, R. D. (1990). *How did humans evolve? Reflections on the uniquely unique species* (Museum of Zoology Special Publication No. 1, pp. 1–38). Ann Arbor: University of Michigan.

Allman, J., & Hasenstaub, A. (1999). Brains, maturation times, and parenting. *Neurobiology of Aging, 20,* 447–454.

Allman, J., McLaughlin, T., & Hakeem, A. (1993). Brain weight and life-span in primate species. *Proceedings of the National Academy of Sciences USA, 90,* 118–122.

Allman, J., Rosin, A., Kumar, R., & Hasenstaub, A. (1998). Parenting and survival in anthropoid primates: Caretakers live longer. *Proceedings of the National Academy of Sciences USA, 95,* 6866–6869.

Alroy, J. (2001, June 8). A multispecies overkill simulation of the end-Pleistocene megafaunal mass extinction. *Science, 292,* 1893–1896.

Altmann, J., Alberts, S. C., Haines, S. A., Dubach, J., Muruthi, P., Coote, T., et al. (1996). Behavior predicts genetic structure in a wild primate group. *Proceedings of the National Academy of Sciences USA, 93,* 5797–5801.

Amodio, D. M., Harmon-Jones, E., Devine, P. G., Curtin, J. J., Hartley, S. L., & Covert, A. E. (2004). Neural signals for detection of unintentional race bias. *Psychological Science, 15,* 88–93.

Anagnostopoulos, T., Green, P. M., Rowley, G., Lewis, C. M., & Giannelli, F. (1999). DNA variation in a 5-Mb region of the X chromosome and estimates of sex-specific/type-specific mutation rates. *American Journal of Human Genetics, 64,* 508–517.

Andersen, R. A., Snyder, L. H., Bradley, D. C., & Xing, J. (1997). Multimodal representation of space in the posterior parietal cortex and its use in planning movements. *Annual Review of Neuroscience, 20,* 303–330.

Anderson, J. R. (1982). Acquisition of cognitive skill. *Psychological Review, 89,* 369–406.

Anderson, J. R. (1990). *The adaptive character of thought.* Hillsdale, NJ: Erlbaum.

Anderson, J. R., & Schooler, L. J. (1991). Reflections of the environment in memory. *Psychological Science, 2,* 396–408.

Anderson, J. R., & Schooler, L. J. (2000). The adaptive nature of memory. In E. Tulving & F. I. M. Craik (Eds.), *The Oxford handbook of memory* (pp. 557–570). New York: Oxford University Press.

Anderson, M. C., Ochsner, K. N., Kuhl, B., Cooper, J., Robertson, E., Gabrieli, S. W., et al. (2004, January 9). Neural systems underlying the suppression of unwanted memories. *Science, 303,* 232–235.

Andersson, M. (1994). *Sexual selection.* Princeton, NJ: Princeton University Press.

Ando, J., Ono, Y., & Wright, M. J. (2001). Genetic structure of spatial and verbal working memory. *Behavior Genetics, 31,* 615–624.

Armstrong, E. (1990). Brains, bodies and metabolism. *Brain, Behavior & Evolution, 36,* 166–176.

Arndt, J., Cook, A., & Routledge, C. (2004). The blueprint of terror management: Understanding the cognitive architecture of psychological defense against awareness of death. In J. Greenberg, S. Koole, & T. Pyszczynski (Eds.), *The handbook of experimental existential psychology* (pp. 35–53). New York: Guilford Press.

Arndt, J., Greenberg, J., & Cook, A. (2002). Mortality salience and the spreading activation of worldview-constructs: Exploring the cognitive architecture of terror management. *Journal of Experimental Psychology: General, 131,* 307–324.

Arndt, J., Greenberg, J., Pyszczynski, T., & Solomon, S. (1997). Subliminal exposure to death-related stimuli increases defense of the cultural worldview. *Psychological Science, 8,* 379–385.

Asfaw, B., Gilbert, W. H., Beyene, Y., Hart, W. K., Renne, P. R., WoldeGabriel, G., et al. (2002, March 21). Remains of *Homo erectus* from Bouri, Middle Awash, Ethiopia. *Nature, 416,* 317–320.

Asfaw, B., White, T., Lovejoy, O., Latimer, B., Simpson, S., & Suwa, G. (1999, April 23). *Australopithecus garhi:* A new species of early hominid from Ethiopia. *Science, 284,* 629–635.

Ashby, F. G., & Waldron, E. M. (2000). The neuropsychological bases of category learning. *Current Directions in Psychological Science, 9,* 10–14.

Ashmore, R. D., Deaux, K., & McLaughlin-Volpe, T. (2004). An organizing framework for collective identity: Articulation and significance of multidimensionality. *Psychological Bulletin, 130,* 80–114.

Atran, S. (1994). Core domains versus scientific theories: Evidence from systematics and Itza-Maya folkbiology. In L. A. Hirschfeld & S. A. Gelman (Eds.), *Mapping the mind: Domain specificity in cognition and culture* (pp. 316–340). New York: Cambridge University Press.

Atran, S. (1998). Folk biology and the anthropology of science: Cognitive universals and cultural particulars. *Behavioral and Brain Sciences, 21,* 547–609.

Au, T. K.-F., & Romo, L. F. (1999). Mechanical causality in children's "folkbiology." In D. L. Medin & S. Atran (Eds.), *Folkbiology* (pp. 355–401). Cambridge, MA: MIT Press/Bradford Book.

Baaré, W. F. C., Hulshoff Pol, H. E., Boomsma, D. I., Posthuma, D., de Geus, E. J. C., Schnack, H. G., et al. (2001). Quantitative genetic modeling of variation in human brain morphology. *Cerebral Cortex, 11,* 816–824.

Baddeley, A. D. (1986). *Working memory.* Oxford, England: Oxford University Press.

Baddeley, A. D. (1994). Working memory: The interface between memory and cognition. In D. L. Schacter & E. Tulving (Eds.), *Memory systems 1994* (pp. 351–367). Cambridge, MA: MIT Press.

Baddeley, A. D. (2000a). The episodic buffer: A new component of working memory? *Trends in Cognitive Sciences, 4,* 417–423.

Baddeley, A. D. (2000b). Short-term and working memory. In E. Tulving & F. I. M. Craik (Eds.), *The Oxford handbook of memory* (pp. 77–92). New York: Oxford University Press.

Baddeley, A. D. (2002). Fractionating the central executive. In D. T. Stuss & R. T. Knight (Eds.), *Principles of frontal lobe function* (pp. 246–260). New York: Oxford University Press.

Baddeley, A. D., Gathercole, S., & Papagno, C. (1998). The phonological loop as a language learning device. *Psychological Review, 105,* 158–173.

Baddeley, A. D., & Hitch, G. J. (1974). Working memory. In G. H. Bower (Ed.), *The psychology of learning and motivation: Advances in research and theory* (Vol. 8, pp. 47–90). New York: Academic Press.

Baddeley, A. D., & Logie, R. H. (1999). Working memory: The multiple-component model. In A. Miyake & P. Shah (Eds.), *Models of working memory: Mechanisms of active maintenance and executive control* (pp. 28–61). Cambridge, England: Cambridge University Press.

Bahn, P. G. (1992). Ancient art. In S. Jones, R. Martin, & D. Pilbeam (Eds.), *The Cambridge encyclopedia of human evolution* (pp. 361–364). New York: Cambridge University Press.

Baker, L. A., Vernon, P. A., & Ho, H.-Z. (1991). The genetic correlation between intelligence and speed of information processing. *Behavior Genetics, 21,* 351–367.

Ball, G. F., & Hulse, S. H. (1998). Birdsong. *American Psychologist, 53,* 37–58.

Baltes, P. B. (1997). On the incomplete architecture of human ontogeny: Selection, optimization, and compensation as foundation of developmental theory. *American Psychologist, 52,* 366–380.

Bandura, A. (1986). *Social foundations of thought and action: A social cognitive theory.* Englewood Cliffs, NJ: Prentice-Hall.

Bao, S., Chan, V. T., & Merzenich, M. M. (2001, July 5). Cortical remodelling induced by activity of ventral tegmental dopamine neurons. *Nature, 412,* 79–83.

Barkow, J. H. (1992). Beneath new culture is old psychology: Gossip and social stratification. In J. H. Barkow, L. Cosmides, & J. Tooby (Eds.), *The adapted mind: Evolutionary psychology and the generation of culture* (pp. 627–637). New York: Oxford University Press.

Baron, J. (1997). The illusion of morality as self-interest: A reason to cooperate in social dilemmas. *Psychological Science, 8,* 330–335.

Baron-Cohen, S. (1995). *Mindblindness: An essay on autism and theory of mind.* Cambridge, MA: MIT Press/Bradford Books.

Baron-Cohen, S. (2000). The cognitive neuroscience of autism: Evolutionary approaches. In M. S. Gazzaniga (Ed.-in-chief), *The new cognitive neurosciences* (2nd ed., pp. 1249–1257). Cambridge, MA: Bradford Books/MIT Press.

Baron-Cohen, S., Ring, H., Moriarty, J., Schmitz, B., Costa, D., & Ell, P. (1994). Recognition of mental state terms: Clinical findings in children with autism and a functional neuroimaging study of normal adults. *British Journal of Psychiatry, 165,* 640–649.

Baron-Cohen, S., Wheelwright, S., Stone, V., & Rutherford, M. (1999). A mathematician, a physicist and a computer scientist with Asperger syndrome: Performance on folk psychology and folk physics tests. *Neurocase, 5,* 475–483.

Barone, P., & Kennedy, H. (2000). Non-uniformity of neocortex: Areal heterogeneity of NADPH-diaphorase reactive neurons in adult macaque monkeys. *Cerebral Cortex, 10,* 160–174.

Barrett, P. T., Daum, I., & Eysenck, H. J. (1990). Sensory nerve conduction and intelligence: A methodological study. *Journal of Psychophysiology, 4,* 1–13.

Barsalou, L. W., Simmons, W. K., Barbey, A. K., & Wilson, C. D. (2003). Grounding conceptual knowledge in modality-specific systems. *Trends in Cognitive Sciences, 7,* 84–91.

Bartels, M., Rietveld, M. J. H., van Baal, G. C. M., & Boomsma, D. I. (2002). Genetic and environmental influences on the development of intelligence. *Behavior Genetics, 32,* 237–249.

Bartley, A. J., Jones, D. W., & Weinberger, D. R. (1997). Genetic variability of human brain size and cortical gyral patterns. *Brain, 120,* 257–269.

Barton, R. A. (1996). Neocortex size and behavioural ecology in primates. *Proceedings of the Royal Society of London B, 263,* 173–177.

Barton, R. A. (1999). The evolutionary ecology of the primate brain. In P. C. Lee (Ed.), *Comparative primate socioecology* (pp. 167–194). Cambridge, England: Cambridge University Press.

Barton, R. A., & Dean, P. (1993). Comparative evidence indicating neural specialization for predatory behaviour in mammals. *Proceedings of the Royal Society of London B, 254,* 63–68.

Barton, R. A., & Harvey, P. H. (2000, June 29). Mosaic evolution of brain structure in mammals. *Nature, 405*, 1055–1057.

Barton, R. A., Purvis, A., & Harvey, P. H. (1995). Evolutionary radiation of visual and olfactory systems in primates, bats and insectivores. *Philosophical Transactions of the Royal Society of London B, 348*, 381–392.

Bates, T. C., & Shieles, A. (2003). Crystallized intelligence as a product of speed and drive for experience: The relationship of inspection time and openness to *g* and Gc. *Intelligence, 31*, 275–287.

Baumeister, R. F., & Leary, M. R. (1995). The need to belong: Desire for interpersonal attachment as a fundamental human motive. *Psychological Bulletin, 117*, 497–529.

Bechara, A., Damasio, H., & Damasio, A. R. (2000). Emotion, decision making and the orbitofrontal cortex. *Cerebral Cortex, 10*, 295–307.

Bechara, A., Damasio, H., Tranel, D., & Damasio, A. R. (1997, February 28). Deciding advantageously before knowing the advantageous strategy. *Science, 275*, 1293–1295.

Behrensmeyer, A. K., Todd, N. E., Potts, R., & McBrinn, G. E. (1997, November 28). Late Pliocene faunal turnover in the Turkana Basin, Kenya and Ethiopia. *Science, 278*, 1589–1594.

Belin, P., Zatorre, R. J., Lafaille, P., Ahad, P., & Pike, B. (2000, January 20). Voice-selective areas in human auditory cortex. *Nature, 403*, 309–312.

Benbow, C. P., & Stanley, J. C. (1996). Inequity in equity: How "equity" can lead to inequity for high-potential students. *Psychology, Public Policy, and Law, 2*, 249–292.

Bentin, S., Sagiv, N., Mecklinger, A., Friederici, A., & von Cramon, Y. D. (2002). Priming visual face-processing mechanisms: Electrophysiological evidence. *Psychological Science, 13*, 190–193.

Bergman, T. J., Beehner, J. C., Cheney, D. L., & Seyfarth, R. M. (2003, November 14). Hierarchical classification by rank and kinship in baboons. *Science, 302*, 1234–1236.

Berlin, B. (1999). How a folkbotanical system can be both natural and comprehensive: One Maya Indian's view of the plant world. In D. L. Medin & S. Atran (Eds.), *Folkbiology* (pp. 71–89). Cambridge, MA: MIT Press/Bradford Book.

Berlin, B., Breedlove, D. E., & Raven, P. H. (1966, October 14). Folk taxonomies and biological classification. *Science, 154*, 273–275.

Berlin, B., Breedlove, D. E., & Raven, P. H. (1973). General principles of classification and nomenclature in folk biology. *American Anthropologist, 75*, 214–242.

Berlinski, D. (2000). *Newton's gift*. New York: Touchstone.

Betzig, L. L. (1986). *Despotism and differential reproduction: A Darwinian view of history*. New York: Aldine.

Betzig, L. (1992). Roman polygyny. *Ethology and Sociobiology, 13*, 309–349.

Betzig, L. (1993). Sex, succession, and stratification in the first six civilizations: How powerful men reproduced, passed power on to their sons, and used power to defend their wealth, women, and children. In L. Ellis (Ed.), *Social stratification and socioeconomic inequality: Vol. 1. A comparative biosocial analysis* (pp. 37–74). Westport, CT: Praeger.

Binet, A. (1905). New methods for the diagnosis of the intellectual level of subnormals. *L'Année Psychologique, 12,* 191–244.

Binet, A., & Simon, T. (1916). *The development of intelligence in children.* Baltimore: Williams & Wilkins.

Bishop, E. G., Cherny, S. S., Corley, R., Plomin, R., DeFries, J. C., & Hewitt, J. K. (2003). Developmental genetic analysis of general cognitive ability from 1 to 12 years in a sample of adoptees, biological siblings, and twins. *Intelligence, 31,* 31–49.

Bishop, K. M., Goudreau, G., & O'Leary, D. M. (2000, April 14). Regulation of area identity in the mammalian neocortex by Emx2 and Pax6. *Science, 288,* 344–349.

Bisley, J. W., & Goldberg, M. E. (2003, January 3). Neuronal activity in the lateral intraparietal area and spatial attention. *Science, 299,* 81–86.

Bjorklund, D. F. (2003). Evolutionary psychology from a developmental systems perspective: Comment on Lickliter and Honeycutt (2003). *Psychological Bulletin, 129,* 836–841.

Bjorklund, D. F., & Bering, J. M. (2003). Big brains, slow development and social complexity: The development and evolutionary origins of social cognition. In M. Brüne, H. Ribbert, & W. Schiefenhövel (Eds.), *The social brain: Evolution and pathology* (pp. 113–151). New York: Wiley.

Bjorklund, D. F., Cormier, C., & Rosenberg, J. S. (in press). The evolution of theory of mind: Big brains, social complexity, and inhibition. In W. Schneider, R. Schumann-Hengsteler, & B. Sodian (Eds.), *Young children's cognitive development: Interrelationships among executive functioning, working memory, verbal ability and theory of mind.* Mahwah, NJ: Erlbaum.

Bjorklund, D. F., & Harnishfeger, K. K. (1995). The evolution of inhibition mechanisms and their role in human cognition and behavior. In F. N. Dempster & C. J. Brainerd (Eds.), *New perspectives on interference and inhibition in cognition* (pp. 141–173). New York: Academic Press.

Bjorklund, D. F., & Pellegrini, A. D. (2000). Child development and evolutionary psychology. *Child Development, 71,* 1687–1708.

Bjorklund, D. F., & Pellegrini, A. D. (2002). *The origins of human nature: Evolutionary developmental psychology.* Washington, DC: American Psychological Association.

Björkqvist, K., Lagerspetz, K. M. J., & Kaukiainen, A. (1992). Do girls manipulate and boys fight? Developmental trends in regard to direct and indirect aggression. *Aggressive Behavior, 18,* 117–127.

Björkqvist, K., Osterman, K., & Lagerspetz, K. M. J. (1994). Sex differences in covert aggression among adults. *Aggressive Behavior, 20,* 27–34.

Black, J. M., Choudhury, S., & Owen, M. (1996). Do barnacle geese benefit from lifelong monogamy? In J. M. Black (Ed.), *Partnerships in birds: The study of monogamy* (pp. 91–117). New York: Oxford University Press.

Blake, R. (1993). Cats perceive biological motion. *Psychological Science, 4,* 54–57.

Bliege Bird, R., & Bird, D. W. (2002). Constraints on knowing or constraints on growing? Fishing and collecting among the children of Mer. *Human Nature, 13,* 239–267.

Bloom, P. (1996). Intention, history, and artifact concepts. *Cognition, 60,* 1–29.

Blurton Jones, N. G., Hawkes, K., & O'Connell, J. F. (1997). Why do Hadza children forage? In N. L. Segal, G. E. Weisfeld, & C. C. Weisfeld (Eds.), *Uniting psychology and biology: Integrative perspectives on human development* (pp. 279–313). Washington, DC: American Psychological Association.

Blurton Jones, N., & Marlowe, F. W. (2002). Selection for delayed maturity: Does it take 20 years to learn to hunt and gather? *Human Nature, 13,* 199–238.

Blythe, P. W., Todd, P. M., & Miller, G. F. (1999). How motion reveals intention: Categorizing social interactions. In G. Gigerenzer, P. M. Todd, & ABC Research Group (Eds.), *Simple heuristics that make us smart* (pp. 257–285). New York: Oxford University Press.

Boag, P. T. (1983). The heritability of external morphology in Darwin's ground finches (*Geospiza*) on Isla Daphne Major, Galápagos. *Evolution, 37,* 877–894.

Boag, P. T., & Grant, P. R. (1978, August 24). Heritability of external morphology in Darwin's finches. *Nature, 274,* 793–794.

Bock, J., & Johnson, S. E. (2004). Subsistence ecology and play among the Okavango Delta peoples of Botswana. *Human Nature, 15,* 63–81.

Bodenhausen, G. V., Macrae, C. N., & Hugenberg, K. (2003). Social cognition. In T. Millon & M. J. Learner (Eds.) & I. B. Weiner (Gen. Ed.), *Handbook of psychology: Vol. 5. Personality and social psychology* (pp. 257–282). New York: Wiley.

Bogin, B. (1999). Evolutionary perspective on human growth. *Annual Review of Anthropology, 28,* 109–153.

Boissiere, M., Knight, J. B., & Sabot, R. H. (1985). Earnings, schooling, ability, and cognitive skills. *American Economic Review, 75,* 1016–1030.

Boone, J. L., & Kessler, K. L. (1999). More status or more children? Social status, fertility reduction, and long-term fitness. *Evolution and Human Behavior, 20,* 257–277.

Borgia, G. (1985a). Bower destruction and sexual competition in the satin bower bird (*Ptilonorhynchus violaceus*). *Behavioral Ecology and Sociobiology, 18,* 91–100.

Borgia, G. (1985b). Bower quality, number of decorations and mating success of male satin bower birds (*Ptilonorhynchus violaceus*): An experimental analysis. *Animal Behaviour, 33,* 266–271.

Borgia, G., & Coleman, S. W. (2000). Co-option of male courtship signals from aggressive display in bowerbirds. *Proceedings of the Royal Society of London B, 267,* 1735–1740.

Bornstein, G. (2003). Intergroup conflict: Individual, group, and collective interests. *Personality and Social Psychology Review, 7,* 129–145.

Bortolini, M. C., Silva Junior, W. A. D., Castro de Guerra, D., Remonatto, G., Mirandola, R., Hutz, M. H., et al. (1999). African-derived South American populations: A history of symmetrical and asymmetrical matings according to sex revealed by bi- and uni-parental genetic markers. *American Journal of Human Biology, 11,* 551–563.

Botvinick, M. M., Braver, T. S., Barch, D. M., Carter, C. S., & Cohen, J. D. (2001). Conflict monitoring and cognitive control. *Psychological Review, 108,* 624–652.

Bouchard, T. J., Jr., Lykken, D. T., McGue, M., Segal, N. L., & Tellegen, A. (1990, October 12). Sources of human psychological differences: The Minnesota study of twins reared apart. *Science, 250,* 223–228.

Bouchard, T. J., Jr., & McGue, M. (1981, May 29). Familial studies of intelligence: A review. *Science, 212,* 1055–1059.

Brace, C. L. (1995). Biocultural interaction and the mechanism of mosaic evolution in the emergence of "modern" morphology. *American Anthropologist, 97,* 711–721.

Bradley, L., & Bryant, P. E. (1983, February 3). Categorizing sounds and learning to read—A causal connection. *Nature, 301,* 419–421.

Bradley, R. H., & Corwyn, R. F. (2002). Socioeconomic status and child development. *Annual Review of Psychology, 53,* 371–399.

Braine, M. D. S. (1978). On the relation between the natural logic of reasoning and standard logic. *Psychological Review, 85,* 1–21.

Brase, G. L., Cosmides, L., & Tooby, J. (1998). Individuation, counting, and statistical inference: The frequency and whole-object representations in judgment under uncertainty. *Journal of Experimental Psychology: General, 127,* 3–21.

Brodmann, K. (1909). *Vergleichende Lokalisationslehre der Grosshirnrinde in ihren Prinzipien dargestellt auf Grund des Zellenbaues* [Comparative localization of the cerebral cortex based on cell composition]. Leipzig, Germany: Barth.

Brose, K., & Tessier-Lavigne, M. (2000). Slit proteins: key regulators of axon guidance, axonal branching, and cell migration. *Current Opinion in Neurobiology, 10,* 95–102.

Brosnan, S. F., & de Waal, F. B. M. (2003, September 18). Monkeys reject unequal pay. *Nature, 425,* 297–299.

Brothers, L. (1990). The social brain: A project for integrating primate behavior and neurophysiology in a new domain. *Concepts in Neuroscience, 1,* 27–51.

Brothers, L., & Ring, B. (1992). A neuroethological framework for the representation of minds. *Journal of Cognitive Neuroscience, 4,* 107–118.

Brown, D. E. (1991). *Human universals.* Philadelphia, PA: Temple University Press.

Brown, R. (1973). *A first language: The early stages.* Cambridge, MA: Harvard University Press.

Browne, J. (2002). *Charles Darwin: The power of place.* New York: Knopf.

Brunswik, E. (1943). Organismic achievement and environmental probability. *Psychological Review, 50,* 255–272.

Buchanan, T. W., Lutz, K., Mirzazade, S., Specht, K., Shah, N. J., Zilles, K., & Jäncke, L. (2000). Recognition of emotional prosody and verbal components of spoken language: An fMRI study. *Cognitive Brain Research, 9,* 227–238.

Buchner, H., Kauert, C., & Radermacher, I. (1995). Short-term changes of finger representation at the somatosensory cortex in humans. *Neuroscience Letters, 198,* 57–59.

Bugental, D. B. (2000). Acquisition of the algorithms of social life: A domain-based approach. *Psychological Bulletin, 126,* 187–219.

Bunge, S. A., Klingberg, T., Jacobsen, R. B., & Gabrieli, J. D. E. (2000). A resource model of the neural basis of executive working memory. *Proceedings of the National Academy of Sciences USA, 97,* 3573–3578.

Buonomano, D. V., & Merzenich, M. M. (1998). Cortical plasticity: From synapses to maps. *Annual Review of Neuroscience, 21,* 149–186.

Burns, N. R., & Nettelbeck, T. (2003). Inspection time in the structure of cognitive abilities: Where does IT fit? *Intelligence, 31,* 237–255.

Burt, C. (1940). *The factors of the mind.* London: University of London Press.

Buss, D. M. (1989). Sex differences in human mate preferences: Evolutionary hypothesis tested in 37 cultures. *Behavioral and Brain Sciences, 12,* 1–49.

Buss, D. M. (1991). Evolutionary personality psychology. *Annual Review of Psychology, 42,* 459–491.

Buss, D. M. (1994). *The evolution of desire: Strategies of human mating.* New York: Basic Books.

Butler, A., & Hodos, W. (1996). *Comparative vertebrate neuroanatomy: Evolution and adaptation.* New York: Wiley Liss.

Byrne, R. (1995). *The thinking ape: Evolutionary origins of intelligence.* New York: Oxford University Press.

Byrne, R. W. (2000). Evolution of primate cognition. *Cognitive Science, 24,* 543–570.

Cabeza, R., & Nyberg, L. (1997). Imaging cognition: An empirical review of PET studies with normal subjects. *Journal of Cognitive Neuroscience, 9,* 1–26.

Cabeza, R., & Nyberg, L. (2000). Imaging cognition II: An empirical review of 275 PET and fMRI studies. *Journal of Cognitive Neuroscience, 12,* 1–47.

Cáceres, M., Lachuer, J., Zapala, M. A., Redmond, J. C., Kudo, L., Geschwind, D. H., et al. (2003). Elevated gene expression levels distinguish human from non-human primate brains. *Proceedings of the National Academy of Sciences USA, 100,* 13030–13035.

Cacioppo, J. T., Berntson, G. G., Adolphs, R., Carter, C. S., Davidson, R. J., McClintock, M. K., et al. (Eds.). (2002). *Foundations in social neuroscience.* Cambridge, MA: Bradford Books/MIT Press.

Callan, D. E., Tajima, K., Callan, A. M., Kubo, R., Masaki, S., & Akahane-Yamada, R. (2003). Learning-induced neural plasticity associated with improved identification performance after training of a difficult second-language phonetic contrast. *NeuroImage, 19,* 113–124.

Calvin, W. H. (2002). Pumping up intelligence: Abrupt climate jumps and the evolution of higher intellectual functions during the ice ages. In R. J. Sternberg & J. C. Kaufman (Eds.), *The evolution of intelligence* (pp. 97–115). Mahwah, NJ: Erlbaum.

Camille, N., Coricelli, G., Sallet, J., Pradat-Diehl, P., Duhamel, J.-R., & Sirigu, A. (2004, May 21). The involvement of the orbitofrontal cortex in the experience of regret. *Science, 304,* 1167–1170.

Campbell, A. (1999). Staying alive: Evolution, culture, and women's intrasexual aggression. *Behavioral and Brain Science, 22,* 203–252.

Campos, J. J., Campos, R. G., & Barrett, K. C. (1989). Emergent themes in the study of emotional development and emotion regulation. *Developmental Psychology, 25,* 394–402.

Canli, T., Sivers, H., Whitfield, S. L., Gotlib, I. H., & Gabrieli, J. D. E. (2002, June 21). Amygdala response to happy faces as a function of extraversion. *Science, 296,* 2191.

Cantalupo, C., & Hopkins, W. D. (2001, November 29). Asymmetric Broca's area in great apes. *Nature, 414,* 505.

Capelli, C., Redhead, N., Abernethy, J. K., Gratrix, F., Wilson, J. F., Moen, T., et al. (2003). A Y chromosome census of the British isles. *Current Biology, 13,* 979–984.

Caporael, L. R. (1997). The evolution of truly social cognition: The core configurations model. *Personality & Social Psychology Review, 1,* 276–298.

Caramazza, A., & Shelton, J. R. (1998). Domain-specific knowledge systems in the brain: The animate–inanimate distinction. *Journal of Cognitive Neuroscience, 10,* 1–34.

Cardon, L. R., Fulker, D. W., DeFries, J. C., & Plomin, R. (1992). Multivariate genetic analysis of specific cognitive abilities in the Colorado adoption project at age 7. *Intelligence, 16,* 383–400.

Carey, S., & Spelke, E. (1994). Domain-specific knowledge and conceptual change. In L. A. Hirschfeld & S. A. Gelman (Eds.), *Mapping the mind: Domain specificity in cognition and culture* (pp. 169–200). New York: Cambridge University Press.

Carpenter, P. A., Just, M. A., & Reichle, E. D. (2000). Working memory and executive function: Evidence from neuroimaging. *Current Opinion in Neurobiology, 10,* 195–199.

Carpenter, P. A., Just, M. A., & Shell, P. (1990). What one intelligence test measures: A theoretical account of processing in the Raven Progressive Matrices Test. *Psychological Review, 97,* 404–431.

Carroll, J. B. (1991). No demonstration that *g* is not unitary, but there's more to the story: Comment on Kranzler and Jensen. *Intelligence, 15,* 423–436.

Carroll, J. B. (1993). *Human cognitive abilities: A survey of factor-analytic studies.* New York: Cambridge University Press.

Carroll, S. B. (2003, April 24). Genetics and the making of *Homo sapiens*. *Nature*, *422*, 849–857.

Carvajal-Carmona, L. G., Soto, I. D., Pineda, N., Ortíz-Barrientos, D., Duque, C., Ospina-Duque, J., et al. (2000). Strong Amerind/White sex bias and a possible Sephardic contribution among the founders of a population in northwest Columbia. *American Journal of Human Genetics*, *67*, 1287–1295.

Case, R. (1992). *The mind's staircase: Exploring the conceptual underpinnings of children's thought and knowledge*. Hillsdale, NJ: Erlbaum.

Caspi, A. (1993). Why maladaptive behaviors persist: Sources of continuity and change across the life course. In D. C. Funder, R. D. Parke, C. Tomlinson-Keasey, & K. Widaman (Eds.), *Studying lives through time: Personality and development* (pp. 343–376). Washington, DC: American Psychological Association.

Catalano, S. M., & Shatz, C. J. (1998, July 24). Activity-dependent cortical target selection by thalamic axons. *Science*, *281*, 559–562.

Catania, K. C. (2000). Cortical organization in insectivora: The parallel evolution of the sensory periphery and the brain. *Brain, Behavior and Evolution*, *55*, 311–321.

Catania, K. C., Lyon, D. C., Mock, O. B., & Kaas, J. H. (1999). Cortical organization in shrews: Evidence from five species. *Journal of Comparative Neurology*, *410*, 55–72.

Cattell, R. B. (1963). Theory of fluid and crystallized intelligence: A critical experiment. *Journal of Educational Psychology*, *54*, 1–22.

Cavaillé, J., Buiting, K., Kiefmann, M., Lalande, M., Brannan, C. I., Horsthemke, B., et al. (2000). Identification of brain-specific and imprinted small nucleolar RNA genes exhibiting an unusual genomic organization. *Proceedings of the National Academy of Sciences*, *97*, 14311–14316.

Cavalli-Sforza, L. L. (1998). The Chinese human genome diversity project. *Proceedings of the National Academy of Sciences*, *95*, 11501–11503.

Caviness, V. S., Jr., Takahashi, T., & Nowakowski, R. S. (1995). Numbers, time and neocortical neuronogenesis: A general developmental and evolutionary model. *Trends in Neurosciences*, *18*, 379–383.

Ceballos, G., & Ehrlich, P. R. (2002, May 3). Mammal population losses and the extinction crisis. *Science*, *296*, 904–907.

Ceci, S. J. (1991). How much does schooling influence general intelligence and its cognitive components? A reassessment of the evidence. *Developmental Psychology*, *27*, 703–722.

Ceci, S. J., & Williams, W. M. (1997). Schooling, intelligence, and income. *American Psychologist*, *52*, 1051–1058.

Chagnon, N. A. (1988, February 26). Life histories, blood revenge, and warfare in a tribal population. *Science*, *239*, 985–992.

Chagnon, N. A. (1997). *Yanomamö* (5th ed.). Fort Worth, TX: Harcourt.

Chan, Y.-M., & Jan, Y. N. (1999). Conservation of neurogenic genes and mechanisms. *Current Opinion in Neurobiology*, *9*, 582–588.

Chang, E. F., & Merzenich, M. M. (2003, April 18). Environmental noise retards auditory cortical development. *Science, 300,* 498–502.

Changizi, M. A. (2001). Principles underlying mammalian neocortical scaling. *Biological Cybernetics, 84,* 207–215.

Changizi, M. A. (2003). *The brain from 25,000 feet: High level explorations of brain complexity, perception and vagueness.* Dordrecht, Holland: Kluwer Academic.

Changizi, M. A., McDannald, M. A., & Widders, D. (2002). Scaling of differentiation in networks: Nervous systems, organisms, ant colonies, ecosystems, businesses, universities, cities, electronic circuits, and Legos. *Journal of Theoretical Biology, 218,* 215–237.

Chen, Z., & Siegler, R. S. (2000). Across the great divide: Bridging the gap between understanding toddlers' and older children's thinking. *Monographs of the Society for Research in Child Development, 65* (No 2, serial no. 261).

Cheng, P., & Holyoak, K. J. (1989). On the natural selection of reasoning theories. *Cognition, 33,* 285–313.

Chenn, A., & Walsh, C. A. (2002, July 19). Regulation of cerebral cortical size by control of cell cycle exit in neural precursors. *Science, 297,* 365–369.

Chiappe, D., & MacDonald, K. (in press). The evolution of domain-general mechanisms in intelligence and learning. *Journal of General Psychology.*

Clark, A. G., Glanowski, S., Nielsen, R., Thomas, P. D., Kejariwal, A., Todd, M. A., et al. (2003, December 12). Inferring nonneutral evolution from human–chimp–mouse orthologous gene trios. *Science, 302,* 1960–1963.

Clark, D. A., Mitra, P. P., & Wang, S. S.-H. (2001, May 10). Scalable architecture in mammalian brains. *Nature, 411,* 189–193.

Clark, J. D., Beyene, Y., WoldeGabriel, G., Hart, W. K., Renne, P. R., Gilbert, H., et al. (2003, June 12). Stratigraphic, chronological and behavioral contexts of Pleistocene *Homo sapiens* from Middle Awash, Ethiopia. *Nature, 423,* 747–752.

Clement, D. (1995). Why is taxonomy utilitarian? *Ethnobiology, 15,* 1–44.

Clement, J. (1982). Students' preconceptions in introductory mechanics. *American Journal of Physics, 50,* 66–71.

Clutton-Brock, J. (1992). Domestication of animals. In S. Jones, R. Martin, & D. Pilbeam (Eds.), *The Cambridge encyclopedia of human evolution* (pp. 380–385). New York: Cambridge University Press.

Clutton-Brock, T. H. (1989). Mammalian mating systems. *Proceedings of the Royal Society of London B, 236,* 339–372.

Clutton-Brock, T. H. (1991). *The evolution of parental care.* Princeton, NJ: Princeton University Press.

Clutton-Brock, T. H. (2002, April 5). Breeding together: Kin selection and mutualism in cooperative vertebrates. *Science, 296,* 69–72.

Clutton-Brock, T. H., & Harvey, P. H. (1980). Primates, brains and ecology. *Journal of Zoology, 190,* 309–323.

Clutton-Brock, T. H., Harvey, P. H., & Rudder, B. (1977, October 27). Sexual dimorphism, socionomic sex ratio and body weight in primates. *Nature, 269,* 797–800.

Clutton-Brock, T. H., & McComb, K. (1993). Experimental tests of copying and mate choice in fallow deer (*Dama dama*). *Behavioral Ecology, 4,* 191–193.

Clutton-Brock, T. H., & Vincent, A. C. J. (1991, May 2). Sexual selection and the potential reproductive rates of males and females. *Nature, 351,* 58–60.

Cohen, J. D., Perlstein, W. M., Braver, T. S., Nystrom, L. E., Noll, D. C., Jonides, J., & Smith, E. E. (1997, April 10). Temporal dynamics of brain activation during a working memory task. *Nature, 386,* 604–608.

Coley, J. D. (1995). Emerging differentiation of folkbiology and folkpsychology: Attributions of biological and psychological properties of living things. *Child Development, 66,* 1856–1874.

Coley, J. D. (2000). On the importance of comparative research: The case of folkbiology. *Child Development, 71,* 82–90.

Coley, J. D., Solomon, G. E. A., & Shafto, P. (2002). The development of folkbiology: A cognitive science perspective on children's understanding of the biological world. In P. H. Kahn, Jr. & S. R. Kellert (Eds.), *Children and nature: Psychological, sociocultural, and evolutionary investigations* (pp. 65–91). Cambridge, MA: MIT Press.

Collette, F., & Van der Linden, M. (2002). Brain imaging of the central executive component of working memory. *Neuroscience and Biobehavioral Reviews, 26,* 105–125.

Collins, W. A., Maccoby, E. E., Steinberg, L., Hetherington, E. M., & Bornstein, M. H. (2000). Contemporary research on parenting: The case for nature and nurture. *American Psychologist, 55,* 218–232.

Collis, K., & Borgia, G. (1992). Age-related effects of testosterone, plumage, and experience on aggression and social dominance in juvenile male satin bowerbirds (*Ptilonorhynchus violaceus*). *Auk, 109,* 422–434.

Colman, A. M. (2003). Cooperation, psychological game theory, and limitations of rationality in social interaction. *Behavioral and Brain Sciences, 26,* 139–198.

Colom, R., Rebollo, I., Palacios, A., Juan-Espinosa, M., & Kyllonen, P. C. (2004). Working memory is (almost) perfectly predicted by *g*. *Intelligence, 32.*

Conner, J. K. (2001). How strong is natural selection? *Trends in Ecology & Evolution, 16,* 215–217.

Conway, A. R. A., Cowan, N., & Bunting, M. F. (2001). The cocktail party phenomenon revisited: The importance of working memory capacity. *Psychonomic Bulletin & Review, 8,* 331–335.

Conway, A. R. A., Cowan, N., Bunting, M. F., Therriault, D. J., & Minkoff, S. R. B. (2002). A latent variable analysis of working memory capacity, short-term memory capacity, processing speed, and general fluid intelligence. *Intelligence, 30,* 163–183.

Conway, A. R. A., & Engle, R. W. (1994). Working memory and retrieval: A resource-dependent inhibition model. *Journal of Experimental Psychology: General, 123*, 354–373.

Cosmides, L. (1989). The logic of social exchange: Has natural selection shaped how humans reason? Studies with the Wason selection task. *Cognition, 31*, 187–276.

Cosmides, L., & Tooby, J. (1994). Origins of domain specificity: The evolution of functional organization. In L. A. Hirschfeld & S. A. Gelman (Eds.), *Mapping the mind: Domain specificity in cognition and culture* (pp. 85–116). New York: Cambridge University Press.

Cosmides, L., & Tooby, J. (2000). Consider the source: The evolution of adaptations for decoupling and metarepresentation. In D. Sperber (Ed.), *Metarepresentations* (pp. 53–115). Oxford, England: Oxford University Press.

Cowan, N. (1988). Evolving conceptions of memory storage, selective attention, and their mutual constraints within the human information-processing system. *Psychological Bulletin, 104*, 163–191.

Cowan, N. (1995). *Attention and memory: An integrated framework*. New York: Oxford University Press.

Cowan, N. (1999). An embedded-process model of working memory. In A. Miyake & P. Shah (Eds.), *Models of working memory: Mechanisms of active maintenance and executive control* (pp. 62–101). Cambridge, England: Cambridge University Press.

Cowan, N. (2001). The magical number 4 in short-term memory: A reconsideration of mental storage capacity. *Behavioral and Brain Sciences, 24*, 87–185.

Cox, D., Meyers, E., & Sinha, P. (2004, April 2). Contextually evoked object-specific responses in human visual cortex. *Science, 304*, 115–117.

Craik, F. I. M., Moroz, T. M., Moscovitch, M., Stuss, D. T., Winocur, G., Tulving, E., & Kapur, S. (1999). In search of self: A positron emission tomography study. *Psychological Science, 10*, 26–34.

Crawford, J. R., Deary, I. J., Allan, K. M., & Gustafsson, J.-E. (1998). Evaluating competing models of the relationship between inspection time and psychometric intelligence. *Intelligence, 26*, 27–42.

Crick, N. R., Casas, J. F., & Mosher, M. (1997). Relational and overt aggression in preschool. *Developmental Psychology, 33*, 579–588.

Crossley, P. H., & Martin, G. R. (1995). The mouse fgf8 gene encodes a family of polypeptides and is expressed in regions that direct outgrowth and patterning in the developing embryo. *Development, 121*, 439–451.

Crossley, P. H., Martinez, S., Ohkubo, Y., & Rubenstein, J. L. R. (2001). Coordinate expression of FGF8, OTX2, BMP4, and SHH in the rostral prosencephalon during development of telencephalic and optic vesicles. *Neuroscience, 108*, 183–206.

Crow, J. F. (1997). The high spontaneous mutation rate: Is it a health risk? *Proceedings of the National Academy of Sciences USA, 94*, 8380–8386.

Crowley, J. C., & Katz, L. C. (2000, November 17). Early development of ocular dominance columns. *Science, 290,* 1321–1324.

Curtis, C. E., & D'Esposito, M. (2003). Persistent activity in the prefrontal cortex during working memory. *Trends in Cognitive Sciences, 7,* 415–423.

Czerlinski, J., Gigerenzer, G., & Goldstein, D. G. (1999). How good are simple heuristics? In G. Gigerenzer, P. M. Todd, & ABC Research Group (Eds.), *Simple heuristics that make us smart* (pp. 97–118). New York: Oxford University Press.

Daly, M., & Wilson, M. (1988). *Homicide.* New York: Aldine de Gruyter.

Damasio, A. R. (1989). Time-locked multiregional retroactivation: A systems-level proposal for the neural substrates of recall and recognition. *Cognition, 33,* 25–62.

Damasio, A. R. (1995). On some functions of the human prefrontal cortex. In J. Grafman, K. J. Holyoak, & F. Boller (Eds.), *Structure and functions of the human prefrontal cortex* (*Annals of the New York Academy of Sciences,* Vol. 769, pp. 241–251). New York: New York Academy of Sciences.

Damasio, A. R. (2003). *Looking for Spinoza: Joy, sorrow, and the feeling brain.* Orlando, FL: Harcourt.

Damasio, A. R., Grabowski, T. J., Bechara, A., Damasio, H., Ponto, L. L. B., Parvizi, J., & Hichwa, R. D. (2000). Subcortical and cortical brain activity during the feeling of self-generated emotions. *Nature Neuroscience, 3,* 1049–1056.

Danion, J.-M., Rizzo, L., & Bruant, A. (1999). Functional mechanisms underlying impaired recognition memory and conscious awareness in patients with schizophrenia. *Archives of General Psychiatry, 56,* 639–644.

Darwin, C. (1846). *Journal of researches into the geology and natural history of the various countries visited by H.M.S. Beagle.* New York: Harper & Brothers.

Darwin, C. (1859). *The origin of species by means of natural selection.* London: John Murray.

Darwin, C. (1871). *The descent of man, and selection in relation to sex* (Vols. 1 & 2). London: John Murray.

Darwin, C. (1998). *The expression of the emotions in man and animals* (3rd ed., with Introduction, afterword, and commentaries by P. Ekman). New York: Oxford University Press. (Original work published 1872)

Darwin, C., & Wallace, A. (1858). On the tendency of species to form varieties, and on the perpetuation of varieties and species by natural means of selection. *Journal of the Linnean Society of London, Zoology, 3,* 45–62.

Darwin, F. (Ed.). (2000). *The autobiography of Charles Darwin.* Amherst, NY: Prometheus Books. (Original work published 1893)

Davis, J. N., & Todd, P. M. (1999). Parental investment by simple decision rules. In G. Gigerenzer, P. M. Todd, & ABC Research Group (Eds.), *Simple heuristics that make us smart* (pp. 309–324). New York: Oxford University Press.

Dawkins, R., & Krebs, J. R. (1979). Arms races between and within species. *Proceedings of the Royal Society of London B, 205,* 489–511.

Deacon, T. W. (1990). Rethinking mammalian brain evolution. *American Zoologist, 30*, 629–705.

Deacon, T. (1997). *The symbolic species: The co-evolution of language and the brain.* New York: Norton.

Dean, C., Leakey, M. G., Reid, D., Schrenk, F., Schwartz, G. T., Stringer, C., & Walker, A. (2001, December 6). Growth processes in teeth distinguish modern humans from *Homo erectus* and earlier hominids. *Nature, 414*, 628–631.

Deary, I. J. (2000). *Looking down on human intelligence: From psychophysics to the brain.* Oxford, England: Oxford University Press.

Deary, I. J. (2001). Human intelligence differences: A recent history. *Trends in Cognitive Sciences, 5*, 127–130.

Deary, I. J., Der, G., & Ford, G. (2001). Reaction times and intelligence differences: A population-based cohort study. *Intelligence, 29*, 389–399.

Deary, I. J., McCrimmon, R. J., & Bradshaw, J. (1997). Visual information processing and intelligence. *Intelligence, 24*, 461–479.

Deary, I. J., Simonotto, E., Marshall, A., Marshall, I., Goddard, N., & Wardlaw, J. M. (2001). The functional anatomy of inspection time: A pilot fMRI study. *Intelligence, 29*, 497–510.

Deary, I. J., & Stough, C. (1996). Intelligence and inspection time: Achievements, prospects, and problems. *American Psychologist, 51*, 599–608.

Deary, I. J., Whalley, L. J., Lemmon, H., Crawford, J. R., & Starr, J. M. (2000). The stability of individual differences in mental ability from childhood to old age: Follow-up of the 1932 Scottish mental survey. *Intelligence, 28*, 49–55.

Deary, I. J., Whalley, L. J., St. Clair, D., Breen, G., Leaper, S., Lemmon, H., et al. (2003). The influence of 4 allele of the apolipoprotein E gene on childhood IQ, nonverbal reasoning in old age, and lifetime cognitive change. *Intelligence, 31*, 85–92.

Deary, I. J., Whiteman, M. C., Whalley, L. J., Fox, H. C., & Starr, J. M. (2004). The impact of childhood intelligence on later life: Following up the Scottish mental surveys of 1932 and 1947. *Journal of Personality and Social Psychology, 86*, 130–147.

Deecke, V. B., Slater, P. J. B., & Ford, J. K. B. (2002, November 14). Selective habituation shapes acoustic predator recognition in harbour seals. *Nature, 420*, 171–173.

DeFries, J. C., Johnson, R. C., Kuse, A. R., McClearn, G. E., Polovina, J., Vandenberg, S. G., & Wilson, J. R. (1979). Familial resemblance for specific cognitive abilities. *Behavior Genetics, 9*, 23–43.

Dehaene, S. (Ed.). (2001). *The cognitive neuroscience of consciousness.* Cambridge, MA: Bradford Books/MIT Press.

Dehaene, S., & Naccache, L. (2001). Towards a cognitive neuroscience of consciousness: Basic evidence and a workspace framework. *Cognition, 79*, 1–37.

Dehaene-Lambertz, G., Dehaene, S., & Hertz-Pannier, L. (2002, December 6). Functional neuroimaging of speech perception in infants. *Science, 298,* 2013–2015.

de Heinzelin, J., Clark, J. D., White, T., Hart, W., Renne, P., WoldeGabriel, G., et al. (1999, April 23). Environment and behavior of 2.5-million-year-old Bouri hominids. *Science, 284,* 625–629.

DeLoache, J. S., Kolstad, D. V., & Anderson, K. N. (1991). Physical similarity and young children's understanding of scale models. *Child Development, 62,* 111–126.

deMenocal, P. B. (2001, April 27). Cultural responses to climatic change during the late Holocene. *Science, 292,* 667–673.

Dennett, D. C. (1987). *The intentional stance.* Cambridge, MA: MIT Press.

Dennett, D. C. (1990). The interpretation of texts, people, and other artifacts. *Philosophy and Phenomenological Research, 50,* 177–194.

Dennett, D. C. (1995). *Darwin's dangerous idea: Evolution and the meaning of life.* New York: Touchstone.

Der, G., & Deary, I. J. (2003). IQ, reaction time and the differentiation hypothesis. *Intelligence, 31,* 491–503.

Desmond, A. (1997). *Huxley: From devil's disciple to evolution's high priest.* Reading, MA: Perseus Books.

Desmond, A., & Moore, J. (1994). *Darwin: Life of a tormented evolutionist.* New York: Norton.

Detterman, D. K., & Daniel, M. H. (1989). Correlations of mental tests with each other and with cognitive variables are highest for low IQ groups. *Intelligence, 13,* 349–359.

Detterman, D. K., & Thompson, L. A. (1997). What is so special about special education? *American Psychologist, 52,* 1082–1090.

Devlin, B., Daniels, M., & Roeder, K. (1997, July 31). The heritability of IQ. *Nature, 388,* 468–471.

Devlin, J. T., Russell, R. P., Davis, M. H., Price, C. J., Moss, H. E., Fadili, M. J., & Tyler, L. K. (2001). Is there an anatomical basis for category-specificity? Semantic memory studies in PET and fMRI. *Neuropsychologia, 40,* 54–75.

Devlin, K. (1998). *The language of mathematics: Making the invisible visible.* New York: W. H. Freeman.

de Waal, F. B. M. (1982). *Chimpanzee politics: Power and sex among apes.* New York: Harper & Row.

de Waal, F. B. M. (1993). Sex differences in chimpanzee (and human) behavior: A matter of social values? In M. Hechter, L. Nadel, & R. E. Michod (Eds.), *The origin of values* (pp. 285–303). New York: Aldine de Gruyter.

de Waal, F. B. M. (2000, July 28). Primates—A natural heritage of conflict resolution. *Science, 289,* 586–590.

de Winter, W., & Oxnard, C. E. (2001, February 8). Evolutionary radiations and convergences in the structural organization of mammalian brains. *Nature, 409,* 710–714.

Diamond, J. M. (1966, March 4). Zoological classification system of a primitive people. *Science, 151,* 1102–1104.

Dickens, W. T., & Flynn, J. R. (2001). Heritability estimates versus large environmental effects: The IQ paradox resolved. *Psychological Review, 108,* 346–369.

Diener, E., & Diener, C. (1996). Most people are happy. *Psychological Science, 7,* 181–185.

Diener, E., & Seligman, M. E. P. (2002). Very happy people. *Psychological Science, 13,* 81–84.

Dinse, H. R., Ragert, P., Pleger, B., Schwenkreis, P., & Tegenthoff, M. (2003, July 4). Pharmacological modulation of perceptual learning and associated cortical reorganization. *Science, 301,* 91–94.

Disbrow, E., Roberts, T., & Krubitzer, L. (2000). Somatotopic organization of cortical fields in the lateral sulcus of Homo sapiens: Evidence for SII and PV. *Journal of Comparative Neurology, 418,* 1–21.

Donoghue, M. J., & Rakic, P. (1999). Molecular evidence for the early specification of presumptive functional domains in the embryonic primate cerebral cortex. *Journal of Neuroscience, 19,* 5967–5979.

Dorit, R. L., Akashi, H., & Gilbert, W. (1995, May 26). Absence of polymorphism at the ZFY locus on the human Y chromosome. *Science, 268,* 1183–1185.

Doupe, A. J., & Kuhl, P. K. (1999). Birdsong and human speech: Common themes and mechanisms. *Annual Review of Neuroscience, 22,* 567–631.

Downing, P. E., Jiang, Y., Shuman, M., & Kanwisher, N. (2001, September 28). A cortical area selective for visual processing of the human body. *Science, 293,* 2470–2473.

Draganski, B., Gaser, C., Busch, V., Schuierer, G., Bogdahn, U., & May, A. (2004, January 22). Changes in grey matter induced by training. *Nature, 427,* 311–312.

Draper, P. (1989). African marriage systems: Perspectives from evolutionary ecology. *Ethology and Sociobiology, 10,* 145–169.

Draper, P., & Harpending, H. (1988). A sociobiological perspective on the development of human reproductive strategies. In K. B. MacDonald (Ed.), *Sociobiological perspectives on human development* (pp. 340–372). New York: Springer-Verlag.

Drigotas, S. M. (2002). The Michelangelo phenomenon and personal well-being. *Journal of Personality, 70,* 59–77.

Driver, J., & Vuilleumier, P. (2001). Perceptual awareness and its loss in unilateral neglect and extinction. *Cognition, 79,* 39–88.

Dukas, R. (Ed.). (1998a). *Cognitive ecology: The evolutionary ecology of information processing and decision making.* Chicago: University of Chicago Press.

Dukas, R. (1998b). Evolutionary ecology of learning. In R. Dukas (Ed.), *Cognitive ecology: The evolutionary ecology of information processing and decision making* (pp. 129–174). Chicago: University of Chicago Press.

Dunbar, R. I. M. (1993). Coevolution of neocortical size, group size and language in humans. *Behavioral and Brain Sciences, 16,* 681–735.

Dunbar, R. I. M. (1995). The mating system of callitrichid primates: I. Conditions for the coevolution of pair bonding and twinning. *Animal Behaviour, 50,* 1057–1070.

Dunbar, R. I. M. (1998). The social brain hypothesis. *Evolutionary Anthropology, 6,* 178–190.

Dunbar, R. (2003, November 14). Evolution of the social brain. *Science, 302,* 1160–1161.

Dunbar, R. I. M., & Bever, J. (1998). Neocortex size predicts group size in carnivores and some insectivores. *Ethology, 104,* 695–708.

Duncan, J. (1995). Attention, intelligence, and frontal lobes. In M. S. Gazzaniga (Ed.), *The cognitive neurosciences* (pp. 721–733). Cambridge, MA: Bradford Books/MIT Press.

Duncan, J. (2001). An adaptive coding model of neural function in prefrontal cortex. *Nature Reviews: Neuroscience, 2,* 820–829.

Duncan, J., Burgess, P., & Emslie, H. (1995). Fluid intelligence after frontal lobe lesions. *Neuropsychologia, 33,* 261–268.

Duncan, J., Emslie, H., & Williams, P., Johnson, R., & Freer, C. (1996). Intelligence and the frontal lobe: The organization of goal-directed behavior. *Cognitive Psychology, 30,* 257–303.

Duncan, J., & Owen, A. M. (2000). Common regions of the human frontal lobe recruited by diverse cognitive demands. *Trends in Neurosciences, 23,* 475–483.

Duncan, J., Rüdiger, J. S., Kolodny, J., Bor, D., Herzog, H., Ahmed, A., et al. (2000, July 21). A neural basis for general intelligence. *Science, 289,* 457–460.

Duyme, M., Dumaret, A.-C., & Tomkiewicz, S. (1999). How can we boost IQs of "dull children"? A late adoption study. *Proceedings of the National Academy of Sciences USA, 96,* 8790–8794.

Düzel, E., Yonelinas, A. P., Mangun, G. R., Heinze, H.-J., & Tulving, E. (1997). Event-related brain potential correlates of two states of conscious awareness in memory. *Proceedings of the National Academy of Sciences USA, 94,* 5973–5978.

Dyer, F. C. (1998). Cognitive ecology of navigation. In R. Dukas (Ed.), *Cognitive ecology: The evolutionary ecology of information processing and decision making* (pp. 201–260). Chicago: University of Chicago Press.

Eccles, J., Wigfield, A., Harold, R. D., & Blumenfeld, P. (1993). Age and gender differences in children's self- and task perceptions during elementary school. *Child Development, 64,* 830–847.

Edelman, G. M. (1987). *Neural Darwinism: The theory of neuronal group selection.* New York: Basic Books.

Eisenberger, N. I., Lieberman, M. D., & Williams, K. D. (2003, October 10). Does rejection hurt? An fMRI study of social exclusion. *Science, 302,* 290–292.

Ekman, P. (1992). Facial expressions of emotion: New findings, new questions. *Psychological Science, 3,* 34–38.

Ekstrom, A. D., Kahana, M. J., Caplan, J. B., Fields, T. A., Isham, E. A., Newman, E. L., & Fried, I. (2003, September 11). Cellular networks underlying human spatial navigation. *Nature, 425,* 184–187.

Elbedour, S., Bouchard, T. J., Jr., & Hur, Y. (1997). Similarity in general mental ability in Bedouin full and half siblings. *Intelligence, 25,* 71–83.

Elfenbein, H. A., & Ambady, N. (2003). Universals and cultural differences in recognizing emotions. *Current Directions in Psychological Science, 12,* 159–164.

Ellis, L. (Ed.). (1993). *Social stratification and socioeconomic inequality: Vol. I. A comparative biosocial analysis.* Westport, CT: Praeger.

Ellis, L. (1994). Social status and health in humans: The nature of the relationship and its possible causes. In L. Ellis (Ed.), *Social stratification and socioeconomic inequality: Vol. II. Reproductive and interpersonal aspects of dominance and status* (pp. 123–144). Westport, CT: Praeger.

Elman, J. L., Bates, E. A., Johnson, M. H., Karmiloff-Smith, A., Parisi, D., & Plunkett, K. (1996). *Rethinking innateness: A connectionist perspective on development.* Cambridge, MA: Bradford Books/MIT Press.

Elton, S., Bishop, L. C., & Wood, B. (2001). Comparative context of Plio-Pleistocene hominid brain evolution. *Journal of Human Evolution, 41,* 1–27.

Embretson, S. E. (1995). The role of working memory capacity and general control processes in intelligence. *Intelligence, 20,* 169–189.

Emlen, S. T. (1995). An evolutionary theory of family. *Proceedings of the National Academy of Sciences USA, 92,* 8092–8099.

Emlen, S. T., & Oring, L. W. (1977, July 15). Ecology, sexual selection, and the evolution of mating systems. *Science, 197,* 215–223.

Enard, W., Khaitovich, P., Klose, J., Zöllner, S., Heissig, F., Giavalisco, P., et al. (2002, April 12). Intra- and interspecific variation in primate gene expression patterns. *Science, 296,* 340–343.

Endler, J. A. (1986). *Natural selection in the wild.* Princeton, NJ: Princeton University Press.

Engle, R. W. (2002). Working memory capacity as executive attention. *Current Directions in Psychological Science, 11,* 19–23.

Engle, R. W., Conway, A. R. A., Tuholski, S. W., & Shisler, R. J. (1995). A resource account of inhibition. *Psychological Science, 6,* 122–125.

Engle, R. W., & Kane, M. J. (2004). Executive attention, working memory capacity, and a two-factor theory of cognitive control. In B. Ross (Ed.), *The psychology of learning and motivation* (Vol. 44, pp. 145–199). San Diego, CA: Academic Press.

Engle, R. W., Kane, M. J., & Tuholski, S. W. (1999). Individual differences in working memory capacity and what they tell us about controlled attention, general fluid intelligence, and functions of the prefrontal cortex. In A. Miyake & P. Shah (Eds.), *Models of working memory: Mechanisms of active maintenance and executive control* (pp. 102–134). Cambridge, England: Cambridge University Press.

Engle, R. W., Tuholski, S. W., Laughlin, J. E., & Conway, A. R. A. (1999). Working memory, short-term memory, and general fluid intelligence: A latent-variable approach. *Journal of Experimental Psychology: General, 128,* 309–331.

Engel, S. A., Glover, G. H., & Wandell, B. A. (1997). Retinotopic organization in human visual cortex and the spatial precision of functional MRI. *Cerebral Cortex, 7,* 181–192.

Ericsson, K. A., Krampe, R. T., & Tesch-Römer, C. (1993). The role of deliberate practice in the acquisition of expert performance. *Psychological Review, 100,* 363–406.

Esposito, G., Kirkby, B. S., van Horn, J. D., Ellmore, T. M., & Berman, K. F. (1999). Context-dependent, neural system-specific neurophysiological concomitants of ageing: Mapping PET correlates during cognitive activation. *Brain, 122,* 963–979.

Evans, G., & Nettelbeck, T. (1993). Inspection time: A flash mask to reduce apparent movement effects. *Personality and Individual Differences, 15,* 91–94.

Evans, J. S. B. T. (2002). Logic and human reasoning: An assessment of the deduction paradigm. *Psychological Bulletin, 128,* 978–996.

Evans, J. S. B. T., & Over, D. E. (1996). *Rationality and reasoning.* Hove, England: Psychology Press.

Evans, P. D., Anderson, J. R., Vallender, E. J., Gilbert, S. L., Malcom, C. M., Dorus, S., & Lahn, B. T. (2004). Adaptive evolution of ASPM, a major determinant of cerebral cortical size in humans. *Human Molecular Genetics, 13,* 489–494.

Eysenck, H. J. (1986). Toward a new model of intelligence. *Personality and Individual Differences, 7,* 731–736.

Falk, D. (1983, September 9). Cerebral cortices by East African early hominids. *Science, 221,* 1072–1074.

Falk, D., Redmond, J. C., Jr., Guyer, J., Conroy, G. C., Recheis, W., Weber, G. W., & Seidler, H. (2000). Early hominid brain evolution: A new look at old endocasts. *Journal of Human Evolution, 38,* 695–717.

Farah, M. J., Meyer, M. M., & McMullen, P. A. (1996). The living/nonliving dissociation is not an artifact: Giving an a priori implausible hypothesis a strong test. *Cognitive Neuropsychology, 13,* 137–154.

Feshbach, N. D. (1969). Sex differences in children's modes of aggressive responses toward outsiders. *Merrill-Palmer Quarterly, 15,* 249–258.

Figueiredo, G. M., Leitão-Filho, H. F., & Begossi, A. (1993). Ethnobotany of Atlantic forest coastal communities: Diversity of plant used in Gamboa. *Human Ecology, 21,* 419–430.

Figueiredo, G. M., Leitão-Filho, H. F., & Begossi, A. (1997). Ethnobotany of Atlantic forest coastal communities: II. Diversity of plant uses at Sepetiba Bay (SE Brazil). *Human Ecology, 25,* 353–360.

Finlay, B. L., & Darlington, R. B. (1995, June 16). Linked regularities in the development and evolution of mammalian brains. *Science, 268,* 1578–1584.

Finlay, B. L., Darlington, R. B., & Nicastro, N. (2001). Developmental structure in brain evolution. *Behavioral and Brain Sciences, 24,* 263–308.

Fischbein, S. (1980). IQ and social class. *Intelligence, 4,* 51–63.

Fiske, S. T. (1993). Controlling other people: The impact of power on stereotyping. *American Psychologist, 48,* 621–628.

Fiske, S. T. (2002). What we know now about bias and intergroup conflict, the problem of the century. *Current Directions in Psychological Science, 11,* 123–128.

Fiske, S. T., & Taylor, S. E. (1991). *Social cognition* (2nd ed.). New York: McGraw-Hill.

Fitch, W. T., & Hauser, M. D. (2004, January 16). Computational constraints on syntactic processing in a nonhuman primate. *Science, 303,* 377–380.

Flashman, L. A., Andreasen, N. C., Flaum, M., & Swayze, V. W., II. (1998). Intelligence and regional brain volumes in normal controls. *Intelligence, 25,* 149–160.

Fleming, A. S., Steiner, M., & Corter, C. (1997). Cortisol, hedonics, and maternal responsiveness in human mothers. *Hormones and Behavior, 32,* 85–98.

Flinn, M. V., & England, B. (1995). Childhood stress and family environment. *Current Anthropology, 36,* 854–866.

Flinn, M. V., Geary, D. C., & Ward, C. V. (in press). Ecological dominance, social competition, and coalitionary arms races: Why humans evolved extraordinary intelligence. *Evolution and Human Behavior.*

Forde, E. M. E., & Humphreys, G. W. (Eds.) (2002). *Category specificity in brain and mind.* East Sussex, England: Psychology Press.

Florence, S. L., & Kaas, J. H. (1995). Large-scale reorganization at multiple levels of the somatosensory pathway follows therapeutic amputation of the hand in monkeys. *Journal of Neuroscience, 15,* 8083–8095.

Flynn, J. R. (1987). Massive IQ gains in 14 nations: What IQ tests really measure. *Psychological Bulletin, 101,* 171–191.

Flynn, J. R. (1998). IQ gains over time: Toward finding the causes. In U. Neisser, (Ed.), *The rising curve: Long-term gains in IQ and related measures* (pp. 25–66). Washington, DC: American Psychological Association.

Fodor, J. A. (1983). *The modularity of mind: An essay on faculty psychology.* Cambridge, MA: MIT Press.

Foley, R. (1987). Hominid species and stone-tool assemblages: How are they related. *Antiquity, 61,* 380–392.

Foley, R. A. (1996). An evolutionary and chronological framework for human social behavior. *Proceedings of the British Academy, 88,* 95–117.

Foley, R. A. (1999). Hominid behavioral evolution: Missing links in comparative primate socioecology. In P. C. Lee (Ed.), *Comparative primate socioecology* (pp. 363–386). Cambridge, England: Cambridge University Press.

Foley, R., & Lahr, M. M. (1997). Mode 3 technologies and the evolution of modern humans. *Cambridge Archaeology Journal, 7,* 3–36.

Fox, C. R. (1999). Strength of evidence, judged probability, and choice under uncertainty. *Cognitive Psychology, 38,* 167–189.

Fox, K., Glazewski, S., & Schulze, S. (2000). Plasticity and stability of somatosensory maps in thalamus and cortex. *Current Opinion in Neurobiology, 10,* 494–497.

Frängsmyr, T. (Ed.). (1983). *Linnaeus: The man and his work.* Berkeley: University of California Press.

Freedman, D. G. (1974). *Human infancy: An evolutionary perspective.* New York: Wiley.

Freedman, D. J., Riesenhuber, M., Poggio, T., & Miller, E. K. (2001, January 12). Categorical representation of visual stimuli in the primate prefrontal cortex. *Science, 291,* 312–316.

Frensch, P. A., & Geary, D. C. (1993). The effects of practice on component processes in complex mental addition. *Journal of Experimental Psychology: Learning, Memory, and Cognition, 19,* 433–456.

Frith, C. D., & Frith, U. (1999, November 26). Interacting minds—A biological basis. *Science, 286,* 1692–1695.

Fry, A. F., & Hale, S. (1996). Processing speed, working memory, and fluid intelligence: Evidence for a developmental cascade. *Psychological Science, 7,* 237–241.

Fry, A. F., & Hale, S. (2000). Relationships among processing speed, working memory, and fluid intelligence in children. *Biological Psychology, 54,* 1–34.

Fukuchi-Shimogori, T., & Grove, E. A. (2001, November 2). Neocortex patterning by the secreted signaling molecule FGF8. *Science, 294,* 1071–1074.

Furuta, Y., Piston, D. W., & Hogan, B. L. (1997). Bone morphogenic proteins (BMPs) as regulators of dorsal forebrain development. *Development, 124,* 2203–2212.

Gabunia, L., Vekua, A., Lordkipanidze, D., Swisher, C. C., III, Ferring, R., Justus, A., et al. (2000, May 12). Earliest Pleistocene hominid cranial remains from Dmanisi, Republic of Georgia: Taxonomy, geological setting, and age. *Science, 288,* 1019–1025.

Gaffan, D., & Heywood, C. A. (1993). A spurious category-specific visual agnosia for living things in normal human and nonhuman primates. *Journal of Cognitive Neuroscience, 5,* 118–128.

Gagné, F., & St Père, F. (2003). When IQ is controlled, does motivation still predict achievement? *Intelligence, 30,* 71–100.

Gainotti, G. (2002). The relationships between anatomical and cognitive locus of lesion in category-specific disorders. In E. M. E. Forde & G. W. Humphreys (Eds.), *Category specificity in brain and mind* (pp. 403–426). East Sussex, England: Psychology Press.

Gallagher, H. L., & Frith, C. D. (2003). Functional imaging of "theory of mind." *Trends in Cognitive Sciences, 7,* 77–83.

Gallistel, C. R. (1990). *The organization of learning.* Cambridge, MA: MIT Press/ Bradford Books.

Gallistel, C. R. (1995). *The replacement of general-purpose theories with adaptive specializations.* In M. S. Gazzaniga (Ed.-in-Chief), The cognitive neurosciences (pp. 1255–1267). Cambridge, MA: Bradford Books/MIT Press.

Gallistel, C. R. (2000). The replacement of general-purpose learning models with adaptively specialized learning modules. In M. S. Gazzaniga (Ed.-in-chief), *The new cognitive neurosciences* (2nd ed., pp. 1179–1191). Cambridge, MA: Bradford Books/MIT Press.

Gallo, L. C., & Matthews, K. A. (2003). Understanding the association between socioeconomic status and physical health: Do negative emotions play a role? *Psychological Bulletin, 129,* 10–51.

Galton, F. (1865). Hereditary character and talent. *MacMillan's Magazine, 11,* 157–166, 318–327.

Galton, F. (1869). *Hereditary genius.* London: MacMillan.

Gangestad, S. W., & Simpson, J. A. (2000). The evolution of human mating: Trade-offs and strategic pluralism. *Behavioral and Brain Sciences, 23,* 573–644.

Gannon, P. J., Holloway, R. L., Broadfield, D. C., & Braun, A. R. (1998, January 9). Asymmetry of chimpanzee planum temporale: Humanlike pattern of Wernicke's brain language area homolog. *Science, 279,* 220–222.

Gannon, P. J., Kheck, N. M., & Hof, P. R. (2001). Language areas of the hominoid brain: A dynamic communicative shift on the upper east side planum. In D. Falk & K. R. Gibson (Eds.), *Evolutionary anatomy of the primate cerebral cortex* (pp. 216–240). Cambridge, England: Cambridge University Press.

Gao, W.-J., & Pallas, S. L. (1999). Cross-modal reorganization of horizontal connectivity in auditory cortex without altering thalamocortical projections. *Journal of Neuroscience, 19,* 7940–7950.

Gardner, H. (1983). *Frames of mind: The theory of multiple intelligences.* New York: Basic Books.

Garlick, D. (2002). Understanding the nature of the general factor of intelligence: The role of individual differences in neural plasticity as an explanatory mechanism. *Psychological Review, 109,* 116–136.

Gaulin, S. J. C. (1992). Evolution of sex differences in spatial ability. *Yearbook of Physical Anthropology, 35,* 125–151.

Gaulin, S. J. C., & Fitzgerald, R. W. (1986). Sex differences in spatial ability: An evolutionary hypothesis and test. *American Naturalist, 127,* 74–88.

Gaulin, S. J. C., & Fitzgerald, R. W. (1989). Sexual selection for spatial-learning ability. *Animal Behaviour, 37,* 322–331.

Gauthier, I., Tarr, M. J., Anderson, A. W., Skudlarski, P., & Gore, J. C. (1999). Activation of the middle fusiform "face area" increases with expertise in recognizing novel objects. *Nature Neuroscience, 2,* 568–573.

Gazzaniga, M. S. (Ed.-in-chief). (2000). *The new cognitive neurosciences* (2nd ed.). Cambridge, MA: Bradford Books/MIT Press.

Geary, D. C. (1992). Evolution of human cognition: Potential relationship to the ontogenetic development of behavior and cognition. *Evolution and Cognition, 1*, 93–100.

Geary, D. C. (1994). *Children's mathematical development: Research and practical applications*. Washington, DC: American Psychological Association.

Geary, D. C. (1995). Reflections of evolution and culture in children's cognition: Implications for mathematical development and instruction. *American Psychologist, 50*, 24–37.

Geary, D. C. (1998). *Male, female: The evolution of human sex differences*. Washington, DC: American Psychological Association.

Geary, D. C. (2000). Evolution and proximate expression of human paternal investment. *Psychological Bulletin, 126*, 55–77.

Geary, D. C. (2001). A Darwinian perspective on mathematics and instruction. In T. Loveless (Ed.), *The great curriculum debate: How should we teach reading and math?* (pp. 85–107). Washington, DC: Brookings Institute.

Geary, D. C. (2002a). Principles of evolutionary educational psychology. *Learning and Individual Differences, 12*, 317–345.

Geary, D. C. (2002b). Sexual selection and human life history. In R. Kail (Ed.), *Advances in child development and behavior* (Vol. 30, pp. 41–101). San Diego, CA: Academic Press.

Geary, D. C. (2002c). Sexual selection and sex differences in social cognition. In A. V. McGillicuddy-De Lisi & R. De Lisi (Eds.), *Biology, society, and behavior: The development of sex differences in cognition* (pp. 23–53). Greenwich, CT: Ablex/Greenwood.

Geary, D. C. (2003). Evolution and development of folk knowledge: Implications for children's learning. *Infancia y Aprendizaje, 26*, 287–308.

Geary, D. C. (in press). Evolution of paternal investment. In D. M. Buss (Ed.), *The evolutionary psychology handbook*. Hoboken, NJ: Wiley.

Geary, D. C., & Bjorklund, D. F. (2000). Evolutionary developmental psychology. *Child Development, 71*, 57–65.

Geary, D. C., Byrd-Craven, J., Hoard, M. K., Vigil, J., & Numtee, C. (2003). Evolution and development of boys' social behavior. *Developmental Review, 23*, 444–470.

Geary, D. C., & Flinn, M. V. (2001). Evolution of human parental behavior and the human family. *Parenting: Science and Practice, 1*, 5–61.

Geary, D. C., & Flinn, M. V. (2002). Sex differences in behavioral and hormonal response to social threat: Commentary on Taylor et al. (2000). *Psychological Review, 109*, 745–750.

Geary, D. C., & Hoard, M. K. (2001). Learning disabilities in arithmetic: Relation to dyscalculia and dyslexia. *Aphasiology, 15*, 635–647.

Geary, D. C., & Huffman, K. J. (2002). Brain and cognitive evolution: Forms of modularity and functions of mind. *Psychological Bulletin, 128,* 667–698.

Geary, D. C., & Widaman, K. F. (1987). Individual differences in cognitive arithmetic. *Journal of Experimental Psychology: General, 116,* 154–171.

Geary, D. C., & Widaman, K. F. (1992). Numerical cognition: On the convergence of componential and psychometric models. *Intelligence, 16,* 47–80.

Gelman, R. (1990). First principles organize attention to and learning about relevant data: Number and animate–inanimate distinction as examples. *Cognitive Science, 14,* 79–106.

Gelman, R., & Gallistel, C. R. (1978). *The child's understanding of number.* Cambridge, MA: Harvard University Press.

Gelman, R., & Williams, E. M. (1998). Enabling constraints for cognitive development and learning: Domain-specificity and epigenesis. In W. Damon (Gen. Ed.) & D. Kuhl & R. S. Siegler (Vol. Eds.), *Handbook of child psychology: Vol. 2. Cognition, perception, and language* (5th ed., pp. 575–630). New York: Wiley.

Gelman, S. A., & Bloom, P. (2000). Young children are sensitive to how an object was created when deciding what to name it. *Cognition, 76,* 91–103.

Gentner, D., & Markman, A. B. (1997). Structure mapping in analogy and similarity. *American Psychologist, 52,* 45–56.

Gentner, T. Q., & Margoliash, D. (2003, August 7). Neuronal populations and single cells representing learned auditory objects. *Nature, 424,* 669–674.

George, N., Dolan, R. J., Fink, G. R., Baylis, G. C., Russell, C., & Driver, J. (1999). Contrast polarity and face recognition in the human fusiform gyrus. *Nature Neuroscience, 2,* 574–580.

Gerlach, C., Law, I., Gade, A., & Paulson, O. B. (1999). Perceptual differentiation and category effects in normal object recognition: A PET study. *Brain, 122,* 2159–2170.

Geschwind, D. H., Miller, B. L., DeCarli, C., & Carmelli, D. (2002). Heritability of lobar brain volumes in twins supports genetic models of cerebral laterality and handedness. *Proceedings of the National Academy of Sciences USA, 99,* 3176–3181.

Geschwind, N., & Levitsky, W. (1968, July 12). Human brain: Left–right asymmetries in temporal speech region. *Science, 161,* 186–187.

Gevins, A., & Smith, M. E. (2000). Neurophysiological measures of working memory and individual differences in cognitive ability and cognitive style. *Cerebral Cortex, 10,* 829–839.

Ghazanfar, A. A., & Logothetis, N. K. (2003, June 26). Facial expressions linked to monkey calls. *Nature, 423,* 937–938.

Gibson, K. R., Rumbaugh, D., & Beran, M. (2001). Bigger is better: Primate brain size in relationship to cognition. In D. Falk & K. R. Gibson (Eds.), *Evolutionary anatomy of the primate cerebral cortex* (pp. 79–97). Cambridge, England: Cambridge University Press.

Giese, M. A., & Poggio, T. (2003). Neural mechanisms for the recognition of biological movements. *Nature Reviews: Neuroscience, 4,* 179–192.

Gigerenzer, G. (2001). The adaptive toolbox. In G. Gigerenzer & R. Selten (Eds.), *Bounded rationality: The adaptive toolbox* (pp. 37–50). Cambridge, MA: MIT Press.

Gigerenzer, G., & Hug, K. (1992). Domain-specific reasoning: Social contracts, cheating, and perspective change. *Cognition, 43,* 127–171.

Gigerenzer, G., & Selten, R. (Eds.). (2001a). *Bounded rationality: The adaptive toolbox.* Cambridge, MA: MIT Press.

Gigerenzer, G., & Selten, R. (2001b). Rethinking rationality. In G. Gigerenzer & R. Selten (Eds.), *Bounded rationality: The adaptive toolbox* (pp. 1–12). Cambridge, MA: MIT Press.

Gigerenzer, G., Todd, P. M., & ABC Research Group. (Eds.). (1999). *Simple heuristics that make us smart.* New York: Oxford University Press.

Gilbert, S. F., Opitz, J. M., & Raff, R. A. (1996). Resynthesizing evolutionary and developmental biology. *Developmental Biology, 173,* 357–372.

Gillan, D. J., Premack, D., & Woodruff, G. (1981). Reasoning in the chimpanzee: I. Analogical reasoning. *Journal of Experimental Psychology: Animal Behavior Processes, 7,* 1–17.

Gilliard, E. T. (1969). *Birds of paradise and bower birds.* London: Weidenfeld and Nicolson.

Goldberg, L. R. (1993). The structure of phenotypic personality traits. *American Psychologist, 48,* 26–34.

Goldman, P. S. (1971). Functional development of the prefrontal cortex in early life and the problem of neuronal plasticity. *Experimental Neurology, 32,* 366–387.

Goldman-Rakic, P. S., & Leung, H.-C. (2002). Functional architecture of the dorsolateral prefrontal cortex in monkeys and humans. In D. T. Stuss & R. T. Knight (Eds.), *Principles of frontal lobe function* (pp. 85–95). New York: Oxford University Press.

Goodall, J. (1986). *The chimpanzees of Gombe: Patterns of behavior.* Cambridge, MA: Belknap Press.

Goodall, J., Bandura, A., Bergmann, E., Busse, C., Matama, H., Mpongo, E., et al. (1979). Inter-community interactions in the chimpanzee population of the Gombe National Park. In D. A. Hamburg & E. R. McCown (Eds.), *The great apes* (pp. 13–53). Menlo Park, CA: Benjamin/Cummings.

Gopnik, A., & Wellman, H. M. (1994). The theory theory. In L. A. Hirschfeld & S. A. Gelman (Eds.), *Mapping the mind: Domain specificity in cognition and culture* (pp. 257–293). New York: Cambridge University Press.

Goren-Inbar, N., Alperson, N., Kislev, M. E., Simchoni, O., Melamed, Y., Ben-Nun, A., & Werker, E. (2004, April 30). Evidence of hominid control of fire at Gesher Benot, Ya'aqov Israel. *Science, 304,* 725–727.

Gottfredson, L. (1997). Why g matters: The complexity of everyday life. *Intelligence, 24,* 79–132.

Gottfredson, L. S. (2004). Intelligence: Is it the epidemiologists' elusive "fundamental cause" of social class inequalities in health? *Journal of Personality and Social Psychology, 86,* 174–199.

Gottlieb, G. (1995). Some conceptual deficiencies in "developmental" behavior genetics. *Human Development, 38,* 131–141.

Gottlieb, G. (2003). On making behavioral genetics truly developmental. *Human Development, 46,* 337–355.

Gottlieb, G., Wahlsten, D., & Lickliter, R. (1998). The significance of biology for human development: A developmental psychobiological systems view. In W. Damon (Ed.-in-chief) & R. M. Lerner (Vol. Ed.), *Handbook of child psychology: Vol. 1. Theoretical models of human development* (5th ed., pp. 233–273). New York: Wiley.

Gould, S. J., & Vrba, E. S. (1982). Exaptation—A missing term in the science of form. *Paleobiology, 8,* 4–15.

Gowlett, J. A. J. (1992). Tools—The Paleolithic record. In S. Jones, R. Martin, & D. Pilbeam (Eds.), *The Cambridge encyclopedia of human evolution* (pp. 350–360). New York: Cambridge University Press.

Grant, B. R., & Grant, P. R. (1989). Natural selection in a population of Darwin's finches. *American Naturalist, 133,* 377–393.

Grant, B. R., & Grant, P. R. (1993). Evolution of Darwin's finches caused by a rare climatic event. *Proceedings of the Royal Society of London B, 251,* 111–117.

Grant, P. R. (1999). *Ecology and evolution of Darwin's finches.* Princeton, NJ: Princeton University Press.

Grant, P. R., & Grant, B. R. (2002a). Adaptive radiation of Darwin's finches. *American Scientist, 90,* 130–139.

Grant, P. R., & Grant, B. R. (2002b, April 26). Unpredictable evolution in a 30-year study of Darwin's finches. *Science, 296,* 707–711.

Gray, J. A. (1987). Perspectives on anxiety and impulsivity: A commentary. *Journal of Research in Personality, 21,* 493–509.

Gray, J. R., Chabris, C. F., & Braver, T. S. (2003). Neural mechanisms of general fluid intelligence. *Nature Neuroscience, 6,* 316–322.

Gray, J. R. (2004). Integration of emotion and cognitive control. *Current Directions in Psychological Science, 13,* 46–48.

Greenberg, J., Pyszczynski, T., Solomon, S., Simon, L., & Breus, M. (1994). Role of consciousness and accessibility of death-related thoughts in mortality salience effects. *Journal of Personality and Social Psychology, 67,* 627–637.

Greene, T., Ernhart, C. B., Ager, J., Sokol, R., Martier, S., & Boyd, T. (1991). Prenatal alcohol exposure and cognitive development in the preschool years. *Neurotoxicology and Teratology, 13,* 57–68.

Greenfield, P. M. (1998). The cultural evolution of IQ. In U. Neisser (Ed.), *The rising curve: Long-term gains in IQ and related measures* (pp. 81–123). Washington, DC: American Psychological Association.

Greeno, J. G., & Simon, H. A. (1988). Problem solving and reasoning. In R. C. Atkinson, R. J. Herrnstein, G. Lindzey, & R. D. Luce (Eds.), *Steven's handbook of experimental psychology* (2nd ed., Vol. 2, pp. 589–672). New York: Wiley.

Greenough, W. T. (1991). Experience as a component of normal development: Evolutionary considerations. *Developmental Psychology, 27,* 14–17.

Greenough, W. T., Black, J. E., & Wallace, C. S. (1987). Experience and brain development. *Child Development, 58,* 539–559.

Grogger, J., & Eide, E. (1995). Changes in college skills and the rise in the college wage premium. *Journal of Human Resources, 30,* 280–310.

Groos, K. (1898). *The play of animals.* New York: D. Appleton and Company.

Grossman, E., Donnelly, M., Price, R., Pickens, D., Morgan, V., Neighbor, G., & Blake, R. (2000). Brain areas involved in perception of biological motion. *Journal of Cognitive Neuroscience, 12,* 711–720.

Grove, E. A., & Fukuchi-Shimogori, T. (2003). Generating the cerebral cortical area map. *Annual Review of Neuroscience, 26,* 355–380.

Grove, E. A., Tole, S., Limon, J., Yip, Y., & Ragsdale, C. W. (1998). The hem of the embryonic cerebral cortex is defined by the expression of multiple Wnt genes and is compromised in Gli3-deficient mice. *Development, 125,* 2315–2325.

Grudnik, J. L., & Kranzler, J. H. (2001). Meta-analysis of the relationship between intelligence and inspection time. *Intelligence, 29,* 523–535.

Guilford, J. P. (1972). Thurstone's primary mental abilities and structure-of-intellect abilities. *Psychological Bulletin, 77,* 129–143.

Gustafsson, J. E. (1984). A unifying model for the structure of intellectual abilities. *Intelligence, 8,* 179–203.

Guthrie, R. D. (2003, November 13). Rapid body size decline in Alaskan Pleistocene horses before extinction. *Nature, 426,* 169–171.

Gutman, L. M., Sameroff, A. J., & Cole, R. (2003). Academic growth curve trajectories in 1st to 12th grade: Effects of multiple social risk factors on preschool child factors. *Developmental Psychology, 39,* 777–790.

Hadamard, J. (1945). *The psychology of invention in the mathematical field.* New York: Dover.

Hagen, E. H. (1999). The functions of postpartum depression. *Evolution and Human Behavior, 20,* 325–359.

Hagen, E. H. (2003). The bargaining model of depression. In P. Hammerstein (Ed.), *The genetic and cultural evolution of cooperation* (pp. 95–123). Cambridge, MA: MIT Press.

Haier, R. J., Siegel, B. V., Jr., Nuechterlein, K. H., Hazlett, E., Wu, J. C., Paek, J., et al. (1988). Cortical glucose metabolic rate correlates of abstract reasoning and attention studied using positron emission tomography. *Intelligence, 12,* 199–217.

Haier, R. J., Siegel, B., Tang, C., Abel, L., & Buchsbaum, M. S. (1992). Intelligence and changes in regional cerebral glucose metabolic rate following learning. *Intelligence, 16,* 415–426.

Haier, R. J., White, N. S., & Alkire, M. T. (2003). Individual differences in general intelligence correlate with brain functioning during nonreasoning tasks. *Intelligence, 31,* 429–441.

Haile-Selassie, Y. (2001, July 12). Late Miocene hominids from the Middle Awash, Ethiopia. *Nature, 412,* 178–181.

Halgren, E., Raij, T., Marinkovic, K., Jousmäki, V., & Hari, R. (2000). Cognitive response profile of the human fusiform face area as determined by MEG. *Cerebral Cortex, 10,* 69–81.

Hamilton, W. D. (1964). The genetical evolution of social behaviour: II. *Journal of Theoretical Biology, 7,* 17–52.

Hamilton, W. D. (1975). Innate social aptitudes of man: An approach from evolutionary genetics. In R. Fox (Ed.), *Biosocial anthropology* (pp. 133–155). New York: Wiley.

Hamilton, W. D. (2001). *Narrow roads of gene land: The collected papers of W. D. Hamilton* (Vol. 2). Oxford, England: Oxford University Press.

Hamilton, W. D., Axelrod, R., & Tanese, R. (1990). Sexual reproduction as an adaptation to resist parasites (A review). *Proceedings of the National Academy of Sciences USA, 87,* 3566–3573.

Hamilton, W. D., & Zuk, M. (1982, October 22). Heritable true fitness and bright birds: A role for parasites? *Science, 218,* 384–387.

Hammer, M. F., Karafet, T. M., Redd, A. J., Jarjanazi, H., Santachiara-Benerecetti, S., Soodyall, H., & Zegura, S. L. (2001). Hierarchical patterns of global human Y-chromosome diversity. *Molecular Biology and Evolution, 18,* 1189–1203.

Harris, J. R. (1995). Where is the child's environment? A group socialization theory of development. *Psychological Review, 102,* 458–489.

Hart, J., Jr., & Gordon, B. (1992, September 3). Neural subsystem for object knowledge. *Nature, 359,* 60–64.

Hartup, W. W., & Stevens, N. (1997). Friendships and adaptation in the life course. *Psychological Bulletin, 121,* 355–370.

Harvey, P. H., & Clutton-Brock, T. H. (1985). Life history variation in primates. *Evolution, 39,* 559–581.

Harvey, P. H., Martin, R. D., & Clutton-Brock, T. H. (1987). Life histories in comparative perspective. In B. B. Smuts, D. L. Cheney, R. M. Seyfarth, R. W. Wrangham, & T. T. Struhsaker (Eds.), *Primate societies* (pp. 181–196). Chicago: University of Chicago Press.

Hasher, L., & Zacks, R. T. (1979). Automatic and effortful processes in memory. *Journal of Experimental Psychology: General, 108,* 356–388.

Hastie, R., & Dawes, R. M. (2001). *Rational choice in an uncertain world: The psychology of judgment and decision making.* Thousand Oaks, CA: Sage.

Hatten, M. E. (2002, September 6). New directions in neuronal migration. *Science, 297,* 1660–1663.

Hauser, M. D. (1996). *The evolution of communication.* Cambridge, MA: MIT Press/Bradford Books.

Hauser, M. D., Chomsky, N., & Fitch, W. T. (2002, November 22). The faculty of language: What is it, who has it, and how did it evolve? *Science, 298,* 1569–1579.

Hawkes, K., O'Connell, J. F., Blurton Jones, N. G., Alvarez, H., & Charnov, E. L. (1998). Grandmothering, menopause, and the evolution of human life histories. *Proceedings of the National Academy of Sciences USA, 95,* 1336–1339.

Hay, D. (1999). The developmental genetics of intelligence. In M. Anderson (Ed.), *The development of intelligence* (pp. 75–104). Hove, England: Psychology Press.

Heath, A. C., Berg, K., Eaves, L. J., Solaas, M. H., Corey, L. A., Sundet, J., et al. (1985, April 25). Education policy and the heritability of educational attainment. *Nature, 314,* 734–736.

Heath, C., Larrick, R. P., & Wu, G. (1999). Goals as reference points. *Cognitive Psychology, 38,* 79–109.

Heckhausen, J., & Schulz, R. (1995). A life-span theory of control. *Psychological Review, 102,* 284–304.

Hed, H. M. E. (1987). Trends in opportunity for natural selection in the Swedish population during the period 1650–1980. *Human Biology, 59,* 785–797.

Henriques, G. (2000). Depression: Disease or behavioral shutdown mechanism? *Journal of Science and Health Policy, 1,* 152–165.

Henriques, G. (2003). The tree of knowledge system and the theoretical unification of psychology. *Review of General Psychology, 7,* 150–182.

Hensch, T. K., & Stryker, M. P. (2004, March 12). Columnar architecture sculpted by GABA circuits in developing cat visual cortex. *Science, 303,* 1678–1681.

Herlihy, D. (1965). Population, plague and social change in rural Pistoia, 1201–1430. *Economic History Review, 18,* 225–244.

Herrnstein, R. J., & Murray, C. (1994). *The bell curve: Intelligence and class structure in American life.* New York: Free Press.

Hewstone, M., Rubin, M., & Willis, H. (2002). Intergroup bias. *Annual Review of Psychology, 53,* 575–604.

Heyes, C. (2003). Four routes of cognitive evolution. *Psychological Review, 110,* 713–727.

Hickling, A. K., & Gelman, S. A. (1995). How does your garden grow? Early conceptualization of seeds and their place in the plant growth cycle. *Child Development, 66,* 856–876.

Higgins, E. T. (1987). Self-discrepancy theory: A theory relating self and affect. *Psychological Review, 94,* 319–340.

Hill, K. (1982). Hunting and human evolution. *Journal of Human Evolution, 11,* 521–544.

Hill, K. (2002). Altruistic cooperation during foraging by the Ache, and the evolved human predisposition to cooperate. *Human Nature, 13,* 105–128.

Hill, K., Boesch, C., Goodall, J., Pusey, A., Williams, J., & Wrangham, R. (2001). Mortality rates among wild chimpanzees. *Journal of Human Evolution, 40,* 437–450.

Hill, K., & Hurtado, A. M. (1996). *Ache life history: The ecology and demography of a foraging people.* New York: Aldine de Gruyter.

Hill, K., & Kaplan, H. (1988). Tradeoffs in male and female reproductive strategies among the Ache: Part 1. In L. Betzig, M. Borgerhoff Mulder, & P. Turke (Eds.), *Human reproductive behaviour: A Darwinian perspective* (pp. 277–289). Cambridge, England: Cambridge University Press.

Hirschfeld, L. A., & Gelman, S. A. (Eds.) (1994). *Mapping the mind: Domain specificity in cognition and culture.* New York: Cambridge University Press.

Hirsh, I. J. (1988). Auditory perception and speech. In R. C. Atkinson, R. J. Herrnstein, G. Lindzey, & R. D. Luce (Eds.), *Steven's handbook of experimental psychology* (2nd ed., pp. 377–408). New York: Wiley.

Ho, H.-Z., Baker, L. A., & Decker, S. N. (1988). Covariation between intelligence and speed of cognitive processing: Genetic and environmental influences. *Behavior Genetics, 18,* 247–261.

Hodges, J. R., Spatt, J., & Patterson, K. (1999). "What" and "how": Evidence for the dissociation of object knowledge and mechanical problem-solving skills in the human brain. *Proceedings of the National Academy of Sciences USA, 96,* 9444–9448.

Hof, P. R., Glezer, I. I., Nimchinsky, E. A., & Erwin, J. M. (2000). Neurochemical and cellular specializations in the mammalian neocortex reflect phylogenetic relationships: Evidence from primates, cetaceans, and artiodactyls. *Brain, Behavior and Evolution, 55,* 300–310.

Hofman, M. A. (2001). Brain evolution in hominids: Are we at the end of the road? In D. Falk & K. R. Gibson (Eds.), *Evolutionary anatomy of the primate cerebral cortex* (pp. 113–127). Cambridge, England: Cambridge University Press.

Hole, F. (1992). Origins of agriculture. In S. Jones, R. Martin, & D. Pilbeam (Eds.), *The Cambridge encyclopedia of human evolution* (pp. 373–379). New York: Cambridge University Press.

Holland, L. Z., & Holland, N. D. (1999). Chordate origins of the vertebrate central nervous system. *Current Opinion in Neurobiology, 9,* 596–602.

Holloway, R., Jr. (1966). Dendritic branching: Some preliminary results of training and complexity in rat visual cortex. *Brain Research, 2,* 393–396.

Holloway, R. L., Jr. (1968). The evolution of the primate brain: Some aspects of quantitative relations. *Brain Research, 7,* 121–172.

Holloway, R. L. (1973a). Endocranial volumes of early African hominids, and the role of the brain in human mosaic evolution. *Journal of Human Evolution, 2,* 449–459.

Holloway, R. L. (1973b, May 11). New endocranial values for the East African early hominids. *Nature, 243,* 97–99.

Holloway, R. (1996). Evolution of the human brain. In A. Lock & C. R. Peters (Eds.), *Handbook of human symbolic evolution* (pp. 74–116). New York: Oxford University Press.

Holloway, R. L. (2002). How much larger is the relative volume of area 10 of the prefrontal cortex in humans? *American Journal of Physical Anthropology, 11,* 399–401.

Holloway, R. L., & de la Coste-Lareymondie, M. C. (1982). Brain endocast asymmetry in pongids and hominids: Some preliminary findings on the paleontology of cerebral dominance. *American Journal of Physical Anthropology, 58,* 101–110.

Holloway, R. L., & Kimbel, W. H. (1986, May 29). Endocast morphology of Hadar hominid AL 162-28. *Nature, 321,* 536–537.

Holyoak, K. J., & Thagard, P. (1997). The analogical mind. *American Psychologist, 52,* 35–44.

Horai, S., Hayasaka, K., Kondo, R., Tsugane, K., & Takahata, N. (1995). Recent African origin of modern humans revealed by complete sequences of hominoid mitochondrial DNAs. *Proceedings of the National Academy of Sciences USA, 92,* 532–536.

Horn, J. L. (1968). Organization of abilities and the development of intelligence. *Psychological Review, 75,* 242–259.

Horn, J. L. (1988). Thinking about human abilities. In J. R. Nesselroade & R. B. Cattell (Eds.), *Handbook of multivariate experimental psychology* (2nd ed., pp. 645–685). New York: Plenum Press.

Horn, J. L., & Cattell, R. B. (1966). Refinement and test of the theory of fluid and crystallized general intelligence. *Journal of Educational Psychology, 57,* 253–270.

Horowitz, D. L. (2001). *The deadly ethnic riot.* Berkeley: University of California Press.

Huffman, K., Molnar, Z., Van Dellen, A., Kahn, D., Blakemore, C., & Krubitzer, L. (1999). Formation of cortical fields on a reduced cortical sheet. *Journal of Neuroscience, 19,* 9939–9952.

Huffman, K. J., Nelson, J., Clarey, J., & Krubitzer, L. (1999). Organization of somatosensory cortex in three species of marsupials, *Dasyurus hallucatus, Dactylopsila trivirgata,* and *Monodelphis domestica:* Neural correlates of morphological specializations. *Journal of Comparative Neurology, 403,* 5–32.

Humphrey, N. K. (1976). The social function of intellect. In P. P. G. Bateson & R. A. Hinde (Eds.), *Growing points in ethology* (pp. 303–317). New York: Cambridge University Press.

Hunt, E. (1978). Mechanics of verbal ability. *Psychological Review, 85,* 109–130.

Hunt, E. (1983, January 14). On the nature of intelligence. *Science, 219,* 141–146.

Hunt, E. (1993). *Thoughts on thought: An analysis of formal models of cognition.* Hillsdale, NJ: Erlbaum.

Hunt, E., Lunneborg, C., & Lewis, J. (1975). What does it mean to be high verbal? *Cognitive Psychology, 7,* 194–227.

Hunt, E., & Minstrell, J. (1994). A cognitive approach to the teaching of physics. In K. McGilly (Ed.), *Classroom lessons: Integrating cognitive theory and classroom practice* (pp. 51–74). Cambridge, MA: MIT Press.

Hunt, T. (1928). The measurement of social intelligence. *Journal of Applied Psychology, 12,* 317–334.

Hunter, J. E., & Hunter, R. F. (1984). Validity and utility of alternative predictors of job performance. *Psychological Bulletin, 96,* 72–98.

Hunter, J. E., & Schmidt, F. L. (1996). Intelligence and job performance: Economic and social implications. *Psychology, Public Policy, and Law, 2,* 447–472.

Huttenlocher, P. R. (1990). Morphometric study of human cerebral cortex development. *Neuropsychologia, 28,* 517–527.

Hutton, U., Wilding, J., & Hudson, R. (1997). The role of attention in the relationship between inspection time and IQ in children. *Intelligence, 24,* 445–460.

Huxley, T. H. (1863). *Evidence as to man's place in nature.* New York: Appleton and Company.

Ilmberger, J., Rau, S., Noachtar, S., Arnold, S., & Winkler, P. (2002). Naming tools and animals: Asymmetries observed during direct electrical cortical stimulation. *Neuropsychologia, 40,* 695–700.

International Human Genome Sequencing Consortium. (2001, February 15). Initial sequencing and analysis of the human genome. *Nature, 409,* 860–921.

Irons, W. (1979). Cultural and biological success. In N. A. Chagnon & W. Irons (Eds.), *Natural selection and social behavior* (pp. 257–272). North Scituate, MA: Duxbury Press.

Isenberg, N., Silbersweig, D., Engelien, A., Emmerich, S., Malavade, K., Beattie, B., & Leon, A. C. (1999). Linguistic threat activates the human amygdala. *Proceedings of the National Academy of Sciences USA, 96,* 10456–10459.

Iverson, J. M., & Goldin-Meadow, S. (1998, November 19). Why people gesture when they speak. *Nature, 396,* 228.

Jackendoff, R. (1992). *Languages of the mind: Essays on mental representation.* Cambridge, MA: MIT Press.

Jacobs, L. F., Gaulin, S. J. C., Sherry, D. F., & Hoffman, G. E. (1990). Evolution of spatial cognition: Sex-specific patterns of spatial behavior predict hippocampal size. *Proceedings of the National Academy of Sciences USA, 87,* 6349–6352.

Jacobs, N., van Gestel, S., Derom C., Thiery, E., Vernon, P., Derom, R., & Vlietinck, R. (2001). Heritability estimates in intelligence in twins: Effect of chorion type. *Behavior Genetics, 31,* 209–217.

Jain, N., Catania, K. C., & Kaas, J. H. (1997, April 3). Deactivation and reactivation of somatosensory cortex after dorsal spinal cord injury. *Nature, 386,* 495–498.

Jenkins, W. M., Merzenich, M. M., & Recanzone, G. (1990). Neocortical representational dynamics in adults primates: Implications for neuropsychology. *Neuropsychologia, 28,* 573–584.

Jensen, A. R. (1982). Reaction time and psychometric g. In H. J. Eysenck (Ed.), *A model for intelligence* (pp. 93–132). New York: Springer-Verlag.

Jensen, A. R. (1987a). Individual differences in the Hick paradigm. In P. A. Vernon (Ed.), *Speed of information processing and intelligence* (pp. 101–175). Norwood, NJ: Ablex.

Jensen, A. R. (1987b). Process differences and individual differences in some cognitive tasks. *Intelligence, 11,* 107–136.

Jensen, A. R. (1992). The importance of intraindividual variation in reaction time. *Intelligence, 13,* 869–881.

Jensen, A. R. (1998). *The g factor: The science of mental ability.* Westport, CT: Praeger.

Jensen, A. R. (2003). Regularities in Spearman's law of diminishing returns. *Intelligence, 31,* 95–105.

Jensen, A. R., Larson, G. E., & Paul, S. M. (1988). Psychometric g and mental processing speed on a semantic verification test. *Personality and Individual Differences, 9,* 243–255.

Jensen, A. R., & Munro, E. (1979). Reaction time, movement time, and intelligence. *Intelligence, 3,* 121–126.

Jerison, H. J. (1973). *Evolution of the brain and intelligence.* New York: Academic Press.

Joffe, T. H. (1997). Social pressures have selected for an extended juvenile period in primates. *Journal of Human Evolution, 32,* 593–605.

John, E. R. (2003). A theory of consciousness. *Current Directions in Psychological Science, 12,* 244–250.

Johnson, J., Im-Bolter, N., & Pascual-Leone, J. (2003). Development of mental attention in gifted and mainstream children: The role of mental capacity, inhibition, and speed of processing. *Child Development, 74,* 1594–1614.

Johnson, W., Bouchard, T. J., Jr., Krueger, R. F., McGue, M., & Gottesman, I. I. (2004). Just one g: Consistent results from three test batteries. *Intelligence, 32,* 95–107.

Johnson-Frey, S. H. (2003). What's so special about human tool use? *Neuron, 39,* 201–204.

Johnson-Laird, P. N. (1983). *Mental models.* Cambridge, England: Cambridge University Press.

Johnson-Laird, P. N., & Byrne, R. M. J. (2002). Conditionals: A theory of meaning, pragmatics, and inference. *Psychological Review, 109,* 646–678.

Jolly, C. J. (1970). The seed eaters: A new model of hominid differentiation based on a baboon analogy. *Man, 5,* 5–26.

Jones, E. G. (1985). *The thalamus.* New York: Plenum Press.

Kaas, J. H. (1982). The segregation of function in the nervous system: Why do the sensory systems have so many subdivisions? *Contributions to Sensory Physiology, 7,* 201–240.

Kaas, J. H. (1991). Plasticity of sensory and motor maps in adults mammals. *Annual Review of Neuroscience, 14,* 137–167.

Kaas, J. H. (2000). Why is brain size so important: Design problems and solutions as neocortex gets bigger or smaller. *Brain and Mind, 1,* 7–23.

Kahneman, D., Slovic, P., & Tversky, A. (Eds.). (1982). *Judgment uncertainty: Heuristics and biases.* Cambridge, England: Cambridge University Press.

Kahneman, D., & Tversky, A. (1982). The simulation heuristic. In D. Kahneman, P. Slovic, & A. Tversky (Eds.), *Judgment uncertainty: Heuristics and biases* (pp. 201–208). Cambridge, England: Cambridge University Press.

Kail, R. (1991). Developmental change in speed of processing during childhood and adolescence. *Psychological Bulletin, 109,* 490–501.

Kampe, K. K. W., Frith, C. D., Dolan, R. J., & Frith, U. (2001, October 11). Reward value of attractiveness and gaze. *Nature, 413,* 589.

Kanaya, T., Scullin, M. H., & Ceci, S. J. (2003). The Flynn effect and U.S. policies: The impact of rising IQ scores on American society via mental retardation diagnosis. *American Psychologist, 58,* 778–790.

Kanazawa, S. (2004). General intelligence as a domain-specific adaptation. *Psychological Review, 111,* 512–523.

Kane, M. J., & Engle, R. W. (2000). Working-memory capacity, proactive interference, and divided attention: Limits on long-term memory retrieval. *Journal of Experimental Psychology: Learning, Memory, and Cognition, 26,* 336–358.

Kane, M. J., & Engle, R. W. (2002). The role of prefrontal cortex in working-memory capacity, executive attention, and general fluid intelligence: An individual-differences perspective. *Psychonomic Bulletin & Review, 9,* 637–671.

Kanwisher, N. (2001). Neural events and perceptual awareness. *Cognition, 79,* 89–113.

Kanwisher, N., McDermott, J., & Chun, M. M. (1997). The fusiform face area: A module in human extrastriate cortex specialized for face perception. *Journal of Neuroscience, 17,* 4302–4311.

Kaplan, H., & Hill, K. (1985). Food sharing among Ache foragers: Tests of explanatory hypotheses. *Current Anthropology, 26,* 223–246.

Kaplan, H., Hill, K., Lancaster, J., & Hurtado, A. M. (2000). A theory of human life history evolution: Diet, intelligence, and longevity. *Evolutionary Anthropology, 9,* 156–185.

Kaplan, H. S., & Robson, A. J. (2002). The emergence of humans: The coevolution of intelligence and longevity with intergenerational transfers. *Proceedings of the National Academy of Sciences USA, 99,* 10221–10226.

Karafet, T. M., Zegura, S. L., Posukh, O., Osipova, L., Bergen, A., Long, J., et al. (1999). Ancestral Asian source(s) of new world Y-chromosome founder haplotypes. *American Journal of Human Genetics, 64,* 817–831.

Karmiloff-Smith, A. (1992). *Beyond modularity: A developmental perspective on cognitive science*. Cambridge, MA: Bradford Books/MIT Press.

Karten, H. J. (1997). Evolutionary developmental biology meets the brain: The origins of the mammalian cortex. *Proceedings of the National Academy of Sciences USA, 94,* 2800–2804.

Kaskan, P. M., & Finlay, B. L. (2001). Encephalization and its developmental structure: How many ways can a brain get big? In D. Falk & K. R. Gibson (Eds.), *Evolutionary anatomy of the primate cerebral cortex* (pp. 14–27). Cambridge, England: Cambridge University Press.

Katz, P. S., & Harris-Warrick, R. H. (1999). The evolution of neuronal circuits underlying species-specific behavior. *Current Opinion in Neurobiology, 9,* 628–633.

Ke, Y., Su, B., Song, X., Lu, D., Chen, L., Li, H., et al. (2001, May 11). African origin of modern humans in East Asia: A tale of 12,000 Y chromosomes. *Nature, 292,* 1151–1153.

Keating, D. P., & Bobbitt, B. L. (1978). Individual and developmental differences in cognitive-processing components of mental ability. *Child Development, 49,* 155–167.

Keating, D. P., List, J. A., & Merriman, W. E. (1985). Cognitive processing and cognitive ability: A multivariate validity investigation. *Intelligence, 9,* 149–170.

Keeley, L. H. (1996). *War before civilization: The myth of the peaceful savage.* New York: Oxford University Press.

Keil, F. C. (1992). The origins of an autonomous biology. In M. R. Gunnar & M. Maratsos (Eds.), *Modularity and constraints in language and cognition: The Minnesota symposia on child psychology* (Vol. 25, pp. 103–137). Hillsdale, NJ: Erlbaum.

Keil, F. C., Levin, D. T., Richman, B. A., & Gutheil, G. (1999). Mechanism and explanation in the development of biological thought: The case of disease. In D. L. Medin & S. Atran (Eds.), *Folkbiology* (pp. 285–319). Cambridge, MA: MIT Press/Bradford Book.

Kempermann, G., Kuhn, H. G., & Gage, F. H. (1997, April 3). More hippocampal neurons in adult mice living in an enriched environment. *Nature, 386,* 493–495.

Kenrick, D. T. (2001). Evolutionary psychology, cognitive science, and dynamical systems: Building an integrative paradigm. *Current Directions in Psychological Science, 10,* 13–17.

Kerns, J. G., Cohen, J. D., MacDonald, A. W., III, Cho, R. Y., Stenger, V. A., & Carter, C. S. (2004, February, 13). Anterior cingulate conflict monitoring and adjustments in control. *Science, 303,* 1023–1026.

Kiang, N. Y.-S., & Peake, W. T. (1988). Physics and physiology of hearing. In R. C. Atkinson, R. J. Herrnstein, G. Lindzey, & R. D. Luce (Eds.), *Steven's handbook of experimental psychology* (2nd ed., pp. 277–326). New York: Wiley.

Killackey, H. P. (1995). Evolution of the human brain: A neuroanatomical perspective. In M. S. Gazzaniga (Ed.), *The cognitive neurosciences* (pp. 1243–1253). Cambridge, MA: Bradford Books/MIT Press.

Kimbel, W. H. (1995). Hominid speciation and Pliocene climatic change. In E. S. Vrba, G. H. Denton, T. C. Partridge, & L. H. Burckle (Eds.), *Paleoclimate and evolution, with emphasis on human origins* (pp. 425–437). New Haven, CT: Yale University Press.

Kingsolver, J. G., Hoekstra, H. E., Hoekstra, J. M., Berrigan, D., Vignieri, S. N., Hill, C. E., et al. (2001). The strength of phenotypic selection in natural populations. *American Naturalist, 157,* 245–261.

Kingston, J. D., Marino, B. D., & Hill, A. (1994, May 13). Isotopic evidence for Neogene hominid paleoenvironments in the Kenya rift valley. *Science, 264,* 955–959.

Kisilevsky, B. S., Hains, S. M. J., Lee, K., Xie, X., Huang, H., Ye, H. H., et al. (2003). Effects of experience on fetal voice recognition. *Psychological Science, 14,* 220–224.

Klindworth, H., & Voland, E. (1995). How did the Krummhörn elite males achieve above-average reproductive success? *Human Nature, 6,* 221–240.

Koechlin, E., Ody, C., & Kouneiher, F. (2003, November 14). The architecture of cognitive control in the human prefrontal cortex. *Science, 302,* 1181–1185.

Kornack, D. R. (2000). Neurogenesis and the evolution of cortical diversity: Mode, tempo, and partitioning during development and persistence in adulthood. *Brain, Behavior and Evolution, 55,* 336–344.

Kornack, D. R., & Rakic, P. (1998). Changes in cell-cycle kinetics during the development and evolution of primate neocortex. *Proceedings of the National Academy of Sciences USA, 95,* 1242–1246.

Kosslyn, S. M., & Thompson, W. L. (2000). Shared mechanisms in visual imagery and visual perception: Insights from cognitive neuroscience. In M. S. Gazzaniga (Ed.-in-chief), *The new cognitive neurosciences* (2nd ed., pp. 975–985). Cambridge, MA: Bradford Books/MIT Press.

Kranzler, J. H., & Jensen, A. R. (1989). Inspection time and intelligence: A meta-analysis. *Intelligence, 13,* 329–347.

Kranzler, J. H., & Jensen, A. R. (1991). The nature of psychometric g: Unitary process or a number of independent processes? *Intelligence, 15,* 397–422.

Krebs, J. R., & Davies, N. B. (1993). *An introduction to behavioural ecology* (3rd ed.). Oxford, England: Blackwell Science.

Krubitzer, L. (1995). The organization of neocortex in mammals: Are species differences really so different? *Trends in Neurosciences, 18,* 408–417.

Krubitzer, L., & Huffman, K. J. (2000). Arealization of the neocortex in mammals: Genetic and epigenetic contributions to the phenotype. *Brain, Behavior and Evolution, 55,* 322–335.

Kudo, H., & Dunbar, R. I. M. (2001). Neocortex size and social network size in primates. *Animal Behaviour, 62,* 711–722.

Kuhl, P. K. (1994). Learning and representation in speech and language. *Current Opinion in Neurobiology, 4,* 812–822.

Kuhl, P. K., Andruski, J. E., Chistovich, I. A., Chistovich, L. A., Kozhevnikova, E. V., Ryskina, V. L., et al. (1997, August 1). Cross-language analysis of phonetic units in language addressed to infants. *Science, 277,* 684–686.

Kuhlmeier, V. A., & Boysen, S. T. (2002). Chimpanzees (*Pan troglodytes*) recognize spatial and object correspondences between a scale model and its referent. *Psychological Science, 13,* 60–63.

Kuncel, N. R., Hezlett, S. A., & Ones, D. S. (2001). A comprehensive meta-analysis of the predictive validity of the Graduate Record Examinations: Implications for graduate student selection and performance. *Psychological Bulletin, 127,* 162–181.

Kunda, Z. (1999). *Social cognition: Making sense of people.* Cambridge, MA: Bradford Books/MIT Press.

Kyllonen, P. C., & Christal, R. E. (1990). Reasoning ability is (little more than) working-memory capacity?! *Intelligence, 14,* 389–433.

La Cerra, P., & Bingham, R. (1998). The adaptive nature of the human neurocognitive architecture: An alternative model. *Proceedings of the National Academy of Sciences USA, 95,* 11290–11294.

Lachman, M. E., & Weaver, S. L. (1998). The sense of control as a moderator of social class differences in health and well-being. *Journal of Personality and Social Psychology, 74,* 763–773.

Landau, B., Gleitman, H., & Spelke, E. (1981, September 11). Spatial knowledge and geometric representations in a child blind from birth. *Science, 213,* 1275–1278.

Langer, E. J. (1975). The illusion of control. *Journal of Personality and Social Psychology, 32,* 311–328.

Lansman, M., Donaldson, G., Hunt, E., & Yantis, S. (1982). Ability factors and cognitive performance. *Intelligence, 6,* 347–386.

Larson, A., & Losos, J. B. (1996). Phylogenetic systematics of adaptation. In M. R. Rose & G. V. Lauder (Eds.), *Adaptation* (pp. 187–220). San Diego, CA: Academic Press.

Larson, G. E., Haier, R. J., LaCasse, L., & Hazen, K. (1995). Evaluation of a "mental effort" hypothesis for correlations between cortical metabolism and intelligence. *Intelligence, 21,* 267–278.

Larson, G. E., & Saccuzzo, D. P. (1989). Cognitive correlates of general intelligence: Toward a process theory of g. *Intelligence, 13,* 5–31.

Lawrence, K., Campbell, R., Swettenham, J., Terstegge, J., Akers, R., Coleman, M., & Skuse, D. (2003). Interpreting gaze in Turner syndrome: Impaired sensitivity to intention and emotion, but preservation of social cueing. *Neuropsychologia, 41,* 894–905.

Laws, K. R., & Neve, C. (1999). A "normal" category-specific advantage for naming living things. *Neuropsychologia, 37,* 1263–1269.

Lazar, I., Darlington, R., Murray, H., Royce, J., & Snipper, A. (1982). Lasting effects of early education: A report from the consortium of longitudinal studies. *Monographs of the Society for Research in Child Development, 47* (Nos. 2–3, serial no. 195).

Lazarus, R. S. (1991). *Emotion and adaptation*. New York: Oxford University Press.

Leadbeater, B. J., Blatt, S. J., & Quinlan, D. M. (1995). Gender-linked vulnerabilities to depressive symptoms, stress, and problem behaviors in adolescents. *Journal of Research on Adolescence, 5,* 1–29.

Leakey, M. G., Feibel, C. S., McDougall, I., & Walker, A. (1995, August 17). New four-million-year-old hominid species from Kanapoi and Allia Bay, Kenya. *Nature, 376,* 565–571.

Leakey, M. G., Feibel, C. S., McDougall, I., Ward, C., & Walker, A. (1998, May 7). New specimens and confirmation of an early age for *Australopithecus anamensis*. *Nature, 393,* 62–66.

Leakey, M. G., Spoor, F., Brown, F. H., Gathogo, P. N., Kiarie, C., Leakey, L. N., & McDougall, I. (2001, March 22). New hominin genus from eastern Africa shows diverse middle Pliocene lineages. *Nature, 410,* 433–440.

Leavens, D. A., & Hopkins, W. D. (1998). Intentional communication by chimpanzees: A cross-sectional study of the use of referential gestures. *Developmental Psychology, 34,* 813–822.

Lee, S. M., Danielian, P. S., Fritzsch, B., & McMahon, A. P. (1997). Evidence that FGF8 signaling from the midbrain–hindbrain junction regulates growth and polarity in the developing midbrain. *Development, 124,* 959–969.

Lee, S. M., Tole, S., Grove, E., & McMahon, A. P. (2000). A local Wnt-3a signal is required for development of the mammalian hippocampus. *Development, 127,* 457–467.

Le Grand, R., Mondloch, C. J., Maurer, D., & Brent, H. P. (2001, April 19). Early visual experience and face processing. *Nature, 410,* 890.

Legree, P. J. (1995). Evidence for an oblique social intelligence factor established with a Likert-based testing procedure. *Intelligence, 21,* 247–266.

Lehrl, S., & Fischer, B. (1988). The basic parameters of human information processing: Their role in the determination of intelligence. *Personality and Individual Differences, 9,* 883–896.

Lenneberg, E. H. (1967). *Biological foundations of language*. New York: Wiley.

Leslie, A. M. (1987). Pretense and representation: The origins of "theory of mind." *Psychological Review, 94,* 412–426.

Levine, B. (1999). Self-regulation and autonoetic consciousness. In E. Tulving (Ed.), *Memory, consciousness, and the brain: The Tallinn conference* (pp. 200–214). Philadelphia: Psychology Press.

Levine, B., Black, S. E., Cabeza, R., Sinden, M., Mcintosh, A. R., Toth, J. P., et al. (1998). Episodic memory and the self in a case of isolated retrograde amnesia. *Brain, 121,* 1951–1973.

Levitt, P. (1995). Experimental approaches that reveal principles of cerebral cortical development. In M. S. Gazzaniga (Ed.-in-chief), *The cognitive neurosciences* (pp. 147–163). Cambridge, MA: Bradford Books/MIT Press.

Levitt, P. (2000). Molecular determinants of regionalization of the forebrain and cerebral cortex. In M. S. Gazzaniga (Ed.-in-chief.), *The new cognitive neurosciences* (2nd ed., pp. 23–32). Cambridge, MA: Bradford Books/MIT Press.

Li, S.-C., Lindenberger, U., Hommel, B., Aschersleben, G., Prinz, W., & Baltes, P. B. (2004). Transformations in the couplings among intellectual abilities and constituent cognitive processes across the life span. *Psychological Science, 15*, 155–163.

Liberman, A. M., & Mattingly, I. G. (1989, January 27). A specialization for speech perception. *Science, 243*, 489–494.

Lichtenstein, S., Slovic, P., & Fischhoff, B., Layman, M., & Combs, B. (1978). Judged frequency of lethal events. *Journal of Experimental Psychology: Human Learning and Memory, 4*, 551–578.

Lickliter, R., & Honeycutt, H. (2003). Developmental dynamics: Toward a biologically plausible evolutionary psychology. *Psychological Bulletin, 129*, 819–835.

Lieberman, M. D., Ochsner, K. N., Gilbert, D. T., & Schacter, D. L. (2003). Do amnesics exhibit cognitive dissonance reduction? The role of explicit memory and attention in attitude change. *Psychological Science, 12*, 135–140.

Lindroth, S. (1983). The two faces of Linnaeus. In T. Frängsmyr (Ed.), *Linnaeus: The man and his work* (pp. 1–62). Berkeley: University of California Press.

Liu, F.-G. R., Miyamoto, M. M., Freire, N. P., Ong, P. Q., Tennant, M. R., Young, T. S., & Gugel, K. F. (2001, March 2). Molecular and morphological supertrees for eutherian (placental) mammals. *Science, 291*, 1786–1789.

Liu, J., Harris, A., & Kanwisher, N. (2002). Stages of processing in face perception: An MEG study. *Nature Neuroscience, 5*, 910–916.

Lloyd-Jones, T. J., & Humphreys, G. W. (1997). Perceptual differentiation as a source of category effects in object processing: Evidence from naming and object decision. *Memory & Cognition, 25*, 18–35.

Lockman, J. J. (2000). A perception–action perspective on tool use development. *Child Development, 71*, 137–144.

Loehlin, J. C. (1998). Whither dysgenics? Comments on Lynn and Preston. In U. Neisser (Ed.), *The rising curve: Long-term gains in IQ and related measures* (pp. 389–398). Washington, DC: American Psychological Association.

Loehlin, J. C. (2002). The IQ paradox: Resolved? Still an open question. *Psychological Review, 109*, 754–758.

Loehlin, J. C., Horn, J. M., & Willerman, L. (1989). Modeling IQ changes: Evidence from the Texas adoption study. *Child Development, 60*, 993–1004.

Logie, R. H. (1995). *Visuo-spatial working memory*. Hove, England: Erlbaum.

Low, A., Bentin, S., Rockstroh, B., Silberman, Y., Gomolla, A., Cohen, R., & Elbert, T. (2003). Semantic categorization in the human brain: Spatiotemporal dynamics revealed by magnetoencephalography. *Psychological Science, 14,* 367–372.

Lubinski, D. (2000). Scientific and social significance of assessing individual differences: "Sinking shafts at a few critical points." *Annual Review of Psychology, 51,* 405–444.

Lubinski, D. (2004). Introduction to special section on cognitive abilities: 100 years after Spearman's (1904) " 'general intelligence,' objectively determined and measured." *Journal of Personality and Social Psychology, 86,* 96–111.

Lubinski, D., Webb, R. M., Morelock, M. J., & Benbow, C. P. (2001). Top 1 in 10,000: A 10-year follow-up of the profoundly gifted. *Journal of Applied Psychology, 86,* 718–729.

Luchins, A. S. (1942). Mechanization in problem solving—The effect of Einstellung. *Psychological Monographs, 54* (No. 6, serial no. 248).

Luciano, M., Smith, G. A., Wright, M. J., Geffen, G. M., Geffen, L. B., & Martin, N. G. (2001). On the heritability of inspection time and its covariance with IQ: A twin study. *Intelligence, 29,* 443–457.

Luciano, M., Wright, M. J., Geffen, G. M., Geffen, L. B., Smith, G. A., Evans, D. M., & Martin, N. G. (2003). A genetic two-factor model of the covariation among a subset of Multidimensional Aptitude Battery and Wechsler Adult Intelligence Scale—Revised subtests. *Intelligence, 31,* 589–605.

Luciano, M., Wright, M. J., Smith, G. A., Geffen, G. M., Geffen, L. B., & Martin, N. G. (2001). Genetic covariance among measures of information processing speed, working memory, and IQ. *Behavior Genetics, 31,* 581–592.

Luo, D., Petrill, S. A., & Thompson, L. A. (1994). An exploration of genetic *g*: Hierarchical factor analysis of cognitive data from the Western Reserve twin project. *Intelligence, 18,* 335–347.

Luo, D., Thompson, L. A., & Detterman, D. K. (2003a). The causal factor underlying the correlation between psychometric *g* and scholastic performance. *Intelligence, 31,* 67–83.

Luo, D., Thompson, L. A., & Detterman, D. K. (2003b). Phenotypic and behavioral genetic covariation between elemental cognitive components and scholastic measures. *Behavior Genetics, 33,* 221–246.

Luria, A. R. (1980). *Higher cortical functions in man* (2nd ed.). New York: Basic Books.

Lyell, C. (1830). *Principles of geology: An attempt to explain the former changes of the earth's surface.* London: John Murray.

Lyell, C. (1839). *Elements of geology.* Philadelphia: James Kay, Jun., and Brother.

Lyell, C. (1867). *Principles of geology* (10th ed., Vol. 1). London: Murray.

Lykken, D., & Tellegen, A. (1996). Happiness is a stochastic phenomenon. *Psychological Science, 7,* 186–189.

Lynn, R. (1996). *Dysgenics: Genetic deterioration in modern populations.* Westport, CT: Praeger.

Lynn, R. (1998). In support of the nutrition theory. In U. Neisser (Ed.), *The rising curve: Long-term gains in IQ and related measures* (pp. 207–215). Washington, DC: American Psychological Association.

Lynn, R., & Hampson, S. (1986). The rise of national intelligence: Evidence from Britain, Japan, and the U.S.A. *Personality and Individual Differences, 7,* 23–32.

Mac Arthur, R. H., & Wilson, E. O. (1967). *The theory of island biogeography.* Princeton, NJ: Princeton University Press.

MacDonald, K. (1992). Warmth as a developmental construct: An evolutionary analysis. *Child Development, 63,* 753–773.

MacDonald, K. (1995). Evolution, the five-factor model, and levels of personality. *Journal of Personality, 63,* 525–567.

Mackintosh, N. J., & Bennett, E. S. (2003). The fractionation of working memory maps onto different components of intelligence. *Intelligence, 31,* 519–531.

Macrae, C. N., & Bodenhausen, G. V. (2000). Social cognition: Thinking categorically about others. *Annual Review of Psychology, 51,* 93–120.

Maguire, E. A., Burgess, N., Donnett, J. G., Frackowiak, R. S. J., Frith, C. D., & O'Keefe, J. (1998, May 8). Knowing where and getting there: A human navigational network. *Science, 280,* 921–924.

Maguire, E. A., Frackowiak, R. S. J., & Frith, C. D. (1996). Learning to find your way: A role for the human hippocampal formation. *Proceedings of the Royal Society of London B, 263,* 1745–1750.

Maguire, E. A., Frackowiak, R. S. J., & Frith, C. D. (1997). Recalling routes around London: Activation of the right hippocampus in taxi drivers. *Journal of Neuroscience, 17,* 7103–7110.

Maguire, E. A., Gadian, D. G., Johnsrude, I. S., Good, C. D., Ashburner, J., Frackowiak, R. S. J., & Frith, C. D. (2000). Navigation-related structural change in the hippocampi of taxi drivers. *Proceedings of the National Academy of Sciences USA, 97,* 4398–4403.

Malt, B. C. (1995). Category coherence in cross-cultural perspective. *Cognitive Psychology, 29,* 85–148.

Malthus, T. R. (1798). *An essay on the principle of population as it affects the future improvement of society with remarks on the speculations of Mr. Godwin, M. Condorcet, and other writers.* London: Printed for J. Johnson, in St. Paul's Church-yard.

Mandler, J. M. (1992). How to build a baby: II. Conceptual primitives. *Psychological Review, 99,* 587–604.

Manktelow, K. (1999). *Reasoning and thinking.* East Sussex, England: Psychology Press.

Manson, J. E., Willett, W. C., Stampfer, M. J., Colditz, G. A., Hunter, D. J., Hankinson, S. E., et al. (1995). Body weight and mortality among women. *New England Journal of Medicine, 333,* 677–685.

Manzanares, M., Wada, H., Itasaki, N., Trainor, P. A., Krumlauf, R., & Holland, P. W. H. (2000, December 14). Conservation and elaboration of Hox gene regulation during evolution of the vertebrate head. *Nature, 408,* 854–857.

Marcus, G. (2004). *The birth of the mind: How a tiny number of genes creates the complexities of human thought.* New York: Basic Books.

Markus, H. (1977). Self-schemata and processing information about the self. *Journal of Personality and Social Psychology, 35,* 63–78.

Martin, P. S. (1967). Prehistoric overkill. In P. S. Martin & H. E. Wright Jr. (Eds.), *Pleistocene extinctions: The search for a cause* (pp. 75–120). New Haven, CT: Yale University Press.

Martin, P. S. (1973, March 9). The discovery of America: The first Americans may have swept the Western Hemisphere and decimated its fauna in 1000 years. *Science, 179,* 969–974.

Matarazzo, J. D. (1972). *Wechsler's measurement and appraisal of adult intelligence* (5th ed.). New York: Oxford University Press.

Matthews, M. H. (1992). *Making sense of place: Children's understanding of large-scale environments.* Savage, MD: Barnes & Noble Books.

Maynard Smith, J., & Price, G. R. (1973, November 2). The logic of animal conflict. *Nature, 246,* 15–18.

Mayr, E. (1974). Behavior programs and evolutionary strategies. *American Scientist, 62,* 650–659.

Mayr, E. (1982). *The growth of biological thought.* Cambridge, MA: Belknap Press.

Mazzocco, M. M. M., & Reiss, A. L. (1997). Normal variation in size of the fMR1 gene is not associated with variation in intellectual performance. *Intelligence, 24,* 355–366.

McCandliss, B. D., Posner, M. I., & Givón, T. (1997). Brain plasticity in learning visual words. *Cognitive Psychology, 33,* 88–110.

McCartney, K., Harris, M. J., & Bernieri, F. (1990). Growing up and growing apart: A developmental meta-analysis of twin studies. *Psychological Bulletin, 107,* 226–237.

McClearn, G. E., Johansson, B., Berg, S., Pedersen, N. L., Ahern, F., Petrill, S. A., & Plomin, R. (1997, June 6). Substantial genetic influence on cognitive abilities in twins 80 or more years old. *Science, 276,* 1560–1563.

McCloskey, M. (1983). Intuitive physics. *Scientific American, 248,* 122–130.

McCrae, R. R., & Costa, P. T., Jr. (1997). Personality trait structure as a human universal. *American Psychologist, 52,* 509–516.

McGarry-Roberts, P. A., Stelmack, R. M., & Campbell, K. B. (1992). Intelligence, reaction time, and event-related potentials. *Intelligence, 16,* 289–313.

McGue, M., Bouchard T. J., Jr., Iacono, W. G., & Lykken, D. T. (1993). Behavioral genetics of cognitive ability: A life-span perspective. In R. Plomin & G. E. McClearn (Eds.), *Nature, nurture, and psychology* (pp. 59–76). Washington, DC: American Psychological Association.

McGue, M., Bouchard, T. J., Jr., Lykken, D. T., & Feuer, D. (1984). Information processing abilities in twins reared apart. *Intelligence, 8,* 239–258.

McHenry, H. M. (1994). Tempo and mode in human evolution. *Proceedings of the National Academy of Sciences USA, 91,* 6780–6786.

McIntyre, J., Zago, M., Berthoz, A., & Lacquaniti, F. (2001). Does the brain model Newton's laws? *Nature Neuroscience, 4,* 693–694.

McNeill, D. (2000). Analogic/analytic representations and cross-linguistic differences in thinking for speaking. *Cognitive Linguistics, 11,* 43–60.

Medin, D. L., & Atran, S. (Eds.). (1999a). *Folkbiology.* Cambridge, MA: MIT Press/ Bradford Book.

Medin, D. L., & Atran, S. (1999b). Introduction. In D. L. Medin & S. Atran (Eds.), *Folkbiology* (pp. 1–15). Cambridge, MA: MIT Press/Bradford Book.

Medin, D. L., Coley, J. D., Storms, G., & Hayes, B. K. (2003). A relevance theory of induction. *Psychonomic Bulletin & Review, 10,* 517–532.

Mercader, J., Panger, M., & Boesch, C. (2002, May 24). Excavation of chimpanzee stone tool site in the African rainforest. *Science, 296,* 1452–1455.

Merriwether, D. A., Huston, S., Iyengar, S., Hamman, R., Norris, J. M., Shetterly, S. M., et al. (1997). Mitochondrial versus nuclear admixture estimates demonstrate a past history of directional mating. *American Journal of Physical Anthropology, 102,* 153–159.

Mesa, N. R., Mondragón, M. C., Soto, I. D., Parra, M. V., Duque, C., Ortíz-Barrientos, D., et al. (2000). Autosomal, mtDNA, and Y-chromosome diversity in Amerinds: Pre- and post-Columbian patterns of gene flow in South America. *American Journal of Human Genetics, 67,* 1277–1286.

Miller, E. K., & Cohen, J. D. (2001). An integration of theory of prefrontal cortex function. *Annual Review of Neuroscience, 24,* 167–202.

Miller, G. F. (2000). *The mating mind: How sexual choice shaped the evolution of human nature.* New York: Doubleday.

Miller, G. H., Magee, J. W., Johnson, B. J., Fogel, M. L., Spooner, N. A., McCulloch, M. T., & Ayliffe, L. K. (1999, January 8). Pleistocene extinction of *Genyornis newtoni:* Human impact on Australian megafauna. *Science, 283,* 205–208.

Milner, A. D., & Goodale, M. A. (1995). *The visual brain in action.* New York: Oxford University Press.

Mitani, J. C., Merriwether, D. A., & Zhang, C. (2000). Male affiliation, cooperation and kinship in wild chimpanzees. *Animal Behaviour, 59,* 885–893.

Mithen, S. (1996). *The prehistory of the mind: The cognitive origins of art and science.* New York: Thames and Hudson.

Miyake, A., & Shah, P. (Eds.). (1999). *Models of working memory: Mechanisms of active maintenance and executive control.* Cambridge, England: Cambridge University Press.

Miyashita-Lin, E. M., Hevner, R., Wassarman, K. M., Martinez, S., & Rubenstein, J. L. R. (1999, August 6). Early neocortical regionalization in the absence of thalamic innervation. *Science, 285*, 906–909.

Moore, C. I., Stern, C. E., Dunbar, C., Kostyk, S. K., Gehi, A., & Corkin, S. (2000). Referred phantom sensations and cortical reorganization after spinal cord injury in humans. *Proceedings of the National Academy of Sciences USA, 97*, 14703–14708.

Morris, J. S., Scott, S. K., & Dolan, R. J. (1999). Saying it with feeling: Neural responses to emotional vocalizations. *Neuropsychologia, 37*, 1155–1163.

Morrison, A. S., Kirshner, J., & Molho, A. (1977). Life cycle events in 15th century Florence: Records of the *Monte Delle Doti. American Journal of Epidemiology, 106*, 487–492.

Moscovitch, M. (1994). Memory and working with memory: Evaluation of a component process model and comparisons with other models. In D. L. Schacter & E. Tulving (Eds.), *Memory systems 1994* (pp. 269–310). Cambridge, MA: MIT Press.

Moscovitch, M. (2000). Theories of memory and consciousness. In E. Tulving & F. I. M. Craik (Eds.), *The Oxford handbook of memory* (pp. 609–625). New York: Oxford University Press.

Moscovitch, M., & Winocur, G. (2002). The frontal cortex and working with memory. In D. T. Stuss & R. T. Knight (Eds.), *Principles of frontal lobe function* (pp. 188–209). New York: Oxford University Press.

Moscovitch, M., Winocur, G., & Behrmann, M. (1997). What is special about face recognition? Nineteen experiments on a person with visual object agnosia and dyslexia but normal face recognition. *Journal of Cognitive Neuroscience, 9*, 555–604.

Moss, C. F., & Shettleworth, S. J. (Eds.). (1996). *Neuroethological studies of cognitive and perceptual processes*. Boulder, CO: Westview Press.

Moss, C. F., & Simmons, J. A. (1996). Perception along the axis of target range in the echolocating bat. In C. F. Moss & S. J. Shettleworth (Eds.), *Neuroethological studies of cognitive and perceptual processes* (pp. 253–279). Boulder, CO: Westview Press.

Mouse Genome Sequencing Consortium. (2002, December 5). Initial sequencing and comparative analysis of the mouse genome. *Nature, 420*, 520–562.

Mousseau, T. A., & Roff, D. A. (1987). Natural selection and the heritability of fitness components. *Heredity, 59*, 181–197.

Murdock, G. P. (1981). *Atlas of world cultures*. Pittsburgh, PA: University of Pittsburgh Press.

Murray, C. (2002). IQ and income inequality in a sample of sibling pairs from advantaged family backgrounds. *American Economic Review, 92*, 339–343.

Murray, C. (2003). *Human accomplishment: The pursuit of excellence in the arts and sciences, 800 B.C. to 1950*. New York: HarperCollins.

Myers, D. G., & Diener, E. (1995). Who is happy? *Psychological Science, 6*, 10–19.

Myers, R. A., & Worm, B. (2003, May 15). Rapid worldwide depletion of predatory fish communities. *Nature, 423,* 280–283.

Nahm, F. K. D., Perret, A., Amaral, D. G., & Albright, T. D. (1997). How do monkeys look at faces? *Journal of Cognitive Neuroscience, 9,* 611–623.

Nakagawa, Y., Johnson, J. E., & O'Leary, D. D. M. (1999). Graded and areal expression patterns of regulatory genes and cadherins in embryonic neocortex independent of thalamocortical input. *Journal of Neuroscience, 19,* 10877–10885.

Nakamura, K., Kawashima, R., Sato, N., Nakamura, A., Sugiura, M., Kato, T., et al. (2000). Functional delineation of the human occipito-temporal areas related to face and scene processing: A PET Study. *Brain, 123,* 1903–1912.

Neiss, M., & Rowe, D. C. (2000). Parental education and child's verbal IQ in adoptive and biological families in the National Longitudinal Study of Adolescent Health. *Behavior Genetics, 30,* 487–495.

Neisser, U. (Ed.). (1998). *The rising curve: Long-term gains in IQ and related measures.* Washington, DC: American Psychological Association.

Neiworth, J. J., Parsons, R. R., & Hassett, J. M. (2004). A test of the generality of perceptually based categories found in infants: Attentional differences toward natural kinds by New World monkeys. *Developmental Science, 7,* 185–193.

Nelson, K. (in press). Evolution and development of human memory systems. In B. J. Ellis & D. F. Bjorklund (Eds.), *Origins of the social mind.* New York: Guilford Publications.

Nettelbeck, T. (2001). Correlation between inspection time and psychometric abilities: A personal interpretation. *Intelligence, 29,* 459–474.

Nettelbeck, T., & Lally, M. (1976). Inspection time and measured intelligence. *British Journal of Psychology, 67,* 17–22.

Nettelbeck, T., & Wilson, C. (2004). The Flynn effect: Smarter not faster. *Intelligence, 32,* 85–93.

Neubauer, A. C. (1997). The mental speed approach to the assessment of intelligence. In J. Kingma & W. Tomic (Eds.), *Advances in cognition and education: Reflections on the concept of intelligence* (pp. 149–173). Greenwich, CT: JAI Press.

Neubauer, A. C., Fink, A., & Schrausser, D. G. (2002). Intelligence and neural efficiency: The influence of task content and sex on the brain–IQ relationship. *Intelligence, 30,* 515–536.

Neubauer, A. C., & Fruedenthaler, H. H. (1994). Reaction times in a sentence-picture verification test and intelligence: Individual strategies and effects of extended practice. *Intelligence, 19,* 193–218.

Neubauer, A. C., Spinath, F. M., Riemann, R., Angleitner, A., & Borkenau, P. (2000). Genetic and environmental influences on two measures of speed of information processing and their relation to psychometric intelligence: Evidence from the German observational study of adult twins. *Intelligence, 28,* 267–289.

Newcomb, A. F., Bukowski, W. M., & Pattee, L. (1993). Children's peer relations: A meta-analytic review of popular, rejected, neglected, controversial, and average sociometric status. *Psychological Bulletin, 113,* 99–128.

Newell, A., & Simon, H. A. (1972). *Human problem solving.* Englewood Cliffs, NJ: Prentice-Hall.

Newton, I. (1995). *The principia.* Amherst, NY: Prometheus Books. [Translated by A. Motte]. (Original work published 1687)

Nimchinsky, E. A., Gilissen, E., Allman, J. M., Perl, D. P., Erwin, J. M., & Hof, P. R. (1999). A neuronal morphologic type unique to humans and great apes. *Proceedings of the National Academy of Sciences USA, 96,* 5268–5273.

Normal, D. A., & Shallice, T. (1986). Attention to action: Willed and automatic control of behavior. In R. J. Davidson, G. E. Schwartz, & D. Shapiro (Eds.), *Consciousness and self-regulation* (Vol. 4, pp. 1–18). New York: Plenum Press.

Northcutt, R. G., & Kaas, J. H. (1995). The emergence and evolution of mammalian neocortex. *Trends in Neurosciences, 18,* 373–379.

Nyberg, L., Forkstam, C., Petersson, K. M., Cabeza, R., & Ingvar, M. (2002). Brain imaging of human memory systems: Between-systems similarities and within-system differences. *Cognitive Brian Research, 13,* 281–292.

Nyborg, H., & Jensen, A. R. (2001). Occupation and income related to psychometric g. *Intelligence, 29,* 45–55.

Oaksford, M., & Chater, N. (1996). Rational explanation of the selection task. *Psychological Review, 103,* 381–391.

Oaksford, M., & Chater, N. (1998). *Rationality in an uncertain world: Essays on the cognitive science of human reasoning.* East Sussex, England: Psychology Press.

Obonsawin, M. C., Crawford, J. R., Page, J., Chalmers, P., Cochrane, R., & Low, G. (2002). Performance on tests of frontal lobe function reflect general intellectual ability. *Neuropsychologia, 40,* 970–977.

Öhman, A. (2002). Automaticity and the amygdala: Nonconscious responses to emotional faces. *Current Directions in Psychological Science, 11,* 62–66.

O'Leary, D. D. M. (1989). Do cortical areas emerge from a protocortex? *Trends in Neuroscience, 12,* 401–406.

O'Leary, D. D. M., Schlaggar, B. L., & Tuttle, R. (1994). Specification of neocortical areas and thalamocortical connections. *Annual Review of Neuroscience, 17,* 419–439.

Ones, D. S., Viswesvaran, C., & Schmidt, F. L. (1993). Comprehensive meta-analysis of integrity test validities: Findings and implications for personnel selection and theories of job performance. *Journal of Applied Psychology Monographs, 78,* 679–703.

Ó Scalaidhe, S. P., Wilson, F. A. W., & Goldman-Rakic, P. S. (1997, November 7). Areal segregation of face-processing neurons in prefrontal cortex. *Science, 278,* 1135–1138.

Ospovat, D. (1979). Darwin after Malthus. *Journal of the History of Biology, 12,* 211–230.

Ospovat, D. (1981). *The development of Darwin's theory: Natural history, natural theology, and natural selection, 1838–1859.* Cambridge, England: Cambridge University Press.

Ovchinnikov, I. V., Götherström, A., Romanova, G. P., Kharitonov, V. M., Lidén, K., & Goodwin, W. (2000, March 30). Molecular analysis of Neanderthal DNA from the northern Caucasus. *Nature, 404,* 490–493.

Owen, R. (1860). Darwin on the origin of species. *Edinburgh Review, 3,* 487–532.

Pääbo, S. (1999). Human evolution. *Trends in Genetics, 15,* M13–M16.

Packer, C., Gilbert, D. A., Pusey, A. E., & O'Brien, S. J. (1991, June 13). A molecular genetic analysis of kinship and cooperation in African lions. *Nature, 351,* 562–565.

Packer, C., Herbst, L., Pusey, A. E., Bygott, J. D., Hanby, J. P., Cairns, S. J., & Mulder, M. B. (1988). Reproductive success of lions. In T. H. Clutton-Brock (Ed.), *Reproductive success: Studies of individual variation in contrasting breeding systems* (pp. 363–383). Chicago: University of Chicago Press.

Pal, S., Shyam, R., & Singh, R. (1997). Genetic analysis of general intelligence, *g*: A twin study. *Personality and Individual Differences, 22,* 779–780.

Pallas, S. L. (2001). Intrinsic and extrinsic factors that shape neocortical specification. *Trends in Neuroscience, 24,* 417–423.

Palleroni, A., & Hauser, M. (2003, February 21). Experience-dependent plasticity for auditory processing in a raptor. *Science, 299,* 1195.

Pandolfi, J. M., Bradbury, R. H., Sala, E., Hughes, T. P., Bjorndal, K. A., Cooke, R. G., et al. (2003, August 15). Global trajectories of the long-term decline of coral reef ecosystems. *Science, 301,* 955–958.

Parker, G. A., & Simmons, L. W. (1996). Parental investment and the control of selection: Predicting the direction of sexual competition. *Proceedings of the Royal Society of London B, 263,* 315–321.

Parker, S. T., & McKinney, M. L. (1999). *Origins of intelligence: The evolution of cognitive development in monkeys, apes, and humans.* Baltimore: Johns Hopkins University Press.

Parks, R. W., Loewenstein, D. A., Dodrill, K. L., Barker, W. W., Yoshii, F., Chang, J. Y., et al. (1988). Cerebral metabolic effects of a verbal fluency test: A PET scan study. *Journal of Clinical and Experimental Neuropsychology, 10,* 565–575.

Pascalis, O., de Haan, M., & Nelson, C. A. (2002, May 17). Is face processing species-specific during the first year of life? *Science, 296,* 1321–1323.

Pascual-Leone, J. (1987). Organismic processes for neo-Piagetian theories: A dialectical causal account of cognitive development. *International Journal of Psychology, 22,* 531–570.

Passingham, R. E., & Rowe, J. B. (2002). Dorsal prefrontal cortex: Maintenance in memory or attentional selection? In D. T. Stuss & R. T. Knight (Eds.), *Principles of frontal lobe function* (pp. 221–232). New York: Oxford University Press.

Pasternak, B., Ember, C. R., & Ember, M. (1997). *Sex, gender, and kinship: A cross-cultural perspective*. Upper Saddle River, NJ: Prentice-Hall.

Paterson, S. J., Brown, J. H., Gsödl, M. K., Johnson, M. H., & Karmiloff-Smith, A. (1999, December 17). Cognitive modularity and genetic disorders. *Science, 286*, 2355–2358.

Pawlowski, B., Lowen, C. B., & Dunbar, R. I. M. (1998). Neocortex size, social skills and mating success in primates. *Behaviour, 135*, 357–368.

Pedersen, N. L., Plomin, R., Nesselroade, J. R., & McClearn, G. E. (1992). A quantitative genetic analysis of cognitive abilities during the second half of the lifespan. *Psychological Science, 3*, 346–353.

Pellegrini, A. D., & Bartini, M. (2001). Dominance in early adolescent boys: Affiliative and aggressive dimensions and possible functions. *Merrill-Palmer Quarterly, 47*, 142–163.

Pellegrino, J. W., & Glaser, R. (1979). Cognitive correlates and components in the analysis of individual differences. *Intelligence, 3*, 187–214.

Pellis, S. M., & Iwaniuk, A. N. (2000). Adult–adult play in primates: Comparative analyses of its origin, distribution and evolution. *Ethology, 106*, 1083–1104.

Pellis, S. M., & Pellis, V. C. (1998). The structure–function interface in the analysis of play fighting. In M. Bekoff & J. A. Byers (Eds.), *Animal play: Evolutionary, comparative, and ecological perspectives* (pp. 115–140). Cambridge, England: Cambridge University Press.

Pennington, B. F., Filipek, P. A., Lefly, D., Chhabildas, N., Kennedy, D. N., Simon, J. H., et al. (2000). A twin MRI study of size variations in human brain. *Journal of Cognitive Neuroscience, 12*, 223–232.

Perani, D., Cappa, S. F., Bettinardi, V., Bressi, S., Gorno-Tempini, M., Matarrese, M., & Fazio, F. (1995). Different neural systems for the recognition of animals and man-made tools. *NeuroReport, 6*, 1637–1641.

Petersen, S. E., Fox, P. T., Posner, M. I., Mintun, M., & Raichle, M. E. (1988, February 18). Positron emission tomographic studies of the cortical anatomy of single-word processing. *Nature, 331*, 585–589.

Petren, K., Grant, B. R., & Grant, P. R. (1999). A phylogeny of Darwin's finches based on microsatellite DNA length variation. *Proceedings of the Royal Society of London B, 266*, 321–329.

Petrill, S. A. (2002). The development of intelligence: Behavioral genetic approaches. In R. J. Sternberg, J. Lautrey, & T. I. Lubart (Eds.), *Models of intelligence: International perspectives* (pp. 81–90). Washington, DC: American Psychological Association.

Petrill, S. A., Ball, B., Eley, T., Hill, L., Plomin, R., McClearn, G. E., et al. (1998). Failure to replicate a QTL association between a DNA marker identified by EST00083 and IQ. *Intelligence, 25*, 179–184.

Petrill, S. A., Luo, D., Thompson, L. A., & Detterman, D. K. (1996). The independent prediction of general intelligence by elementary cognitive tasks: Genetic and environmental influences. *Behavior Genetics, 26*, 135–147.

Petrill, S. A., Luo, D., Thompson, L. A., & Detterman, D. K. (2001). Inspection time and the relationship among elementary cognitive tasks, general intelligence, and specific cognitive abilities. *Intelligence, 29,* 487–496.

Pfennig, D. W., & Collins, J. P. (1993, April 29). Kinship affects morphogenesis in cannibalistic salamanders. *Nature, 362,* 836–838.

Phelps, E. A., O'Connor, K. J., Cunningham, W. A., Funayama, E. S., Gatenby, J. C., Gore, J. C., & Banaji, M. R. (2000). Performance on indirect measures of race evaluation predicts amygdala activation. *Journal of Cognitive Neuroscience, 12,* 729–738.

Piao, X., Hill, R. S., Bodell, A., Chang, B. S., Basel-Vanagaite, L., Straussberg, R., et al. (2004, March 26). G protein-coupled receptor-dependent development of human frontal cortex. *Science, 303,* 2033–2036.

Picton, T. W., Alain, C., & McIntosh, A. R. (2002). The theatre of the mind: Physiological study of the human frontal lobes. In D. T. Stuss & R. T. Knight (Eds.), *Principles of frontal lobe function* (pp. 109–126). New York: Oxford University Press.

Pinker, S. (1994). *The language instinct.* New York: William Morrow.

Pinker, S. (1997). *How the mind works.* New York: Norton.

Pinker, S. (1999). *Words and rules: The ingredients of language.* New York: Basic Books.

Pinker, S. (2002). *The blank slate: The modern denial of human nature.* New York: Viking.

Pinker, S., & Bloom, P. (1990). Natural language and natural selection. *Behavioral and Brain Sciences, 13,* 707–784.

Pinker, S., & Jackendoff, R. (in press). The faculty of language: What's special about it? *Cognition.*

Plomin, R. (2002). General cognitive ability. In R. Plomin, J. C. DeFries, I. W. Craig, & P. McGuffin (Eds.), *Behavioral genetics in the postgenomic era* (pp. 183–201). Washington, DC: American Psychological Association.

Plomin, R., & Craig, I. (2001). Genetics, environment and cognitive abilities: Review and work in progress towards a genome scan for quantitative trait locus associations using DNA pooling. *British Journal of Psychiatry, 178*(suppl. 40), S41–S48.

Plomin, R., & DeFries, J. C. (1980). Genetics and intelligence: Recent data. *Intelligence, 4,* 15–24.

Plomin, R., DeFries, J. C., Craig, I. W., & McGuffin, P. (Eds.) (2002). *Behavioral genetics in the postgenomic era.* Washington, DC: American Psychological Association.

Plomin, R., DeFries, J. C., & Loehlin, J. C. (1977). Genotype–environment interaction and correlation in the analysis of human behavior. *Psychological Bulletin, 84,* 309–322.

Plomin, R., DeFries, J. C., McClearn, G. E., & McGuffin, P. (2001). *Behavioral genetics* (4th ed.). New York: Worth Publishers.

Plomin, R., Fulker, D. W., Corley, R., & DeFries, J. C. (1997). Nature, nurture, and cognitive development from 1 to 16 years: A parent–offspring adoption study. *Psychological Science, 8*, 442–447.

Plomin, R., Hill, L., Craig, I. W., McGuffin, P., Purcell, S., Sham, P., et al. (2001). A genome-wide scan of 1842 DNA markers for allelic associations with general cognitive ability: A five-stage design using DNA pooling and extreme selected groups. *Behavioral Genetics, 31*, 497–509.

Plomin, R., McClearn, G. E., Smith, D. L., Skuder, P., Vignetti, S., Chorney, M. J., et al. (1995). Allelic associations between 100 DNA markers and high versus low IQ. *Intelligence, 21*, 31–48.

Plomin, R., & Neiderhisher, J. (1991). Quantitative genetics, molecular genetics, and intelligence. *Intelligence, 15*, 369–387.

Plomin, R., & Spinath, F. M. (2002). Genetics and general cognitive ability (*g*). *Trends in Cognitive Sciences, 6*, 169–176.

Plutchik, R. (2001). The nature of emotions. *American Scientist, 89*, 344–350.

Plutchik, R. (2002). *Emotions and life: Perspectives from psychology, biology, and evolution*. Washington, DC: American Psychological Association.

Polley, D. B., Kvašòák, E., & Frostig, R. D. (2004, May 6). Naturalistic experience transforms sensory maps in the adult cortex of caged animals. *Nature, 429*, 67–71.

Poremba, A., Malloy, M., Saunders, R. C., Carson, R. E., Herscovitch, P., & Mishkin, M. (2004, January 29). Species-specific calls evoke asymmetric activity in the monkey's temporal poles. *Nature, 427*, 448–451.

Porter, R. H., & Winberg, J. (1999). Unique salience of maternal breast odors for newborn infants. *Neuroscience and Biobehavioral Reviews, 23*, 439–449.

Posner, M. I. (1994). Attention: The mechanisms of consciousness. *Proceedings of the National Academy of Sciences USA, 91*, 7398–7403.

Posner, M. I., Boies, S. J., Eichelman, W. H., & Taylor, R. L. (1969). Retention of visual and name codes of single letters. *Journal of Experimental Psychology Monograph, 79*, 1–16.

Posner, M. I., & DiGirolamo, G. J. (2000). Attention and cognitive neuroscience: An overview. In M. S. Gazzaniga (Ed.-in-chief), *The new cognitive neurosciences* (2nd ed., pp. 623–631). Cambridge, MA: Bradford Books/MIT Press.

Posner, M. I., & MacLeod, P. (1982). Information processing models: In search of elementary operations. *Annual Review of Psychology, 33*, 477–514.

Posner, M. I., & Rothbart, M. K. (1998). Attention, self-regulation and consciousness. *Philosophical Transactions of the Royal Society of London—Series B: Biological Sciences, 353*, 1915–1927.

Posthuma, D., de Geus, E. J. C., Baaré, W. F. C., Hulshoff Pol, H. E., Kahn, R. S., & Boomsma, D. I. (2002). The association between brain volume and intelligence is of genetic origin. *Nature Neuroscience, 5*, 83–84.

Posthuma, D., de Geus, E. J. C., & Boomsma, D. I. (2002). Genetic contributions to anatomical, behavioral, and neurophysiological indices of cognition. In

R. Plomin, J. C. DeFries, I. W. Craig, & P. McGuffin (2002). *Behavioral genetics in the postgenomic era* (pp. 141–161). Washington, DC: American Psychological Association.

Posthuma, D., de Geus, E. J. C., Neale, M. C., Hulshoff Pol, H. E., Baaré, W. F. C., Kahn, R. S., & Boomsma, D. (2000). Multivariate genetic analysis of brain structure in an extended twin design. *Behavior Genetics, 30,* 311–319.

Potts, R. (1998). Variability selection in hominid evolution. *Evolutionary Anthropology, 7,* 81–96.

Poucet, B. (1993). Spatial cognitive maps in animals: New hypotheses on their structure and neural mechanisms. *Psychological Review, 100,* 163–182.

Povinelli, D. J. (2000). *Folk physics for apes: The chimpanzees theory of how the world works.* New York: Oxford University Press.

Povinelli, D. J., & Bering, J. M. (2002). The mentality of apes revisited. *Current Directions in Psychological Science, 11,* 115–119.

Povinelli, D. J., & Preuss, T. M. (1995). Theory of mind: Evolutionary history of a cognitive specialization. *Trends in Neuroscience, 18,* 418–424.

Povinelli, D. J., & Vonk, J. (2003). Chimpanzee minds: Suspiciously human? *Trends in Cognitive Sciences, 7,* 157–160.

Prabhakaran, V., Narayanan, K., Zhao, Z., & Gabrieli, J. D. E. (2000). Integration of diverse information in working memory within the frontal lobe. *Nature Neuroscience, 3,* 85–90.

Prabhakaran, V., Smith, J. A. L., Desmond, J. E., Glover, G. H., & Gabrieli, J. D. E. (1997). Neural substrates of fluid reasoning: An fMRI study of neocortical activation during performance of the Raven's progressive matrices test. *Cognitive Psychology, 33,* 43–63.

Pratto, F. (1996). Sexual politics: The gender gap in the bedroom, the cupboard, and the cabinet. In D. M. Buss & N. M. Malamuth (Eds.), *Sex, power, conflict: Evolutionary and feminist perspectives* (pp. 179–230). New York: Oxford University Press.

Premack, D., & Premack, A. J. (1995). Origins of human social competence. In M. S. Gazzaniga (Ed.), *The cognitive neurosciences* (pp. 205–218). Cambridge, MA: Bradford Books/MIT Press.

Premack, D., & Woodruff, G. (1978). Does the chimpanzee have a theory of mind? *Behavioral and Brain Sciences, 1,* 515–526.

Preuss, T. M. (2000a). Taking the measure of diversity: Comparative alternatives to the model-animal paradigm in cortical neuroscience. *Brain, Behavior and Evolution, 55,* 287–299.

Preuss, T. M. (2000b). What's human about the human brain? In M. S. Gazzaniga (Ed.-in-chief), *The new cognitive neurosciences* (2nd ed., pp. 1219–1234). Cambridge, MA: Bradford Books/MIT Press.

Preuss, T. M. (2001). The discovery of cerebral diversity: An unwelcome scientific revolution. In D. Falk & K. Gibson (Eds.), *Evolutionary anatomy of the primate cerebral cortex* (pp. 138–164). Cambridge, England: Cambridge University Press.

Preuss, T. M. (2003). Specialization of the human visual system—The monkey model meets human reality. In J. H. Kaas & C. E. Collins (Eds.), *The primate visual system* (pp. 231–259). Boca Raton, FL: CRC Press.

Preuss, T. M. (2004). What is it like to be a human? In M. S. Gazzaniga (Ed.-in-chief), *The cognitive neurosciences* (3rd ed.). Cambridge, MA: Bradford Books/MIT Press.

Preuss, T. M., & Kaas, J. H. (1999). Human brain evolution. In M. J. Zigmond, F. E. Bloom, S. C. Landis, J. L. Roberts, & L. R. Squire (Eds.), *Fundamental neuroscience* (pp. 1283–1311). San Diego, CA: Academic Press.

Preuss, T. M., Qi, H., & Kaas, J. H. (1999). Distinctive compartmental organization of human primary visual cortex. *Proceedings of the National Academy of Sciences USA, 96,* 11601–11606.

Price, C. J., & Friston, K. J. (2002). Functional imaging studies of category specificity. In E. M. E. Forde & G. W. Humphreys (Eds.), *Category specificity in brain and mind* (pp. 427–447). East Sussex, England: Psychology Press.

Price, G. R. (1970, August 1). Selection and covariance. *Nature, 227,* 520–521.

Puelles, L., Kuwana, E., Puelles, E., Bulfone, A., Shimamura, K., Keleher, J., et al. (2000). Pallial and subpallial derivatives in the embryonic chick and mouse telencephalon, traced by the expression of the genes *Dlx-2, Emx-1, Nkx-2.1, Pax-6,* and *Tbr-1. Journal of Comparative Neurology, 424,* 409–438.

Pugh, K. R., Shaywitz, B. A., Shaywitz, S. E., Shankweiler, D. P., Katz, L., Fletcher, J. M., et al. (1997). Predicting reading performance from neuroimaging profiles: The cerebral basis of phonological effects in printed word identification. *Journal of Experimental Psychology: Human Perception and Performance, 23,* 299–318.

Pusey, A., Williams, J., & Goodall, J. (1997, August 8). The influence of dominance rank on the reproductive success of female chimpanzees. *Science, 277,* 828–831.

Quartz, S. R., & Sejnowski, T. J. (1997). The neural basis of cognitive development: A constructivist manifesto. *Behavioral and Brain Sciences, 20,* 537–596.

Raby, P. (2001). *Alfred Russel Wallace: A life.* Princeton, NJ: Princeton University Press.

Ragsdale, C. W., & Grove, E. A. (2001). Patterning the mammalian cerebral cortex. *Current Opinion in Neurobiology, 11,* 50–58.

Raichle, M. E., Fiez, J. A., Videen, T. O., MacLeod, A. M. K., Pardo, J. V., & Petersen, S. E. (1994). Practice-related changes in human brain functional anatomy during non-motor learning. *Cerebral Cortex, 4,* 8–26.

Rakic, P. (1976, June 10). Prenatal genesis of connections subserving ocular dominance in the rhesus monkey. *Nature, 261,* 467–471.

Rakic, P. (1988, July 8). Specification of cerebral cortical areas. *Science, 241,* 170–176.

Rakic, P. (1995). A small step for the cell, a giant leap for mankind: A hypothesis of neocortical expansion during evolution. *Trends in Neurosciences, 18,* 383–388.

Rakic, P. (1998). Brain development: VI. Radial migration and cortical evolution. *American Journal of Psychiatry, 155,* 1150–1151.

Rakic, P. (2000). Setting the stage for cognition: Genesis of the primate cerebral cortex. In M. S. Gazzaniga (Ed.-in-chief), *The new cognitive neurosciences* (2nd ed., pp. 7–21). Cambridge, MA: Bradford Books/MIT Press.

Rakic, P., & Kornack, D. R. (2001). Neocortical expansion and elaboration during primate evolution: A view from neuroembryology. In D. Falk & K. R. Gibson (Eds.), *Evolutionary anatomy of the primate cerebral cortex* (pp. 30–56). Cambridge, England: Cambridge University Press.

Ramachandran, V. S. (1993). Behavioral and magnetoencephalographic correlates of plasticity in the adult human brain. *Proceedings of the National Academy of Sciences USA, 90,* 10413–10420.

Ramey, C. T., & Ramey, S. L. (1998a). Early intervention and early experience. *American Psychologist, 53,* 109–120.

Ramey, C. T., & Ramey, S. L. (1998b). In defense of special education. *American Psychologist, 53,* 1159–1160.

Ranganath, C., & Rainer, G. (2003). Neural mechanisms for detecting and remembering novel events. *Nature Reviews: Neuroscience, 4,* 193–202.

Rauschecker, J. P., Tian, B., & Hauser, M. (1995, April 7). Processing of complex sounds in the macaque nonprimary auditory cortex. *Science, 268,* 111–114.

Raven, J. C., Court, J. H., & Raven, J. (1993). *Manual for Raven's Progressive Matrices and Vocabulary Scales.* London: H. K. Lewis & Co.

Raz, N., Torres, I. J., Spencer, W. D., Millman, D., Baertschi, J. C., & Sarpel, G. (1993). Neuroanatomical correlates of age-sensitive and age-invariant cognitive abilities: An in vivo MRI investigation. *Intelligence, 17,* 407–422.

Reber, A. S. (1993). *Implicit learning and tacit knowledge: An essay on the cognitive unconscious.* New York: Oxford University Press.

Recanzone, G. H., Merzenich, M. M., Jenkins, W. M., Grajski, K. A., & Dinse, H. R. (1992). Topographic reorganization of the hand representation in cortical area 3b of owl monkeys trained in a frequency discrimination task. *Journal of Neurophysiology, 67,* 1031–1056.

Ree, M. J., & Earles, J. A. (1993). *g* is to psychology what carbon is to chemistry: A reply to Sternberg and Wagner, McClelland, and Calfee. *Current Directions in Psychological Science, 2,* 11–12.

Reed, T. E., & Jensen, A. R. (1991). Arm nerve conduction velocity (NCV), brain NCV, reaction time, and intelligence. *Intelligence, 15,* 33–47.

Reed, T. E., & Jensen, A. R. (1992). Conduction velocity in a brain nerve pathway of normal adults correlates with intelligence level. *Intelligence, 16,* 259–272.

Reed, T. E., & Jensen, A. R. (1993). A somatosensory latency between thalamus and cortex also correlates with level of intelligence. *Intelligence, 17,* 443–450.

Rees, G., Kreiman, G., & Koch, C. (2002). Neural correlates of consciousness in humans. *Nature Reviews: Neuroscience, 3,* 261–270.

Reichert, H., & Simeone, A. (1999). Conserved usage of gap and homeotic genes in patterning the CNS. *Current Opinion in Neurobiology, 9,* 589–595.

Reid, I. (1998). *Class in Britain.* Cambridge, England: Polity Press.

Reifers, F., Bohli, H., Walsh, E. C., Crossley, P. H., Stainier, D. Y. R., & Brand, M. (1998). Fgf8 is mutated in zebrafish acerebellar (ace) mutants and is required for maintenance of midbrain–hindbrain boundary development and somatogenesis. *Development, 125,* 2381–2395.

Reisberg, D., Rappaport, I., & O'Shaughnessy, M. (1984). Limits of working memory: The digit digit-span. *Journal of Experimental Psychology: Learning, Memory, and Cognition, 10,* 203–221.

Reynolds, C. R., Chastain, R. L., Kaufman, A. S., & McLean, J. E. (1987). Demographic characteristics and IQ among adults: Analysis of the WAIS–R standardization sample as a function of the stratification variables. *Journal of School Psychology, 25,* 323–342.

Reynolds, J. D. (1987). Mating system and nesting biology of the red-necked phalarope *Phalaropus lobatus:* What constrains polyandry? *Isis, 129,* 225–242.

Reynolds, J. D., & Székely, T. (1997). The evolution of parental care in shorebirds: Life histories, ecology, and sexual selection. *Behavioral Ecology, 8,* 126–134.

Reznick, J. S., & Corley, R. (1999). What twins can tell us about the development of intelligence—A case study. In M. Anderson (Ed.), *The development of intelligence* (pp. 105–136). Hove, England: Psychology Press.

Rietveld, M. J. H., van Baal, G. C. M., Dolan, C. V., & Boomsma, D. I. (2000). Genetic factor analyses of specific cognitive abilities in 5-year-old Dutch children. *Behavior Genetics, 30,* 29–40.

Rilling, J. K., & Insel, T. R. (1998). Evolution of the cerebellum in primates: Differences in relative volume among monkeys, apes and humans. *Brain, Behavior and Evolution, 52,* 308–314.

Rilling, J. K., & Insel, T. R. (1999). The primate neocortex in comparative perspective using magnetic resonance imaging. *Journal of Human Evolution, 37,* 191–223.

Riss, D., & Goodall, J. (1977). The recent rise to the alpha-rank in a population of free-living chimpanzees. *Folia Primatologica, 27,* 134–151.

Rivera-Batiz, F. L. (1992). Quantitative literacy and the likelihood of employment among young adults in the United States. *Journal of Human Resources, 27,* 313–328.

Roberts, R. D., & Stankov, L. (1999). Individual differences in speed of mental processing and human cognitive abilities: Toward a taxonomic model. *Learning and Individual Differences, 11,* 1–120.

Roberts, R. G., Flannery, T. F., Ayliffe, L. K., Yoshida, H., Olley, J. M., Prideaux, G. J., et al. (2001, June 8). New ages for last Australian megafauna: Continent-wide extinction about 46,000 years ago. *Science, 292,* 1888–1892.

Rodin, J. (1986, September 19). Aging and health: Effects of the sense of control. *Science, 233,* 1271–1276.

Roe, A. (1956). *Psychology of occupations*. New York: Wiley.

Roe, A. W., Pallas, S. L., Hahm, J. O., & Sur, M. (1990, November 9). A map of visual space induced in primary auditory cortex. *Science, 250,* 818–820.

Roe, A. W., Pallas, S. L., Kwon, Y. H., & Sur, M. (1992). Visual projections routed to the auditory pathway in ferrets: Receptive fields of visual neurons in the primary auditory cortex. *Journal of Neuroscience, 12,* 3561–3664.

Roff, D. A. (1992). *The evolution of life histories: Theory and analysis.* New York: Chapman & Hall.

Rolfhus, E. L., & Ackerman, P. L. (1999). Assessing individual differences in knowledge: Knowledge, intelligence, and related traits. *Journal of Educational Psychology, 91,* 511–526.

Röricht, S., Meyer, B.-U., Niehaus, L., & Brandt, S. A. (1999). Long-term reorganization of motor cortex outputs after arm amputation. *Neurology, 53,* 106–111.

Rosen, V. M., & Engle, R. W. (1998). Working memory capacity and suppression. *Journal of Memory and Language, 39,* 418–436.

Rosenthal, R., Hall, J. A., DiMatteo, M. R., Rogers, P. L., & Archer, D. (1979). *Sensitivity to nonverbal communication: The PONS test.* Baltimore: Johns Hopkins University Press.

Rosenzweig, M. R., & Bennett, E. L. (1972). Cerebral changes in rats exposed individually to an enriched environment. *Journal of Comparative and Physiological Psychology, 80,* 304–313.

Rosenzweig, M. R., Krech, D., Bennett, E. L., & Diamond, M. C. (1962). Effects of environmental complexity and training on brain chemistry and anatomy. *Journal of Comparative and Physiological Psychology, 55,* 429–437.

Rosenzweig, M. R., Krech, D., Bennett, E. L., & Zolman, J. F. (1962). Variation in environmental complexity and brain measures. *Journal of Comparative and Physiological Psychology, 55,* 1092–1095.

Roser, M., & Gazzaniga, M. S. (2004). Automatic brains—Interpretive minds. *Current Directions in Psychological Science, 13,* 56–59.

Rothbaum, F., Weisz, J. R., & Snyder, S. S. (1982). Changing the world and changing the self: A two-process model of perceived control. *Journal of Personality and Social Psychology, 42,* 5–37.

Rowe, D. C. (1994). *The limits of family influence: Genes, experience, and behavior.* New York: Guilford Press.

Rowe, D. C. (2002). Assessing genotype–environment interactions and correlations in the postgenomic era. In R. Plomin, J. C. DeFries, I. W. Craig, & P. McGuffin (Eds.), *Behavioral genetics in the postgenomic era* (pp. 71–86). Washington, DC: American Psychological Association.

Rowe, D. C., Jacobson, K. C., & Van den Oord, E. J. C. G. (1999). Genetic and environmental influences on vocabulary IQ: Parental education level as moderator. *Child Development, 70,* 1151–1162.

Rowe, D. C., & Rodgers, J. L. (2002). Expanding variance and the case of historical change in IQ means: A critique of Dickens and Flynn (2001). *Psychological Review, 109,* 759–763.

Rowe, D. C., Vesterdal, W. J., & Rodgers, J. L. (1999). Herrnstein's syllogism: Genetic and shared environmental influences in IQ, education, and income. *Intelligence, 26,* 405–423.

Rowe, J. B., Toni, I., Josephs, O., Frackowiak, R. S. J., & Passingham, R. E. (2000, June 2). The prefrontal cortex: Response selection or maintenance within working memory? *Science, 288,* 1656–1660.

Rozin, P. (1976). The evolution of intelligence and access to the cognitive unconscious. In J. M. Sprague & A. N. Epstein (Eds.), *Progress in psychobiology and physiological psychology* (Vol. 6, pp. 245–280). New York: Academic Press.

Rozin, P., & Schull, J. (1988). The adaptive-evolutionary point of view in experimental psychology. In R. C. Atkinson, R. J. Herrnstein, G. Lindzey, & R. D. Luce (Eds.), *Steven's handbook of experimental psychology* (2nd ed., Vol. 1, pp. 503–546). New York: Wiley.

Rubenstein, J. L., Anderson, S., Shi, L., Miyashita, L. E., Bulfone, A., & Hevner, R. (1999). Genetic control of cortical regionalization and connectivity. *Cerebral Cortex, 9,* 524–532.

Rubenstein, J. L. R., Shimamura, K., Martinez, S., & Puelles, L. (1998). Regionalization of the prosencephalic neural plate. *Annual Review of Neuroscience, 21,* 445–447.

Ruchkin, D. S., Grafman, J., Cameron, K., & Berndt, R. S. (2003). Working memory retention systems: A state of activated long-term memory. *Behavioral and Brain Sciences, 26,* 709–777.

Ruff, C. B., Trinkaus, E., & Holliday, T. W. (1997, May 8). Body mass and encephalization in Pleistocene *Homo. Nature, 387,* 173–176.

Rushton, J. P., & Ankney, C. D. (1996). Brain size and cognitive ability: Correlations with age, sex, social class, and race. *Psychonomic Bulletin & Review, 3,* 21–36.

Rutherford, S., & D'Hondt, S. (2000, November 2). Early onset and tropical forcing of 100,000-year Pleistocene glacial cycles. *Nature, 408,* 72–75.

Sabbagh, M. A., & Taylor, M. (2000). Neural correlates of theory-of-mind reasoning: An event-related potential study. *Psychological Science, 11,* 46–50.

Sacchett, C., & Humphreys, G. W. (1992). Calling a squirrel a squirrel but a canoe a wigwam: A category-specific deficit for artefactual objects and body parts. *Cognitive Neuropsychology, 9,* 73–86.

Salthouse, T. A. (1991). Mediation of adult age differences in cognition by reductions in working memory and speed of processing. *Psychological Science, 2,* 179–183.

Salthouse, T. A. (1996). The processing-speed theory of adult age differences in cognition. *Psychological Review, 103,* 403–428.

Saltzman, W. (2003). Reproductive competition among female common marmosets (*Callithrix jacchus*): Proximate and ultimate causes. In C. B. Jones (Ed.), *Sexual selection and reproductive competition in primates: New perspectives and directions* (pp. 197–229). Norman, OK: American Society of Primatologists.

Sanfey, A. G., Rilling, J. K., Aronson, J. A., Nystrom, L. E., & Cohen, J. D. (2003, June 13). The neural basis of economic decision-making in the ultimatum game. *Science, 300*, 1755–1758.

Santos, L. R., & Caramazza, A. (2002). The domain-specific hypothesis: A developmental and comparative perspective on category-specific deficits. In E. M. E. Forde & G. W. Humphreys (Eds.), *Category specificity in brain and mind* (pp. 1–23). East Sussex, England: Psychology Press.

Sapolsky, R. M. (1993). The physiology of dominance in stable versus unstable social hierarchies. In W. A. Mason & S. P. Mendoza (Eds.), *Primate social conflict* (pp. 171–204). Albany: State University of New York Press.

Sato, A., O'Huigin, C., Figueroa, F., Grant, P. R., Grant, B. R., Tichy, H., & Klein, J. (1999). Phylogeny of Darwin's finches as revealed by mtDNA sequences. *Proceedings of the National Academy of Sciences USA, 96*, 5101–5106.

Sattler, J. M. (1974). *Assessment of children's intelligence.* Philadelphia: W. B. Saunders.

Sawaguchi, T. (1997). Possible involvement of sexual selection in neocortical evolution of monkeys and apes. *Folia Primatologica, 68*, 95–99.

Scarr, S. (1992). Developmental theories of the 1990s: Developmental and individual differences. *Child Development, 63*, 1–19.

Scarr, S., & McCartney, K. (1983). How people make their own environments: A theory of genotype→environment effects. *Child Development, 54*, 424–435.

Scarr, S., & Weinberg, R. A. (1977). Intellectual similarities within families of both adopted and biological children. *Intelligence, 1*, 170–191.

Scarr, S., & Weinberg, R. A. (1983). The Minnesota adoption studies: Genetic differences and malleability. *Child Development, 54*, 260–267.

Scarr-Salapatek, S. (1971, December 24). Race, social class, and IQ. *Science, 174*, 1285–1295.

Schiff, W., & Oldak, R. (1990). Accuracy of judging time to arrival: Effects of modality, trajectory, and gender. *Journal of Experimental Psychology: Human Perception and Performance, 16*, 303–316.

Schlagger, B. L., & O'Leary, D. D. M. (1991, June 14). Potential of visual cortex to develop an array of functional units unique to somatosensory cortex. *Science, 252*, 1556–1560.

Schmidt, F. L., & Hunter, J. E. (1993). Tacit knowledge, practical intelligence, general mental ability, and job knowledge. *Current Directions in Psychological Science, 2*, 8–9.

Schmidt, F. L., & Hunter, J. E. (1998). The validity and utility of selection methods in personnel psychology: Practical and theoretical implications of 85 years of research findings. *Psychological Bulletin, 124*, 262–274.

Schmidt, F. L., & Hunter, J. (2004). General mental ability in the world of work: Occupational attainment and job performance. *Journal of Personality and Social Psychology, 86,* 162–173.

Schneider, D. J. (1973). Implicit personality theory: A review. *Psychological Bulletin, 79,* 294–309.

Schofield, R., Reher, D., & Bideau, A. (Eds.). (1991). *The decline of mortality in Europe.* Oxford, England: Oxford University Press.

Schultz, H. (1991). Social differences in mortality in the eighteenth century: An analysis of Berlin church registers. *International Review of Social History, 36,* 232–248.

Schultz, R. T., Gauthier, I., Klin, A., Fulbright, R. K., Anderson, A. W., Volkmar, F., et al. (2000). Abnormal ventral temporal cortical activity during face discrimination among individuals with autism and Asperger syndrome. *Archives of General Psychiatry, 57,* 331–340.

Schulz, R., & Heckhausen, J. (1996). A life span model of successful aging. *American Psychologist, 51,* 702–714.

Schusterman, R. J., Reichmuth, C. J., & Kastak, D. (2000). How animals classify friends and foes. *Current Directions in Psychological Science, 9,* 1–6.

Schyns, P. G., Bonnar, L., & Gosselin, F. (2002). Show me the features! Understanding recognition from the use of visual information. *Psychological Science, 13,* 402–409.

Scullin, M. H., Peters, E., Williams, W. M., & Ceci, S. J. (2000). The role of IQ and education in predicting later labor market outcomes: Implications for affirmative action. *Psychology, Policy, and Law, 6,* 63–89.

Segal, N. L. (1993). Twin, sibling and adoption methods: Tests of evolutionary hypotheses. *American Psychologist, 48,* 943–956.

Segal, N. L. (2000). Virtual twins: New findings on within-family environmental influences on intelligence. *Journal of Educational Psychology, 92,* 442–448.

Segal, N. L., & Hershberger, S. L. (1999). Cooperation and competition in adolescent twins: Findings from a prisoner's dilemma game. *Evolution and Human Behavior, 20,* 29–51.

Segal, N. L., & Hill, E. M. (in press). Developmental behavioral genetics and evolutionary psychology: Tying the theoretical and empirical threads. In B. J. Ellis & D. F. Bjorklund (Eds.), *Origins of the social mind.* New York: Guilford.

Seielstad, M. T., Minch, E., & Cavalli-Sforza, L. L. (1998). Genetic evidence for a higher female migration rate in humans. *Nature Genetics, 20,* 278–280.

Seligman, M. E. P. (1991). *Learned optimism.* New York: Knopf.

Selten, R. (2001). What is bounded rationality? In G. Gigerenzer & R. Selten (Eds.), *Bounded rationality: The adaptive toolbox* (pp. 13–36). Cambridge, MA: MIT Press.

Semaw, S., Rogers, M. J., Quade, J., Renne, P. R., Butler, R. F., Dominquez-Rodrigo, M., et al. (2003). 2.6-million-year-old stone tools and associated bones from

OGS-6 and OGS-7, Gona, Afar, Ethiopia. *Journal of Human Evolution, 45,* 169–177.

Semendeferi, K. (2001). Advances in the study of hominoid brain evolution: Magnetic resonance imaging (MRI) and 3-D reconstruction. In D. Falk & K. R. Gibson (Eds.), *Evolutionary anatomy of the primate cerebral cortex* (pp. 257–289). Cambridge, England: Cambridge University Press.

Semendeferi, K., Armstrong, E., Schleicher, A., Zilles, K., & van Hoesen, G. W. (1998). Limbic frontal cortex in hominoids: A comparative study of area 13. *American Journal of Physical Anthropology, 106,* 129–155.

Semendeferi, K., Armstrong, E., Schleicher, A., Zilles, K., & van Hoesen, G. W. (2001). Prefrontal cortex in humans and apes: A comparative study of area 10. *American Journal of Physical Anthropology, 114,* 224–241.

Semendeferi, K., & Damasio, H. (2000). The brain and its main anatomical subdivisions in living hominoids using magnetic resonance imaging. *Journal of Human Evolution, 38,* 317–332.

Semendeferi, K., Damasio, H., Frank, R., & van Hoesen, G. W. (1997). The evolution of the frontal lobes: A volumetric analysis based on three-dimensional reconstruction of magnetic resonance scans of human and ape brains. *Journal of Human Evolution, 32,* 375–388.

Semendeferi, K., Lu, A., Schenker, N., & Damasio, H. (2002). Humans and great apes share a large frontal cortex. *Nature Neuroscience, 5,* 272–276.

Semino, O., Passarino, G., Oefner, P. J., Lin, A. A., Arbuzova, S., Beckman, L. E., et al. (2000, November 10). The genetic legacy of Paleolithic *Homo sapiens* in extant Europeans: A Y chromosome perspective. *Science, 290,* 1155–1159.

Shallice, T. (2002). Fractionation of the supervisory system. In D. T. Stuss & R. T. Knight (Eds.), *Principles of frontal lobe function* (pp. 261–277). New York: Oxford University Press.

Shapiro, D. H., Jr., Schwartz, C. E., & Astin, J. A. (1996). Controlling ourselves, controlling our world: Psychology's role in understanding positive and negative consequences of seeking and gaining control. *American Psychologist, 51,* 1213–1230.

Sharma, J., Angelucci, A., & Sur, M. (2000, April 20). Induction of visual orientation modules in auditory cortex. *Nature, 404,* 841–847.

Shaywitz., B. A., Shaywitz, S. E., Blachman, B. A., Pugh, K. R., Fulbright, R. K., Skudlarski, P., et al. (2004). Development of left occipitotemporal systems for skilled reading in children after a phonologically-based intervention. *Biological Psychiatry, 55,* 926–933.

Shea, D. L., Lubinski, D., & Benbow, C. P. (2001). Importance of assessing spatial ability in intellectually talented young adolescents: A 20-year longitudinal study. *Journal of Educational Psychology, 93,* 604–614.

Sheeran, P., & Orbell, S. (2000). Self-schemas and the theory of planned behaviour. *European Journal of Social Psychology, 30,* 533–550.

Shepard, R. N. (1994). Perceptual–cognitive universals as reflections of the world. *Psychonomic Bulletin & Review, 1*, 2–28.

Sherif, M., Harvey, O. J., White, B. J., Hood, W. R., & Sherif, C. W. (1961). *Intergroup conflict and cooperation: The Robbers Cave experiment.* Normal: Institute of Group Relations, University of Oklahoma.

Sherry, D. F., Forbes, M. R. L., Khurgel, M., & Ivy, G. O. (1993). Females have a larger hippocampus than males in the brood-parasitic brown-headed cowbird. *Proceedings of the National Academy of Sciences USA, 90*, 7839–7843.

Siegal, M., & Varley, R. (2002). Neural systems involved in "theory of mind." *Nature Reviews: Neuroscience, 3*, 463–471.

Siegler, R. S. (1996). *Emerging minds: The process of change in children's thinking.* New York: Oxford University Press.

Sigala, N., & Logothetis, N. K. (2002, January 17). Visual categorization shapes feature selectivity in the primate temporal cortex. *Nature, 415*, 318–320.

Silk, J. B. (1987). Social behavior in evolutionary perspective. In B. B. Smuts, D. L. Cheney, R. M. Seyfarth, R. W. Wrangham, & T. T. Struhsaker (Eds.), *Primate societies* (pp. 318–329). Chicago: University of Chicago Press.

Silk, J. B. (1993). The evolution of social conflict among female primates. In W. A. Mason & S. P. Mendoza (Eds.), *Primate social conflict* (pp. 49–83). Albany: State University of New York Press.

Silk, J. B., Alberts, S. C., & Altmann, J. (2003, November 14). Social bonds of female baboons enhance infant survival. *Science, 302*, 1231–1234.

Silverman, I., & Eals, M. (1992). Sex differences in spatial abilities: Evolutionary theory and data. In J. H. Barkow, L. Cosmides, & J. Tooby (Eds.), *The adapted mind: Evolutionary psychology and the generation of culture* (pp. 533–549). New York: Oxford University Press.

Simon, H. A. (1955). A behavioral model of rational choice. *Quarterly Journal of Economics, 59*, 99–118.

Simon, H. A. (1956). Rational choice and the structure of the environment. *Psychological Review, 63*, 129–138.

Simon, H. A. (1990a). Invariants of human behavior. *Annual Review of Psychology, 41*, 1–19.

Simon, H. A. (1990b, December 21). A mechanism for social selection and successful altruism. *Science, 250*, 1665–1668.

Simonton, D. K. (1999). *Origins of genius: Darwinian perspective on creativity.* New York: Oxford University Press.

Simonton, D. K. (2003). Scientific creativity as constrained stochastic behavior: The integration of product, person, and process perspectives. *Psychological Bulletin, 129*, 475–494.

Singh, D. (1993). Adaptive significance of female physical attractiveness: Role of waist-to-hip ratio. *Journal of Personality and Social Psychology, 65*, 293–307.

Skinner, B. F. (1938). *The behavior of organisms: An experimental analysis.* New York: D. Appleton-Century Company.

Skuder, P., Plomin, R., McClearn, G. E., Smith, D. L., Vignetti, S., Chorney, M. J., et al. (1995). A polymorphism in mitochondrial DNA associated with IQ? *Intelligence, 21,* 1–11.

Smith, E. E. (2000). Neural bases of human working memory. *Current Directions in Psychological Science, 9,* 45–49.

Smith, E. E., & Jonides, J. (1999, March 12). Storage and executive processes in the frontal lobes. *Science, 283,* 1657–1661.

Smith, P. K. (1982). Does play matter? Functional and evolutionary aspects of animal and human play. *Behavioral and Brain Sciences, 5,* 139–184.

Sokolov, E. N. (1963). *Perception and the conditioned reflex.* New York: Pergamon Press.

Solomon, S., Greenberg, J., Schimel, J., Arndt, J., & Pyszczynski, T. (2004). Human awareness of mortality and the evolution of culture. In M. Schaller & C. S. Crandall (Eds.), *The psychological foundations of culture* (pp. 15–40). Mahwah, NJ: Erlbaum.

Spearman, C. (1904). General intelligence, objectively determined and measured. *American Journal of Psychology, 15,* 201–293.

Spearman, C. (1927). *The abilities of man.* London: MacMillan.

Spelke, E. S., Breinlinger, K., Macomber, J., & Jacobson, K. (1992). Origins of knowledge. *Psychological Review, 99,* 605–632.

Sperber, D. (1994). The modularity of thought and the epidemiology of representations. In L. A. Hirschfeld & S. A. Gelman (Eds.), *Mapping the mind: Domain specificity in cognition and culture* (pp. 39–67). New York: Cambridge University Press.

Spitz, H. H. (1986). *The raising of intelligence: A selected history of attempts to raise retarded intelligence.* Hillsdale, NJ: Erlbaum.

Spitz, H. H. (1999). Attempts to raise intelligence. In M. Anderson (Ed.), *The development of intelligence* (pp. 275–293). Hove, England: Psychology Press.

Sporns, O., Tononi, G., & Edelman, G. M. (2000). Connectivity and complexity: The relationship between neuroanatomy and brain dynamics. *Neural Networks, 13,* 909–922.

Stadler, M. A., & Frensch, P. A. (Eds.). (1997). *Handbook of implicit learning.* Thousand Oaks, CA: Sage.

Stajkovic, A. D., & Luthans, F. (1998). Self-efficacy and work-related performance: A meta-analysis. *Psychological Bulletin, 124,* 240–261.

Stanovich, K. E. (1999). *Who is rational? Studies of individual differences in reasoning.* Mahwah, NJ: Erlbaum.

Stanovich, K. E., & West, R. F. (2000). Individual differences in reasoning: Implications for the rationality debate? *Behavioral and Brain Sciences, 23,* 645–726.

Stearns, S. C. (1992). *The evolution of life histories.* New York: Oxford University Press.

Stedman, H. H., Kozyak, B. W., Nelson, A., Thesler, D. M., Su, L. T., Low, D. W., et al. (2004, March 25). Myosin gene mutation correlates with anatomical changes in the human lineage. *Nature, 428,* 415–418.

Steele, C. M. (1997). A threat in the air: How stereotypes shape intellectual identity and performance. *American Psychologist, 52,* 613–629.

Stephan, K. E., Marshall, J. C., Friston, K. J., Rowe, J. B., Ritzl, A., Zilles, K., & Fink, G. R. (2003, July 18). Lateralized cognitive processes and lateralized task control in the human brain. *Science, 301,* 384–386.

Stephan, W. G. (1985). Intergroup relations. In G. Lindzey & E. Aronson (Eds.), *Handbook of social psychology: Vol. 2. Special fields and applications* (pp. 599–658). New York: Random House.

Sterck, E. H. M., Watts, D. P., & van Schaik, C. P. (1997). The evolution of female social relationships in nonhuman primates. *Behavioral Ecology and Sociobiology, 41,* 291–309.

Sternberg, R. J. (1977). *Intelligence, information processing, and analogical reasoning: The componential analysis of human abilities.* Hillsdale, NJ: Erlbaum.

Sternberg, R. J. (1984). Toward a triarchic theory of human intelligence. *Behavioral and Brain Sciences, 7,* 269–315.

Sternberg, R. J. (1997). Inspection time for inspection time: Reply to Deary and Stough. *American Psychologist, 52,* 1144–1147.

Sternberg, R. J. (2000, July 21). The holey grail of general intelligence. *Science, 289,* 399–401.

Sternberg, R. J., & Gardner, M. K. (1983). Unities in inductive reasoning. *Journal of Experimental Psychology: General, 112,* 80–116.

Sternberg, S. (1966, August 5). High-speed scanning in human memory. *Science, 153,* 652–654.

Stevenson, H. W., Parker, T., Wilkinson, A., Hegion, A., & Fish, E. (1976). Longitudinal study of individual differences in cognitive development and scholastic achievement. *Journal of Educational Psychology, 68,* 377–400.

Stiles, J. (2000). Neural plasticity and cognitive development. *Developmental Neuropsychology, 18,* 237–272.

Stone, V. E., Cosmides, L., Tooby, J., & Knight, R. T. (2002). Selective impairment of reasoning about social exchange in a patient with bilateral limbic system damage. *Proceedings of the National Academy of Sciences USA, 99,* 11531–11536.

Stoolmiller, M. (1999). Implications of the restricted range of family environments for estimates of heritability and nonshared environment in behavior-genetic adoption studies. *Psychological Bulletin, 125,* 392–409.

Stott, R. (2003). *Darwin and the barnacle: The story of one tiny creature and history's most spectacular scientific breakthrough.* New York: Norton.

Strathern, P. (2001). *Mendeleyev's dream: The quest for the elements.* New York: St. Martin's Press.

Strathman, A., Gleicher, F., Boninger, D. S., & Edwards, C. S. (1994). The consideration of future consequences: Weighing immediate and distant outcomes of behavior. *Journal of Personality and Social Psychology, 66,* 742–752.

Streissguth, A. P., Barr, H. M., Sampson, P. D., Darby, B. L., & Martin, D. C. (1989). IQ at age 4 in relation to maternal alcohol use and smoking during pregnancy. *Developmental Psychology, 25,* 3–11.

Stringer, C. B. (1992). Evolution of early humans. In S. Jones, R. Martin, & D. Pilbeam (Eds.), *The Cambridge encyclopedia of human evolution* (pp. 241–251). New York: Cambridge University Press.

Stuss, D. T., & Levine, B. (2002). Adult clinical neuropsychology: Lessons from studies of the frontal lobes. *Annual Review of Psychology, 53,* 401–433.

Suddendorf, T., & Busby, J. (2003). Mental time travel in animals? *Trends in Cognitive Sciences, 7,* 391–396.

Sugiyama, L. S., Tooby, J., & Cosmides, L. (2002). Cross-cultural evidence of cognitive adaptations for social exchange among the Shiwiar of Ecuadorian Amazonia. *Proceedings of the National Academy of Sciences USA, 99,* 11537–11542.

Sundet, J. M., Tambs, K., Magnus, P., & Berg, K. (1988). On the question of secular trends in the heritability of intelligence test scores: A study of Norwegian twins. *Intelligence, 12,* 47–59.

Supèr, H., & Uylings, H. B. M. (2001). The early differentiation of the neocortex: A hypothesis on neocortical evolution. *Cerebral Cortex, 11,* 1101–1109.

Süß, H. M., Oberauer, K., Wittmann, W. W., Wilhelm, O., & Schulze, R. (2002). Working-memory capacity explains reasoning ability—and a little bit more. *Intelligence, 30,* 261–288.

Svensson, E., & Sheldon, B. C. (1998). The social context of life history evolution. *Oikos, 83,* 466–477.

Swanson, L. W. (2003). *Brain architecture: Understanding the basic plan.* New York: Oxford University Press.

Swisher, C. C., III, Rink, W. J., Antón, S. C., Schwarcz, H. P., Curtis, G. H., Suprijo, A., & Widiasmoro (1996, December 13). Latest *Homo erectus* of Java: Potential contemporaneity with *Homo sapiens* in Southeast Asia. *Science, 274,* 1870–1874.

Taketoshi, O., & Nishijo, H. (2000). Neurophysiological basis of emotion in primates: Neuronal responses in the monkey amygdala and anterior cingulate cortex. In M. S. Gazzaniga (Ed.-in-chief), *The new cognitive neurosciences* (2nd ed., pp. 1099–1131). Cambridge, MA: Bradford Books/MIT Press.

Talcott, J. B., Witton, C., McLean, M. F., Hansen, P. C., Rees, A., Green, G. G. R., & Stein, J. F. (2000). Dynamic sensory sensitivity and children's word decoding skills. *Proceedings of the National Academy of Sciences USA, 97,* 2952–2957.

Tambs, K., Sundet, J. M., Magnus, P., & Berg, K. (1989). Genetic and environmental contributions to the covariance between occupational status, educational attainment, and IQ: A study of twins. *Behavior Genetics, 19,* 209–222.

Taylor, S. E. (1982). The availability bias in social perception and interaction. In D. Kahneman, P. Slovic, & A. Tversky (Eds.), *Judgment uncertainty: Heuristics and biases* (pp. 190–200). Cambridge, England: Cambridge University Press.

Taylor, S. E., & Brown, J. D. (1988). Illusion and well-being: A social psychological perspective on mental health. *Psychological Bulletin, 103,* 193–210.

Taylor, S. E., Klein, L. C., Lewis, B. P., Gruenewald, T. L., Gurung, R. A. R., & Updegraff, J. A. (2000). Biobehavioral responses to stress in females: Tend-and-befriend, not fight-or-flight. *Psychological Review, 107,* 411–429.

Teaford, M. F., & Ungar, P. S. (2000). Diet and the evolution of the earliest human ancestors. *Proceedings of the National Academy of Sciences USA, 97,* 13506–13511.

Teasdale, T. W., & Owen, D. R. (1989). Continuing secular increases in intelligence and a stable prevalence of high intelligence levels. *Intelligence, 13,* 255–262.

Teasdale, T. W., & Owen, D. R. (2000). Forty-year secular trends in cognitive abilities. *Intelligence, 28,* 115–120.

Templeton, A. R. (2002, March 7). Out of Africa again and again. *Nature, 416,* 45–51.

Terman, L. M. (1916). *The measurement of intelligence.* Boston: Houghton Mifflin.

Terman, L. M. (1959). *Genetic studies of genius* (Vols. 1–5). Stanford, CA: Stanford University Press. (Original work published 1925)

Thompson, L. A., Detterman, D. K., & Plomin, R. (1991). Associations between cognitive abilities and scholastic achievement: Genetic overlap but environmental differences. *Psychological Sciences, 2,* 158–165.

Thompson, P. M., Cannon, T. D., Narr, K. L., van Erp, T., Poutanen, V.-P., Huttunen, M., et al. (2001). Genetic influences on brain structure. *Nature Neuroscience, 4,* 1–6.

Thompson, S. C., Armstrong, W., & Thomas, C. (1998). Illusions of control, underestimations, and accuracy: A control heuristic explanation. *Psychological Bulletin, 123,* 143–161.

Thomson, G. H. (1951). *The factor analysis of human ability.* Boston: Houghton Mifflin.

Thomson, R., Pritchard, J. K., Shen, P., Oefner, P. J., & Feldman, M. W. (2000). Recent common ancestry of human Y chromosomes: Evidence from DNA sequence data. *Proceedings of the National Academy of Sciences USA, 97,* 7360–7365.

Thorndike, R. L., Hagen, E. P., & Sattler, J. M. (1986). *The Stanford–Binet Intelligence Scale* (4th ed.). Chicago: Riverside.

Thurstone, L. L. (1938). Primary mental abilities. *Psychometric Monographs* (No. 1).

Thurstone, L. L., & Thurstone, T. G. (1941). Factorial studies of intelligence. *Psychometric Monographs* (No. 2).

Tiger, L. (1969). *Men in groups.* New York: Random House.

Timberlake, W. (1994). Behavior systems, associationism, and Pavlovian conditioning. *Psychonomic Bulletin & Review, 1,* 405–420.

Tobias, P. V. (1987). The brain of *Homo habilis*: A new level of organization in cerebral evolution. *Journal of Human Evolution, 16,* 741–761.

Todd, P. M. (2000). The ecological rationality of mechanisms evolved to make up minds. *American Behavioral Scientist, 43,* 940–956.

Todd, P. M. (2001). Fast and frugal heuristics for environmentally bounded minds. In G. Gigerenzer & R. Selten (Eds.), *Bounded rationality: The adaptive toolbox* (pp. 51–70). Cambridge, MA: MIT Press.

Todd, P. M., & Miller, G. F. (1999). From pride to prejudice to persuasion: Satisficing in mate choice. In G. Gigerenzer, P. M. Todd, & ABC Research Group (Eds.), *Simple heuristics that make us smart* (pp. 287–308). New York: Oxford University Press.

Tomasello, M., & Call, J. (1997). *Primate cognition.* New York: Oxford University Press.

Tomasello, M., Call, J., & Hare, B. (2003). Chimpanzees understand psychological states—The question is which ones and to what extent. *Trends in Cognitive Sciences, 7,* 153–156.

Tooby, J., & Cosmides, L. (1992). The psychological foundation of culture. In J. H. Barkow, L. Cosmides, & J. Tooby (Eds.), *The adapted mind: Evolutionary psychology and the generation of culture* (pp. 19–136). New York: Oxford University Press.

Tooby, J., & Cosmides, L. (1995). Mapping the evolved functional organization of mind and brain. In M. S. Gazzaniga (Ed.), *The cognitive neurosciences* (pp. 1185–1197). Cambridge, MA: Bradford Books/MIT Press.

Tooby, J., Cosmides, L., & Barrett, H. C. (2003). The second law of thermodynamics is the first law of psychology: Evolutionary developmental psychology and the theory of tandem, coordinated inheritances: Comment on Lickliter and Honeycutt (2003). *Psychological Bulletin, 129,* 858–865.

Trinkaus, E. (1992). Evolution of human manipulation. In S. Jones, R. Martin, & D. Pilbeam (Eds.), *The Cambridge encyclopedia of human evolution* (pp. 346–349). New York: Cambridge University Press.

Trivers, R. L. (1971). The evolution of reciprocal altruism. *Quarterly Review of Biology, 46,* 35–57.

Trivers, R. L. (1972). Parental investment and sexual selection. In B. Campbell (Ed.), *Sexual selection and the descent of man 1871–1971* (pp. 136–179). Chicago: Aldine.

Trivers, R. L. (1974). Parent–offspring conflict. *American Zoologist, 14,* 249–264.

Tucker, A. S., Yamada, G., Grigoriou, M., Pachnis, V., & Sharpe, P. T. (1999). Fgf-8 determines rostral–caudal polarity in the first brachial arch. *Development, 126,* 51–61.

Tucker, D. M., Luu, P., & Pribram, K. H. (1995). Social and emotional self-regulation. In J. Grafman, K. J. Holyoak, & F. Boller (Eds.), *Structure and functions of the human prefrontal cortex* (*Annals of the New York Academy of Sciences,* Vol. 769, pp. 213–239). New York: New York Academy of Sciences.

Tudge, C. (2000). *The variety of life: A survey and celebration of all of the creatures that ever lived.* New York: Oxford University Press.

Tudhope, A. W., Chilcott, C. P., McCulloch, M. T., Cook, E. R., Chappell, J., Ellam, R. M., et al. (2001, February 23). Variability in the El Niño–southern oscillation through a glacial–interglacial cycle. *Science, 291,* 1511–1517.

Tulving, E. (1983). *Elements of episodic memory.* Oxford, England: Clarendon Press.

Tulving, E. (1985). Memory and consciousness. *Canadian Psychology, 25,* 1–12.

Tulving, E. (1993). What is episodic memory? *Current Directions in Psychological Science, 2,* 67–70.

Tulving, E. (2000). Concepts of memory. In E. Tulving & F. I. M. Craik (Eds.), *The Oxford handbook of memory* (pp. 33–43). New York: Oxford University Press.

Tulving, E. (2002). Episodic memory: From mind to brain. *Annual Review of Psychology, 53,* 1–25.

Tulving, E., & Craik, F. I. M. (Eds.). (2000). *The Oxford handbook of memory.* New York: Oxford University Press.

Tulving, E., Kapur, S., Craik, F. I. M., Moscovitch, M., & Houle, S. (1994). Hemispheric encoding/retrieval asymmetry in episodic memory: Positron emission tomography findings. *Proceedings of the National Academy of Sciences USA, 91,* 2016–2020.

Turkheimer, E., Goldsmith, H. H., & Gottesman, I. I. (1995). Commentary. *Human Development, 38,* 142–153.

Turkheimer, E., Haley, A., Waldron, M., D'Onofrio, D., & Gottesman, I. I. (2003). Socioeconomic status modifies heritability of IQ in young children. *Psychological Science, 14,* 623–628.

Turkheimer, E., & Waldron, M. (2000). Nonshared environment: A theoretical, methodological, and quantitative review. *Psychological Bulletin, 126,* 78–108.

Turner, A., & Wood, B. (1993). Comparative palaeontological context for the evolution of the early hominid masticatory system. *Journal of Human Evolution, 24,* 301–318.

Tversky, A., & Kahneman, D. (1974, September 27). Judgment under uncertainty: Heuristics and biases. *Science, 185,* 1124–1131.

Tversky, A., & Koehler, D. J. (1994). Support theory: A nonextensional representation of subjective probability. *Psychological Review, 101,* 547–567.

Underhill, P. A., Jin, L., Zemans, R., Oefner, P. J., & Cavalli-Sforza, L. L. (1996). A pre-Columbian Y chromosome-specific transition and its implications for human evolutionary history. *Proceedings of the National Academy of Sciences USA, 93,* 196–200.

Underhill, P. A., Passarino, G., Lin, A. A., Shen, P., Lahr, M. M., Foley, R. A., et al. (2001). The phylogeography of Y chromosome binary haplotypes and the origins of modern human populations. *Annals of Human Genetics, 65,* 43–62.

Underhill, P. A., Shen, P., Lin, A. A., Jin, L., Passarino, G., Yang, W. H., et al. (2000). Y chromosome sequence variation and the history of human populations. *Nature Genetics, 26,* 358–361.

United Nations. (1985). *Socio-economic differentials in child mortality in developing countries*. New York: Author.

Vallin, J. (1991). Mortality in Europe from 1720 to 1914: Long-term trends and changes in patterns by age and sex. In R. Schofield, D. Reher, & A. Bideau (Eds.), *The decline of mortality in Europe* (pp. 38–67). Oxford, England: Oxford University Press.

Vanduffel, W., Fize, D., Peuskens, H., Denys, K., Sunaert, S., Todd, J. T., & Orban, G. A. (2002, October 11). Extracting 3D from motion: Differences in human and monkey intraparietal cortex. *Science, 298,* 413–415.

VanLehn, K. (1989). Problem solving and cognitive skill acquisition. In M. I. Posner (Ed.), *Foundations of cognitive science* (pp. 527–579). Cambridge, MA: MIT Press/Bradford Book.

Van Valen, L. (1973). A new evolutionary law. *Evolutionary Theory, 1,* 1–30.

Venter, J. C., Adams, M. D., Myers, E. W., Li, P. W., Mural, R. J., Su Hon, G. G., et al. (2001, February 16). The sequence of the human genome. *Science, 291,* 1304–1351.

Verbeek, P., & de Waal, F. B. M. (2002). The primate relationship with nature: Biophilia as a general pattern. In P. H. Kahn, Jr. & S. R. Kellert (Eds.), *Children and nature: Psychological, sociocultural, and evolutionary investigations* (pp. 1–27). Cambridge, MA: MIT Press.

Vernon, P. A. (1987). *Speed of information processing and intelligence.* Norwood, NJ: Ablex.

Vernon, P. A. (1989). The heritability of measures of speed of information-processing. *Personality and Individual Differences, 10,* 573–576.

Vernon, P. A., & Mori, M. (1992). Intelligence, reaction times, and peripheral nerve conduction velocity. *Intelligence, 16,* 273–288.

Vernon, P. A., Wickett, J. C., Bazana, P. G., & Stelmack, R. M. (2000). The neuropsychology and psychophysiology of human intelligence. In R. J. Sternberg (Ed.), *Handbook of intelligence* (pp. 245–264). Cambridge, England: Cambridge University Press.

Vernon, P. E. (1965). Ability factors and environmental influences. *American Psychologist, 20,* 723–733.

Vogt, B. A. (1987). Cingulate cortex. In G. Adelman (Ed.), *Encyclopedia of neuroscience* (Vol. 1, pp. 244–245). Boston: Birkhäuser.

Voland, E. (1988). Differential infant and child mortality in evolutionary perspective: Data from late 17th to 19th century Ostfriesland (Germany). In L. Betzig, M. Borgerhoff Mulder, & P. Turke (Eds.), *Human reproductive behaviour: A Darwinian perspective* (pp. 253–261). Cambridge, England: Cambridge University Press.

Vouloumanos, A., & Werker, J. F. (in press). Tuned to the signal: The privileged status of speech for young infants. *Developmental Science.*

Vrba, E. S. (1974, July 5). Chronological and ecological implications of the fossil Bovidae at the Sterkfontein Australopithecine site. *Nature, 250,* 19–23.

Vrba, E. S. (1975, March 27). Some evidence of chronology and palaeoecology of Sterkfontein, Swartkrans and Kromdraai from the fossil Bovidae. *Nature, 254*, 301–304.

Vrba, E. S. (1995a). On the connections between paleoclimate and evolution. In E. S. Vrba, G. H. Denton, T. C. Partridge, & L. H. Burckle (Eds.), *Paleoclimate and evolution, with emphasis on human origins* (pp. 24–45). New Haven, CT: Yale University Press.

Vrba, E. S. (1995b). The fossil record of African antelopes (Mammalia, Bovidae) in relation to human evolution and paleoclimate. In E. S. Vrba, G. H. Denton, T. C. Partridge, & L. H. Burckle (Eds.), *Paleoclimate and evolution, with emphasis on human origins* (pp. 385–424). New Haven, CT: Yale University Press.

Vrba, E. S., Denton, G. H., Partridge, T. C., & Burckle, L. H. (Eds.). (1995). *Paleoclimate and evolution, with emphasis on human origins*. New Haven, CT: Yale University Press.

Wagner, R. K. (1997). Intelligence, training, and employment. *American Psychologist, 52*, 1059–1069.

Wagner, R. K., Torgesen, J. K., & Rashotte, C. A. (1994). Development of reading-related phonological processing abilities: New evidence of bidirectional causality from a latent variable longitudinal study. *Developmental Psychology, 30*, 73–87.

Walberg, H. J. (1984). Improving the productivity of America's schools. *Educational Leadership, 41*, 19–27.

Wallace, A. R. (1855). On the law which has regulated the introduction of new species. *Annals and Magazine of Natural History, 16*, 184–196.

Wallace, A. R. (1869). Geological climate and origin of species. *London Quarterly Review, 126*, 187–205.

Wallace, A. R. (1887/2000). [Personal letter reprinted]. In Darwin, F. (Ed.) (2000). *The autobiography of Charles Darwin*. Amherst, NY: Prometheus Books. (Original work published 1893)

Wallace, A. R. (1911). *The world of life: A manifestation of creative power, directive mind and ultimate purpose*. New York: Moffat, Yard & Company.

Wallis, J. D., Anderson, K. C., & Miller, E. K. (2001, June 21). Single neurons in prefrontal cortex encode abstract rules. *Nature, 411*, 953–956.

Walsh, P. D., Abernethy, K. A., Bermejo, M., Beyers, R., de Wachter, P., Akou, M. E., et al. (2003, April 10). Catastrophic ape decline in western equatorial Africa. *Nature, 422*, 611–614.

Waltz, J. A., Knowlton, B. J., Holyoak, K. J., Boone, K. B., Mishkin, F. S., Santo, M. d. M., et al. (1999). A system for relational reasoning in human prefrontal cortex. *Psychological Science, 10*, 119–125.

Wang, X., Merzenich, M. M., Sameshima, K., & Jenkins, W. M. (1995, November 2). Remodeling of hand representation in adult cortex determined by timing of tactile stimulation. *Nature, 378*, 71–75.

Warrington, E. K., James, M., & Maciejewski, C. (1986). The WAIS as a lateralizing and localizing diagnostic instrument: A study of 656 patients with unilateral cerebral lesions. *Neuropsychologia, 24,* 223–239.

Warrington, E. K., & Shallice, T. (1984). Category-specific semantic impairments. *Brain, 107,* 829–854.

Wason, P. C. (1966). Reasoning. In B. M. Foss (Ed.), *New horizons in psychology* (Vol. 1, pp. 106–137). Harmandsworth, England: Penguin.

Watanabe, M. (2002). Integration across multiple cognitive and motivational domains in monkey prefrontal cortex. In D. T. Stuss & R. T. Knight (Eds.), *Principles of frontal lobe function* (pp. 326–337). New York: Oxford University Press.

Watson, N. V., & Kimura, D. (1991). Nontrivial sex differences in throwing and intercepting: Relation to psychometrically-defined spatial functions. *Personality and Individual Differences, 12,* 375–385.

Webb, R. M., Lubinski, D., & Benbow, C. P. (2002). Mathematically facile adolescents with math–science aspirations: New perspectives on their educational and vocational development. *Journal of Educational Psychology, 94,* 785–794.

Wechsler, D. (1949). *Manual for the Wechsler Intelligence Scale for Children.* New York: Psychological Corporation.

Wechsler, D. (1955). *Manual for the Wechsler Adult Intelligence Scale.* New York: Psychological Corporation.

Wechsler, D. (1981). *Manual for the Wechsler Adult Intelligence Scale—Revised.* New York: Psychological Corporation.

Weinberg, R. A., Scarr, S., & Waldman, I. D. (1992). The Minnesota transracial adoption study: A follow-up of IQ test performance at adolescence. *Intelligence, 16,* 117–135.

Weiner, J. (1995). *The beak of the finch.* New York: Vintage Books.

Weisfeld, G. E., Czilli, T., Phillips, K. A., Gall, J. A., & Lichtman, C. M. (2003). Possible olfaction-based mechanisms in human kin recognition and inbreeding avoidance. *Journal of Experimental Child Psychology, 85,* 279–295.

Wells, R. S., Yuldasheva, N., Ruzibakiev, R., Underhill, P. A., Evseeva, I., Blue-Smith, J., et al. (2001). The Eurasian heartland: A continental perspective on Y-chromosome diversity. *Proceedings of the National Academy of Sciences USA, 98,* 10244–10249.

Werker, J. F., & Tees, R. C. (1992). The organization and reorganization of human speech perception. *Annual Review of Neuroscience, 15,* 377–402.

West, J. (1986). *Alcohol and brain development.* London: Oxford University Press.

West, S. A., Pen, I., & Griffin, A. S. (2002, April 5). Cooperation and competition between relatives. *Science, 296,* 72–75.

West-Eberhard, M. J. (1975). The evolution of social behavior by kin selection. *Quarterly Review of Biology, 50,* 1–33.

West-Eberhard, M. J. (1983). Sexual selection, social competition, and speciation. *Quarterly Review of Biology, 58,* 222–234.

Westendorp, R. G. J., & Kirkwood, T. B. L. (1998, December 31). Human longevity at the cost of reproductive success. *Nature, 396,* 743–746.

Wheeler, M. A. (2000). Episodic memory and autonoetic awareness. In E. Tulving & F. I. M. Craik (Eds.), *The Oxford handbook of memory* (pp. 597–608). New York: Oxford University Press.

Wheeler, M. A., Stuss, D. T., & Tulving, E. (1997). Toward a theory of episodic memory: The frontal lobes and autonoetic consciousness. *Psychological Bulletin, 121,* 331–354.

Wheeler, M. E., & Fiske, S. T. (in press). Controlling racial prejudice and stereotyping: Changing social cognitive goals affects human amygdala and stereotype activation. *Psychological Science.*

Whissell, C. (1996). Mate selection in popular women's fiction. *Human Nature, 7,* 427–447.

White, L. E., Coppola, D. M., & Fitzpatrick, D. (2001, June 28). The contribution of sensory experience to the maturation of orientation selectivity in ferret visual cortex. *Nature, 411,* 1049–1052.

White, M. (1998). *Newton: The last sorcerer.* Reading, MA: Perseus Books.

White, T. D. (1995). African omnivores: Global climatic change and Plio-Pleistocene hominids and suids. In E. S. Vrba, G. H. Denton, T. C. Partridge, & L. H. Burckle (Eds.), *Paleoclimate and evolution, with emphasis on human origins* (pp. 369–384). New Haven, CT: Yale University Press.

White, T. D. (2003, March 28). Early hominids—Diversity or distortion. *Science, 299,* 1994–1995, 1997.

White, T. D., Asfaw, B., DeGusta, D., Gilbert, H., Richards, G. D., Suwa, G., & Howell, F. C. (2003, June 12). Pleistocene *Homo sapiens* from Middle Awash, Ethiopia. *Science, 423,* 742–747.

Wickett, J. C., Vernon, P. A., & Lee, D. H. (2000). Relationships between factors of intelligence and brain volume. *Personality and Individual Differences, 29,* 1095–1122.

Wiesel, T. N. (1982, October 14). Postnatal development of the visual cortex and the influence of environment. *Nature, 299,* 583–591.

Wiesel, T. N., & Hubel, D. H. (1965). Comparison of the effects of unilateral and bilateral eye closure on cortical unit responses in kittens. *Journal of Neurophysiology, 28,* 1029–1040.

Williams, G. C. (1957). Pleiotropy, natural selection and the evolution of senescence. *Evolution, 11,* 398–411.

Williams, G. C. (1966). *Adaptation and natural selection: A critique of some current evolutionary thought.* Princeton, NJ: Princeton University Press.

Williams, G. C. (1975). *Sex and evolution.* Princeton, NJ: Princeton University Press.

Wilson, D. S., Near, D., & Miller, R. R. (1996). Machiavellianism: A synthesis of the evolutionary and psychological literatures. *Psychological Bulletin, 119,* 285–299.

Wilson, J. F., Weiss, D. A., Richards, M., Thomas, M. G., Bradman, N., & Goldstein, D. B. (2001). Genetic evidence for different male and female roles during cultural transitions in the British isles. *Proceedings of the National Academy of Sciences USA, 98*, 5078–5083.

Wilson, M. L., Hauser, M. D., & Wrangham, R. W. (2001). Does participation in intergroup conflict depend on numerical assessment, range location, or rank for wild chimpanzees? *Animal Behaviour, 61*, 1203–1216.

Wilson, R. S. (1983). The Louisville twin study: Developmental synchronies in behavior. *Child Development, 54*, 298–316.

Wissler, C. (1901). The correlation of mental and physical tests. *Psychological Monographs, 3*(No. 6, serial no. 16).

Witelson, S. F., Kigar, D. L., & Harvey, T. (1999). The exceptional brain of Albert Einstein. *Lancet, 353*, 2149–2153.

Witte, O. W. (1998). Lesion-induced plasticity as a potential mechanism for recovery and rehabilitative training. *Current Opinion in Neurology, 11*, 655–662.

Witting, L. (2000). Population cycles caused by selection by density dependent competitive interactions. *Bulletin of Mathematical Biology, 62*, 1109–1136.

Wolpoff, M. H., Hawks, J., & Caspari, R. (2000). Multiregional, not multiple origins. *American Journal of Physical Anthropology, 112*, 129–136.

Wolpoff, M. H., Hawks, J., Frayer, D. W., & Hunley, K. (2001, January 12). Modern human ancestry at the peripheries: A test of the replacement theory. *Science, 291*, 293–297.

Wood, B. (1992, February 27). Origin and evolution of the genus *Homo*. *Nature, 355*, 783–790.

Wood, B., & Collard, M. (1999, April 2). The human genus. *Science, 284*, 65–71.

Wood, J. N., & Grafman, J. (2003). Human prefrontal cortex: Processing and representational perspectives. *Nature Reviews: Neuroscience, 4*, 139–147.

Wrangham, R. W. (1980). An ecological model of female-bonded primate groups. *Behaviour, 75*, 262–300.

Wrangham, R. W. (1986). Ecology and social relationships in two species of chimpanzee. In D. I. Rubenstein & R. W. Wrangham (Eds.), *Ecological aspects of social evolution: Birds and mammals* (pp. 352–378). Princeton, NJ: Princeton University Press.

Wrangham, R. W. (1999). Evolution of coalitionary killing. *Yearbook of Physical Anthropology, 42*, 1–30.

Wrangham, R. W., Holland Jones, J., Laden, G., Pilbeam, D., & Conklin-Brittain, N. (1999). The raw and stolen: Cooking and the ecology of human origins. *Current Anthropology, 40*, 567–594.

Wrangham, R. W., & Peterson, D. (1996). *Demonic males*. New York: Houghton Mifflin Company.

Wyckoff, G., Wang, W., & Wu, C. (2000, January 20). Rapid evolution of male reproductive genes in the descent of man. *Nature, 403*, 304–309.

Yamasaki, H., LaBar, K. S., & McCarthy, G. (2002). Dissociable prefrontal brain systems for attention and emotion. *Proceedings of the National Academy of Sciences USA, 99,* 11447–11451.

Zahavi, A. (1975). Mate selection—A selection for a handicap. *Journal of Theoretical Biology, 53,* 205–214.

Zerjal, T., Xue, Y., Bertorelle, G., Wells, R. S., Bao, W., Zhu, S., et al. (2003). The genetic legacy of the Mongols. *American Journal of Human Genetics, 72,* 717–721.

Zhang, J. (2003). Evolution of the human ASPM gene, a major determinant of brain size. *Genetics, 165,* 2063–2070.

Zhu, R. X., Hoffman, K. A., Potts, R., Deng, C. L., Pan, Y. X., Guo, B., et al. (2001, September 27). Earliest presence of humans in northeast Asia. *Science, 413,* 413–417.

Zilles, K., Armstrong, E., Moser, K. H., Schleicher, A., & Stephan, H. (1989). Gyrification in the cerebral cortex of primates. *Brain, Behavior and Evolution, 34,* 143–150.

Zilles, K., Armstrong, E., Schleicher, A., & Kretschmann, H.-J. (1988). The human pattern of gyrification in the cerebral cortex. *Anatomy and Embryology, 179,* 173–179.

Zilles, K., Dabringhaus, A., Geyer, S., Amunts, K., Qu, M., Schleicher, A., et al. (1996). Structural asymmetries in the human forebrain and the forebrain of non-human primates and rats. *Neuroscience and Biobehavioral Reviews, 20,* 593–605.

AUTHOR INDEX

Barrett, P. T., 262
Barsalou, L. W., 205
Bartels, M., 282
Bartini, M., 65
Bartley, A. J., 286
Barton, R. A., 32, 57, 58, 61, 63, 98, 99,
    103, 104, 107, 117, 118, 119,
    128, 147, 149, 209, 225, 227,
    247, 288
Bates, N., 59
Bates, T. C., 267, 269, 277, 295
Baumeister, R. F., 122, 140, 334
Bazana, P. G., 262
Bechara, A., 218, 243, 244
Beehner, J. C., 30, 120, 132
Begossi, A., 147
Behrensmeyer, A. K., 55
Behrmann, M., 131
Beier, M. E., 207, 268
Belin, P., 133, 136
Benbow, C. P., 21, 253, 311, 314
Bennett, E. L., 10, 109
Bennett, E. S., 266, 267, 295
Bentin, S., 132, 141
Beran, M., 49, 230
Berg, K., 280, 315
Bergman, T. J., 30, 120, 132, 142
Bering, J. M., 9, 66, 127, 128, 136, 222
Berlin, B., 11, 144, 145
Berlinski, D., 311
Berman, K. F., 271
Berndt, R. S., 205, 263
Bernieri, F., 281
Berthoz, A., 148
Betzig, L. L., 61, 75, 174, 308
Bever, J., 32, 43, 104, 247
Bideau, A., 308
Binet, A., 257, 302
Bingham, R., 87, 107
Bird, D. W., 157
Bishop, E., 18, 281, 282
Bishop, K. M., 96
Bishop, L. C., 56
Bisley, J. W., 211
Bjorklund, D. F., 12, 13, 64, 66, 78, 85,
    122, 156, 195, 196, 197, 204,
    219, 221, 248, 325, 334
Björkqvist, K., 69
Black, J. E., 85, 156
Black, J. M., 174, 175
Blake, R., 117, 119, 123

Blatt, S. J., 69
Bloom, P., 63, 155, 159, 227
Blumenfeld, P., 335
Blurton Jones, N., 65, 157
Blythe, P. W., 175
Boag, P. T., 27, 290
Bobbitt, B. L., 260, 261
Bodenhausen, G. V., 139, 143, 240, 246,
    247, 250
Boesch, C., 152
Bogin, B., 65
Boies, S. J., 259
Boissiere, M., 320
Boninger, D. S., 234
Bonnar, L., 167
Boomsma, D. I., 282
Boone, J. L., 228
Borgia, G., 40, 42
Borkenau, P., 267
Bornstein, G., 137, 247, 248, 251
Bornstein, M. H., 293
Bortolini, M. C., 71
Botvinick, M. M., 215, 216, 243
Bouchard, T. J., Jr., 18, 256, 281, 282,
    284, 292, 293, 305
Boyle, M. O., 207, 268
Boysen, S. T., 149
Brace, C. L., 53, 290
Bradley, D. C., 148, 211
Bradley, L., 326, 330
Bradley, R. H., 75
Bradshaw, J., 264
Braine, M. D. S., 195
Brandt, S. A., 107
Brase, P., 177
Braun, A. R., 102, 136
Braver, T. S., 211, 215, 271
Breedlove, D. E., 11, 144, 145
Breinlinger, K., 128
Brent, H. P., 156
Breus, M., 247
Broadfield, D. C., 102, 136
Brock, 62
Brodmann, K., xii, 89, 95, 211, 212, 212,
    229, 232
Brose, K., 93
Brosnan, S. F., 180, 181
Brothers, L., 4, 63, 77, 128, 131, 227,
    246
Brown, D. E., 20, 67, 69, 71, 137, 310
Brown, J. D., 72, 242, 250

Brown, J. H., 87
Brown, R., 156, 208
Browne, D. E., 139
Browne, J., 188, 192, 196
Bruant, A., 210
Brunswik, E., 171
Bryant, P. E., 326, 330
Buchanan, T. W., 133
Buchner, H., 107, 108, 155
Buchsbaum, M. S., 274, 327
Bugental, D. B., 11, 66, 130, 131, 142, 310
Bukowski, W. M., 180
Bunge, S. A., 214
Bunting, M. F., 207, 208, 266, 269
Buonomano, D. V., 10, 107, 108, 109, 117, 121, 155
Burckle, L. H., 54
Burgess, P., 273
Burns, N. R., 269
Burt, C., 255
Busby, J., 210, 220, 249
Buss, D. M., 40, 66, 68, 73, 75, 174
Butler, A., 90
Byrd-Craven, J., 157, 248, 334
Byrne, R., 128, 228
Byrne, R. M. J., 195

Cabeza, R., 125, 133, 217
Cáceres, M., 93, 94, 107, 341
Cacioppo, J. T., 240
Call, J., 12, 127, 128, 135, 225, 226, 228
Callen, D. E., 327
Calvin, W. H., 56
Cameron, K., 205, 263
Camille, N., 218
Campbell, A., 68
Campbell, K. B., 262
Campos, J. J., 79, 236, 239
Campos, R. G., 79, 239
Canli, T., 133
Cantalupo, C., 102, 136
Capelli, C., 71
Caporael, L. R., 20, 66, 122, 130, 131, 137, 164, 310
Caramazza, A., 128, 146, 147, 148, 159, 241
Cardon, L. R., 282, 283
Carey, C., 147

Carey, S., 77, 144, 332
Carmelli, D., 286
Carpenter, P. A., 204, 214, 266, 273
Carroll, J. B., 17, 19, 254, 256, 260, 262, 267, 302, 304
Carroll, S. B., 63
Carter, C. S., 215
Carvajal-Carmona, L. G., 71, 248, 308
Casas, J. F., 69, 334
Caspari, R., 49
Caspi, A., 313
Catalano, S. M., 97
Catania, K. C., 61, 98, 99, 107
Cattell, R. B., 17, 19, 186, 256, 266, 267, 275, 277, 279, 300, 302, 303, 304, 328, 337
Cavaillé, J., 92
Cavalli-Sforza, L. L., 47, 70, 71
Caviness, V. S., Jr., 101
Ceballos, G., 59
Ceci, S. J., 21, 296, 298, 317, 320, 336
Chabris, C. F., 211, 271
Chagnon, N. A., 63, 65, 67, 68, 71, 72, 76, 139, 143
Chamov, E. L., 65
Chan, V. T., 109, 159
Chan, Y.-M., 92, 93
Chang, E. F., 110
Changizi, M. A., 105, 106, 278
Chastain, R. L., 317
Chater, N., 169, 195
Chen, Z., 158
Cheney, D. L., 30, 120, 132
Cheng, P., 180
Chenn, A., 101
Chiappe, D., 127, 170
Chomsky, N., 84
Choudhury, S., 174
Christal, R. E., 17, 266, 304
Chun, M. M., 132, 172, 205
Cianciolo, A. T., 323, 324, 325, 328
Clarey, J., 9, 100, 147
Clark, A. G., 94
Clark, D. A., 32, 103, 104, 105, 107, 134, 247, 288
Clark, J. D., 58, 224
Clement, D., 147
Clement, J., 226, 333
Clutton-Brock, J., 53, 290
Clutton-Brock, T., 32, 34, 52, 57, 65, 67, 71, 103, 138

Cohen, J. D., 180, 205, 207, 211, 212, 214, 215, 216, 217, 219, 230, 236, 237, 263, 278, 326
Cole, R., 314
Coleman, S. W., 40
Coley, J. D., 77, 147, 153, 154, 186, 332
Collard, M., 6, 46, 47, 50, 52, 81
Collette, F., 211, 214
Collins, J. P., 137
Collins, W. A., 293
Collis, K., 42
Colman, A. M., 239, 250
Colom, R., 266
Combs, B., 177
Conklin-Brittain, N., 6, 58, 152
Conner, J. K., 26
Conway, A. R., 207, 208, 266, 268–269, 269, 276
Cook, A., 248
Coppola, D. M., 9, 110
Corley, R., 282, 283
Cormier, C., 196, 204
Corter, C., 137
Corwyn, R. F., 75
Cosmides, L., 63, 85, 113, 115, 121, 123, 124, 140, 154, 158–159, 160, 168, 169, 170, 172, 177, 179, 180, 195, 196, 198, 227, 234, 310, 341
Costa, P. T., Jr., 75
Court, J. H., 194, 257
Cowan, N., 78, 202, 205, 207, 208, 209, 266, 269, 276–277, 285, 304
Cox, D., 132
Craig, I., 280, 289
Craik, F. I. M., 202, 210, 214, 217, 219
Crawford, J. R., 257, 264
Crick, N. R., 69, 334
Crossley, P. H., 96
Crow, G. F., 24
Crowley, J. C., 110
Curtis, C. E., 214, 216, 232
Czerlinski, J., 177
Czilli, T., 137–138

Daly, M., 67
Damasio, A., 20, 77, 79, 80, 133, 134, 166, 172, 180, 181, 205, 207, 216, 218, 235, 236–238, 239, 243, 246, 263, 311, 322

Damasio, H., 65, 133, 135, 218, 229
Daniel, M. H., 257
Danielian, P. S., 93
Daniels, M., 291
Danion, J.-M., 210
Darby, B. L., 292
Darlington, R., 295
Darlington, R. B., 9, 103, 104, 105, 107, 287
Darwin, C., xi, 3, 5, 8, 13, 22, 23, 24n, 26, 29, 32, 33, 35, 36, 40, 41, 42, 43, 44, 56, 60, 63, 67, 80, 83, 84, 87, 89, 94, 115, 122, 125, 127, 188, 189, 191, 192, 193, 194, 197, 216, 223, 229, 311, 332–333
Darwin, F., 188, 189
Daum, I., 262
Davies, N. B., 34, 44
Davis, J. N., 177
Dawes, R. M., 169
Dawkins, R., 4, 115, 170, 198, 223, 225
Deacon, T., 103, 105, 107, 229, 230, 231, 234
Dean, C., 47, 62
Dean, P., 57, 98, 117, 119, 147
Deary, I. J., 17, 254, 257, 261, 262, 263, 264, 264–265, 265, 269, 270, 271, 274, 276, 277, 278, 289, 304, 313
Deaux, K., 131, 243
DeCarli, C., 286
Decker, S. N., 284
Deecke, V. B., 118
DeFries, J. C., 24, 280, 281, 282, 283
de Geus, E. J. C., 282
de Haan, M., 158
Dehaene, S., 14, 133, 204, 207, 214, 215, 232, 234, 235, 237, 249, 326
Dehaene-Lambertz, G., 133
de Heinzelin, J., 58, 152
de la Coste-Lareymondie, M. C., 49, 51, 231, 232, 287
DeLoache, J. S., 158
DeMenocal, P. B., 54, 63
Dennett, D. C., 5, 24, 117, 155, 166, 168, 204, 227, 234, 235, 237, 238, 240, 250
Denton, G. H., 54
Der, G., 261
Desmond, A., 187, 188, 197, 245, 271
D'Esposito, M., 214, 216, 232

Detterman, D. K., 257, 264, 283, 284, 295, 315
Devlin, B., 291
Devlin, J. T., 146
Devlin, K., 331
de Waal, F. B. M., 32, 39, 67, 137, 142, 144, 177, 180, 181, 228
de Winter, W., 9, 103, 104, 105, 107, 288
D'Hondt, S., 54
Diamond, M. C., 10, 109
Dickens, W. T., 298
Diener, C., 76
Diener, E., 76, 80
DiGirolamo, G. J., 211
DiMatteo, M. R., 132, 204
Dinse, H. R., 107, 109, 121
Disbrow, E., 90, 92
Dolan, C. V., 282
Dolan, R. J., 133
Donaldson, G., 260
D'Onofrio, D., 291
Donoghue, M. J., 96
Dorit, R. L., 71
Doupe, A. J., 90, 94, 123, 136, 140, 156, 159, 208
Downing, P. E., 133, 159
Draganski, B., 109
Draper, P., 68
Drigotas, S. F., 244
Driver, J., 207, 211
Dubin, M., 213
Dukas, R., 61, 87, 98, 148, 202, 209
Dumaret, A.-C., 295
Dunbar, R., 32, 34, 121
Dunbar, R. I. M., 10, 30, 31, 32, 43, 63, 63–64, 67, 81, 98, 104, 122, 128, 130, 134, 177, 178, 227, 246, 247, 251, 300
Duncan, J., 18, 19, 21–22, 211, 214, 215, 232, 271, 273, 276, 277, 302, 305, 326, 327, 337
Duyme, M., 295, 298
Düzel, E., 210, 217
Dyer, F. C., 115, 151, 209

Eals, M., 209, 225
Earles, J. A., 316
Eccles, J., 335
Edelman, G. M., 22, 111, 326

Edwards, C. S., 234
Ehrlich, P. R., 59
Eichelman, W. H., 259
Eide, E., 320
Eisenberger, N. I., 239, 243, 249
Ekman, P., 80
Ekstrom, A. D., 150
Elbedour, S., 281
Elfenbein, H. A., 140, 159
Ellis, L., 73
Ellmore, T. M., 271
Elman, J. L., 85, 87
Elton, S., 56
Ember, C. R., 69
Ember, M., 69
Embretson, S. E., 17, 266, 276, 304, 325
Emlen, S. T., 33, 34
Emslie, H., 273
Enard, W., 93
Endler, J. A., 23, 25
Engel, S. A., 90
England, B., 69
Engle, R. W., 14, 17, 18, 19, 207, 208, 214, 215, 219, 232, 236, 249, 266, 267, 268, 269, 271, 272, 274, 276, 277, 304, 325, 326, 327, 328
Ericsson, K. A., 335
Erwin, J. M., 98
Esposito, G., 271, 278
Evans, G., 264
Evans, J. S. B. T., 5, 13, 14, 166, 166n, 168, 182, 195, 197, 199, 204, 234, 239, 248, 275, 323
Evans, P. D., 94, 101, 102
Eysenck, H. J., 260, 262

Falk, D., 49, 50, 51, 56
Farah, M. J., 146, 147
Feibel, C. S., 47
Feldman, M. W., 47
Feshbach, N. D., 69
Feuer, D., 284
Figueiredo, G. M., 147
Fink, A., 274
Finlay, B. L., 9, 103, 104, 105, 107, 287
Fischbein, S., 294, 296
Fischer, B., 267
Fischhoff, B., 177
Fish, E., 314

Fiske, S. T., 72, 73, 131, 137, 138, 139, 142, 143, 159, 240, 241, 242, 243, 244, 245, 246, 247, 250
Fitch, W. T., 84, 135
Fitzgerald, R. W., 35, 37, 121
Fitzpatrick, D., 9, 110
Flashman, L. A., 270
Flaum, M., 270
Fleming, A. S., 137
Flinn, M. V., 11, 43, 63, 69, 69, 73, 81, 128, 132, 133, 136, 139, 158, 227, 247
Florence, S. L., 108
Flynn, J. R., 18, 296, 298
Fodor, J. A., 113
Foley, R., 6–7, 39, 58, 118, 152, 177, 224
Forbes, M. R. L., 38
Ford, G., 261
Ford, J. K. B., 118
Forde, E. M. E., 146
Forkstam, C., 217
Fox, C. R., 176
Fox, H. C., 313
Fox, K., 107
Fox, P. T., 215
Frackowiak, R. S. J., 150, 214
Frängsmyr, T., 311
Frank, R., 229
Frayer, D. W., 47
Freedman, D. G., 12, 122, 123, 156, 158
Freedman, D. J., 120
Freer, C., 273
Frensch, P. A., 186, 325
Freudenthaler, H. H., 261
Friederici, A., 132
Friston, K. J., 146, 151
Frith, C. D., 132, 133, 134, 135, 150, 228, 233, 237, 245, 249
Frith, U., 132, 133, 134, 135, 245
Fritzsch, B., 93
Frostig, R. D., 117, 121
Fry, A. F., 207, 268, 276, 304, 325
Fukuchi-Shimogori, T., 9, 92, 96, 99
Fulker, D. W., 282, 283
Furuta, Y., 96

Gabrieli, J. D. E., 133, 134, 214, 219, 271
Gabunia, L., 47
Gade, A., 146

Gaffan, D., 146, 147
Gage, F. H., 109
Gagné, F., 314
Gainotti, G., 146
Gall, J. A., 138
Gallagher, H. L., 228, 233, 237, 249
Gallistel, C. R., 85, 115, 121, 123, 128, 144, 148, 154, 157, 158, 159, 169, 170, 198, 209
Gallo, L. C., 241
Galton, F., 16, 254, 280, 302
Gangestad, S. W., 174
Gannon, P. J., 102, 136, 231
Gao, W.-J., 97
Gardner, H., 11, 20, 128, 130, 259, 311, 329
Gardner, M. K., 259, 260
Garlick, D., 22, 329, 337
Gathercole, S., 208
Gaulin, S. J. C., 35, 37, 44, 121
Gauthier, I., 141
Gazzaniga, M. S., 202, 218
Geary, D. C., xi, xii, 3, 8, 10, 11, 15, 16, 21, 33, 34, 35, 38, 40, 43, 60, 63, 64, 65, 66, 67, 68, 69, 72, 73, 81, 82, 85, 86, 88, 91, 112, 114, 115–116, 117, 121, 122, 124, 127, 128, 132, 133, 136, 139, 156, 157, 158, 159, 160, 164, 171, 177, 186, 202, 211, 220, 225, 226, 227, 228, 235, 237, 247, 248, 249, 260, 279, 299, 300, 308, 312, 323, 325, 329, 330, 331, 334
Gelman, R., 10, 77, 85, 111, 120, 122, 128, 144, 145, 147, 153, 158, 160, 204, 332, 334
Gelman, S. A., 10, 77, 128, 147, 155
Gentner, D., 197
Gentner, T. Q., 95
George, N., 132, 140–141
Gerlach, C., 146
Geschwind, D. H., 286
Geschwind, N., 136
Gevins, A., 22, 328, 272, 337
Ghazanfar, A. A., 135
Giannelli, F., 71
Gibson, K. R., 49, 230
Giese, M. A., 120, 134
Gigerenzer, G., 13, 164, 171, 172, 175, 177, 180, 198, 203, 211, 244

Gilbert, D. A., 39, 139
Gilbert, D. T., 244
Gilbert, S. F., 92
Gilbert, W., 71
Gillan, D. J., 197
Gilliard, E. T., 35, 40
Givón, T., 327
Glaser, R., 259
Glazewski, S., 107
Gleicher, F., 234
Gleitman, H., 158
Glezer, I. I., 98
Glover, G. H., 90, 271
Goldberg, L. R., 335
Goldberg, M. E., 211
Goldin-Meadow, S., 140
Goldman, P. S., 108
Goldman-Rakic, P. S., 133, 214
Goldsmith, H. H., 280
Goldstein, D. G., 177
Goodale, M. A., 148
Goodall, J., 32, 39, 124, 132, 134, 178,
    224, 225, 228
Gopnik, A., 131
Gordon, B., 146, 159
Gordon, H. L., 134
Gore, J. C., 141
Goren-Inbar, N., 58
Gosselin, F., 167
Gotlib, I. H., 133
Gottesman, I. I., 256, 280, 291
Gottfredson, L., 18, 21, 84, 253, 257,
    267, 302, 313, 316, 317, 318,
    319, 327, 336
Gottlieb, G., 10, 280
Gould, S. J., 210
Gowlett, J. A. J., 152
Grafman, J., 205, 212, 214, 230, 263
Grajski, K. A., 109
Grant, B. R., 26, 27, 28, 29, 193
Grant, P. R., 5, 26, 27, 28, 29, 193, 194
Gray, J. A., 80, 166, 169
Gray, J. R., 211, 271, 277
Green, M., 115
Green, P. M., 71
Greenberg, J., 137, 247, 248, 340
Greene, T., 292
Greenfield, P. M., 298
Greeno, J. G., 171, 183, 184, 186, 235
Greenough, W. T., 10, 12, 85, 109, 110,
    111, 122, 156

Griffin, A. S., 138
Grigoriou, M., 96
Grogger, J., 320
Groos, K., 62, 64
Grossman, E., 133, 158
Groudreau, G., 96
Grove, E. A., 9, 92, 96, 97, 99
Grudnik, J. L., 264
Gsödl, M. K., 87
Gudmundsson, G. A., 115
Guilford, J. P., 255
Gustafsson, J. E., 256, 264
Gutheil, G., 144
Guthrie, R. D., 59
Gutman, L. M., 314, 315

Hadamard, J., 311, 312
Hagen, E. H., 80
Hagen, E. P., 257
Hahm, J. O., 97
Haier, R. J., 18, 271, 272, 274, 278, 327
Haile-Selassie, Y., 46
Hakeem, A., 63
Hale, S., 207, 268, 276, 304, 325
Haley, A., 291
Halgren, E., 132–133
Hall, J. A., 132, 204
Hamilton, W. D., 23, 39, 39, 63, 115,
    116, 137, 138
Hammer, M. F., 71, 72
Hampson, S., 296, 298
Hari, R., 133
Harnishfeger, K. K., 13, 78, 195, 197,
    204, 219, 221
Harold, R. D., 335
Harpending, H., 68
Harris, A., 132, 167
Harris, J. R., 66, 281
Harris, M. J., 281
Harris-Warrick, R. H., 92
Hart, J., Jr., 146, 159
Hartup, N. A., 65–66, 180
Harvey, O. J., 139
Harvey, P. H., 52, 57, 71, 98, 103, 104,
    225, 288
Harvey, T., 311
Hasenstaub, A., 62, 63, 64
Hasher, L., 202–203, 203
Hassett, J. M., 120
Hastie, R., 169

Lubinski, D., 21, 254, 311, 313, 314, 316, 319, 321, 336
Luchins, A. S., 182, 183
Luciano, M., 207, 284, 285, 286
Lunneborg, C., 253
Luo, D., 264, 282, 283, 284, 315, 316
Luria, A. R., 211, 273
Luthans, F., 319
Luu, P., 133, 216
Lyell, C., 83, 188, 189
Lykken, D. T., 76, 281, 282, 284
Lynn, R., 291, 296, 297–298, 298, 299
Lyon, D. C., 98

MacArthur, R. H., 60, 189
Maccoby, E. E., 293
MacDonald, K., 12, 75, 127, 156, 170
Maciejewski, C., 273
Mackintosh, N. J., 266, 267, 295
MacLeod, P., 259
Macomber, J., 128
Macrae, C. N., 139, 143, 240
Magnus, P., 280, 315
Maguire, E. A., 150, 151, 155, 159
Malt, B. C., 144, 145
Malthus, T. R., 60, 61, 142, 188, 189, 191, 193, 216, 228
Mandler, J. M., 158
Mangun, G. R., 210
Manktelow, K., 195
Manson, J. E., 299
Manzanares, M., 92
Marcus, G., 89, 113, 134
Margoliash, D., 95
Marinkovic, K., 132–133
Marino, B. D., 55
Markman, A. B., 197
Markus, H., 130, 244, 250
Marlowe, F. W., 157
Martin, D. C., 292
Martin, G. R., 96
Martin, P. S., 57, 58, 59, 60, 224
Martin, R. D., 103
Martinez, S., 93, 96
Matarazzo, J. D., 313
Matthews, K. A., 241
Matthews, M. H., 149, 158
Mattingly, I. G., 116–118
Maurer, D., 156

Maynard Smith, J., 12, 115, 124, 170, 198, 300, 310, 336
Mayr, E., 24, 30
Mazzaocco, M. M. M., 289
McBrinn, G. E., 55
McCandliss, B. D., 327
McCarthy, G., 233
McCartney, K., 122, 281, 281–282, 282, 295
McClearn, G. E., 24, 281, 282, 284
McCloskey, M., 226, 333
McComb, K., 32
McCrae, R. R., 75
McCrimmon, R. J., 264
McDannald, M. A., 106
McDermott, J., 132, 172, 205
McDougal, I., 47
McGarry-Roberts, P. A., 262
McGue, M., 18, 256, 281, 282, 284, 292, 293, 305
McGuffin, P., 24, 280
McHenry, H. M., 46, 47, 50, 51, 52
McIntosh, A. R., 234
McIntyre, J., 148
McKinney, M. L., 135, 225
McLaughlin, T., 63
McLaughlin-Volpe, T., 131, 243
McLean, J. E., 317
McMahon, A. P., 93, 96
McMullen, P. A., 146
McNeill, D., 140, 159
Mecklinger, A., 132
Medin, D. L., 128, 144, 145, 154, 186, 195, 241
Mercader, J., 152
Merriman, W. E., 260
Merriwether, D. A., 39, 71
Merzenich, M. M., 10, 107, 108, 109, 110, 117, 121, 155, 159
Mesa, N. R., 71
Meyer, B.-U., 107
Meyer, M. M., 146
Meyers, E., 132
Miller, B. L., 286
Miller, E. K., 120, 205, 207, 212, 214, 215, 216, 217, 219, 230, 236, 237, 263, 278, 326
Miller, G. F., 70, 174, 175
Miller, G. H., 59
Miller, R. R., 75
Milner, A. D., 148

Minch, E., 70
Minkoff, S. R. B., 208, 266
Minstrell, J., 333
Mintun, M., 215
Mitani, J. C., 39
Mithen, S., 10, 128
Mitra, P. P., 32, 103, 134, 247, 288
Miyake, A., 14, 79, 202, 207, 249
Miyashita-Lin, E. M., 96, 99, 124
Mock, O. B., 98
Molho, A., 57
Molnar, Z., 97
Mondloch, C. J., 156
Montiel, J., 90
Moore, C. I., 107
Moore, J., 187, 188, 197
Morales, D., 90
Morelock, M. J., 314
Mori, M., 262
Morris, J. S., 133
Morrison, A. S., 57, 76
Moscovitch, M., 14, 131, 211, 214, 216, 217, 223, 235, 237, 243, 249
Moser, K. H., 230
Mosher, M., 69, 334
Moss, C. F., 98, 148
Mouse Genome Sequencing Consortium, 90
Mousseau, T. A., 5, 25, 44, 290, 305
Munro, E., 261, 304
Murdock, G. P., 72, 149, 154, 155
Murray, C., 18, 20–21, 21, 253, 254, 280, 313, 316, 320, 335, 336
Murray, H., 295
Myers, D. G., 76
Myers, R. A., 59

Naccache, L., 14, 207, 214, 215, 232, 234, 235, 237, 249, 326
Nahm, F. K. D., 135
Nakagawa, Y., 96
Nakamura, K., 133, 141, 150, 159
Narayanan, K., 134, 218–219
Near, D., 75
Neiderhisher, J., 289
Neiss, M., 18, 293
Neisser, U., 298
Neiworth, J. J., 120
Nelson, C. A., 158
Nelson, J., 9, 98, 99, 100, 147

Nelson, K., 203
Nesselroade, J. R., 282
Nettelbeck, T., 17, 263, 264, 269, 297
Neubauer, A. C., 261, 262, 267, 274, 283, 284, 285
Neve, C., 146
Newcomb, A. F., 180
Newell, A., 78, 79, 182, 183, 186, 189, 235
Newton, I., 311, 312, 322, 332, 333
Nicastro, N., 9, 103
Niehaus, L., 107
Nimchinsky, E. A., 98, 231, 232, 233
Nishijo, H., 233
Noachtar, S., 146
Noll, D. C., 211
Normal, D. A., 214
Northcutt, R. G., 90, 102
Nowakowski, R. S., 101
Numtee, C., 157, 248, 334
Nyberg, L., 125, 133, 217
Nyborg, H., 317, 320
Nystrom, L. E., 180, 211

Oaksford, M., 169, 195
Oberauer, K., 204, 266
Obonsawin, M. C., 272
O'Brien, S. J., 39, 139
Ochsner, K. N., 244
O'Connell, J. F., 65, 157
Ody, C., 214
Oefner, P. J., 47, 71
Ohkubo, Y., 96
Öhman, A., 80, 133, 142, 172, 179, 181, 239
Oldak, R., 149
O'Leary, D. D. M., 9, 95, 96, 97
Ones, D. S., 318, 319
Ono, Y., 285
Opitz, J. M., 92
Orbell, S., 244
Oring, L. W., 34
Ó Scalaidhe, S. P., 133
O'Shaughnessy, M., 209
Ospovat, D., 187, 188
Osterman, K., 69
Ovchinnikov, I. V., 47
Over, D. E., 168, 195
Owen, A. M., 22, 327, 337
Owen, D. R., 18, 296, 297, 298

Sattler, J. M., 257
Sawaguchi, T., 33, 43, 63, 104, 122
Scarr, S., 12, 122, 156, 281, 282, 291, 293, 294, 295, 296, 298
Scarr-Salapatek, S., 294
Schacter, D. L., 244
Schenker, N., 65, 135, 229
Schiff, W., 149
Schimel, J., 137, 340
Schlagger, B. L., 9, 96, 97
Schleicher, A., 229, 230
Schmidt, F. L., 21, 316, 317, 318, 319, 321, 336
Schneider, D. J., 245
Schofield, R., 308
Schooler, L. J., 203
Schrausser, D. G., 274
Schull, J., 330
Schultz, H., 76, 308
Schultz, R. T., 141
Schulz, R., 16, 72, 78, 240, 242
Schulze, R., 204, 266
Schulze, S., 107
Schusterman, R. J., 119
Schwartz, C. E., 72, 242
Schwenkreis, P., 107
Schyns, P. G., 167, 172
Scott, S. K., 133
Scullin, M. H., 21, 296, 317
Segal, N. L., 63, 70, 280, 281, 282, 293
Seielstad, M. T., 70, 71
Sejnowski, T. J., 87, 102, 288
Seligman, M. E. P., 80, 242
Selten, R., 13, 164, 171, 172, 173, 175, 198, 203, 211, 244
Semaw, S., 58
Semendeferi, K., 65, 135, 229, 232
Semino, O., 47, 72
Seyfarth, R. M., 30, 120, 132
Shafto, P., 147
Shah, P., 14, 79, 202, 207, 249
Shallice, T., 146, 147, 214, 215, 232, 326
Shapiro, D. H., Jr., 72, 242
Sharma, J., 97
Sharpe, P. T., 96
Shatz, C. J., 97
Shaywitz, B. A., 330
Shea, D. L., 311
Sheeran, P., 244
Sheldon, B. C., 68
Shell, P., 204, 266

Shelton, J. R., 128, 146, 147, 148, 159, 241
Shen, P., 47
Shepard, R. N., 94, 115, 148, 154, 159, 169
Sherif, M., 139, 143
Sherry, D. F., 37, 38
Shettleworth, S. J., 98
Shieles, A., 267, 269, 277, 295
Shimámura, K., 93
Shisler, R. J., 207, 269
Shuman, M., 133
Shyam, R., 281
Siegal, M., 134, 142
Siegel, B., 274, 327
Siegler, R. S., 158, 203
Sigala, N., 120
Silk, J. B., 30, 132, 134, 139, 178
Silverman, I., 209, 225
Simeone, A., 92, 93
Simmons, J. A., 98, 148
Simmons, L. W., 34
Simmons, W. K., 205
Simon, H. A., 12, 13, 74, 78, 79, 164, 167, 171, 172, 173, 175, 177, 179, 182, 183, 184, 186, 189, 198, 203, 211, 235, 242, 244, 312
Simon, L., 247
Simon, T., 257, 302
Simonotto, E., 265
Simonton, D. K., 195, 335
Simpson, J. A., 174
Singh, D., 73
Singh, R., 281
Sinha, P., 132
Sivers, H., 133
Skinner, B. F., 173
Skuder, P., 289
Skudlarski, P., 141
Slater, P. J. B., 118
Slovic, P., 176, 177
Smith, E. E., 214, 219, 232, 286
Smith, G. A., 284
Smith, J. A. L., 271
Smith, M. E., 22, 272, 328, 337
Smith, P. K., 64
Snipper, A., 295
Snyder, L. H., 148, 211
Snyder, S. S., 240
Sokolov, E. N., 207
Solomon, G. E. A., 147

Tononi, G., 22, 326
Tooby, J., 85, 113, 115, 121, 123, 154,
    158–159, 160, 168, 169, 170,
    172, 177, 180, 195, 196, 198,
    234, 308, 310, 341
Torgesen, J. K., 330
Tranel, D., 133, 218
Trinkaus, E., 6, 45, 57, 152, 290
Trivers, R. L., 33, 34, 40, 63, 67, 68, 69,
    70, 74, 124, 140, 180, 236
Tsugane, K., 46
Tucker, A. S., 96
Tucker, D. M., 133, 134, 142, 216
Tudge, C., 332
Tudhope, A. W., 54
Tuholski, S. W., 207, 266, 267, 268, 269
Tulving, E., 11, 14, 16, 20, 130, 134,
    200, 202, 202–203, 203, 209,
    210, 214, 217, 218, 219, 221,
    222, 227, 233, 234, 235, 236,
    237, 243, 249, 250, 311, 322
Turkheimer, E., 280, 291, 294, 295, 296,
    298
Turner, A., 55
Tuttle, R., 96
Tversky, A., 171, 176, 246

Underhill, P. A., 47, 49, 56, 70, 71, 248
Ungar, P. S., 57
United Nations, 61, 69, 76, 308
Uylings, H. B. M., 90

Vallin, J., 76
Van Baal, G. C. M., 282
Van den Oord, E. J. C. G., 291
Van der Linden, M., 211, 214
Vanduffel, W., 151
Van Hoesen, G. W., 229
Van Horn, J. D., 271
VanLehn, K., 183, 186
VanSchaik, C. P., 30
VanValen, L., 116
Varley, R., 134, 142
Venter, J. C., 93, 289
Verbeek, P., 144
Vernon, P. A., 260, 262, 264–265, 265,
    270, 274, 276, 278, 284, 305
Vernon, P. E., 255, 304
Vesterdal, W. J., 316, 321

Vigil, J., 157, 334
Vincent, A. C. J., 34
Viswesvaran, C., 319
Vogt, B. A., 231
Voland, E., 76
Von Cramon, Y. D., 132
Vonk, J., 135
Vouloumanos, A., 85, 156
Vrba, E. S., 6, 44, 54, 55, 56, 81, 84,
    103, 210, 222, 223
Vuilleumier, P., 207, 211

Wagner, R. K., 316, 330
Wahlsen, D., 10
Walberg, H. J., 21, 313, 314, 336
Waldman, I. D., 293
Waldron, E. M., 120
Waldron, M., 291, 295
Walker, A., 47
Wallace, A. R., 3, 5, 8, 13, 22, 23, 24n,
    26, 58, 60, 83, 85, 89, 92, 127,
    189, 191, 193, 194, 216, 224,
    332–333
Wallace, D. S., 156
Wallis, J. D., 216
Walsh, C. A., 101
Walsh, P. D., 59
Waltz, J. A., 214
Wandell, B. A., 90
Wang, S., 70
Wang, S. S.-H., 32, 103, 134, 247, 288
Wang, X., 109
Ward, C., 47, 81
Warrington, E. K., 146, 147, 273
Wason, P. C., 195
Wassarman, K. M., 96
Watanabe, M., 216
Watson, N. V., 149
Watts, D. P., 30
Weaver, S. L., 241
Webb, R. M., 21, 314, 317
Wechsler, D., 257, 273, 317
Weinberg, R. A., 281, 282, 293, 295
Weinberger, D. R., 286
Weiner, J., 28
Weisfeld, G. E., 137–138
Weisz, J. R., 240
Wellman, H. M., 131
Wells, R. S., 71
Werker, J. F., 85, 156

SUBJECT INDEX

Attentional control, *continued*
    as core cognitive competency in
        fluid intelligence, 19
    and executive control, 14, 15, 219,
        249
    and fluid intelligence, 273, 274, 276
    in goal achievement, 178
    in intelligence studies, 271
    and IQ, 321
    and prefrontal cortex, 211, 232, 249
    and working memory, 19, 21, 78, 79,
        207, 236, 238, 253, 268–269,
        271–272, 301,
        316, 321–322, 325, 327–328,
            337, 340
    and working memory/gF, 232, 268,
        305, 312, 318
    See also Inhibition; Working
        memory
Attentional focus, 14, 17, 18, 256, 304,
    326
    and working memory, 17, 18
Australopithecines, 6
    and brain morphology, 51
    brain volume of, 81
    diets of, 57–58, 59
    and human evolutionary history, 127
Australopithecus, 6, 46
Australopithecus afarensis, 46, 47, 48
    diets of, 57–58
    and evolutionary change in brain
        volume, 49, 50, 50–51, 52
Australopithecus africanus, 46, 47, 48
    and brain morphology, 51
    brain volume for, 50, 50–51, 52, 81
    EQ for, 53
    weight of, 52
Australopithecus anamensis, 46, 47, 48
Australopithecus garhi, 46, 47, 48
    brain volume for, 50, 50–51, 52, 81
    diets of, 57–58
    EQ for, 53
Autism, 160, 340
Automatization of complex tasks, 272
Autonoetic awareness, 16, 130, 210,
    217–219, 219, 227
Autonoetic mental models, 16, 210–211,
    234, 235, 236, 250, 312, 336,
    337, 339–340
    and conscious awareness of informa-
        tion, 301

    and intelligence, 300, 301, 302
    and problem solving, 19, 245
    processes and systems in support of,
        19
    and responses to variant conditions,
        20
    and novel information patterns, 21
    and self-awareness, 19
    and simulation heuristic, 246
    and social competition, 308
    See also Self-awareness
Availability heuristic, 177
Awareness
    autonetic, 16, 130, 210, 217–219,
        219, 227
    noetic, 210
    See also Self-awareness

Baboons (*Papio*), 30, 120
Barnacle geese (*Branta leucopsis*), 174–
    175, 176, 195, 198
Bats (*Eptesicus*), echolocation of, 148
Beetle (*Chiasognathus grantii*), male and
    female of, 36
Behavioral biases, 4
    evolution of, xi
Behavioral heuristics, 13
Behavioral traits, evolutionary analysis of,
    44
Behavior-cognition-ecology links. *See*
    Cognition-behavior-ecology links
Behavior genetic studies, on general intel-
    ligence, 291–295
Bell Curve, The (Herrnstein and Murray),
    18
Biases, 4
    attributional, 78
    in behavioral responding, 179
    in folk biology, 147, 333
    evolution of (behavioral), xi
    toward forms of social information
        processed, 132
    of infants toward human characteris-
        tics, 122
    kin, 138
    toward out-group, 78, 247 (*see also*
        In-group-out-group psychology)
    toward wanting to learn, 334
Biological organisms, dynamic relations
    among, 115

Biological resources, 4, 20, 73, 309
Bird song, 35, 121
    starlings' response to, 95
Bonobos (*Pan paniscus*), 46, 135, 231,
    232
Bounded rationality, 12–13, 171–174,
    198, 204
    and barnacle geese, 174–175
    and heuristics, 177
    in reasoning, 195
Bowerbirds (*Chlamydera, Ptilonorhynchus*),
    40, 42
Brain
    development, 95–97
    within evolutionary frame, 127
    function of, 123
    genes involved in, 289
    of human and of chimpanzee, 126
        in rates of gene expression, 341
        (*see also* Chimpanzees)
    plasticity in, 8
    regions of processing social informa-
        tion (human), 132–134
    See also Brain evolution, Mind,
        Neocortex
Brain correlates of intelligence, 258–269
Brain evolution, 49, 84, 229–233, 236
    and brain organization, 8–9, 51, 89
        and comparative ecology, 97–102
        and comparative genetics, 92–95
        and comparative neurobiology,
            89–92
        and development of neocortex,
            95–97
    Darwin on, xi, 122–123
    Darwin vs. Wallace on, 83, 89
    and encephalization quotient (EQ),
        6, 52–53, 54, 81, 128 (*see also*
        Encephalization quotient)
    expansion of prefrontal cortex,
        229–230
    genetic and experiential influences
        in, 8, 9
    and modules, 84
    and plasticity, 85–89
    and reorganization of prefrontal cor-
        tex and anterior cingulate cortex,
        231–232
    and selection pressures, 6–7 (*see also*
        Selection pressures)
    and sexual selection, 42–43

and significant evolutionary behav-
    iors, 163
in volume (size), 6, 49–52, 59, 81
    (*see also* Brain volume)
Brain imaging, and metabolic patterns
    during cognitive processing,
    273–274
Brain injury
    and cheater-detection competencies,
        180–181
    and general intelligence, 272–273
    and living-nonliving categorization,
        146
    as loss of ability to function, 322
    to right prefrontal cortex, 217
    and sense of self or mental time
        travel, 14, 217–218
Brain mechanisms
    in intelligence, 277–278
    and learning, 327–328
Brain morphology, for neocortex, 51
Brain organization or structure
    and evolution, 8–9, 89
        and comparative ecology, 97–
            102
        and comparative genetics, 92–95
        and comparative neurobiology,
            89–92
        and development of neocortex,
            95–97
    experiential modification of, 9–10,
        102–103, 107
        and allometry, 103–107
        injury, 107–109
        learning, 109
    and heredity, 286–289
    nature vs. nurture in, 123
    prenatal, 122
Brain proportion, 105
Brain regions
    experience-dependent or experience-
        independent architecture of, 110
    and general intelligence, 270–272
    and inspection-time tasks, 265
    See also Amygdala; Anterior cingu-
        late cortex; Dorsolateral pre-
        frontal cortex; Frontal pole;
        Hippocampus; Neocortex; Pre-
        frontal cortex; Somatosensory
        cortex; Thalamus
Brain specialization, 104–105

Brain systems, 211–217
　for episodic memory and autonoetic
　　awareness, 217–219
　social context of, 61
Brain volume (size)
　of australopithecine species, 81
　and climate change, 55–56, 222–223
　decline in, 291
　and ecological conditions, 223–224,
　　226
　evolutionary changes in, 6, 44, 49–
　　52, 81
　　and diet, 59
　factors associated with, 64
　and foraging and hunting competen-
　　cies, 59
　and heredity, 286–289
　of human vs. chimpanzee, 106
　and intelligence measures, 270
　and organization, 49–52
　and population fluctuations, 228
　and social relationships, 134
　and specializations, 49
Breeding of pigeons, as natural-selection
　　analogy, 197
Broca's area, 50, 51, 102, 125

Callionymus lyra, 41
Cat, body representations in somatosen-
　　sory cortex of, 100
Categorization, neural correlates for,
　　146–147
Category formation, 120
　as folk competency, 225
　of plants and animals in traditional
　　societies, 144–145
　rule-based, 10, 116, 117, 119–120,
　　124, 142, 153, 155, 156, 160
　for social activities, 157
　for tools, 155
　by traditional hunting societies vs.
　　college students, 153
　See also In-group/out-group social
　　psychology
Central executive, 14, 207–208, 219,
　　265–266
　and adapting to change, 221–222
　and heuristic-based processes, 215
　and slave systems, 208, 209

in working memory, 207, 208,
　265–266
　See also Executive control
Central nervous system (CNS), 89
　common subdivisions of, 92–93
　constraint or conservation in archi-
　　tecture of, 90
Cerebrotypes, 104
Chamaeleon bifurcus, 36
Cheater detection competencies, 180–181
Chick (*Gallus domesticus*), 93
Children, developmental experience of,
　　157–158. *See also* Developmental
　　period or experience
Chimpanzees (*Pan troglodytes*)
　anterior cingulate cortex of, 231
　and brain morphology, 51, 126
　　hemispheric asymmetry of pla-
　　　num temporale, 136
　brain volume for, 50
　　and number of neurons (vs. hu-
　　　man), 106, 230–231
　and category formation, 225
　coalitional behavior of, 38, 39
　and common ancestor, 46
　comparison of genes in, 94
　EQ for, 53
　and expression of genes, 93
　as extant relative, 127
　frontal cortex size(s) of, 135
　and frontal pole, 232
　left-right asymmetry lacking in, 231
　and levels of gene expression and
　　neural activity, 107
　locational understanding of, 149
　opportunistic hunting of, 224
　sexual politics of, 43
　and social competencies, 135
　and tool use, 148, 149, 152,
　　225–226
　and understanding of physical phe-
　　nomena, 152–153
　See also Apes
Choice, intersexual, 33, 40–42, 67, 68
　female, 68, 71
　male, 68
Climatic conditions
　increased body size from, 84 (see
　　also Turnover pulse hypothesis)
　in problem-solving evolution,
　　222–223

Climatic selection pressures, 5, 26–30
    and EQ, 54–56
Coalitional behavior, 30–32
    competition, 38–40, 138–139
    kin-based, 68, 71–72
    in lions, 39
    as strategy for individual, 40
    as uniquely human, 228
    See also In-group/out-group social
        psychology
Cognition, 202, 235–236
    and academic learning, 323–327
Cognition–behavior–ecology links, 171,
        198, 202–203, 211
    bounded rationality in, 204
Cognitive abilities, genetic influences on,
        282–284
Cognitive competencies, in intrasexual
        competition, 35
Cognitive correlates of intelligence,
        258–269
Cognitive evolution, and sexual selec-
        tion, 42–43
Cognitive mechanisms
    and control, 78
    in intelligence, 276–277
Cognitive module, 114
    in folk biology, 144–146
    in folk physics, 148–150
    in folk psychology, 131–132,
        136–137
Cognitive processes
    and behavioral engagement, 164
    implicit, 164, 165
    See also Bounded rationality; Heu-
        ristic(s); Motivation to control;
        Problem solving
Cognitive research, divided from neurobi-
        ological research, 126
Cognitive systems, 14, 202, 249
    central executive, 14, 207–208, 219,
        265–266 (*see also* Central exec-
        utive)
    cross-species differences in, 209
    explicit, 166, 202, 204–205, 272
    and explicit awareness of implicit
        processes, 205–207
    implicit, 166, 202–204, 272
    plasticity in, 8, 85–89 (*see also* Plas-
        ticity of mind and brain)
    and self-awareness, 209–211

shift from explicit to implicit, 272
    slave systems, 14, 208–209, 265–266
    social context of, 61
Cognitive tradition, 253
    reviews on, 254
Cognitive traits, evolutionary analysis of,
        44
Common ancestor
    of Asian men, 75
    comparison of species with, 35, 37
    of humans, australopithecines and
        chimpanzees/bonobos, 46, 50–51
Comparative ecology, 97–102
Comparative genetics, 92–95
Comparative neurobiology, 89–92
Competition
    between-group, 63
    boys' group-level, 157
    and changes in information patterns,
        227
    coalitional, 38–40, 138–139
    female-female, 43, 67, 68, 69
    intrasexual, 33, 34–40, 67, 68
    male-male, 67, 68, 71, 72, 119, 248,
        308, 330
    social, 7, 66, 339 (*see also* Social
        competition)
    within-species, 60
    See also In-group/out-group social
        psychology
Complex social dynamics, and heuristics,
        179–182
Conditioning, operant, 173
Conditioning, Pavlovian, and bounded
        rationality, 172
Conflict, and acquisition of resources, 66
Conscientiousness, 319
Conscious, 3, 4, 11, 13, 15, 77, 120, 134,
        142, 144, 172, 177, 182, 202,
        205, 206, 207, 216, 219, 233,
        234, 239, 244, 248, 249, 250,
        263, 277, 333, 339
Conscious, as related to problem solving,
        5, 13–16, 166–170, 182–197
    See also Problem solving, Mental
        time travel
Conscious awareness, 14, 15, 17, 18, 137,
        158, 164, 172, 175, 177, 198,
        204, 205, 207, 219, 232, 234,
        235, 237, 244, 247, 248, 249,
        276, 278, 304, 325

and parental investment, 64
and soft modularity, 155–158
Diminishing returns, law of, 257, 258, 261, 303
Dorsolateral prefrontal cortex, 22
asymmetry of, 231–232
and autonoetic mental models, 19
cognitive functions dependent on, 327
evolutionary expansion of, 232
and executive functions, 214
and goal achievement, 215, 326
heritability of, 289
and intelligence, 17–18, 270, 271, 272, 289
general fluid intelligence, 275, 277, 278, 305
and language, 231
in learning, 328
verbal and spatial information processed by, 286
Dragonet (*Callionymus lyra*), male, 40

Ecological conditions, in problem-solving evolution, 223–226
Ecological dominance, 3, 7, 60–61
competencies supporting, 225
cooperative relationships needed for, 62–63
emergence of, 45
and modules for folk knowledge, 224
and motivation to control, 20
and plasticity, 121
population expansion from, 63, 228
and selection pressures, 81–82
and social complexity, 61–63
and social dynamics, 63–66
social selection pressures as following, 134–135
social competition, 60–61, 227, 228, 247
and tool use, 12
See also Hunting and foraging
Ecological selection pressures, 5–6, 26–30, 250
and EQ, 56–59
shift from, 45
vs. social, 81–82
Ecological systems, functional, 144
and folk biology, 144–148

and folk physics, 148–153
and soft modularity, 153–155
Ecological variability, 115–116
Ecology, comparative, 97–102
Education
and gap between folk knowledge and academic competence, 22, 337
See also Academic learning and achievement
Einstein, Albert, 311–312
Electrophysiological methods, on processing speed, 264–265
Encephalization quotient (EQ), 6, 52–53, 54
of australopithecine species, 81
and climatic pressures, 54–56
and climatic variation, 222–223
decline in, 53, 290–291, 298
and ecological pressures or conditions, 56–59, 223–224, 226
evolution of, 6, 52–53, 54, 81, 128
factors associated with, 64
and population fluctuations, 228
of prefrontal cortex, 232
and selection pressures, 290–291
climatic pressures, 54–56, 222–223
ecological pressures, 56–59, 223–224, 226
social pressures, 60–70, 227–228
Environmental enrichment interventions and IQ, 295–296, 298
Environmental influences
on general intelligence, 18, 291–296, 305
and Flynn effect, 298
inequality in opportunity from, 296
See also Developmental period or experience
Epigenesis, 85
Episodic buffer, 134, 145, 209, 210, 218–219, 238
Episodic memory, 14, 209, 210, 217–219
and autonoetic awareness, 219
and prefrontal cortex, 211, 218
Errors in judgment
from cognitive biases, 176
in reasoning, 197
Essence, 11, 145, 153, 225
Euclid, 331

Eutheria (mammal), 90, 91
Evolution
    Darwin on, xi, 83, 89, 94, 122–123, 125, 229 (see also Darwin, Charles)
    and heritability, 290–291, 305
    hominid, 6, 80–82
        adaptation and selection in, 54–72
        and brain, 49–54, 103
        origins of, 46–49
    and intelligence, 279, 305
    as metatheory, xi, xii, 5
    and problem solving, 220–221
        and brain evolution, 229–233
        selection pressures in, 221–228
    and social competition, 19–20, 308
        and general intelligence, 310–311
        and modularity, 311–312
        and motivation to control, 309–310
Evolutionary arms race. See Arms race, evolutionary
Evolutionary change, rapidity of, 24
Exchanges, social, 179–182
Executive competencies, and motivation to control, 321–322
Executive control, 14, 15, 214–217, 219
    and brain volume increase, 233
    and cognitive systems, 249
    and ecological control, 226
    and evolutionary expansion of prefrontal cortex, 236
    and modular systems, 301
    and selection pressures, 220
    and sense of self, 219
    See also Attentional control; Central executive; Working memory
Executive functions (systems), 7, 15, 310
    brain regions in support of, 214
    and prefrontal cortex, 211, 211–212, 214, 216, 219, 220
Exoskeleton, as plasticity analogy, 10, 116–119, 122, 124, 156–157, 160, 169, 340
    and bounded rationality, 171–172, 179
    and conscious awareness, 205
    in information search, 178, 179
    and local ecology, 154
    and social relationships, 140

Experiential modification, of brain organization, 9–10, 102–103, 107
    and allometry, 103–107
    injury, 107–109
    learning, 109–111
Explicit cognitive systems, 166, 202, 204–205, 272
Extinction
    and climatic changes, 55
    of megafauna (due to human agency), 58–59, 60

Facial expressions, 80
    and bounded rationality, 172, 179
    brain function and behavioral responses to, 279
    complexity in interpretation of, 169–170
    fear-signaling, 239
    and individual-level modules, 11
    as information patterns, xii (see also Information patterns)
    universal and regional in, 140
Factor analysis, 255
Failure, attribution of, 242
Fair play, 180
    and capuchin monkeys (Cebus apella), 180, 181
    and Ultimatum Game, 181
Family environment, and general intelligence, 293–294
Family relationships, 67, 68–69
Family studies
    on brain structure, 286
    on intelligence, 281–282, 294
Fatherhood, 67. See also Paternal investment
Feelings, 79, 239. See also Affective
Female choice, 68, 71
Female–female competition, 43, 67, 68, 69
Ferrets (Mustela putorius furo), light-deprivation experiments on, 110
Fetal alcohol syndrome (FAS), 292
FGF8, 96
Finches (Geospiza)
    on Galápagos islands, 26–30, 44
    ground finches, 193–194
Fluid intelligence (general fluid intelligence, gF), 17, 256, 275, 304–305
    and academic learning, 322–328

and autonoetic mental models, 340
brain mechanisms for, 277–278
and brain regions, 271
cognitive mechanisms in, 276–277
cognitive processes and brain systems in, 17, 19
and evolution, 279
and glucose utilization, 274
in initial phase of learning, 328
and learning process, 21–22
first step, 337
and mental models, 301–302
and novel competencies, 21–22
and prefrontal cortex, 273
and resource control, 310
secular trends in (Flynn effect), 296–299
and selection pressures, 300
and socioeconomic status, 307
and speed of processing, 285
and status, 21
and working memory, 266–267, 268
heritability of, 285–286
Flynn effect, 296–299
Folk biology, 4, 7, 144–148, 159, 308, 309
and autonoetic mental models, 236
and brain/cognition research, 160
competencies of, 225–226
vs. other primates, 226
in Darwin/Wallace investigations, 188
and developmental period, 158
evolved, 59
and human thought, 331
as modular, 11–12, 77, 128, 129, 153–154, 204, 311
and ecological dominance, 224
and motivation of Darwin and Wallace, 22
and natural selection, 332–333
and soft modularity, 12
in taxonomy of mind, 10, 129
Folk decision-making heuristics, 177
Folk heuristics, 177
Folk knowledge
vs. academic knowledge, 22, 332–333, 334, 337
anchors in, 340

as crystallized intelligence, 19, 302–303
and ecological dominance, 62
heuristics in, 176–177
and human intellectual history, 22, 331–332
and modular plasticity, 328–329
as necessary but not sufficient, 22, 337
and Newton, 312, 322
social-dynamics reasoning based on, 239
as starting point, 322
Folk physics, 4, 7, 148–153, 159, 308, 309
and autonoetic mental models, 236
competencies of, 225–226
vs. other primates, 226
and developmental period, 158
and human thought, 331
as modular, 12, 77, 128, 129, 154–155, 204, 311
and ecological dominance, 224
in taxonomy of mind, 10, 129
Folk psychology, 4, 7, 159, 308, 309
and developmental period, 158
group, 136–139
and human thought, 331
individual, 131–136
as modular, 11, 12, 77, 122, 128, 129, 159, 160, 204, 311
and reading or writing, 329–330
and social cognition, 16, 240
and social dynamics, 63
in taxonomy of mind, 10, 129
Friendships, 11, 65–66, 139, 143
Frontal pole, 220, 231–232, 232–233, 233, 243
Fruit fly (Drosophila), 93
Functional ecological systems. See Ecological systems, functional
Functional modules, 114, 130, 164, 175–176
Functional social systems. See Social systems, functional
Functional taxonomy of human mind, 10–12, 127–130
Future orientation
and brain-injured patient, 218
brain regions for, 233
drawbacks of, 340–341
as evolutionary side-effect, 210

Heritable individual differences, 5
    in competencies leading to survival
        and success, 76
    as natural selection backbone, 24,
        25–26
    personality differences, 75
Heuristic(s), 13, 119, 168, 169, 171,
    176–182, 198
    in predator–prey relationship, 198
    in problem solving, 184, 186
    in reasoning, 195
    schemata as, 186
    simulation, 246
    under uncertainty, 169, 170, 198
Heuristic-based folk systems, inhibition
    of, 197, 198–199
Heuristic-based processes
    and central executive, 215
    decision-making, 279
Hierarchical theories, of human intellec-
    tual ability, 255, 256
High intelligence, 277, 279, 314. See also
    General intelligence; Genius;
    Intelligence
Hippocampus, 90, 109, 275
    and crystallized knowledge, 267
    of female vs. male cowbird
        (*Molothrus ater ater*), 38
    and folk physics, 151
    and geometric location, 150
    and intelligence measures, 270
    of male vs. female meadow voles
        (*Microtus pennsylvanicus*), 37
    and memories, 216
    in taxi drivers, 155
Hominid evolution, 6, 80–82
    adaptation and selection in, 54–72
    and brain, 49–54, 103
    origins of, 46–49
Hominids, 45
    and fire, 58
    as superpredators, 57, 58, 224
    and tool use, 152
Homo ergaster/erectus, 45, 46, 47, 48, 49,
    81
    brain volume of, 50, 55–56, 81
    and cortex areas, 231
    developmental period of, 62
    ecological dominance achieved by,
        224
    and EQ, 53, 58

and evolutionary arms race, 152
extinction of, 136
food extraction by, 60
and heritability of brain structure,
    287
and human evolutionary history, 127
hunting competencies of, 59
migration of, 47, 63
and stone tools, 58
Homo (Australopithecus?) habilis, 46, 47,
    48
    brain morphology of, 51
    brain volume of, 50, 52, 55–56, 81
    EQ of, 53
    and tool use, 51, 58, 152
Homo heidelbergensis, 46
    stone tools of, 58
    and tool specialization, 224
Homo neanderthalensis, 46, 47, 47–49
    and human evolutionary history,
        127
    stone tools of, 58
Homo sapiens, 45, 46, 47, 48
    brain volume for, 50
    and EQ, 53, 58
    food extraction by, 60
    hunting competencies of, 59
Homunculus question, 215
Honest indicators, 40
Hostile attribution bias, 245–246
Host–parasite relationships, 115–116
Human face
    as information pattern, 8, 77, 111–
        113, 141, 279
    stages in categorization of, 132
    See also Facial expressions
Human intellectual history, 331–332
Humans
    anterior cingulate cortex of, 231
    as ecologically dominant, 3 (*see also*
        Ecological dominance)
    female–female competition in, 43
    motivation to control in, 3–4 (*see
        also* Motivation to control)
    as social species, 66 (*see also* Social
        dynamics; Social relationships)
    See also Hominids
Humming birds (*Spathura underwoodi*),
    40, 41
Hunting, 224–225, 226. *See also*
    Predator–prey relationships

Hunting and foraging
    and development of brain and cognition, 61
    development period needed for, 157
    See also Ecological dominance
Huxley, T. H., xi, 8, 125, 126, 229
    and ideal self, 245
Hybrid radial units, 102

Ideal self, 245
Ideologies, social, 137, 138, 139
    of in-group, 248
    as uniquely human, 228
Ill-structured problems, 187
Immune system defenses, 116
"Impetus" and folk physics, 333
Implicit cognitive systems, 166, 202–204, 272
Inclusive fitness, 138
Income, and general intelligence, 319–321
Individual differences
    advantage in discrimination of, 124
    and discovery of natural selection, 191, 192, 193, 197
    and heredity of general intelligence, 280
    in mental abilities, 253, 259
        and *g*, 255
    in natural selection, 5, 23
    and plasticity, 169
    in reproductive success, 35
Individual folk psychology, 131–136
Inductive reasoning, in Wallace's route to natural selection, 192–193
Infant, odor of mother recognized by, 137
Inference, 239, 301
    biases in, 176
    and conscious awareness, 325
    inhibition required for, 197
    and working memory, 266–267
    See also Problem solving, controlled; Reasoning
Information patterns
    and autonoetic mental models, 21
    awareness of, 205
    and brain-behavior link, 163
    and classification of plants and animals, 145 (*see also* Category formation)

    in cognition–behavior–ecology links, 198
    in evolution of brain and mind, xii, 159, 171
    and evolution of cognitive competencies, 15
    in group-level competition and dynamics, 227
    and implicit processes, 203
    invariant, 170–171
    and modular control systems, 77
    of physical space, 150
    variant
        and developmental period, 160
        and plasticity, 12, 121 (*see also* Plasticity of mind and brain)
    variant and invariant, 8, 10, 87, 111–113, 124, 159, 169–170, 299
        explicit and implicit cognitive mechanisms for, 167, 168
        and extent of variance, 116
        and general intelligence, 279
        and nature vs. nurture debate, 123
        and plasticity, 115
In-group/out-group social psychology, 139, 143–144, 247–248
    competition-based, 157
In-groups, 11
Inhibition
    and brain damage, 218
    and central executive, 208, 219
    and cognition resource use, 328
    of heuristic-based responding, 204, 233, 248
    of heuristic folk-based systems, 197, 198–199
    of irrelevant brain systems, 278
    of irrelevant information or associations, 208, 211, 214–215, 219, 276, 304
    in logical reasoning or rational analysis, 196, 197, 198–199, 204, 248
    and prefrontal cortex, 211, 214–215
    of unneeded brain regions, 274
    See also Attentional control
Injury, and brain organization, 107–109. *See also* Brain injury
Inspection time, 263–265, 269
    and academic achievement, 316

Integrity, 319
Intellectual history, 331–332
Intelligence (IQ)
　　and bounded rationality of barnacle geese, 175
　　characteristics of high intelligence, 277, 279, 314
　　cognitive and brain correlates of, 258–269
　　and evolution, 279, 305
　　and glucose utilization patterns, 274
　　and law of diminishing returns, 257, 258, 261
　　performance characteristics of, 275–276
　　and reasoning, 194
　　See also Crystallized intelligence; Fluid intelligence; General intelligence
Intelligence tests, 257–258, 301–302
　　school-performance prediction as goal of, 302
　　and self-awareness, 19
　　See also IQ test scores
Intelligent design, Huxley's argument against, 126
Interbreeeding model of human evolution, 49, 72
Intersexual choice, 33, 40–42, 67, 68
Interventions, for improving cognitive competencies, 295–296, 298
Intrapersonal intelligence, 130
Intrasexual competition, 33, 34–40, 67, 68. *See also* Population genetics
Intuition, heuristics as, 176–177
In utero speech of mother, 122
IQ QTL Project, 289
IQ test scores, 20, 253, 257–258
　　and academic achievement, 313–314, 315
　　and brain size, 270
　　and fluid intelligence, 302
　　and Flynn effect, 297
　　and implicit problem solving, 272
　　and income, 321
　　and life experiences, 313
　　and life outcomes, 336
　　and prefrontal functioning, 272
　　and processing speed, 260, 261, 264, 265
　　and selection pressures, 290–291

and spatial problem-solving task, 327
　　See also Intelligence tests
Island biogeography, 60
Itza-Maya hunters, animal taxonomies by, 153–154

Job performance, and general intelligence, 318

Killer whales (*Orcinus orca*), and seals (*Phoca vitulina*), 118
Kinship-biased relationships, 63, 137–138
　　coalitions, 68, 71–72
Knowledge, declarative, 186, 209–210
Knowledge gap (folk knowledge vs. academic competencies), 22, 332–333, 334, 337
Knowledge-lean domains, 183–186
Knowledge-rich domains, 186–194

Language, 19, 102, 134
　　and constraints on processing, 87
　　and Einstein on scientific thought, 312
　　and focus on auditory system, 209
　　genetic influences on, 283
　　and phonological buffer, 227
　　and plasticity, 85
　　and soft modularity, 156
　　understanding of gained, 125
　　universal and regional in, 140
Learning
　　academic, 21–22, 303, 322 (*see also* Academic learning and achievement)
　　and brain organization, 109–111
Linnaeus (Carl von Linné), 311, 332
Lion (*Panthera leo*), coalitional behavior of, 38–39
Logic, and reasoning, 195–196. *See also* Reasoning
Long-term memory, 17, 203, 205, 275, 326
Lyell, Charles, 83, 188

Macroevolution, 3, 29
Male, Female: The Evolution of Human Sex Differences (Geary), xi

Male choice, 68

Male–male competition, 67, 68, 72, 248, 308
  dynamics of social competition in, 119
  in spy novels, 330
  and variance in Y chromosome genes, 71
  See also Population genetics

Malthus, Thomas, 60, 188–189, 191, 216, 228

Mammals
  evolutionary lines of, 90, 91
  male vs. female reproductive rates of, 34
  male-male competition among, 34–35

Marriage patterns, 71–72

Maternal effects, 291–292

Mating, 33–34, 121

Means–ends analysis, 183. See also Problem solving, controlled

Memories, 203

Memory systems, 203–204
  of brain-damaged patients, 217–218
  cross-species differences in, 209
  episodic, 14, 209, 210, 211, 217–219, 219
  long-term, 17, 203, 205, 275, 326
  semantic, 210
  short-term, 17, 269, 278, 283–284, 285, 304, 316
  working, 14, 15, 78, 304 (see also Working memory)
  working with, 216

Mental abilities, and psychometrics, 16–17, 254–258

Mental effort, and metabolic activity, 273–274

Mental models, 5, 13, 16, 202
  autonoetic, 16, 20, 210–211, 234, 235, 236, 250, 312, 336, 337, 339–340 (see also Autonoetic mental models)
  chimpanzees' lack of, 226
  and fluid intelligence, 301–302
  in folk biology, 145
  in folk physics, 149–150
  and general intelligence, 322
  and reasoning, 195–197, 199
  See also Simulations

Mental representations. See Representations

Mental simulations. See Simulations

Mental time travel, 14, 130, 210–211, 221–222, 227–228, 235, 249, 322
  for hunting, 224
  See also Simulations

Metabolic activity, and mental effort, 273–274

Metatheria (mammal), 90, 91

Microevolution, 3

Mind. See also Brain
  Darwin on evolution of, xi
  within evolutionary frame, 127

Mind, human
  function of, 123
  functional taxonomy of, 10–12, 129

Mind organization, nature vs. nurture in, 123

Mitochondrial DNA (mtDNA), 70

Modular domains, 10–11
  ecological, 144–155
  social, 130–144
  taxonomy of, 128, 129, 340

Modularity, 84, 311–312, 328
  and crystallized intelligence, 302–303
  within dorsolateral prefrontal cortex, 231
  forms of, 113–115
  modular competencies, 20
    and motivation to control, 322
  modular systems, 74, 77, 131, 299–300
  modules, 84, 113, 128–130
    cognitive, 114, 144–146, 148–150
    and conscious-psychological simulations, 240
    folk biological, 144–146, 153–154, 205
    folk physical, 148–150, 154–155, 205
    folk psychological, 205
    functional, 114, 130, 164, 175–176
    higher- and lower-level, 113, 134
    neural, 114
    perceptual, 114
  soft, 10, 12, 111–122, 160 (see also Soft modularity)
  and variant or invariant information patterns, 299–300

Modular plasticity, 328–329. *See also*
    Plasticity of mind and brain
Monkeys
    and brain organization comparison
        (rhesus macaques), 97–98, 101
    category formation by, 120
    coalitional behavior of females of,
        30
    competencies of, 225
    and fair play, 180
    monogamy and paternal investment
        of, 34
    neocortical areas of, 91
    primary visual cortex of, 106
    and similarity in phonetic processing
        (rhesus macaques), 136
    social dynamics and brain evolution
        in, 104–105
    and theory of mind, 135
    tool use by, 225–226
Mothers, odor of infant recognized by,
    137
Motivation to control, 3–4, 7, 11, 45,
        72–77, 82, 164–170, 233–234,
        309–312, 330–331, 335–336, 339
    and academic vs. folk knowledge,
        332–333, 334
    and brain–behavior link, 164
    and conscious-psychological
        mechanisms, 241
    and control-related behaviors, 250
    evolution of, 19–20
    evolutionary function of, 79–80
    evolutionary pressures behind, 335
    and evolution of intelligence, 305
    and executive competencies,
        321–322
    and folk psychology, 240
    functions associated with, 220
    and general intelligence, 20
    and intellectual history, 331–332
    and mental models, 234–240
    modules and mechanisms for, 77–79
    as organizing relationships, 20
    in organizing social ecology, 123
    and perfect world, 16
    and self-awareness, 15, 20, 249, 311
Motivation to learn, 334–335
Mouse, 90, 91, 93, 94, 101
Mutations, individual differences
    through, 24

National Longitudinal Study of Youth
    (NLSY), 313, 317, 320, 321
Natural decision-making heuristics, 177
Natural selection, 3, 5, 23
    and climatic or ecological selection
        pressures, 26–30
    Darwin and Wallace on, 83
    Darwin and Wallace problem
        solving to find, 188–194
    and folk biology, 332–333
    and humans as ecologically
        dominant, 3
    mechanisms of, 23–26
    reasoning about, 13, 24, 196–197
    and social selection pressures, 30–32
    as struggle with other humans, 60
    as well understood, 43–44
Nature vs. nurture, 8, 123. *See also* Envi-
    ronmental influences; Genetic in-
    fluences; Heredity; Heritability
Neanderthals. *See Homo neanderthalensis*
Neocortex
    allometric expansion of, 104, 107
    cause of evolutionary expansion of,
        9–10
    and complexity of social relation-
        ships, 43
    and complex social groups, 32
    and cooperative groups, 246–247
    damage to, 146, 180–181
    development of, 95–97
    homologous areas of, 90
    human
        areas of, 213
        of Einstein, 311
        gene contributing to large size of,
            101
        and general intelligence, 17, 49
        map of, 212
        outer surface of left hemisphere
            of, 49, 50
    human vs. chimpanzee, 93
    incidental expansion of, 102, 103
    and inherent constraint vs. develop-
        mental experiences, 86
    and language, 87
    as modifiable through developmental
        experience, 104
    morphology of, 51
    organization of, 9
    prenatal development of, 97

for hunting and foraging, 157
and individual differences, 169
and information patterns, 115
and knowledge construction, 22
and language, 140
as sensitivity to variation, 113
in social competition, 159
and theory of mind, 141
in tool use, 154–155, 159
and variation within constraints,
160
Platypus (*Ornithorhynchus anatinus*), 90,
91
Play, 157
rough-and-tumble, 64
See also Games; Sports
Politics, 67
Polygyny, 72
Population crashes, 60, 188–189, 228. *See
also* Multhus
Population genetics, 49, 70–72
Positron emission tomography (PET),
274
Possum (opossum), 91, 98
Postpartum depression, 80
Predator–prey relationships, 115, 116
as evolutionary arms races, 4
heuristics in, 198
hunting as, 225
modular perspective of, 148–149
and visuospatial sketch pad,
208–209
Prefrontal cortex, 14, 15, 136, 211–212,
213, 243, 249
in cheater detection, 181
evolutionary expansion of, 229–230,
232, 236
evolutionary reorganization of, 231
and executive functions, 211, 211–
212, 214, 216, 219, 220
and glucose metabolism, 274
heritability in structure of, 289
and inspection time, 265
and intelligence measures, 272, 272–
273, 278
and mental simulations, 237
and representations, 249
right, 217–218, 232, 233, 239
and specialization, 214
See also Dorsolateral prefrontal
cortex, Neocortex

Prenatal brain development, 9
and comparative genetics, 92
of neocortex, 95–97
regional differences in, 105
Prenatal brain organization, 122
Prenatal environment, and general
intelligence, 291–293
Prenatal neocortical development, 103
Primates
anterior cingulate cortex of, 231
complex social activities of, 228
fruit-eating vs. leaf-eating, 118
social complexity and brain size
in, 63
and status, 241
Principia, The (Newton), 311, 312
Principles of Geology (Lyell), 83, 188
Problem solving, 235, 301
and central executive, 219
conscious and explicit, 5 (*see also*
Problem solving, controlled)
and human evolution, 15–16
and brain evolution, 229–233
and motivation to control/general
intelligence, 82
for unpredictability, 170
Problem solving, controlled, 5, 13, 168,
182, 238, 249–250
and autonoetic mental models, 19,
245
and brain regions, 215, 233
and cognitive systems, 202 (*see also*
Cognitive systems)
and evolutionary expansion of
prefrontal cortex, 236
and fluid intelligence, 276, 305
and general intelligence, 248
and human evolution, 220–221
selection pressures in, 221–228
inhibition required in, 197
and IQ scores, 272
in knowledge-lean domains,
183–186
in knowledge-rich domains, 186–194
synchronization in, 216–217
See also Simulations
Problem space, 183, 186
in Darwin/Wallace reasoning,
193–194
and divine explanation of origin of
species, 188

Processing speed. *See* Speed of processing
Propositions, 195–196
Protocortex hypothesis, 96
Protomap hypothesis, 95
Prototheria (mammal), 90, 91
Psychometric *g*, 303. See also Crystallized
      intelligence; Fluid intelligence;
      Intelligence; Intelligence tests
Psychometrics, 253
    and crystallized intelligence,
       302–303
    intelligence tests, 256–257 (*see also*
       Intelligence tests; IQ test scoess)
    and mental abilities, 16–17
       organization of, 254–256
    reviews on, 254

Quoll, northern (*Dasyurus hallucatus*), 98

Raccoon (*Procyon lotor*)
    body representations in somato-
       sensory cortex of, 100
    forepaws neocortical areas of, 9, 99
Radial units, 95, 99, 101
    hybrid, 102
Rational analysis, and general intelli-
      gence, 248. *See also* Reasoning
Rationality, bounded. *See* Bounded
      rationality
Rats (*Rattus norvegicus*), 97, 100, 109
Raven's Progressive Matrices Test, 257
Reaction time, as related to IQ, 259–263
    and motor response, 263–264
Reading, 5, 21
    and folk psychology, 329–330
    learning of, 326–327
Reasoning, 194–195, 239, 249–250,
      301
    and central executive, 219
    as core cognitive competency in
       fluid intelligence, 17–18
    and mental models, 195–197, 199
    about natural selection, 196–197
Reciprocal social exchanges, 179–182
Regional activation, in intelligence
      studies, 271–272
Relational aggression, 334
Replacement model of human evolution,
      49, 72

Representations, 14, 77, 79, 208, 249
    of chimpanzees, 149
    conscious-psychological, 77–78, 79
    content of, 79
    in folk biological knowledge
      meaning-based, 114
    in problem solving, 183, 186
    in reasoning, 195
    See also Conscious; Mental models;
      Simulations
Reproductive rate, sex differences in,
      34, 71
Resource control, 76, 78, 309, 310, 339.
      See also Motivation to control
Resource distribution, as plasticity form,
      10, 116, 117, 120–121, 155, 160
Resources
    biological, 4, 20, 73, 309
    physical, 4, 20, 73, 309
    social, 4, 73, 309
    symbolic, 20, 309
Right prefrontal cortex, 217–218
Rule-based category formation, as plastic-
      ity form, 10, 116, 117, 119–120,
      124, 156, 160
    and folk biology, 153
    and social parsing, 142
    and tool use, 155
Rules, abstract, 216
Rules of engagement, 119
    and social grammar, 142
Rules of thumb, 184

s (specific mental abilities), 255
Satisficing, 173, 174, 175, 242
Schemata, 186
    in Darwin/Wallace discovery, 190
    of person, 131, 245–246, 250
    of self, 130, 244–245, 250
Schizophrenia, 341
Scientific breakthroughs, 312
Seals, and killer whales, 118
Selection pressures, 5–6, 15, 44, 221–
      228, 300
    climatic, 5, 26–30, 54–56, 222–223
    ecological, 5–6, 26–30, 45, 56–59,
      81–82, 223–226, 250
    and ecological dominance, 6–7,
      223–226
    and EQ of humans, 53

and executive control, 220
and fluid intelligence, 300
and general intelligence, 305
and heritability, 290
issue of relative importance of, 81–82
and mind/brain evolution, 84, 87
in problem-solving evolution,
221–228
social, 6, 30–32, 45, 227–228, 250,
300, 308 (*see also* Social selection
pressures)
Self
attributions about, 78
sense of, 134
as part of time-continuum, 227
as social being, 135, 249
and social relationships, 322
Self-awareness, 209–211, 238
as autonoetic awareness, 15–16, 19,
210, 250
brain areas in, 233
and conscious awareness of information, 301
and conscious-psychological control
mechanisms, 235
fluid intelligence separate from, 302
and motivation to control, 15, 20,
249, 311
of self as continuous through time,
130, 227
of self as social being, 11, 77, 130,
237
as uniquely human, 15, 237
and social relationships, 77, 322
and theory of mind, 238
See also Autonoetic awareness
Self-efficacy, 241–242
Self-regulation of behavior, and autonoetic awareness, 210, 227
Self schema, 130, 244–245, 250
Semantic memory, 210
Sense of self. *See* Self
Sensitivity to affective states, 20
Sex differences
in competition for mates vs. parental
investment, 33–34
and nerve-conduction-velocity effect
on IQ, 262
in reproductive rate, 34, 71
in traits supporting intrasexual
competition, 35, 36

Sexual reproduction, individual
differences through, 23
Sexual selection, 4, 23, 72, 197
Darwin on, xi
effects of (voles), 37
and parenting, 66–67
and population genetics, 70–72
and social dynamics, 32–33
brain and cognitive evolution
from, 42–43
and intersexual choice, 40–42
and intrasexual competition,
34–40
and mating or parenting, 33–34
as well understood, 43–44
Shiwiar hunter-horticulturalists, cheating
detection by, 180
Short-term memory, 269, 278, 285, 304
and academic achievement, 316
genetic influences on, 283–284
and intelligence, 17, 265, 304, 316
Simulated behavioral strategies, 238
Simulation heuristic, 246
Simulations, 13, 14, 16, 79, 149, 150,
183, 189, 195–197, 199, 202,
234–240, 246, 248, 249, 250,
301, 309, 310, 311, 312, 340, 341
conscious-psychological, 5, 16, 240
of potential future relationships
among groups, 248
See also Mental models
Skinner, B. F., 173
Slave systems, 14, 208–209, 265–266
Social activities, evolutionary basis of,
334
Social cognition, 240–241, 243–244, 250
and control-related conscious-
psychological mechanisms,
241–243
and folk psychology, 16, 240–248
and group-related social behaviors,
246–248
and person schema (others),
245–246
and selection pressures, 240, 241,
246
and self schema, 244–245
Social competencies, 70
and developmental period, 64–65,
158
in male–male competition, 69

Social competencies, *continued*
    and reproductive prospects, 43
    and social competition, 66
    and social or reproductive dynamics, 72
    survival and success from, 76
Social competition, 7, 339
    and children's social activities, 334
    and co-evolutionary arms race, 228
    and ecological dominance, 60–61, 227, 228, 247
    and evolution, 19–20, 308
        and general intelligence, 310–311
        and modularity, 311–312
        and motivation to control, 309–310
    heuristics in, 198
    plasticity of, 159
    and social competencies, 66
    See also Competition; In-group/out-group social psychology; Population genetics; Selection pressures
Social complexity, and ecological dominance, 61–63
Social conditions, in problem-solving evolution, 227–228
Social cooperation, and ecological dominance, 62
Social deception, and brain specialization, 104
Social dynamics
    complex, 179–182
    and ecological dominance, 63–66
    and fluid intelligence, 302, 305
    and high-status job demands, 318–319
    and logical reasoning, 239, 250
    for men, 67
    and neocortical volumes, 104
    and sexual selection, 32–33
        brain and cognitive evolution from, 42–43
        and intersexual choice, 40–42
        and intrasexual competition, 34–40
        and mating or parenting, 33–34
    and survival and reproductive activities, 66
    See also Social competition

Social ecology, 30–32
Social exclusion, 239
Social networking
    as strategy for individual, 40
    See also Coalitional behavior
Social outcomes, and general intelligence, 20–21, 312–313, 321–322, 336
    education, 313–316
    income, 319–321
    work, 316–319
Social parsing, 136–137, 142
Social relationships
    autonoetic mental models for, 340
    complexity of and group size, 31, 32
    and developmental period, 158
    and discrimination of individual differences, 124
    forms of, 66
    and infant's bias toward human characteristics, 122
    and sense of self, 322
Social resources, 4, 20, 73, 309
Social rules, 250
Social selection pressures, 6, 30–32, 45, 224–228, 250, 300, 308
    and control-related behaviors, 250
    vs. ecological, 81–82
    and EQ, 60–70
    as following ecological dominance, 134–135
    and group psychology, 247, 248
    shift to, 45
    and social cognition, 240–241, 246
    See also Folk psychology; In-group/out-group social psychology
Social systems, functional, 130–131
    and group folk psychology, 136–139
    and individual folk psychology, 131–136
    and soft modularity, 140–144
Social variability, 115–116
Socioeconomic status (SES), 21, 75–76, 241, 307, 309, 336
    and general intelligence, 307, 321
        genetic contribution to, 294, 313
Soft modularity, 10, 12, 111–122, 160
    and development, 155–158
    and forms of plasticity, 116–121
    and functional ecological systems, 153–155

Unpredictability
  behavioral, 336
  during co-evolutionary arms race,
    170

Variability, ecological and social,
    115–116
Variation, and natural selection, 27–28
Visual representation, for Darwin, 193
Visuospatial sketch pad, 14, 208, 208–
    209, 227
Voles, intrasexual competition of, 35, 37

Wallace, Alfred, 3, 8
  on evolution of mind and brain,
    83, 89
  and folk biology, 311
  on Malthus, 189
  motivation of, 22
  and natural selection, 23, 26
  observations and inferences of, 24
  problem solving by, 188–194, 216
  on uniqueness of human mind, 127
Warfare, 72
Water jars example, 183, 184, 185, 186
Wechsler Adult Intelligence Scale
    (WAIS)
  and location of brain injuries, 273
  representative standardization sample
    for, 317
Wernicke's area, 50, 102

Work, and general intelligence, 316–319.
    See also Socioeconomic status
Working memory, 14, 15, 78, 275, 276,
    304
  and academic achievement, 316
  and autonoetic mental models, 340
  central executive in, 207, 208, 265–
    266 (*see also* Central executive)
  and cognitive systems, 249
  in complex arithmetic problems, 186
  components of, 268–269
  as core cognitive competency in
    fluid intelligence, 17–18, 19
  and crystallized intelligence, 267
  and episodic buffer, 134
  and fluid intelligence, 266–267, 268,
    269, 286
  and folk-biological module, 145
  and heredity, 285–286
  and information-processing speed,
    207
  and motivation to control/general
    intelligence, 82
  and sense of self, 219
  for simulation of social and
    behavioral strategies, 79
  See also Attentional control; Central
    executive; Executive control;
    Executive functions
Writing, and folk psychology, 329–330

Yanomamö, 63

ABOUT THE AUTHOR

David C. Geary received his PhD in developmental psychology in 1986 from the University of California at Riverside, after which he held faculty positions at the University of Texas at El Paso and the University of Missouri, first at the Rolla campus and then in Columbia. Dr. Geary is department chair and professor of psychological sciences at the University of Missouri and from 2000 to 2003 was Middlebush Professor of Psychological Sciences. He has published more than 100 articles and chapters across a wide range of topics, including cognitive and developmental psychology, education, evolutionary biology, and medicine. His first two books, *Children's Mathematical Development* (1994) and *Male, Female: The Evolution of Human Sex Differences* (1998), were published by the American Psychological Association. He has given invited addresses in a variety of departments (anthropology, biology, behavior genetics, computer science, education, government, mathematics, neuroscience, physics, and psychology) and universities throughout the United States as well as in Belgium, Canada, Germany, and Italy. In addition to these activities, he was one of the primary contributors to the *Mathematics Framework for California Public Schools: Kindergarten Through Grade Twelve*. Among many distinctions is the Chancellor's Award for Outstanding Research and Creative Activity in the Social and Behavioral Sciences (1996).